Interpreting Bach
at the Keyboard

Interpreting Bach at the Keyboard

PAUL BADURA-SKODA

Translated by
ALFRED CLAYTON

CLARENDON PRESS · OXFORD

Oxford University Press, Great Clarendon Street, Oxford OX2 6DP

Oxford New York

Athens Auckland Bangkok Bogota Bombay
Buenos Aires Calcutta Cape Town Dar es Salaam
Delhi Florence Hong Kong Istanbul Karachi
Kuala Lumpur Madras Madrid Melbourne
Mexico City Nairobi Paris Singapore
Taipei Tokyo Toronto

and associated companies in
Berlin Ibadan

Oxford is a trade mark of Oxford University Press

Published in the United States by
Oxford University Press Inc., New York

First published in German by Laaber Verlag 1990
English translation © Oxford University Press 1993
First published 1993
Paperback edition 1995

British Library Cataloguing in Publication Data
Data available

Library of Congress Cataloging in Publication Data
Interpreting Bach at the keyboard
Paul Badura-Skoda; translated by Alfred Clayton.
Translation of: Bach–Intepretation.
Includes bibliographical references and index.
1. Bach, Johann Sebastian, 1685–1750. Harpsichord music.
2. Harpsichord music—Interpretation (Phrasing, dynamics, etc.)
3. Performance practice (Music)—18th century. I. Title.
ML410.B1B24513 1995 786'.146'092—dc20 95–15754
ISBN 0–19–816576–5

3 5 7 9 10 8 6 4 2

Printed in Great Britain
on acid-free paper by
St. Edmundsbury Press,
Bury St. Edmunds, Suffolk

To my wife Eva,

without whose help and encouragement
this book could not have been written.

PREFACE

The ever-increasing number of performances of Bach's music is a sign of its enduring vitality. Yet there now exists a diversity of interpretation of a magnitude that probably applies to no other composer. None of these methods can immediately be termed right or wrong. Too much depends on local and social conditions, and indeed on the attitudes and identities of performers and audiences. In general terms it is possible to distinguish three main tendencies in Bach interpretation, and these in turn could easily be subdivided:

1. Historically minded musicians pretend that they and their audiences are living in the time of Bach.

2. Performers who have a predilection for the style of the nineteenth century like to operate with large masses of sound, thereby emphasizing specific expressive elements. They seem to be blissfully unaware of the results of musicological research.

3. Performers who prefer the style of the twentieth century aim at a compromise. Their wish to perform Bach's music using the resources available today means that they are not afraid of making use of adaptations, though these are often even more remote from the original sonorities than nineteenth-century 'romantic' performances.

We should not forget those 'pseudo-historians' whose view of Bach is often diametrically opposed to that of Bach scholarship, which can after all look back on more than a hundred years of serious, solid work. They attempt to create the impression that they are drawing on sources and documents that have hitherto escaped the notice of previous scholars, and that this justifies a view of Bach that is completely at variance with the one handed down to us by Bach's sons and pupils. Occasionally such 'pseudo-authentic' performances can be totally compelling, as in the case of Glenn Gould, whose pianistic mastery and great literary gifts helped him to put across his often eccentric ideas. Glenn Gould may have fascinated his listeners, but Wilhelm Furtwängler, whose style somehow combined the second and third of the interpretational categories suggested above, possessed the ability to move his audience. His performances were imbued with a 'spiritual magic', a passionate immersion in the music that silenced objections to the lack of stylistic accuracy. The Bach scholar Hermann Keller once expressed it thus: 'I know that much of it is quite wrong from a historical standpoint, but nevertheless it makes a profound impression on me.'

In spite of such exceptions I believe that as far as the modern performer is concerned there can in fact be only one task: to recognize and respect Bach's musical and intellectual intentions as well as he can, and, by using the means available to us today, be it voices trained in the old or the modern style, or early or modern instruments, to convey them to a late-twentieth-century audience in such a way as to bring about *Gemütsergötzung* in the original meaning of the word, that is, the pleasure and spiritual enrichment to be derived from experiencing the greatness of Bach's music. In order to reach this goal it is above all necessary to bridge the traditional divide between musicology and practical music-making. I am convinced that this is possible, for I believe that the application of knowledge is not inimical to intuition and inspiration. Rather, knowledge can and should be an enrichment. However, good intentions are often more important than detailed historical knowledge. In other words, a truly enthusiastic amateur church choir can sometimes perform Bach more 'correctly' than an ensemble of uninspired professionals. I am also deeply convinced that the performance that comes closest to the intentions of the composer (not only in the case of Bach) is the one which will move the audience in the most profound way. I pursued my research with this in mind, and in setting out the results of my investigations I am also concerned to demonstrate the extent to which this knowledge can be applied today.

Bach's unsurpassed mastery of the art of counterpoint has repeatedly caused him to be viewed exclusively as a designer of 'abstract' musical configurations, and this not only in his canons and fugues. Even Beethoven's famous statement that he should not be called *Bach*, a stream, but *Meer*, the ocean—an ocean, that is, of contrapuntal art—points in this direction. Hans Gál's fitting description of the canons of the *Musical Offering* may be applied to the whole of Bach's work:

The involved scholastic devices to be found in some of these amazing compositions might give an impression of ingenuity for its own sake, if judged on a superficial impression. But this is certainly not the case. When Bach put his mind to tricky problems like these, he did it in the spirit of the masters of the fifteenth and sixteenth centuries who developed this kind of technique: as a discipline and a stimulus towards the utmost concentration under conditions of extreme technical difficulty. The essential fact is that the result is not mathematics but music, a flow of impeccably controlled events, and that even under the severest restriction of space the inventive imagination always succeeds in creating a fluent, expressive composition. For a master's inventiveness, the technical problem is not an obstruction but a stimulation.[1]

---

[1] Pref. to *J. S. Bach, Musical Offering* (London, 1952), p. iv.

This book is the result of an intensive, though not exclusive, preoccupation with the works of Johann Sebastian Bach spanning more than three decades. As a practical musician I have always felt the need to study the theoretical sources dealing with the performance practice of Bach's time, for I wished to understand Bach's music and that of his contemporaries and successors in all its complexity in order to be able to play it with empathy and conviction. The knowledge thus acquired, together with the practical experience gained in the concert-hall, slowly began to make me wish to convey these insights to other musicians and music-lovers. Later still I realized that this striving to convey information in an instructive manner was quite in keeping with Bach's attitude, for he was very much concerned to teach in a way that transcended the mere giving of lessons, particularly in his keyboard works. The dedications and titles of some of his works are a clear indication of this. Thus the Inventions were composed as an 'honest guide by which lovers of the clavier, and particularly those desirous of learning' were introduced not only to the art of polyphonic playing, but also given 'a strong foretaste of composition'. The motto of the *Orgel-Büchlein* was:

> To the glory of God in the highest,
> And instruction for my fellow man.[2]

The only sizeable keyboard and organ works to be published in his lifetime appeared under the modest title of *Clavier-Übung* (Keyboard Practice).

The second part of the present book is devoted to ornamentation. Considerable space has been allocated to this subject, not only because of its significance for baroque music in general, but also because the last decades have witnessed a certain stagnation in the assimilation of new insights and historical facts. This has given rise to the false impression that the problem of how to play Bach's ornaments has been solved once and for all, and in a 'historically accurate' manner at that. In fact this attitude has led to a wholly monotonous manner of playing Bach's ornaments based on a handful of rules taught at most of the world's conservatories. In reality these widespread habits do not correspond to the baroque style at all, for in many cases they are more or less a gross over-simplification. Interpretation of this kind sometimes takes its bearings from partially valid insights and a partial knowledge of the sources, though it makes the mistake of confusing a part with the whole. That is, it deduces a general law from an exegesis that may well be correct in a particular instance, and on the basis of this applies simplified rules without taking into account the context. Of course, this is a phenomenon that also occurs in other disciplines.

Fortunately a change seems to be taking place in the attitude to baroque

---

[2] Fac. of the autograph (Leipzig, 1981).

performance practice in general and the problem of ornamentation in particular. Nikolaus Harnoncourt has recently observed: 'Not everything is nowadays taken for granted. The arrogance of performers whose certainty is based on nothing but misunderstood tradition has largely given way to an attitude of open-minded enquiry'.[3] Even if this (probably rather too optimistic) statement holds true only for a small circle of open-minded musicians, the time has perhaps come to show those who are interested in the subject how to play Bach's ornaments in a manner that is historically justified. In the eighteenth century it was believed that ornaments should never be 'stuck on' at certain points. Rather, they were above all intended 'to link notes'.[4]

In view of the sheer multitude of problems facing the modern performer it would be foolhardy to deal with every single aspect of Bach interpretation within the space of one book. However, as it seems necessary to fill some of the more obvious and glaring gaps, I have decided to concentrate principally on those problems most in need of being solved. These include ornamentation, certain rhythmic matters, articulation, and the choice or treatment of the appropriate keyboard instruments.

The decision to concentrate on a relatively small number of areas was prompted by another factor. The recent past has witnessed the publication of several good works devoted to the question of Bach interpretation which outline a sensible compromise between historical insight and modern performance practice. Apart from Frederick Neumann's detailed study of baroque ornamentation and Bodky's book, which is still worth reading, even though its findings are in part outdated, the studies by Christoph Albrecht, Karl Hochreiter, and Helmuth Perl are of particular interest (see Bibliography). Jean-Claude Veilhan's *Die Musik des Barock und ihre Regeln* is a very good short survey. Not wishing to repeat what has already been said in these works, I have decided to discuss only those aspects to which they did not accord detailed attention.

I pursued research in two main directions:

1. to determine the influences on Bach, be they treatises or compositions from various periods and in various styles;
2. to describe the influence of Bach as a composer and teacher both in his own time and subsequently.

Bach's influence on his century was much greater than has hitherto been assumed. The idea that he was wholly forgotten until being 'rediscovered' in the nineteenth century has little basis in fact. However, the most important

---

[3] *Musik als Klangrede*, 2nd edn. (Salzburg and Vienna, 1983), 162.
[4] See Johann Adam Hiller, *Anweisung zum musikalisch-zierlichen Gesange* (Leipzig, 1780); repr. (Leipzig, 1976).

sources for the performance of Bach are the works themselves. Those who study them attentively will soon notice that Bach's way of thinking was much more modern than that of most of his contemporaries. He was at pains to express his musical intentions as clearly as possible with the notational resources at his disposal. He would continually revise the same work, and in so doing would choose different kinds of notation, or, by applying different ornamentation, would express in an almost didactic manner the possibilities at his disposal for free interpretation within a strict framework. In cases where he later made improvements or corrected errors, we can learn much about his compositional intentions and the idiosyncrasies of his style. All this requires thought, empathy, indeed the retracing of the compositional process. This study is neither easy reading, nor does it seek to provide comprehensive advice. Rather, the reader is repeatedly invited to think for himself and occasionally even to reach conclusions which differ from my own. However, this was what I set out to do. I am not concerned to offer patent solutions, or 'predigested' instructions on how to perform the music, but I am concerned to stimulate 're-creation' in future Bach interpretation. To clarify matters I have occasionally repeated a quotation or an idea, sometimes because it has led me in a different direction and always because it makes for ease of reference—few readers will want to read the book from end to end like a novel, and many may wish to consult only those sections which are of particular interest to them.

The manuscript of the book was completed in 1986, and for this reason certain important publications devoted to eighteenth-century performance practice could not be taken into consideration.

Finally I should like to thank the scholars and librarians who have helped me to acquire microfilms and photocopies of source material. I am particularly indebted to my wife, who not only contributed to its structure by suggesting improvements and pointing out aspects which I had omitted to discuss, but also edited the whole text. This book, unlike the study on Mozart interpretation which we published jointly in 1957, does not bear both our names. The reason for this is the fact that I wrote the greater part, my wife merely contributing Chapter 6 and parts of Chapters 3, 9, 11, and 20. It is at her wish that the book is published under my name alone. I should also like to thank Dr Reingard Nickl, who provided editorial help, Gisela Roithner, who always managed to decipher my handwriting, and Renée La Roche, for advice on technical matters connected with the harpsichord. Last but not least, I owe a debt of gratitude to the staff of the Johann-Sebastian-Bach-Institut in Göttingen, and Dr Yoshitake Kobayashi in particular, who provided invaluable advice of various kinds. I am especially grateful to Dr Alfred Dürr and Dr Klaus Hofmann, who were kind enough to read the manuscript, thereby correcting a number of mistakes. I also thank the Fonds zur Förderung der Wissenschaftlichen Forschung for its financial support.

My special thanks go to the translator of this book, Dr Alfred Clayton, who took endless trouble to secure a most precise translation without sacrificing the fluidity of style. He even managed to convey the sense of some of my puns! I also thank the editorial staff of Oxford University Press, to whom I owe many valuable suggestions.

CONTENTS

ABBREVIATIONS

BGA	Bach-Gesamtausgabe: *J. S. Bach: Werke*, ed. Bach-Gesellschaft (Leipzig, 1851–99): the 'old' Bach complete edition
BJb	*Bach-Jahrbuch*
BWV	Number in *Thematisch-systematisches Verzeichnis der musikalischen Werke Johann Sebastian Bachs: Bach-Werke-Verzeichnis*, ed. W. Schmieder (Leipzig, 1950)
MGG	*Musik in Geschichte und Gegenwart*, ed. F. Blume (Kassel and Basle, 1949–79)
NBA	Neue Bach-Ausgabe: *J. S. Bach: Neue Ausgabe sämtlicher Werke*, ed. Johann-Sebastian-Bach-Institut, Göttingen, and Bach-Archiv, Leipzig (Kassel, Basle, and Leipzig, 1954–): the 'new' Bach complete edition
NZfM	*Neue Zeitschrift für Musik*
ÖMZ	*Österreichische Musikzeitschrift*
WTC I	J. S. Bach, *The Well-Tempered Clavier*, Book I
WTC II	J. S. Bach, *The Well-Tempered Clavier*, Book II

Note: Unless otherwise specified, 'Partita' refers to one of the six Partitas in Bach's *Clavier-Übung*, Part I.

A NOTE ON TERMINOLOGY

British terminology for note durations is used throughout this book. The American equivalents are given below.

semibreve	whole-note
minim	half-note
crotchet	quarter-note
quaver	eighth-note
semiquaver	sixteenth-note
demisemiquaver	thirty-second-note
hemidemisemiquaver	sixty-fourth-note

PART I

General Problems of Interpretation

1

An Authentic Eighteenth-Century Performance Source: C. F. Colt's Organ-Barrels

What would we not give to possess eighteenth-century gramophone records, if not by one of the great masters, then at least by a professional performer! Such a performance would tell us more than the treatises, for all their rules and regulations, which often left the simplest things unsaid because they were apparently familiar to everyone.

The fulfilment of such a wish would seem to be a Utopian dream, for Edison's phonograph, the first recording apparatus, was invented about a hundred years 'too late'. However, authentic eighteenth-century recordings have survived in the shape of a handful of musical clocks and barrel-organs, which, by some miracle, have remained in playable condition. Such mechanical instruments should be compared less with records than with the kind of electronic music produced on synthesizers. They are not the result of live performances, but laboriously 'assembled', note by note and pin by pin. This means that, apart from some unavoidable rhythmic imprecision caused by bent pins, nothing is the result of chance. There are practically no wrong notes. The price one pays for this is an almost total lack of spontaneity, and often a rather mannered style with which the maker sought to overcome it.

I should like at this point to describe the events which led me to make these observations. About thirty years ago, when I first visited C. F. Colt (he later became my friend 'Mick') in Bethersden, Kent, I was primarily interested in his important collection of early harpsichords and pianos. It is difficult to describe how surprised and delighted I was when from among his treasures Colt produced a medium-sized barrel-organ in working order and proceeded to play an eighteenth-century march. In a way this machine could be compared to a record-player, and for a time it even made me forget Colt's collection of keyboard instruments. By an even greater stroke of luck it was accompanied by a fairly comprehensive collection of barrels ranging from 'pop' to 'classical', in this case from folk-melodies and folk-dances to Handel's organ concertos. A surprising aspect was the extremely conservative nature of the 'serious' music. If, as we now think, this barrel-organ by Henry Holland can really be assigned to the last decades of the eighteenth century, then the music which was 'modern' at the time, such as that of Johann Christian Bach, was conspicuous by its absence.

Colt's organ with its barrels differed from other surviving mechanical organs and musical clocks with regard to its Handel repertoire. In addition to movements from Handel's operas (e.g. a gavotte from *Ottone* and minuets from *Arianna*, *Rodelinda*, and *Samson*) it included (and in this respect it was probably unique) two organ concertos—Op. 4 No. 2 in B flat major and Op. 4 No. 5 in F major. At the time I listened for hours to these 'recordings'. It was moving to watch Mick turning the small squeaking mechanism until he was exhausted, sometimes repeating a passage at my request. From a modern standpoint it was certainly not an elevating musical experience. The tone of the pipes was not very good, and the unchanging dynamics, despite occasional variations in registration, were wearily monotonous. Yet these tunes must have been familiar to all sorts of English listeners, and it says something about the enormous popularity of Handel that they included several of his works. Whereas Handel never fell out of favour in England, it is unfortunately wishful thinking to imagine that German or Flemish organ-barrels at the end of the eighteenth century might have played extracts from Bach's cantatas. Searching for such barrels would be a vain endeavour.

Many years have passed since this first encounter. In the mean time Colt's barrels have been lubricated and restored, and their artistic and historical significance has been investigated and assessed by several noted musicologists and musicians.[1] A record that includes pieces by Handel and some folk-songs appeared in 1985.[2] Although I left the musicological evaluation to others, I had the pleasure of being the first performer able to draw some conclusions from the little barrel-organ. These observations certainly influenced my view of eighteenth-century style. At the time Colt very kindly provided me with tapes of almost the entire repertoire, so that I was able to listen to it undisturbed at home. When the tapes arrived the well-known conductor Charles Mackerras (not as yet elevated to knighthood) happened to be staying with us. I still remember how we listened to them and the lively discussion which ensued. Mackerras of course knew far more about early English music than I did, and was thus able to point out certain differences between the original and the arrangements which would probably have escaped my notice.

[1] David Fuller, *G. F. Handel, Two Ornamented Organ Concertos, Op. 4 Nos. 2 and 5, as Played by an Early Barrel Organ* (Hackensack, NJ, 1980), 'Mechanical Instruments as a Source for the Study of *notes inégales*', *Bulletin of the Musical Box Society International*, 20 (1974), and 'Analyzing the Performance of a Barrel Organ', *The Organ Yearbook*, 11 (1980); Arthur W. J. G. Ord-Hume, 'Ornamentation in Mechanical Music', *Early Music*, 11 (1983), 185–93.

[2] *Handel, un enrégistrement d'epoque* (sleeve-note by Olivier Roux), Erato, Paris ERA 9274, RC 250.

All the pieces were in fact arrangements, and all, including the folk-tunes, were richly embellished. The application of 'trills' and 'fancy-work' is a common feature of almost all musical clocks. (Even today I distinctly remember a melody from *La Traviata* in a musical-box version from my earliest childhood which had a similar number of trills and arpeggios.) However, it must be said in defence of the English arranger of the pieces by Handel that he added embellishments with taste and with a certain 'English' reticence. As a rule the embellishments were profuse, yet they were applied only to the main melody.

What then were our observations (which, incidentally, have been confirmed on a number of occasions since)? First of all we were struck by the fact the music was played too quickly. Most of the tempos were fast, and some pieces were taken at breakneck speed.

Readers will no doubt want to know whether it is in fact possible to determine tempos from a barrel turned by hand, and whether the speed of the music corresponds to the rotational speed of the barrel. How can changes in this relationship be measured? It is in fact easier to do this than one might think, even though it is impossible to achieve total accuracy. Evidently the mechanism is designed to produce the 'correct' tempo only at the slowest possible rotational speed, that is, the slowest possible regular speed still able to supply the pipes with enough air.[3] If one exceeds this slowest possible speed, the music becomes a mere caricature of itself, and it is impossible to hear anything clearly. Yet even at slow rotational speeds the tempos still seemed to be too fast. One could of course be content merely to register this fact. However, a practical musician immediately wishes to know the reasons for it, and its bearing on performance practice.

The first explanation is of course that in the eighteenth century music was generally played faster than it is today. Yet this is only one of several possibilities. Another explanation might be that it was simply a question of cramming as much music as possible on one barrel, possibly for financial reasons. The majority of those who bought them were probably not very rich. This aspect is often overlooked today, though not so long ago a 78 r.p.m. record was limited to a maximum of four and a half minutes, so that even famous musicians had to select incredibly fast tempos in order to 'compress' a piece on to one side.

Back to the organ-barrels. A third reason for the amazingly fast speeds, particularly with regard to the ornaments, may have been a wish to demonstrate that mechanical 'fingers' are faster than human ones. (Welte piano-rolls provide a recent parallel. Unlike in the case of records and tapes, the speed can be increased without raising the pitch or altering the tone-colour. Thus, while making a record of Emil Sauer's Welte roll of Liszt's

---

[3] See Fuller, pref. to *G. F. Handel: Two Ornamented Organ Concertos*.

Réminiscences de Don Juan, some Soviet engineers amused themselves by increasing the speed dramatically, so that Sauer completely eclipsed Horowitz. In actual fact Sauer tended to take quite leisurely tempos, as Viennese audiences well remember.)

A fourth possible explanation escaped our notice at the time. The organ had not yet been restored, and air was escaping through the defective mechanism (leaking valves and bellows), so that one had to turn the handle fairly fast in order to maintain enough air pressure in the pipes. When I last visited Colt in Bethersden shortly before he died, he once again played some Handel on the organ, which in the mean time had been carefully restored. The tempos were still fast, though not as exaggerated as before, and coincided more with my own view of the music. The illusion that one was listening to a virtuoso organist was enhanced by the presence of four different stops.

This experience showed that it is wise to think twice before jumping to conclusions. Yet the differences in tempo noted before and after the organ had been restored were relatively small. That our initial observations concerning the surprisingly fast tempos were largely correct is corroborated by the following.

Another mechanical organ once existed whereby the second possibility (hurried tempos for the sake of economy) certainly did not apply. This was the Earl of Bute's great 'machine organ' in Luton Park. Built in 1762–3, it was unfortunately destroyed by fire in 1843 together with its fifty-eight barrels. This was a great loss, for, with a second, smaller, instrument for the Earl's country house (neither the organ nor the barrels have survived), it had four barrels with works by Corelli, seven with works by Vivaldi, and no fewer than thirty-six (!) with vocal and instrumental works by Handel, all recorded by John Christopher Smith the younger (1712–95), whose father had been Handel's copyist and amanuensis for twenty-four years.[4] Though the organ was destroyed by fire, a book by Alexander Cumming dating from 1812 has survived.[5] This contains a catalogue of all the barrels with precise information about the duration of each movement. On the basis of the identifiable pieces, William Malloch calculated metronome markings by dividing the duration in each case by the number of bars. This was possible because according to Cumming *no cuts* had been made in the works concerned. Gaps between movements (sometimes of over a minute)[6] indicated that the barrel-maker had not deliberately compressed the tempos. Malloch compared his results with various modern recordings and came to conclusions similar to ours: the majority of movements were played substantially faster than we are

---

[4] See William Malloch, 'The Earl of Bute's Machine Organ: A Touchstone of Taste', *Early Music*, 11 (1983), 172–83.

[5] *A sketch of the properties of the Machine Organ Invented, Constructed, and Made by Mr. Cumming, for the Earl of Bute, and a Catalogue of the Music on the Various Barrels, Numbered from One to Sixty-Four* (London, 1812), mentioned in Malloch, 'The Earl of Bute's Machine Organ', p. 182 n. 1.

[6] On barrel 23, even 2 min. 56 sec.; see Malloch, 'The Earl of Bute's Machine Organ', p. 174.

accustomed to today (on average in a ratio of three to four, according to Malloch). Yet an acceleration of this magnitude seems fairly implausible. Even if one assumes that Malloch based his observations on the slowest recordings of baroque works, a ratio of three to four would change an Allegro moderato ($\quarternote$ = 126) into an Allegro assai quasi presto ($\quarternote$ = c.168). Neither players nor listeners would be able to make much sense of this. Of course, we must not forget that these reconstructions are conjectural. As the barrels themselves are no longer in existence, it is impossible to substantiate the claim that the pieces had no cuts. In the case of da capo forms in particular we do not know whether the first section was repeated in its entirety. A shortened da capo would naturally give us a slower overall tempo calculated on the basis of duration divided by number of bars. (Malloch is of course aware of this problem.) If, however, we employ other eighteenth-century ways of calculating tempo, such as Quantz's comparison with a pulse of eighty beats per minute (see p. 292 n. 67), then the acceleration compared with modern practice would be about ten to fifteen per cent. This smaller increase in tempo still makes it possible to articulate clearly, a basic requirement of the age, and to hear the small note-values distinctly, as is demanded by all the theorists.

However, a handful of movements on the Earl of Bute's barrels were just as fast as or even slower than modern renditions (barrel 49, No. 4, 'Sound an Alarm' and chorus from *Judas Maccabeus*, 4 minutes 17 seconds, Allegro a tempo giusto 6/8, $\dottedquarternote$ = 61).

Of particular interest to Bach scholarship are those Vivaldi concertos in the collection that Bach also transcribed for harpsichord or organ. For example, the Largo from the E major Violin Concerto Op. 3 No. 12 (the second movement of Bach's transcription for solo harpsichord in C major, BWV 976) lasts 2 minutes 42 seconds at $\quarternote$ = 50. In the B minor Concerto for four violins (Bach's A minor Concerto for four harpsichords, BWV 1065), the Allegro lasts 3 minutes 42 seconds at $\quarternote$ = 112, the Largo, 40 seconds at $\quarternote$ = 72, the Larghetto 1 minute 10 seconds at $\quarternote$ = 72, and the final Allegro 3 minutes 15 seconds at $\dottedquarternote$ = 77; and the Allegro and Larghetto from the A minor Concerto for two violins Op. 3 No. 8, R. 522 (Bach's A minor Organ Concerto, BWV 593) last respectively 3 minutes 27 seconds at $\quarternote$ = 109 and 2 minutes 51 seconds at $\eighthnote$ = 97. In the case of Handel's Organ Concerto Op. 4 No. 5, which is also on one of Colt's barrels, the tempos are approximately the same if the first Allegro is 'synchronized', though the introductory Larghetto is somewhat faster ($\quarternote$ = c.94 instead of $\quarternote$ = 75) on Colt's barrel.

What are the first conclusions of our investigation into the performance practice of the age of Bach and Handel? In very general terms we can say that music was often played more quickly in the eighteenth century than it is today. Quantz's tempo indications and those of other 'early metronomes' (such as pendulums) point to the same thing, as do Beethoven's 'insanely' fast metronome markings. Beethoven was indeed a child of the eighteenth century. The statement in the 'Nekrolog' that Bach preferred very lively tempos is of importance in this connection (see p. 16). That such an observation was considered worth making four years after Bach's death is in itself noteworthy. And it must be seen in the context of an age in which tempos were demonstrably faster than they are today.

In addition to the fast tempos we were struck by a second peculiarity of Colt's barrels: the rigorously strict time. Of course it is easier for a barrel-maker to maintain a uniform tempo than for a performer; he merely has to position the barlines on the drawing-board. But as this particular maker was evidently a master of his craft he could surely have achieved a more lively performance by means of agogic fluctuation (retardation and acceleration). The fact that he did not do so suggests that strict time was considered more important than agogic freedom. There are practically no concluding ritardandos; the pieces race straight to the end, a feature that often has a charm of its own.

This strict maintenance of a given tempo made a deep impression on me. Yet in contrast to this rigorous adherence to strict time there were numerous rhythmic irregularities *within* the beats, which were hardly noticeable. This conveyed the impression of slight inebriation. Another observation later proved to be without foundation. In the case of groups of notes of equal length (e.g. groups of 4 + 4 semiquavers) it seemed that slight irregularities on the lines of *notes inégales* had been introduced on Colt's barrels. A subsequent examination showed that these were not intentional, being merely the result of slightly bent pins or warped wooden barrels.[7] Other kinds of rhythmic freedom, for example with regard to dotting, may well have been intentional.

The dotted rhythms were a surprise, particularly in the introduction of the B flat major Concerto Op. 4 No. 2, which is in the style of a French overture (though the tempo marking is not 'Grave', but 'A tempo ordinario, e staccato'). The kind of 'French' over-dotting expected by early and modern theorists was virtually non-existent.[8] The notated values [♩ ♪♫♫] were not played [♩. ♪♫♫], but only slightly emphasized, like badly executed quintuplets—[♩ ♪♫♫]. On account of the astonishingly fast tempo (on the recording ♩ = 80–4) and the distinct break after the long note the performance none the less gave the impression of being 'baroque' performance practice.[9] With regard to Handel's overtures this observation indicates that his notated rhythms were on the whole to be played as written, and that the widespread practice of extreme over-dotting (which goes back to Dolmetsch) probably does not reflect eighteenth-century practice.

[7] See Fuller, 'Mechanical Instruments', and Ord-Hume, 'Ornamentation in Mechanical Music', p. 185.

[8] See Graham Pont, 'Handel's Overtures for Harpsichord or Organ: An Unrecognized genre', *Early Music*, 11 (1983), 309–22 (on Colt's mechanical organ see p. 319).

[9] Alfred Cortot used to apply almost imperceptible over-dotting in Chopin, e.g. in the introduction to the Fantasie Op. 49 and in the central section of the 3rd movement of the Sonata Op. 58.

It would have been of interest to know whether the barrel-maker, when transcribing the common Handelian rhythm of ♩ ♪♫♫♩ , would have interpreted the quaver as a quaver or as a semiquaver. I have been unable to find an example of this kind. However, it is important to note that in other movements dotted rhythms are usually sharpened, and that even equal quavers are over-dotted.[10] This is noticeable in the case of the Larghetto introduction of the F major Organ Concerto (see Ex. 1.1; see also Ex. 1.3).

Ex. 1.1. Handel, Organ Concerto Op. 4 No. 5, first movement, Larghetto

Bars 34–44, original notation

[10] The problem has recently been debated with some acrimony. With regard to the question of whether or not rhythmic notation should be performed as written, Graham Pont has suggested a sensible compromise, particularly in his most recent and comprehensive study, 'Handel and Regularization: A Third Alternative', *Early Music*, 13 (1985), 500–5.

Bars 34–40 as executed on Colt's barrel

At the time we were mainly concerned with the ornamentation, as regards both the execution of appoggiaturas, trills, and turns, and their free application where they were not in the original. The latter was evident only in a few works, such as the Handel organ concertos. In the majority of cases the lack of notated music made it impossible to distinguish between the composer's text and the barrel-maker's additions. With regard to the first category, the execution of the ornaments was in accordance with the strict eighteenth-century rules formulated by French and English theorists. The vast majority of long and short trills (always fast) began on the upper auxiliary, even in places where we would nowadays tend to begin on the main note, for instance in descending passages which without trills would probably be played legato. Of course, turns also began on the upper note. Appoggiaturas were mainly long and always played on the down-beat (*on* and not *before* the beat).

There was one very striking feature: though numerically in the minority, there were quite a few ornaments which began on the main note: trills, *Pralltriller*, mordents, snaps (*Schneller*), and snapped turns (*geschnellte Doppelschläge*). Obviously ornamentation practice at this time was not as rigid as we are often led to believe.

However, I was at the time and still am principally interested in Bach interpretation. Did any of these observations have a bearing on Bach, and if so, to what extent? The principal benefit from this fascinating encounter with the organ-barrels was the fact that they represented a living baroque tradition, even if they were made at least a generation after Bach and Handel. Neither the *galant* style, nor the rococo and early classical styles seemed to have had a significant influence. In spite of all objections on artistic grounds, it was an important source. Scholars will have to devote more time to these and other surviving barrels. For example, it would be of interest to establish the extent to which the various barrel-makers agreed or differed in the interpretation of the same work.[11] I do not know whether sufficient evidence has in fact survived for such an assessment. In any case, one is well advised to treat the barrels as one source among many, albeit an important one.

Viewed in this way, the principles of interpretation which were common to all schools may be applied to Bach, for example: strict time; with some reservations, a flowing, 'lively' tempo; and the practice of beginning long and short trills on the auxiliary where this does not impair the melodic line or the legato phrasing necessary in some passages, and where it does not lead to forbidden consecutives (e.g. fifths). On occasion additional ornaments should be added. Free embellishment is to some extent confirmed by other pieces by Handel. In the case of Bach, however, we must exercise extreme caution. After all, Scheibe accused him of having written out virtually everything in full. In this connection I ought to add that the many embellishments on these barrels are a characteristic feature of mechanical instruments. They compensate for the fact that such instruments are incapable of amplifying a held note by means of dynamics, vibrato, or tone-colour. For this reason even simple folk-songs, which were probably sung without ornaments at the time, are richly embellished. Thus in the case of Handel's organ concertos, for example, it would be rash to assume this to be anything more than the musical-clock style or to deduce that it is perhaps a quasi-authentic way of performing Handel.[12]

But back to the 'essential' ornaments. For a long time it has been my main concern as a performer, scholar, and teacher to prove that Bach was more 'musical' than many a modern performance would lead us to suspect. With regard to ornaments this suggests that his embellishments were governed by the melodic context and the laws of voice-leading, even where this involved a departure from contemporary rules. Colt's organ-barrels gave me unexpected support in this respect. For example, even though most of the trills begin on the upper auxiliary, there are quite a few trills and *Pralltriller* that start on the

---

[11] Though somewhat neglected in German-speaking countries, this has recently been thoroughly researched by British and American musicologists. Ord-Hume's pioneering work is of particular importance, and his study *Barrel-Organ* (London, 1978) can be regarded as a standard work on the subject. In his latest book, *Joseph Haydn and the Mechanical Organ* (Cardiff, 1982), he reveals the existence of three surviving organs with music by Haydn. The Musical Box Society International is dedicated to encouraging research on the subject. See also Ernst Simon, *Mechanische Musikinstrumente früherer Zeiten und ihre Musik* (Wiesbaden, 1960); Quentin Durward Bowers, *Encyclopedia of Automatic Musical Instruments* (New York, 1972); and David Fuller, 'An Introduction to Automatic Instruments', *Early Music*, 11 (1983), 164–6.

[12] To Fuller's credit he did not fall into this trap. His commentary judiciously weighs up the pros and contras of such interpretations.

main note. This is not merely an 'interpretation', but an incontrovertible fact determined by the arrangement of the pins on the barrels. And then of course Colt's mechanical organ is not an isolated case. French musicologists have examined similar barrels and have made similar observations with regard to fast tempos, strict time, and ornamentation. Françoise Cossart-Cotte examined the ornamentation, rhythm, and tempo on about 500 'musical documents' of this kind from the end of the eighteenth century. She summed up her findings thus. 'The ornamentation was treated with a great measure of freedom. The rhythm of the melody as a whole remains vigorous and strict, though complex. The performer moves freely between the strong beats . . . In the accompaniment the alterations follow the harmony. The tempos are very fast, though not impossible.'[13]

We shall now briefly examine some of the ornaments transcribed by David Fuller from the two Handel organ concertos preserved on Colt's barrels (see Ex. 1.2; for the original see the last four bars of Ex. 1.1*a*). In addition to a simple mordent the first system contains three suffixed trills beginning on the auxiliary, and a simple mordent. Yet the trills that embellish the resolutions of the two dissonant notes C and F in the two concluding bars begin on the main note.

Ex. 1.2. Handel, Organ Concerto Op. 4 No. 5, end of second movement

[13] '"Documents sonores" de la fin du XVIIIe siècle: leurs enseignements pour l'interprétation', *L'Interprétation de la musique française aux XVIIème et XVIIIème siècles* (Paris, 1974), 139–41.

Ex. 1.3. Handel, Organ Concerto Op. 4 No. 2, first movement, bars 46–9

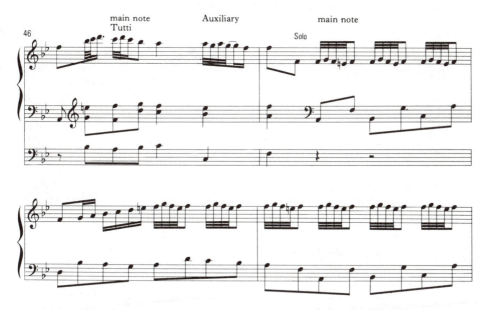

In the Exx. 1.3 and 1.4 the ornaments begin either on the auxiliary, or, 'contrary to the rules', on the main note.[14] What do these examples prove? They provide irrefutable evidence that certain ornaments were played in the late Baroque era which did not occur in the treatises. After all, eighteenth-century English theory was just as strict as French or North German theory with regard to beginning long and short trills on the auxiliary. However, what was right for the Anglo-Saxons might also have been right for the Saxons. In other words, even in central Germany players in the eighteenth century probably allowed themselves a certain degree of freedom in ornamentation, beginning a trill or a *Pralltriller* on the main note if the melodic context of a phrase made it seem appropriate, all the more so since the seventeenth-century German and Italian tradition of beginning trills and *Pralltriller* on the main note was still very much in use and the French style was only slow to gain acceptance.

[14] The notation in the top system of Ex. 1.3, the embellishments of which are surprisingly similar to those on Colt's barrel, stems from a MS of *c.*1760: Rowe Library, King's College, Cambridge, MS 251 (Fuller, *G. F. Handel: Two Ornamented Organ Concertos*, p. vi).

Ex. 1.4. Handel, Organ Concerto Op. 4 No. 2, last movement, bars 1–10, after D. Fuller, *G. F. Handel, Two Ornamented Organ Concertos*

2

Studies in Rhythm

INTRODUCTION

Whole books could and should be written about Bach's rhythm.[1] To date the literature that has accumulated on this subject is unfortunately rather small, and at times it is also misleading. There are of course a number of studies and polemics on the various aspects of rhythm in performance, but far too little has been written about the nature of Bach's rhythm as such. In restricting myself to certain aspects that are of importance for the performer, I am aware that I am merely concentrating on the tip of an iceberg, the greater part of which still remains to be discovered.

In contrast to composers of the Classical period, who, as is well known, often based their sonatas and symphonies on a number of rhythmically contrasting motifs and themes, baroque composers tended to construct movements upon rhythmically uniform motifs. This procedure is often referred to as 'uniform rhythm'. In fact even large-scale movements are pervaded by a constant rhythmic pattern embracing all the motifs. Where different motifs or themes are introduced within one movement in concertos by Corelli, Vivaldi, or Handel, to name only a few baroque composers, they are clearly subordinated to the tutti themes and only rarely introduce rhythmic contrast. Bach, whose rhythms are more varied than those of most of his contemporaries (with the exception of Domenico Scarlatti), also adheres

---

[1] Aspects of general interest are dealt with in Gustav Becking, *Der musikalische Rhythmus als Erkenntnisquelle* (Augsburg, 1928); Curt Sachs, *Rhythm and Tempo* (New York, 1958); and Robert Donington, *Tempo and Rhythm in Bach's Organ Music* (London and New York, 1960) and *Baroque Music: Style and Performance* (London, 1983). The latter contains an interesting compilation of quotations from 17th- and 18th-cent. theoretical works. There are also specialized studies by Anna Gertrud Huber, *Takt, Rhythmus, Tempo in den Werken von Johann Sebastian Bach* (Zurich, 1958) and Rudolf Steglich, *Tanzrhythmen in der Musik Johann Sebastian Bachs* (Wolfenbüttel and Zurich, 1960). See also the relevant sections of the books and articles by Bodky, Harnoncourt, Perl, O'Donnell, Frederick Neumann, and Pont listed in the Bibliography. Problems of rhythm are the central issue in Anthony Newman, *A Performing Guide to Baroque Music with Special Emphasis on the Music of J. S. Bach* (New York, 1985), though his conclusions must be treated with caution. George Houle, *Meter in Music 1600–1800: Notation, Perception and Performance* (Bloomington, Ind., 1987) is a particularly valuable contribution to this subject.

to this compositional principle, which means that a subsidiary theme, such as an idea assigned to solo violin or solo harpsichord, can be accompanied or enveloped by motifs from the introductory tutti theme, or that various themes can be combined in double fugues. This formal principle leads to the even flow characteristic of baroque music, a feature that has sometimes been poetically compared with an undulating ocean.

STRICT TIME: RIGIDITY OR FLEXIBILITY?

The rhythmically uniform style of composition alluded to above thus implies an even style of performance. Clearly, in works of the age of Bach the metre must in general be observed even more strictly than in music of the Classical period. Contemporary pronouncements on playing and conducting agree that the ability to maintain strict time is one of the most important qualities a musician ought to possess.

Thus Georg Muffat (1698) demanded 'that the tempo corresponding to the character of the piece' be maintained 'in constant uniformity, neither slower nor quicker, as long as the piece is being played'.[2] Johann Joachim Quantz was of the same opinion:

The leader of an orchestra must also know how to keep perfect time. He must be able to pay the most exact attention to the value of the notes, and particularly to the short semiquaver and demisemiquaver rests, so that he neither rushes nor drags. For if he makes a mistake in this regard, he misleads all the others, and produces confusion in the ensemble. After short rests it would be less harmful to begin later and then rush the following short notes a little than to anticipate them.[3]

In this connection it is worth recalling the reference to Bach's conducting quoted above: 'With regard to conducting he was very precise. The tempo, which he usually took very fast, was extremely steady.'[4] A century before Bach, Heinrich Schütz had perceived 'regular' time to be 'as it were the soul of music': 'The conductor should stand by the organ next to the soloists and give a regular, slow and appropriate beat (which is as it were both the soul and life of all music)'.[5] It is revealing to compare the 'slow beat' mentioned here with the remarks about Bach's conducting cited above.

---

[2] *Florilegium secundum* (Passau, 1698), p. 23; ed. H. Rietsch, Denkmäler der Tonkunst in Österreich, ii/2 (1895) (reprint vol. 4).

[3] *Versuch einer Anweisung, die Flöte traversiere zu spielen* (Berlin, 1752); trans. as *On Playing the Flute* (London, 1966; refs. are to New York pbk. edn., 1975), p. 208.

[4] 'Nekrolog', *Bach-Dokumente*, iii. 87.

[5] Pref. to *Auferstehungs-historia* (Dresden, 1628); repr. Leipzig, n.d.). The beat is also referred to as 'the soul of the music' by Martin Heinrich Fuhrmann, *Musicalischer Trichter* (Frankfurt an der Spree [Berlin], 1706); Johann Gottfried Walther, *Praecepta der musicalischen Composition* (Weimar, 1708), p. 33; and Leopold Mozart, *Versuch einer gründlichen Violinschule* (Augsburg, 1756), p. 27; trans. E. Knocker as *A Treatise on the Fundamental Principles of Violin Playing* (London, 1948).

There are, of course, moments in every piece where the rhythmic flow is compressed, interrupted, or brought to a standstill. To what extent does this apply to baroque music? It is a fact that in the music of Bach and his contemporaries notated modifications to tempo are very rare indeed. In addition, the age of Bach evidently had no great liking for ritardandos. Toccatas and fantasias, which we shall discuss later, are an exception to this rule, as are recitatives. Final ritardandos, if indeed they occurred, were certainly much less pronounced than is the custom today. This view is based on contemporary theory, and is corroborated by surviving eighteenth-century organ-barrels.

Yet it would be wrong to equate the maintenance of a regular beat with twentieth-century motoric rhythms. Between the firm 'pillars' of the beats there was a large degree of freedom. With the exception of pieces in *perpetuum mobile* style, there were all kinds of rubato, 'breathing pauses', breaks, and thematic dovetailing running counter to the beat. Bach's music in particular is 'long-winded', but even the strongest lungs have to be able to breathe somewhere. These 'pauses for breath' are most noticeable in the numerous works for wind instruments, such as concerto or cantata movements for solo flute, solo oboe, and so on. In practice the most suitable place for taking a breath usually proves to be between the first and second notes of a passage in semiquavers or triplets, which in fact corresponds to Bach's 'normal phrasing'. Longer pauses for breath (with a ritardando) are possible and indeed occasionally necessary at the natural caesuras within a form, for example the end of the middle section of a da capo aria, where cadenza-like runs or coloraturas often demand a fairly free treatment of the metre in any case.[6] Of course one should also 'breathe' between the end of a tutti theme and the following solo episode (but without a ritardando), even in solo keyboard music (see Ex. 2.1).

Ex. 2.1. Italian Concerto, BWV 971, first movement, bars 27–32: suggested execution with a 'pause for breath' in bar 30 (when playing a two-manual harpsichord without a coupler it is of course unnecessary to shorten the crotchet f^1 and a^1)

---

[6] This is confirmed by C. P. E. Bach: 'In slow or moderate tempos, caesurae are usually extended beyond their normal length . . . This applies to fermate, cadences, etc., as well as caesurae. It is customary to drag a bit and depart somewhat from a strict observance of the bar, for the note before the rest as well as

Making a break between the first and second notes of a melody is also to be recommended where the tempo changes from slow to fast. Thus, in passing from the Andante to the Allegro in the Sinfonia of Partita No. 2, it is advisable to retain the slow tempo on the final G major chord and not to embark on the faster tempo until the two semiquavers which follow. It is perhaps no accident that in the manuscript of *WTC* I, the 'Allegro' marking in the second prelude (C minor) is quite clearly over the *second* note of bar 35 (a fact no critical commentary has ever considered worth mentioning).

Naturally, the more or less strict maintenance of the metre depends on the basic rhythmic character of a work. An arioso allows one greater rhetorical freedom, more rubato, that is, than, for example, a gavotte or a minuet. The greatest 'agogic' freedom is permissible in freely structured forms such as the instrumental *stylus phantasticus* of the toccata and the fantasia. Works of this kind had their origins in instrumental improvisation, such as the free invention of preludes. Frescobaldi's often-cited directions in the prefaces to the toccatas concerning rhythmically free performance are equally applicable to many works of his pupil Froberger. It is possible to demonstrate the latter's influence on German composers in general and on Buxtehude and Bach in particular. Yet in the case of Bach, even in his toccatas, some caution is advisable.

A relative degree of independence of the beat also applies in the case of recitative, no matter whether it is vocal or instrumental.

At least it can be seen in accompanied recitatives that tempo and metre must be frequently changed in order to rouse and still the rapidly alternating affections. Hence, the metric signature is in many such cases more a convention of notation than a binding factor in performance. It is a distinct merit of the fantasia that, unhampered by such trappings, it can accomplish the aims of the recitative at the keyboard with complete, unmeasured freedom.[7]

A great measure of freedom is required. The experienced singer is aware of this, but the modern instrumentalist is often misled by the fact that recitatives are always notated in what amounts to 4/4 time. In passages *not* notated in this way, such as the recitative in the second prelude of *WTC* I (bar 34), industrious editors are at pains to preserve the 'four-beat' bar (see Ex. 2.2). Why? The NBA editors consider this to be a Bachian slip of the pen.

Despite this freedom, the relationships between the note-values must be approximately preserved, even in recitative. Thus it would be incorrect to play quavers faster than semiquavers. For the performer the most important task with regard to rhythm consists in recognizing the groupings of notes and

the rest itself is extended beyond its notated length.' (*Versuch über die wahre Art, das Clavier zu spielen* (Berlin, 1753 and 1762); trans. W. J. Mitchell as *Essay on the True Art of Playing Keyboard Instruments* (London, 1949), 375). On flexibility in baroque tempo see pp. 202 ff. See also Donington, *Baroque Music*, pp. 20 f.

[7] C. P. E. Bach, *Essay*, p. 153.

Ex. 2.2. *WTC* I, Prelude in C minor, bar 34

The manuscript and most of the copies

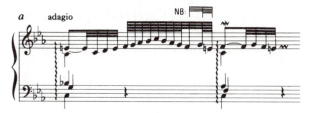

All editions except for Willard A. Palmer's edition (Sherman Oaks, Calif., 1981)

beats in all their diversity, and making them intelligible to the listener by means of greater or lesser accentuation, tension and relaxation, breathing and articulation, and by combining and separating them. This task is more complex in Bach than in many other composers in so far as the rhythmic patterns in his music are extremely diverse.

EMPHASIS, DECLAMATION, AND PERIOD STRUCTURE

At the beginning of a work by Bach there is the time signature, the significance of which has hardly changed since his time. (Metre and its relationship to tempo are discussed in greater detail in the next chapter.)

The basic rhythm in duple or triple time, no matter how it is notated, must be 'scanned', that is, a distinction needs to be made between strong and weak beats. Thus, in triple time, especially in dance movements, the first beat of the bar is far stronger than the last two. In 4/4 time, however, the first and third beats are 'strong' (the third is not quite as strong as the first), and the second and fourth are 'weak' (in the language of Bach's time, *schlecht* or *schlicht*). Though this rule is simple and is postulated by virtually every theorist,[8] it is

---

[8] e.g. C. P. E. Bach, *Essay*, p. 156. The nonsensical remarks on this subject in recent encyclopaedias of music (*MGG*, xi. 410 f. and *The New Grove Dictionary of Music*, ed. S. Sadie, London, 1980, 'Rhythm') are unbelievable. The latter states: 'Bach's music lacks differentiated nuances of emphasis; its rhythm moves evenly, 'objectively', without personal additive . . .' The author of this article excludes dance music and seems to be referring to polyphony, but the view he expresses merely reflects the kind of 'sewing-machine'

largely ignored nowadays, though one sometimes hears exaggerated accentuation. The principle of correct declamation also applies to smaller metrical subdivisions, such as groups of four quavers in 3/2 (the F major Prelude of *WTC* II), where the differences in emphasis might be graphically expressed thus:[9]  Correct declamation should also be applied to different

note values. It often corresponds to the metre of classical verse, as Bach's contemporaries Mattheson and Walther, and more recently Anna Gertrud Huber have pointed out. For example:

Such differences in emphasis originated in vocal declamation, which can also be applied to instrumental works. Composers have at all times been at pains to achieve the proper declamation of the words they set to music. If at all possible, verbal emphasis and musical accent were intended to coincide. In the case of purely instrumental works the distinction between 'strong' and 'weak' was self-evident in the eighteenth century, particularly in dance movements. In the minuet, for example, the second and third beats were played lightly, whereas in the sarabande the second beat often had a slight secondary emphasis, the main emphasis in both cases being on the first beat. In Germany words were added to instrumental themes for didactic purposes as late as the nineteenth century. Good examples from the time of Bach are provided by Johann Gottfried Walther in his *Praecepta der musicalischen Composition*:[11]

1. 2. 3. 4. 5. 6. 7. 8.
- ∪ - ∪ - ∪ - ∪

Mei – ne See – le ruft und schrey-et.

. . . according to their inherent value the first, third, fifth, and seventh notes are long; the second, fourth, sixth, and eighth short . . . The speech rhythm is subordinated to the barline. Thus the following arrangement is incorrect:

1. 2. 3. 4. 5. 6. 7. 8.   1.
- ∪ - ∪ - ∪ - ∪   -

Mei – ne See – le ruft und schrey– et.

music often heard 30 years ago. This befits the 20th cent. better than the 18th, though not even Prokofiev should be subjected to it. At any rate, it has nothing whatsoever to do with Bach.

[9] The scansion symbols for long and short quantities were transferred by Hugo Riemann and Arnold Schoenberg to musical notation, in which they express 'stressed' and 'unstressed' notes.

[10] In the case of the other rhythmic patterns, such as iambic (∪ –), trochee (– ∪), etc., this kind of declamatory underlay is impossible.

[11] (Reprint, Leipzig, 1955), p. 23.

For triple time Walther adduces similar correspondences between accent length and the position of the note within the bar.

This theory of accent length is peculiarly useful both in vocal and instrumental music, for hence derives the stylish restraint of the voice and the fingers whereby, that is, one emphasizes a note which is long, quantitatively speaking; whereas a note that is short, quantitatively speaking, is played slightly shorter and more softly.[12]

Walther's 'long–short' terminology suggests that he was thinking of *notes inégales* (see below, pp. 68 f.). Yet this is unlikely. Rather, it is a case of the quantities of spoken verse being applied to music. What may well have been long and short in Ancient Greece became stressed and unstressed (or strong and weak) in European languages, as every poetry reading proves. The same holds true of music. But as unstressed notes cannot be produced on the harpsichord through finger-pressure, the only means available is the abbreviation of note-values, for instance on the lines of the example above:

or very rarely thus: .

In orchestral or choral music 'long' and 'short' can only be taken to signify a difference in emphasis, for otherwise performances would be a chaotic affair. That this was so is confirmed by Johann Philipp Kirnberger, whose ideas derived from Bach himself. In the second part of his *Kunst des reinen Satzes* (1776–9) he discusses the important fact that larger musical units can also be perceived in terms of strong and weak: 'Both in duple and triple time there are melodies in which, clearly, whole bars are alternately strong and weak, so that one senses a whole bar as one beat.' In this case 'two bars must of necessity be taken together to make a single bar, the first part of which is long, and the second short.'[13] Obviously whole bars cannot be lengthened or abbreviated, for otherwise keeping time would be an illusion.

With regard to rhythm in performance, the first, relatively easy, task confronting the performer is to make the listener aware of the metre. To do this he must strive, especially at the beginning of a piece, to distinguish between strong and weak by means of articulation ('weighting', or emphasis and 'non-emphasis'); see Exx. 2.3–2.5. To my dismay I have often heard these subjects played as in Ex. 2.6. Of course the rhythm required by Bach sooner or later falls into place somehow or other, though the beginning is 'lost'. Particularly in cases where a theme (such as that of the G sharp minor

[12] *Musicalisches Lexicon* (Leipzig, 1732), quoted in Perl, *Rhythmische Phrasierung*, pp. 28 f.
[13] Quoted in Perl, *Rhythmische Phrasierung*, pp. 110 f.

Fugue of *WTC* II) is made up of equal note-values, the rhythm ought to be more clearly emphasized in the opening bars than later on.

Ex. 2.3. *WTC* I, Fugue in D minor, subject

Ex. 2.4. *WTC* II, Fugue in G sharp minor, subject

Ex. 2.5. *WTC* I, Fugue in B flat major, subject

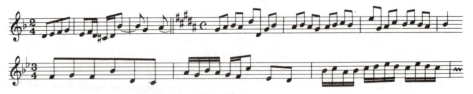

Ex. 2.6. Wrong articulation of preceding Examples

In the Praeambulum of Partita No. 5 the 3/4 metre demands that the first beats of bars 1 and 2 be firmly emphasized (see Ex. 2.7), for otherwise the listener will misinterpret them and hear an incorrect upbeat (Ex. 2.8). If the two G major chords are wrongly stressed, the opening might also be interpreted as the down-beat of a 3/2 bar. However, the rhythmic ambiguity

Ex. 2.7. Partita No. 5, BWV 829, Praeambulum, bars 1–4

Ex. 2.8

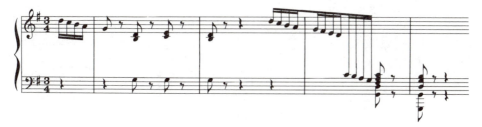

of this theme may in fact be intentional (cf. the Polonaise of the B minor Orchestral Suite).

In the case of simple dance forms whose character has changed little over the centuries, strong and weak beats should be clearly distinguished. It is of interest in this respect to compare bars 1–8 of the Gavotte from the G minor English Suite (Ex. 2.9) with the theme of the third movement of Mozart's B flat major Sonata K. 281/189*f* (Ex. 2.10). In spite of the stylistic differences they have much in common, for instance the 2 × 4 bar period structure typical of dance forms. In both cases a very slight break should therefore be made after the first phrase, about as long as a good singer would require to breathe if he sang the first four bars in one breath. The second common element is the ambiguous rhythm of the gavotte. As the opening half-bar coincides with a relatively strong beat, the listener is initially uncertain whether it is an up-beat or a down-beat. After all, the first barline could well be two crotchets to the

Ex. 2.9. English Suite No. 3, BWV 808, Gavotte, bars 1–8

Ex. 2.10. Mozart, Piano Sonata K. 281/189*f*, Rondeau, bars 1–8.

right.[14] This rhythmic ambiguity has a charm of its own.[15] Only as the movement proceeds does it become clear, especially in the case of Mozart, that the beginning was an up-beat. If Mozart had composed bars 3 and 4 differently, for instance as in Ex. 2.11, the theme would have started on the down-beat.

Ex. 2.11

[14] On this point Alfred Dürr commented: '1. There are many examples—at least in non-dance music—in which Bach simply moves a theme two crotchets to the left or to the right. This qualifies the above observations. 2. At the beginning of a piece within a suite such as the Gavotte of BWV 808, around 1720 it was immediately apparent that it was a gavotte, a dance which, as is well known, begins with two crotchets. It was something that was virtually impossible to misunderstand.' There are good examples of rebarrings in Robert Marshall, *The Compositional Process of J. S. Bach*, i (Princeton, 1972), pp. 71–4.

[15] Common to both themes is the fact that they are works of genius that create 'themes for eternity' from a handful of notes. Both are dance themes, but whereas Bach creates a large, unified gesture, Mozart presents a finely chiselled *galant* theme that delights in small subdivisions.

Bach would probably have considered the agglomeration of 'little sighs', particularly in bars 3 and 4, to be too rococo (though he also wrote some *galant* pieces adorned with sighs, such as the *Capriccio sopra la lontananza del suo fratello dilettissimo* in B flat, BWV 992, and the slow movements of the trio sonata in the *Musical Offering*, BWV 1079). In fact one only has to eliminate a number of the Mozartian sighs or suspensions in this theme to arrive at what is almost a Bachian theme, a sign of how close in fact the two geniuses were (see Ex. 2.12). In the case of the 'real' Bach gavotte, in addition to the overall division into 4 + 4 bars, it is above all a question of recognizing and sensing the rhythmic tensions (see Ex. 2.13). Here the stroke of genius is the reversal of 'long–short–short' to 'short–short–long' in bar 3, which must be sensed as a rhythmic retardation. A minor eighteenth-century composer would probably have continued as in Ex. 2.14. This would still be an attractive 'French' gavotte, but it would not be Bach.

Ex. 2.12

Ex. 2.13. English Suite No. 3, BWV 808, Gavotte I, bars 1–8

Meaning of signs:
- = tenuto or 'strong' note
= = tenuto and emphasized note, slightly stronger than –
∪ = unstressed, 'weak' note
⏞ = staccato, not too short

Ex. 2.14

Yet gavotte notation with an up-beat of two crotchets does not always indicate that a movement should begin unstressed. An interesting example of such 'false barlines' is provided by the Air from Partita No. 6 (see Ex. 2.15).[16]

Ex. 2.15. Partita No. 6, BWV 830, Air, bars 1–12

Here stressing the down-beats would result in unmusical accentuation (Ex. 2.16). Why then did Bach arrange them in this way? Surely because after four and a half bars the rhythm continues differently. In modern notation this change of

Ex. 2.16

---

[16] I am grateful to Klaus Hofmann for pointing out to me that this effect is linked to the harmony. The tonic triad in root position has so much more weight than the 2 ensuing 6th chords (dominant minor, subdominant) that we hear it as a strong beat. (Furthermore, there is the familiar gambit of a descending 4th in the bass.) There is a serious error in NBA, bar 29: the *d* in both hands should be *e*.

Ex. 2.17

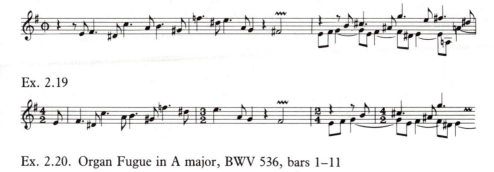

accent could be clarified by means of the notation shown in Ex. 2.17. A conflict between what is notated and what is heard often arises when a piece begins with a long rest (see Ex. 2.18). Initially, rests of this kind cannot be perceived by the player and the listener. We hear the version shown in Ex. 2.19. The rhythmic ambivalence in the A major Organ Fugue, BWV 536, the beginning of which can be heard both in terms of 3/4 (as notated) and 3/2, is particularly attractive (see Ex. 2.20).

Ex. 2.18. Partita No. 6, BWV 830, Gigue, bars 1–3

Ex. 2.19

Ex. 2.20. Organ Fugue in A major, BWV 536, bars 1–11

With regard to period structure, apart from simple dances, unfigured chorales occupy an important place in Bach's output by virtue of their popular, rhythmically uncomplicated quality. With the exception of the fermatas these are song-like movements with a very simple period structure, mostly of 4 + 4 bars. It is common knowledge that many chorales are adaptations of German folk-songs, which originally were rhythmically freer and more varied than the chorales. However, in the course of about two hundred years this diversity gradually disappeared to be replaced by a simplified, march-like style, probably as a result of the practical problems involved when they were sung by large congregations. The rhythmic impoverishment was almost compensated for by the evolution of harmonic sophistication. Bach's four-part chorale harmonizations, which his son Carl Philipp Emanuel assembled into a collection, are some of his most beautiful works and should be in every Bach library. The richness of invention is inexhaustible, and one is continually amazed by striking and unexpected progressions. The rhythmic structure of the chorales would be easy to render in performance were it not for the fermatas. There is often disagreement today about whether or not they should be held. Some performers confuse them with 'long-term car-parks', though most conductors with 'No Waiting' signs. They race through them as if a traffic warden were about to give them a parking-ticket. However, these fermatas should not be ignored, if only because the majority of the chorales in Bach's cantatas and Passions are stylized *congregational* singing. We may safely assume that this has hardly changed in the course of time. A more or less lengthy pause has always been made at the chorale fermata in order to breathe. Apart from such practical considerations, I do not, as a musician, like the undesirable march-like character thus evoked.

The lack of pauses in many a performance is no doubt due to the fact that even respected Bach conductors tend to jump to conclusions about the original chorales on the basis of the chorale preludes. There is no doubt that chorales in these works should be played without a break, for the other voices do not have fermatas. On the other hand, there are also chorale preludes with elaborated *Versettln* (organ versets) between the phrases, which could be an argument in favour of (occasional) pauses for breath in the congregational chorales.[17]

It is particularly important to convey a sense of period structure in slow dance movements. Few musicians are aware that the eight-bar period predominates even in the case of allemandes and sarabandes bristling with notes, and that in the majority of instances the first section consists of exactly eight bars. In order to phrase the music correctly it is important to think of larger units 'in one breath'. In his study *Tanzrhythmen in der Musik Johann Sebastian Bachs* Steglich demonstrated this with reference to the Allemande of the E major French Suite (see Ex. 2.21). This 'conjoining of what belongs together' will also help the performer to avoid the pitfalls of unduly slow tempos.

---

[17] Neumann, *Ornamentation*, p. 546, is also in favour of (brief) fermatas in chorales. See also Christoph Albrecht, *Interpretationsfragen. Probleme der kirchenmusikalischen Aufführungspraxis von Johann Walter bis Max Reger (1524–1916)* (Berlin, 1981), 176 f.

Ex. 2.21. French Suite No. 6, BWV 817, Allemande, bars 1–4, in Steglich's interpretation (*Tanzrhythmen*, chapter 2, note 1)

THE INTERACTION OF RHYTHM AND DYNAMICS IN POLYPHONIC WORKS

Staggered Lines of Tension

The rhythmic possibilities in works of a polyphonic character are more complex than those in the dance and song forms discussed above. Here one of the most important principles (which few performers understand) is that of 'complementary rhythm'. Good polyphonic pieces have always been composed in such a way that as a rule accents and 'non-accents' in the various voices do not coincide. Rather, with the exception of final cadences, they are staggered. This means that while the tension increases in one voice, it decreases in another. The principle is particularly evident in the case of strettos as in the D sharp minor Fugue of *WTC* I (Ex. 2.22).

For this reason it is important, in terms of dynamics, to shape the course of a theme correctly right from the start, especially in the many instances where this goes against the time signature, such as the opening of the same fugue (Ex. 2.23).[18] One must resist the temptation to turn this into an up-beat (see

[18] Hofmann comments: 'Stylistically the D sharp minor Fugue is an example of the *stylus gravis* (*motecticus*, *antico*), a mensural style lacking accented beats. When writing in this style at the time of Bach, composers had to make a conscious effort to suppress or repress the accented beat (by introducing counter accents, etc., or deliberate irregularities).'

Ex. 2.22. *WTC* I, Fugue in D sharp minor, bars 50–1

Ex. 2.23. *WTC* I, Fugue in D sharp minor, bars 1–3

Chapter 10, pp. 224 f. and 236). Nevertheless the underlying 4/4 time is not altogether abrogated, remaining in the background as a kind of safeguard. The immense variety of tension in polyphonic pieces is demonstrated by two telling examples from the E flat Prelude in *WTC* I, quoted by Peter Williams (see Ex. 2.24).

Ex. 2.24. *WTC* I, Prelude in E flat major, bars 10–14, 25–8, after Peter Williams, 'A New Approach to Bach's Well-tempered Clavier', *Early Music*, 11 (1983)

The Relationship between Rhythm and Personality in Bach's Music: the
Symbolism of Faith and of the Cross

One reason for the growing interest in the music of Bach may be the fact that
even listeners who know little about music history intuitively sense that it has
an elemental strength which induces reassurance, confidence, and courage.
These works are not only the utterances of a musical genius, but also of a
stable, non-neurotic character, of someone who drew his strength from an
unshakeable faith in God.[19] This strength, which can as it were be sensed in
every note, finds particular expression in the rhythm. Clearly, the performer
must sense and re-create it in order, as a medium (or intermediary), to convey
it to the listener. Let us consider some of Bach's themes from this angle.

Ex. 2.25. Organ Fugue in C major, BWV 564, subject

   1. *C major Organ Fugue, BWV 564.* This subject (Ex. 2.25) consists of a
rhythmically striking head-motif and its *Fortspinnung* or continuation. The
thematic core is the ascending major triad C–E–G–C, or C–E–G–F–A–C
enriched by the subdominant harmony in bar 3, to which is added the
neighbour-note d^2 of the *Fortspinnung*. Themes of this kind have always been
symbolic of strength, and it is thus no accident that the choral fugue in
Cantata No. 50, *Nun ist das Heil und die Kraft* exhibits a melodic affinity to the
subject of this fugue (see Ex. 2.26). When performing the fugue it hardly
needs to be said that the theme should be played in the style of a fanfare, non
legato that is, so that the rests in bars 2, 4, and 6 are charged with tension and
not felt to be breaks. The notes in these bars should really be stressed, but as
this is obviously impossible on the organ, g^1, a^1, and c^2 must be held slightly
longer than the remaining quavers in order to increase the amount of sound.
   2. *A minor Fugue, WTC II.* At the beginning of this fugue (Ex. 2.27) the
unique feature is the rhythmic design, not the melodic invention. The head-
motif itself was an old formula often elaborated in the Baroque era. It

[19] Graphological studies of the handwriting of the great composers have shown that Bach and Joseph
Haydn are among the handful of creative musicians who display no neurotic features. It would of course be
quite wrong to see this as the sole positive criterion of creative power or musical greatness. Geniuses who
were ill or unstable have written some of the greatest masterpieces. One only has to think of Wagner or
Gustav Mahler, who freed themselves of their illnesses in their works. (See also Epilogue, pp. 521 ff.)

Ex. 2.26. Cantata No. 50, *Nun ist das Heil und die Kraft*, bars 1–8

Ex. 2.27. *WTC* II, Fugue in A minor, bars 1–4

contained both a symbol of the Cross and a symbol of pain: if lines are drawn to link the first and fourth, and second and third notes, a St Andrew's cross results (see Ex. 2.28). Furthermore, for centuries the descending diminished seventh (here f^1–$g\sharp$) was considered to be a symbol of pain. Thus it is not surprising that it occurs in Handel's *Messiah* (the chorus 'And with His Stripes we are Healed', Isaiah 53: 5; see Ex. 2.29) and, half a century after Bach, in Mozart's Requiem (the Kyrie double fugue; Ex. 2.30).

Ex. 2.28

Ex. 2.29. Handel, *Messiah*, No. 22, bars 1–8

Ex. 2.30. Mozart, Requiem, Kyrie double fugue, bars 1–4

All this was common musico-symbolic cultural property. However, what distinguishes Bach's theme from the versions of Handel and Mozart is the rhythm of the continuation. After a pregnant pause (being a 'starting-point', the g♯ should be emphasized or slightly lengthened), there are two more 'crosses' in rhythmic diminution, and a further acceleration to an eighth of the original note-values (demisemiquavers instead of crotchets). This rapid figuration is also permeated with Cross symbolism (E–A–C–F♯, etc.).[20]

Ex. 2.31. *WTC* II, Fugue in E major, bars 1–3

3. *E major Fugue*, WTC *II*. The rhythm of this theme (Ex. 2.31) is more unchanging than that of the two quoted above, but this does not diminish its vigour. It would be easy to apply the words 'Credo in unum deum', as in the related theme from the B minor Mass (Ex. 2.32). For this reason it would be quite wrong to play it gently and in a lingering manner (though this is often done).

In this context it seems appropriate to mention the significance of the concepts of symbolism, figure, and affection in the music of the Baroque era. Symbols and figures presuppose extramusical knowledge, whereas the 'affections' make a more or less direct appeal to the senses. (In reality it is often impossible to make a strict distinction between the three concepts.) The difference between symbols and figures is that in the case of symbols the

---

[20] The substantial literature on the subject of symbolism in Bach, which has been mentioned only in passing, ranges from Albert Schweitzer to Arnold Schmitz and Friedrich Smend. Of recent pubs. the best are H. Heinrich Eggebrecht, *Bachs 'Kunst der Fuge'. Erscheinung und Deutung*, 2nd edn. (Munich, 1985), and 'Affekt und Symbolik' in Albrecht, *Interpretationsfragen*, pp. 157–66.

Ex. 2.32. Mass in B minor, Credo, No. 12, bars 1–7.

meaning is to a large extent deduced in an intellectual manner, and is not immediately apparent in musical terms, whereas figures, which usually derive from the rhetorical tradition, can be directly perceived by the senses.[21] Thus large numerical groupings cannot be heard, for instance the number of symbols 14 and 41 ('Bach' and 'J. S. Bach' according to the numerical alphabet in which a = 1, b = 2, etc.). However, it is possible to hear the diminished fourth (*quarta falsa* or *saltus duriusculus*) as an image of what is 'false and hard'; the *gradatio* (climax) for climaxes; ascending lines ('They went up to the Mount of Olives'); or chorale quotations, the textual significance of which was obvious to all. On the borderline between symbol and figure are the Cross symbols mentioned above or B–A–C–H themes, which can only express 'Bach' in German. Bach used figures in a manner reminiscent of Wagnerian leitmotifs a century later; they too revealed complex relationships with the help of memory.

DEVIATIONS FROM REGULAR METRE IN HOMOPHONIC MUSIC

Whereas the metre can be interrupted or partly abrogated by staggered thematic entries or strettos in fugues and other polyphonic pieces, it is usually more persistent in dance movements. Nevertheless, Bach's music frequently deviates from the regular metre. It is the performer's task to recognize this fact, and to play such passages correctly.

By far the most common deviation in triple time is the hemiola. This occurs in 3/8, for example, when there are rhythmic patterns that are felt to constitute three groups of two quavers (i.e. three crotchets). There is an instance of this in the Prelude of the English Suite No. 3 (Ex. 2.33). Sometimes hemiolas are also placed across a barline, as in bars 3–4 of the Gigue of English Suite No. 1 (Ex. 2.34) The opposite happens when 6/4 bars

---

[21] See Eggebrecht, *Bachs 'Kunst der Fuge'*, p. 87.

Ex. 2.33. English Suite No. 3, BWV 808, bars 29–31

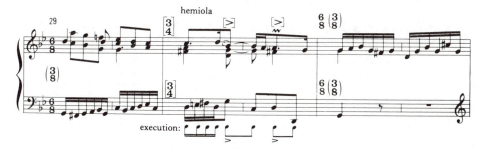

Ex. 2.34. English Suite No. 1, BWV 806, Gigue, bars 1–4

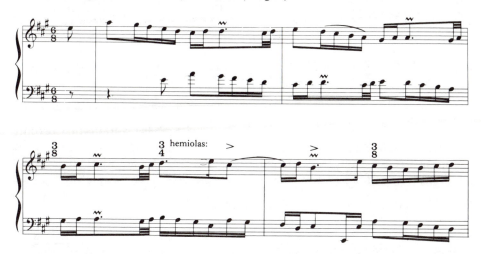

(two groups of three crotchets) are inserted into 3/2 metre, as at the end of the Courante from Partita No. 2 (Ex. 2.35).

Playing such passages poses no problems. However, the Bach performer is faced with a more difficult and interesting task when hemiolas occur in only one of two voices (the other maintaining the basic metre). Good examples of

Ex. 2.35. Partita No. 2, BWV 826, Courante, bars 23–4

Ex. 2.36. Partita No. 2, BWV 826, Rondeau, bars 25–32

this are found in the Rondeau of Partita No. 2 (Ex. 2.36), and in the Corrente of Partita No. 6 (Ex. 2.37). The rhythmic combinations in the Corrente of the C minor French Suite are particularly delightful. In addition to 'normal' hemiolas (units of 3/2), such as bars 14–15 and 36–7 (see Ex. 2.38), there are

Ex. 2.37. Partita No. 6, BWV 830, Corrente, bars 11–15

Ex. 2.38. French Suite No. 2, BWV 813, Corrente, bars 36–8

also, in bars 46[22] and 54, hemiolas in the bass against upper-voice figuration that can be played in 3/8 or in 3/4 (Ex. 2.39). This does not mean that the 3/8 passages ought to be specially emphasized, for the peculiar charm of the piece is precisely the fact that the figuration contradicts the metre.

Ex. 2.39. French Suite No. 2, BWV 813, Corrente, bars 46–55

The Sarabande of the French Overture contains a particularly sophisticated example of rhythmic design. Here, in the top and middle voices, a hemiola follows the main motif in bars 2 and 3. At the same time the lower voice, in imitation of the beginning, maintains 3/4, and in addition, in bar 4, prepares for the continuation of the period (bar 5 of the top voice; see Ex. 2.40).

Ex. 2.40. French Overture, BWV 831, Sarabande, bars 1–5

---

[22] This subtle nuance does not appear in the earlier versions of the suite.

Ex. 2.41. Partita No. 5, BWV 829, Minuet, bars 1–5 (NBA mistakenly gives the third note of bar 5 as $f\sharp^2$)

From this toying with various rhythmic possibilities it is but a small step to the rhythmic witticism in the Minuet of the G major Partita (Ex. 2.41). In the first three bars the listener is lulled into believing that he is hearing 6/8, though bar 4 makes it clear that it was 3/4 all along. Bar 4 should thus be a revelation. For this reason the performer should not play the preceding 'deceptive bars' in 'genuine' 6/8 time, but in such a way that the minuet tempo is still faintly audible. This can be achieved by slightly emphasizing the penultimate quaver (Ex. 2.42). Such differences in emphasis are also possible

Ex. 2.42. Partita No. 5, BWV 829, Minuet, bars 1–5

on good harpsichords. On a two-manual harpsichord the double-stemmed notes could be played on the first manual and the rest on the second, both lightly. A buff or lute stop sounds rather attractive here. The final 'explanation' in the minuet first comes towards the end (bars 41–4), where the two rhythms are heard simultaneously for the first and only time and, in accordance with the old rhetorical principle, the knot is 'untied' (see Ex. 2.43).

Ex. 2.43. Partita No. 5, BWV 829, Minuet, bars 41–4

An even bolder and more original passage occurs in the Sarabande of the same partita (bars 24–8), where the undisguised four-beat groups in the bass are only 'held in check' by the persistence of 3/4 in the upper voice (see Ex. 2.44).

Ex. 2.44. Partita No. 5, BWV 829, Sarabande, bars 24–8

In the Corrente (3/2) of Partita No. 4 Bach even goes so far as to make a point of imitation enter at the 'wrong' interval of five crotchets (Ex. 2.45). This Corrente is altogether a curiosity from a rhythmic point of view, for in spite of the 3/2 time signature the first and last bars of both halves are in 6/4 time. In between the two metres are perpetually in conflict.[23]

Ex. 2.45. Partita No. 4, BWV 828, Corrente, bars 33–6

A passage in the Rejouissance of the Fourth Orchestral Suite in D major, BWV 1069, is almost Brahmsian in character. In bars 21 and 41 the accompanying middle voices emphasize the 3/4 dance rhythm, whilst the melody instruments are given three statements of a counter-rhythm in 4/4, which is freely imitated in the bass. This counter-rhythm must of course be accentuated quite clearly (see Ex. 2.46).

Such subtleties also occur in movements in duple and quadruple time. There is a good example in the Allemanda of Partita No. 6, where, in bars 5–6 and 11–12, 4/4 is 'contradicted' by a 'dotted motif' in 6/4 time (see Ex. 2.47).

---

[23] See Steglich, *Tanzrhythmen*, pp. 18–19.

Ex. 2.46. Orchestral Suite No. 4, BWV 1069, Rejouissance, bars 21–5

Ex. 2.47. Partita No. 6, BWV 830, Allemanda, bars 5–7

Similarly, in the B flat minor Fugue of *WTC* I, the 3/2 metre of the episode in bars 6–9 contradicts the alla breve time signature.

Lack of space makes it impossible to proceed from these small units to an investigation of larger rhythmic groupings (regular and irregular periods and groups of bars, etc.), though the above remarks may encourage the Bach performer to explore for himself the richness and diversity of Bach's rhythmic forms, which are often interlinked with number symbolism.

RHYTHMIC NOTATION THAT DIFFERS FROM MODERN PRACTICE

Although it is gratifying to see that familiarity with baroque performance practice has increased significantly in the last few decades, there are still quite a few musicians who play Bach 'as it is written', thus committing numerous errors. They (still) do not know that certain kinds of notation did not signify what they do today. The blame for mistakes of this kind must be put on those modern editions which print early texts without a commentary, thus giving the impression that there are no performance problems. This lack of 'directions for use' in prefaces and footnotes affects ornamentation, articulation, and also rhythm. Compared with modern notation, there were differences in the assimilation of triplets and in the value of the dots, which, from our point of view, were notated imprecisely.

Should Dotted Notes be Assimilated to Triplets?

Because baroque composers tried to avoid triplets where unequal note-values such as ♩ ♪♩ ♫ ♪♩ were involved, they used time signatures such as 3/4, 6/8, 9/8, and so on from the start, or alternatively employed dotted rhythms (♫ ♫) to denote triplets. This kind of notation, which remained widespread until Schubert and Chopin, suffered from the disadvantage that it was not always possible to tell whether triplets or 'real' dotting was intended. There were different views on the matter even in the eighteenth century. C. P. E. Bach was in favour of assimilating dotted notes to triplets, even when two notes were written against three (see Ex. 2.48).[24] But Quantz was against it: 'Hence you must not strike the short note after the dot with the third note of the triplet, but after it. Otherwise it will sound like six-eight or twelve-eight time.' In fact, he even demanded that the note after the dot should be played later than notated: 'If you were to play all the dotted notes found beneath the triplets in accordance with their ordinary value, the expression would be very lame and insipid, rather than brilliant and majestic.'[25]

Ex. 2.48. From C. P. E. Bach, *Essay*, p. 160

This in particular shows that Quantz was not thinking of the same musical context as C. P. E. Bach. With regard to J. S. Bach, Agricola claimed in a review of Löhlein's *Clavier-Schule* (1765) that he had instructed his pupils to

---

[24] 'With the advent of an increased use of triplets in common or 4/4 time, as well as in 2/4 and 3/4, many pieces have appeared which might be more conveniently written in 12/8, 9/8, or 6/8. The performance of other lengths against these notes is shown in Figure 177. The unaccented appoggiatura, which is often disagreeable and always difficult, can be avoided in the ways illustrated in these examples.' (*Essay*, p. 160).

[25] *On Playing the Flute*, p. 68.

play dotted rhythms beneath triplets exactly as notated (i.e. unlike C. P. E. Bach).[26] The controversy about whether or not dotted notes should be synchronized with triplets continues unabated. The most important arguments for and against synchronization have been discussed by Eta Harich-Schneider and Erwin R. Jacobi.[27]

The fact that even experts can hold such diametrically opposed views on the subject of 'variable dotting' suggests that simple answers are not always available. David Fuller's study 'The "Dotted Style" in Bach, Handel and Scarlatti' provides a reasoned assessment of certain problematical cases, including *The Art of Fugue*.[28] I am grateful to Dr Alfred Dürr, who helped to formulate the editorial policy of the NBA, for the following comments on this question:

With regard to the 'triplet problem', two things have to be taken into consideration. The first is Bach's own notation, and the second is the possibility of reproducing it in printed form. With regard to Bach's own notation, much does in fact seem to suggest assimilation. The matter might be summarized as follows. Assimilation may often be deduced from the way the notes are written—and particularly from the way in which the editions that Bach himself saw into print arrange them. In the majority of cases, however, the written notes can be interpreted in more than one way, and they can never be seen as providing unambiguous proof of non-assimilation (exceptions probably prove the rule). We are no doubt in agreement on these points.

The origin of the 'mathematical' decision was not primarily Bach's own notation, but the question of how to reproduce clearly in print his largely ambiguous written notation. For this reason I would be unable to tell you where Bach does not assimilate. However, there are countless instances where one asks oneself how in heaven's name such a passage can be printed *in an assimilated form*. Here are a few examples of what I mean.

Let us turn first to the aria 'Du bist geboren mir zugute' from the cantata *Also hat Gott die Welt geliebt*, BWV 68, (fourth movement, NBA I/14, pp. 49–54). Here it seems appropriate to assimilate the semiquavers to the preceding rests, for instance in bar 6:

(thus ♪ = ♪)

So far, so good. But what happens in bar 12? The notation would have to be as follows:

[26] *Bach-Dokumente*, ii. 206.

[27] Harich-Schneider, 'Über die Angleichung nachschlagender Sechzehntel an Triolen', *Die Musikforschung*, 12 (1959), 35–59; Jacobi, '"Über die Angleichung nachschlagender Sechzehntel an Triolen": Bemerkungen und Hinweise zum gleichnamigen Artikel von Eta Harich-Schneider', ibid. 13 (1960), 268–81.

[28] In *Bach, Handel, Scarlatti: Tercentenary Essays*, ed. P. Williams (Cambridge, 1985), 99–118.

But is this what is meant, right in the middle of triplets? For it would mean that ♪♪ would have to be sung as ♪♪♪. Should it not perhaps be sung thus ♩ ♪♪? Yet this would be notationally absurd, for then the signs would have to be grouped thus:

Or what about bar 18? Should ↗♪ be understood as triplets? If so, the semiquaver rest would disappear! As a result, quaver and semiquaver would be assimilated:

I also recommend similar passages in the aria 'Ach Herr, was ist ein Menschenkind' from the cantata *Unser Mund sei voll Lachens*, BWV 110 (fourth movement, NBA I/1, pp. 116–18). The alternating triple and duple rhythm may well be intentional. In individual cases, however, one can only arrive at tentative conclusions, as when one compares the continuo rhythm of bars 5 and 7 with the corresponding oboe part. How is one to print this?? All in all I believe the following to be true. That notes should be assimilated seems plausible. The question of how they are to be assimilated seems to be so difficult in many cases that I am of the opinion that the NBA should not take a patronizing attitude in this matter. And so I believe that the best thing is still:

1. 'Mathematical' printing;
2. Information in the preface;
3. Information also in works such as your book, not as criticism of the NBA, but as a guide to interpreting it.

Only in this way can we educate performers to think for themselves, performers who are not at the mercy of the subjective decisions of a printed edition.

In spite of Agricola's claim, I have found only a single work by Bach in which playing the semiquaver after the third note of the triplet seems to have been intended and where it is artistically convincing. This is the third movement of the C minor Sonata for violin and obbligato harpsichord (Ex. 2.49). Of his

Ex. 2.49. Sonata No. 4 for violin and harpsichord, BWV 1017, third movement, bars 1–4

own accord a violinist who only has the violin part in front of him would hardly play the dotted notes as 'lame' triplets. Furthermore, the movement ends with both instruments joining in semiquaver figuration, which hints at polyrhythm. In fact, this movement seems to prefigure the Andante of Mozart's C major Violin Sonata K. 296, where polyrhythm is proved by the insertion of four semiquavers in the theme itself (see Ex. 2.50).[29]

Ex. 2.50. Mozart, Violin Sonata K. 296, Andante, bars 34–8

Apart from the above exception, in the majority of passages in Bach where triplets and dotted rhythms coincide, the dotted rhythms should be assimilated to triplets as recommended by C. P. E. Bach. This is suggested not only by musical logic, but above all by the way in which many manuscripts and first editions are arranged graphically;[30] examples include the E minor Fugue in *WTC* II, the Allemande of Partita No. 5, and the Gavotte of Partita No. 6. The Corrente of Partita No. 1 is notated as in Ex. 2.51. The rhythm here is the same as in Contrapunctus 12 of *The Art of Fugue*, where Bach chose unambiguous notation (Ex. 2.52).

However, it is not always possible to rely on the graphic alignment of notes in printed editions. In the Courante of the E flat major French Suite, the manuscript of which has not survived, it would seem that semiquavers played

---

[29] In 'Bach-Interpretation zwischen Scylla und Charybdis', *ÖMZ*, 42 (1987), 66, Eduard Melkus made the same comparison between Mozart and Bach. Triplet synchronization also occurs in other works by Mozart, e.g. in the Andante of the Piano Sonata K. 279/189*d* and in the B flat major Piano Concerto K. 450, 1st movement, bar 76: see Eva and Paul Badura-Skoda, *Mozart-Interpretation* (Vienna, 1957), p. 62; enlarged Eng. trans., *Interpreting Mozart on the Keyboard* (London, 1962), p. 50. In Schubert triplet synchronization in dotted rhythm is a rule with very few exceptions. It also occurs occasionally in Beethoven, e.g. in the Andante of the 5th Symphony, bars 14, 18, 19 (but surely not in the 'Moonlight' Sonata, Op. 27 No. 2).

[30] But in many MSS, above all in drafts, there is hardly any relationship between the graphic arrangement of the notes and the intended rhythmic execution. There is no reason to suppose that Agricola was lying. Dürr comments: 'Might it not be the case that Bach either changed his mind as he grew older, or only wished to tell Agricola that this is how it should really be done (though composers are often rather lax about it)?'

Ex. 2.51. Partita No. 1, BWV 825, Corrente, bars 1–4

Ex. 2.52. *The Art of Fugue*, Contrapunctus 12, bars 9–12

[short appoggiatura, *port de voix*]

after the last triplet note of the kind described by Agricola and Quantz were intended (see Ex. 2.53). The NBA points out in a footnote and in the preface that these dotted rhythms should be played as triplets.[31] Assimilation to triplets is just as important in keyboard and organ works (e.g. the E minor Sonata, BWV 528, third movement) as in orchestral works. Christoph Albrecht cites a telling example from the Ouverture of the D major Orchestral Suite, BWV 1069 (Ex. 2.54). Here it would be totally absurd if the third trumpet were to play a 'delayed' semiquaver.

Ex. 2.53. French Suite No. 4, BWV 815, Courante, bars 1–3

Another instructive example cited by Albrecht comes from the last of the 'Schübler' chorales, *Kommst du nun, Jesu,* in which all forms of assimilation occur. In the pedal line triplets are surely intended throughout (Ex. 2.55).

---

[31] The Henle and Wiener Urtext edns. (see App. 1) align the triplets and the dotted notes, following the alignment in the Gerber copy.

Ex. 2.54. Orchestral Suite No. 4, BWV 1069, Ouverture, bars 89–92, after Albrecht, *Interpretationsfragen*

Ex. 2.55. Chorale prelude *Kommst du nun, Jesu*, BWV 650, bars 13–17, after Albrecht, *Interpretationsfragen*, p. 129.

The melody would be seriously distorted if one were to play it in any rhythm other than that shown in Ex. 2.56. However, this is something of an exception. Usually Bach is careful to make a distinction between triplets and duplets, as in the Allemande of Partita No. 5 (Ex. 2.57). The duplets in this piece are in reality written-out appoggiaturas. However, if the a^1 in bar 5 had

Ex. 2.56

Ex. 2.57. Partita No. 5, BWV 829, Allemande, bars 5–6

been notated as a grace-note, its length would have been ambiguous. In bar 5 (and in bars 4 and 17–20) Bach could easily have written dotted semiquavers (𝅘𝅥𝅯) if he had wanted them to be played as triplets. Thus it seems more likely that he wished to express different rhythms by using different notation; see also bar 25, where the triplets are similarly interrupted (Ex. 2.58; it is of course true that in the first edition the second duplet note is always beneath the second triplet note, which could have been intentional). Similar considerations suggest that even quaver duplets should be played in bar 2 of the D major Prelude in *WTC* II. Otherwise Bach could have saved himself the trouble of writing the double time signature ₵ 12/8, and in bar 2, as in the rest of the prelude, could simply have written dotted quavers and semiquavers (see Ex. 2.59).[32]

Ex. 2.58. Partita No. 5, BWV 829, Allemande, bar 25

The 'tripletization' of duple note-values is fashionable nowadays, particularly in Britain. For example, Howard Ferguson, in his otherwise extremely perceptive book *Keyboard Interpretation*[33] suggests that in the Gavotte of Partita No. 6 the rhythm 𝅘𝅥𝅮𝅘𝅥𝅮 should be played as 𝅘𝅥𝅮𝅘𝅥𝅮𝅘𝅥𝅮. But why should Bach

---

[32] Some years ago this formed the topic of an entertaining exchange of letters with Walter Emery. In his excellent study *Editions and Musicians* (London, 1957), p. 42, he made out a case for triplets (crotchet + quaver) in bars 2 and 4 of this prelude on the grounds that even quavers would lead to consecutive 5ths in bar 18. I demonstrated that triplets would also lead to consecutive 5ths in this bar. He retorted: 'Yes, but your 5ths are worse than mine.'

[33] London, 1975, p. 91.

Ex. 2.59. *WTC* II, Prelude in D major, bars 1–7

have gone to the trouble of writing this rhythm in a different way if triplet notation, which predominates in this Gavotte, would also have been possible? The rhythmic distinction was most probably intentional here, and possibly it should even be carried a step further, for instance ♫ ♩.

Ferguson is also in favour of triplet rhythms in the two gigues in the D minor French Suite and the E minor Partita, which are not notated in triple time, on the grounds that a gigue should be in ternary rhythm.[34] Despite the reference to an example from Froberger's E minor Suite in which the binary notation of the Gigue was changed to ternary rhythm in a later copy (1660–70), I believe that this interpretation cannot be applied to Bach. First, it is clear from a remark by Quantz that a gigue does not necessarily have to be in 6/8 time.[35] In addition to this, it seems to me that it is problematical to alter the ♪♪♪♪♪ rhythm to $\frac{6}{8}$ ♪ ♪♪ ♪♪♪ or even to $\frac{6}{8}$ ♪♪♪ ♪♪♪ , for Bach surely did not wish to mystify contemporary performers. Finally, the rhythm of bar 11 cannot be turned into triplets at all: ♪♪♪♪ . Furthermore, notation in ternary rhythm (6/8 or 12/8) would have been perfectly feasible in this gigue if Bach had wished such an execution.[36] In the E minor Partita Bach had already notated the Tempo di Gavotta (which comes immediately before the Gigue) in

[34] *Keyboard Interpretation*, pp. 96 f. The Gigue of Partita No. 1 is also in 4/4, something that is usually overlooked.

[35] *On Playing the Flute*, p. 291.

[36] See Erwin Bodky, *The Interpretation of Bach's Keyboard Works* (Cambridge, Mass., 1960), p. 188.

gigue rhythm. He can hardly have wanted to duplicate the same rhythm in two successive movements.

A good example of intentional polyrhythm occurs in the finale of the E major Sonata for violin and harpsichord. The main theme, in semiquavers, is contrasted with a subsidiary theme in triplets, as in bars 42–5 (Ex. 2.60).

Ex. 2.60. Sonata No. 3 for violin and harpsichord, BWV 1016, last movement, bars 42–5

However, the accompaniment of the triplet theme maintains the duplet rhythm of the main theme (Ex. 2.61). To assimilate the accompaniment to triplets, as is sometimes suggested, would rob the passage of its charm, and would not make musical sense (see e.g. the semiquavers in bar 37, which could hardly be changed into triplets).

Ex. 2.61. Sonata No. 3 for violin and harpsichord, BWV 1016, last movement, bars 34–7

Finally there are quite a number of pieces which are wholly based on the contrast between triplets and equal semiquavers. These include the triplet version of Invention No. 1 and the F sharp minor Prelude of *WTC* II (Ex. 2.62).

If the groups of four were turned into triplets, for example ♩ ♩♩ ♩ in place of ♪♪♪♪ , the result would sound very much like jazz. Furthermore, if Bach had wanted this rhythm he could easily have written the F sharp minor Prelude in 18/16 time.

Ex. 2.62. *WTC* II, Prelude in F sharp minor, bars 1–3

Dotted Rests not Notated in the Baroque Era

The practice of dotting rests was unknown in the Baroque era, and only gradually came into use after about 1750. Thus certain up-beats to dotted rhythms were apparently notated as if they were to be played undotted. However, in reality this was a convention in operation everywhere in Europe. Thus, the common eighteenth-century notation shown in Ex. 2.63*a* should in fact be played like as in Ex. 2.63*b* (a further possible sharpening of the dot is discussed below).

Ex. 2.63

Mozart was obviously well aware of this. In his arrangement of the chorus 'Surely He hath Borne our Grief' from Handel's *Messiah* (No. 21), he changed notation *a* to *b*. This was not an alteration of the rhythm, but merely a clarification of imprecise notation.[37] Bach's contemporary Quantz described this convention thus:[38]

If demisemiquavers follow a long note and a short rest, they must be played very rapidly, both in the Adagio and in the Allegro. Hence, before playing the quick notes, you must wait to the very end of the time reserved for them, so that you do not lose the beat.

If in slow alla breve or common time a semiquaver rest appears on the downbeat, and dotted notes follow, the rest must be regarded as if it were dotted, or as if it were followed by another rest of half the value, and the following note as if it were of half the value.

[37] A footnote in the Hallische Händel-Ausgabe (I/17. 102 n.) indicates the correct execution. See also David Fuller, 'Dotted Rhythms', *The New Grove*. Anthony Hicks gives the same information in the pref. to the Henle edn. of the 8 great suites. (But see p. 9 n. 10.) This baroque notional practice (a seemingly long up-beat after a rest) continued in use well into the Classical period, e.g. in Haydn's Sonata in E flat major, Hob. xvi/52 (Washington, Library of Congress), 1st movement, bars 47 and 68 (MS) (ed. P. Badura-Skoda (Vienna, 1958), 6).

[38] *On Playing the Flute*, p. 226.

It would no doubt be right to apply this to the 'Grave adagio' section of the Sinfonia in Bach's C minor Partita (see Ex. 2.64).

Ex. 2.64. Partita No. 2, BWV 826, Sinfonia, bars 1–2

At this point some readers may object that on occasion Bach did in fact use dotted rests. If there are dots after the rests in the G minor Prelude of *WTC* II (Ex. 2.65), why are there none in Partita No. 2? The answer is that these dots do not stem from Bach. Unfortunately, as we shall be forced to remark below, even the best Urtext editions are unreliable. In this case the editors have simply modernized Bach's notation *tacitly*, without mentioning why they departed from the original. In reality Bach placed demisemiquaver rests after

Ex. 2.65. *WTC* II, Prelude in G minor, bars 1–2 [as in all printed editions]

the semiquaver rests, which was the only way of notating short up-beats after rests that was known to him (see Ex. 2.66). Such cumbersome notation shows that in his later works Bach was indeed concerned to notate his intentions as precisely as possible. This prelude displays the same rhythmic structure as the introductory chorus of the earlier *Trauer-Ode* (Cantata No. 198), composed in 1727 (Ex. 2.67). Here Bach still made use of the earlier notation, though no doubt the same rhythm was intended. The similarity between the two works is also a valuable indication that the prelude is a passionate expression of suffering and pain.

Ex. 2.66. *WTC* II, Prelude in G minor, bars 1–2, Bach's original notation [appears in no printed edition]

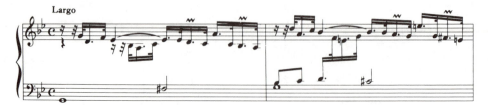

Ex. 2.67. Cantata No. 198, opening chorus

Yet even in the case of this kind of notation one should be wary of applying the 'lengthening of rests in dotted rhythms' rule in a purely mechanical manner. In the above examples it is primarily the overture style which suggests a dotted execution. By adding the title 'Sinfonia, Grave adagio' in Partita No. 2, Bach stipulated the rhythmic pattern where this was the rule. It is of course another matter when similar rhythmic notation occurs in cantabile movements that are not in the overture style, such as the second subject of the F sharp minor Fugue of *WTC* II (Ex. 2.68). Curtailing the length of the first note would be quite out of place.

Ex. 2.68. *WTC* II, Fugue in F sharp minor, bars 20–2

Problems of Over-Dotting

The notated double dot did not come into general use until after Bach. This explains why the single dot could have various meanings, depending on the context in which it occurred. In the first instance it meant the same as it does today, lengthening a note by half its value. According to Quantz this applied particularly to dotted minims and crotchets.[39] But for dotted quavers and smaller notes he demanded a shorter execution, equivalent to our double or triple dot (see Ex. 2.69). According to the generally accepted convention, an

Ex. 2.69. After Quantz, *On Playing the Flute*, p. 67

As notated:

Rhythmically altered
in performance:

Ex. 2.70

or:

articulatory rest was usually inserted before the short note, as in Ex. 2.70. The only way of notating over-dotting 'correctly' in the modern sense was by means of an additive method that Bach employed on rare occasions, for instance at the end of the Allemande of Partita No. 2 (Ex. 2.71), or by spelling out the articulatory rest, as at the end of the Sarabande from Partita No. 5 in

---

[39] *On Playing the Flute*, p. 66.

Ex. 2.71. Partita No. 2, BWV 826, Allemande, bars 31–2

Ex. 2.72. Partita No. 5, BWV 829, Sarabande, bars 38–40, version corrected by Bach

the version corrected by Bach (Ex. 2.72). At the point marked 'NB' there was originally a dotted crotchet followed by a quaver.

In his typically fastidious manner, C. P. E. Bach says of dotting:[40]

Short notes which follow dotted ones are always shorter in execution than their notated length. Hence it is superfluous to place strokes or dots over them. Figure VII illustrates their execution. Occasionally the division must agree with the notated values.

To be sure, he modifies this rule significantly in the second part of the *Essay*:

Because proper exactness is often lacking in the notation of dotted notes a general rule of performance has been established which, however, suffers many exceptions. According to this rule, the notes which follow the dots are to be played in the most rapid manner; and they often should be. But sometimes notes in other parts, with which these must enter, are so divided that a modification of the rule is required. Again, a suave affect, which will not survive the essentially defiant character of dotted notes, obliges the performer slightly to shorten the dotted note. Hence, if only one kind of execution is adopted as the basic principle of performance, the other kinds will be lost.[41]

[40] *Essay*, p. 157.   [41] *Essay*, p. 372.

What then was the rule, and what was the exception? Quantz and C. P. E. Bach, who were both in the service of Frederick the Great,[42] disagreed even with regard to dotted crotchets followed by quavers. It is not difficult to understand why there is still controversy about double and triple dotting.

The tendency to excessive over-dotting goes back to Arnold Dolmetsch, who went too far in this respect.[43] For example, he suggested the exaggerated interpretation of the E flat minor Prelude from *WTC* I shown in Ex. 2.73. A performance in which notes are chopped off in this way would sound simply appalling. This is not to imply that the quaver up-beats in this prelude must be played precisely as notated. I would suggest a slight, almost imperceptible shortening (approximately a quintuplet quaver), which would do justice to the rhetorical pathos at this juncture. An imperceptible lengthening of dotted notes has also been observed on eighteenth-century organ-barrels, where excessive over-dotting does not occur (see Chapter 1, pp. 8 f.).

Ex. 2.73. After Dolmetsch, *Interpretation*, p. 64

The question as to where one should and where one should not use double dotting has recently led to heated controversy. Frederick Neumann has argued strongly against double dotting in a number of articles,[44] and this has aroused some disagreement. Fuller and O'Donnell have adduced arguments to the contrary that are in part well documented, and which for this reason must be taken seriously.[45] In his latest work on this subject, *Essays in Performance Practice*,[46] Neumann has come up with new and more convincing

---

[42] Whether Frederick II really deserves the epithet 'the Great' is open to doubt. His parsimony was proverbial. For example, Bach received nothing for his performance in Potsdam. Nor did the king acknowledge the dedication of the *Musical Offering*.

[43] *The Interpretation of the Music of the XVII and XVIII Centuries* (London, 1946).

[44] 'La note pointée et la soi-disant "manière française"', *Revue de musicologie*, 51 (1965), 66 (translated as 'The Dotted Note and the So-Called French Style', *Early Music*, 5 (1977), 310–24; reprint in *Essays in Performance Practice* (Ann Arbor, 1982), 73–98); 'Facts and Fiction about Overdotting', *Musical Quarterly*, 63 (1977), 155–85.

[45] David Fuller, 'Dotting, the "French Style" and Frederick Neumann's Counter-Reformation', *Early music*, 5 (1977), 517; John O'Donnell, 'The French Style and the Overtures of Bach', *Early Music*, 7 (1979), 190, 336, and 8 (1980), 79. See also Graham Pont, 'French Overtures at the Keyboard: How Handel Rendered the playing of them', *Musicology*, 6 (1980), 29; and 'Handel and Regularization'. Pont is in agreement with Neumann, at least with regard to the interpretation of Handel.

[46] Ann Arbor, Mich., 1984.

arguments. He is now willing on occasion to admit the validity of double dotting.

There can be no doubt whatever that Bach employed the dot in both straightforward and over-dotted applications, not only in the so-called French overture. First, in many works the dot signifies the same as it does today. Typical examples of the straightforward dot occur in the F minor prelude of *WTC* I, bars 13 f., and the Allemande of the D minor English Suite, where no sensible musician would wish to interrupt the natural flow of the melody by double dotting (see Ex. 2.74).[47] Conversely, there are many places where only

Ex. 2.74. English Suite No. 6, BWV 811, Allemande, bars 1–4

double dotting produces rhythms that make musical sense, as in the extracts from the keyboard works quoted in Exx. 2.75–2.77.[48] The vertical alignment of the notes in Exx. 2.75 and 2.76 corresponds exactly to the original edition and reproduces its inconsistencies in rhythmic notation, inconsistencies which are typical of baroque music. It is of course legitimate to question the extent to which a printed edition can accurately reproduce Bach's notation and intentions. However, most experts agree that there is a close connection between the sources (in part no longer extant) and the handful of printed editions that appeared in Bach's lifetime. As Wolfgang Wiemer noted in *Die wiederhergestellte Ordnung in J. S. Bachs Kunst der Fuge*,[49] some of the first

[47] As we shall see in the case of the Praeambulum in the *Clavier-büchlein* for W. F. Bach, BWV 924 (p. 334), the held bass note D should be restruck at least at the beginning of bars 2 and 3. The 2nd ornament in bar 3 is probably a mordent ($c\#^1$–b–$c\#^1$). At any rate the ornaments in this bar should probably begin on $c\#^1$ on account of the d–$c\#^1$ dissonance.

[48] Albrecht (*Interpretationsfragen*, p. 130) adduces a similar ex. from the orchestral parts of Cantata No. 127, *Herr Jesu Christ*.

[49] Wiesbaden, 1977.

Ex. 2.75. Partita No. 3, BWV 827, Allemande, bar 2

Ex. 2.76. Partita No. 6, BWV 830, Allemanda, bars 3–4

Ex. 2.77. Partita No. 6, BWV 830, Sarabande, bars 32–3

editions, being engravings, were straightforward copies of the autograph manuscripts. 'Because the engraver conscientiously transferred Bach's original to the plate, this resulted in a printed version that was very close indeed to the manuscript, even with regard to minute details (spacing, note-heads, height, beams, accidentals, rests . . . etc).[50]

In Ex. 2.77 the bass proves that double dotting was intended in bars 32 and 33. If performed as written, this would almost lead to consecutive octaves with the treble (a–g).

In the Sarabande of Partita No. 5, bar 13 (Ex. 2.78), the rhythms should in fact be slightly exaggerated, that is with slightly shortened semiquavers. Bar

[50] Ibid. pp. 9–10. Christoph Wolff's valuable study of printing techniques as they apply to Bach is in the accompanying vol. to the fac. edn. of *Clavier-Übung*, pts. I–IV (Leipzig and Dresden, 1983). See also the review in *BJb*, 73 (1987), 185.

Ex. 2.78. Partita No. 5, BWV 829, Sarabande, bars 13–16

6, which is rhythmically related, should surely be played with double-dotted crotchets, as in Ex. 2.79. The style and character of this sarabande is similar to that of the Fifth French Suite. In view of what has been said there can hardly be any doubt that the melody of this should also be played dotted throughout (see Ex. 2.80). However, the suggested double dotting could also be executed in a more elegant, 'softer' manner.

Ex. 2.79. Partita No. 5, BWV 829, Sarabande, bars 6–8

If this sarabande were the work of a French contemporary of Bach, I would not hesitate to dot the middle line as well. However, Bach was more precise with regard to rhythmic notation than many of his contemporaries. The very fact that he wrote equal quavers in bar 7 in all the surviving versions, when he could easily have aligned them with the upper voice, is an argument against dotting.

Hans Klotz's comparison of the Offertory of Couperin's *Messe pour les paroisses* (Ex. 2.81*a*) and Bach's E flat major Organ Prelude, BWV 552 (*Clavier-Übung*, Part III; Ex. 2.81*b*) is of interest in this context. The similarity between the two is probably a sign that Bach was familiar with French practice, though favouring more precise rhythmic notation, including articulating rests before short notes. Couperin himself commented on this manner of playing dotted rhythms:

To my mind there are mistakes in the way we notate music which derive from the way we notate language. Our pieces are not notated as they are played. For this reason

Ex. 2.80. French Suite No. 5, BWV 816, Sarabande, bars 1–8

Ex. 2.81. Comparison of *a* Couperin, *Messe pour les paroisses*, Offertory and *b* Bach, Organ Prelude in E flat major, BWV 552, after Hans Klotz, *L'Interprétation de la musique française au 17e et 18e siècles* (Paris, 1974), 163

foreigners do not play our music as well as their own, whereas the Italians notate their music in the true rhythmic values, as they have imagined them. For example, we play ascending or descending quavers as if they were dotted, and yet we notate them as if they were of equal value. Habit has got the better of us, and we continue to adhere to this practice.[51]

[51] *L'Art de toucher de clavecin* (Paris, 1716, 2nd edn., 1717; reprint, Wiesbaden, n.d.), p. 23.

The fact that Bach notated these rhythms in a way that was 'almost' correct (as we have seen, he was unable to write double or triple dots) makes it seem probable that he intended passages in equal note-values to be played undotted. Even in his overtures such equal note-values occasionally occur, for instance in the French Overture, BWV 831, bars 13 and 158, or in the 'Ouvertüre' (variation 16) of the Goldberg Variations, bars 8–9 (Ex. 2.82), where the dots over the notes do not only signify that they should be played detached, but are also an indication that they are not *notes inégales*. A contemporary theoretical treatise states: 'If there is a dot below or above quavers or semiquavers they must be played equal and detached.'[52]

Ex. 2.82. Goldberg Variations, variation 16, bars 8–9

Ex. 2.83. Partita No. 2, BWV 826, Sinfonia, bars 5–6

However, there are a handful of instances in Bach where dotted rhythms were probably intended despite notation in equal values. Ex. 2.83 shows part of the Sinfonia of Partita No. 2; as the principal motif of the introduction concludes with a dotted rhythm elsewhere, it is difficult to see why an exception should be made here. The same applies to the Sarabande of Partita

[52] Claude Denis, *Nouveau système de musique pratique* (Paris, 1747), quoted in Jean-Claude Veilhan, *Die Musik des Barock* (Paris, 1977), p. 25. See also Quantz, *On Playing the Flute*, p. 124 and J. Hotteterre ('Le romain'), *L'Art de préluder sur la flûte traversière, sur la flûte-à-bec, sur le haubois, et autres instruments de dessus* (Paris, 1719).

Ex. 2.84. Partita No. 6, BWV 830, Sarabande, bars 30–1

No. 6, bars 30–1 (see Ex. 2.84). Conversely, even in a work that is decidedly 'French' in character over-dotting is occasionally eschewed, the notes being played as written. This is shown by the fifth fugue of *WTC* I (Ex. 2.85). As

Ex. 2.85. *WTC* I, Fugue in D major, bars 3–4

Tovey[53] and Palmer[54] demonstrated in their editions, unacceptable consecutive octaves ($f\sharp$–d) would result if bar 4 were over-dotted. Furthermore, in this fugue Bach always wrote the semiquaver directly below or above the seventh demisemiquaver. Thus I believe that the dotting should also be 'normal' in bars 9–10 and 17–19 and not delayed. Should it be played as in the Busoni

---

[53] *Bach, 48 Preludes and Fugues, Book I*, ed. Donald Francis Tovey (London, 1924), 31. But in bar 22 Tovey prefers double dotting, not without good reason. There are clearly no easy answers.

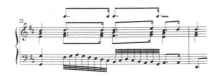

[54] *J. S. Bach, Das wohltemperierte Klavier I*, ed. Willard A. Palmer (Sherman Oaks, Calif. 1982). Palmer admits the validity of double dotting, though with some reservations.

edition? Of course not. It is quite possible to shorten the semiquavers to quintuplet (or even sextuplet) semiquavers, if one starts the demisemiquaver motifs slightly more slowly and then accelerates, in other words, if one plays rubato (see below, pp. 63 f.).

As we have seen, Quantz and C. P. E. Bach do not always agree. When a dotted note or a note with a rest is followed by two or more short notes, Quantz says that the latter should be delayed and shortened,[55] but C. P. E. Bach says that they should be played as notated (see Ex. 2.86).[56]

Ex. 2.86. After C. P. E. Bach, *Essay*, p. 158.

In the third edition of the *Essay* he adds the following remark:[57]

When four or more short notes follow a dot, their number ensures that they are short enough. The same applies to these examples:

When the tempo is not too slow, the same applies to these examples:

When a dotted quaver is followed by three demisemiquavers, as in the above example, one would render them as triplets in modern notation. However, this would be erroneous in terms of baroque style. Thus there is no difference nowadays in the execution of *a* and *b* in Ex. 2.87. It is clear that *a* does not imply triplets, partly on account of the vertical alignment with normal demisemiquavers (see Ex. 2.82 above, or the Ouverture of Partita No. 4, bar

Ex. 2.87

[55] *On Playing the Flute*, p. 226.

[56] *Essay*, p. 157. The music exx. are given in the treble clef, except for fascimiles. In the original they are in the soprano clef.

[57] Ibid. Translation amended.

15. In fact Bach repeatedly exchanged one notation for the other). However, passages of this kind are rarely intended to be played as written. Depending on the affection, the first note is often very slightly lengthened and the following ones shortened correspondingly. This practice is known as 'rubato'.

RUBATO, SYNCOPATION, *NOTES INÉGALES*

Rubato can be only imperfectly reproduced by our notational system. In Ex. 2.88, for instance, the second version already seems rather exaggerated.

Ex. 2.88

Rubato of this kind is appropriate in the Allemande of Partita No. 6. The beat must be strictly maintained, and the quavers in the lower voices played evenly (see Ex. 2.89). Even when the rhythm is reversed, that is, with the dotted note at the end, Quantz[58] and C. P. E. Bach recommend accelerating the short note:

Short notes, when they precede dotted ones, are also played more rapidly than their notation indicates. All of the short notes in the last example, even the sixteenths, when the tempo is not too slow, follow this rule. It would be better practice to add a beam to all the notes.

It is only generally true that the short notes described here should be played rapidly, for there are exceptions. The melodies in which they appear should be carefully examined.[59]

Ex. 2.89. Partita No. 6, BWV 830, Allemanda, bars 1–2

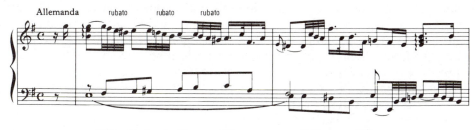

---

[58] *On Playing the Flute*, p. 226.   [59] *Essay*, p. 158.

This form of acceleration is often to be recommended in J. S. Bach, for example at the beginning of the Sarabande of Partita No. 4 (Ex. 2.90). The same is true of the Allemande of Partita No. 3, BWV 827 (see Ex. 2.91). It is significant that in the earlier version of the partita in the *Notenbuch* for Anna Magdalena Bach this bar was rhythmically more primitive, consisting of four dactyls (see Ex. 2.92).

Ex. 2.90. Partita No. 4, BWV 828, Sarabande, bars 1–2

Ex. 2.91. Partita No. 3, BWV 827, Allemande, bars 11–12

Ex. 2.92. Partita No. 3, BWV 827, Allemande, bar 11, earlier version

Concepts such as rubato, syncopation and *notes inégales* are actually all concerned with one thing: minute rhythmic inflections within very small units against a constant beat. Even syncopation is a kind of rubato, because the 'purloined' (or, better still, 'borrowed') time-value is returned at some point along the line. When playing syncopations performers often make the mistake of relating the syncopated voice too closely to the beat. In a performance of the Corrente of Partita No. 6 one hears, as it were, the thought process shown in Ex. 2.93 at work. But this destroys the sense of the melodic line, which in fact should make the e^1 in bar 1 and the c^2 in bar 2 sound like down-beats (Ex. 2.94). Even in rubato proper the main thing, as Mozart once said, is that 'the left

Ex. 2.93. Partita No. 6, BWV 830, Corrente, bars 1–4

Ex. 2.94

hand does not know what the right hand is doing'; that rhythmically the left hand must not be allowed to yield.[60] With regard to ensemble playing, C. P. E. Bach described it thus: 'In order to avoid vagueness, rests as well as dots must be given their exact value except at fermate and cadences. Yet certain purposeful violations of the beat are often exceptionally beautiful . . . but in large ensembles made up of motley players the manipulations must be addressed to the bar alone without touching on the broader pace.'[61]

In the third edition of the *Essay* C. P. E. Bach added a more detailed description of rubato, which can be applied without reservation to his father's music, and also to that of Chopin:

On entering a fermata expressive of languidness, tenderness, or sadness, it is customary to broaden slightly. This brings us to the tempo rubato. Its indication is simply the presence of more or fewer notes than are contained in the normal division of the bar. A whole bar, part of one, or several bars may be, so to speak, distorted in this manner . . . When the execution is such that one hand seems to play against the bar and the other strictly with it, it may be said that the performer is doing everything that can be required of him. It is only rarely that all parts are struck simultaneously . . . Proper execution of this tempo demands great critical faculties and a high order of sensibility. He who possesses these will not find it difficult to fashion a performance whose complete freedom will show no trace of coercion . . . for without a fitting sensitivity, no amount of pains will succeed in contriving a correct rubato. As soon as the upper part begins slavishly to follow the bar, the essence of the rubato is lost, for then all other parts must be played in time. Other instrumentalists and singers, when they are accompanied, can introduce the tempo much more easily than the solo keyboardist . . . My keyboard pieces contain many rubato passages. The division and indication of these is about as satisfactory as can be expected. He who has mastered the tempo rubato need not be fettered by the numerals which divide notes into groups

---

[60] Letter of 23 October 1777. See E. and P. Badura-Skoda, *Interpreting Mozart*, p. 43.
[61] *Essay*, pp. 150–1.

of 5, 7, 11, etc. According to his disposition but always with appropriate freedom he may add or omit notes.[62]

Probably the most beautiful written-out rubatos in all keyboard music are those in the Andante of the Italian Concerto, BWV 971. With the aid of rhythmic notation of unparalleled subtlety, Bach wrote down the free rhythms that a contemporary singer or instrumentalist schooled in the Italian style might have improvised in performance. There is a noteworthy rhythmic analysis of this movement in a study by Boris de Schloezer.[63] In the extracts shown in Ex. 2.95, in order to make it easier to understand the rubato, I have added the 'normal' notation above Bach's original. To be sure, even Bach's notation cannot wholly render the infinite subtleties which characterize great artistry in performance. A sensitive harpsichordist will emphasize the bb^2 in Ex. 2.95a by playing it 'just a shade early' in order to be able to sustain it slightly longer. This rhythmic flexibility enables good harpsichordists to overcome the relatively inflexible dynamics of their instrument and still play cantabile. However, this does not mean that other instrumentalists or singers should eschew rubato.

The injunction to play short note-values faster than written, which occurs repeatedly in eighteenth-century treatises, is another indication of where to employ rubato. The opening runs in the Ouverture of Partita No. 4 belong to this category (see Ex. 2.96). The first D in the left hand is thus held slightly longer than written, and the run delayed accordingly. This in turn is made up for by subsequent acceleration, so that the third beat arrives punctually. A characteristic feature of overtures, fast runs of this kind are known as 'tirades'. There is contemporary evidence that the dotted rhythms in French overtures were exaggerated, and that they were played with correspondingly detached articulation. At the end of a bar written quavers, semiquavers, and demisemiquavers were often played simultaneously, that is, as demisemiquavers.[64] However, recent commentators have questioned this performance style, particularly in the case of Handel's overtures (see p. 55). Bach's notation in the B minor Overture (Orchestral Suite) BWV 1067 is of interest in

this connection. In bars 1 and 11 he wrote ¢ 𝅘𝅥 𝄽 𝅘𝅥𝅰𝅘𝅥𝅯 𝅘𝅥𝅘𝅥𝅮 𝄽 𝅘𝅥𝅰𝅘𝅥𝅯 in the middle

---

[62] *Essay*, pp. 161–2.

[63] *Entwurf einer Musikästhetik. Zum Verständnis von Johann Sebastian Bach* (Hamburg and Munich, 1964; 1st pub. in French, Paris, 1947), 163 f.

[64] See Quantz, *On Playing the Flute*, p. 290: 'In this metre [¢] . . . the quavers that follow the dotted crotchets . . . must not be played with their literal value, but must be executed in a very short and sharp manner. The dotted note is played with emphasis, and the bow is detached during the dot. All dotted notes are treated in the same manner if time allows; and if three or more demisemiquavers follow a dot or a rest, they are not always played with their literal value, especially in slow pieces, but are executed at the extreme end of the time allotted to them, and with the greatest possible speed, as is frequently the case in overtures, entrées, and furies. Each of these quick notes must receive its separate bow-stroke, and slurring is rarely used.'

Ex. 2.95. Italian Concerto, second movement: examples of rubato

(Cont. over)

Ex. 2.95 (*cont.*):

Ex. 2.96. Partita No. 4, BWV 828, Ouverture, bars 1–2

strings, but in the rest of the introduction he used the traditional notation of dotted crotchets followed by quavers.

Many Bach performers fight shy of *notes inégales*, not without good reason. If most of the equal note-values in Bach were turned into unequal ones, as some advocates of this style suggest, it would result in a kind of musical stammering which most of us would find meaningless. As in the case of double dotting, this has led to much unjustified exaggeration. There is not even general agreement on whether *notes inégales* should be 'long–short' or 'short–long'. In her study 'Zur heutigen Aufführungspraxis der Barockmusik',[65] Isolde Ahlgrimm rightly criticizes such exaggerations, citing solid historical evidence in support of her views. After all, Bach's 'champion' Birnbaum made a point of praising 'the quite unusual skill with which he plays every note clearly and evenly throughout, even at the highest speed'.[66] In other words, he observed equality and not inequality.

Nevertheless we should not 'throw out the baby with the bathwater' by rejecting *inégalité* of any kind. Anyone who has listened to a half-speed tape

---

[65] *Organa Austriaca* 2 (Vienna, 1979), 2 ff.
[66] *Bach-Dokumente*, ii. 300. See also pp. 489 f. below.

recording of evenly played fast runs has made the sobering discovery that what sounded even at a fast tempo sounded quite uneven and uncontrolled, indeed amateurish, when played slowly. However, if one were able to master consciously these unintentional augmentations and diminutions, one would have at one's disposal a means of improving 'declamation' and of playing more clearly. A minute inequality of the notes produced in this way might even create the effect of equality, for strong and weak notes could be emphasized accordingly. Yet such differences would only be audible in slow, expressive pieces. Here we are dealing with a kind of 'mini-rubato' in the service of expressivity, to which Quantz is probably referring when he states that in the case of equal note-values in pieces in moderate tempo or adagio the strong notes (i.e. the first, third, fifth, and seventh) should be played slightly longer and with a stronger tone than the weak ones (the second, fourth, sixth, and eighth; see Ex. 2.97).[67] Discreetly applied, this can sound more 'pleasing' than exactly equal notes. In the same paragraph Quantz lists a number of exceptions in which all notes should be of equal length. These include very fast passage-work, vocal coloratura, repeated notes, staccato passages, slurs above more than two notes, and quavers in gigues. In fact even in music influenced by the French style *inégalité* is the exception rather than the rule.

Ex. 2.97. After Quantz, *On Playing the Flute*, p. 123

CONCLUDING REMARKS

Almost all rhythmic processes may be understood as a temporal conjunction of various elements that join or diverge according to the context. In our music there is often an antithesis between the steady beat (an imperfect image or imitation of the heartbeat, which is not nearly so regular) and elements that wish to proceed in a free manner: melody, free declamation, or the dance in its more sophisticated forms. In polyphony this leads to a remarkable phenomenon. Initially nothing seems freer than the motion of the various voices, which seem to be pursuing their melodic curves independently, like birds gyrating on the wing. However, if this seemingly free counterpoint is to become music, its freedom must be counterbalanced by an attendant striving for harmony capable of combining these lines. They can be united to form a coherent whole only by a common denominator. The greater the complexity

[67] *On Playing the Flute*, p. 123.

of the various movements, the stricter is the required unifying principle. In music for more than one performer, this to all intents and purposes can only be the beat, something regular, that is, against which everything else is set and on which it is based. We have already compared music to the flight of a bird. In this context a flock of birds on the wing offers a further musical parallel, for there can be no talk of independence. Are we not reminded of a symphony orchestra when a flock of birds, as though informed by one will, moves along steadily in a straight line, draws irregular figures in the air, or lands and flies away simultaneously? Sometimes the 'conductor' is plain for all to see, but often he is not. And yet behavioural research has shown that the impulse, even if we do not perceive it, comes from a leader bird, as in the case of a chamber orchestra without a conductor, where the leader usually assumes this role.

We must return to practical matters. Rhythmic problems have in fact remained the same ever since the advent of ensemble playing. There have always been works in which all the performers have submitted themselves willingly to the beat, for instance simple kinds of dance and march music, and those in which they have refused to submit to it, such as bel canto and jazz, where solo voices deviate from the beat. The striving to make the barline inaudible is especially apparent in polyphonic music, where in points of imitation, for example, the stress in the individual voices comes at different places. Between the two extremes of 'submission' and 'protest' there are of course many intermediate levels. In baroque music, for example, these are the many stylized dance movements, which can contain remarkably free forms based on simple periods.

Of the basic metres, only duple and quadruple time can be traced back to the heartbeat or to the other fundamental movement, walking at an even pace. Walking and the heartbeat have in common the fact that there is always a stronger and a weaker impulse. This is the fundamental rhythm. It is a remarkable fact that when we are confronted with completely equal 'inorganic' beats produced by mechanical means we hear them in terms of the 'strong–weak' idea, almost always as 2/4 or 4/4, and hardly ever as 3/4 or 5/4 (except in cases where the apparatus itself is imperfectly adjusted!). This explains why triple time has always been sensed to be something special: on the one hand as the highest level of abstraction, the medieval *tempus perfectum*, a symbol of the Holy Trinity; and on the other hand as a dance such as the waltz or the minuet, which also has an intellectual 'pleasure principle': the delight in an asymmetry that is only resolved in the larger unit ($2 \times 3, 4 \times 3$).

Finally, there is also large-scale rhythm, the numerical proportions between the individual sections of longer works, which in Bach often merge with mathematics and number mysticism. Such structures are often determined by the course of the modulations or the thematic material. They should be consciously (and not only intuitively) elucidated by the performer and rendered accordingly.

3

In Search of the Correct Bach Tempo

INTRODUCTION

Choosing the correct tempo is a matter of the utmost importance. Mozart once remarked that it is the most crucial thing in music.[1] Yet for a long time I was unable to write about tempos in Bach. It was not that I did not have a clear idea about the speed at which his works ought to be played. However, my research is concerned with facts, not with subjective emotions. True, in Bach's lifetime various treatises dealt with the question of tempo, though a hundred years before the invention of the metronome they were usually content to give a rough indication of the *relative* speed, for instance that a certain tempo should be taken at a 'lively' pace, and that another should be 'less lively'. The rare attempts to define tempo in 'absolute' terms with the help of time, pulse, or pendulum measurements apply to works which are stylistically so far removed from Bach that it is not really possible to transfer the results to his music.[2] How can I prove that my tempos are more correct than those of a pianist who plays adagio movements and sarabandes twice as slowly as I do? The modern differences in tempo are clearly due to the almost complete lack of precise contemporary tempo indications in Bach's works.

Of course, there is a great divergence in tempo in almost every work that is still played today. Be it in the concert-hall, in the opera, or on record, there is hardly a masterpiece of the last two hundred years which is not performed at a wide variety of speeds. This seems rather odd in view of the fact that ever since the invention of the metronome shortly after 1800 composers have made full use of the ability to define tempos exactly. What is the origin of all these different tempos? I believe it to be of importance to pause to consider this matter, for some of the answers may help to clarify the subject of Bach's tempos.

[1] In a letter of 24 Oct. 1777 to his father Mozart wrote of Nanette Stein: '. . . she will never acquire the most essential, the most difficult and the chief requisite in music, which is, time [tempo] . . .'. Emily Anderson, ed. and trans., *The Letters of Mozart and his Family*, 3rd edn. (London, 1985), 340.

[2] On this subject see the interesting article by Hellmuth-Christian Wolff, 'Das Metronom des Louis-Léon Pajot 1735', *Festskrift Jens Peter Larsen* (Copenhagen, 1972), pp. 205–17.

The principal reason for the discrepancies in tempo in modern musical life is probably the fact that many musicians simply ignore composers' metronome or tempo marks. As far as they are concerned, a composer's idea of tempo is not binding. Yet even the small minority of musicians who strive to observe a composer's tempo marks often only manage to approximate to the authentic tempos. Why is this? Sometimes, though only sometimes, a composer's tempo marks are simply detrimental to a work. For example, Max Reger declared that some of his metronome marks indicated speeds that were too fast. Some composers in fact eschew metronome marks altogether in order not to be misunderstood. Yet it is simply unthinkable that *all* composers erred in their metronome markings or possessed incorrectly adjusted metronomes, as is sometimes claimed. The frequent tempo discrepancies between composer and performer must have their origins elsewhere.

A recurrent feature of all investigations into tempo of this kind, from Beethoven, Chopin, Schumann, and Brahms to Bartók and Hindemith, is the fact that in performance it is always the *slow* movements which tend to be considerably slower than the authentic tempos. To give one example among many, the slow movement of Brahms's Second Piano Concerto, which has a metronome marking of ♩ = 84, is played on most gramophone recordings at a tempo of ♩ = c.56, a third more slowly.[3] No wonder that Brahms is often described as the 'phlegmatic North German'. Performers seem to be unaware of the fact that the theme of this movement derives from the song 'Immer leiser wird mein Schlummer' (Ever lighter becomes my slumber), for they usually play 'Ever deeper . . .'. As the expression of emotion is principally assigned to slow movements, the performer tries to play every note in an eloquent and stirring manner. But with this (wholly legitimate) end in mind he may all too easily lose the sense of the 'larger line', and fail to 'see the wood for the trees'. Such performers take the understandable view that it is better to adopt a wrong (though consciously adopted) tempo than a correct tempo that is rattled off mechanically.

However, a composer sees expression in the context of the whole. Often he simply does not want individual notes to be fraught with meaning. Rather, to use a linguistic comparison, he wishes the phrases as a whole to be eloquent, and not the individual words or letters. This is aptly known as the 'telescopic view', the art of looking at something down a telescope the wrong way round. It is of course perfectly possible that a composer performer may, in the heat of

---

[3] It was difficult to persuade Brahms to add metronome markings to his works, for he wished to retain a certain amount of leeway to cater for mood, form, instrument, and concert-hall. In the case of the 2nd Piano Concerto he made a rare exception, supplying all movements with metronome markings (he was very proud of this fact). In a letter to Clara Schumann he suggested that with regard to the metronome markings she should write down the tempos she considered best over a period of time, and compare them at a later date. See Berthold Litzmann, ed., *Clara Schumann, Johannes Brahms: Briefe aus den Jahren 1853–1896* (Leipzig, 1927), i. 359–61.

the moment, take his own original tempo marking more slowly, but he will hardly ever employ the grotesquely slow tempos that some performers unfortunately apply in works by Chopin, Schumann, or Brahms.

Admittedly, not all the metronome marks of the great composers are really feasible. Beethoven 'in his deafness', for example, sometimes imagined tempos that do not take into account such factors as starting transients, the acoustics of concert-halls, practicability, the limits of the listener's acoustical perception, and so on. Especially in his fast movements one can on occasion reduce his metronome markings by about ten to fifteen per cent without doing injustice to his intentions. On the other hand, there have been and are composers whose prescribed tempos are 'valid' for almost all performers. Among them are Bizet, Hindemith, and Frank Martin, and to some extent Stravinsky. That it is easy to understand the tempos stipulated by these composers is probably due to the clear structure of the melodic phrases, and to the fact that dance-like rhythms play a large role in their music. Dances have always had tempos of their own determined by the movement of the body. This is probably the reason why the tradition of tempos applied to Johann Strauss's waltzes and dances is largely undisputed and continues in existence to this day.

With regard to Bach, these modern insights suggest that we will not go far wrong if, in his numerous pieces in dance form, we attempt to discern the kind of step involved. Not only Bach's gavottes, courantes, sarabandes, minuets, passepieds, and polonaises should be understood as stylized dances, but also some of his fugues (e.g. *WTC* II, fugues in C sharp minor and G sharp minor, which are both like gigues). Sometimes whole concerto movements and even chorale preludes are in dance style (e.g. BWV 608, 648, 674, 679, 695, 734). Yet the general observation mentioned above, that slow movements should be moulded in 'one breath' and that they must not be played too slowly, also applies to J. S. Bach.

Historical research into eighteenth-century tempo reveals a colourful state of affairs. Even if, as almost all research has shown, people generally played faster in the period between the Baroque and Classical eras, and above all more 'lightly' than today, there must also have been substantial differences in tempo, though these were determined not so much individually, as they are today, as by local and cultural traditions. In a little-known book, *Tempobezeichnungen. Ursprung—Wandel im 17. und 18. Jahrhundert*,[4] Irmgard Hermann-Bengen discusses the tempo definitions of the time. For example, the tempo marking for an allemande could range from 'auff das langsamste' to 'presto'. Thus, according to Hermann-Bengen Corelli wrote allemandes with 'largo', 'vivace', 'allegro', and 'presto' markings.[5] Vivaldi also wrote 'presto'

---

[4] Tutzing, 1959.   [5] *Tempobezeichnungen*, pp. 106, 119.

allemandes, and relatively fast allemande markings also occur in Couperin.[6] Even in the case of such a distinctive dance as the gavotte there was little agreement in Bach's lifetime. Brossard (1703) says that gavottes were 'quelques fois gays, quelques fois graves' (sometimes merry, and sometimes grave),[7] and Walther (1732) that they were 'manchmal hurtig, bisweilen aber auch langsam tractirt werden' (sometimes fast, but occasionally also slow).[8]

Fortunately, in the case of Bach, there is a tradition handed down by his pupils and his pupils' pupils. According to this, his allemandes were of the slow type and his gavottes of the fast variety (see below, pp. 85 ff.).

Eighteenth-century tempos, as we have had occasion to remark, were usually faster than today. For example, Jens Peter Larsen and others have established tempos for Handel's *Messiah* that strike us as excessively fast.[9] In the autograph scores of the oratorios *Judas Maccabeus* (1746) and *Solomon* (1748) Handel noted the duration at the end of each act. The total duration for *Judas Maccabeus* is 40 + 40 + 25 = 105 minutes, and for *Solomon* 50 + 40 + 40 = 130 minutes. In comparison, Sir Charles Mackerras's early recording of *Judas Maccabeus* took 56 + 55 + 40 = 151 minutes,[10] though in the mean time his tempos have increased significantly—so much so, in fact, that he is now often criticized on this account. Bach's first biographer, Johann Nikolaus Forkel, expanded the quotation about Bach's tempos from the 'Nekrolog' cited above (p. 16) to include a reference to Bach's manner of playing the clavichord, the harpsichord, and the organ: 'In the performance of his own pieces he usually adopted a very lively tempo, though he was able, in addition to this liveliness, to add so much variety to his performance that each work, in his hands, was as it were as eloquent as speech.'[11]

Yes, but *how* lively, *how* fast? The sources fail to give us answers to these questions. We would be much the wiser if, in the eighteenth century, the great composers, as most of their modern counterparts are in the habit of doing,[12] had at least given us the approximate duration of their works. Unfortunately, apart from the Handel scores mentioned above, we have little

---

[6] *Tempobezeichnungen*, pp. 125 ff.

[7] Sebastien de Brossard, 'Gavotta', *Dictionaire de musique* (Paris, 1703; facsimile, Amsterdam, 1964).

[8] Johann Gottfried Walther, *Musikalisches Lexicon* (1732; facsimile ed. Richard Schaal, Kassel, 1953), p. 274.

[9] Jens Peter Larsen, 'Tempoprobleme bei Händel, dargestellt am Messias', *Händel-Konferenzbericht Halle 1959* (Leipzig, 1961), 141 ff.

[10] Archiv-Produktion 2723 050. See Klaus Miehling, 'Die Wahrheit über die Interpretation der vor- und frühmetronomischen Tempoangaben', *ÖMZ* 44 (1989), 81–9. The article also makes reference to other important authentic tempo marks from the Baroque era.

[11] *Über Johann Sebastian Bachs Leben, Kunst und Kunstwerke* (Leipzig, 1802; repr. Berlin, 1968), 40; Eng. trans., p. 312.

[12] In the case of certain modern composers the stated duration of the piece in minutes is usually slightly longer than a performance calculated on the basis of the metronome markings. Perhaps the 22nd cent. will deduce on the basis of this that our metronomes were incorrectly adjusted. One of the reasons for this discrepancy could be the fact that a composer receives more royalties for a piece that lasts 11 mins. than for one that lasts a mere 9 mins. He thus indicates a longer duration.

of this kind to go by, if we disregard a few markings by some rather obscure Frenchmen, the tempo measurements on English barrel-organs (see pp. 7 ff.),[13] and what Quantz had to say on the subject.

TEMPO: INFORMATION SUPPLIED BY BACH'S CONTEMPORARIES

Johann Joachim Quantz, the cultured flute teacher of the Prussian king, was only twelve years younger than J. S. Bach. He too came from central Germany. In his treatise he gave what is probably the most thorough account of the problem of tempo. He considered '. . . it necessary to give an idea of how the approximate tempo required for individual pieces can be determined',[14] but immediately emphasized that this was no easy matter. However, because the choice of the correct tempo played such an important role in music, he wished to formulate certain rules, taking his bearings from the pulse-beat of a healthy person '. . . with approximately eighty beats to a minute'.[15] There are of course many people whose pulse-beat is much slower than this, yet Quantz was virtually the only one of Bach's *German* contemporaries who attempted to give precise tempo indications.

In common time:
In an Allegro assai, the time of a pulse beat for each minim;
In an Allegretto, a pulse beat for each crotchet;
In an Adagio cantabile, a pulse beat for each quaver;
And in an Adagio assai, two pulse beats for each quaver.

In alla breve time there is:
In an Allegro, a pulse beat for each semibreve;
In an Allegretto, a pulse beat for each minim;
In an Adagio cantabile, a pulse beat for each crotchet;
And in an Adagio assai, two pulse beats for each crotchet.[16]

Quantz also noted:

There are, however, certain main categories from which the others can be derived. I will divide these tempos, as they occur in concerto, trio, and solo, into four classes, and will use these classes as the basis [for determining the others]. They are based on common or four-four time, and are as follows: (1) the *Allegro assai*, (2) the *Allegretto*, (3) the *Adagio cantabile*, (4) the *Adagio assai*.[17]

Quantz included Allegro di molto and Presto under *Allegro assai*; Allegro ma non tanto, non troppo, non presto, moderato, and so on under *Allegretto*; Arioso, Larghetto, Soave, Dolce, Poco andante, Affettuoso, Pomposo,

---

[13] George Houle's *Metre in Music* became available to me after the present book had been completed, and could therefore not be taken into account.
[14] *On Playing the Flute*, pp. 282–3.
[15] *On Playing the Flute*, p. 288.
[16] *On Playing the Flute*, pp. 285–6.
[17] *On Playing the Flute*, p. 284.

Maestoso, alla siciliana, and Adagio spirituoso under *Adagio cantabile*; and Adagio pesante, Lento, Largo assai, Mesto, Grave, and so on under *Adagio assai*. He added: 'Each of these titles, to be sure, has an individual meaning of its own, but it refers more to the expression of the dominant passions in each piece than to the tempo proper. If the aforementioned four principal categories are clearly grasped, the tempos of the others can be learned more easily, since the differences are slight.'

Quantz then gives certain rules that are obviously meant to be taken with a pinch of salt, for it is impossible to adhere to them. In fact they are practically useless, as Curt Sachs remarked and Erwin Bodky demonstrated in detail. For example, Bach's Gigue in the French Suite in C minor, BWV 813, is undoubtedly a fast gigue related in style to the canarie (a dance with dotted rhythms in very fast tempo). For this type of dance Quantz arrives at a tempo of $\downarrow$.= 160,[18] which we would regard as impossible. However, at this point Michel L'Affilard comes to our rescue.[19] He arrives at a tempo of $\downarrow$.= 106, or in similar gigues $\downarrow$.= 116 in 3/8 and $\downarrow$.= 100 in 6/8. We would still consider this to be on the fast side, but we could play and listen to it. In a preceding section Quantz himself noted the extent to which Italian markings also signify the affection of a piece. Thus, in the first half of the eighteenth century they cannot be seen as mere tempo indications. Elsewhere Quantz states that the tempo of Italian dance movements was much more arbitrary than that of similar French works, and that above all in cantabile arioso pieces the tempo had to be deduced from the affection of the work. Like Quantz, C. P. E. Bach mentions the fact that the fashionable Italian markings such as 'Allegro' and 'Adagio' did not merely indicate the tempo, but were more a way of determining the character of a piece.

BACH'S TEMPO MARKS

Tempo marks left by J. S. Bach such as 'Vivace ed allegro' (B minor Mass) and 'Allegro e presto' (G major Toccata, BWV 916) combine concepts which according to modern usage would seem to indicate different speeds. In the Baroque era their combination still seemed feasible. They were to be taken literally inasmuch as they indicated the desired affections (the Italian words *vivace* and *allegro* signify 'lively' and 'cheerful').

J. S. Bach adopted the normal Italian tempo marks in his arrangements of Italian concertos. He also used such marks in a number of other works, though unfortunately not often enough. With regard to the keyboard works,

---

[18] *On Playing the Flute*, p. 291. Quantz is referring to French dance music (ballet) and not to stylized keyboard forms.
[19] *Principes très faciles pour bien apprendre la musique* (Paris, 1694), cited in Veilhan, *Die Musik des Barock*, pp. 73 and 79.

Erwin Bodky has compiled a list of all the tempo marks found in autograph manuscripts and printed editions published by Bach himself.[20] The list is not quite complete, for in recent years important new sources have come to light. Thus the C minor Partita contains a tempo mark Bodky did not know—in a newly discovered source there are tempo indications in bars 28 ('allegro') and 29 ('adagio') of the Sinfonia. Of particular interest are Bach's holograph annotations in his personal copy of the first printed edition of *Clavier-Übung*, Part IV, which contains the Goldberg Variations. These were brought to light about 1970. Here, in the seventh variation, Bach added the indication 'al Tempo di Giga'. Why Bach should have added an indication in order to influence the tempo at this particular point, but otherwise included few marks of this kind, is an interesting question. Might it have been that without this indication it was possible to play this 6/8 rhythm more slowly in the eighteenth century, namely in a 'pastoral' siciliano tempo? After all, not all sicilianos were slow (one of Quantz's *Adagio cantabile* tempos was alla siciliana); some in fact were rather lively. Alessandro Scarlatti wrote several arias headed 'Allegro' and 'Siciliana', and Bach's cousin J. G. Walther mentions Sicilian canzonettas which were 'like gigues' and almost always in 12/8 or 6/8 time.[21]

Robert Marshall has compiled the most comprehensive list to date of the tempo indications used by Bach. It is based on virtually all the available vocal and instrumental sources. Marshall described the results of his research in an article, 'Tempo and Dynamic Indications in the Bach Sources',[22] in which he lists not only all tempo indications, but also the frequency of their occurrence. He cites no less than forty-five different tempo indications, the great majority being of Italian origin (see Table 1). The fact that Bach added 'assai', 'un poco', and 'ma non' on many occasions shows that he strove to differentiate between tempos in a way that was unusual in the Baroque era. This is already apparent in the early works, such as the *Capriccio sopra la lontananza del suo fratello dilettissimo*, BWV 992, or in the Mühlhausen cantatas Nos. 131, 106, and 71. Bach's six basic tempos (their frequency defines them as such) are given by Marshall as Adagio, Largo, Andante, Allegro, Vivace, and Presto.

Going by contemporary usage, Largo should really have been slower than Adagio. Marshall cites the explanation given in Walther's *Lexicon*:

Adagio: 'gemächlich, langsam' ('leisurely, slow')
Largo: 'sehr langsam, den Tact gleichsam erweiternd' ('very slow, as if expanding the
    measure')
Andante: 'alle Noten fein gleich . . . executirt . . . und etwas geschwinder als adagio'
    ('all the notes executed nice and evenly . . . and somewhat quicker than adagio')
Allegro: 'frölich, lustig, wohl belebt oder erweckt; sehr offt auch: geschwinde und
    flüchtig: manchmal aber auch, einen gemässigten, obschon frölichen und belebten

---

[20] *Interpretation*, pp. 100–1.   [21] *Musicalisches Lexicon*, p. 139.
[22] In *Bach, Handel, Scarlatti*, ed. P. Williams, pp. 259 f.

TABLE 1. *Tempo and* Affekt *Designations in the Bach Sources*[a]

Term	Earliest observed appearance Year	BWV	Number of appearances 1	2–5	25 +
1 *Adagio*	1704	992			x
2 *adagio assai*	c.1707	106		x	
3 *Adagio mà non tanto*	1721	1051			
4 *Adagio o vero Largo*	Cöthen?	1061	x		
5 *adagißimo*	c.1704?	565		x	
6 *adagiosissimo*	1704	992		x	
7 *Affettuoso*	1708	71 (libretto)		x	
8 *Allabreve*	1733	232		x	
9 *Allegro*	1705?	535a			x
10 *Allegro assai*	1720	1005			
11 *Allegro e presto*	Weimar?	916	x		
12 *allegro ma non presto*	c.1726	1039	x		
13 *Allegro ma non tanto*	c.1735	1027		x	
14 *Allegro moderato*	c.1735	1027		x	
15 *Allegro poco*	1704	992	x		
16 *Andante*	1707	131			x
17 *Andante un poco*	c.1725	1015	x		
18 *Animose*	1708	71 (libretto)	x		
19 *cantabile*	1721	1050		x	
20 *con discretione*	c.1710	912	x		
21 *dolce*	c.1727–30	527		x	
22 *Fort gai*	c.1725	818a	x		
23 *gay*	1714	61	x		
24 *Grave*	c.1713–14	596			
25 *Larghetto*	1708	71		x	
26 *Largo*	1707	131			x
27 *Largo ma non tanto*	Cöthen?	1043	x		
28 *Lente*	1707	131		x	
29 *Lentement*	c.1738	1067	x		
30 *Lento*	c.1707	106	x		
31 *moderato*	1736	244	x		
32 *molt'adagio*	c.1704?	565		x	
33 *molt'allegro*	1731	36	x		
34 *più presto*	1713	208	x		
35 *prestissimo*	c.1704?	565		x	
36 *Presto*	c.1706–10?	911			x
37 *Spirituoso*	1714	21	x		

TABLE 1. (*cont.*):

Term	Earliest observed appearance		Number of appearances		
	Year	BWV	1	2–5	25 +
38 *Tardò*	1707	524	x		
39 *Tempo di (Borea, Gavotta, Giga, Minuetta)*	Cöthen	173*a*			
40 *tres viste*	*c*.1730	995	x		
41 *un poc'allegro*	1707	131			
42 *un poco Adagio*	Cöthen	1019*a*	x		
43 *vistement*	*c*.1725	809	x		
44 *Vivace*	1707	131			x
45 *Vivace è allegro*	1723	24		x	

[a] After Marshall, 'Tempo and Dynamic Indications', p. 268.

Tact' ('happy, merry, quite lively or awake; very often also quick or fleeting; but sometimes also a moderate but happy, lively measure')
Vivace: 'lebhafft. Vivacissimo. sehr lebhafft' ('lively; Vivacissimo, very lively')
Presto: 'geschwind' ('quick')[23]

In his evaluation of Bach's tempo indications, Marshall reaches conclusions that are different from ours, particularly because Bach often modified 'Adagio' to make it even slower 'Adagissimo', 'Adagississimo', 'Adagio assai', 'Molto adagio'), whereas on occasion he changed 'Largo' to 'Larghetto', or 'Largo ma non tanto'. In this respect Marshall's arguments are not quite convincing, for these modifications occur too infrequently in Bach's work to enable us to draw conclusions or derive rules from them. For example, 'Largo ma non tanto' occurs only once, in BWV 1043. In some cases a movement has two different tempo indications. Thus, in the 'Qui tollis' of the B minor Mass, we find 'Adagio' at the top of the violin 1 part, and 'Lente' in the cello and continuo parts. Yet even an indication such as 'Lente' proves little, for the 'Qui tollis' is certainly not a very slow piece (note particularly the flute figuration). In the second movement of the C major Concerto for two harpsichords, BWV 1061, in point of fact it makes no great difference as far as the performer is concerned whether he understands the indication 'Adagio o vero Largo', to mean 'flowing, restrained largo', or indeed 'a somewhat slow adagio'.

Marshall demonstrates that different tempo indications in one movement do not always have to signify the same tempo, pointing to the last movement

[23] Walther, *Musicalisches Lexicon*, cited in Marshall, 'Tempo and Dynamic Indications'.

of the G major Sonata, which exists in two versions, namely as the Trio Sonata for flute, violin, and continuo, BWV 1039, and as the Viola da Gamba Sonata with obbligato harpsichord, BWV 1027. The movement is headed 'Presto' in the trio sonata and 'Allegro moderato' in the viola da gamba sonata, probably for technical reasons. Similarly, some of Bach's arrangements for lute could well be played at a slower tempo, even if there are no tempo indications to prove it.

Furthermore, Marshall convincingly demonstrates that Allegro was tacitly taken to be the basic tempo of many first movements, and that in his youth Bach, in his early keyboard and organ works, preferred extreme tempo indications in both fast and slow movements, possibly in order to be better able to demonstrate his virtuosity. A unique indication 'con discretione' in the D major Toccata, BWV 912, signifies 'in free rhythm'. 'One usually tends, in such pieces, to write the words: ceci se joue à discretion, or, in Italian, con discrezione, in order to signify that one is not bound to the time signature, but can play as fast or as slowly as one wishes.'[24]

The concept of cantabile, as Marshall rightly notes, is in a sense half-way between tempo and dynamics. On the one hand there is the 'Cantabile ma un poco Adagio' in the alternative (BWV 1019*a*) to the third movement of the G major Violin Sonata with obbligato harpsichord, BWV 1019; and on the other the dynamic marking 'Cantabile' in the third movement of the Fifth Brandenburg Concerto (bar 148), which is intended to emphasize the entry of the violins.

As we have seen, in Bach's works tempo indications are the exception rather than the rule. Most of his music has come down to us without tempo marks. Bach assumed that the player would be able to deduce the right tempo from the time signature, the rhythmic patterns, the choice and disposition of certain note-values, the text underlay, and titles of movements. In many works the intended tempo is fairly obvious, even today. Thus every musical conductor will perform the chorus 'Sind Blitze, sind Donner in Wolken verschwunden'[25] as fast and tempestuously as a sudden thunderstorm, whereas he will take the 'funeral bells' of 'Ach, Golgatha, unsel'ges Golgatha'[26] slowly. Dance-like pieces such as the march or the polonaise will pose few problems for the modern performer, because their character has remained the same for centuries. Difficulties are presented by the numerous pieces where no firm clues are provided either by a text or the expressive character. Here we are forced to fall back on two contributory features:

1. The metre and the notation of note-values;
2. Titles that to some extent function as tempo indications, such as 'Overture', 'Allemande', 'Corrente', 'Sarabande', 'Passepied', 'Gigue'.

[24] Johann Mattheson, *Der vollkommene, Capellmeister* (Hamburg, 1739), 10.
[25] *St Matthew Passion*, NBA No. 27b, BGA No. 33.
[26] *St Matthew Passion*, NBA No. 59, BGA No. 69.

With regard to the first feature, a great deal of information is supplied by Johann Philipp Kirnberger, who was in touch with the Bach circle. The article 'Takt' (Metre) by his pupil J. A. P. Schulz in Johann Georg Sulzer's music lexicon[27] and the second part of his *Kunst des reinen Satzes* deal with the subject in some detail, particularly the chapters entitled 'Von der Bewegung' (Concerning Movement) and 'Von dem Tackte' (Concerning Metre).[28] Kirnberger was principally concerned with the distribution of accents within the various kinds of metre, and with the relationship between notational form and *tempo giusto*, the correct fundamental tempo.

Every kind of metre has its own *tempo giusto* . . . This principle comes from the following: 'With regard to metre, the greater time signatures, such as alla breve, 3/2 and 6/4 are heavier and slower than the short time signatures such as 2/4, 3/4, and 6/8, and these in turn not as lively as 3/8 and 6/16.' (Kirnberger 1776, pp. 106 f.)

The *tempo giusto*, even in the case of dance movements, can be modified by the character of the movement concerned.

Kirnberger systematizes the various metres in a manner that demonstrates the distribution of accents:

Simple duple time
(1) 2/1 time or *O* : tripled, 6/2 time
(2) 2/2 time or 𝄴 :– –   6/4 time
(3) 2/4 time   – –   6/8 time
(4) 2/8 time   – –   6/16 time

Simple quadruple time
(1) 4/2 time or *O* : tripled, 12/4 time
(2) 4/4 time or **C** :– – 12/8 time
(3) 4/8 time   – –   12/16 time

Simple triple time
(1) 3/1 time or **3** : tripled, 9/2 time
(2) 3/2 time   – –   9/4 time
(3) 3/4 time   – –   9/8 time
(4) 3/8 time   – –   9/16 time
(5) 3/16 time   – –   9/32 time (Kirnberger 1776, II, p. 117.)

Triple time has the same tempo as simple time. Thus three quavers in 9/8 correspond to one crotchet in 3/4 time. The unchanged basic beat determines all the proportions.

Kirnberger characterizes the various time signatures as follows:

2/2, alla breve 𝄵 or **2**: 'very heavy and emphatic, but twice as fast as is suggested by the note-values'.
6/4 'slightly more regular' than alla breve.

---

[27] *Allgemeine Theorie der schönen Künste* (Leipzig, 1771–4).
[28] Berlin and Königsberg, 1776–9. I am indebted to Helmuth Perl for valuable information on this subject.

2/4 has 'the movement' (i.e. tempo and accentual pattern) of alla breve, but is played more lightly (Kirnberger 1776, p. 118).[29]

Of particular interest is the following remark by Kirnberger:[30]

12/16 time is played more lightly than 12/8. 'There was certainly a reason why the elder Bach wrote fugue A in 12/8, and fugue B in 12/16.'

Thus the C sharp minor Fugue of *WTC* II should be played considerably faster than the Fughetta BWV 961 (suggested tempo for the fugue ♪ = c.132–8, and for the fughetta ♩. = c.108).

J. A. P. Schulz contributed to Sulzer's *Allgemeine Theorie* an interesting article, 'Taktart' (Metre), on the relationship between tempo and time signature:

There is a vast difference, and this should be apparent to everyone, between playing a piece on the violin, regardless of the tempo, with the whole weight of the bow, or lightly and merely with the tip. Here we do not mean artificial interpretation, but one rooted in the character of the piece itself, without which the music would be uniform in a stiff and boring way. This must be discerned if it is to be properly rendered. Now every experienced musician has got into the habit of playing long notes, such as semibreves and minims, heavy and strong; and short notes, such as quavers and semiquavers, lightly and not so strong. . . .

If now a piece is to have a light execution, but at the same time a slow movement, then the composer will select, in accordance with the nature of the light or lighter execution, a metre of short or shorter beats and use the word 'andante', or 'largo' or 'adagio' etc. to signify that the slowness of the piece is to exceed the natural movement of the metre; and conversely, if a piece is to be played heavily and at the same time have a rapid movement, then he will select a heavy metre in accordance with the nature of the performance, and label it 'vivace', 'allegro' or 'presto', and so on.[31]

Let us attempt to apply some of this to the music of J. S. Bach. In very general terms notation in large note-values (e.g. semibreves and minims, as in the C sharp minor Fugue from *WTC* I) is 'heavier' than notation in smaller

---

[29] Quoted in Helmuth Perl, *Rhythmische Phrasierung in der Musik des 18. Jahrhunderts* (Wilhelmshaven, 1984), 107–8.

[30] Quoted in Perl, *Rhythmische Phrasierung.*

[31] Johann Georg Sulzer, *Allgemeine Theorie der schönen Künste* (2nd revised edn., Leipzig, 1794), pp. 490–502. On Kirnberger's comments about alla breve and the various kinds of triple metre, see App. 4.

note-values, such as the fugues in C major and F minor of *WTC* II, which should surely be played in a lively manner. The E minor Duet, which begins with a demisemiquaver run, should of course be played at a lively tempo. Suggested tempo: ♪= *c*.132–8 (see Ex. 3.1).

Ex. 3.1. Duet No. 1, BWV 802, bars 1–4

On a number of occasions Bach changed one form of notation to another, for instance in the Gigue of the E minor Partita (Ex. 3.2) and Contrapunctus 11 from *The Art of Fugue* (Ex. 3.3). In fact in both cases the version in larger note values seems more 'sublime' and more substantial. Was this linked with a change in Bach's idea of the tempo in the direction of 'slightly slower' speeds?

Ex. 3.2. Partita No. 6, BWV 830, Gigue, opening

In this connection it is of interest that the last movement of the Italian Concerto is in alla breve and not, as might have been expected in such a sparkling piece, in 2/4. Perhaps the reason for this is the music of bars 3 and 4, the similarity of which to the beginning of the chorale 'In dir ist Freude' is surely no accident (see Ex. 3.4). Quaver notation would not do justice to the declamation, not even visually (Ex. 3.5).

The extremely rare combination (in the eighteenth century) of 3/4 and 'alla breve' occurs in the middle section of the aria 'Es ist vollbracht' in the *St John*

Passion.[32] The sepulchral music of the 'molto adagio' opening section is set against the triumphant middle section, 'Der Held aus Juda siegt mit Macht' (a

Ex. 3.3. *The Art of Fugue*, Contrapunctus 11, opening

a   Original notation:
Contrapunctus

b   Later notation:
Contrapunctus

Ex. 3.4. Italian Concerto, third movement, bars 1–5

Ex. 3.5

---

[32] NBA No. 30, BGA No. 58.

foretaste of the Resurrection?). Here 'alla breve' signifies not only a much faster tempo, but also the rhythmic grouping of larger units.[33]

Of course, one should not overestimate the significance of time signatures. 3/2 can occasionally be faster than 2/4. Moreover, in Bach the signatures ₵, ₵, and ₵ are often interchangeable. This is the reason why it was possible, in the chorus 'Ehre sei Gott in der Höhe' (Christmas Oratorio, No. 21), for the instrumental parts to be notated in ₵ in the autograph, but the chorus in ₵ (a fact most modern editions fail to mention).[34] In the orchestral suites, BWV 1066–9, it is often the case that orchestral parts are notated in ₵ and ₵ in the same movement.[35]

Composers and copyists in the age of Bach were very imprecise when it came to ₵ and ₵. Thus Bach's contemporary Johann David Heinichen noted that '. . . the indications ₂ ₵ ₵ ₵ are found indiscriminately in pieces that are by nature fast, and those that are slow'.[36]

DANCES IN BACH'S SUITES AND PARTITAS

In trying to determine Bach's historically correct tempos there is, as we have seen, another important clue—the titles of movements, especially in the case of suites. Bach's 'great-grand-pupil' Griepenkerl, whose views derived from an oral tradition transmitted via his teacher Forkel, and from Bach's contemporary Mattheson, is still a good source of information in this regard. In the preface to the volume of partitas in the old Peters edition he provided a detailed description of Bach's suite movements. Aspects concerned with tempo are as follows:

The Allemande has a serious German character. It is written in 4/4 and has two sections, which are repeated. . . . Its tempo most closely approximates to our allegro moderato. Its execution is legato, grave, and serious. But this is only true of German allemandes, for the French and Italians have seldom captured its true spirit.

The Courante (corrente) has very strict rules as a dance. However, if merely played, it is allowed greater freedom so long as its uninterrupted figuration does justice to its name. It should really be written in 3/2, though composers quite often depart from this, as in the case of Partita No. 5 . . . which is written in 3/8. It has two sections, which are repeated. A rapid allegro is well suited to it . . . Mattheson says: 'The courante has something hearty, desirous, cheerful, which is all found by hope.'

J. S. Bach's courantes sometimes contain peculiar and very delightful changes of

---

[33] Probably first pointed out by Erich Leinsdorf in *The Composer's Advocate* (New Haven and London, 1981), 77. In the 17th cent. the indication ₵ 3/2 was fairly common. See Houle, *Metre in Music*, p. 21.

[34] See Perl, *Rhythmische Phrasierung*, p. 105.

[35] See NBA, Critical Report on the orchestral suites (overtures).

[36] *Der General-Baß in der Composition* (Dresden, 1728), p. 350.

the metric accent, particularly in the English Suites . . . which the performer should take note of.

The Aria. Where this name occurs in old instrumental compositions, it designates a short, cantabile piece with a striking melody which is often much embellished, as in the suites of Handel. Its character is calm serenity and its movement is that of our andante. The aria has two sections, which are repeated. The first of these is usually shorter than the second, though both can have the same number of bars, namely four, eight, or sixteen.

The Sarabande, originally a Spanish dance, is written in 3/4 or 3/2, begins on the down-beat, and has two sections, usually of eight bars, which are both repeated. It requires a slow movement . . . Its character is a certain grandeur in the expression of all the more profound feelings of sublimity, dignity, and majesty. Religious texts could even be added to some of J. S. Bach's sarabandes. Everything that is petty must carefully be avoided, and for this reason it cannot tolerate runs.

The Minuet. . . . It is written in 3/4 and consists of two sections, each eight bars in length, both of which are repeated. The main caesura in each section is in the middle, the subsidiary caesuras are located at the last crotchet of bars 2 and 6. . . . The character of the minuet is decent, moderate gaiety with noble simplicity and without affectation, which is the reason why quavers were its fastest notes. A second minuet used to be added to the first. This was sometimes called trio and then had to be for three voices.

The Gavotte has two sections, each eight bars in length, which are both repeated. Yet this length is not wholly adhered to when the gavotte is only designed to be played. It is written in 4/4 time alla breve (₵) and only two beats are given when conducting. It begins on the up-beat with the third crotchet and consists of two-bar sections, which thus always begin on the third beat. The fastest notes are quavers. Its movement is moderately gay, its character exultant joy. It has a hopping, not a running nature, yet it is pleasing. The second gavotte is usually called a musette. . . . The quavers that occur in it must be slurred, not detached. It is based on a continuous or continually recurring bass note, as on the bagpipes or the hurdy-gurdy. Its nature is soft, ingratiating song with naïve rustic simplicity.

The Passepied is similar in character to the minuet, though it is more lively. It is written in 3/8 and semiquavers are its shortest notes. The caesuras are as in the kind of minuet which begins on the up-beat. . . . Charming frivolity is its main character, which at times reaches to a temperate, noble, and charming gaiety. Mattheson says: 'The passepied does not have the fervour, passion or heat of the Gigue'. . . . Its movement is usually a rapid allegretto or a moderate allegro.

The Loure is a short piece full of gravity, dignity, indeed grandeur, coupled with noble reticence. It is in 3/4 time, and the movement is slow (lento). It begins on the up-beat and consists of two sections, each of 8, 12, or even 16 bars. The loure in 6/4 is played twice as fast as the one in 3/4. The caesura is after the first dotted crotchet of each bar. In order to make it perceptible one has to play the following quaver as a semiquaver. Mattheson states that the loure is a kind of gigue, of which more below. . . .

The Gigue (giga), as music for dancing, is a small, gay piece in 6/8, 12/8, or 12/16. It has two sections which are repeated . . . and in which the notes are largely of the same duration. In gigues only designed to be played, these laws are significantly disregarded. Thus in J. S. Bach's suites there are gigues in 9/16, 4/2, 4/4, and 3/8 time . . . Mattheson is of the opinion that there are four kinds of gigue, which he characterizes as follows:

1. Normal English gigues have a heated and fleeting fervour, a passion that soon evaporates.
2. Loures or slow and dotted gigues have a proud and puffed-up nature, which is why the Spaniards love them.
3. The canaries must be very eager and fast, and at the same time sound rather simple.
4. Italian gigues, which are played on the violin, force themselves, as it were, to be extremely fast and fleeting, though in a flowing, not a furious manner, rather like the swiftly moving arrow of a stream.[37]

Griepenkerl was one of the first editors to add metronome markings to Bach's works. Here he demonstrated that he was still a child of the eighteenth century: fresh, and in part very fast tempos predominate, particularly in the case of allemandes, sarabandes, and gigues.

TEMPO IN BACH'S OVERTURES

John O'Donnell has made an ingenious attempt to reconstruct some of Bach's tempos despite the lack of hard and fast tempo marks.[38] Proceeding from the fact that the form of the French overture remained unchanged for about a century, and that it was cultivated everywhere in central Europe, O'Donnell first examined all the French sources with reliable tempo indications. These included Loulié's *chronomètre* of 1696 (a forerunner of the metronome); Saint-Lambert's comparisons with a man's 'measured step' (1702); the *Principes* of Michel L'Affilard (5th edn., 1705); and the exact durations stipulated for the movements of de Lalande's Te Deum (1684). On the basis of this O'Donnell came to the conclusion that in France there was a surprising degree of conformity. The introductory 'grave' section in dotted rhythm was about ♩ = 57–76, as for instance in La Chapelle's 'Entrée de ballet' of 1737 (see Ex. 3.6). The following section (often in fugal style) was usually in the same or in a

Ex. 3.6. La Chapelle, 'Entrée de ballet', bars 1–9

---

[37] *Klavierwerke von Joh. Seb. Bach*, vol. viii (Leipzig, *c*.1835), ed. F. K. Griepenkerl sen.
[38] 'The French Style'.

slightly faster tempo, though it gave the impression of being faster because there were more notes per bar and because, instead of two slow beats, there were four of about twice the speed ($\downarrow$ = 112–27). But if the second section was in triple time (e.g. 6/4), then it was considerably faster than the first.

Proceeding from these clearly ascertainable tempos, O'Donnell attempted to apply them to Bach's overtures. Bearing in mind that the Germans were in the habit of performing their music in a 'heavier' manner than the French, he came to the following conclusions:

'Ouverture' (variation 16) of the Goldberg Variations: section 1 $\downarrow$ = 53, section 2 $\downarrow$. = 53.
'Ouvertures', orchestral suites Nos. 1 and 3 (BWV 1066 and 1068): section 1 ('Grave') $\downarrow$ = 56, section 2 $\downarrow$ = 112, that is, practically 'l'istesso tempo'.

Bach's only recorded comment on the subject of time and tempo could also be interpreted in this light. It is preserved in a thorough-bass tutor evidently written down by one of his pupils:

But mark my words: nowadays duple time is written in two ways, $\overline{\underline{\mathbf{C2}}}$. The second is used by the French in such pieces which are to sound fast and fresh, and the Germans copy the French. Otherwise the Germans and Italians usually retain the first way, especially in sacred music, and employ a slow beat. If it is to be fast the composer makes a point of adding 'allegro' or 'presto'; if it is to be slow this is expressed by adding 'adagio' or 'lento'.[39]

It is a curious fact that, whereas the original tempos of the French are wholly suited to the music concerned, the tempos O'Donnell suggests for Bach seem incredibly fast in the grave sections, and decidedly 'cosy' in the allegro sections. Of course O'Donnell is also aware that many of his readers will consider these grave tempos to be extremely fast. He puts the blame on twentieth-century listening habits. But the problem cannot be solved that easily. If Bach specialists such as Leonhardt or Kirkpatrick play the opening Grave almost twice as slowly, but otherwise prefer the 'right' tempos in French music, it seems likely that O'Donnell may have made an error in his calculations. At this point the organ-barrels discussed in Chapter 1 come in useful. Fuller gives the speed of the overture of Handel's B flat major Organ Concerto, Op. 4, No. 2, whose rhythmic structure is similar to Bach, as $\downarrow$ = 72 (see p. 4, n. 1). On the record of the mechanical organ it is $\downarrow$ = 76–80, and in the allegro section $\downarrow$ = c.112. This cannot simply be bad twentieth-century taste. Whereas the grave tempos calculated by O'Donnell are not felt to be 'very slow' (forte lente) in Muffat's sense of the word,[40] the organ-barrel tempos are just about tolerable. A second observation speaks against the overly fast tempo of the introductory sections. In the autograph of the first

---

[39] Quoted from Philipp Spitta, *Johann Sebastian Bach* (Leipzig, 1873 and 1880), ii. 917; Eng. trans., iii. 319.
[40] See O'Donnell, 'The French Style', p. 196 n. 10.

violin part of the Third Orchestral Suite in D major, BWV 1068, the beginning of the second section (bar 24b) is headed 'viste' (i.e. 'vite' or fast). This indication would be pointless if the tempo remained practically the same.

It seems that O'Donnell, for all his perceptive calculations, made the mistake of underestimating the difference between the rich rhythmic and harmonic character of the music of Bach (and of Handel) on the one hand and that of the less ornate French models on the other. It is true that in Bach the introductory sections should be played in terms of slow minims. The opening bars usually have only two stresses each and could still be performed in the 'French' manner described by O'Donnell. But soon the stresses increase to four (i.e. two subdivided), and the music can no longer be played at this speed. This suggests a compromise between two and 'real' four. The tempo felt to be 'correct' also lies between the tempo demanded by O'Donnell and one that is twice as slow; for example, instead of $\downarrow = c.50$ ($\downarrow = 100$) this suggests $\downarrow = c.75$, a range of between 63 and 80.[41] The fast sections on the other hand can be played at O'Donnell's tempo or even faster.

The difficulty of reaching a satisfactory solution in one of the kinds of movement described above shows that the problem of correct Bach tempo, for lack of unambiguous evidence, is impossible to solve. In addition to O'Donnell, Helmut Perl has recently examined the question of tempo. The chapter 'Tempo und Takt' of his book *Rhythmische Phrasierung* is well worth reading, for it quotes important sources and makes some noteworthy suggestions (with metronome markings) concerning the tempo of the E minor Flute Sonata, BWV 1034, the G major Trio Sonata, BWV 1038, and the flute sonatas in B minor, BWV 1030, and A major, BWV 1032. The tempos are convincing, though there is no real evidence for them.

Perl sums up the factors that contribute to the 'right' tempo thus:

The prescribed metre including the proportions;
the use of dance rhythms;
the note-values;
the compositional style;
the tempo marking;
the affection;
the technique of the instrument;[42]
the room and the scoring.[43]

In the following an attempt is made to correct certain widespread misconceptions:

1. *Adagio*, up to about 1800, was not a particularly slow tempo. The word originally came from *ad agio*, which corresponds roughly to 'at ease, easygoing

[41] Quantz (*On Playing the Flute*, p. 292) gives a metronome marking of $\downarrow = 80$ for the Entrée (Ouverture).
[42] A presto on a lute would seem rather easy-going to a violinist or a pianist.
[43] *Rhythmische Phrasierung*, p. 102.

and agreeable', or to *à l'aise* in French. Thus 'molt'adagio', which often occurs in Bach, is certainly not meant to be slower than our modern adagio.

2. *Andante*, in the eighteenth century, signified 'walking' in the sense of flowing execution,[44] and was often considered to be a moderately *fast* tempo. Thus 'molto andante' signifies 'faster'. What Couperin says in *L'Art de toucher le clavecin* probably also applies to Bach: 'Cantabile pieces should not be played as slowly on the clavecin as on other instruments on account of the short duration of its notes. Rhythm and style can be preserved regardless of the greater or lesser slowness.'[45]

3. *Vivace* was not a tempo indication in its own right, but an epithet signifying 'lively'.

4. *Presto*, in Bach's time, was not the embodiment of the fastest possible movement, but was often equated with allegro. O'Donnell gives ♩ = 120 as the norm for a Bach presto.[46] This rather moderate tempo would be suitable in something like the last movement of the Italian Concerto. Unlike O'Donnell I am of the opinion that Bach's presto must have been faster than his allegro, for otherwise, in the second prelude of *WTC* I these two different tempo indications, which occur consecutively, would be meaningless. Here my suggested tempo would be: 'allegro' (opening and conclusion), ♩ = *c*.138 (with ritardando in the final bar); 'presto' (bars 28 ff.), ♩ = 80.

5. *Minuet* (menuet, minuet, menuetto, minuetta, etc.) was a *moderately fast to very fast* dance in France. The tempo ranged from ♩ = 160 (Quantz) to ♩. = 70 (L'Affilard). In the case of Bach and Handel, however, the minuet had a greater 'range downwards', that is to say, the tempo could also be slower. For the Minuet of Partita No. 1 I recommend ♩. = *c*.58, and for that of Partita No. 4 ♩ = 138. Surprisingly, the slowest minuets I have come across are on Colt's organ-barrels: one from Handel's *Samson* is at ♩ = 144, one from *Rodelinda* ♩ = 138, and from *Arianna* ♩ = 98! This multiplicity in itself shows that it is impossible to arrive at correct solutions by merely applying old rules in a mechanical manner.

6. *Sarabandes* are usually played too slowly nowadays. In 1705 L'Affilard gave ♩ = 84 for placid sarabandes.[47] This is probably too fast for Bach's sarabandes. I would like to suggest a range between ♩ = 48 (for richly embellished sarabandes) and ♩ = 72 (simple sarabandes).

Finally we must quote what is probably the most precise authentic tempo indication of the eighteenth century. In Dom François Bédos de Celles's *L'Art du facteur d'orgues* (1766–78), Père Engramelle, while discussing the production of an organ-barrel, cites the example of a 'Romance' by M. Balbastre, a minor mid-eighteenth-century French composer (see Ex. 3.7). According to

---

[44] Suggested tempo for the Andante of the Italian Concerto: ♩ = 76; on modern pianos and in large halls, slightly slower.

[45] (Wiesbaden, n.d.), p. 24.

[46] 'The French Style', pp. 191 f.   [47] Perl, *Rhythmische Phrasierung*, p. 118.

Ex. 3.7. Balbastre, Romance, from Bédos, *L'Art du facteur d'orgues*

»Romance de Mr. Balbastre«

Engramelle, Balbastre normally played this piece, which he marked as slow, in 2 minutes and 45 seconds. 'One multiplies the 68 bars of the Romance by 4 crotchets per bar and obtains 272 crotchets, which must be executed in 206 rotations of the barrel.'[48] We are particularly grateful to Père Engramelle for this seemingly superfluous remark, because it clarifies which parts were repeated (otherwise the time indicated would tell us nothing). This indicates that for a 'slow' Romance $\downarrow = 99$ was the authentic tempo selected by the composer himself. What a pity that Bach did not know someone like Dom Bédos!

Many of the questions relating to Bach's tempos are, as we have seen, incapable of being answered conclusively on account of the lack of precise evidence. This means that we are forced to fall back on imprecise theoretical statements and approximate values. I would like to be able to adduce only arguments that can be substantiated historically, and to eschew speculation, but the fact remains that it is impossible to demonstrate the exact tempo for any of Bach's works. However, the sum total of the research into this subject shows that *lively* tempos are more appropriate to Bach's music than those that drag in a sentimental manner, or those that are solemn and boring.

---

[48] *L'Art du facteur d'orgues* (Paris, 1766–78), fac. repr. of pt. IV (Kassel, 1936), vol. i, pp. 514 ff., vol. ii, Table 119. As Bédos admitted, the passage about the construction of mechanical organs is by Engramelle. However, as the work was published under Bédos's name, he is often given the credit for it.

4

Bach's Articulation

INTRODUCTION

If I were asked to name the most serious and most common fault in modern performances of Bach, I would reply without hesitation: 'non-existent or incorrect articulation'. Non-existent articulation is tantamount to rattling off the music and playing the notes with no sense of their inner coherence. Incorrect articulation, on the other hand, can obscure the meaning of a passage, and in extreme cases make a nonsense of it, just as wrong punctuation can produce the opposite of the intended meaning. In his keyboard tutor of 1789, Daniel Türk compared the sentence 'Er verlor sein Leben, nicht nur sein Vermögen' (He lost his life, not only his fortune) with 'Er verlor sein Leben nicht, nur sein Vermögen' (He lost his life not, only his fortune), where a wrongly placed comma inverts the meaning.[1]

One can also speak of non-existent articulation when the performer plays staccato or legato throughout. This amounts to a kind of computer language without punctuation which the layman simply cannot understand. C. P. E. Bach poked fun at such players: 'There are some who play stickily, as if they had glue between their fingers. Their touch is lethargic; they hold the notes too long. Others, in an attempt to correct this, leave the keys too soon, as if they were red-hot. Both are wrong.'[2] The keys of Glenn Gould's Steinway must have been particularly hot when he played Bach's C minor Fugue from *WTC* II with staccato articulation (see Ex. 4.1). This staccato is wrong for three reasons:

1. The subject is vocal in character.
2. Apart from the leap of a fifth in the middle, it consists entirely of small intervals, which suggest legato at a slow tempo.
3. At the chosen tempo the subject is quiet and sustained in character, and this, according to the doctrine of the affections, suggests legato playing.

[1] *Clavierschule* (Leipzig and Halle, 1789), fac. repr. (Kassel, 1962), 340.
[2] *Essay*, p. 149.

Ex. 4.1. *WTC* II, Fugue in C minor, bars 1–3

Gould's articulation:

Of course, Gould knew what he was doing, but he simply had no scruples about disregarding historical considerations whenever he thought he could dazzle his audience with a modern interpretation. In this he undoubtedly succeeded, world-wide. In the case of this particular fugue his 'pointillist' performance, which is reminiscent of Anton von Webern, attained to a kind of pellucid clarity. However, this has little to do with Bach's intentions, which we do after all know fairly well nowadays.[3]

The unarticulated style of many keyboard players probably stems from the fact that, particularly in his keyboard works (including those for organ), Bach hardly ever provided articulation marks, in this regard placing his trust in the player's education. It is true that modern Urtext editions have done away with the stylistically misleading arrangements of the nineteenth century. However, by presenting a bare text without some accompanying 'instructions for use' they have done a disservice to practical musicians. Creative (or 're-creative') performance and historical style are seldom taught nowadays, and even good musicians are sometimes at a loss when confronted with unmarked texts. Depending on their talents and training they either play in a shapeless, amorphous manner or distort the music grotesquely. In both cases the result is musically nonsense or, at best, a caricature.

The reasons for this failure can often be traced back to teachers, who ought in fact to familiarize pupils from the start with the significance of articulation and, as long as the latter are incapable of doing so themselves, should add articulation and breathing marks in all the voices of keyboard works by Bach and his contemporaries. Yet even more mature performers cannot circumvent the task of marking the articulation of each voice individually, as if the piece were a string trio or quartet. In this regard string players have a certain advantage over keyboard players, for in order to be able to play securely they have to work out all the bowings in advance. This automatically produces

---

[3] One cannot really object to modern distortions of works of art, e.g. Dali's variations on the Mona Lisa, even when they are lacking in good taste. But in the case of Glenn Gould many of his admirers are still convinced that he was playing in the spirit of Bach. It must be said in Gould's defence that, as far as I know, he never claimed that his performances were historically authentic.

articulation, even if it is sometimes incorrect (in Bach they tend to apply too much legato and not enough breathing pauses).

It should in fact not be difficult to elucidate the correct execution (or, better still, several possible correct executions) that Bach would have approved of. As a starting-point one can use the passages in Bach's keyboard, chamber, and orchestral works that have been precisely marked. Equally instructive with regard to articulation and declamation is the text underlay in vocal works.

To be sure, with regard to articulation it is rarely possible to rely on even the best editions of Bach, for they convey the impression of a kind of regularity that seldom exists in Bach's own notation. In many cases Bach's slurring is difficult to decipher because his slurs, as those of Haydn, are usually too short and are placed arbitrarily above groups of notes. The Sarabande of the C minor Partita is a case in point. Ex. 4.2 shows a facsimile of part of the first edition. Virtually every edition prints bars 13–16 with the articulation shown in Ex. 4.3*a*, but in view of the large melodic leaps involved this is surely wrong. Bach probably intended the articulation shown in Ex. 4.3*b*, which in bars 2 and 4 corresponds more closely to the original, even in graphic terms. A similar articulation exists in the first movement of Cantata No. 98 (first violin).

Ex. 4.2. Partita No. 2, BWV 826, Sarabande, bars 12–16, first edition

Of course, scholars have known this for a long time. Nevertheless, it is a remarkable fact that before 1980 little research was devoted specifically to Bach's articulation. Most musicians ignored the results in any case. For this reason a short survey of the most important studies on the subject of articulation may prove helpful.

Albert Schweitzer's monumental Bach biography was a pioneering achievement.[4] The modern performer will still find it valuable and stimulating, though some of the views expressed are out of date and untenable. Schweitzer's study was followed some decades later by Hermann Keller's *Phrasierung und Artikulation*,[5] which contains three chapters devoted to

---

[4] *J. S. Bach* (Leipzig, 1908), trans. Ernest Newman (London, 1911).   [5] Kassel, 1955.

Ex. 4.3. Partita No. 2, BWV 826, Sarabande, bars 13–16

articulation in Bach. Bodky's *Interpretation* gives a good account of articulation problems in Bach's keyboard works. For instance, his observation that in Bach a one-note up-beat is never linked to the next note by a slur solves all sorts of problems. The articulation tables in the appendix are particularly valuable, for they demonstrate both parallels and incongruities in articulation with the help of numerous examples.[6] Georg von Dadelsen has also written on this subject lucidly, though on a high scholarly level.[7] Harnoncourt,[8] Hochreither,[9] and in particular Perl[10] have also made a number of interesting comments on the subject. Hochreither cites a valuable, but virtually unknown study by Hans-Peter Schmitz that also contains important remarks on articulation.[11] Recently Willard A. Palmer's edition of *WTC* I[12] has made a valuable contribution to the subject. In addition to the (mainly) good slurs and staccato markings in the text, it contains an articulation table (in an appendix) that provides a survey of the fugue subjects based on the most important editions and recordings.

Josef Rainerius Fuchs's study of Bach's articulation marks in organ and keyboard works is the most comprehensive to date.[13] Dietrich Kilian's essay

---

[6] pp. 201–22, 382–98.

[7] 'Die Crux der Nebensache: editorische und praktische Bemerkungen zu Bachs Artikulation', *BJb*, 64 (1978), 95–112.

[8] *Musik als Klangrede*, pp. 48 ff.

[9] *Zur Aufführungspraxis des Vokal- und Instrumentalwerkes Joh. Seb. Bachs* (Kassel, 1983), 126–31.

[10] *Rhythmische Phrasierung*, pp. 92 ff., 150 ff., 158 ff.

[11] *Prinzipien der Aufführungspraxis alter Musik* (Berlin, 1950), 22, 27.

[12] Alfred edn. (Sherman Oaks, Calif., 1982). See App. 1.

[13] *Studien zu Artikulationsangaben in Orgel- und Klavierwerken Joh. Seb. Bachs* (Neuhausen and Stuttgart, 1985).

'Zur Artikulation bei Bach', is a valuable contribution to the subject.[14] A book by Ludger Lohmann appeared in 1986.[15] A previous article, 'Zur Artikulation bei Bach' published in *Ars organi* in 1983,[16] led to an interesting exchange of views with Hans Klotz in the same journal.[17] The most recent contribution to the subject is a book by John Butt.[18]

With regard to Bach's articulation, a simple rule emerges. This is that stepwise passages should on the whole be played legato, whereas larger intervals and leaps should be detached.[19] The rule can be of great help, though of course there are all kinds of nuances, exceptions, and modifications dictated by the various affections. Another rule involves taking into account the harmony, and in particular the fact that dissonances are linked to their resolutions. The only exception to this is occasionally found in the case of syncopated passages, which, with regard to articulation, often create a kind of state of flux. Octave leaps should almost never be played legato.[20] Similarly, broken triads, especially in allegro or forte passages, should usually be played non-legato or staccato. (This does not apply to arpeggios; see below). Non-legato and finger-staccato are appropriate in toccata-like virtuoso pieces. On the harpsichord and the piano different styles of playing should be employed in fast movements which suggest a non-legato reminiscent of the lute or the guitar, such as the Courante of the E major French Suite, BWV 817, or the episodes in the Prelude of Partita No. 5, BWV 829. A lute stop or a combination of lute and buff stops makes it possible to separate notes on the harpsichord even when playing legato, whereas finger-staccato is necessary on the fortepiano.

Articulation often helps to clarify rhythmical and metrical relationships. Let us briefly examine the beginnings of Inventions Nos. 3 (Ex. 4.4) and 4 (Ex. 4.5). Both Inventions are in 3/8, and both begin with a semiquaver ascent from the tonic. The sole rhythmic difference is the up-beat character of the first two notes of the D major Invention. This 'anapaest' can only be made audible if the up-beats are detached and played 'lightly'. But if, as is often unfortunately the case, one were to include the initial notes in the legato, the listener would automatically hear the beginning as a down-beat, as in Invention No. 4 (Ex. 4.6).[21]

---

[14] In *Beiträge zur Bachforschung*, vol. ii (Nationale Forschungs- und Gedenkstätten Johann Seb. Bach der DDR, Leipzig, 1983).

[15] *Studien zu Artikulationsangaben bei den Tasteninstrumenten des 16.–18. Jahrhunderts* (Regensburg, 1986).

[16] Vol. 31, pp. 35–42.

[17] Vol. 31 (1983), pp. 94–7, 159–61, 251–4.

[18] *Bach Interpretation: Articulation Marks in Primary Sources in J. S. Bach* (Cambridge, 1990).

[19] Bach himself applied this rule in the F minor Invention, BWV 780.

[20] A rare exception to this rule is the fugue in the Capriccio BWV 992, where the legato octave leaps imitate the sound of the post-horn.

[21] On this subject see ch. 2.

Ex. 4.4. Invention No. 3, BWV 774, bars 1–4

Ex. 4.5. Invention No. 4, BWV 775, bars 1–4

Ex. 4.6

WALKING BASSES: NON-LEGATO

A typical feature of baroque slow movements is the 'walking bass', usually in even quavers. Examples are the B minor Prelude, of *WTC* I (Ex. 4.7),[22] the Andante in the Sinfonia of the C minor Partita (Ex. 4.8),[23] and the Corrente of the E minor Partita (Ex. 4.9).[24]

Ex. 4.7. *WTC* I, Prelude in B minor, bars 1–3

[22] The 'andante' tempo indication that Bach himself supplied in this prelude is often misunderstood by modern performers. In the eighteenth century andante was not a slow tempo, but a flowing, 'onward-moving' one. In terms of Quantz's pulse measurement it is not the quaver, but the crotchet which should be regarded as the pulse unit (= *c*.80).

[23] '*Andante*, from the verb *andare* (go, walk), tells the continuo that all notes have to be equal and clearly detached.' (S. de Brossard, quoted in Veilhan, *Die Musik des Barock*, p. 63).

[24] Concerning the declamation of the upper voice ch. 2, pp. 19 f., and p. 65.

Ex. 4.8. Partita No. 2, BWV 826, Sinfonia, bars 8–9

Ex. 4.9. Partita No. 6, BWV 830, Corrente, bars 1–5

Walking basses should usually be played slightly detached, as a good cellist or viola da gamba player would render them; *détaché* (*louré*), that is, as an expressive melodic line with staccato or non-legato that is not too short.[25] Such notes can also be thought of as tenuto semiquavers followed by semiquaver rests. At a faster tempo (D major Prelude, *WTC* I) these bass notes become correspondingly shorter. C. P. E. Bach no doubt meant this when he wrote: 'Notes which are neither detached, connected, nor fully held are sounded for half their value, unless the abbreviation Ten. (hold) is written over them, in which case they must be held fully. Crotchets and quavers in moderate and slow tempos are usually performed in this semidetached manner. They must not be played weakly, but with fire and a slight accentuation.'[26]

Taken out of context, this pronouncement can easily be misunderstood (and often is). C. P. E. Bach's reduction of the note-value by half is an extreme case. Eighteenth-century French composers for the organ recommend only a *slight* reduction in the note value (cf. the discussion between Lohmann and Klotz mentioned on p. 96). The fact that most eighteenth-century music contains no articulation marks has recently led to the emergence of a historical style of performance in which most of the notes are shortened. This sounds ugly and choppy, and, though an understandable reaction to the exaggerated legato playing of the past, is musically unbearable and often historically untenable. Only a few pages earlier C. P. E. Bach states that 'rests as well as

---

[25] In my edns. I denote this kind of singing staccato with a tenuto line over the dot.
[26] *Essay*, p. 157.

notes must be given their exact value', that one should 'learn to think in terms of song', and that 'the tenderness of adagios' is expressed 'by broad, slurred notes'.[27] On the other hand, staccato should 'in general' be employed in brisk movements, as long as it corresponds to the 'affection' of the piece. C. P. E. Bach makes a point of saying: 'I use the expression, "in general", advisedly, for I am well aware that all kinds of execution may appear in any tempo.'[28]

In the case of J. S. Bach staccato is often employed in 'energetic' movements, and especially in the case of leaps (see below). Another general aspect of eighteenth-century staccato for which I have found little confirmation, except in Becking's study, is perhaps worth mentioning. Staccato in Haydn and Mozart should on the whole be 'shorter' and 'lighter' than in Bach; in other words, Bach's staccato is hardly ever as 'sharp' as Mozart's sometimes is. The difference in sonority between the harpsichord and the fortepiano underlines this, for on the harpsichord even the shortest note has a certain resonance, whereas on the fortepiano it is immediately dampened.[29]

ARTICULATION PROBLEMS ASSOCIATED WITH 'BACH RHYTHM'[30] (FIGURA CORTA)

The following remarks demonstrate that rhythm, tempo, and articulation are often closely interlinked and that they must be seen in the context in which they occur.

The 'short–short–long' (anapaest) or 'long–short–short–long' (dactyl) rhythm that occurs so frequently in Bach requires various kinds of articulation dependent on the tempo and the affection. In an 'ingratiating' adagio it is usually played legato, but at a faster tempo it is imbued with energy and should often be played non-legato or staccato. Examples of this are found in the Brandenburg Concertos. On a Bach trumpet the characteristic trumpet motifs in the Second Brandenburg Concerto can to all intents and purposes only be played detached (see Exx. 4.10 and 4.11). In the case of the strings *détaché* down–up–down bowing is more appropriate to this rhythm than slurring the two semiquavers, which Bach rarely indicated for such motifs in an

---

[27] *Essay*, pp. 149–51. Quantz's comments are similar: 'Each note must be expressed with its true value' (*On Playing the Flute*, p. 123). See also the similar remark about correct performance quoted on p. 16 above.

[28] *Essay*, pp. 149.

[29] In the case of stringed instruments the change in bowing technique since the time of Tartini and Leopold Mozart has led to a different sonority. According to Eduard Melkus, the use, in Bach's time, of a bow that was less taut meant that one played closer to the strings. As a result 'staccato' was weightier and longer than in later periods. Modern 'off-string' playing first became fashionable in the 20th century. See Eduard Melkus, 'Bach Interpretation', pp. 67 f.

[30] This term, though widely used by practical musicians, is historically inaccurate in view of the fact that the *figura corta* formula (see below, p. 278) was a common feature of late baroque music. However, it is difficult to find a more suggestive phrase.

allegro (see Ex. 4.12), an exception being the third movement of the D minor harpsichord concerto.

Ex. 4.10. Brandenburg Concerto No. 2, BWV 1047, first movement, bars 1–3

Ex. 4.11. Brandenburg Concerto No. 2, BWV 1047, third movement, bars 1–6

Ex. 4.12. Brandenburg Concerto No. 3, BWV 1048, first movement, bars 1–3, Violin 1 part

In keyboard works similar passages should also be played staccato. Unfortunately 'keyboard players' are continually tempted to apply a drab kind of legato to such rhythms. To articulate thus ♫♫♪ is simply not as good as ♫♫♪. A few examples should make this clear. Ex. 4.13 shows the articulation

Ex. 4.13. Chromatic Fugue, bars 1–13, articulation by Paul Badura-Skoda

that I recommend for the opening of the Chromatic Fugue, BWV 903 (note the treatment of the first countersubject, bars 8 ff.). For the beginning of the A minor Fugue of *WTC* I (Ex. 4.14) I recommend articulation *a* rather than *b*. The opening of the Courante of Partita No. 4 should be played as in Ex. 4.15.

Ex. 4.14. *WTC* I, Fugue in A minor, bars 1–6

Ex. 4.15. Partita No. 4, BWV 828, Courante, bars 1–3

In the case of organ music, reverberation in large churches affects articulatory clarity, and thus staccato articulation in the *figura corta* is even more necessary than on the harpsichord or piano, as for instance in the

Fantasia 'con imitazione' in B minor (Ex. 4.16) and in the chorale prelude *Erschienen ist der herrliche Tag* from the *Orgel-Büchlein* (Ex. 4.17). Lifting fingers between the notes in this way in order to obtain clear articulation is

Ex. 4.16. Fantasia 'con imitazione', BWV 563, bars 1–3

Ex. 4.17. Chorale prelude *Erschienen ist der herrliche Tag*, BWV 629, bars 1–4

demanded, among others, by Dom Bédos in his monumental work *L'Art du facteur d'orgues*. Though written a generation after Bach, this still exudes the spirit of the Baroque era.

All notes consist of two basic elements, the attack (*tenue*) and the rest (*silence*). Together they make up the full note-value. The attack always occupies the first part of the note, whereas the rest concludes it. These two parts of a note have a defined length in music, which should be reflected exactly in notation. Thus not only the value of the audible portion of each note must be given, but also that of its attendant rest, which serves to separate them, and thus constitutes musical articulation. Without such rests the effect would be as bad as that of bagpipes, whose most noticeable shortcoming is the fact that there is no articulation.[31]

On the other hand, the B flat minor Prelude of *WTC* I, which has the character of a *tombeau* or funeral procession, should surely be performed slowly and legato. Edwin Fischer played this work in an inimitable way, and his recording of the work is still a valid and masterly interpretation (see Ex. 4.18). A borderline case between staccato and legato that combines quavers and semiquavers is the second fugue of *WTC* I (Ex. 4.19). In his edition (which is of historical interest in that it claims to be based on Beethoven's interpretations)

---

[31] Bédos, *L'Art du facteur d'orgues*, i. 498 f.

Carl Czerny added staccato dots to this subject, thereby distorting the meaning by turning it into a scherzando (see Ex. 4.19). Yet the underlying idea of slightly separating the notes and thus preserving the coherence of the

Ex. 4.18. *WTC* I, Prelude in B flat minor, bars 1–4

Ex. 4.19. *WTC* I, Fugue in C minor, bars 1–3

Ex. 4.20. *WTC* I, Fugue in C minor, bars 1–3, unpublished articulation marks by Paul Badura-Skoda

short motifs is actually correct, because up-beats of one note should always be separated (see p. 95). Perhaps Beethoven played it like this and Czerny merely misunderstood him. However, ♫ ♪ would also be justified.

MIXED ARTICULATION

The following section is devoted to 'mixed' articulation, the frequent combination of staccato and legato. As a starting-point let us consider an oboe part (the introduction to the aria 'Hochgelobter Gottessohn' from Cantata No. 6, *Bleib bei uns, denn es will Abend werden,* to which Bach himself added articulation marks (Ex. 4.21). The astonishing liveliness of Bach's articulation, which adheres (with certain exceptions) to the principle that stepwise motion is slurred and leaps are detached, should serve as a model for the performance of many keyboard works. In particular I intend to examine certain fugue subjects (and their continuations), because it is of paramount importance to articulate them correctly. Once the subject of a fugue has been correctly executed, the most important problem of playing the fugue has virtually been solved.[32] If a musician is able to articulate fugue subjects and countersubjects well, he will be unlikely to encounter difficulties in other forms, be they polyphonic or homophonic.

Ex. 4.21. Cantata No. 6, aria 'Hochgelobter Gottessohn', introduction, oboe part, after Kilian, 'Zur Artikulation bei Bach'

---

[32] An exemplary instance of clear and convincing articulation is Jean Guillou's recording of the *Musical Offering*, BWV 1079, on the organ of St Bavo, Haarlem, Holland (FESTIVO, Stereo 507, Bodegraven, Holland). Cf. also an older recording by Guillou on the organ of the Luther-Kirche, Berlin (Philips 6,504.069).

Many of the fugue subjects in Bach's instrumental music are vocal in character, for example the B flat minor Fugue of *WTC* I (Ex. 4.22). The affinity to the introductory chorus of Cantata No. 64, *Sehet, welch eine Liebe*,[33] is obvious (see Ex. 4.23). The complete text of this movement is: 'Sehet, welch eine Liebe hat uns der Vater erzeiget, daß wir Kinder Gottes heißen' (Behold, what manner of love the Father hath bestowed upon us, that we should be called the sons of God). This rather cheerful and positive exclamation is reflected in Bach's active and vigorous rhythm. But why did he choose a 'serious' minor key? Here, as so often, Bach was engaged in 'musical

Ex. 4.22. *WTC* I, Fugue in B flat minor, bars 1–6

Ex. 4.23. Cantata No. 64, opening chorus, bars 1–10

---

[33] Alfred Heuß has questioned the authenticity of this cantata. See 'Die im Dezember gesendeten Bach-Kantaten', *Zeitschrift für Musik*, 101 (1934), 191. However, there are arguments in its favour, especially in regard to the 1st movement.

theology', for in order to enable us to become the sons of God (salvation, a joyful event) Christ had to die on the cross (a tragedy). The cross symbol described by the first four notes expresses this in an unmistakable manner. The related subject of the B flat minor Fugue should be construed similarly (Ex. 4.24).

Ex. 4.24

It is a matter for debate to what extent knowledge of this kind can help us to perform Bach's music. In the final analysis performance is not the result of knowledge, but of musicality, which in turn requires emotional involvement. For this reason I believe that an agnostic who intuitively 'senses' such religious dimensions might well be a better Bach performer than, say, a Protestant theologian or a Bach scholar with no artistic talent. The words of St Paul (1 Corinthians 13) are also true of music: 'Though I speak with the tongues of men and of angels and have not charity [i.e. empathy or inner sympathy], I am become as sounding brass, or a tinkling cymbal.'[34]

The D major Fugue of *WTC* II is also 'vocal' in character (see Ex. 4.25). Here it would be quite possible to add a text, for instance 'Es steht geschrieben: Wir sind erlöst' (For it is written: We are redeemed). The antecedent should surely be played marcato, though the consequent (i.e. the second phrase) should be sung and played legato or quasi legato (Ex. 4.26).

Ex. 4.25. *WTC* II, Fugue in D major, bars 1–4

Ex. 4.26

---

[34] Translator's note: in Luther's trans. of the Bible the word 'charity' is rendered as *Liebe*.

This phrasing should also be maintained in the numerous strettos on the second motif, which can only be made clear to the listener if played as in Ex. 4.27.

Ex. 4.27. *WTC* II, Fugue in D major, bars 34–41

One of the few fugue subjects to which Bach himself added a few articulation marks is that of the finale of the C major Concerto for two harpsichords (see Ex. 4.28). The unmarked opening motif should surely be played detached (the semiquavers non-legato), though probably not as short as the staccato in bars 3 and 4. (In passing it is worth noting the interesting structure of the melody: 2 + 3 + 3 minims.) We can make use of these authentic marks in the fugue subject of the Toccata of Partita No. 6 (see Ex. 4.29). The similar second half of this theme should also be played detached, though on account of its essentially elegiac character it should probably be slightly longer than in the more energetic C major fugue of BWV 1061. Bach's own markings in the G major Viola da Gamba Sonata BWV 1027 may serve as a model for the first motif (see p. 315). The performer is strongly

Ex. 4.28. Concerto in C major for two harpsichords, BWV 1061, last movement

Ex. 4.29. Partita No. 6, BWV 830, Toccata, bars 26–32

Ex. 4.30

urged not to commit the common error of shortening the last note of the motif when releasing it (Ex. 4.30). C. P. E. Bach distinguishes between two notations of pairs of slurred notes. Normally the first note is emphasized, but the second should not be shortened. Only in the case where the second note is marked staccato[35]

the last note of each slur is detached. The finger must be raised immediately after it has struck the key.

C. P. E. Bach warns the player not to change the rhythm as seen above. Obviously the correct execution of the dotted second notes should be as in Ex. 4.31. Incidentally, Mozart and Schubert used that notation if they wanted the second note to be shortened.

Ex. 4.31

Since Bach never wrote a staccato-dot on the second note, it is both unnecessary and undesirable to shorten the last note of the sigh-motif,

---

[35] *Essay*, p. 157.

because the ensuing rest ensures clear articulation, and the coherence of the passage as a whole needs to be preserved. Only correct articulation (without shortening the third note of the motif) can make the later strettos comprehensible, for the listener may otherwise misunderstand the voice-leading (see Ex. 4.32).

Ex. 4.32. Partita No. 6, BWV 830, Toccata, bars 60–2

The fugato in the Ouverture of Partita No. 4 is usually played staccato, as in Ex. 4.33. This is perfectly possible, of course. However, later on in the movement (bars 63–7 and 70) Bach wrote out a legato version in which virtually every note is sustained (see Ex. 4.34). For this reason I suggest playing legato right from the start in order to avoid inconsistent articulation within the movement.

Ex. 4.33. Partita No. 4, BWV 828, Ouverture

Ex. 4.34. Partita No. 4, BWV 828, Ouverture, bars 67–8, 70

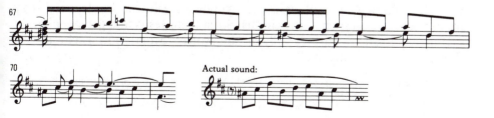

Slurred pairs of notes often occur in Bach's music. They resemble sighs, or the *anticipatione della Sillaba*.[36] The subtle difference between the two is the fact that in the case of the sigh the first note of a pair is usually a dissonance, whereas in that of the *anticipatione* it is a consonance.

A characteristic chain of sighs occurs in bars 66–7 of the Chromatic Fugue (see Ex. 4.35). The *anticipatione* predominates in the wind parts of the chorus that concludes Part I of the *St Matthew Passion* (see Ex. 4.36). In both cases, as in the majority of short slurs, the first note of a pair should be emphasized (strong), whereas the second should diminish slightly.[37] (On the piano this can be achieved by a stroking movement of the arched second or third finger.)

Ex. 4.35. Chromatic Fugue, bars 64–7

Ex. 4.36. *St Matthew Passion*, chorus NBA No. 29, BGA No. 35

It may safely be assumed that such articulation should be applied to unmarked notes of this kind, as in the F sharp minor Fugue of *WTC* I (Ex. 4.37). These chains of sighs are symbols of pain can be deduced from various vocal works, such as the chorus 'So ist mein Jesus nun gefangen' in the *St Matthew Passion*, bars 27–30, at the words 'Mond und Licht ist vor Schmerzen untergegangen'.[38]

---

[36] Also known as *subsumptio postpositiva*. See Hochreither, *Zur Aufführungspraxis.* pp. 108–9.
[37] See also pp. 69 and 392 ff.
[38] NBA No. 27a, BGA No. 33. See Leinsdorf, *The Composer's Advocate*, pp. 33–4.

Ex. 4.37. *WTC* I, Fugue in F sharp minor, bars 8–9

At this juncture we should briefly examine the possibility of transferring from one genre to another the articulation of similar or identical passages. In the second movement of the Concerto for two violins, Bach notated a typically violinistic kind of articulation for the semiquavers, which he transferred to the version for two harpsichords (Ex. 4.38). We will not go far wrong if we apply the same articulation to similar sequential motifs, for instance in the second movement of the C major Concerto for two harpsichords (Ex. 4.39). In the case of chorale preludes that are transcriptions of cantata movements, organists will take their bearings from the phrasing of the original, as in the case of the unmarked 'Schübler' chorale *Kommst du nun, Jesu, vom Himmel herunter*, which is based on the second movement of Cantata No. 137, *Lobe den Herrn* (Ex. 4.40). In the Gigue of Partita No. 1, many players tend to slur pairs of notes. However, in view of the fact that this figuration is rhythmically and

Ex. 4.38. Concerto for two violins, BWV 1043, second movement, bars 3–4

Ex. 4.39. Concerto for two harpsichords, BWV 1061, second movement, bars 25–9

or reversed:

Ex. 4.40. Chorale prelude *Kommst du nun, Jesu, vom Himmel herunter*, BWV 650

melodically related to the bass-line of the famous Air of the Third Orchestral Suite, slightly detached melody-notes would seem more in keeping with the style (see Ex. 4.41). String players would play the two-note motifs with alternate up- and down-bows.

Ex. 4.41. Partita No. 1, BWV 825, Gigue, bars 1–4

STACCATO

At the beginning of this chapter I criticized the indiscriminate use of staccato. However, this is not to say that staccato should be avoided altogether. In some cases it is certainly appropriate, for example in the G major Fugue of *WTC* I (Ex. 4.42) or the Corrente from Partita No. 5 (Ex. 4.43). Both these themes

Ex. 4.42. *WTC* II, Fugue in G major, bars 1–10

Ex. 4.43. Partita No. 5, BWV 829, Corrente, bars 1–8

were evidently inspired by flute music. Those who have heard a good performance of the Fourth Brandenburg Concerto (also in G major!), will take pleasure in imitating the delicate staccato of recorders on the harpsichord or piano (Ex. 4.44). Bach's manner of playing (drawing in the finger and sliding it off the front of the key) is to be recommended when playing staccato (and *non legato*) on keyboard instruments.

Ex. 4.44. Brandenburg Concerto No. 4, BWV 1049, first movement, bars 1–12

In contrast to this soft, 'evanescent' staccato, there is the vigorous kind that predominates in certain gigues and similar fast movements. A typical example of this is in the Gigue of the French Suite in C minor, which is in the style of a canarie (Ex. 4.45). In this connection Quantz writes: 'The gigue and canarie have the same tempo . . . The gigue is played with a short and light bow-stroke, and the canarie, which is always in dotted notes, with a short and sharp bow-stroke.'[39]

Ex. 4.45. French Suite No. 2, BWV 813, Gigue, bars 1–9, earlier version

There is another kind of 'staccato gigue' in the closing fugue of the D major Harpsichord Toccata (see Ex. 4.46). The Gigue of the G major French Suite is similar (Ex. 4.47). The Allegro section of the first movement of the French Overture has Bach's own staccato marks, which tacitly suggest legato for the semiquavers (see Ex. 4.48). In the Capriccio of Partita No. 2, the tenths (Ex. 4.49) should probably be played just as exuberantly as in the similar passage in the finale of Beethoven's Piano Concerto No. 1, Op. 15 (bars 192 ff.).

Ex. 4.46. Harpsichord Toccata in D major, BWV 916

Ex. 4.47. French Suite No. 5, BWV 816, Gigue, bars 1–4

[39] *On Playing the Flute*, p. 291.

Ex. 4.48. French Overture, BWV 831, first movement, bars 20–4

Ex. 4.49. Partita No. 2, BWV 826, Capriccio, bars 81–4

The 'scourging' figure that frequently occurs in Bach (not only in the sacred music) should undoubtedly be played staccato, as in the accompaniment of the recitative 'Erbarm es Gott' from the *St Matthew Passion* (Ex. 4.50).[40] This is a typical example of Bach's word-painting, the importance of which (and of musical symbolism) was pointed out by Albert Schweitzer. (It has also been discussed by Bodky[41] and Albrecht[42].) The same rhythm also occurs in the G minor Prelude of *WTC* I and in the second movement of the E minor Partita. Handel employed this rhythmic idea in aria No. 21 of the *Messiah*, 'He gave his back to the smiters'.

With regard to staccato, a distinction between the dot and the stroke was made even in Bach's day, as we discover from Quantz.[43] It was actually the

---

[40] In bar 4 of this section the word *Wunden* would almost certainly have had an appoggiatura (going by 18th-cent. rules of recitative).

[41] *Interpretation*, pp. 223–58.   [42] *Interpretationsfragen*, pp. 155–6.

[43] *On Playing the Flute*, p. 223. There is a great deal of valuable information in Quantz's treatise on the subject of articulation, particularly on the bow-strokes of stringed instruments, e.g. that fast movements 'require a lively, very light, nicely detached, and very short bow-stroke' (p. 231), and that a slow, melancholy piece, i.e. Adagio assai or Lento, 'requires the greatest moderation of tone, and the longest, most tranquil, and heaviest bow-stroke' (p. 231). He also states 'that in the accompaniment, particularly in lively pieces, a short and articulated bow-stroke, wielded in the French manner, produces a much better effect than a long and dragging Italian stroke' (p. 230). Dance music in the French style, e.g. sarabandes, must be 'played seriously, with a heavy yet short and sharp bow-stroke, more detached than slurred. That which is delicate and singing is rarely found in it. Dotted notes are played heavily, but the notes following them briefly and sharply. Fast pieces must be executed in a gay, hopping, and springing manner with a very short bow stroke, always marked with an interior stress. In this fashion the dancers are continually inspired and encouraged to leap, and at the same time what they wish to represent is made comprehensible and tangible to the spectators; for dancing without music is like food in a painting' (p. 290).

Ex. 4.50. *St Matthew Passion*, recitative NBA No. 51, BGA No. 60, bars 1–4

distinction we draw today: the stroke signifies marcato. However, the two marks often overlap. In the D minor Fugue of *WTC* I Bach seems to have meant staccato dots. But the five strokes in the theme of the D minor Harpsichord Concerto, BWV 1052 (autograph) probably suggest that the notes should be vigorous and detached (see Ex. 4.51).[44] This is a typical

Ex. 4.51. Harpsichord Concerto in D minor, BWV 1052, first movement, bars 1–7

[44] Hans Klotz, *Die Ornamentik der Klavier- und Orgelwerke von J. S. Bach* (Kassel, 1984), 178 ff., is of the opinion that in Bach strokes should be construed as a very slight shortening of the note-value on the lines of Couperin's 'aspiration'. This may be correct in the case of keyboard works, though it is improbable in the case of strings. A 3rd interpretation (accent stroke on sustained notes) is given by Telemann in *Singe-, Spiel- und Generalbass-Übungen* (Hamburg, 1733–4), No. 14.

baroque concerto theme in which the *détaché* bow-stroke mentioned above should be applied. It is surely no accident that this type of 'bowing' also predominates at the beginning of the Italian Concerto, a work which is as it were an arrangement of an imaginary orchestral work for two-manual harpsichord. As is the case with stringed instruments, other kinds of articulation appear later. This work enjoyed great popularity early in the nineteenth century, when it was considered to be a Classical sonata. Some editions from this period add a 'romantic' legato slur between the first two notes, which is wholly out of keeping with the style. It is a remarkable fact that this articulation is still heard today. However, a good 'Italian' performance can dispense with such slurs, though a slur on the appoggiaturas in bars 4 and 8 might be possible (see Ex. 4.52).

Ex. 4.52. Italian Concerto, first movement, bars 1–8

LEGATO

The examples examined above are certainly not exhaustive, for we have not yet dealt with the most important kind of execution, legato. Despite all these subtleties of articulation Bach is primarily a 'legato composer'. His great cantabile lines, both in vocal and instrumental works, should naturally be played in a broadly flowing legato manner.[45] We only have to think of the great arias from the Passions, of the aria 'Qui sedes' in the Gloria of the B minor Mass, or of the great melodic arches in the violin sonatas, such as that in the first movement of the E major Sonata with obbligato harpsichord, BWV 1016. With regard to the organ works, many of the quiet chorale preludes should be played legato, as should certain keyboard works, including many of the allemandes and sarabandes and the arioso passages in *WTC*, for instance in the two C sharp minor preludes.

---

[45] Ernst Ludwig Gerber, in the art. on C. G. Schröter published in *Historisch-Biographisches Lexikon der Tonkünstler* (1792), p. 455, stated: 'Those who were acquainted with the excellent legato style of playing that Bach employed on the organ could never conceive a liking for the style of Schröter, who always played staccato on the instrument'. As is well known, Gerber's father was a faithful pupil and great admirer of J. S. Bach.

Legato should be employed in fugues that are vocal in character, such as the C sharp minor Fugue of *WTC* I (Ex. 4.53) or the B major Fugue of *WTC* II (Ex. 4.54).[46] It hardly needs to be said that in the C sharp minor fugue the later 'coloratura' subject, which is reminiscent of certain choral movements, should also be played legato (Ex. 4.55). However, this does not mean that

Ex. 4.53. *WTC* I, Fugue in C sharp minor, bars 1–8

Ex. 4.54. *WTC* II, Fugue in B major, bars 1–8

Ex. 4.55. *WTC* I, Fugue in C sharp minor, bars 36–40

vocal melismas were automatically sung legato. When executing coloratura passages of this kind instrumentalists should remember that in Bach's lifetime articulation was frequently applied within melismas (see John Butt, *Bach*

---

[46] The kind of slurring shown in the B major Fugue does not imply a break between the slurs at the barlines, but continuous legato. The same is true of similar original bar-to-bar slurs in Bach, Haydn, and Mozart. See the original slurs in Invention No. 3 (Ex. 4.4).

Interpretation, 30–4). Even today singers faced with the problem of achieving clarity in fast coloratura passages sung on one vowel solve the difficulty by inserting an almost imperceptible 'h' between the notes.

And finally, the main subject of *The Art of Fugue* is also decidedly cantabile and legato in character (Ex. 4.56). Again, it hardly needs to be said that the 'basic' legato style recommended here does not imply that all notes should be linked in the same way, without 'breathing-pauses' or declamation. Thus, in Ex. 4.56, bars 6–8 of the alto voice should be articulated as shown in Ex. 4.57. The periodic four-bar phrases in these fugues also suggest cantabile execution.

Ex. 4.56. *The Art of Fugue*, Contrapunctus 1, bars 1–8

Ex. 4.57

There is in fact no dearth of contemporary evidence for legato execution on the harpsichord and organ. Isolde Ahlgrimm cites important seventeenth- and eighteenth-century evidence, including the following:

Saint-Lambert: 'On the organ . . . notes are played very legato . . . The instrument has no need of the effort required in the case of the clavecin in order to mitigate the dryness of the instrument.' (*Les Principes*, p. 63).

François Couperin: 'In all one plays on the clavecin one should observe a perfect legato.' (*L'Art*, p. 33)

Rameau: 'When one notices that the hand is fully trained, one gradually reduces the height of the seat until the elbows are slightly lower than the keyboard. This forces the player to hold the hand so that it clings to the keys, and this finally secures for his attack all the legato it is capable of.' (*Pièces de clavessin*, p. 19)

Quantz writes of 'the natural weakness' of the harpsichord, 'which is that the tones cannot be joined to one another as upon other instruments . . . and that one must attempt, through one's touch, to 'obviate' this 'as much as possible'.[47]

But how does one play legato? From my own experience as a pianist, harpsichordist, and teacher I can safely say that this manner of execution, which is perhaps the most difficult encountered on keyboard instruments, can be mastered only when several factors are combined. Three principles are primarily involved:

1. the actual slurring or linking of the notes;
2. the correct touch, or 'pressure' on the keys;
3. sensing and moulding the lines of tension.

I shall explore legato execution in greater detail in Chapter 7. At this juncture only one more point needs to be made. This is that the basis of legato (as of all good execution) is a relaxed body and state of mind. As Edwin Fischer used to say, 'a pressed note does not carry'.

A characteristic form of legato notation in Bach's keyboard music, which is known as 'legatissimo', *überbinden*, or *style luthé*, deserves to be mentioned separately.[48] It is distinguished by the fact that, within a single melodic line, individual notes are often held longer in order to fill out the harmony, thus creating the impression of two- or three-part writing (complementary voice-leading). The Allemande of the C minor French Suite contains a typical example (Ex. 4.58).[49] In the later version a further held note was added (Ex. 4.59). In reality this is a single melodic line that could also have been notated as in Ex. 4.60. Other examples of the *style luthé* occur in the Allemande of the A minor Partita (see Ex. 4.61) and in the Allemande of the B flat major Partita (Ex. 4.62). The last example is particularly instructive, because Bach chose simpler notation in the parallel passage at the end (see

Ex. 4.58. French Suite No. 2, BWV 813, Allemande, bars 1–2

---

[47] 'Zur heutigen Aufführungspraxis', pp. 1–3. The quotations from Quantz are from *On Playing the Flute*, p. 259.

[48] One might also term this manner of playing 'ultra-legato'.

[49] Klotz, *Ornamentik*, p. 183, gives a similar ex. of such a 'liaison' in 2 versions of the C major Organ Prelude, BWV 545 and 545*a*.

Ex. 4.59. French Suite No. 2, BWV 813, Allemande, bars 1–2, later version

Ex. 4.60

Ex. 4.61. Partita No. 3, BWV 827, Allemande, bars 3 and 14

Ex. 4.62. Partita No. 1, BWV 825, Allemande, bars 17–18

Ex. 4.63); undoubtedly the same execution was intended as in bars 17–18 (see Ex. 4.64).[50]

Ex. 4.63. Partita No. 1, BWV 825, Allemande, bars 37–8

Ex. 4.64

In contrast to this 'ultra-legato', in which two or more notated parts constitute a single melodic line, there are the many themes in which Bach seems to be teasing a two-part texture from a single voice, such as the fugue subject of the E minor Toccata for harpsichord (Ex. 4.65). Themes of this kind convey the impression of 'real' two-part writing, as in Ex. 4.66. This does not mean that this fugue subject should be played legatissimo. In fact the opposite is the case: the latent two-part writing is best heard if played non-legato (*détaché*). Bach makes good use of this way of 'spelling out' chords in the works for solo violin or cello.

Ex. 4.65. Harpsichord Toccata in E minor, BWV 914, bars 71–5

[50] About a cent. later Beethoven 'reinvented' this kind of 'ultra-legato'. See the beginning of the Piano Sonata Op. 109:

Ex. 4.66

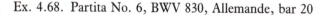

LEGATO AND NON-LEGATO IN ARPEGGIOS AND BROKEN CHORDS

Many of the arpeggios in Bach's keyboard music should also be played legato. Usually the arpeggio consists of a more or less rapid succession of notes outlining the chord from bass to treble (and sometimes back again). The affection and the type of composition can also have an influence on how broken chords are played. Some of the ways in which it is possible to articulate such figuration are examined below. (See also Chapter 18 on arpeggios.)

Legato and Legatissimo Execution

Ex. 4.67. Chromatic Fantasia, arpeggiated passage, bars 28–31

Ex. 4.68. Partita No. 6, BWV 830, Allemande, bar 20

Later version

Earlier version in the *Notenbüchlein* for Anna Magdalena Bach: execution

The chord should also be held where this is not specifically notated, as for instance, at the beginning of the Toccata of the E minor Partita (Ex. 4.69). On instruments with variable dynamic attack (the clavichord, fortepiano, and modern piano) it is important in such arpeggios to emphasize the outer parts and to 'thin out' the harmonic padding, that is, to play more delicately, especially in the lower register. (Bach's scoring demonstrates that the outer parts tended to be emphasized, even in polyphonic movements. This was a common stylistic feature of the epoch.[51]) The character of the arpeggios is determined primarily by their speed. The delicate final arpeggio of the Allemande of Partita No. 6 stands in contrast to the energetic nature of Exx. 4.67 and 4.69. (See also Chapter 18, Arpeggios.)

Ex. 4.69. Partita No. 6, BWV 830, Toccata, bars 1–2: suggested execution

Energetic Detached Execution in Toccata Passages

At the toccata-like beginning of the Chromatic Fantasia in D minor, non-legato attack is recommended for the semiquaver figures from bar 3 onwards (see Ex. 4.70). At the beginning of the C minor Fantasia, BWV 906, the descending broken triad should not be played legato, especially on modern pianos, as it does not consist of consecutive seconds. However, on the harpsichord it may be played legato so long as this does not blur the incisive quality of the rhythm (Ex. 4.71).

---

[51] See Hochreither, *Zur Aufführungspraxis*, pp. 118 f.

Ex. 4.70. Chromatic Fantasia, bars 1–8

Ex. 4.71. Fantasia in C minor, BWV 906, bars 1–2

In the Style of a Lute

Though written for lute, on which articulation is wholly impossible, the Prelude in C minor, BWV 999, is often played on the piano. In this case the performer should imitate a lute (see Ex. 4.72). See also Exx. 4.73 and 4.74, which display similar characteristics.

Ex. 4.72. Prelude in C minor, BWV 999, bars 1–3

Ex. 4.73. Partita No. 1, BWV 825, Allemande, bars 1–3

Ex. 4.74. Chromatic Fugue, bars 49–52

On a fortepiano or modern piano, finger-staccato combined with frequent pedalling ('semi-pedal') produces a charming effect. Here non legato is also possible on the harpsichord. But the desired plucking effect can also be achieved in legato by selecting a lute stop. As only a handful of German harpsichords from the time of Bach have survived, it is difficult to say how common lute stops were. On the other hand, we know that Bach had a *Lautenwerk* or lute harpsichord which sounded almost exactly like a lute.

A special role is played by figured broken chords, which should usually be played legato. An example of this is the C sharp major Prelude of *WTC* II (Ex. 4.75), though here the first two semiquavers could well be separated.

Ex. 4.75. *WTC* II, Prelude in C sharp major, bars 1–3

Similarly, there are arpeggios (which should also be played legato) with added non-harmonic notes (acciaccaturas). The Organ Fantasia in G major (*Pièce d'orgue*), BWV 572, is a good example of this (see Ex. 4.76). In contrast, the acciaccaturas in the Sarabande of the E minor Partita should be rapid and 'sharp'. The appoggiatura B in bar 1 is of course one of the acciaccaturas on to the A minor seventh chord, and must not be played slowly, as is sometimes the case (Ex. 4.77). In central and northern Germany oblique lines through chords signified acciaccaturas, whereas in southern Germany, Vienna, and

Ex. 4.76. Organ Fantasia in G major, BWV 572, bars 186–7

Ex. 4.77. Partita No. 6, BWV 830, Sarabande, bars 1–2

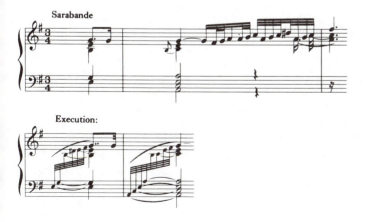

Italy they merely signified an arpeggio. In other words, there are no non-harmonic notes in an arpeggio notated in this way. Performers are largely ignorant of this fact, and nowadays this often leads to incorrect 'Bachian' interpretations of Haydn and Mozart.

Finally, another kind of articulation occurs in Bach's works which, remarkably, has been neglected both in theory and in practice. This is rhythmic articulation by graphic means: the way the notes are grouped and beamed. It should be self-evident that notes which are separated visually should also be kept apart aurally, in both legato and non-legato. In Exx. 4.78 and 4.79 the breaks are determined by the change of manual. Taking his cue from such passages, Wilhelm Rust, the editor-in-chief of the old BGA, printed similar groupings in the last movement of Bach's C minor Concerto for two harpsichords, BWV 1060 (see Ex. 4.80). Though not authentic, the thinking behind this is acceptable. Incidentally, this kind of articulation frequently occurs in Mozart.

Ex. 4.78. Italian Concerto, first movement, bars 56–60

Ex. 4.79. French Overture, BWV 831, Echo, bars 58–62

By studying Bach's manuscripts the performer can learn from the composer's own articulation signs how the majority of his unmarked pieces should be played. He will then find, both to his own satisfaction and to that of his listeners, that properly articulated music breathes, as it were, and gains a new lease of life.

Ex. 4.80. Concerto in C minor for two harpsichords, BWV 1060, last movement, bars 10–14

5

Dynamics

INTRODUCTION

The paucity of dynamic marks in baroque music makes it necessary for every musician to determine the dynamics he intends to apply. First some remarks concerning dynamics on the harpsichord. Shaping the dynamics of the melodic lines is only marginally possible on the harpsichord, though it must not be overlooked. François Couperin says of this:

As the notes of the clavecin are each of them fixed, and as a result can neither increase nor decrease in volume, it seemed almost inconceivable hitherto that one might imbue this instrument with a soul. However, through the effort with which I have moulded the little talent Heaven has given me, I will try to explain how I have acquired the good fortune of being able to move people with taste.

The emotive expression I mean owes its effect to the timely application of 'interruption' (*cessation*) and 'delay' (*suspension*) according to the character required by the melodies of the preludes and pieces. These two kinds of embellishments (*agréments*) in their contradictory quality leave the ear in doubt to such an extent that where bowed instruments swell their notes, the notes of the clavecin, by a contrary effect, convey the same effect to the ear. In the table of ornaments of my first volume I already explained, by means of note-values and rests, aspiration [accented abbreviation of the note], and suspension [delayed entry of a note], but I hope that the idea that I have given of it, however brief, will not be without use for sensitive people.[1]

Other means of emphasis on the harpsichord are an increase in the number of voices, the application of fast ornaments (e.g. mordents), and a slight lengthening of expressive notes and corresponding shortening of unimportant notes (rubato).

Common to all keyboard instruments is the concern with emphasis, 'non-emphasis', and the increasing and decreasing dynamics of melodic lines. All this is easier to put into practice on the fortepiano and the clavichord than on the harpsichord. Rhythm, melody, and harmony are subject to their own laws which can of course come into conflict. With regard to rhythm, it is important

[1] *L'Art*, p. 14.

to distinguish between strong and weak beats. In 4/4 1 and 3 are stronger than 2 and 4, in 3/4 2 and 3 are weaker than 1. Furthermore, it is a fact that longer notes are 'stronger' than short ones. With regard to harmony, there is the old rule that dissonances should be emphasized, and that the ensuing consonances should be weaker.

Yet the most important feature of cantabile legato is 'melodic dynamics'. Here keyboard players should take their cue from singers. C. P. E. Bach says:

> Above all, lose no opportunity to hear artistic singing. In so doing, the player will learn to think in terms of song. Indeed, it is good practice to sing instrumental melodies in order to reach an understanding of their correct performance. This way of learning is of far greater value than the reading of voluminous tomes or listening to learned discourses. In these one meets such terms as Nature, Taste, Song, and Melody.[2]

Only those who sing themselves, or who observe singers closely, know that in long notes the voice swells slightly; that high notes, on account of the greater tension of the vocal cords and so on, are louder and more intense than low ones; that a beautiful vocal phrase usually begins and ends in a relaxed manner, reaching its dynamic peak half-way through. But above all a singer knows that it is necessary to breathe and articulate (or declaim) well. It is of the utmost importance for him to discern the right breathing pauses in the music or the text. Where phrases follow each other directly the singer has very little time to breathe, and this necessitates a short rhythmic retardation that is often made up for by subsequent acceleration. Far from being felt as obtrusive, such pauses permit the music to 'breathe', and impart to it an 'eloquent' kind of expression that differs markedly from the monotonous way in which music is often rattled off on the piano. Above all, a good singer must take an interest in the relationship between the words and the music. Often it is only the text which 'explains' the affection or the emotional expression of an aria or a song, especially where the music does not express its essence in an unambiguous manner. Bach adapted a number of cantata movements in his instrumental works. Knowledge of the original text can give the keyboard player valuable insights into the emotional content of this and similar pieces.

With regard to increasing and decreasing dynamics in the case of single notes, wind instruments are closest to the voice. It is instructive to study an example provided by Quantz, who, using a slow movement of a flute sonata, expressed these inner melodic dynamics with the help of a system of abbreviations. Karl Hochreither has transcribed this example, part of which is cited here in Ex. 5.1, into modern notation.[3] At first these dynamics seem exaggerated, at least on paper. However, if we regard the dynamic values in relative terms, substituting 'stronger' for 'forte' and 'weaker' or 'unstressed' for 'piano', the shaping of the line seems to be perfect. Of particular interest

---

[2] *Essay*, pp. 151–2.   [3] See also Perl, *Rhythmische Phrasierung*, pp. 251–4.

Ex. 5.1. Quantz's dynamic markings in the slow movement of a flute sonata, transcribed in Hochreither, *Zur Aufführungspraxis*, p. 121

are the unstressed passing appoggiaturas in bars 1 and 2. Here most modern performers would place the emphasis quite differently.

Robert Marshall has compiled a very useful list of all dynamic marks found in Bach's works.[4] As the vast majority appear only in vocal pieces, few keyboard players will be aware of the subtle way in which Bach sometimes expressed his intentions. Among baroque composers he is unique in this respect as well.

Few musicians know that in Bach *pp* (in agreement with Walther's *Musicalisches Lexicon*[5]) does not signify 'pianissimo', but 'più piano'. In the

---

[4] 'Tempo and Dynamic Indications', p. 261.   [5] pp. 257 f.

first movement of the D major Harpsichord Concerto, BWV 1054 (the keyboard version of the E major Violin Concerto), bars 17–19 and 35–7 of the viola part are marked '*p–pp*–pianissimo', which practically amounts to a diminuendo.

As an intermediate mark between 'piano' and 'forte' Bach used the expressions 'poco piano', 'mezo forte' (sic), and 'poco forte'. It is also noteworthy that Bach repeatedly wrote 'poco forte' in contrast to the predominant 'piano' in places where a tutti ritornello motif subsequently appeared in the accompanying parts and was to be emphasized, as in the oboe part of the duet 'Gott du hast es wohl gefüget' from the Weimar Christmas Cantata No. 63 or in the aria 'Mein Erlöser und Erhalter' from Cantata No. 69, *Lobe den Herrn, meine Seele*. In this connection Bach's use of the indication 'poco forte', which occurs twice (bars 37 and 59) in the first movement of the C major Concerto for three harpsichords, BWV 1064, deserves to be mentioned. It is a sign of a dynamic differentiation that is relatively rare in baroque notation.[6]

Marshall also points out that music bearing the indication 'poco piano' should be played more loudly or more softly than a normal *p* in accordance with the context and the affection. The most interesting subtlety occurs in the first movement of the Second Brandenburg Concerto: by adding 'forte' in bars 45 and 51–4 and similar passages Bach set off the predominant thematic lines against the rest, which are marked 'piano'—a wholly modern kind of notation. The first movement of the Fifth Brandenburg Concerto also contains examples of subtle dynamics, for instance in bars 31, 50, 71, and 100.

TERRACE DYNAMICS

'Terrace dynamics' is a concept which is occasionally misunderstood and sometimes misused. In orchestral works (such as overtures, suites, and especially concerti grossi) terrace dynamics came into being by the alternation of tutti and solo (or concertino) passages. It would of course be wrong to suppose that within a 'terrace' one should be inflexible in the use of forte or piano, though it would be equally wrong to introduce crescendos or decrescendos designed to turn the terraces into slopes.

We should treat the concept of terrace dynamics with caution, for the term was coined only about a hundred years ago. In fact, the Baroque era probably made far greater use of dynamics than we now like to suppose. As early as 1619 Michael Praetorius wrote that the violinist presented 'affections' on his instrument in 'bowing and applying pressure loudly or quietly'.[7] The use of

---

[6] I am grateful to Klaus Hofmann for pointing out that the indication 'poco forte' is not infrequent in baroque violin music.

[7] *Syntagma musicum*, ii (Wolfenbüttel, 1619), 69.

dynamics in accordance with the 'affection' was even more important in vocal music. Only on the harpsichord and the organ was it impossible to achieve dynamic gradations by means of melodic inflection. This was possible only by a change of manual or registration, the increase or decrease in the number of voices, and other artificial means such as those indicated by Couperin (see above p. 130). In the age of Bach this was occasionally felt to be a disadvantage. Like many other commentators, C. P. E. Bach noted that in this regard the fortepiano was superior to the harpsichord:

We shall open the subject of performance by discussing volume. Of all the instruments that are used in the playing of thorough bass the single-manual harpsichord is the most perplexing with regard to *forte* and *piano*. To make amends for the imperfection of the instrument in this respect the number of parts must be increased or reduced. . . . Some resort to a highly detached touch in order to express a *piano*, but the performance suffers tremendously by this; and even the most detached staccato performance requires pressure. . . . The fine invention of our celebrated Holefeld which makes it possible to increase or decrease the registration by means of pedals, while playing, has made the harpsichord, particularly the single-manual kind, a much-improved instrument, and, fortunately, eliminated all difficulties connected with the performance of a *piano*. If only all harpsichords were similarly constructed as a tribute to good taste! . . . But aside from this invention, the clavichord and fortepiano enjoy great advantages over the harpsichord and organ because of the many ways in which their volume can be gradually changed.[8]

However, even in the case of the harpsichord and the organ, changes of manual were often more concerned with changes in tone-colour than with dynamics.

The dynamic differences between the terraces were fairly small by modern standards, so in order to pander to the modern listener used to less subtle fare it will often be necessary to emphasize some of the contrasts. Yet even Quantz stated that excesses should be avoided:

The Forte and Piano must never be unduly exaggerated. The instruments must not be handled with more force than their constitution permits, since the ear will be most disagreeably affected, especially in a small place. You must always be able, in case of necessity, to express an additional Fortissimo or Pianissimo. It may often happen that you must unexpectedly bring out or soften a note, even if nothing is indicated. And this opportunity will be lost if you always play with the greatest loudness or softness. There are also many more degrees of moderation between the Fortissimo and the Pianissimo than can be expressed by words; these degrees must be executed with great discretion, and can only be learned through feeling and judgement from the execution of a good soloist. The Fortissimo, or the greatest volume of tone, can be achieved

---

[8] *Essay*, pp. 368–9. The possibility of engaging and disengaging stops by means of pedals was particularly favoured by English harpsichord makers in the 2nd half of the 18th cent. The Venetian swell, which made it possible to achieve differences in the dynamic level *within* a register (again by means of a pedal), came into use at about the same time.

most conveniently with the lowest part of the bow, playing rather close to the bridge, and the Pianissimo, or the utmost softness of tone, with the tip of the bow, rather far from the bridge.[9]

Terrace dynamics are often employed on the organ and on two-manual harpsichords. In fugues, for instance, certain episodes should be played on the quieter manual. Once again it is Quantz who provides interesting information on how to play fugue subjects:

The *principal subject* (*thema*), particularly in a fugue, must be vigorously stressed in each part whenever it appears unexpectedly, especially if it begins with long notes. Neither a flattering style of playing nor extempore additions are permissible in it. If in the continuation of the fugue no rests precede its entry, you may moderate the volume of the preceding notes somewhat. You must proceed in the same manner with notes that resemble the principal ideas, or are inserted as new ideas in the middle of the piece, whether in the tutti or during the solo of a concertante part.[10]

These comments are in marked contrast to the habit of playing longer string notes so that they start as it were from nothing. Wilfried Bruchhäuser rightly notes that in the Baroque era instrumentation was nothing more than a kind of registration. 'Registrational orchestration shares with the models of its origins the direct presence of starting transients. In the case of the organ and the harpsichord the note is there, or it is not. Similar things were expected of other instruments. Gradually creeping into a note and other hypertrophic sensitization processes first appeared in the late Romantic period.'[11]

ECHO DYNAMICS

Echo effects were very popular in the Baroque era (and earlier): 'In the repetition of the same or of similar ideas consisting of half or whole bars, whether at the same level or in transposition the repetition of the idea may be played somewhat more softly than the first statement.'[12] In works with dynamic marks J. S. Bach on occasion makes use of an echo effect, though very sparingly. In *Clavier-Übung*, Part II, it occurs in only two movements, namely the first movement of the Italian Concerto, BWV 971, and the last movement of the French Overture, BWV 831. The *St Matthew Passion* contains only one echo effect, in the final chorus, with telling poetic effect— 'Ruhe sanft'. Bach's reticence in this respect is quite understandable: echo

---

[9] *On Playing the Flute*, pp. 274–5.
[10] *On Playing the Flute*, p. 277.
[11] 'Zur Aufführungspraxis der Werke Johann Sebastian Bachs—Forschung–Tradition–Willkür', *Bach-Tage Berlin* (Neuhausen and Stuttgart, 1985), 100.
[12] Quantz, *On Playing the Flute*, p. 277.

effects often prettify and detract from the monumental impression, as if in a Greek temple one wished to 'loosen up' the regularity of Doric columns by adding a few Corinthian capitals. Echoes can also significantly interrupt the flow of a work. For this reason they should be used sparingly in unmarked works. They might be applied in the fugal subject of the C minor Toccata, BWV 911, bars 34–5 and parallel passages; in the Corrente of the E minor Partita, BWV 830, bars 31–2 and 91–3; and, possibly, in the D minor Organ Toccata, BWV 565, bars 6–7. They should not be applied to the Chromatic Fantasia, bar 4 or bar 15, which are not exact repetitions of the preceding ideas. Here some editions print dynamic marks and variants which claim to stem from Wilhelm Friedemann Bach, but these are later additions foreign to the style of J. S. Bach.

WHEN SHOULD ONE PLAY PIANO, AND WHEN SHOULD ONE PLAY FORTE?

As Bach's music is more subtle and complex than that of his contemporaries, there is reason to believe that this had an effect on his use of dynamics and registration. This view is supported by Forkel's remarks that Bach 'was able to make his performances as varied as a conversation', and that he had drawn forth sounds from the organ, by means of unusual registrations, which even the organ-builder himself had considered impossible.

To all this came his personal way of combining the various voices of the organ, or his art of registration. It was so unusual that many organ-builders and organists were startled when they witnessed his registrations. They were of the opinion that such a combination of stops could not possibly sound good; but were most surprised afterwards to note that the organ sounded best in this way, having acquired a strange, unusual quality which their own manner of registration could not bring forth.[13]

Bach was obviously inspired by the instrument of the moment, and of course by the harpsichords, lute harpsichords, clavichords, or fortepianos at his disposal. A good example of an unusual registration, which, exceptionally, Bach in fact wrote down, is found in the chorale prelude *Gott durch Deine Güte*, BWV 600, from the *Orgel-Büchlein*, where he stipulated that the chorale should be played by an eight-foot trumpet pedal, and the real bass voice (*Prinzipal*) by the left hand. According to Alfred Dürr this is a practice that already occurs in the organ works of Scheidt.

It is disconcerting to hear performers 'rattling off' pieces with contrasting themes such as the first movements of English Suite No. 6 and of Partitas Nos. 4 and 6, at the same dynamic level (usually forte). Such performers have

---

[13] *Bachs Leben*, p. 44; Eng. trans., *The Bach Reader*, p. 314.

obviously not taken the trouble to glean the relevant information from similarly structured movements in which Bach added dynamic indications.

Our most important sources of information are of course the three works for two-manual harpsichord in which Bach himself provided detailed dynamic marks, namely the Italian Concerto, BWV 971, the French Overture, BWV 831, and, indirectly, the Goldberg Variations. In the latter, in place of dynamic marks, there are indications on the use of the two manuals. (The second manual is usually used as a soft register.) At first sight this does not seem to add up to very much, but it is actually a great deal for a composer of Bach's time. Domenico Scarlatti, for example, only added dynamic marks to a single sonata, K. 70 (Longo 50, Fadini 30).[14]

Most famous of all are the dynamic indications in the Italian Concerto. The first movement, composed in the Italian concerto form often found in Vivaldi, Corelli, and Marcello (but also in the First Brandenburg Concerto), distinguishes between the 'tutti', which employs all the available stops and is repeated in total or in part, and the 'solo' episodes, which in a real concerto were assigned to the solo violin, or the concertino, a group of soloists. From this point of view Bach's registration is not altogether successful, because the solo passages are played at the same forte as the tutti, with the sole difference that the accompaniment is now played piano and the texture as a whole is thinner and more delicate. This minor blemish—it is as if six violins in unison were playing the solo part in a violin concerto—is naturally bound up with the nature of the instrument itself. Changing the registration in the course of a movement, for instance switching off the four-foot stop at the entry of the first solo passage, would have been too time-consuming, necessitating an involuntary pause, and was thus not viable musically. In the opening movements of English Suites Nos. 2–6, Bach is clearly at pains to refashion the tutti–solo contrast into a texture of this kind.

The second movement, with its decidedly 'Italian' cantilena, is an ideal transcription for a keyboard instrument of an imaginary solo concerto movement. The forte in the solo part was probably not intended to be as loud as the 'orchestral' tutti in the first and last movements. Experience shows that such solo cantilenas should be played with one or two eight-foot stops, without an additional four-foot stop, and the accompaniment as quietly as possible on the second manual. Pianists should not hesitate to play the vocal part with a full and expressive tone. The only difficulty on the harpsichord occurs at the end of the movement, where the dynamic level has a natural tendency to decrease, something that cannot be rendered on this instrument. The resolution of the suspension in the final chord of the left hand is invariably too loud.

---

[14] Personal communication from Emilia Fadini, ed. of the Scarlatti complete edn. (Ricordi).

In the third movement, a Presto, Bach departed furthest from the orchestral concerto model, composing one of the most brilliant of all 'keyboard' pieces. The way in which he makes a dynamic distinction in the second theme between main and subsidiary voices by occasionally assigning the forte register to the left hand and the piano register to the right (e.g. in bar 25) is remarkable. So is the incongruence of the registration in the third theme (the second episode). On its first appearance (bar 77) both hands play piano, whereas the second time round (bars 155–71) the bass figure is marked 'forte'. I believe that this departure from the schema is wholly intentional. Applied to other works, it signifies that it is not always necessary to use the same registration for similar passages.

The B minor French Overture, BWV 831, is a mine of information about the right application of forte and piano registration. In the first movement the first and last sections should be played using all the stops available. The Allegro section, an ingenious combination of fugal and concerto forms, makes a clear distinction between the forte of the fugal sections and the piano of the episodes, which should of course be played on the second manual. These dynamics should also be applied in the case of similarly constructed overtures, for instance in that of Partita No. 4, bar 33 (Ex. 5.2). There the second theme, which enters at this point, is similar in style to soft Christmas music.

Ex. 5.2. Partita No. 4, BWV 828, Ouverture, bars 33–5

In such cases it sometimes happens that at the end of an episode one hand is still playing piano whilst the other is already playing forte the 'precursor' of a fugal ritornello, as for example in bar 89 of the first movement of the French Overture. The dynamic indications in the other movements of this work are very instructive, for example in the ternary dance forms, where the trio (e.g. Gavotte II) should normally be played more quietly than the outer sections. Naturally Bach's 'forte' does not mean the same in all eight or eleven movements[15] of this, his largest solo suite. It can be interpreted on the harpsichord as follows: first manual, eight-foot stop; first and second manuals, coupled eight-foot stops, or a 'tutti' encompassing a four-foot stop. Sixteen-

---

[15] Modern edns. print Gavotte I, II, etc. as separate movements. Strictly speaking this is an error.

foot stops were so unusual on eighteenth-century harpsichords that this register is only mentioned here in passing. Finally, the last movement of the French Overture, entitled 'Echo', makes great demands on the harpsichordist with regard to switching swiftly from one manual to the other.

In statistical terms there are far more 'forte' marks in Bach's keyboard works than any other dynamic indications. This is probably linked to the 'joyful' baroque attitude to life. Unmarked works should normally also begin forte. This, incidentally, also holds true of Haydn and Mozart.

The Goldberg Variations, with their stipulations on the use of one or two manuals, are a mine of information about dynamic marks, though of a different kind. It is fascinating to note that Bach repeatedly leaves it to the player to decide whether to play a variation on one or two manuals, that is, with a homogeneous or a 'divided' sound; for example, the seventh variation is headed 'a 1 ovvero 2 Clav'. There are interesting suggestions for registration in Ralph Kirkpatrick's edition of this work (p. xxvi).[16] However, they stem from a time which relished the use of the sixteen-foot stop on Pleyel harpsichords and similar instruments.

The organ works also provide valuable hints on where to play piano and forte. Thus Bach, in the final movement of his variations on 'O Gott, du frommer Gott', BWV 767, gave detailed instructions for changing manuals by adding 'piano' and 'forte' marks. According to Hans Klotz, this corresponds exactly to the alternation between 'Grand Clavier' and 'Positif' in the 'Dialogues sur les Grands Jeux' by French composers such as Couperin and de Grigny,[17] which in turn suggests that Bach used the reed chorus. Those who have studied these models should not find it difficult to decide whether a piece ought to be played in a tender and cantabile way or in a vigorously forthright manner. The presence of all the voices virtually always signifies forte. Klotz is surely right when he says that it is primarily the structure of a keyboard or organ work from which changes of manual, and thus dynamic gradations, should be deduced:

A change of manual, if it is at all justified musically, can be regarded as authentic if both the end of a *Hauptwerk* passage, and the beginning of a new one

(*a*) are stylistically unobjectionable in all voices,
(*b*) are physically and technically possible, and
(*c*) can be applied consistently in all parallel passages.

On the basis of these criteria Bach's preludes and fugues divide into two groups. In the first group a change of manual immediately poses so many problems that the idea

---

[16] See App. 1.
[17] *Studien zu Bachs Registrierkunst* (Wiesbaden, 1983), 60. George B. Stauffer's essay 'Über Bachs Orgelregistrierpraxis', *BJb*, 67 (1981) was reissued in slightly modified form as 'Bach's Organ Registration Reconsidered' in the collection of essays *J. S. Bach as Organist: His Instruments, Music and Performance Practices*, ed. George B. Stauffer and Ernest May (Bloomington, Ind., 1986), 193 ff. Klotz disagrees with some of Stauffer's views.

must be dismissed at once. In the second group the conditions are fulfilled so exactly that it is no longer a matter of chance, and virtually certain that Bach himself was thinking in terms of more than one manual.[18]

The discussion of Bach's art of registration in the last chapter of Klotz's book is extremely interesting, and should also prove stimulating to harpsichordists and pianists.

It hardly needs to be said that the numerous dynamic marks in nineteenth-century editions of Bach were mostly added by ignorant and sentimental 'romantics' acting in a wholly arbitrary manner. They should simply be ignored.[19] Murmuring in a weak sort of way is out of place in Bach's music. If in doubt, play forte (but please ensure that it is a singing forte).

DYNAMIC GRADATIONS, CONCLUDING CRESCENDOS

The following remark by Quantz on the execution of tied notes is instructive: 'In ligatures or tied notes that consist of crotchets or minims, the volume of the tone may be allowed to swell, since the other parts have dissonances. Dissonances in general, in whatever part they are found, always require special emphasis.'[20]

Do crescendo and decrescendo play a role in Bach's music? Though there are no large-scale written-out crescendos in the nineteenth-century sense, one nevertheless notices an inner dynamic which is the result of harmonic tension, a thickening of the polyphonic web, and an increase in the number of voices. Karl Hochreither has observed that in some choral fugues (e.g. the first movement of Cantata No. 76, *Die Himmel erzählen die Ehre Gottes*) an architectonic intensification transcending the additive process is achieved by an increase in the number of parts—in this case the trumpet adds a fifth voice.[21] Hochreither rightly observes: 'Inevitably, however, singers and instrumentalists will demonstrate a greater degree of intensity from exposition to exposition. It would be artificial to leave it at mere addition, and . . . thus to deny the restrospective intensifying effect of 'additional registration'.[22] Of interest in this connection is the entry of the oboe in the Wedding Cantata No. 202, *Weichet nur, betrübte Schatten.*[23]

A common feature of Bach's keyboard music is a concluding climax brought about by an increase in the number of voices. The third prelude from *WTC* I, which is in two parts, finishes with seven-part chords, and in the A

---

[18] *Bachs Registrierkunst*, p. 85.
[19] In such cases a Viennese conductor used to say 'Net amol ignoriern' (Don't even bother to ignore it).
[20] *On Playing the Flute*, p. 277.
[21] *Zur Aufführungspraxis*, pp. 118 f.   [22] *Zur Aufführungspraxis*, pp. 110 f.
[23] I am grateful to Alfred Dürr for this information. He pointed out that as early as 1938 Werner Neumann had made similar observations in *J. S. Bachs Chorfuge* (Leipzig, 1938; end edn., 1950).

minor Fugue from *WTC* I the four-part texture becomes a six-part one at the end. This practice is particularly apparent in the Chromatic Fugue, BWV 903. At two 'points of congestion' (bars 94 and 135) the three parts increase to eight.[24] Furthermore, the last four bars are in six parts, with octaves in the left hand, a rare device in Bach. In spite of such concluding intensification modern performances of Bach fugues often end with a diminuendo, for instance in the great C sharp minor Fugue of *WTC* I. In my opinion this desire to 'let the sound die away' is based on an incorrect interpretation of the long concluding pedal-note. Bass notes tied over several bars do in fact die away to a *pianissimo* on stringed keyboard instruments. However, striking a pedal-note once and then holding it applies only to performances on the organ. On other keyboard instruments the bass note must normally be restruck after two or three bars. 'The performer may break a long tied note by restriking the key.'[25] This also applies to long held notes in the upper register, for example at the end of the C sharp minor Fugue of *WTC* I. 'If the bass alone has the held note, the accompanist may repeat solely the bass note just as it dies out. But this must not be done "against the beat", as the expression goes. In a duple bar the repetitions may occur at the beginning and in the middle, according to its divisions and the pace. In a triple bar only the downbeat is played.'[26] Quantz was even more adamant about restriking bass notes, 'for without the fundamental note the dissonances are transformed into consonances by the ear, destroying the desired effect.'[27] In the *WTC* there are numerous places where a long held note in the bass can be restruck—in Book I, for instance, in preludes No. 7 (bars 1–3), No. 12 (bars 17–21), and No. 16 (bars 18–19) and at the end of fugues No. 1, No. 2, No. 4, and No. 20.

The problem of 'long notes' is dealt with differently by François Couperin. He recommends using trills or long mordents, whereas C. P. E. Bach makes a point of warning against the application of trills on such notes:

Why must the finest legato passages be ruined so often by inept playing? Indeed, most errors are committed in just such places [long and held notes]. Trills are introduced in an attempt to rescue these passages from oblivion. . . . It is apparent that those guilty of these faults can neither think lyrically nor grant each tone its proper weight and length. Tones will sing on the harpsichord as well as on the clavichord if they are not detached from each other, although one instrument may be better constructed for this purpose than another. . . . Even when the tempo is too slow or the instrument not good enough to sustain tones properly, it is better to sacrifice a little of the clear flow of a legato passage than to disrupt it with trills, for a correct performance will be ample compensation for the lack of sonority.[28]

[24] Some eds. disregard the sources and add a 'linking' passing note b on the last crotchet of bar 93, thereby destroying the 'congestion' effect.

[25] C. P. E. Bach, *Essay*, p. 159.

[26] C. P. E. Bach, *Essay*, p. 374.

[27] *On Playing the Flute*, p. 263.

[28] *Essay*, p. 106.

However, C. P. E. Bach later states that, in order to enhance the cantabile quality of an Adagio, singers sometimes discreetly applied trills and mordents.

Of course Bach also wrote diminuendo endings. They are structurally appropriate in quiet and delicate pieces that are cantabile in character, such as the C sharp minor Prelude of *WTC* I, or in certain allemandes, but almost always inappropriate in fugues. At the end of the Chromatic Fantasia, there is a kind of elaborated diminuendo: the melody descends nearly two octaves, and the character of the phrases changes from confidence $(d^2-g^1-bb^1)$ to resignation $(d^2-d^1-g\sharp^1)$. Yet even here, in view of the full final chord, the diminuendo should not, in my opinion, be exaggerated.

Just as an increase in the number of voices suggests a crescendo, a reduction in the number of voices signifies a decrease in the dynamic level, not as a diminuendo, but in the shape of a sudden change of registration. Thus, in the Chromatic Fugue, the two lute-like episodes (beginning at bars 49 and 97) are best played with a restrained second manual registration (a lute stop, if possible), or non legato at the piano with 'semi-pedal'. The following fugal entries should not be prepared for by a crescendo, but played subito forte (first manual). Compare the remark by Quantz quoted above concerning the preparation of (forte) fugal entries by means of a diminuendo.

We may, indeed we should apply dynamics to Bach's keyboard music, but we ought to bear in mind the limitations imposed by the structure of the music. It is wrong to begin a Bach fugue like a purring kitten, and to end like a roaring lion.

In connection with the concluding climax, holding the final chord also plays an important role. The common habit of abbreviating the last chord is to be deplored. That Bach was not merely complying with a convention when he notated many final chords in long sustained notes, often with fermatas to boot, is shown by the fact that he also wrote numerous short final chords. Examples from the *WTC* include Book I, preludes No. 2, No. 11, No. 13, and No. 21 and fugues No. 10 and No. 15; Book II, preludes No. 4, No. 7, and No. 8, and fugues No. 4, No. 11, and No. 16. Christoph Albrecht warns against the opposite mistake (more common among organists) of lengthening short final notes:

Finally, in quite a number of pieces even the last note still poses problems. If a piece ends with a long note, especially if it lasts a full bar, it should be held for at least the full extent of its value. Nobody will object to it being prolonged, provided that this is not out of keeping with the rest of the piece, no matter whether or not the composer has added a fermata. On the other hand, it is wrong for a performer to depart from the text in final bars where the metre is carefully written out, and, ostensibly for the sake of a more effective ending, to hold a short final chord longer than it is notated, for example in Bach's B minor Prelude, BWV 544

or in the C major Fugue, BWV 564.

If Bach had considered a long final chord desirable, he could have considerably simplified the troublesome notation of the final bars.[29]

In conclusion it should be mentioned that the recent past has witnessed the rise of the strange habit of 'emasculating' the final rhythms on the strong beat, the so-called masculine endings, by adding free and wholly unjustified long appoggiaturas or trills. If this practice continues, Beethoven's Fifth Symphony will be played as in Ex. 5.3 a hundred years from now. Further comment on this subject is superfluous.

Ex. 5.3

[29] *Interpretationsfragen*, p. 126.

Problems of Sonority

INSTRUMENTS IN THE AGE OF BACH

It may be taken for granted that J. S. Bach was intimately acquainted with the rich variety of instruments in use in his time. It may also be taken for granted that Bach was not always wholly satisfied with these instruments, particularly when the ones at his disposal were of poor quality or in need of repair. This may have been one of the reasons why he acquired a rather large collection of instruments, as is shown by the catalogue of his estate.

Extract from the catalogue of Bach's estate:

Particulars [*Specificatio*] of the estate of the late Johann Sebastian Bach, formerly cantor at St Thomas's School in Leipzig, who died on 28 July 1750.

Chapter VI

Instruments

1 veneered clavecin, which is to remain in the family if at all possible	80	–	–
1 Clavesin	50	–	–
1 ditto	50	–	–
1 ditto	50	–	–
1 ditto smaller	20	–	–
1 Lauten Werck [lute harpsichord]	30	–	–
1 ditto	30	–	–
1 Stainer violin	8	–	–
1 lower-quality violin	2	–	–
1 ditto piccolo	1	8	–
1 Braccie [viola]	5	–	–
1 ditto	5	–	–
1 ditto	–	16	–
1 Bassettgen [small bass]	6	–	–
1 Violoncello	6	–	–
1 ditto	–	16	–
1 Viola da Gamba	3	–	–
1 Lute	21	–	–

1 Spinettgen [small spinet]	3	– –
Summa summarum	371	16 –[1]

The collection was rather valuable, particularly when we bear in mind that the valuations were usually kept deliberately low for the benefit of the heirs.

We will have reason to return to the catalogue of Bach's estate on a number of occasions. Elsewhere the *Specificatio* mentions the fact that Bach's youngest son, Johann Christian, received '3. Clavire nebst Pedal' during his father's lifetime. Two of these 'Clavire' may have been clavichords; and the pedal may either have been an instrument in its own right placed beneath the harpsichord, or combined with a clavichord or a harpsichord. However, it is also conceivable that one of the three 'Clavire' was a fortepiano. At any rate, it is a remarkable fact that Chapter VI of the *Specificatio* lists seven wing-shaped keyboard instruments, but does not mention a clavichord. Alfred Dürr is of the opinion that this is because Anna Magdalena Bach may have claimed a clavichord as her personal property. Even if this were the case, it is still surprising that no clavichord is mentioned in the list.

CHURCH AND CHAMBER ORGANS

Bach was primarily an organist. Thus it is perhaps surprising that the catalogue of the estate does not list a chamber organ. In Leipzig he presumably did not need to practise at home in view of the proximity of St Thomas's Church.

As an organist Bach certainly had a number of predilections when it came to the combination of different sonorities. Thus, as Klotz has demonstrated, he did not like all Silbermann organs, for, in spite of their excellent workmanship, they did not always have a specification that came up to his expectations. Did he consider them to be too *rococo* in character? Further, Bach might not have been satisfied with Silbermann's unequal temperament. According to Klotz, he evidently liked a wide variety of sonorities, not only reed stops of all kinds, but also more delicate shades such as the Viola da gamba, Salizional, Gemshorn, and Quintadena stops and the bright *Glockenspiel* stop. And he was particularly enchanted by the sound of the full organ. That he also praised recondite stops such as the thirty-two-foot of the organ in Hamburg's St Catherine's Church is an established fact, as is his enthusiasm for the large number of reed stops on this organ. As a composer of contrapuntal works he no doubt liked to combine different stops. For further information, the reader is referred to Hans Klotz's excellent book *Studien zu*

---

[1] *Bach-Dokumente*, ii. 492 f. and 504.

Bachs Registrierkunst, and to the relevant publications by Robert Marshall[2] and George Stauffer.[3]

STRINGED AND PLUCKED INSTRUMENTS

Though Bach's fame was primarily due to his organ playing, he was evidently not only able to play all kinds of keyboard instruments, but also the violin. With regard to stringed instruments, Bach is known to have bewailed the lack of an intermediate member of the violin family. At his behest a very large viola, or 'tenor violin' was constructed (or reconstructed). This has gone down in history as the 'viola pomposa', and was evidently the instrument for which he wrote his violoncello piccolo parts.[4] In addition to this Bach still made use of the violino piccolo, for example in the First Brandenburg Concerto (an instrument of this kind is also listed in the catalogue of the estate). Finally, in the eighteenth century, there were still a greater number of bass stringed instruments in use than today. The so-called *bassettl* was presumably a small cello (in the catalogue of Bach's estate it is termed *bassettgen*). It has been suggested that it may possibly have been played like a viola pomposa. Then it was not a small double bass, and thus may well have been identical with the instrument Bach termed 'violoncello piccolo'.[5]

Merely of historical interest to violinists are the claims advanced by Arnold Schering and Albert Schweitzer, who suggested that Bach made use of a curved bow that enabled the performer to play in three and four parts at once, that is, making it possible to avoid arpeggiating the four-part chords such as those in the Chaconne of Bach's D minor Solo Partita. Though this idea was debated for decades, it was convincingly refuted by Andreas Moser[6] as early as 1920, and more recently, in 1956, by Eduard Melkus.[7] Towards the end of his life even Albert Schweitzer was convinced by the latter's arguments that the so-called 'Bach bow' was the result of an incorrect interpretation of the sources. Just as the so-called 'Bach trumpet' was an invention of the nineteenth century, the curved bow, though used in the nineteenth and early twentieth century (especially by the famous violinist Ole Bull), was most likely unknown to J. S. Bach and his friend, the Dresden court musician

---

[2] 'Organ or "Klavier"? Instrumental Prescriptions in the Sources of Bach's Keyboard Works', in *J. S. Bach as Organist*, ed. G. Stauffer and E. May, 212 ff.

[3] 'Bach's Organ Registration Reconsidered'. This is a modified version of Stauffer's earlier essay 'Über Bachs Orgelregistrierpraxis' in *BJb*, 1981.

[4] See Heinrich Besseler, 'Zum Problem der Tenorgeige', *Musikalische Gegenwartsfragen*, i (Heidelberg, 1949); W. Schrammek, 'Viola pomposa und Violoncello piccolo bei Johann Sebastian Bach', *Bericht über die Internationale Konferenz zum III. Internationalen Bachfest der DDR in Leipzig 1975* (Leipzig, 1977), pp. 345 ff.

[5] See Ulrich Drüner, 'Violoncello piccolo und Viola pomposa bei Bach', *BJb*, 73 (1987).

[6] 'Zu Joh. Seb. Bachs Sonaten und Partiten für Violine allein', *BJb*, 17 (1920), 52 ff.

[7] 'Zur Frage des Bach-Bogens', *ÖMZ*, 11 (1956), 99 ff. See also Melkus, 'Bach-Interpretation'.

Pisendel. Apart from Telmanyi, Tossy Spivakovsky was probably the last great violinist who, despite the refutation of this theory, continued to promote the idea of the curved 'Bach bow' in theory and practice, even after the Second World War,[8] and performed Bach's Chaconne with such a bow. His recording and that of Telmanyi are certainly of historical interest. However, few modern violinists would want to imitate the harmonium-like sound of the chords of the chaconne theme.

It is a different matter with regard to the welcome revival of certain other stringed instruments of Bach's time. Whereas the viola da gamba has come back into its own since the beginning of the century, and is nowadays an indispensable part of Bach performances, only a handful of musicians are able to play the viola d'amore. This mirrors the fact that Bach rarely had such a player at his disposal, and, with the exception of two cantatas, employed it only in the *St John Passion*. And even here, at a later performance, its place had to be taken by violins playing with mutes.[9] As the viola d'amore literature is rather small, and as the tuning of the instrument's twelve or fourteen strings (six or seven are sympathetic strings) can be very time-consuming, learning to play the viola d'amore is nowadays often not considered to be worth the effort. (There is no convincing evidence to suggest that the viola d'amore in Bach's day did not possess sympathetic strings. However, the number of normal and sympathetic strings varied.) The revival of the theorbo is of greater importance for performances of Bach's works, even if we take into account the fact that in Bach's autographs, as in the case of most other baroque composers, the instrument is never expressly stipulated. Yet it is an established fact that in the eighteenth century it was still in use as a thorough-bass instrument. At this time the collective term 'lute' also served to describe archlutes with two pegboxes, and theorbos. In other words, 'archlute' could also signify 'theorbo'. The catalogue of Bach's estate does not list a theorbo or an archlute, and mentions only a lute (and two lute harpsichords). Should this really be taken to mean that Bach was no longer interested in the larger lutes, using them neither as accompanying nor as continuo instruments? After all, theorbos were louder and thus of greater value than lutes in larger ensembles. As a matter of fact J. S. Bach employed a lute on several occasions, and he was a close friend of the Saxon court lute-maker Johann Christian Hoffmann, who mentioned him in his will.

With regard to Bach's use of wind instruments, much has been written on the subject in the last few decades, and we refer the reader to the work of Menke, Barnes, Tarr, and Hochreither. However, it is worth mentioning that in the first Leipzig cantatas Bach was already using the oboe d'amore, which had been invented shortly before 1720. This again demonstrates Bach's particular interest in innovations in the field of instrument-making.

[8] See Spivakovsky, 'Polyphony in Bach's Works for Solo Violin', *Music Review*, 28 (1967).
[9] I am grateful to Alfred Dürr for this piece of information.

STRINGED KEYBOARD INSTRUMENTS

Lute Harpsichords (Lautenwerke)

J. S. Bach may be termed the inventor not only of the viola pomposa, but also of a new keyboard instrument. Around 1720 he commissioned a cabinet-maker in Cöthen to build a lute harpsichord (*Lautenclavicymbel* or *Lauten Werck*); the instrument was made to specifications supplied by Bach, and cost 60 thaler.[10] Another instrument of this type was constructed two decades later at his behest by Hildebrand, a pupil of Silbermann. This instrument was described thus by Jacob Adlung: 'In the year 1740 or thereabouts a lute harpsichord was made in Leipzig by Mr Zacharias Hildebrand to specifica-tions supplied by Mr Johann Sebastian Bach. . . . It had two sets of gut strings and a so-called "Octävchen" (small octave) of brass strings . . . In actual fact it sounded . . . more like a theorbo than a lute.'[11]

Bach's lute harpsichord probably had a softer and quieter sound than a normal harpsichord. The instrument looked like a harpsichord, and did not possess a lute body of the kind suggested by the instrument by Rudolf Richter shown at the Stuttgart exhibition '300 Jahre J. S. Bach'.[12] Agricola remembered seeing Bach's lute harpsichord around 1740, noting that it looked like a normal harpsichord, though it had a smaller compass and gut strings. Richter has since made another lute harpsichord that is probably much closer to the instrument devised by Bach. Other reproductions on these lines have been made by the Ammer brothers (in 1931–2) and by Martin Sassmann (in 1962).[13]

It is easy to forget the fact that in Bach's lifetime there were far more different kinds of stringed keyboard instruments than we are willing to admit. Today Bach is associated with only two stringed keyboard instruments, the harpsichord and the clavichord, and the fortepiano is rarely mentioned. Yet it would be more correct to speak of at least three groups of such instruments. Harpsichords and clavichords were not standardized instruments, being made to order for individual customers. Also, different 'hammer-harpsichords' existed and it is incorrect to exclude completely from Bach performances the historical fortepiano as invented by Cristofori as early as 1698 (not 1709, as is sometimes stated) and built by Gottfried Silbermann in 1732 at the very latest, and most probably about ten years earlier (though in a not yet satisfying version).

[10] See Rudolf Bunge, 'Johann Sebastian Bachs Kapelle zu Cöthen und deren nachgelassene Instrumente', *BJb*, 2 (1905), 29.

[11] *Musica mechanica organoedi*, ed. J. L. Albrecht (Berlin, 1768), ii. 139.

[12] Catalogue no. 224.

[13] See Uta Henning, 'The Most Beautiful Among the Claviers', *Early Music*, 10 (1982), 480 f.

Harpsichords

The harpsichord proper (cembalo, *Clavicymbel*, *Kielflügel*, clavecin) is a stringed keyboard instrument on which the strings are plucked by plectra (usually raven's or other quills). On the basis of this definition the harpsichord group in the wider sense includes spinets, *spinettini* (Bach's *Spinettgen*), virginals, and *épinettes*, all names for variously shaped though usually small, square or broad-format instruments. Cristofori even made an oval spinet, which is now preserved in the Instrument Museum of Leipzig University. The upright harpsichord, or *clavicytherium*, outwardly a twin brother of the later pyramid piano, should also be mentioned here. Yet in the seventeenth and eighteenth century the harpsichord in the narrower sense of the word (or 'instrument', as it was often simply called) was always large and wing-shaped.

Just as the word 'clavier' was used as a collective term for keyboard instruments in general in the eighteenth century, the Italian term 'cembalo' was for a long time a generalized word for wing-shaped stringed keyboard instruments. Thus it is a well-known fact that Mozart wrote 'cembalo' at the beginning of the piano part in the score of his concertos at a time when he was already using his own fortepiano for subscription concerts in Vienna. Both Beethoven (the autograph of the A major Piano Sonata Op. 101 contains the marking 'una corda- due corde-tutto il cembalo') and Schubert (in an early work, D 28) used the word 'cembalo' even though they meant the fortepiano. In the nineteenth century people in Paris still spoke of 'clavecinistes' when the latter were clearly playing Beethoven's 'Hammerklavier' Sonata or works by Liszt on fortepianos. In Italy, a little book published in Naples as late as 1850 provided information on how one could best replace the leather of 'i martelli dei cembali' (the 'hammers of harpsichords'). In Italy in particular the fortepiano, with very few exceptions, was termed 'cembalo' throughout most of the eighteenth century.[14] We will return to this general meaning of the word 'cembalo' or 'clavecin' below.[15]

Harpsichords or 'cembalos' in the narrower sense of the word could have one or two manuals, occasionally even three. They could have a small or large compass, and a greater or lesser number of stops. None of Bach's instruments mentioned in the catalogue of the estate has survived, unless one of the harpsichords was identical with the so-called Berlin 'Bach harpsichord' (see

[14] In his article 'Pianoforte' in the *New Grove*, xiv. 682, Edwin Ripin gives the impression that somehow or other Cristofori used the modern term when referring to his new 'harpsichord with hammers'. This is quite erroneous. Cristofori always considered fortepianos to be also 'cembali', though 'cembali' that could be played loudly and softly. Cristofori's name for the fortepiano shown to the Marchese Maffei was 'gravecembalo, che fa il pian' e il forte'.

[15] With regard to this and the following section see Eva Badura-Skoda, 'Prolegomena to a History of the Viennese Fortepiano', *Israel Studies in Musicology*, 2 (1980), 77 f., and 'Zur Frühgeschichte des Hammerklaviers', *Festschrift Hellmut Federhofer zum 75. Geburtstag*, ed. C. Mahling (Tutzing, 1988). See also *Atti del XIV Congresso della Società Internazionale di Musicologia, Bologna, 1987*, ii, Study Session XII (Turin, 1990), 283–96.

below). Unfortunately the important question of what Bach's favourite harpsichord may have been cannot be precisely answered.

It used to be said that in Bach's lifetime there was no specifically German style of harpsichord-making, and that German harpsichords of this period were merely copies of French, Flemish, or Italian instruments. One reason for this assumption was the fact that for a long time only relatively few harpsichords made in Germany were known to be extant. However, a number of harpsichords have since come to light, and these have enabled us to modify our views on this matter. An unsigned harpsichord now in Berlin, which probably once belonged to Wilhelm Friedemann Bach, was for a long time taken to be a 'Bach harpsichord'.[16] Friedrich Ernst, sometime restorer of this collection, cast doubt on its authenticity, though it now appears that he was wrong.[17] Hubert Henkel has described a harpsichord by Harass now in the Schlossmuseum in Sondershausen. He was able to demonstrate that it was so similar to the harpsichord in the Berlin collection that both instruments can probably be ascribed to the Thuringian maker Harass (1665–1714). The possibility that the 'Bach harpsichord' once belonged not only to Friedemann, but previously to J. S. Bach, may now seriously be entertained. It has two manuals and three choirs of strings, and originally had a sixteen-foot and a four-foot stop in the lower, and an eight-foot in the upper manual and a coupler. It was rebuilt with sixteen-foot and eight-foot stops in the lower manual, and with eight-foot and four-foot stops in the upper manual. This rebuilding may have happened at an early stage, that is, before 1714 (according to Krickeberg and Rase).

There are two other unsigned harpsichords in Berlin which may with some justice be called 'Bach harpsichords'. In 1718 Bach was permitted to order a harpsichord for the court of Cöthen. The instrument chosen, certainly with Bach's approval, came from the workshop of the Berlin court instrument-maker Michael Mietke. Heinrich Besseler suggested that Bach travelled to Berlin in 1718 to order the harpsichord personally.[18] On this occasion he may well have met the Margrave of Brandenburg and played the Mietke instruments in his possession. This remains a hypothesis. It has been possible to prove only that Bach travelled to Berlin in 1719 to evaluate the completed Mietke harpsichord and to take it back with him to Cöthen. It must have been a valuable instrument, for it cost the Prince of Anhalt-Cöthen more than 100 thalers—Bach was paid 130 thalers to cover the costs of the instrument, transport, and travel; and transport and travel cannot possibly have amounted to more than 30 thalers. This harpsichord was almost certainly a two-manual

---

[16] No. 316 of the Instrument Collection of the Staatliches Institut für Musikforschung, Berlin.

[17] See Dieter Krickeberg and Horst Rase, 'Beiträge zur Kenntnis des mittel- und norddeutschen Cembalobaus um 1700', *Studia Organologica: Festschrift John Henry van der Meer* (Wissenschaftliche Beibände zum Anzeiger des Germanischen Nationalmuseums; Tutzing, 1987).

[18] 'Markgraf Christian Ludwig von Brandenburg', *BJb*, 43 (1956), 18–35.

instrument, and may even have had a sixteen-foot stop. We have no reliable information on this point, for the instrument has disappeared without trace. It may however have been similar to the two-manual 'black' unsigned harpsichord which is still (or again) in Schloss Charlottenburg (see Fig. 1). Research carried out by Dieter Krickeberg and Sheridan Germann suggests that it was made by Michael Mietke, probably for the Electress (and later Queen) Sophie Charlotte, who was very musical. It no doubt stood in the music-room of the palace and had a compass of F_1-e^3 (originally only F_1-c^3 without $F\sharp_1$ and $G\sharp_1$), eight-foot and four-foot stops on the lower manual, an eight-foot stop on the upper manual, and a coupler. However, in Cöthen, according to Alfred Dürr, Bach always seems to have required a compass of G_1-d^3 in his keyboard works, which nearly corresponds to the compass of the 'black' harpsichord in Berlin before it was rebuilt. The compass of $G_1—d^3$, rather than F_1-c^3, may very well have been what Bach wanted in the case of

FIG. 1. The two-manual harpsichord by Michael Mietke (court instrument-maker in Berlin, d. 1719) made for Queen Sophie Charlotte and kept at the palace of Charlottenburg in Berlin. Shortly before he died, Mietke made a similar instrument for the court at Cöthen. J. S. Bach personally took delivery of the instrument in Berlin in 1719

the Cöthen instrument, and he may well have stipulated it when ordering it from Mietke.

In addition to the two-manual 'black harpsichord' (the chinoiserie on a black background is attributed to Dagly) Mietke probably made another harpsichord for Sophie Charlotte's palace. This instrument, the basic colour of which is white, has become famous on account of the valuable painting by Dagly.[19] It has recently been established that in the course of his career Mietke also made two instruments with a sixteen-foot stop, both of which, unlike the instruments destined for the court of Sophie Charlotte, were probably signed. Krickeberg believes that one of these may well have been ordered by Bach for the court at Cöthen.

The fact that Bach himself probably chose a harpsichord by Michael Mietke for the court at Cöthen, or at any rate evaluated the instrument and brought it back to Cöthen, is an important piece of information. The Fifth Brandenburg Concerto, which was written shortly afterwards, was probably composed with this instrument in mind. Thus the kind of harpsichord Bach preferred was evidently a two-manual instrument with a compass of more than five octaves (probably G_1–c^3). It was probably in the German style, and similar to Mietke's 'black' harpsichord. Bach may also have thought highly of harpsichords by Johann Heinrich Harass, Gottfried Silbermann, Johann Christoph Fleischer, Johann Nikolaus Bach, Zacharias Hildebrand, and Heinrich Gräbner. It is certain that he owned 'excellent instruments'. Ernst Ludwig Gerber, writing of his father Heinrich Nicolaus Gerber in his *Lexikon*, stated: 'Bach played the latter [*WTC*] to him three times with his inimitable mastery; and my father considered his happiest hours to have been those when Bach, under the pretext of not wanting to teach, sat down at one of his excellent [*sic*!] instruments and made these hours seem but minutes.'[20]

Presumably most German harpsichords of the age of Bach had a disposition of an eight-foot and a four-foot stop on the lower manual and an eight-foot stop on the upper manual, possibly with a lute or buff stop, and a coupler. The question of whether one of Bach's own harpsichords may have had a sixteen-foot stop after all is again open and will no doubt be discussed afresh in the near future by Krickeberg and others.

As only a small handful of German harpsichords from the eighteenth century have survived, almost none of them in good or even playable condition, it has become customary in the twentieth century to play Bach on

---

[19] In a thorough and exhaustive article, 'The Mietkes, the Margrave and Bach', in *Bach, Handel, Scarlatti*, ed. P. Williams, Sheridan Germann suggests that Bach, when visiting the margrave, may have played the white 1-manual harpsichord (painted by Dagly). However, Dieter Krickeberg has demonstrated convincingly why Bach probably played the 2-manual black harpsichord rather than the 1-manual white one: see 'Michael Mietke—ein Cembalobauer aus dem Umkreis von J. S. Bach', *Köthener Bach-Hefte*, 3 (Cöthen, 1985), and 'Der Berliner Cembalobauer Michael Mietke, die Hohenzollern und Bach', *Programmbuch der Berliner Bachtage* (Berlin, 1986), pp. 17–28.

[20] *Historisch-Biographisches Lexikon*, p. 492.

historical instruments (or reproductions) from other countries. Today French and Dutch harpsichords are still very much in favour with harpsichordists and makers of reproductions. However, we believe that English instruments, such as those by Kirckman or Shudi, the design and disposition of which is closer to eighteenth-century German ones, probably approximate more to Bach's ideal sonority with their carrying power and their cantabile and yet clear tone. Our knowledge of German harpsichord-building in the age of Bach has increased markedly in recent years. Thus harpsichordists are encouraged to choose exact copies of a Mietke or a Harass harpsichord.

Hämmerwerke *or* Hämmerpantalone

Keyboard instruments in existence after 1700 included the *Hämmerpantalone* or *Hämmerwerke*, named after the 'pantaleon', an instrument invented by Pantaleon Hebenstreit around 1695. From about 1720 onwards this term often referred to a combination of an enlarged dulcimer or cimbalon and a hammer action with a keyboard. Until recently it tended to be forgotten that, although Hebenstreit himself played his instrument with hammer sticks, that is, without a keyboard, shortly before or after 1720 the pantaleon was made both with and without a keyboard.[21] On the basis of the descriptions of its sound, the instrument most nearly resembled an unrefined and rather loud *Tangentenflügel* (tangent piano), or a somewhat imperfect 'fortepiano sounding like a harpsichord'. Gottfried Silbermann had made a pantaleon for Hebenstreit in Strasbourg as early as 1703/4, and around 1720 was making instruments of this kind in Saxony, initially at Hebenstreit's behest. Hebenstreit, who by then had not only a highly paid position at the Dresden court, but also the royal privilege to his instrument, subsequently accused Silbermann of making these instruments without his permission, and felt moved to complain to the king in 1726.[22]

In 1758 Jacob Adlung, in his *Anleitung zur musikalischen Gelahrtheit*, described the *Hämmerpantalon* thus:

The main body of a *Hämmerwerk* or *Hämmerpantalon* is similar to that of the clavecin, and when upright, to the *clavicytherium*. However, the action functions with the help of wooden or horn hammers attached to metal or wooden sticks. These sticks cause the strings to sound either from below through the sound-board [presumably this means between the sound-board and the strings] or fall on to the strings from above; and the ones we have here are all like the latter. Most of the ones to be seen here were made by Fickert in Zeiz . . . Fickert's instruments have a head-piece that contains the

---

[21] See Eva Badura-Skoda, 'Besaitete Tasteninstrumente um und nach 1700: Hämmerpantalone, Lautenwerk und Cembal d'amour' (forthcoming).

[22] Hebenstreit was acquainted not only with Silbermann, but also with J. S. Bach, whose son W. Friedemann he is known to have helped. See Alfred Berner, 'Hebenstreit, Pantaleon', *MGG*.

keyboard and the hammers and covers the wrest plank, which is the reason why it has to be removed when one wishes to tune the instrument.[23]

This demonstrates that these pantaleons or *Hämmerwerke* were supplied with keyboards, which meant that they could be played by every keyboard player. Whether or not this was the case with Kuhnau's instrument of 1706, which he mentioned in a letter to Mattheson in 1718, is an unsolved question.[24] Christoph Gottlieb Schröter noted in 1763 that the pantaleon was in widespread use, and claimed: 'I know of more than twenty towns and villages where, since 1721, instead of the usual *clavicymbel*, such keyboard instruments with hammers and strikers have been made, which, when the string is struck from above, are known by their makers and buyers as pantaleon.'[25]

At any rate, the instrument to which the following advertisement in the *Leipziger Postzeitung* of 23 October 1731 referred certainly had a keyboard:

Lovers of the noble art of music are advised that the maker of organs and instruments by the name of Friedrich Fickern in the town of Zeitz has once again invented and made a new musical instrument, which is called *Cymbal-Clavir*. It is in the shape of a sixteen-foot harpsichord, and with four choirs of wire strings. In gravity and force it surpasses the loudest harpsichord, and remains in tune as long as a good clavichord without the least adjustment. It is also easy to play, for the little hammers fall 2½ inches down on the strings. Furthermore it has several innovations: (1) an agreeable moderato mechanism, as if one were playing with little padded hammers; (2) one can also, by means of a stop, prevent the intermingling of notes while playing, just as the strip of cloth in the tangent of a *clavicymbel* silences the string. This instrument, which may be had for an affordable price, has the qualities of the cymbal invented by the most famous Pandalon [*sic*], and has been admired and approved by many virtuosos.[26]

Even if we are currently unable to describe the sound of the *Hämmerpantalone*, because no instrument seems to have survived in its original state, and none has been copied by a maker since, it is interesting to note that many harpsichords and fortepianos in Bach's time had a stop or register known as 'Pantalon'. Its precise nature remains unclear.

---

[23] p. 559, §249.

[24] Johann Mattheson, *Critica musica*, ii (Hamburg, 1722–5; facs. Amsterdam, 1964), 236. See Eva Badura-Skoda, 'Besaitete Tasteninstrumente um und nach 1700: Hämmerpantalone, Lautenwerk und Cembal d'amour'.

[25] See Marpurg, *Kritische Briefe über die Tonkunst*, letter cxxxix (Berlin, 20 Aug. 1763). 1743, the date assigned to Schröter's publication by Hubert Henkel, 'Bach und das Hammerklavier', *Beiträge zur Bachforschung*, ii (Leipzig, 1983), p. 58, is incorrect.

[26] Quoted in Christian Ahrens, 'Zur Geschichte von Clavichord, Cembalo und Hammerklavier', *Ausstellungskatalog der 10. Tage alter Musik in Herne* (Herne, 1985), p. 59.

Clavichords

Clavichords are so well known that it is hardly necessary to describe their construction. They are the smallest and in tone the most delicate keyboard instruments, and the only ones on which a note can be modified after the key has been struck. The thin metal strings are caused to speak not by plucking, as on the harpsichord, but by a metal pin or 'tangent' that strikes the string and divides it like a bridge, lifting it slightly as long as a finger remains on the key. This makes *Bebung* possible, a tonal resource similar to string vibrato.

Like harpsichords, clavichords differed greatly with regard to structure and quality in Bach's time. The instrument was usually a portable square box that could be placed on a table. Fretted clavichords were often very small, usually significantly smaller than unfretted instruments. According to Walther's *Musicalisches Lexicon*, the latter first appeared in 1709. Each key now possessed a string or a pair of strings, so that every conceivable chord became possible, something which, as is well known, was not always possible on a fretted instrument. Unfretted clavichords were often larger and made in various sizes, whereby the materials used and the quality probably differed greatly. This is the only way to explain the fact that there were great differences between the prices of clavichords in the middle of the century. Gottfried Silbermann's instruments were particularly famous. Older fretted clavichords were cheaper and simpler, but they had a more robust sound than the later unfretted instruments, whose tone is described as delicate, soft, capable of subtle inflections, and soulful. For this reason it became the favourite instrument of the composers of the epoch of *Empfindsamkeit*. C. P. E. Bach is said to have possessed an especially valuable Silbermann clavichord of unique quality. This may well have been the reason for his special predilection for the instrument.

The so-called pantalon or pantaleon stop on the clavichord divided the strings from the damper, thus permitting them to vibrate. This suggests that the pantalon stop, which occurs in descriptions of old German fortepianos, means the same as the 'forte' stop in the eighteenth century, namely the dividing of the strings from the damper (although Adlung equates the pantaleon stop with 'harpsichord stops', small metal plates that strike the strings). It seems that small fortepianos were sometimes built without dampers.[27] This was surely a reminiscence of the sound of Hebenstreit's pantaleon.

Cembal d'amour

Silbermann's *cembal d'amour* was another interesting keyboard instrument from the age of Bach that is practically unknown today. Though it looked like

----

[27] See Laurence Libin, 'Early Pianos Without Dampers', *Atti del XIV Congresso*, pp. 287 f.

a harpsichord, it was apparently a member of the clavichord family. To judge by the various descriptions of it, the action of the *cembal d'amour* was based on that of the clavichord. Silbermann constructed it before 1721 for the wife of the Dresden court poet König, who was the court harpsichordist and had asked him 'to think of an instrument that had the power and capabilities of a small harpsichord, while preserving the tenderness of a clavichord'.[28]

Ernst Ludwig Gerber described the *cembal d'amour* thus:

A second invention [Gerber had referred to Silbermann's 'Piano-Fort' as the first] that the worthy Silbermann made all alone is the *cembal d'amour*. This has exactly the same keys and tangents as the clavier [clavichord], and also approximates to the form of the latter. Yet its strings are twice as long as those of the clavier, for they are struck by the tangent in the middle and must produce the same note on both sides. For this reason there are bridges and sound-boards on both sides. In the middle the string rests on a small U-shaped prong covered with cloth, in the middle of which the tangent touches the string and, by raising it from the cloth, produces the double note from both sides. . . . The advantages of this instrument compared to the normal clavichord are: (1) greater volume; (2) an increase in the duration of a note; and (3) greater dynamic variety.'[29]

In June 1724 the *cembal d'amour* was described in the *Breslauer Sammlungen*.[30] However, in 1725 Mattheson commented on this description thus: 'The description itself tells us little, for we have not been told what advantages it possesses compared to other instruments, and what the great art of its maker consists of. Which the renowned Herr Sécretaire König intends to take the trouble to do in detail if he has the time, and to compare the Florentine and the Freyberg instruments.'[31] The 'Florentine and Freyberg' instruments were of course the novel harpsichord with hammers of Cristofori and probably Gottfried Silbermann's newest cembalo with tangents. After Bach's death a *cembal d'amour* was offered for sale in Leipzig, which suggests that Bach might have known and played an instrument of this kind.

The question of when and where the first tangent piano was built is still a matter for debate, though recent research suggests that square instruments of this kind may have existed before 1700.[32] Presumably the first model of a *clavecin à maillets* that Jean Marius described to the Académie Française in 1716 was a kind of tangent piano, that is, it functioned without an escapement, but had small hammers as tangents (which only partly justifies the name *Hammerklavier*). It is still unclear whether, as is sometimes claimed in eighteenth-century German literature (notably by Bossler), the wing-shaped tangent piano was first built by Jacob Späth in Regensburg around 1750, or whether it was already in existence earlier in Bach's lifetime.

[28] Quoted in W. Müller, *Gottfried Silbermann: Persönlichkeit und Werk* (Leipzig, 1982), 36.
[29] 'Silbermann (Gottfried)', *Historisch-Biographisches Lexikon*, pp. 516 f.
[30] Vol. 5, p. 697.   [31] *Critica musica*, ii. 380.
[32] See Stewart Pollens, 'An Early Tangent Piano', *Atti del XIV Congresso*, pp. 286 f.

Fortepianos

Until recently it was commonly believed that the first fortepiano was made by Cristofori in Florence as late as about 1709. This date has had to be revised as a result of research first carried out by Mario Fabbri. We now know that Cristofori invented his hammer action before 1700 (presumably around 1698) and developed a 'cembalo che fa il piano e il forte' (literally 'harpsichord which makes piano and forte'). This redating of the invention of the fortepiano to a decade earlier is of great interest with regard to Domenico Scarlatti's youth, though it probably had little influence on Bach's student years. Bach probably grew up in ignorance of this 'new-fangled harpsichord'. However, at about the age of 30 or 35 he may well have been confronted with the first fortepianos made by Cristofori or Silbermann on the occasion of his visit to Dresden to compete with Marchand. This date has not been confirmed, but it is certainly a possibility.

Fortepianos, with regard to both their form and the nomenclature employed, were referred to as *cembali* (harpsichords) in Bach's lifetime. Serviceable hammer actions, as developed by Cristofori and Silbermann, were first built into wing-shaped cases. Later (perhaps from about 1740) Silbermann's pupil Friederici and others began to make square instruments. 'Piano-forte' (or 'forte-piano'), the names that began to be used for this novel kind of harpsichord after about 1745, were wholly unknown in the first three decades of the eighteenth century in Italy and Germany. It is important to remember this, for we really have no precise idea of what was meant by the numerous 'clavecins', 'cembali', or 'novel clavessins' mentioned in court and civic archives, in Silbermann and Bach documents, and in other contemporary records. For example, in Mattheson's *Critica musica*, where an article by Maffei (translated by the Dresden court poet König) appeared in 1725 under the title 'A description of a newly invented clavicein, on which piano and forte may be obtained', Cristofori's fortepiano is always referred to as a 'new kind of harpsichord' or 'instrument'. Maffei's article is of interest on account of the objections to this new and extraordinary harpsichord, which did not have 'a sound as loud as that of other harpsichords'. 'But', Maffei continues, 'the greatest objection to this instrument is based on the fact that normally not everyone was able to play it at once'.[33] This is understandable, for even today those who have never touched an eighteenth-century fortepiano have difficulty in learning how to play the instrument. Good harpsichordists and pianists usually need to practise on the instrument for several days or even weeks in order to master its technique. For this reason alone we must assume that when Bach arrived in Potsdam in 1747, he must have been fairly familiar with the Silbermann fortepianos, for otherwise he would have been unable to

[33] *Critica musica*, ii. 337.

play to the king on one immediately after his arrival. On the subject of the fortepiano C. P. E. Bach also noted: 'The more recent fortepiano, when it is sturdy and well-built, has many fine qualities, although its touch must be carefully worked out, a task which is not without difficulties.'[34]

Agricola gave the following account of Bach's attitude to Silbermann's 'piano-fort' instruments:

Mr. Gottfried Silbermann had at first built *two* of these instruments. One of them was seen and played by the late Kapellmeister Mr. Johann Sebastian Bach. He had praised, indeed admired, its tone; but he had complained that it was too weak in the high register, and was too hard to play. This was taken greatly amiss by Mr. Silbermann, who could not bear to have any fault found in his handiworks. He was therefore angry at Mr. Bach for a long time. And yet his conscience told him that Mr. Bach was not wrong. He therefore decided—greatly to his credit be it said—not to deliver any more of these instruments, but instead to think all the harder about how to eliminate the faults Mr. J. S. Bach had observed. *He worked for many years on this. And that this was the real cause of this postponement I have the less doubt since I myself heard it frankly acknowledged by Mr. Silbermann.* Finally, when Mr. Silbermann had really achieved many improvements, notably in respect to the action [*Tractament*], he sold one again to the Court of the Prince of Rudolstadt. [This is presumably the one which Herr Schröter had in mind in the 141st Critical Letter, p. 102.] Shortly thereafter His Majesty the King of Prussia had one of these instruments ordered, and when it met with His Majesty's Most Gracious approval, he had several more ordered from Mr. Silbermann. Those who, like me, had seen one of the old instruments, saw and heard on all these instruments quite easily how much effort Herr Silbermann must have expended on improving them. Mr. Silbermann had also the laudable ambition to show one of these instruments of his later workmanship to the late Kapellmeister Bach and to have it examined by him; and he had received, in turn, complete approval from him.[35]

This detailed report has led some scholars to think that Agricola may have been present when Bach tried out Silbermann's first 'piano-fort' model, or that this event was at least chronologically close to Agricola's sojourn in Leipzig as Bach's pupil (1738–41).[36] However, it is wrong to draw this inference. Agricola says that Silbermann himself told him that Bach had criticized his instruments. Thus the improved instrument must have been in existence between 1738 and 1741 at the latest. Agricola must have met Silbermann before the end of 1741 and he may in fact have met him in 1738 or 1739. When Agricola states that he saw the improved Silbermann instruments,

---

[34] *Essay*, p. 36.

[35] *Bach-Dokumente*, iii. 194; Eng. trans. in Hans T. David and Arthur Mendel, *The Bach Reader* (New York, 1945; 2nd edn., London, 1966), p. 259. Italics by the author.

[36] e.g. Christoph Wolff, in his article on Bach and the fortepiano (see Bibliography), who states: 'The information is so detailed and like an eyewitness report that this must have occurred at about the time of Agricola's sojourn in Leipzig as Bach's pupil (1738–1741)'. Wolff then deduces, wrongly in my opinion, that Bach first saw Silbermann's first attempt at an instrument known as 'piano-fort' between 1738 and 1741, and thus the improved Silbermann instrument in 1745–6.

which were the result of many years' work, *and* 'one of the old instruments', it may be assumed that this 'old' fortepiano really was old. It could have been standing somewhere in Leipzig for five, ten, or even twenty years when Agricola saw it. (The reference to Schröter's report is no more than a supposition, and cannot serve as proof for the chronology, especially in view of the fact that Schröter's report first appeared in 1763.)

Silbermann evidently first combined the adjectives 'piano' and 'forte' to form a noun in 1732, applying it to his new instrument. In the fifth volume of Zedler's *Universal Lexikon*, which appeared in 1733, the entry for 'Cembal d'amour' states at the end: 'Furthermore, the famous Herr Silbermann has recently invented another new instrument, which he [*sic!*] terms piano-fort, and last year [1732] delivered to His Royal Highness the Crown Prince of Poland and Lithuania etc. and Elector of Saxony. It is said to have been graciously received on account of its extremely pleasant sound.'[37]

The word 'recently' does not, however, invalidate a daring hypothesis, namely that Silbermann's first attempts to make fortepianos may have been considerably earlier than 1731–2. To show a new instrument to one's musician friends did not mean making it public to the extent that the author of a *Universal Lexikon* would have heard about it.[38] Rather, the lexicographer's remarks could be taken to mean that Silbermann had made a fortepiano around 1720 (with which Bach was not satisfied), and that it was only around 1731–2 that he made fortepianos with which he was entirely satisfied, and which he was proud to present to the world at large and the Dresden court under a new name, 'piano-fort'. This at least is suggested in a dedicatory poem by Erselius of 1735, and a report in *Curiosa Saxonica* (1736).[39] Thus it may be possible to assume that Silbermann made his first two fortepianos as early as 1725, or even 1720 (prior to the *cembal d'amour* perhaps), and that he was so discouraged by Bach's criticism that he only returned to the construction of a fortepiano action after having seen a Cristofori fortepiano around 1730, having carefully studied the Florentine instrument. It was only now that he made his improved and masterly instruments, proudly giving them a name of their own ('piano-fort'), and presenting them to the 'world', that is, to the king and the members of the royal chapel in Dresden, but also to well-known Leipzig citizens, including Johann Sebastian Bach and the author of the article in Zedler's *Universal Lexikon*. Of course, this is no more than a hypothesis, yet more probable than the assumption that Silbermann completed his first two fortepianos as late as 1732.

As we have seen, he delivered one of these instruments in 1732 to the Saxon

---

[37] See Müller, *Gottfried Silbermann*, p. 39.

[38] We know far too little about Bach's travels. It is not wholly impossible that on his journey to Dresden in 1720 (?) he may have visited Görlitz, where he is said to have played the organ, and Silbermann's workshop in Freiberg.

[39] Cf. Müller, *Gottfried Silbermann*, pp. 38 f.

Crown Prince in Dresden; he may have sent the other to Leipzig, where Bach, after the end of state mourning for King August the Strong, once again conducted his collegium musicum. In June 1733 a Leipzig newspaper carried an advertisement of a forthcoming collegium musicum concert. It stated:

After His Royal Highness and His Grace the Elector has graciously conceded that the Collegia Musica lately discontinued may now be resumed, a start will be made with a pleasing concert given by Bach's Collegio Musico tomorrow, Wednesday 17 June, in Zimmermann's Garden on Grimmischen Stein-Wege at 4 p.m., to be continued on a weekly basis, *featuring a new clavicymbel, the like of which has never been heard before here*, and amateurs of music as well as virtuosi are invited to attend.[40]

The Leipzig newspaper noted that 'it started with a beautiful concerto . . . with a new *clavicymbel*, the like of which has never been heard here before'.[41] That the new term 'piano-fort' does not appear, and that there is talk of a *clavicymbel*, is understandable. Bach, the Leipzig journalist, and other musicians were used to referring to pianos with hammer actions as 'cembalo', *clavessin*, *clavicymbel*, or 'instrument'. After all, Cristofori, Maffei, and König had done the same. It was a long time before every musician was familiar with Silbermann's new name.

It should not surprise us that Bach was reluctant to use the single substantive 'piano-forte'. In 1749, at the end of his life, when he received a payment of 115 *Reichsthaler* for a fortepiano which was most probably made by Silbermann, he stated in a receipt that the money was for an 'instrument named Piano et Forte'.[42] The same term is used in Gottfried Silbermann's inscription in the fortepiano preserved in the palace of Sanssouci (see p. 166 n. 50).

Combination Instruments

In the eighteenth century different kinds of keyboard instruments were often combined. For example, the *claviorganum* combined a chamber organ and a harpsichord. In 1742 the following advertisement appeared in the *Leipziger Post-Zeitung*: 'A new clavecin with three manuals, of which the lower 2 have 4 choirs of strings with different stops, the third manual a *cymbal* with small hammers and different stops.'[43] A similar two-manual instrument by

---

[40] *Nachricht auch Frag- und Anzeiger*, 16 June 1733, quoted in *Bach-Dokumente*, ii. 237 f (author's italics). On the advertisements, which were probably devised by Bach himself, see Werner Neumann, 'Einige neue Quellen zu Bachs Herausgabe eigener und zum Mitvertrieb fremder Werke', *Festschrift Walther Vetter* (Leipzig, 1969), 165 ff. See also E. Badura-Skoda, 'Komponierte J. S. Bach "Hammerklavier-Konzerte"?', *BJb*, 77 (1991), 117–29.

[41] See Herbert Heyde, 'Der Instrumentenbau in Leipzig zur Zeit Johann Sebastian Bachs', *300 Jahre Johann Sebastian Bach* (Tutzing, 1985), 73–88.

[42] See *Bach-Dokumente*, iii. 633 (addenda to vol. i).

[43] C. Ahrens, 'Zur Geschichte von Clavichord, Cembalo und Hammerklavier', *Ausstellungskatalog der 10. Tage alter Musik in Herne* (Herne, 1985), 44–68, at 61.

Cristofori's pupil Giovanni Ferrini was built around the same time. It is now again in playable condition and in a private collection in Bologna. Its upper manual belongs to a fortepiano and its lower manual to a harpsichord. The conjunction of harpsichord and fortepiano sonorities makes possible not only the combination of eight-foot stops and lute registers on the harpsichord— and thus of loud and soft—but also, through the fortepiano's flexible dynamics, a much greater variety of tone-colour. Repetitions of single bars (echo effects) or repeats of whole movements of a suite enabled the listener to judge the advantages of the two instruments in succession or conjunction. It reminds us of the mixed sonorities of C. P. E. Bach's Concerto for harpsichord and fortepiano.

Finally a brief word about contemporary pedal instruments. Every organist needed pedals on which to practise. Both clavichords and harpsichords and, later, fortepianos were sometimes supplied with pedal-boards (in which case the same strings were played on the manuals and the pedals). On the other hand there were also pedal instruments in their own right (better, though more expensive solutions), in which the pedal-board was attached to its own strings in a case of its own. This independent instrument was placed under the harpsichord so that both could be played together. Silbermann's pupil Zacharias Hildebrand, who constructed the lute harpsichord at Bach's behest, made a pedal instrument, which was offered for sale on 9 July 1763 in the *Leipziger Intelligenzblatt*: 'For sale: A very beautiful clavecin, with 2 keyboards and a 16' pedal. The keys are of ivory, and the instrument is outwardly beautifully veneered.'[44]

BACH'S ATTITUDE TO STRINGED KEYBOARD INSTRUMENTS

For a long time early fortepianos were to all intents and purposes excluded from 'authentic' Bach performances, though in the recent past they have come back into favour. The fortepiano tended to be excluded because it was generally believed that Bach became acquainted with the instrument too late to have composed for it and that he was not particularly satisfied with it. It was popularly believed that fortepianos had not reached perfection in Bach's lifetime. This view of the fortepiano, which now seems untenable, can be traced back to Bach's first biographer, Nikolaus Forkel, who, around 1800, characterized Bach's attitude to the various keyboard instruments thus:

He preferred to play the clavichord. Wing-shaped harpsichords, although they enable the player to employ a range of nuances, he deemed to be without soul, and during his lifetime the fortepiano was still in the process of being developed, and still too coarse

---

[44] See Herbert Heyde, 'Der Instrumentenbau in Leipzig zur Zeit Johann Sebastian Bachs', *300 Jahre Johann Sebastian Bach* (Tutzing, 1985), p. 76.

to satisfy him. He thus regarded the clavichord to be the best instrument on which to study, and for the purposes of private music-making. He found it best adapted to express his most subtle thoughts, and did not believe that a harpsichord or fortepiano could produce such variety in the gradations of sound as on this, an admittedly soft, but on a small scale extremely flexible instrument.[45]

Forkel's words seem to mirror the views of C. P. E. Bach, a great lover of the clavichord, who supplied him with most of his information. This is particularly true of his evaluation of the clavichord. As Robert Marshall has demonstrated, J. S. Bach, unlike his son, in fact considered the clavichord in the main to be a practice instrument only.[46]

In regard to the assessment of the harpsichord, Forkel's statement can only be considered a historically untenable exaggeration. In Beethoven's lifetime, when this biography of Bach was written, the harpsichord was in fact deemed to be a soulless, old-fashioned instrument. However, if Bach had really considered it to be unsatisfactory, he would hardly have written so many works expressly intended for it, such as the second part of the *Clavier-Übung*, the Goldberg Variations, the violin sonatas with keyboard accompaniment, and so on. In contrast to this, not a single work by Bach seems to have been composed specifically for the clavichord. This does not exclude the possibility that Bach and his pupils may have used the sensitive and expressive clavichord for domestic music-making. But it may well be that C. P. E. Bach, who was presumably the source of Forkel's information, attributed to his father his own predilection for this instrument.

J. S. Bach's frequent use of the harpsichord is also demonstrated by the fact that in addition to two lute harpsichords and a *spinettino* the catalogue of his estate mentions no fewer than five 'clavecins'. (One of these may well have been a fortepiano; in the eighteenth century the generic term for such instruments continued to be 'cembalo' or 'clavecin'.) That clavichords are missing from the catalogue can only partially be explained by the fact that Johann Christian Bach was given these instruments by his father before he died, or that they were portable, and thus removed from the estate before it became subject to death duty. After all, a Stainer violin was also portable. Alfred Dürr has attempted to explain the lack of clavichords in the catalogue by suggesting that a clavichord belonged to Anna Magdalena Bach.[47] Yet even if this were true, it would not point to a great predilection for the instrument on Bach's part.

If Forkel's assertion that Bach considered the harpsichord to be without soul is questionable, then we should also cast doubt on his negative comments about the fortepiano. Recent research into the history of the fortepiano may help to dispel some old prejudices. A document that has recently come to light

[45] *Bachs Leben*, p. 39; Eng. trans., p. 311.   [46] See 'Organ or "Klavier"?'.

[47] 'Tastenumfang und Chronologie in Bachs Klavierwerken', *Festschrift G. von Dadelsen* (Stuttgart, 1978), 73.

(the receipt for payment of a valuable fortepiano mentioned above) makes it seem likely that Bach was more intimate with the Silbermann fortepiano and its maker than was thought. We now know that Bach and Silbermann corresponded. Letters from Bach existed in Silbermann's estate, though they are no longer extant.[48]

Yet the most important source of information on this point is the Silbermann instrument itself. It is one of the ironies of history that of the many stringed keyboard instruments that Bach played on in his lifetime none seems to have survived, with the exception of the fortepianos by Gottfried Silbermann now in Potsdam (see Figs. 2, 3, and 4). A report states that Bach tried out all the instruments in the royal palace. Bach's visit to Frederick the Great in Potsdam on 7 and 8 May 1747 is in fact one of the best documented episodes of his life. The king had a predilection for Silbermann's fortepianos

FIG. 2. Fortepiano by Gottfried Silbermann once owned by Frederick the Great, now kept in the Neues Palais at Potsdam

[48] See Müller, *Gottfried Silbermann*, p. 402.

FIG. 3. Fortepiano by Gottfried Silbermann once owned by Frederick the Great, dated 1746, now kept in the palace of Sanssouci

Fig. 4. Fortepiano by Gottfried Silbermann (see Fig. 3), detail

and purchased a number of them for his own use.[49] On this occasion Bach improvised two fugues on a fortepiano. The three-part ricercar of the *Musical Offering* which Bach dedicated to the king is probably the first of the two fugues, which he wrote down from memory. It can with some justice be described as 'composition for the fortepiano'.

Much has been written about Gottfried Silbermann's fortepianos, though few scholars seem to have had the opportunity of playing his instruments. This may be one of the reasons for the many misconceptions and prejudices. The Silbermann fortepiano in the Germanisches Nationalmuseum in Nuremberg has not been restored, and thus cannot be played. It simply gives us a visual impression of the instrument. However, while visiting Potsdam to give a concert, I sought permission to play on the recently restored Silbermann fortepiano in the palace of Sanssouci. The authorities acceded to my request, and thus, on 23 May 1984, I was able to spend an hour with this instrument,

---

[49] According to Agricola he had 7, and Forkel even claims he had 15 instruments by Silbermann.

which stands in the *Konzertzimmer* (concert-room).[50] Its compass extends from F_1 to d^3. It has two choirs of strings throughout and a *Stosszungen* (jack) action which is remarkably similar to that of Cristofori. At the right and left ends of the keyboard there are levers to raise the dampers. This is the sole difference from Cristofori's fortepiano, where the dampers cannot be raised, and doubtless reflects the influence of the pantaleon instruments that Silbermann had made for Hebenstreit. (He probably fitted keyboards to the pantaleon and sold the instruments without Hebenstreit's permission. The latter considered this to be in breach of the royal privilege and in 1726 sued Silbermann for damages.) It means that pedalling in the later sense of the word is impossible, though one can raise the dampers for longer passages, a registration effect that leads to an intermingling of the harmonies. This can sound delightful in tender pieces such as the first prelude of *WTC* I. In spite of the name 'Fortepedal' later applied to this lever, it is quite clear that it was never used for playing longer passages loudly, as Friedrich Ernst assumed,[51] even when we bear in mind that the resonance of the early fortepiano was much, much shorter than that of the modern piano.

Silbermann's fortepiano also possesses a manually operated *Verschiebung* (una corda or soft pedal), which according to the restorer, Martin-Christian Schmidt, corresponds to a transposing mechanism in the fortepiano in the Neues Palais. Furthermore, the Silbermann fortepiano in the Neues Palais also has a *Veränderung*, which Schmidt terms 'harpsichord stop'. To the right and the left of the damper-rail there are strips of ivory (each about 2×100 mm.). In the treble the two last segments are covered with a thin layer of brass. The sound of this 'accessory' does in fact come remarkably close to that of a harpsichord. The old pantaleon stop described by Adlung and others may have corresponded more to the lifting of the damper and not to this 'harpsichord' accessory, though Adlung asserted the opposite.

Apart from the possibility of using a knee-lever or pedal to lift its dampers, the Silbermann instrument in the palace of Sanssouci is fairly similar with regard to touch and sound to the fortepianos built by Johann Andreas Stein

---

[50] Inventory no. V 13. Height 92.5 cm. (without stand, 27 cm.), width 92.5 cm., length 232 cm. The body is of oak, and the stand with its turnings and 6 legs is of alder-wood. In 1983 the instrument was restored by Martin-Christian Schmidt. According to Schmidt, the following is written under the wrest-plank: 'Dieses Instrument: Piano et Forte genandt, ist von dem Königl. Polnischen und Churf. Sächsischen Hof- und Land-Orgelmacher und Instrumentenbauer, Herrn Gottfried Silbermann gefertiget worden. Freyberg in Meissen den 11. Juni Anno Christi 1746.' (This instrument, called Piano et Forte, was made by Mr Gottfried Silbermann, Royal Polish and Electoral Saxon court and state organ-builder and instrument-maker . . .) The 2nd Silbermann fortepiano to have survived in Potsdam is now in the Neues Palais, in the concert-room of Frederick the Great's apartments. Unfortunately I have not been able to examine it. According to information supplied by the director of the Staatliche Schlösser und Gärten Potsdam-Sanssouci collection, it has the inventory no. V 12, height 93 cm. (without stand, 25 cm.), width 95 cm., and length 232 cm. The body is of oak, the carved stand of lime-wood covered with gold leaf. It has a range of F_1–e^3.

[51] 'Bach und das Pianoforte', *BJb*, 48 (1961), 69.

about thirty years later. However, the *Stosszungen* (jack) action is inferior in terms of 'technical' sensitivity to the 'Viennese' action later developed by Stein. But Stein's piano even resembles Silbermann's instruments externally, which is actually not very surprising, for Stein was trained by a nephew of Silbermann in Strasbourg, who in turn had become acquainted with the instruments of his uncle Gottfried in Freiberg.

Compared with that of a clavichord, the action of a Silbermann fortepiano is rather heavy. But compared with the modern piano and many eighteenth-century tracker-action organs the action still seems light to our fingers; in fact, it seems very light indeed. (It is difficult to compare with the touch of a harpsichord, which can vary greatly, and, depending on the kinds of quill employed and the number of stops, can be heavier or lighter than a hammer action.)

I admit that on the basis of Forkel's report and other negative remarks, I did not approach the Silbermann instrument with great expectations about its sound. Rather, I expected to be confronted with an imperfect instrument with a tinny and thin tone, with weak treble notes, and with an insensitive, sluggish action. I was all the more surprised to find a fully developed fortepiano which in its own way is almost on a par with the later Stein instrument from Augsburg, known to have elicited an enthusiastic response from Mozart in 1777. The Silbermann fortepiano has an eloquent, fluty tone and sounds enchanting. True, the action is slightly 'sticky', but still fluent and light enough to permit the execution of fast trills and mordents without difficulty.[52]

The main difference between the Silbermann fortepiano and later South German, French, or English instruments of the age of Mozart is, as we have seen, the absence of a pedal action. That the pedal had to be operated 'manually' does not seem to have worried musicians who were accustomed to the harpsichord. As late as 1776 Johann Heinrich Silbermann, Gottfried Silbermann's nephew, was making very similar instruments.[53] In the nineteenth century Carl Czerny made a point of mentioning that the use of the pedal was never 'obbligato' in Mozart's keyboard music.[54] Having to play legato with their fingers only is a salutary lesson for modern pianists.

Bach would have been a bad musician if he had failed to appreciate the qualities and the beautiful sound of this new fortepiano. A composer who evidently followed new developments in instrument-building with the greatest of interest would hardly have ignored an important innovation like the fortepiano. Thus Agricola's account of Bach's dealings with Silbermann seems

---

[52] This sluggishness may also be due to the way the instrument is adjusted. Some time after this, at the Metropolitan Museum in New York, I had the opportunity to play the Cristofori instrument of 1720, the action of which is almost identical. It responded more lightly and precisely than the Silbermann instrument, and in this can certainly be compared to a Stein action.

[53] A well-preserved Strasbourg wing-shaped Silbermann instrument of this kind is now in the Musical Instrument Collection of the Staatliches Institut für Musikforschung (Preußischer Kulturbesitz), Berlin.

[54] *Complete Theoretical and Practical Piano Forte School. Op. 500*, iii (London, 1839), p. 100.

altogether credible. It is merely debatable whether he first became acquainted with Silbermann's improved fortepiano as early as 1732, or as late as 1740.

Of course, all old and modern fortepianos sound slightly colourless and sober compared with the splendid and intoxicating sound of the best harpsichords with their varied sonorities and stops. But the sound of the piano has a beauty of its own, and in the case of the early fortepianos its timbre is still similar to that of other eighteenth-century keyboard instruments. But clavichords and fortepianos are superior to harpsichords in one respect: expressivity. The 'cantabile execution' Bach repeatedly demanded (e.g. in the preface to the Inventions) means in the final analysis that in every melodic line there ought to be strong and weak and intense and relaxed notes. Such accents and 'non-accents' can be expressed only imperfectly with the help of touch on the harpsichord, on account of its relatively unyielding action. Other means of enlivening the dynamic range, such as an imperceptible lengthening and shortening of notes, the application of embellishments, and an increase in the number of voices, have to make up for the lack of genuine dynamic gradations. However, the clavichord and the fortepiano enable the performer to play in a direct and 'natural' manner. Bach surely noticed this advantage just as much as we do. Thus it is difficult to disagree with Christoph Wolff when, in the preface to the NBA edition of the ricercar mentioned above and in the editorial notes on the *Musical Offering*, he construes the sigh-motifs and crescendo figuration as evidence that Bach was thinking in terms of the Silbermann fortepiano.

However, many other works written before 1747 contain passages that are equally expressive. Though most of Partita No. 3 sounds beautiful and convincing on the harpsichord, a point is reached in the particularly expressive Sarabande where the dynamic possibilities of the instrument are exhausted, a fact of which every musical harpsichordist is acutely aware. A string player or singer would play the beginning of this movement as in Ex. 6.1. Doubtless the clavichord (which cannot be used in the concert-hall) and the fortepiano are more appropriate than the best harpsichord to this musical idea, which was probably conceived in vocal terms. This is also true of some of the preludes of *WTC* II. In passages where points of imitation in the middle and lower voices have to be emphasized, the fortepiano proves to be superior to the harpsichord. In addition to fugues and canons, such passages occur in the Allemande of the Sixth English suite in D minor (BWV 811), where the opening theme appears in the lower voice (bars 5–7), and in the Sarabande of the French Overture (BWV 831), with its imitations in bars 2, 5, and so on (see Ex. 2.40).

In addition to the expressive shaping of melodies, the fortepiano is superior to the harpsichord in that it makes it possible to play crescendos. A 'Mannheim crescendo' is surely inappropriate in Bach's music. However, there are in his works a number of written-out crescendos. Good examples

Ex. 6.1. Partita No. 3, BWV 827, Sarabande, bars 1–4

are the endings of certain fugues where the number of voices is augmented, upward-striving lines such as the ending of the C major Concerto for two harpsichords, BWV 1061 (which ascends four octaves), and passages in some other concerto movements.

Another characteristic of fortepiano tone that is often ignored in modern analyses deserves to be mentioned here. This is the fact that an increase in the intensity of touch leads to an increase not only in dynamics, but also in the number of overtones. This means that loud chords or passages on a Silbermann or Stein fortepiano are so fraught with overtones that one almost has the impression that an additional four-foot stop is being used. In this way the variable dynamics of the fortepiano provide the possibility of a kind of registration which also approximates to the harpsichord. Many old fortepianos even have lute stops and other *Veränderungen* (means of changing the tone-quality) which further enhance this similarity.

The question of the keyboard instruments Bach acquired during his lifetime and owned at the time of his death has been discussed in great detail. The catalogue of the estate reveals that one of the first five 'clavecins' in the list must have been particularly valuable, for it had a remarkably high estimated value of 80 thalers, though it was described as a 'fournirt [veneered] Clavecin', which means that its value cannot have been due to artwork. Furthermore, there is the comment that, if possible, it was to remain in the family. What could this valuable instrument have been? Was it perhaps a two-manual harpsichord with a sixteen-foot stop or an additional pedal harpsichord? Recently it has been suggested that the instrument in question may have been a Hildebrand or Silbermann fortepiano. After all, Silbermann's instruments were always rather valuable and correspondingly expensive. The suggestion is a legitimate one, especially in view of the fact that the catalogue of the estate was drawn up not by a musician, but by a civic or legal clerk who was surely as ignorant of the difference between a harpsichord and a fortepiano as of the new term 'piano-fort'. The 'veneered clavecin' may also have been a combination instrument like the ones advertised in the *Leipziger Post-Zeitung* in 1742 and 1743. Combination instruments were not as rare as is normally supposed.

ONCE MORE TO THE QUESTION: HARPSICHORD OR PIANO?

Let me start by making it clear from the outset that anyone who expects me to adopt an unequivocal stance in favour of one of the two instruments will be disappointed. As a musician who is equally at home with eighteenth-century and twentieth-century keyboard instruments, it is a question not of 'either-or', but of 'both'. After all, we do not play early music in order to take ourselves back in time, but because it pleases and moves us here and now. The twentieth century, in contrast to the nineteenth, has seen a welcome increase in the number of keyboard instruments available to us on account of the revival of harpsichords, fortepianos, positive organs, and so on. This has come about not for purely historical reasons, but because we admire the sound of these instruments for their own sake. It is of course possible to play well on every instrument, provided that it is of good quality and well tuned. It would be a sorry state of affairs if we were only able or allowed to play on a small handful of instruments. Bach himself, who wrote immortal works for all the instruments he played and who was always adapting his own music for all sorts of occasions in the shape of parodies and transcriptions, was certainly not narrow-minded in this regard.

What then is the purpose of historical research of this kind? Here I can only restate what I have said repeatedly above: that music performed 'correctly', in a manner that also corresponds to the historical sonorities, usually sounds more beautiful and meaningful. From this standpoint historical instruments (or copies of them) have an incontrovertible advantage over those of later periods, provided they are of high quality and in good condition. However, this advantage is not a good enough reason to exclude from performances instruments that were subsequently invented. We are thus led to ask whether or not Bach interpretation is possible on the modern piano.

The attitude towards this has definitely changed in the course of the twentieth century.[55] At the beginning of the century the modern piano was considered to be an instrument equal, if not superior, to the harpsichord. In the last fifty years it has had an increasingly bad press in Bach literature. Its sound was said to be thick and colourless, and it was considered to be too loud and penetrating in relation to other instruments employed in the Baroque era. Furthermore, it was said to lead the player astray into crescendo and decrescendo dynamics that had nothing to do with the baroque aesthetic, and was thus ill suited to Bach interpretation. For example, in an article of 1972 Peter Schmiedel wrote:

The piano speaks the language of our time. Should we therefore translate Bach into the language we understand? It will either turn out to be a lifeless acoustic happening,

---

[55] On this subject see the valuable essay by Josef Dichler, 'Bach auf dem modernen Hammerklavier', *ÖMZ* (1962), 574–9, and Max Cooke's excellent pamphlet *Bach at the Piano* (Melbourne, 1985).

because the sonority is incapable of re-creating the original intellectual content, which ranges from the sensory event to the inner experience of form. We must relinquish from the outset the all-pervasive inner unity described above. It may be possible to convey some idea of the inner form, but it is not established by the acoustic structure, remaining isolated from it in the realm of pure 'meaning', and therefore abstract and dead. Or a new significance that derives from modern performance practice is imparted to the abstract and empty structure, a significance which the latter was never intended to convey, and for which the old formal accoutrements are altogether too small.[56]

And Werner Neumann has summarized the change in attitude with regard to the piano thus:

Since 1900 the debate about which keyboard instrument should be used has witnessed, in continually changing guises, a theory propounded by advocates of the piano and directed against the harpsichord. As formulated by Peter Raabe (*Stein Festschrift*, 1935) this theory states: 'If Bach had known the modern grand piano, he would not have insisted on his works being played on the imperfect instruments that preceded it.' An attempt is often made to bolster up this wholly untenable view of [the harpsichord as] an imperfect precursor of the piano by an equally questionable hypothesis, namely that certain advanced works by Bach transcend the expressive resources of the instruments at his disposal, obviously having been written for an ideal instrument of the future. It is a hypothesis that seems more in keeping with the romantic than with the baroque idea of music.[57]

Around 1970, from a musicological point of view, it seemed that the piano was no longer an instrument on which it was possible to play Bach. Even today it seems that certain musicologists and many harpsichordists would like to prohibit Bach performances on modern grand pianos, and enforce this ban with fines and prison sentences. However, if one were to ban the piano, would it not be logical to banish modern stringed and wind instruments used in Bach performances from concert-halls and churches? Not to mention all women's voices in choirs? Whether or not this would be beneficial for Bach is a moot point.

With regard to the piano, we must counter the undoubtedly correct statement 'Bach certainly had good harpsichords which suited his require-ments' with a question: 'Do we have instruments that are equally good?' The answer is an emphatic 'no'. Despite the welcome growth of the harpsichord movement, we are still far from a situation where every larger concert-hall has a reasonably good harpsichord. For this reason almost all famous harpsichord-ists travel with their own instruments, a practice that does not exactly make their nomadic lives any easier, and in particular poses almost insoluble

---

[56] 'Zum Gebrauch des Cembalos und des Klaviers bei der heutigen Interpretation Bachscher Werke', *BJb*, 58 (1972), 103.
[57] 'Probleme der Aufführungspraxis im Spiegel der Geschichte der Neuen Bachgesellschaft', *BJb*, 53 (1967), 100–20.

problems on trips overseas. Even where there are good harpsichords, as for instance in instrument museums, we are confronted repeatedly with instruments which have a beautiful tone, but are wholly unsuited to Bach with regard to touch and the kind of stops available, for the majority are old French or Flemish instruments, or Italian harpsichords from the sixteenth and seventeenth centuries. The difference between these and eighteenth-century German instruments is almost as great as the one between an imaginary Bach harpsichord and a modern grand piano. Furthermore, there is no unanimity on what the ideal Bach harpsichord was in the past, or on what it should look or sound like today. The pioneer of the harpsichord movement, Wanda Landowska, who adduced ingenious and sound arguments in favour of the use of the harpsichord in Bach performances,[58] possessed a Pleyel harpsichord which (unintentionally) was an unhistorical nineteenth-century creation, standing in relation to old harpsichords like an elephant to a gazelle. Other modern harpsichords often sound like wire crates or frying-pans when compared with old harpsichords or good modern copies. One reason for many of these defects is the problem of maintenance. Faced with a lack of tuners and technicians, concert-halls and conservatories can keep only harpsichords able to survive the rigours of modern concert and educational life. They have to be robustly built, so that the action does not have to be regulated every week and the instrument does not go out of tune with every change in the weather. Even the best modern copies of old harpsichords often achieve this stability only at the price of a loss in beauty of tone. Even if we wanted to, we could not banish the piano from modern Bach performances. The question is, do we want to banish it?

As far as the record-buying and concert-going public is concerned, Bach played on modern grand pianos is still very popular, even today. Few music-lovers would be willing to forgo performances of the *WTC* by pianists such as Edwin Fischer, Sviatoslav Richter, Friedrich Gulda, Jörg Demus, Glenn Gould, and others who play (or played) the modern piano. In these interpretations, does the inner form, as Schmiedel says, really remain 'abstract and dead'? I very much doubt it. Even more open to doubt is the idea that a good harpsichord, even in inartistic and unmusical hands, allows the spirit of baroque music to come to life in a magical way, as it were.

In the article quoted above, Werner Neumann does not deny the piano its right to rival the harpsichord:

For musico-sociological reasons alone it would be absurd to want to exclude the millions of people who possess the most common keyboard instrument from the experience of playing Bach. In the concert-hall, however, pianists will still have to demonstrate how far their ability to play this universal instrument does justice to the

[58] 'Bach's Keyboard Instruments', in *Landowska on Music*, ed. and trans. D. Restout (New York, 1964), 139.

specific tonal structure of a work by Bach. It is an undertaking which from the historian's viewpoint can only be considered to be a transcription.[59]

Whereas this comment is quite correct, it would be quite wrong to ascribe to the concept of 'transcription' the negative idea of something which is a substitute or second-rate, as is frequently the case. With regard to keyboard music, the greater part of our repertoire, played on modern instruments, is similarly a transcription, from Haydn and Mozart to Chopin and early Brahms or Liszt, all of whom had quite different keyboard instruments at their disposal. In a wider sense, however, almost all great music is transcription. In most cases a musical idea can be realized in terms of sonority only by means of adaptation and arrangement.

Bach himself was one of the greatest transcribers of all time, both of his own works and of those of others. Norman Carrell's study of this subject, *Bach the Borrower*,[60] and (in more concise form) Georg von Dadelsen's article in the *Festschrift für Alfred Dürr*,[61] list hundreds of adaptations and transcriptions. If Bach transcribed a work for solo violin so that it could also be played on the organ, the lute, and the harpsichord, and if he had no hestitation in transcribing an oboe part for flute, harpsichord, or a stringed instrument, he would surely not have objected to 'transcriptions' of his keyboard works for the modern grand piano. More important for the performance of any music than a particular 'sonority' are musicality, the understanding and shaping of musical structure, the choice of something approaching the correct tempo, the convincing and stylish execution of articulation and ornamentation, the perception of the affection, emotional content, musical symbolism, and so on.[62] Overestimating the importance of sonority seems in fact to be a modern malaise. For centuries tone-colour was considered to be of secondary importance, a factor which rarely had anything to do with the substance of the music. In the case of much early music we do not even know whether it was sung or played on instruments, to say nothing of the question of which instruments were used. Bach's transcriptions would seem to partake of this spirit. Of course, this does not amount to a *carte blanche* for every arbitrary transcription.

In one respect the modern piano's relative lack of overtones, in conjunction with its capacity for differentiated dynamics, is even an advantage. In some polyphonic pieces it is often easier on a modern piano than on a harpsichord to achieve plastic execution which renders fugal entries, points of imitation, and strettos audible. The choice of varying degrees of loudness when playing several voices simultaneously even makes it possible to achieve slight

---

[59] 'Probleme', p. 107. [60] London, 1967.

[61] 'Anmerkungen zu Bachs Parodieverfahren', *Bachiana et alia Musicologica. Festschrift Alfred Dürr*, ed. Wolfgang Rehm (Kassel, 1983), pp. 52–7.

[62] In his *MGG* art. 'Bach, Johann Sebastian', Friedrich Blume provides a good summary of the virtually impenetrable complexity of Bach's music with regard to affection, symbolism, and numerical relationships.

differences in tone-colour (louder = brighter, softer = darker) which are not possible on other keyboard instruments, with the possible exception of the organ.

Another reason why I think the modern grand piano is a legitimate instrument with a future in performances of Bach is the fact that his music often contains accents implied by the inner structure which have to be 'suggested' rather than played on the harpsichord. These can be brought out even more on modern pianos than on fortepianos and clavichords. A typical example of an intrinsic accent is the subject of the A major Fugue from *WTC* I (Ex. 6.2). The first note followed by a rest is, in purely structural terms, like an explosion. In fact it must project its energy across the rest to the next triplet figure. Every string player would play the first note marcato. As is well known, Carl Czerny incorporated in his edition of the *WTC* (a historical achievement of great interest) his memories of Beethoven's performances. I have no doubt that the dynamic marks supplied by Czerny went back to the way Beethoven played this work (see Ex. 6.3). This is of course an exaggeration from the point of view of the style of Bach, but may in fact be the best way of making it clear to the listener that the subject (especially in later entries) does not begin after the long rest.

Ex. 6.2. *WTC* I, Fugue in A major, bars 1–4

Ex. 6.3. *WTC* I, Fugue in A major, bars 1–4, ed. Czerny

On the basis of these findings we may restate the old question: 'What would Bach have thought of the modern concert grand?' The probable answer would be neither naïve—'He would have considered it to be the fulfilment of his secret wishes'—nor arrogant—'He would have considered it to be an unmusical monstrosity'. We may now assume with greater insight and for better reasons that Bach would have recognized both the advantages and weaknesses of the instrument. Its undisputed advantages include the great dynamic range and the capacity for cantabile tone in the middle and high treble register. Its disadvantages, on the other hand, include its relatively colourless, 'grey' tone. Even in the case of more brilliant modern instruments, Bach might well have criticized the tone as being too thick and drab, and, especially in the lower register, as being too unclear and opaque. Like all other eighteenth-century keyboard players, Bach would no doubt have considered the action to be too heavy.

Yet Bach would also have recognized the precision and flexibility of the modern piano action, and the fact that the instrument makes possible the execution of very rapid repeated notes in trills and other ornaments. His main objection to the modern piano would doubtless have been that it does not blend well with other instruments and is almost wholly unsuited for continuo playing in the orchestra on account of its lack of overtones. But despite these objections he would probably have recognized that it was a mature instrument with great scope for virtuoso and expressive playing. He would probably have acquiesced in the use of the modern piano for most of his 'keyboard' works, with the proviso that dynamic extremes be avoided. He might even have allowed occasional octave doublings in the bass on the lines of those he wrote out (exceptionally) in the E major Sonata for violin and obbligato harpsichord, BWV 1016, but, it is to be hoped, not the well-known 'Busoni basses' in the lowest register.

What role should be assigned to the modern pedal? Whereas it can be very useful, when playing Bach, to do without the pedal altogether—in order to emphasize articulation and finger-legato—the total rejection of the pedal sometimes advocated today seems rather pointless. The manner in which the sound is suddenly 'cut off' by modern dampers produces a dryness of tone which was never heard on eighteenth-century harpsichords or fortepianos. On larger harpsichords in particular there was a considerable interval between the key being released and the point when the strings and the sound-board ceased to vibrate.

In pieces with arpeggiated triads, for example, the sound of a good early harpsichord was very similar to that of a modern piano when the pianist makes a discreet use of the pedal. The pedal is the 'stop' peculiar to the modern piano, and with its help magical sounds can be evoked. It is the piano's only substitute for the harpsichord's many stops.

It would also be just as wrong to try to 'play the harpsichord' on the modern piano as it is, conversely, to 'play the piano' on the harpsichord (this can sound terrible). A pianist who eschews the pedal is like a violinist who does not use vibrato, for on the piano a note played with pedal creates a vibrato effect. Performers of baroque and rococo music are fully aware of the fact that violin vibrato was used in the eighteenth century, particularly by virtuosos, though less frequently than today. Geminiani describes vibrato in his famous violin treatise of 1751, stating that it should be used 'as often as possible'.[63] It has always been one of a performer's primary concerns to draw the most beautiful sounds possible from his instrument.

I have already mentioned the intermingling of different harmonies on early fortepianos. Whilst it is hardly ever appropriate to play a piece by Bach on the modern piano with the pedal depressed for long stretches at a time, Bach and his contemporaries often write movements of the 'musette' type with pedal-points in the bass that imitate the sound of hurdy-gurdies or bagpipes on the harpsichord. Movements of this kind are Gavotte II 'ou la Musette' from English Suite No. 3, BWV 808, Gavotte II from English Suite No. 6, BWV 811, and, to a slightly lesser extent, Minuet II from the B flat Partita, BWV 825. Here some strong 'over-pedalling' on the piano probably comes closer to the original than the harpsichord. There is no need to be afraid of using the pedal!

To sum up. In comparison with the tonal ideal of the nineteenth and twentieth centuries all eighteenth-century musical instruments had a brighter, clearer, more transparent, but also thinner and quieter sound than later ones. Conversely, where music is pure poetry in sound, listeners have always tended to forget the instrument and even the performer, because it speaks to us on a level that is more profound than a merely sensual response to sound. I and other musicians experience this every time we hear Edwin Fischer's moving performance of the B flat minor Prelude from *WTC* I. This is deeply felt music of mourning that speaks directly to the heart. Therefore, without wishing to belittle our quest for the correct instrument, I would like to conclude by saying that the sonority is not the most important element. Bach himself adapted his works for all sorts of instruments, without taking into account the original sonority. In the end it was not the instrument or the voice that he considered important, but the spirit that infused the player or singer. 'Let everything that hath breath praise the LORD.'[64]

---

[63] *The Art of Playing on the Violin* (London, 1751), p. 8.   [64] Psalm 150.

7

Problems of Harpsichord and Piano Technique, and of Expressive Playing

INTRODUCTION

Because we are concerned with performances on harpsichords, fortepianos, and modern pianos, it seems apposite to describe the similarities and differences between the ways these instruments are played.[1] Common to all of them is a certain resistance in the action that has to be overcome in order to produce a sound. On the harpsichord this resistance stems from the greater or lesser degree of rigidity of the quill plectra and can be quite considerable when all the stops are in use. On the fortepiano, be it early or modern, the reason for this resistance is the (now much greater) weight of the hammer and the 'aftertouch', which is similar to that of the harpsichord. In passing it is worth mentioning that on the clavichord there is no escapement resistance until the tangent strikes the vibrating string.

However, this is about as far as the similarities go. On the harpsichord the speed at which a key is depressed makes little or no difference to the intensity of a note, whereas on the fortepiano it is the variable speed at which the key is struck, and nothing else, that makes possible the many gradations in volume between *pp* and *ff*. This in turn brings with it the following phenomenon: the faster the acceleration of a hammer, the greater, according to the laws of kinetic energy, the resistance of its mass. This means that when the speed is doubled, the (apparent) weight of the hammer increases fourfold, and when it is quadrupled, it increases sixteenfold. Because of the extremely light hammers employed, this increase does not play a significant role on eighteenth-century fortepianos. On modern pianos, however, it can amount to several kilograms, for instance in the thundering octaves of a work by Liszt or Brahms. It is easy to understand that fingers and wrists alone were no longer strong enough to surmount resistance of this magnitude, and that in the

---

[1] See my art. 'Playing the Early Piano', *Early Music*, 12 (1984), 477–80. The reader is also referred to Richard Troeger, *Technique and Interpretation on the Harpsichord and Clavichord* (Bloomington, Ind., 1987).

course of the nineteenth century a 'weight' technique was developed which requires the performer to play from the arm and even from the shoulders.

The modern 'weight' technique is totally alien to the eighteenth century. When applied to harpsichords or fortepianos it produces an unwelcome knocking sound and an appalling tone. All eminent harpsichordists have rightly protested about pianists who play the harpsichord in this way (i.e. with their usual arm-weight technique).[2] Eta Harich-Schneider has described the different techniques in her textbook, which is as relevant as ever:

Harpsichordists are continually being asked why one cannot play the harpsichord by gradual pressure applied by the fingertips, as on the piano—and why we always employ a sharp attack from the knuckles. But it should be self-evident to every instrumentalist that actions as different as those of the piano and the harpsichord also require a different kind of touch!

Just before the string is plucked there is a short, but very noticeable resistance of the key against the finger. This resistance must be 'struck through' by the speed of the descending finger. When several stops are in use the combined resistance of several quill plectra has to be overcome simultaneously. An increase in the number of stops requires a corresponding increase in the swiftness of touch. 'Slowly depressing' the key as on a piano can lead to the stops being heard consecutively. The finger breaks into the key like a poor skater through thin ice.

Thus harpsichord touch emanates from the knuckles, with a motionless hand and a light arm, consisting of a very swift blow which strikes through all the registers and a subsequent short moment of repose on the key. This combination of a strong snap and light fingers, with the attendant necessity to exclude the use of the arm, is difficult for all beginners, be they children or adults. The old masters were well aware of this difficulty, and in order to overcome it, suggested that beginners should use instruments with soft quills. From Diruta onwards, every textbook contains a warning about hard quills and badly regulated instruments which inevitably ruin the players' touch. Diruta makes a telling comparison to describe a soft, relaxed touch (for which a softly quilled instrument is a precondition).

'Let me give an example to illustrate the manner in which one should hold one's hands over the keys lightly and gently. If you are angry and box someone's ears, you need a lot of force. However, if you wish to be tender and caressing, no force is needed. Your hand is held as lightly as when stroking a little child.'

Rameau stated in his *Code de musique pratique*: 'First you need a soft (or softly quilled) instrument, so that its resistance does not force the fingers (which are still weak in their movements) to derive their strength from the whole hand. As the freedom of movement increases, so does the acquired strength, and correspondingly one can increase the resistance of the keys by using harder quills to pluck the strings'.[3]

---

[2] See W. Landowska, 'Bach's Keyboard Instruments', *Landowska on Music*, pp. 168 ff.
[3] *Die Kunst des Cembalospiels*, 2nd edn. (Kassel, 1939), 21–2.

THE POSITION OF BODY, HANDS, AND FINGERS

The second chapter of Eta Harich-Schneider's *Die Kunst des Cembalospiels* contains a description of posture and touch which deserves to be studied closely. I quote from it here because some keyboard players may not have access to it, and because a few additional remarks on playing early fortepianos are desirable.

From a pianist we expect a technique that elicits all the tonal resources of the modern piano, a technique that involves relaxation on the one hand and a display of force on the other if, that is, his playing is to have a fully orchestral effect. Naturally his posture must reflect these requirements. Before beginning to play, his body will appear both relaxed, and ready to exert the necessary force from his back and shoulders. The posture of the harpsichordist, on the other hand, is less relaxed. It is a state of quiet tension: he does not play using the whole of his bodily strength. Rather, the decisive features of his technique are discipline and balance. He sits up straight, he 'carries' his arms—many old pictures show the harpsichordist holding his arms in a light and controlled manner, using only his fingers in the manner of engraving tools to 'etch' his music on the keys. This posture should not, for example, be regarded merely as the expression of a kind of conventional grace. Rather, it is necessary for the correct handling of the instrument. It is thus not surprising that the sources describing this posture are numerous and detailed.[4]

Harich-Schneider does not quote the following observations from Couperin's *L'Art de toucher le clavecin*:

If one wishes to sit at the right height, then the bottom of the elbow, the wrists, and the fingers must describe a straight line. For this reason one should select a chair which makes it possible to satisfy these demands.

Young people, according to the speed they grow up, should have a more or less high cushion placed under their feet, so that these do not sway in the air and can keep the body in the proper balance.

The distance that a fully grown person should be from the clavecin is about nine inches [about 1/4 metre]. Young people should be closer. The middle of the body should be directed towards the clavecin.

When sitting at the clavecin, one should turn the body a little to the right; the knees should not be pressed together; the feet should be parallel, but the right foot pointing outwards.

One can cure oneself from making faces by placing a mirror on the music-stand of the spinet or clavecin.

One should not stare at a certain object, nor should one stare blankly. Finally, one should look at the audience, if there is one, as if one were not occupied elsewhere. This advice is of course only intended for those who play without the help of music.

The first lessons should be given on the spinet or on a single manual of the clavecin, both of them softly quilled. This point is of the greatest importance, for beautiful

[4] p. 16.

playing depends more on the flexibility and free movement of the fingers than on their strength. If one allows a child to play on two manuals right from the start, it is forced, in order to draw music from the strings, to exert its little hands more than is appropriate, and this leads to bad posture and hard execution. A soft touch makes it necessary to hold the fingers as close as possible to the keys. Apart from what experience teaches us, it must seem obvious that a hand which falls from above produces a drier tone than when it strikes the keys from close to, and that (in the former) the quill will produce a harder tone on the string.

People who learn the instrument late in life or have been badly taught, since their sinews have grown hard or may have become accustomed to bad habits, must ensure that before they sit down at the clavecin their fingers are supple or made supple. This means that they should stretch out their fingers in all directions, or have someone to stretch them. This also raises one's spirits and one feels freer.[5]

These remarks are equally valid when applied to the correct fortepiano posture. According to C. P. E. Bach one should sit slightly higher.[6] With regard to the posture of the fingers themselves, the old tutors are in complete agreement: they should always be curved. C. P. E. Bach starts out from the same natural hand-position as Chopin did about a century later (in his incomplete piano method): 'The hand should be placed on the keyboard in such a way that the second, third, and fourth fingers come to rest in a slightly curved position on the black keys.' In the *Essay* he states: 'Hence, the first principal rule: Black keys are seldom taken by the little finger and only out of necessity by the thumb.'[7]

The remarks on Bach's fingering in Forkel's biography are of particular interest. Furthermore, they are undoubtedly trustworthy, for Forkel no doubt questioned Bach's two eldest sons closely on this matter:

Sebastian Bach's manner of holding the hand at the keyboard entails bending all five fingers so that the fingertips are in a straight line. These then fit the level line of adjacent keys so that no finger need first be drawn closer if and when required. Rather, each finger hovers over the key that it is to depress. The following is bound up with this position of the hand.

(1) No finger may fall or (as often happens) be thrown on to its key. It may only be applied with a certain feeling of inner strength and control over the movement.

(2) The strength or the amount of pressure thus applied to the keys must be maintained at the same level. This is not achieved by lifting the finger vertically from the key, but by gradually drawing back the fingertips towards the palm of the hand, so that the finger slides off the front part of the key.

(3) When moving from one key to the next the degree of strength or pressure applied to the first note is very swiftly thrown on to the next finger by means of this sliding movement. Thus the two notes cannot be torn apart, nor can one note continue to sound after the second has been struck.

Thus the touch is, as C. P. E. Bach says, neither too long nor too short, but exactly as it ought to be. . . . Bach is also said to have played with a finger movement that was

<hr />

[5] pp. 10 ff.   [6] See *Essay*, p. 42.   [7] p. 45.

so light and small as to be almost imperceptible. Only the front joints of the fingers moved. The hand retained its curved form even in the most difficult passages, and the fingers were lifted only slightly from the keys, hardly more than in the case of trills. When one finger was employed, the other remained in a state of repose. The other parts of his body were even less involved in his playing, something that is often lacking in the case of players whose hands have not been trained to be light.[8]

We shall return below to the practice of drawing the fingers forward to slide off the keys, which, it seems, was not taught by the French.

Scheibe, when describing Bach's organ playing, made a similar observation about the combination of steady posture and great virtuosity:

His artistry on the keyboard and the organ is extraordinary. At present there is only one other musician who is roughly his equal. I have heard this great man play on several occasions. One is surprised by his skill, and it is difficult to understand how his fingers and feet can possibly cross, stretch out, and execute the greatest leaps so curiously and nimbly without hitting a single wrong note, and, despite such vigorous movement, without engaging in bodily contortions.[9]

However, we should not expect that he adhered wholly to the 'classical harpsichord posture' with its steady and almost motionless wrists. Even Bach must have raised his arm to cross hands in certain passages, and to play the octaves at the end of the Chromatic Fugue. The active use of arms and elbows applies still more in the case of Domenico Scarlatti, whose music can at times be played only by using 'modern' keyboard technique. (Anyone who has heard the unforgettable Scarlatti performances by Fernando Valenti, a pupil of Kirkpatrick, will be aware that it is also possible to play percussive repeated chords on the harpsichord.) Moreover, recent research has established that Scarlatti came across Cristofori's fortepiano in his youth and that he had several fortepianos at his disposal at the Spanish court.[10] It is therefore quite possible that many of his sonatas were in fact composed for the fortepiano.

The controlled use of finger-technique is not only important on the harpsichord; it is also the Alpha and Omega of eighteenth-century fortepiano technique. However, even in Haydn and Mozart the arm is employed repeatedly for chords and octaves. A widespread error among pianists, which is the result of heavy modern actions, is the use of wrist staccato for single notes. This always sounds rather 'wooden' on early instruments. The old harpsichord technique should be employed instead:

In view of the fact that it is necessary to play the harpsichord using the kind of finger-snapping described above, without the help of the arm, it is obvious that staccato and the various degrees of non-legato do not differ with regard to the movement

[8] *Bachs Leben*, pp. 32 ff.; Eng. trans., pp. 307–8.
[9] *Der critische Musicus* (Hamburg, 1737), quoted in *Bach-Dokumente*, ii. 286.
[10] See Eva Badura-Skoda, 'Domenico Scarlatti und das Hammerklavier', *ÖMZ*, 40 (1985), 525; Ralph Kirkpatrick, *Domenico Scarlatti* (Princeton, NJ, 1953; rev. 1955, 1982), p. 178.

employed. Arm or wrist staccato, or even the well-known non-legato that emanates from the arm, is excluded from harpsichord technique. The difference between the types of touch is simply the duration of the note, that is, whether the tip of the finger is raised quickly or slowly from the key. Visually the movement of the hand and arm has the same quiet and controlled appearance as in legatissimo. Of course, the harpsichord requires a conscious cultivation of various modifications of touch, because the possibilities of varying the dynamics by touch are so few.[11]

On the harpsichord, as on the piano, an uneven curved position of the fingers leads to uneven playing, especially in scales. Quantz had this to say:

If you accustom yourself at the very beginning to curving all the fingers inwards, each one as far as the others, you are less likely to make this mistake. In the performance of these running passages, however, you must not raise the fingers immediately after striking the key, but rather draw the tips of the fingers back towards yourself to the foremost part of the key, until they glide away from it. Running passages are produced most distinctly in this manner. I appeal here to the example of one of the greatest of all players on the keyboard, who practised and taught in this way.[12]

Drawing in the fingers in this way seems to have been characteristic of the old German and Dutch style of playing. According to Friedrich Ernst, the technique of sliding the finger off the key was the reason for the worn keys found in the middle register of early harpsichords.[13] It used to be easier to play in this way because the front halves of the keys are significantly shorter on old keyboard instruments (about 3.5 cm.) than on modern ones (about 5 cm.).

This style of playing is characteristic of the harpsichord, but it can also be used on historical and modern pianos. The 'sliding-off' (*Abzug*) technique was something of a revelation as far as I was concerned, for it does in fact make possible clearly articulated fingering in non-legato and legato, even in fast passages. This is often of value even in Haydn, Mozart, and Beethoven.

When playing legato, on the other hand, I do not find the style so useful, despite the legatissimo mentioned by Quantz. This kind of 'sliding-off' suggests itself only in places where a finger has to cross another one (for example, 3 over 4 or 4 over 5 in 'Chopin fingering'). C. P. E. Bach describes passing a longer finger over a shorter one as well as the frequent use of the thumb (with an appeal to his 'deceased father'), and the passing of the thumb under the fingers.[14] He specifically demands that the player should use 'arched' fingers and 'relaxed' muscles[15] and places particular value on the art of correct fingering, to which he devotes no fewer than thirty-eight pages (still worth reading today) of his textbook.

---

[11] Harich-Schneider, *Die Kunst des Cembalospiels*, p. 26.

[12] *On Playing the Flute*, p. 260. The last remark refers to J. S. Bach, whom Quantz identifies in the index.

[13] *Der Flügel Johann Sebastian Bachs* (Frankfurt-on-Main and New York, 1955), 46.

[14] *Essay*, pp. 42–6.   [15] *Essay*, p. 42.

PROBLEMS OF TOUCH IN BACH

The keyboard player's equivalent of the bow-stroke of a string player, or the embouchure of a wind player, is good touch, no matter which instrument he is using. Touch is the soul of music-making, and good touch adapts itself to the instrument like a good rider to a horse. Both consciously and intuitively, it senses the 'soul' of an instrument and understands how to draw from it the secrets of its most beautiful tone. Yet at the same time it mirrors the player's personality. We recognize certain great performers by their inimitable touch.[16] Even experts are often surprised by the fact that supposedly 'mechanical' instruments can suddenly acquire a 'soul' in the hands of the artist. Yet these are indeed measurable acoustical processes. In purely physical terms the tone that results from touch is solely dependent on the speed with which the key or the escapement mechanism is struck or released. (In the case of hammer actions, an increase in the speed at which the key is struck entails a greater acceleration of the hammer, and thus an increase in volume.)

A sensitive keyboard player is aware of the tonal resources at his disposal, moulding them to suit both the work and his own personality. A performer who is not at least 'mentally' close to the string will either strike too hard and produce a 'wooden' sound or produce a kind of 'rustling' that does not exploit the resonance to the full. Only a gifted performer can preserve the delicate balance of the principal melodic and the accompanying subsidiary voices, be it in homophonic or polyphonic writing. All this requires a great deal of subtlety, something that emanates not only from the fingers, but in part from deep down in the subconscious.

With regard to touch, a second principle of good musicianship needs to be explained. No matter which keyboard instrument we choose, we must try to draw from it (or 'bring out') the best, most beautiful, and indeed most magical sound that we can. In this regard there is widespread misunderstanding about playing Bach on the modern piano, for many pianists attempt to 'play the harpsichord', or at least to imitate the sound of the latter. (This is understandable, for every musician is aware that the rounded romantic piano sound produced by a plentiful use of the pedal was unknown to Bach.) However, this often leads to musically unsatisfactory and indeed quite ugly results. An oboist would never attempt to imitate the clarinet, and a trumpeter would never try to imitate the bassoon. If we are going to play Bach on the piano we must try to bring out the positive qualities of this instrument and produce a beautiful tone. And then the intelligent application of the pedal also

---

[16] Even a layman, when listening to their recordings, can tell the difference between the sounds produced by Horowitz, Cortot, and Edwin Fischer on the piano, or by Landowska, Leonhardt, and George Malcolm on the harpsichord.

contributes to beautiful piano playing. To eschew this unique feature of the piano would be tantamount to rejecting its most beautiful tonal resource. Teachers who forbid their pupils to use the pedal on the piano because it is a sonority unavailable to the harpsichord forget that on historical harpsichords every note continues to sound for a moment after it has been dampened, which to the ears of a pianist sounds like the discreet application of the pedal. Besides, the harpsichord has a number of attractive registers of which there are no equivalents on the piano. The only registrations possible on the piano are the effects produced by the two pedals and of course the almost limitless possibility of dynamic gradation. It would be easier for a violinist to eschew vibrato,[17] something that is often stylistically valid in Bach, than for a pianist to do without the beneficial effect of the pedal, especially in cantabile pieces. Even in the case of a single note, the sound of the piano, in itself somewhat colourless, is tonally enriched by the sympathetic vibration of other strings. Of course, the pedal must be used sparingly and released frequently in order not to endanger the clarity of the musical lines. Exceptions to the sparing use of the pedal are the movements in which hurdy-gurdies, musettes, or bagpipes are imitated on the harpsichord. Here one can achieve the desired effect on the piano much better than on the harpsichord by a powerful dose of 'over-pedalling'.

Another way of imitating the harpsichord on the piano, often intentional and usually unsuccesful, is to play aggressively and far too loud in order to enrich the overtones present or to achieve a kind of 'sweeping' sonority. It is true that loud notes on the piano are richer in overtones and brighter than soft notes. However, they are coupled with a hammering and percussive effect that is quite foreign to the harpsichord. Moreover, playing the piano in an aggressive manner produces the kind of jangling sound that has always been considered ugly.[18] The rediscovery of authentic instruments and performance styles has taught us that eighteenth-century performances were brighter, more lively, and clearer than modern ones, and also a great deal quieter. If we are going to play instruments that are louder than authentic ones, then this is something we should not exaggerate. It is perfectly possible to play quietly and yet clearly and brightly on modern instruments. In so doing it is important that this softer tone should be full of character and energy. At any rate, an 'unstable' and blurred tone with an ill-defined beginning should be ruled out. Clarity is primarily achieved by finger-articulation and appropriate phrasing. To say that the pedal should be used with the greatest economy and occasionally not at all in fast and clearly structured movements does not contradict what has been said above.

---

[17] On the subject of violin vibrato in Bach see Melkus, 'Bach-Interpretation', pp. 71 f.

[18] 'I can't stand this damn pounding', Schubert wrote in a letter to his parents on 25 (28?) July 1825. Chopin warned against playing the piano as loudly as the Germans. See Edith J. Hipkins, *How Chopin Played* (London, 1937), p. 7.

In fact piano tone is not quite as colourless as if often believed. Thus a pianistic harpsichord imitation can occasionally be achieved by plucking the notes by means of finger-staccato and pedalling very briefly. In the twentieth century Spanish composers have shown that it is possible to imitate the guitar or the lute in this manner. Lutes and harpsichord lute stops were also popular in Bach's time.

And what about touch on the harpsichord?

Nothing can sound as ugly, thin, and inadequate as a harpsichord played with bad touch. . . . In none of the sources from the sixteenth to the eighteenth century is there the slightest support for the view that flat, uniform harpsichord playing with no indication of dynamic curves and no cantabile was felt to be the particular charm of this instrument. On the contrary, we find a unanimous acknowledgement of a certain, albeit weak, capacity for modification, the meagreness of which lends a certain fascination to the task of 'infusing with soul' (as the early masters call it) this inflexible instrument. The treatises repeatedly state that one should improve one's technique and ear by practising the clavichord, in order to make the harpsichord sing as much as possible, and not to play in a monochrome manner.[19]

Exactly the same view is expressed by Quantz:

On each instrument the tone may be produced in different ways, and the same is true of the harpsichord, although it might appear that on this instrument everything depends not upon the player but only upon the instrument itself. Experience shows, however, that if two musicians play the same instrument, one produces a better tone than the other. The reason for this must be the touch peculiar to each person. In this regard it is necessary that each finger strikes the key with equal force and emphasis, and with the proper weight; that the strings are given sufficient time to make their vibrations unhindered; and that the fingers are not depressed too sluggishly, but are rather given, through a snap (*Schneller*), a certain force that will make the vibrations of the string longer in duration, and sustain the tone longer. In this fashion you will obviate as much as possible the natural weakness of the instrument, which is that the tones cannot be joined to one another as upon other instruments.

Recently Kenneth Gilbert has commented:

The basic treatises of Couperin (*L'Art de toucher le Clavecin*, 1716), Saint-Lambert (*Les Principes du clavecin*, 1702), Rameau (*De la mécanique des doigts sur le clavecin*, 1724), Marpurg (*Die Kunst das Klavier zu spielen*, 1750, Paris edition, 1755), and Corrette (*Le Maître de clavecin*, 1753) should be read and read again by harpsichordists who are fortunate enough to have access to good instruments based on the classical models. For it is only on such an instrument, with its light, crisp touch and clear sound, that these writings can be fully applied and have real meaning for us. The early authors are in complete accord about the proper harpsichord touch, but it is of no great use to study their writings, and then to expect to be able to apply them to an

---

[19] Harich-Schneider, *Die Kunst des Cembalospiels*, p. 13.

instrument with a heavy action, bearing little or no resemblance to a classical harpsichord.[20]

Richard Troeger's *Technique and Interpretation on the Harpsichord and Clavichord* is the most comprehensive study on playing the harpsichord and the clavichord to date.

PLAYING LEGATO AND CANTABILE

As indicated in Chapter 4, there are three basic rules of legato playing. These are:

1. the actual linking of notes;
2. the correct pressure or touch;
3. the dynamic shaping of the line(s).

Usually only the first of these requirements is observed. Yet a really beautiful, singing legato materializes only when all three are combined.

Linking the Notes

When linking notes much depends, of course, on the moment at which the player raises his fingers, or slides off the previous 'note'. Here we may distinguish between normal legato and legatissimo. Rameau describes both: 'From the finger with which we started we move to its neighbour, and so on. We observe that the one that has just struck a key releases it at the moment its neighbour strikes the next. Lifting one finger and applying another must occur simultaneously.'[21] Furthermore, 'a slur that links two different notes . . . means that the finger may only be lifted from the first note after the second has been struck.'[22]

Such slurring must be practised separately, preferably by subdividing each note into two halves and lifting the fingers in syncopation. Raising the fingers should be practised with the fingertips at right angles to the key, like a nail being hammered into a board. The fingers should be lifted even more swiftly than when striking the key, as though it were a 'negative' fortissimo. Lifting the fingers without extending them is in fact an unnatural movement. However, the advantage is that the raised finger is ready to play again immediately without losing time. It remains in this position until required. This forceful raising of the fingers is often neglected in modern piano teaching because the weight of the key presses the fingers up in any case. However, this

---

[20] Introduction to *Couperin, Pièces de clavecin, Livre I* (Paris, 1969), p. xx.

[21] Quoted in Harich-Schneider, *Die Kunst des Cembalospiels*, p. 27.

[22] *Pièces de clavessin avec une méthode pour la méchanique des doigts* (Paris, 1724), large table of ornaments; fac. table, ed. E. R. Jacobi (Kassel, 1958).

produces a one-sided and indeed incorrect development of the muscles, and this can prove detrimental to harpsichord, fortepiano, or clavichord technique.

Richard Troeger has described yet another way of playing legato, which entails releasing the key shortly *before* the next note is struck. This 'articulated' kind of legato takes advantage of the fact that the string continues to vibrate for a moment after the key has been released. It is indispensable for polyphonic passages in which the same finger is obliged to play two successive notes.

Touch

In legato the correct kind of touch is really pressure, as C. P. E. Bach rightly remarked. It is also valid for the harpsichord. 'The first note [of a legato phrase] is accented by means of gentle pressure, but not by a sharp attack or a rapid release.'[23] 'Attack and touch are one and the same thing. Everything depends on their force and duration.'[24]

The pressure varies constantly, depending on the instrument selected and the degree of force required by the musical context. In the case of melody-notes the pressure required is surprisingly great. Masters of cantabile tone, such as Edwin Fischer and Wilhelm Kempff, instructed their pupils to press sustained melody-notes so strongly that the white under the finger-nails becomes visible. Finger-pressure also varies according to the length or brevity of a melody-note, and from almost every instrument to another. On the clavichord it is possible for a 'long, affettuoso tone' to be 'performed with a vibrato [*Bebung*]. The finger that depresses and holds the key is gently shaken'.[25] Even on the fortepiano and the modern piano a similar kind of 'rocking' prevents a hard touch as it were retrospectively. Of course the pressure applied to accompanying lines will be proportionately less.

Shaping the Line(s)

However, the most important thing is to 'retrace' the dynamics of melodic lines with their moments of greater and lesser tension, and their rhythmically strong and weak notes. All the mechanical slurring and the best touch in the world are insufficient to convey the cantabile character of a line if the relationship of the accents is wrong. This principle of performance, which has already been discussed above (Chapter 5), will be examined in greater detail in Chapters 9 and 10.

---

[23] *Essay*, p. 158. This in fact contradicts Harich-Schneider's remarks on the subject (p. 178 above).
[24] *Essay*, p. 154.   [25] C. P. E. Bach, *Essay*, p. 156.

8

The Urtext Problem: An Imaginary Interview

A CONVERSATION BETWEEN DR C., THE MUSIC CRITIC, AND PAUL BADURA-SKODA (B.-S.)

DR C. Professor Badura-Skoda, for decades you have been studying the problems associated with musical texts. I have taken the trouble to look up some of your essays and, in addition to the 'Urtext' chapter of the book on Mozart written jointly with your wife, I have found the following articles on the subject. 'Fehlende Takte und korrumpierte Stellen in klassischen Meisterwerken',[1] 'Um den Chopin'schen Urtext',[2] 'Unbekannte Eigenschriften bekannter Schubert-Werke',[3] 'War Beethoven unfehlbar?',[4] 'Fehlende und überzählige Takte bei Beethoven und Schubert',[5] 'Text und Interpretationsprobleme in Beethovens Klavierkonzerten'.[6] Last but not least, there are your many Urtext editions of Haydn, Mozart, Beethoven, Schubert, and Chopin. Would it be right to say that textual criticism is your favourite hobby?

B.-S. No, in fact, my favourite hobby is chess. The search for the authentic text means more to me than a hobby; it is a matter of musical life and death. Incidentally, you have forgotten to mention what is possibly my most important essay on the subject, which deals with a disputed textual problem in Beethoven's 'Hammerklavier' Sonata.[7]

DR C. To my chagrin I don't know it, but then I wasn't trying to list all your publications. But why do you describe this kind of research as a matter of musical life and death? Aren't you satisfied, as your colleagues are, with good modern Urtext editions, which provide all the information you require?

---

[1] NZfM, 119 (1958), 635–42.
[2] NZfM, 121 (1960), 82–8.
[3] NZfM, 122 (1961), 502.
[4] Hifi-Stereophonie, 12 (1973), 148 f.
[5] ÖMZ, 33 (1978), 284 ff.
[6] Piano Jahrbuch (1983), 9 ff.
[7] 'Noch einmal zur Frage Ais oder A in der Hammerklaviersonate op. 106 von Beethoven', Gedenkschrift für Günter Henle (Munich, 1980), 53–81; Eng. trans. by Thomas Grey and Alfred Clayton, 'Once more on the question: A-sharp or A-natural in Beethoven's "Hammerklavier" Sonata op. 106', in Conventions in Eighteenth- and Nineteenth-Century Music (Pendragon Press, 1992).

B.-S. Your final question sounds slightly reproachful, almost as if you were suggesting that I'm a bit of a smart alec. In some ways, of course, what you say is quite justified. There are in fact quite a number of good Urtext editions these days. However, there are still unfortunately quite a few which certainly do not deserve the epithet 'Urtext' in any shape or form. Who can tell the difference between what is good and bad unless it is someone who knows the works thoroughly, and who, like me, has examined numerous manuscripts (or photocopies of them), manuscript copies, and first and early editions?

DR C. You seem to be claiming a special place among performing musicians with regard to musical philology.

B.-S. Of course not. My colleagues Malcolm Frager, Alfred Brendel, and, of the older generation, Rudolf Serkin, pursued research of exactly the same kind, and published their findings. There are also a small number of violinists and conductors who are similarly motivated, for example Eduard Melkus, Erich Leinsdorf, and Max Rudolf.

DR C. Well, what is the real difference between a good and a bad Urtext edition?

B.-S. In the first place it is the selection of the best sources (based on a comprehensive knowledge of the material), and the editor's thoroughness. Secondly, it rests on the aims of the edition itself. Certain people always use the word 'Urtext' to denote the first version that the composer committed to paper. Strictly speaking they are right, of course. Yet this is not always the point of an 'Urtext' edition. Some editors consider the final version (*Fassung letzter Hand*) to be the only legitimate one, and others again produce a 'composite mixture' that is often entirely subjective.

DR C. You surprise me. Isn't there a single version sanctioned by the composer, which one should simply reproduce in an Urtext edition as closely as possible? For example, are there several versions of Chopin Ballades and Bach Inventions?

B.-S. In the case of the F major Ballade there are for example three different endings that Chopin had published simultaneously in Paris, Leipzig, and London. And in the case of Bach's first Invention there exists, in addition to the familiar version, a later one with triplets, which a record company once turned down when I wanted to record it.

DR C. I happen to know about the different endings to Chopin's F major Ballade. Yet the melody and the harmony are the same in all these versions, and thus the listener hardly notices differences such as fuller chords or a lower bass note. Is this enough to enable us to speak of different versions? After all, the differences between the various versions of Bruckner symphonies, or of certain operas such as *Tannhäuser*, are much more substantial. In the case of piano music your research can only be of importance for a small circle of specialists. Do you really believe that a handful of variants can decisively alter the character of a work, or that they can actually lead to a better performance?

B.-S. Naturally the identity of a work survives intact even if the composer has made a number of smaller modifications. The same is true of someone who has 'improved' his nose by plastic surgery.

In reality his personality remains the same. Yet the feeling that his fellow human beings no longer consider him ugly or inferior can in fact change his character. The same can be true of musical changes within a work. A small modification can influence the character of the whole. That modifications in piano works are not as substantial as in operas, where far more performers are involved, is obvious. None the less we must not underestimate them. In a poem, for example, two altered lines can make a crucial difference. They would not be noticed in a play.

DR C. But instances where there are several equally valid versions are the exception, aren't they? Surely you are not suggesting that the French Suites . . .

B.-S. There are at least two quite different versions about which editors have been arguing for a hundred years . . .

DR C. . . . or the Chromatic Fantasia and Fugue . . .

B.-S. . . . and here the four most important manuscripts differ quite significantly . . .

DR C. . . . or the Italian Concerto are works whose texts are still in dispute?

B.-S. Yes, in the case of the Italian Concerto, the manuscript of which is no longer extant (luckily, I'm almost inclined to add), there really is something that approximates to a definitive version, and this has been printed in the Neue Bach-Ausgabe. Unambiguous and correct versions on which most Urtext editions agree (apart from printing errors) are few and far between. This is usually only the case when a work was neither revised nor printed during the composer's lifetime. Most Mozart piano concertos and the late Schubert sonatas belong to this category. In the case of Bach, who was always revising his works and making significant changes in the process, we must as a rule take into account more than one version. For example, the first prelude of the second part of the *Well-Tempered Clavier* was originally several bars shorter. The characteristic demisemiquaver figure of the beginning only appears in later copies, not in the autograph. It is an afterthought, though one without which it is difficult to imagine the prelude today. Only in cases where the loss of the main source means that a work of Bach only survives in a single contemporary copy are we absolved of the need to study and evaluate the sources. We only have to take into account the probability of copyist's errors.

DR C. That's all well and good. However, this work of 'studying and evaluating', as you call it, has in many cases been done by qualified editors, hasn't it? So I can't understand why you spend so much time and energy on checking the work of specialists and, one might say, on handing down marks. Wouldn't it have been better to devote these thousands of hours of research to practising the piano or to composing?

B.-S. . . . in order to become a kind of keyboard sportsman with the fastest octaves? No, I'd prefer to become a professional chess player, if it comes to that. But let's go back to the study of sources. If you make light of my demand for the correct text, then you forget that when I prepare a piece for performance I need above all else a firm basis in order to be able to identify with the composer's intentions. My Urtext research began as a child, when I found two completely different figurations in two editions of Beethoven's 'Appassionata'. My teachers were only able to give me emotionally based answers that failed to satisfy me. Thus I set out to discover the 'original text' on my own, without suspecting the difficulties I was destined to encounter. The search for an authentic text is far more labour-intensive than a layman might imagine. Sometimes there are relatively few problems, especially when one lives in a large city like Vienna, where there are good archives and libraries with good holdings of autographs and photostats. But often the search for the sources is extremely difficult, and at times it seems quite impossible. Luckily my wife is a musicologist, and thanks to her I found out more quickly and with greater ease than my colleagues how to discover which sources have survived, how to locate and study them, indeed how to obtain access to manuscripts and first editions.

A lot could also be said on the subject of printing errors. You are no doubt aware of how minute alterations can change the meaning of words. There is after all a difference between 'loving' and 'loafing', or between 'playing' and 'praying'. Such comparisons are misleading inasmuch as every intelligent reader can correct mistakes of this kind by referring to the context in which they occur. Yet even in language there are cases where the sense of a sentence can be reversed by the omission of the word 'not', or by incorrect punctuation.

It is much the same in music, where a single wrong note can make a decisive difference. In the second movement of the last B flat sonata the old Schubert complete edition had a $c\sharp^2$ in the top voice in bar 5—which was simply a printer's error—instead of Schubert's b^1. It was very disconcerting. Yet Artur Schnabel played this $c\sharp$, and it sounded awful.

DR C. I know that record. In spite of this single bizarre note I still consider Schnabel's recording of the B flat major Sonata to be a moving example of an inspired performance. Such wonderful, deeply felt phrasing. Such unique rubato, such subtle pauses towards the end . . .

B.-S. You're right. I also admire Artur Schnabel. He was one of the greatest pianists, and he had a purity and depth of emotion, a subtle sense of form, and a many-coloured, singing tone that few of his contemporaries possessed, with the exception of Edwin Fischer. His greatness is not diminished by the occasional wrong note. In a way there are important and unimportant wrong notes. Even complete editions are not immune to mistakes of both categories. When Mozart's C minor Piano Concerto was published by the Neue Mozart-Ausgabe about twenty-five years ago, I wrote a long letter to the editorial board proving that the edition contained about eighty unimportant and about fifteen serious mistakes.

DR C. The editor can't have been very happy about this communication.

B.-S. I'm sorry I had to write that letter. When you read the long letters containing lists of mistakes that Beethoven, for example, sent to his publishers, some of them plastered with some pretty coarse insults, you will perhaps admit that for many composers an exact text was something that was very important, and that for us it cannot be a luxury, but a duty and a necessity to take the old masters seriously. If one has the gift to do so, one can 'draw' good music out of a bad edition, just as one can still see a landscape through a dirty window. But we all prefer a clean window, don't we?

DR C. If I've understood you correctly, a good edition as you see it should reproduce the intentions of the composer as clearly and as unequivocally as possible. It should also give the text in its pure, unadulterated form.

B.-S. I couldn't have put it better myself. In the majority of cases an exact reproduction of the text that includes any relevant variants is in fact sufficient, particularly in cases where the text itself cannot be misunderstood. Even composers are human. Though fidelity to the original is of paramount importance, obvious mistakes ought to be corrected, though they should not be left uncommented. Yet in the case of early music an editor must bear in mind that certain notational conventions are not the same today as they were two or three centuries ago. An appropriate adaptation to modern notation is nowadays considered to be self-evident, for instance treble clefs in place of soprano or alto clefs, modern usage with regard to accidentals, and the layout of the score. This is good as far as it goes, though it is insufficient. More should be modernized, or explanations provided. It seems illogical to print old-fashioned rhythmic notation in modern Bach editions without supplying an explanation of their significance. It is tantamount to misleading players who are only acquainted with modern notational conventions. 'Instructions for use' are urgently required.

DR C. You yourself have provided such 'instructions for use' in your editions of certain works by Haydn[8] and Mozart.[9] Haven't you sunk to the level of the much-despised editions of the nineteenth century?

B.-S. Certainly not! My additions are clearly marked. Every user sees

[8] *Joseph Haydn, 4 sonates pour clavier*, performing edn. (Paris, 1984).
[9] *W. A. Mozart, Fantasie in D minor*, performing edn. (Paris, 1987).

immediately what the composer wrote, and what I have added. Those who disagree with my performing suggestions are perfectly free to perform the Urtext differently. Most of the older editions contain no information whatsoever about what the composer wrote, and what the editor added. Furthermore, editors of the old school often made quite arbitrary changes to a work, altering dynamics, phrasing, and even notes as they saw fit. Bach and Chopin were probably the most frequent victims, followed by Mozart and Domenico Scarlatti (the Longo edition).

DR C. What is your attitude to instructive Bach editions, both old and new?

B.-S. With regard to most of the older ones I am tempted to quote the Bible— 'If the blind lead the blind, both shall fall into the ditch'.

DR C. Would you also call Busoni blind?

B.-S. Certainly not. His organ transcriptions are works of genius and, like those of Liszt, were designed to acquaint a larger public with Bach's organ works, which at the time were almost unknown. But his edition of the keyboard works, despite some valuable insights, often evades the substance of Bach's music. In those days historical performance practice, authentic instruments, and baroque rhythm and affections were uncharted territory as far as most practical musicians were concerned. Even Bartók knew very little about this. Thus I would describe the Busoni and to an extent the Petri editions as 'distortions of genius'. In the case of the others (Mugellini, Bülow, Germer, etc.) there is no such saving grace; their editions simply distort the original.

DR C. A few moments ago you spoke of different versions of one and the same work. Should we not term the chronologically latest version as the most perfect one from the composer's point of view, and thus disregard the other, less perfect ones? After all, who wants to have the second or third best?

B.-S. It would be nice if it were that easy. In theory you're right, of course. But in Bach's case in particular a *Fassung letzter Hand* or final version has only been established in a minority of cases.[10] Many later changes are adaptations determined by circumstances. If we were only willing to accept the final version as 'authentic' we would in future have to restrict performances of the violin concertos in E major and D minor to the later versions for one or two harpsichords and the first movement of the Third Brandenburg Concerto to the version for winds that Bach adapted for use in a later cantata (No. 174).[11] In all these cases the first version is neither devalued nor displaced by the later version. If this were so, one would only be allowed to play Beethoven's Violin Concerto in the later piano version.

[10] See Dadelsen, 'Die Crux der Nebensache'; 'Die "Fassung letzter Hand" in der Musik'; *Über Bach und anderes* (Laaber, 1983); 'Von den Quellen zur Neuen Bach-Ausgabe', *300 Jahre Johann Sebastian Bach: Eine Ausstellung der Internationalen Bach-Akademie, Stuttgart* (Tutzing, 1985), 29–50.

[11] See Bruchhäuser, 'Zur Aufführungspraxis', pp. 93 ff.

DR C. So what should an editor do? Print the best version that can be established on the basis of various criteria in the main body of the text, and mention the variants in all cases?

B.-S. Quite right. And where there are too many variants, as in the case of certain inventions, movements of suites, and preludes, the work should simply be printed twice or even three times, as is done by the NBA and certain other modern editions.

DR C. Several versions of a single work were also printed in the old Bach complete edition. What do you think of that edition?

B.-S. It was a remarkable achievement for its time. The old Bach complete edition was considerably better than the old Mozart or Beethoven complete editions, which appeared slightly later. Bach's text was on the whole reproduced in unadulterated form, insofar as this was at all possible on the basis of the sources available at the time.

DR C. Well, why do we need a new complete edition?

B.-S. Because musicology in general and Bach research in particular have made tremendous progress over the last hundred years. After all, if you wanted to find out about mathematics and physics, you wouldn't consult a lexicon published in 1890 or consider it to be the only relevant source of information.

DR C. I agree with you as regards nuclear physics, but surely the situation is different in music. Once Bach's text has been established and accurately reproduced . . .

B.-S. . . . then it is inaccessible for many modern musicians, who can no longer read soprano, alto, or tenor clefs. However, this is only a superficial matter. Many autographs that a century ago were considered to be by Bach have been identified as copies made by pupils or members of his family. We are now able to identify most of the copyists on the basis of palaeographic and paper research. We are now able to establish where, for example, Bach began to write a violin part of a cantata, and at what point he passed it to one of his sons or pupils. The authenticity or spuriousness of autographs, the newly discovered sources unknown at the time, and new insights into the chronology of the works and Bach's parody technique—all these factors taken together mean that we can no longer rely on old editions, however good they might be. For example, the editors of the Bach complete edition did not know the London autograph of the second part of the *Well-Tempered Clavier*. Nor did they know Gerber's copy of the French Suites . . .

DR C. . . . but Hans Bischoff knew this.

B.-S. Yes, in fact he was incredibly accurate. His edition of Bach's keyboard works,[12] in its way a monument of German thoroughness, is still of great importance today, because he was the first to include all important variants

---

[12] Pub. Steingräber (Leipzig, 1881). An Eng. trans. of the commentaries is pub. by Kalmus (New York), together with a photographic repro. of the text.

in the preface or in footnotes. He also clearly distinguished between his performance indications (which on the whole did not derive from Bach) and the original text by using thin and small type, so that it is impossible to confuse the two.

DR C. An almost modern approach, as modern, for example, as that of Rosalyn Tureck, who also states in the preface to her edition of the Italian Concerto that all ornaments added by the editor are given in small type.[13]

B.-S. The comparison is not a good one. Tureck says this, but unlike Bischoff, she does not adhere to this principle. For example, look at the beginning of the second movement, or the final chord of the last movement, where several mordents that Bach did not write are included in large type.

DR C. [*leafing through the Tureck edition*]. Well, I confess that I had only read the preface. But in fact these ornaments, which are certainly not by Bach, are printed in even larger type than the authentic ornaments, for instance here in bars 16 to 18, upper system, of the second movement. However, this may simply be a printer's error. But don't you think that, despite your criticism of this aspect, the Tureck edition of the Italian Concerto represents an almost ideal combination of musicology and practical musicianship? The editor makes a point of mentioning her musicological studies and insights, and her experience of modern and historical keyboard instruments, which all contributed to her edition. Tureck expressly states that this is the first edition to give Bach's text in unadulterated form.

B.-S. Isn't she laying it on a bit? If what she says were true, all previous editors, including the NBA with its decades of research work, would have been failures. Look, if a professional musicologist comes up with a sensational claim such as, for example, that in the second movement of the Italian Concerto the alto voice should be freely embellished throughout, then he or she should adduce some evidence to support it. I know of no Italian or German treatise written during Bach's lifetime that suggests the embellishment of accompanying (in contrast to imitative) inner voices. Thus one might expect from Dr Tureck some evidence or explanation for such a claim . . .

CR C. Doesn't she point to the fact that the thirds in the lower system of the Andante have two tails throughout, thus proving that they are two distinct voices?

B.-S. This is simply a naïve remark and doesn't prove anything. Everyone who is acquainted with the keyboard music of the eighteenth century knows that it was common notational practice to add two tails to all thirds, sixths, and so on. This even occurs in Haydn and Mozart. If what she says were true, one could also, in the Italian Concerto, set about enriching the accompaniment of bars 30 f., 46 f., and 129 f. of the first movement with ornaments.

---

[13] *Concerto in the Italian Style* (Tureck/Bach Urtext Series; New York, 1983).

DR C. But Tureck points to bar 17 of the second movement, where, in the first edition, there really is a *Pralltriller* sign in the middle voice . . .

B.-S. . . . which is almost certainly a mistake. The NBA Critical Report describes this ornament as an engraver's error . . .

DR C. How is it possible to distinguish between Bach's intentions and an engraver's error?

B.-S. There are at least four criteria which enable us to do this. I'll try to explain what I mean. Let us take the example of an imaginary violin or oboe concerto in the Italian style. In movements of this kind the solo instrument was accompanied by a string orchestra that had to supply a sonorous harmonic background. The slow movements of Bach's violin concertos clearly belong to this category. It is hard to imagine that someone in the accompanying orchestra would have dared to disturb the soloist's cantabile line by adding trills and *fioriture*. Secondly, in other solo movements of this type Bach did not add ornaments to the alto voice. Examples of this are the Allemande of Partita No. 4, BWV 828, and the chorale prelude *O Mensch, bewein dein Sünde groß*, from the *Orgel-Büchlein*, BWV 622, both of which have richly embellished treble voices. But thirdly and most importantly, in this bar of the Italian Concerto a *Pralltriller* in the alto voice leads to consecutive fifths with the ornament of the treble voice (not consecutive fourths, as Dr Tureck claims). Finally there is a fourth point. It is extremely unlikely that the engraver of the first edition, who printed all the rest of Bach's *Pralltriller* signs incorrectly,[14] should have hit on the correct graphic form precisely at this point . . .

DR C. Isn't there a manuscript of the Italian Concerto copied by someone called O'Kelly?

B.-S. Johann Christoph Oley. He was German, in fact, and not Irish. We owe several important copies of Bach's works to his pen. His copy of the Italian Concerto is the only source that has preserved an early version of the work. Of course, Oley has no *Pralltriller* sign in the lower system of bar 17. On top of everything else, Dr Tureck's suggested execution of this apocryphal ornament is wrong.

DR C. How can you say that about a world-famous Bach performer?

B.-S. Because the *Pralltriller* formula she adduces is not found in a single treatise before 1757, seven years after Bach died. The *Pralltriller* or half-trill (*mezzo trillo*) is in reality a short form of the 'tied trill' (*tremblement lié*). If this ornament is preceded by the note c, as in this case, then it must always begin on bb. All the early theorists agree on this point.

DR C. Well, we should not only talk about one particular edition. What is your opinion of the most well-known recent editions of Bach?

B.-S. Of course I don't know all of them. As I see it the NBA is the best,

---

[14] On this subject see ch. 13, p. 313.

followed by the Wiener Urtextausgabe, and the Peters, Henle, Schott, and Editio Musica editions. Willard A. Palmer's edition of Bach's keyboard works[15] is pleasing to the eye and textually often very accurate, though I feel that his suggestions on the subject of ornamentation are occasionally rather old-fashioned.

DR C. Would you describe the NBA as infallible?

B.-S. Not really. The NBA has some excellent and some less successful volumes. Thus the volume containing the Partitas (*Clavier-Übung*, Part I) has some serious mistakes. According to Robert Marshall[16] the old BGA edition of the B minor Mass in some respects reproduces Bach's intentions more accurately than the NBA. Yet even the less successful volumes are still on a much higher level than most of the old editions. It is particularly praiseworthy that the volumes containing the music tie in with the critical reports. They should be used in conjunction.

DR C. But surely there are other good modern Urtext editions, such as the widely used Henle edition . . .

B.-S. . . . to which there are two sides, in a way, particularly in the case of Bach. Since 1975 it has been on the highest level, including brief editorial notes and variants. Prior to this, unfortunately, it had fairly arbitrary readings, no variants, and either no editorial reports at all, or ones that were too short. It is to be hoped that the publisher will soon publish better editions of Bach. The early ones (e.g. of the *Well-Tempered Clavier*) do his reputation no good.

DR C. . . . and the other new editions?

B.-S. . . . can often be judged by the name of the editor. In the case of the Peters edition Kroll, Landshoff, Kreutz, Keller, and Soldan were usually good, conscientious editors, even if they did not always have access to enough source material in the modern sense. The latest editions of the harpsichord concertos edited by Hans-Joachim Schulze are good. The same is true of the Schott editions, which are in part by the same editors (e.g. Kreutz), though they edited different works than in the Peters edition.

DR C. . . . and the Wiener Urtext edition?

B.-S. . . . sometimes approaches the NBA with regard to archival work and clear presentation. Recently Editio Musica Budapest has produced some good work, though it contains more imperfections and mistakes than the other editions mentioned.

DR C. I note that the editions you praise most are often the most expensive ones. What is the reason for that?

B.-S. There are two reasons why music has become so expensive in the recent past. First, the enormous increase in production costs, and secondly, the reduction in the number of copies sold on account of the shameless

---

[15] Alfred edn., Sherman Oaks, Calif.

[16] *The Music of Johann Sebastian Bach. The Sources, the Style, the Significance* (New York, 1989).

disregard of copyright laws by most musicians. I know hardly a single music student who appears for his or her lesson without a pile of photocopies under his arm (of course only in countries where photocopying is cheap and readily available). For this reason . . .

DR C. Copyright? Surely the old masters are no longer protected by copyright . . .

B.-S. Let me finish. The works themselves are no longer protected, but the musical text and the critical apparatus of an Urtext edition certainly are. What I was trying to say is that music publishers usually do not survive on the proceeds of selling music, but from the royalties that accrue from the performance of copyright works. I happen to be of the opinion that a musician should not be stingy when it comes to buying music. The best edition is just about good enough when we are dealing with the works of the great masters. A really good edition maintains its value even decades later, it is a faithful companion.

DR C. . . . until what purports to be a better 'companion' turns up. Let us go back to the Tureck edition of the Italian Concerto. Tureck claims in the preface that as early as bars 13–14 she has restored the original text, which all previous editors have changed to bring it into line with the parallel passage in bars 175–6 . . .

B.-S. . . . and 73–4, so . . .

DR C. . . . but now you're interrupting me! . . . which all previous editors have changed and falsified . . .

B.-S. . . . yes, but not without stating what they were doing in footnotes or critical report. In the other Bach concertos initial and final tuttis of a movement are identical, which means that it is very probable that this discrepancy goes back to an engraver's error that Bach overlooked. After all, one could also change the passage the other way round:

In all three passages, in fact. Oley actually did this in his copy, probably after having compared his version with the first edition. Bach's earlier version originally read thus:

DR C. Fascinating. I have just one more question about the ornamentation of the first movement. Why does the Tureck edition always print long trill signs where the Wiener Urtextausgabe, Peters, and NBA have *Praller*?

B.-S. Because she takes her bearings from a copy in the British Library corrected by Bach, MS Hirsch III 38, K8 g7.

DR C. If Bach himself added these trills, isn't Dr Tureck justified in reproducing them in facsimile form, so to speak?

B.-S. Unfortunately the facts of the case are difficult to explain in one sentence. Are you in a hurry?

DR C. Not really. I ought to be at a concert, but this is beginning to interest me. A series of authentic Bach corrections which the NBA seems to have ignored! But please be brief.

B.-S. I'll try. For reasons that are irrelevant in this context, Bach assigned the engraving of the piece to a publisher who had no previous experience of this kind of work. For this reason the engraver of the first edition printed meaningless straight lines at places where Bach must have written his usual trill sign, namely a short wavy line, in the autograph (which unfortunately is no longer extant). Look:

In order to transform these meaningless lines into legible ornaments Bach in his copy added a *t* at the beginning and a wavy line at the end:

However, this meant that in the last bar of the first page, and also in bars 91 f. and 147 f., seemingly long trills were placed above short semiquavers—which is quite absurd. However, a corrected new edition appeared shortly afterwards. Look at the corresponding passages:

DR C. Undoubtedly *Pralltriller* symbols. But how do we know that the corrections on the plates were really made by Bach himself?

B.-S. Who else could it have been? Actually, there is a neat piece of evidence for this. In the rest of the *Clavier-Übung* (i.e. in parts I, II/2, III, and IV) the *tr* sign never appears at all, only the short or long wavy line.

Incidentally, Tureck was fully aware of the superiority of the second edition. In bar 43 of the Andante, where there is a mordent, she follows this source and not the first edition mentioned above, where Bach failed to correct an incorrect trill sign. Bach originally overlooked a few other mistakes as well.

DR C. Why was that?

B.-S. Surely one of the reasons must have been his failing eyesight.

DR C. Ah yes, I remember reading in a contemporary report about Bach's *blödes Gesicht* (stupid face), which can easily be misunderstood today. It simply meant that his eyesight was bad. One final question on the Tureck edition. She stipulates that many chords should be played arpeggiated because Bach evidently did not use the arpeggio symbol in his works.

B.-S. That's an unfortunate way of putting it. Dr Tureck is of course aware of the fact that Bach used the arpeggio sign on a number of occasions, for example at the beginning of the French Overture, which in the first edition follows directly upon the Italian Concerto. What she probably wanted to say is that on many occasions one should arpeggiate chords when this is not expressly stipulated. She is surely right in this. Yet to linger on the bottom note of the chord, as she suggests, is not to be recommended. Baroque treatises hardly ever mention improvised arpeggios, perhaps because it was as self-evident as the use of the pedal on the modern piano. Arpeggios were expressly recommended in the Baroque era only with regard to accompanying recitatives.

DR C. Thank you for this interview. You have convinced me that the problems involved in editing Bach are often difficult to solve, and that it is probably better to place one's trust in professional musicologists than in outsiders.

For details of recommended editions of Bach's keyboard works, see Appendix 1.

9

Rendering the Structure as a Whole

In an interesting, though largely subjective, review of Erwin Bodky's book on Bach, Glenn Gould accused the author of having written only about fugue subjects, and not about the performance of whole fugues, and criticized him for not having addressed himself to the question of how Bach achieved the cohesion of large scale works.[1] This criticism is justified, though it could be levelled at all the authors of eighteenth-century treatises. Despite the thoroughness with which C. P. E. Bach and Quantz deal with everything that pertains to good execution, they fail to tell us how they envisaged the structure of fugues, sonatas, suites, or concerto movements in terms of performance. True, Leopold Mozart speaks on a number of occasions of the continuous line, the *filo* of a composition, though he does not tell us how to grasp this connecting 'thread' or where, for example, the moments of greatest and least tension are, and so on.

There must be a reason why the writers of treatises remained silent when it came to the overall structure or shape of a piece. In fact, there are several reasons. Primarily it is because to describe large-scale structures and to discuss ways of performing them would not have fitted into the framework of a manual. The problems were too complicated, and were difficult to put in words. It was much easier to demonstrate what one meant.

Eggebrecht's analysis of the first ten bars of Bach's *Art of Fugue* gives an idea of how difficult it is to write in some detail about a certain work of art. He needed four pages for this (excellent) structural analysis of the beginning of Contrapunctus 1.[2] However, he does not even touch upon the question of how these structures should be played on a harpsichord or some other instrument, which notes should and should not be emphasized or played legato or detached, and how the structure determines the bowing or the points where a singer ought to take a breath. And of course all the kinds of analysis in use today, with the possible exception of the Schenkerian method, fail to reveal the means with which the performer can present the structural architecture intended by the composer. Why was Furtwängler usually a more impressive

---

[1] *The Glenn Gould Reader* (New York, 1985), 28 ff.   [2] *Bachs 'Kunst der Fuge'*, pp. 65 ff.

conductor than many of his famous colleagues? Precisely because like hardly any other musician of our time he penetrated the secrets of how to portray the total structure of a work of music. There have been many attempts to account for the fact that he was more successful than other musicians in shaping works as a whole, even in extremely slow tempos. Was it his great art of moulding transitions? In his performances works and movements did not fall apart into separate sections, and he was always able to convey a sense of the whole.

In the following I shall attempt, despite the difficulties indicated, to say something about the structure of Bach's works and about the task of how the 'fundamental line' of a work can be discerned and shaped. A performer must be able to grasp it if he wishes to do justice to his task. Naturally this can only scratch the surface of the subject.

In quite general terms, 'fundamental line' or *filo conduttore* refers to the ability to grasp a work in its totality, no matter whether it is large or small, and in performances not to 'stop short' at minor details. (Many a performer who clings to them creates the impression that he cannot see the wood for trees.) As I have stated elsewhere,[3] the aim is to give the listener a kind of 'telescopic view'. Just as one can only clearly perceive the proportions of a cathedral from some distance away, the musician needs a kind of distance in time, which in the case of larger instrumental works (i.e. works that have to be shaped without the help of a text) can be achieved only by repeated listening and with the help of memory. For the player this overall view does not mean that he should play 'al fresco', as it were, and neglect to shape smaller musical units. This would merely result in superficiality or incomprehensibility. However, if a building is to stand firm, the bricks and the smaller building-blocks must be properly shaped and fit together well.

The comparison with firmly anchored building-blocks of large buildings also helps us to understand better the principle of maintaining strict time. Bars are in fact nothing but musical building-blocks that make it possible to construct larger structures consisting of similar units. Adhering strictly to the length of the bars thus corresponds to the use of similarly large stones or columns in a palace. As we have seen (pp. 17 f.), only in the case of structurally motivated breaks, such as pauses and imperfect cadences—that is, in the succession of different parts within a whole—should there be a broadening of the tempo and caesuras, which make it easier for the listener to understand the piece. In architecture one might compare such breaks with the addition of portals, towers, wings, and so on, which often entail a break with the rest of the material.

One of the first problems in the presentation of the 'fundamental line', particularly for players of keyboard instruments, is to liberate oneself from the

[3] Analysis of Beethoven's 'Hammerklavier' Sonata, Op. 106, in Paul Badura-Skoda and Jörg Demus, *Beethovens 32 Klaviersonaten* (Wiesbaden, 1970), 174.

tendency to play music as a succession of dots or chords, and to think in terms of lines. The predominance of chordal writing in much keyboard music tempts us to assign the greatest importance to 'vertical' presentation. This way of playing is of course detrimental to the presentation of the linear aspect. Simultaneous events (depicted vertically on the staves) are naturally easier to control than the linear 'progression in time', which is always poised between 'not yet' and 'no longer'. Singers and players of melody instruments have an easier task in this respect, for on the whole they have to deal with a single line not directly encumbered with harmony—melody and rhythm unfold horizontally in time. However, as every good musician knows, harmonies first come alive as they progress and on account of the tension usually determined by the voice-leading and the tonal function. A good example of lines within a 'harmonic' piece that must be treated 'horizontally' is the Adagio of the First Brandenburg Concerto. In vertical and chordal terms the dissonance ab–a♮ would be insupportable. However, as a combination of two lines (b–a–b, g–ab–g) it has an austere Bachian beauty (see Ex. 9.1).

Ex. 9.1. Brandenburg Concerto No. 1, BWV 1046, Adagio, bars 9–10

Nowhere is the necessity of thinking in 'horizontal' terms instead of merely juxtaposing chords 'vertically' more important and striking than in that peculiarly compelling and perhaps greatest invention of Western music, the I–IV–V–I cadential formula. As a means of structuring perfect and imperfect cadences, cadential formulas were of course in existence long before Bach. However, the advent of various systems of equal temperament enabled Bach, as the first great composer, to expand tonality and its inherent tensions, because during his lifetime it first became possible to play in all keys on keyboard instruments without some of the harmonies sounding very much out of tune. Not only the title and contents of the *WTC* demonstrate this, but also some of those works which, within a single piece, traverse the whole tonal spectrum, such as the spiral canon in the *Musical Offering*, which, starting out from C minor, is restated a tone higher every time, in D minor, E minor, F sharp minor, and so on, until it returns to C minor an octave higher.[4] The

---

[4] The question of whether Bach envisaged equal or irregular temperament for *WTC* remains a moot point. In the recent past the majority of harpsichordists have tended to hold the view that the kind of

Chromatic Fantasia, BWV 903, and the G minor Organ Fantasia, BWV 542, also modulate to distant keys. But works of this kind are more the exception in Bach. In general he restricted himself to traversing the given tonal possibilities of a certain work.

Modulation within a movement is perhaps the most important and most easily perceivable means of understanding structures, which must be presented accordingly. If a work is in the major mode, J. S. Bach almost always moves first to the nearest key, the dominant (in C major this is G major). When the dominant is reached there is often a short break or pause for breath, though sometimes Bach fashions a seamless transition by interlocking the conclusion of one section with the beginning of the next. Yet even here some slight articulation is necessary to ensure that the music does not sound like the rattling of mill-wheels or an industrious robot. It must be apparent to the listener that the transition from one section to the next is a structural feature.[5]

From the dominant Bach usually modulates to more distant keys. In C major the dominant, G major, is often followed by A minor (the relative minor) or D minor (the supertonic), and on occasion by F major (the subdominant). Bach rarely touches on keys that are foreign to the scale, such as (in C major) B flat major and D major, keys whose tonic chords include a B♭ or an F♯ and thus do not directly belong to C major. The further Bach moves away from the tonal centre, the greater the harmonic tension; it is as if a rubber band were attached to the tonic. Performers and listeners should be aware of this. The most distant key in diatonic terms is the mediant, which in C major is E minor. This key implies a greater degree of tension than a harmonic progression which, having touched on D minor or A minor, returns to the tonic. The return to the tonic, and occasionally its establishment by dominant or tonic pedal-points, are usually the last harmonic and structural 'events' within a work by Bach. In the minor mode the relationships are of course different. The first modulations are to the dominant and the relative major. In C minor these would be G major (or minor) and E flat major.

It would be naïve to assume that recognizing and making audible the modulations might in itself solve the problem of how to shape the structure. Thematic development, high and low notes, texture, and above all the use of dissonances and their resolution are elements that contribute to tension and thus to structure. Apart from suspended dissonances (e.g. a fourth resolving

unequal irregular temperament suggested by Kirnberger is the only possibility (see H. A. Kellner, 'Neue Perspektiven der Bach-Forschung—das Rätsel von Bachs Cembalostimmung', *ÖMZ*, 40 (1985), 73 ff.). However, critical opinion has once again begun to favour equal temperament. See Rudolf Rasch, 'Does "Well-Tempered" mean "Equal-Tempered"?', *Bach, Handel, Scarlatti*, ed. P. Williams. Serge Cordier's study *Piano bien tempéré et justesse orchestrale* (Paris, 1982) also contains valuable information on this subject.

[5] Konrad Wolff, *Masters of the Keyboard* (Bloomington, Ind., 1983), 12 f., contains some excellent comments on the subject of structure and modulation.

on to a third), seventh and ninth chords with their superimposed thirds play an important role. In Bach's time (and still in the age of Haydn, Mozart, and Beethoven) ninths chords in particular were considered to be hard and 'shocking' dissonances whose very presence was an indication of great tension. Two examples illustrate this. In the otherwise euphonious E major Fugue of *WTC* II, which begins in the strict Palestrina style, the isolated (i.e. unprepared ninth of the dominant ninth chord in G sharp minor (bar 33), e^2, must have sounded disturbing to Bach's contemporaries, partly because it is also in the most distant key, the mediant (Ex. 9.2). Here Bach departs from the 'classical' convention (surely intentionally), writing something that was stylistically as novel as if Mozart had written twelve-note-rows in a symphony (something he actually did in the finale of the G minor Symphony K. 550). This is surely the climax of the E major Fugue. Thus the ninth chord must be emphasized with regard to dynamics and agogics, that is, by holding back the tempo slightly and bringing out the dissonance $d\sharp$–e^2 in what amounts to an expression of pain.

Ex. 9.2. *WTC* II, Fugue in E major, bars 32–5

The second example comes from the Chromatic Fugue. Four ninth chords (bars 94, 135, 139, 158) have the effect of massive pillars that crown the concluding bars of the fugue (Ex. 9.3). It is immediately apparent that these ninth chords abruptly augment the three-part texture of the fugue, which is otherwise adhered to strictly. In the first two instances the chord is preceded by a rhythmic and melodic agglomeration. The theme literally comes to a halt, and can overcome the obstacle only through a kind of extra effort (by an increase in the number of parts). The agglomeration is particularly noticeable before the second ninth chord. Here the theme leaps upwards a tenth (contrary to all the rules) from the tenor to the treble. (In view of such audacity we must pity the narrow-mindedness of those editors who failed to notice that the first extract prepares this leap with more modest means (bar 93). When will pianists and harpsichordists finally stop playing Bülow's Bach 'improvements'? His text reads as shown in Ex. 9.4. It is only before the last ninth chord that the theme manages to overcome the preceding obstacles. This 'supreme effort' leads not only to the highest of the three staggered chords, but also and simultaneously to the 'thundering octaves' in the left

Ex. 9.3. Chromatic Fugue, bars 93–5, 134–40, 187–91

Ex. 9.4. Chromatic Fugue, bars 93–4, ed. Bülow

hand, which are unique in Bach.[6] Pianists bent on improving Bach introduce octaves 18 bars prior to this (bar 140) or even earlier. In this case the final octaves really ought to be 'tripled' in order to preserve the intensification of the ending (see Ex. 9.5).

Ex. 9.5. Chromatic Fugue, bars 158–9

The horizontal treatment of harmony also requires the correct maintenance of note-values. Here keyboard players are often not as good as string players. For instance, with regard to the frequent anticipatory formula shown in Ex. 9.6, harpsichordists and pianists usually shorten the value of the lower note in the right hand unwittingly, playing inaccurately as in Ex. 9.7. This markedly reduces the harmonic tension, because the short moment of friction between the leading-note and the anticipation of the tonic is omitted (see Ex. 9.8). This rule also applies when the anticipation, ab^1, is shortened to become a semiquaver.

Ex. 9.6. *WTC* I, Prelude in A flat major, bars 34–5

---

[6] Later octave passages in Partitas No. 1 (end of the Praeludium) and No. 5 (end of the Gigue) and in the first movement of the E major Sonata for violin and harpsichord are considerably tamer.

The same is true of suspensions frequently notated carefully by Bach. In the Ouverture of the D major Partita, bars 94–6, most players 'swallow' the

Ex. 9.7

Ex. 9.8

dissonances (see Ex. 9.9). Instead of the notated dissonances d–c♯, c♯–b, and b–a one usually hears only one note (Ex. 9.10). This robs the harmonic line, which is built up on dissonances and their resolution, of its tension and forward motion.

Ex. 9.9. Partita No. 4, BWV 828, Ouverture, bars 93–6

Ex. 9.10

An important role is played by the question of thematic development, particularly in the case of fugues. It is axiomatic that the exposition is intended to be expanded and developed as the fugue progresses. But then, according to Dürr, there are fugues whose 'fundamental line' is quite different, for instance a return to the beginning (Organ Fugue in E minor, BWV 548; Fugue in C sharp major, *WTC* I); a continual intensification

(Fugue in D sharp minor, *WTC* I, and most fugues with more than one subject), and so on. Bach's chamber works and fugal movements also make use of the variation and transformation of themes in a very forward-looking manner.

C. P. E. Bach mentions another means of understanding and presenting musical structure: 'Above all, lose no opportunity to hear artistic singing. In so doing, the keyboardist will *learn to think in terms of song*. Indeed, it is good practice to sing instrumental melodies in order to reach an understanding of their correct performance.'[7] In encouraging the player to think in terms of song, C. P. E. Bach had in mind not only a cantabile style of performance, but also an imaginary verbal articulation of a rhetorical kind. In fact, that music had to follow the laws of rhetoric was a baroque axiom. In this regard Quantz says:

Musical execution may be compared with the delivery of an orator. The orator and the musician have, at bottom, the same aim in regard to both the preparation and the final execution of their productions, namely to make themselves masters of their listeners, to arouse or still their passions, and to transport them now to this sentiment, now to that. Thus it is advantageous to both, if each has some knowledge of the duties of the other. . . . As to delivery, we demand that an orator have an audible, clear, and true voice; that he have distinct and perfectly true pronunciation, not confusing some letters with others, or swallowing them; that he aim at a pleasing variety in voice and language; that he avoid monotony in the discourse, rather allowing the tone of the syllables and words to be heard now loudly, now softly, now quickly, now slowly; and that he raise his voice in words requiring emphasis, subdue it in others. He must express each sentiment with an appropriate vocal inflexion, and in general adapt himself to the place where he speaks, to the listeners before him, and to the content of the discourse he delivers. Thus he must know, for example, how to make the proper distinction between a funeral oration, a panegyric, a jocular discourse, &c. Finally, he must assume a good outward bearing.[8]

J. S. Bach no doubt obeyed these rhetorical rules in performance. Matthias Claudius's fine account (in a letter) of C. P. E. Bach's playing could just as well have been written about his father: 'I can best describe his playing of the Adagio by respectfully asking you to think of an orator who has not memorized his speeches. Rather, he is full of the contents of his oration, and does not hurry to bring something forth, calmly permitting one wave after another to stream out of the fullness of his heart, without making this in any way artificial.'[9]

J. S. Bach observed the ancient rules of rhetoric not only in performance, but also in composition. These rules were common intellectual property in the eighteenth century, and as early as 1880 the great Bach biographer, Philipp

---

[7] *Essay*, pp. 151–2 (my italics).   [8] *On Playing the Flute*, p. 119.
[9] Ernst Fritz Schmid, *Carl Philipp Emanuel Bach und seine Kammermusik* (Kassel, 1931), p. 60.

Spitta, demonstrated that Bach's preface to the Inventions and Sinfonias (1723) was based on rhetorical principles:

When at the beginning of 1723 he gathered together the 'Inventions and Sinfonias' to form a self-contained work, he gave it the following title: 'Honest Guide by which lovers of the clavier, and particularly those desirous of learning, are shown a plain way not only (1) to play neatly in two parts, but also, as they progress, (2) to treat three obbligato parts correctly and well, and, at the same time, to acquire good ideas (*inventiones*) and properly to elaborate them, and most of all to learn a singing style of playing, and simultaneously to obtain a strong foretaste of composition.' He primarily wished to provide a work for the instruction of keyboard players, though with and through mechanical practice he was concerned to further their artistry both with regard to the extempore invention of such importance to the execution of the figured bass, and to composition itself. Having been a sixth-former (*Primaner*) at the Michaelisschule in Lüneburg, Bach had not forgotten his rhetoric. He knew that arrangement (*collocatio*) and expression (*elocutio*) belonged to invention (*inventio*). Thus the remark about ideas (*inventiones*) is immediately followed by a reference to their elaboration (*collocatio*) and a singing style of playing (*elocutio*), although a different sequence would have seemed more appropriate. Classical rhetoric also informs the desire to demonstrate how to play 'neatly in two parts' on the one hand, and to treat three parts 'correctly and well' on the other. However, the three-part works should of course be played just as 'neatly' as the two-part ones, and these in turn 'correctly and well'. Quite obviously this is a reference to *emendatum* (correctness), *perspicuum* (neatness), and *ornatum* (the quality of being pleasing and graceful), the three main requirements of the Roman rhetoricians.[10]

Observations of this kind can also be of use to the performer. Thus the elaboration of thematic material (*collocatio*) will require rather more tension than its exposition. Even the ornaments in a piece may be assigned a rhetorical role. They belong both to the concept of expression (*elocutio*) and to *ornatum*, the graceful execution of an idea. Studies of the subject include Isolde Ahlgrimm's 'Bach und die Rhetorik'[11] and Ursula Kirkendale's 'The Source for Bach's Musical Offering: The Institutio oratoria of Quintilian'.[12] There is of course considerable controversy about the extent to which Bach adhered to rhetorical rules when composing.

---

[10] *Johann Sebastian Bach*, ii. 665 f.; Eng. trans., ii. 55–6.

[11] *ÖMZ*, 9 (1954), 342.

[12] *Journal of the American Musicological Society*, 33 (1980), 88–141. The author argues convincingly that 'Bach obviously modelled his work on classical rhetoric. A direct comparison between Quintilian's rhetorical schema and Bach's work (in Spitta's sequence) often suggested striking analogies, particularly when taking into account Bach's titles and the baroque theory of figures and affections.' Ursula Kirkendale's claims seem more plausible in view of the significance of rhetoric in Bach's lifetime, which is difficult to understand today, and even more so in the light of the fact that Bach knew the edn. of Quintilian owned by a Leipzig friend. It was not commonly known that Bach intended the *Musical Offering* to be a contribution to Mizler's Societät der Musicalischen Wissenschaften. (*Frankfurter Allgemeine Zeitung*, 1 June 1979). By understanding the relationship between rhetoric and formal structure, Kirkendale was able to determine the sequence of the pieces in the *Musical Offering*, a previously unsolved problem.

Opinions differ even more when it comes to assessing the extent to which Bach made use of number symbolism.[13] When, in the *St Matthew Passion*, the question 'Is it I [who will betray thee]?' is repeated eleven times,[14] this has a numerical basis in fact, for Judas of course does not ask the question. Yet the idea that Bach based almost all his works on cabbalistic numerals is open to doubt, especially in the periods when he had to provide one or more cantatas per week. At any rate it is of no importance to the performer whether a theme contains thirteen or fourteen notes. However, some hidden numerical relationships may none the less have been intentional, if we are willing to believe certain studies of the subject.[15]

One important principle of performance has hardly been mentioned so far. This is the recognition of the affection expressed by the music. Few people would nowadays be prepared to subscribe to the old view that many of Bach's works are 'absolute' music that simply aim at being 'sonorous form'. Rather, all his works express something: the 'affection'. This is the emotional dimension that provides a foundation for the music itself. Thus there is a big difference between a work that 'bubbles' along like a murmuring stream and one in which the affection is intended to move heaven and earth. Those who are in doubt about whether, in instrumental works, they have understood the expressive intent, should acquaint themselves with the texts of vocal works of similar musical substance, especially arias. In the 'Coffee' Cantata, for example, we will find the 'murmuring waves', or in the chorale *Jesus bleibet meine Freude* (Cantata No. 147), which has become popular through Myra Hess's masterly transcription.[16] On the other hand, the aria 'Es ist vollbracht' from the *St John Passion* is full of dramatic contrast. Christ's last words, 'Es ist vollbracht', are set off against the triumphal central section, 'Der Held aus Juda siegt mit Macht', which is followed by a return to the beginning of the

[13] 'At the start of Cantata No. 28, after 12 introductory bars (13 including the final bar), whilst the treble sings "Gottlob, nun geht das Jahr zu Ende", there are exactly 365 notes in the score. This could of course have been a mere accident. However, not only the days of the year appear in number form. So do the months. The voice part has 31, the basso continuo 30 notes, a falling fifth occurs 28 times. The number . . . of the days of the week is reflected in the seven accompanying parts and the number of words.' Bernhard Billeter, 'Zahlensymbolik bei Bach', *Schweizerische musikpädagogische Blätter*, 76 (1988), 82.

[14] NBA No. 9c, BGA No. 15.

[15] These include Friedrich Smend, *Bach bei seinem Namen gerufen* (Kassel, 1950); Harry Hahn, *Symbol und Glaube im 1. Teil des Wohltemperierten Klaviers von J. S. Bach* (Wiesbaden, 1973); Wiemer, *Die wiederhergestellte Ordnung*; Ulrich Siegele, *Bachs theologischer Formbegriff und das Duett F-Dur* (Neuhausen and Stuttgart, 1978); Ludwig Prautsch, 'Figuren und Symbole in der "Kunst der Fuge"', *Bach-Tage Berlin*, 75 ff.; Herbert Anton Kellner, 'Neue Perspektiven der Bach-Forschung', p. 73 f. The tendency to discern in Bach's works all kinds of numerical secrets is criticized by Alfred Dürr, 'Neue Forschungen zu Bachs "Kunst der Fuge"', *Die Musikforschung* (1979), 153 f., and Eggebrecht, *Bachs 'Kunst der Fuge'*, pp. 20 f. In this connection it should be pointed out that the subject of the D sharp minor Fugue of *WTC* I has 13 notes, an 'unpleasant' number, and the theme of Arietta in Beethoven's Sonata Op. 111 has twice 25 melody notes. It would be that much more interesting from a numerical point of view if it had only 25 + 24 notes $(5^2 + (2^3 \times 3) = 7^2)$.

[16] Not as famous, though on the same artistic level, is a transcription of this cantata movement by Wilhelm Kempff.

aria. Here the original meaning is changed; Christ's Passion becomes a symbol of victory, of the overcoming of the self and the world that is the message of St John's Gospel (see Ex. 9.11). Those who can understand and sense this dramatic struggle between life and death will not hesitate to introduce great contrast in performances of Bach's instrumental works when the affection make this seem apposite.

In the final analysis the 'fundamental line' is nothing more and nothing less than the full inner presence of the performer, who at every moment identifies with the work and its message.

Ex. 9.11. *St John Passion*, aria, NBA No. 58, BGA No. 30, bars 39–41

Prelude in E flat minor and Fugue in D sharp minor, *WTC* I, BWV 853. An Analysis for Performance

The primary purpose of this book is to pave the way for stylistically authentic performances of Bach. Yet analytical knowledge is worthless if it is not brought together to form a whole, a synthesis of all the different aspects in the shape of a performance that strikes the listener as organic, a performance that no longer displays traces of long and laborious study. In the final analysis art emanates from the subconscious, from the wealth of imagination seeking communion with others.

For this reason I will attempt to demonstrate a way of arriving at this synthesis in the case of an important work by Bach. Of course, I am perfectly aware of the fact that there can be no such thing as the one and only correct way of performing a masterpiece composed several centuries ago. There are far too many variables and 'unknown quantities'. However, it is quite possible to work towards an interpretation that corresponds to the intentions of the composer, and which is thus ideal. My analysis for performance should be seen in this light. Much of what at first sight may seem subjective opinion is based on insights that in their turn are based on many years of historical study. Finally, no one should feel obliged to agree with my interpretation in its entirety.

Nevertheless, the synthesis, which in the actual performance of a work combines separate aspects such as harmony, melody, rhythm, and affection to form a whole, is of crucial importance. For this reason I have placed this chapter at the centre of my book. It means that the important area of ornamentation, which forms the subject of its second part, makes a slightly premature appearance. The choice of this work is deliberate. One of Bach's greatest works for the keyboard, it is also a classic example of the most frequent problems of interpretation.

PRELUDE IN E FLAT MINOR

The Affection

One of the performer's most important tasks is to recognize a work's 'affection' (to use the word current in Bach's day), to understand it, and to convey it to the listener. That this entails understanding and defining the structure of a work of art should be just as self-evident as the performer's striving for musical mastery and technical command of his instrument. The structure is the 'bearer' of the message and its expressive intent. So long as the message is comprehensible there is no reason why the performer should especially emphasize in performance the formal pattern revealed by analysis. A comparison with language may help to clarify this. A knowledge of grammatical rules and vocabulary is a prerequisite for verbal communication, yet we hardly ever think of grammar, unless of course we are speaking a foreign language with which we are not wholly familiar. Even where language itself becomes art, for example in poetry, the structures affect us only in an unconscious manner. Few people would scrutinize the metre and the rhymes before reading a poem by Goethe in order to be able to understand it 'better'. Yet in music such attempts continue to be made. However, just as it would be wrong in the case of a poem to try to make the rhythm of the lines comprehensible to the listener by means of conscious stresses, in music it would be a mistake to try to draw the listener's attention to certain structures, for instance by exaggerating fugal entries. In the case of fugues in particular, the fact that the harpsichord and organ are at a disadvantage compared with the clavichord and fortepiano on account of the action, which militates against the use of dynamic accents, is often a blessing in disguise.

The situation is rather different in passages where the structure itself is the bearer of the message or expressive intent, such as fugal strettos, where the collision of the various voices creates a conflict that needs to be heard and felt. To a lesser extent this also applies to imitation and canon. Thus the performer, like the student of a foreign language, must learn structures, punctuation, lines of tension, and so on. He should also become acquainted with the significance of figures and symbols.[1] Subsequently, however, he should 'forget' grammar and indeed everything connected with structure and technique in order to concentrate fully on conveying the contents of the work to his listeners.

There can be little doubt about the affection of the prelude. It depicts intense pain, and is expressed with an unrestrained passion that rarely occurs in Bach's music. The solemn dotted rhythm, the 'jagged' melody that initially consists only of leaps, and the incredibly expressive and dissonant harmony

---

[1] See Eggebrecht, *Bachs 'Kunst der Fuge'*, pp. 76 and 86 f.

with its numerous minor and diminished seventh chords all emphasize the work's tragic and agitated character. We can only guess at the emotions that led to the composition of this exceptional work. In his lectures on Bach Wilhelm Fischer suggested that the sudden death of Bach's first wife Maria Barbara, which must have affected him deeply, may have been the event that prompted him to write this piece. (Maria Barbara, to whom he had been married for thirteen years, died on 7 July 1720 while he was away from home on a visit to Carlsbad with the Prince of Cöthen, and was buried before he returned.[2]) Not even the music of the Passions contains an example of such 'acute' pain. Of course, such ideas stem from the Romantic philosophy of art, and we should treat them with a certain amount of circumspection.

Bearing the affection in mind, we arrive at our first conclusion. This piece should not be played in a soft and melancholy manner, or slowly and legato. The opposite is the case. The chords, which should be played in a strictly rhythmical manner, seem to be in a 'frenzy', and thus the tempo should not be too slow, nor should the melody be played quietly. It would be quite wrong to play the opening phrases legato as in Ex. 10.1, as so often happens, even if Czerny recommended it. The reader will no doubt ask: Why not? The answer is: because we are dealing with a melodic pattern that is decidedly vocal in character (like arioso, recitative), and in which every note corresponds to a clearly articulated syllable. There are numerous examples of this, including 'Erbarm es Gott' from the *St Matthew Passion* NBA No. 51, BGA No. 60— words that could easily be used as text underlay for the principal motif of this prelude.[3]

In this context the performer is faced with another problem. Although the dotted motif is felt to be the first beat of a bar, the prelude in fact begins two

Ex. 10.1. Bars 1–4, ed. Czerny

---

[2] In the autograph of the *Clavier-Büchlein* for W. F. Bach (begun 22 Jan. 1720) this prelude as copied by Friedemann is on pp. 51 ff. It breaks off at bar 35, to be followed immediately by the F minor Prelude (p. 54). The most plausible explanation for this sudden interruption is that the F minor Prelude had been copied in at an earlier date, and that the E flat minor Prelude was entered later, the allotted space of 3 pages proving to be insufficient. This suggests that the E flat minor Prelude may well have been written in summer 1720. However, Alfred Dürr is of the opinion that the entries in the *Clavier-Büchlein* are of a later date (1721?, 1722?), because the versions of the 4 last preludes correspond to the final versions and not to the early Forkel versions.

[3] Vocal movements resembling the prelude in expressive intent occur not only in Bach; e.g. in Mozart, Donna Anna's aria 'Or sai, che onore' (*Don Giovanni*) is similar, the affection being one of wounded pride.

beats earlier. The down-beat with c♭, the melodic goal of the up-beat motif, is felt to be the first bar yet is in fact bar 2. Bach probably wrote out the bar in full in order to be able to begin in E flat minor (all the preludes in *WTC* begin on the tonic) and to create a starting-point for the ensuing four-bar periods.[4] The problem is relatively simple for the performer if he prefaces an imaginary text 'Welch große Qual' with the word 'Seht!' ('Ah! The piercing pain doth tear my heart'). (See Ex. 10.2).

Ex. 10.2

I consider this prelude to be like a dramatic soprano aria with solo violin and cello as obbligato accompanying instruments. As I have said elsewhere (p. 55), up-beat quavers of this kind, in keeping with the affection, can be very slightly shortened (to quaver quintuplets), but not to semiquavers, which would make it impossible to understand the 'text'.

Two other points emerge from the use of an imaginary text of the kind indicated above.

1. The accompaniment must be subordinated to the melodic line in order to avoid giving the wrong aural impression, as for instance in Ex. 10.3.

Ex. 10.3

2. The main stress is always at the end of the motif, something Albert Schweitzer once pointed out (see Ex. 10.4).[5]

Ex. 10.4

a Incorrect:

b Correct:

---

[4] The situation in the C sharp minor Prelude of *WTC* II is very similar, and the 1st bar of the melody is almost identical.

[5] *J. S. Bach*, p. 349; Eng. trans., i. 356.

Furthermore, in order to grasp the meaning of the theme, I believe it is important to understand the gradual accretion of semiquavers as variations of the basic rhythm. The 'basic form' (Ex. 10.5) turns into Ex. 10.6. Even more semiquavers are added later, though they do not obscure the basic rhythm; for instance Ex. 10.7 evolves out of Ex. 10.8. This invention of a flowing melodic line (effectively a diminution) can be explained by the fact that an unchanging dotted melody is too monotonous and unsingable and, in terms of the emotional subject-matter, by the fact that the initial 'sobbing' dissolves into 'weeping'.

Ex. 10.5

Ex. 10.6

Ex. 10.7

Ex. 10.8

As in the majority of arias, the emotional and dynamic climax coincides with the highest note, c^3, in bar 11. It is remarkable that this climax should occur at such an early stage. However, it enables us to deduce that this 'aria', like Pamina's G minor counterpart in Mozart's *Die Zauberflöte* of seventy years later, moves from despair to resignation. True, a number of subsidiary climaxes reaching up to $c♭^3$ follow (e.g. in bars 28 and 35). Nevertheless, the descending curve after bar 11 is unmistakable. Even on the harpsichord the ending, with its gradual descent to the lower register, has the effect of a diminuendo, and is related to the melodic descent at the end of the Chromatic Fantasia.

The means with which Bach prepares the climactic effect in bar 11 are remarkable. After the second-highest melody note has been briefly touched upon in bar 2, and then in bars 8–9, the c^3 seems to be the result of an upward melodic motion. Moreover, it is precisely at this juncture that the diminished-seventh chord is heard for the first time. The baroque (and later the classical and romantic) doctrine of musical figures considered this chord to be a symbol of tragedy or terror. An example is the exclamation 'Barrabam!' ('Barabbas!') in the *St Matthew Passion*.[6] This meaning derives from the fact that the diminished-seventh chord is the only one 'proper to the key' that does not have a perfect fifth, consisting of two interlocking diminished fifths (a symbol of imperfection, of evil—the *diabolus in musica*). It is fascinating to observe how the chord is prepared with the help of two passing chords (see Ex. 10.9). The db^2 in the preceding chord could be termed a 'melodic' passing note, and the c^1 in the bass a 'harmonic' passing note. The combination of these two passing notes creates a kind of modern linear dissonance rarely found in eighteenth-century music.

Ex. 10.9

Another feature of a soprano aria is the singer's licence to add or not to add further embellishments. In the *WTC* Bach emphasized this 'circumscribed freedom' by adding or letting his pupils add additional ornaments, not only in his own autograph, but also in copies made by his students. Unfortunately the majority of 'philo-illogical' Urtext editions simply omit to mention many of the later copies.[7]

Finally, in singing, the correct affection encompasses a degree of rhetorical freedom achieved by the use of rubato. While adhering strictly to the basic rhythm, the semiquaver coloraturas in the 'soprano' and 'cello' parts in particular must, by means of retardation and acceleration, sound as if they were being improvised in a natural manner. Here it is particularly important to understand the difference between agogics (modification of the tempo) and rubato (freedom between the beats). Agogics can in fact be applied in this prelude, namely at the harmonic pivots, the cadences in B flat minor (bars 15–

---

[6] NBA No. 45a, BGA No. 54.

[7] Two exx. from *WTC* II may serve to illustrate this. Prelude in C sharp minor: the turn over the 1st melody note of bar 2 (Altnikol I = P 430) is only given in the old Kroll edn. Prelude in F minor: the *Pralltriller* sign over bar 1 and some parallel passages (Schwencke = P 203, Altnikol II = P 402) is rarely mentioned. Alfred Dürr comments: 'In the case of some ornaments that go beyond the autograph—if it exists—it is possible to prove that they were added later, presumably after 1750.' However, they could still go back to Bach.

16) and A flat minor (bars 19–20), the interrupted cadence in bars 28–9, and the broadening-out towards the end.

Ornamentation

This prelude is a good example of the fact that the three different signs for the trill—short wavy line, long wavy line, and *t* or *tr*—were interchangeable. The short wavy lines in bars 14, 19, and 29 are almost certainly not *Pralltriller*, but long trills, whereas the *tr* sign in bar 15 can signify only a short *Pralltriller*. That Bach used different notations within a single piece is most unusual. Presumably he added the *tr* sign in bar 15 at a later stage, probably in order to point out that this kind of cadential formula should always be embellished. As we have observed elsewhere, it is the context that determines the choice of a particular ornament. (This rule is true not only for Bach, but also for Haydn, Mozart, Chopin, and others.)

With regard to the frequent arpeggio signs, this prelude is an exceptional work. As is well known, in the Baroque and early Classical periods many chords were arpeggiated as and when the performer saw fit. A chord in which all the notes are struck at once often produces a hard, thick sound. Even in the Romantic era (e.g. in Schumann, Chopin, and Brahms) far more chords were arpeggiated than the notation would lead us to believe.

What in fact does the notation selected by Bach mean? Probably not that the other chords in this prelude should not be arpeggiated. That this would be misguided is best demonstrated with reference to the prelude's coda. From bar 30 to bar 34 the autograph has no arpeggio signs. However, they are included in the following reliable sources: bars 30–4 in the copy made by Anna Magdalena Bach, the first chord in Schwencke P 203, and bars 31–4 in Gerber's copy.

If many chords were arpeggiated in any case, why, we are moved to ask, did Bach go to the trouble of notating so many arpeggio signs from bar 4 onwards? The most likely answer to this is that the arpeggio played such a crucial role in the work that Bach did not wish to leave it to the whim of the player, preferring unusually to stipulate its use precisely. Where arpeggios are not notated, especially in the first three bars, they are optional. The performer had (and still has) the choice of striking the full chord simultaneously or arpeggiating it.

Information on the use of arpeggios is rare in eighteenth-century literature—if something was self-evident it was often mentioned in passing or not at all. In eighteenth-century treatises there is little about the free arpeggiation of chords, and even the manner of performance of arpeggio signs has not been conclusively established. Only in the case of recitatives was the arpeggiation of chords expressly recommended, even when there are no signs, though according to C. P. E. Bach this applied only to the harpsichord and not to the organ.[8]

Is there any evidence to suggest that J. S. Bach wished for free arpeggiation in works other than recitatives? The answer is yes. At the beginning of the Sarabande of the E minor Partita, BWV 830, Bach wrote acciaccaturas in the chords without adding a wavy arpeggio line. But an acciaccatura (non-harmonic passing note) can only be played in the course of an arpeggio. The strange chord in bar 28 of the Scherzo of the A minor Partita, BWV 827, makes sense only when it is arpeggiated. Further indirect evidence for the improvised arpeggiation of chords transpires from a comparison of the beginnings of the works in *Clavier-Übung*, Part II. Both the Italian Concerto, BWV 971, and the French Overture, BWV 831, begin with a four-part forte chord in the left hand. However, only the French Overture has an arpeggio sign. In view of the structural similarity, it is not quite clear why the opening chord of the Italian Concerto should not also be played with an energetic arpeggio, unless we are seeking to draw a specious distinction between the 'French' and 'Italian' styles. Of course it would be perfectly possible to construe this initial accent of an imagined orchestral entry as a 'starting shot', that is, without an arpeggio.[9]

Finally, we return to the affection, the emotional content of this prelude. After the passionate climaxes in bars 11, 19–20, and 26–9 the work's energy is as it were exhausted. The last four bars—in a low register—no longer have the power to generate large leaps, ending in a kind of resignation, in an acceptance of the inevitable. On the piano this will suggest a diminuendo, on the harpsichord perhaps the use of the upper manual. The end of this prelude suggests an inner affinity with that of the Chromatic Fantasia, BWV 903. This also has a melodic descent in the final bars and a full final major chord, which as it were brings the motion to an end.

FUGUE IN D SHARP MINOR

General Remarks on the Performance of Fugues

Even good musicians sometimes make the mistake of regarding Bach's fugues as 'abstract' music that is primarily a play of pure form. In reality Bach's fugues are just as much imbued with poetic expression (paired with intellectual discipline in regard to the formal design) as Petrarch's sonnets, Beethoven's sonatas, and Schubert's or Schumann's songs and character pieces. The poetic expression is not restricted to the fugue subjects, but extends to countersubjects and episodes. In some fugues the latter play a role similar to the episodes in rondo form. Every voice of a Bach fugue is replete

---

[8] *Essay*, pp. 420 ff.   [9] Klaus Hofmann, personal communication.

with melodic expression, and as in a poem or a Schubert impromptu there are varying degrees of expressivity. The fugue subjects are of particular importance for the expression of an individual voice, though not to the extent that other and equally important voices are relegated to a subsidiary role. In this connection it is interesting to note that Bach's fugues differ from textbook fugues in that in the majority of cases there is no break before the entry of a subject. Rather, the voice 'runs into' the subject, and sometimes it 'arrives' only at the second note of the subject.

Such observations suggest that it would be quite wrong to emphasize or to 'chisel out' fugue subjects whenever they occur. It was once said of an organist that he did not play fugues, but only fugue subjects. (This of course was a backhanded compliment.) Thus it is correct to see every voice as a melodic unity, as if it were assigned to a cello, a viola, or a violin for the duration of the fugue. For the keyboard player it is sometimes of use to play only a single voice, such as the alto, expressively, rather than the whole of the fugal texture. Another useful exercise (for pianists) is to play one part (e.g. the alto) forte and the other parts piano or mezzo-piano. As we have seen in Chapter 4, one should imitate string players and write in phrasing marks, slurs, *détaché* marks, and breathing breaks for every voice. It should be borne in mind that in Bach short staccato is extremely rare.

I have appended a text of this fugue in which I have attempted to add recommended articulation based on my experience and knowledge of the style. The music sometimes looks rather cluttered. This is unfortunately unavoidable wherever, in keyboard music, three or more voices are compressed on to two staves. Bach himself, in certain keyboard fugues such as the six-part ricercar of the *Musical Offering* and in the *Art of Fugue*,[10] chose to print the works in score with six or four staves. Unfortunately, very few keyboard players are able to play them from the score.

But the expressive melodic and correctly articulated execution of the individual voice does not in itself solve all the problems of fugue interpretation. Of course, the parts have to be dynamically adjusted; contrapuntal and harmonic features have to be taken into account, as does the structure of the fugue as a whole. In point of fact this is no more and no less than what would be required in the case of a Mozart or Beethoven sonata, where the player also has to be aware of the main and subsidiary voices (the latter just as expressive, though not as strong as in Bach), and of where the development section, the recapitulation, and the coda begin.

An important aspect of contrapuntal writing is the use of complementary rhythm (see p. 30) and the non-synchronous distribution of accents (not only in fugues, of course). This means that while one voice is being emphasized, the complementary voice is not, a principle that makes it possible to ensure

---

[10] The incomplete final fugue was notated on 2 staves only. It is thus conceivable that the lost original versions of the other fugues were originally notated on 2 systems.

the clear audibility of the voices while preserving a relative degree of independence. Exx. 10.10–10.13 serve to illustrate this. Ex. 10.11 shows an instance of free imitation. The high long $d\sharp^2$ begins as a consonance, becoming a dissonance on the third beat of the bar. After the upward leap of a fourth, the consonance $c\sharp^2 - a\sharp^1$ becomes the dissonance $b\sharp^1 - a\sharp^1$, which requires a soft resolution on to $g\textup{x}$.) In Ex. 10.12, the consonant bb^1 in the upper voice is accented because of its length. It becomes a dissonance in bar 15, resolving unaccented on the consonant a^1. The solo in the middle voice in bar 15 begins as a consonant note (c^1 is a fifth above the bass F) and rises melodically and harmonically to the climax on gb^1 over the ninth chord, in a sharp accented dissonance that resolves on to f^1. Ex. 10.13 shows the same line of tension as in Ex. 10.12, probably an involuntary reminiscence on Beethoven's part.

Ex. 10.10. Partita No. 6, BWV 830, Gigue, bars 3–5

Ex. 10.11. *WTC* I, Fugue in D sharp minor, bars 5–6

Ex. 10.12. *WTC* I, Prelude in E flat minor, bars 14–16

Ex. 10.13. Beethoven, Piano Sonata Op. 110, third movement, bars 20–1

Of course, even in polyphonic movements accents sometimes occur in all voices simultaneously. This is particularly evident in the case of cadential patterns, which determine not only the harmonic structure of a fugue, but also the formal design, the work's 'corner-stones' (these also include the cadences).

The feature that distinguishes Bach's fugues from those of his predecessors (and of many of his successors) is the harmonic richness and the resultant formal consistency. Everything—even the most complicated combination of themes, strettos, augmentations, and so on—seems to be subject to or on a par with the harmonic design in a natural and seemingly effortless manner, as if it were the easiest thing in the world. It is possible to listen to a Bach fugue without the slightest knowledge of counterpoint, and yet to experience a beautiful and eventful piece of music. Schumann in his writings noted this quality and paid tribute to it. The later composers who were closest to Bach in this regard were Mozart (in the C minor Fugue K. 426 and K. 546), Bruckner, and Max Reger. Similarly, Alban Berg made good use of the principle of different forms employed simultaneously. In his works forms such as fugue, canon, and sonata overlap with a rich, late romantic harmony, and at the same time are subject to the laws of dodecaphony.[11] In many works number symbolism may have been to Bach what twelve-note technique was to Berg: a self-imposed additional discipline that has nothing to do with musical form in the primary sense. It matters little whether a movement is 39, 40, or 41 bars in length, or whether a row has ten or twelve notes. And yet this interlocking of various kinds of artistic representation leads to a greater intensity of expression that even the untutored ear will sense to be deeper and operative in three or more dimensions. The two composers even have in common the game of using the musical letters of their names.[12]

The subject of the D sharp minor Fugue: Meaning and Affection

The principal feature of the fugue subject is the motion from the fifth to the minor sixth and back to the fifth. The minor sixth above the fifth has always been considered to be one of the most expressive of melodic forms, especially when depicting some kind of pain—it was a symbol of distress, of having been forsaken by God, of the deepest despair. It is probably no accident that this subject displays an affinity to Luther's chorale 'Aus tiefer Not schrei ich zu

---

[11] With regard to the fundamental and yet 'invisible' structure, Bach might well have agreed with Berg's remarks about *Wozzeck*: 'However much one knows about what this opera contains in the way of musical forms, how everything is strictly and logically "worked out", and what artistry there is in every single detail . . . from the moment the curtain rises to the moment it descends for the last time, there should be no one in the audience who notices anything of the various fugues and inventions, suites and sonata movements, variations and passacaglias—no one who is filled with anything more than the idea of this opera, which goes further than Wozzeck's personal fate. And in this—I believe—I have been successful!' (Willi Reich, *Alban Berg* (Zurich, 1963), p. 61; Eng. trans. p. 66).

[12] Cf. the motto of Berg's Chamber Concerto and the name symbolism in the Lyric Suite.

Dir' ('Out of the depths I cry unto thee'), which in turn goes back to earlier sacred melodies (see Ex. 10.14).[13] In the baroque doctrine of figures this sequence of intervals and semitone motion (fifth–minor sixth–fifth) was termed 'pathopoietic' ('causing suffering').[14]

Ex. 10.14

The second half of the subject, which ascends only a fourth from the tonic, sounds like a coda to the first melody curve on a smaller scale. As I have stated elsewhere (see pp. 29 f.), the barlines do not correspond to the melodic and rhythmic pattern. Rather, the subject consists of a group of three and two minims. Also of note is the fact that, unlike the chorale, the expressive minor sixth occurs on an unaccented short note, which signifies a slightly muted expression of pain. However, the performer ought to be aware of the fact that the minor sixth, despite its rhythmic position, must be sensed as the subject's melodic climax.[15]

With regard to the articulation of the subject, both the melisma from the second to the eighth (or ninth) notes and the end of the subject should be played legato. Bach provided an unmistakable hint that there should be a break in the leap of a fourth in the second half of the subject in the later variant, bars 19–22 (see Ex. 10.15). Clearly he would not have written out this variant of the subject if the caesura had not been present in latent form at the very beginning. Thus it only remains to be decided whether the first leap in the subject ought to be played *détaché* or legato. Both are possible. A break is suggested by the parallelism of the two halves of the subject, a slur by the ligature in the case of the inversion of the subject in the bass at the beginning of bar 39 (see Ex. 10.16). The extensions of the slurs indicated by dots in Ex. 10.16 refer to performances on keyboard instruments. String players would change bowing a note earlier—of course without a musically perceptible break. However, a very slight break after the slur is also possible

---

[13] Eggebrecht (*Bachs 'Kunst der Fuge'*, p. 50) points out that Bach set this chorale in Cantata No. 38 and in the chorale prelude BWV 686, always with the 2-note melisma on the word 'schrei', something that does not occur in the original version of the chorale.

[14] See Eggebrecht, *Bachs 'Kunst der Fuge'*, pp. 18, 26, 76.

[15] See my comments on the same problem in the 2nd movement of Haydn's F major Piano Sonata, Hob. xvi/23, *Joseph Haydn, 4 sonates pour clavier* (Paris, 1984).

on keyboard instruments. Furthermore, it is important to play the initial *d♯* so firmly that it is not misconstrued as an up-beat. Thus the interpretation shown in Ex. 10.17 would be wrong. With regard to the inversion of the subject,

Ex. 10.15

Ex. 10.16

which is heard for the first time in bar 30 (Ex. 10.18*a*), it is noteworthy that Bach was certainly not concerned to achieve a 'mathematically exact' mirror image; the 'correct' version is shown in Ex. 10.18*b*. As far as Bach was concerned, harmonic coherence and logic were more important than a strict adherence to abstract techniques. Here he was obviously concerned to elaborate the key of F sharp major. Both this and the inversion of the subject have the effect of light in chiaroscuro, particularly the upward line (c♯–d♯–e♯–f♯) at the end of the inverted subject, which is in direct contrast to the original.

Ex. 10.17

Ex. 10.18

A special feature of this fugue is Bach's free augmentation by 'one-and-a-half-times' of the subject, in which only certain notes increase in length, for instance in bars 24–7 (see Ex. 10.19). Intervallic changes in the interests of the harmony and free rhythmic variants are both features that recur in *The Art of*

Ex. 10.19

Fugue, composed decades later. This partial augmentation prepares the way in psychological terms for the 'real' augmentation of the subject which is the goal and climax of the fugue (Ex. 10.20).

Ex. 10.20

More than the subject itself, the countersubjects (which unusually for Bach are not strict) consist largely of stepwise and scalar motion (see Ex. 10.21). Small intervals are the essence of a freely flowing melody. The upper voice creates a kind of euphony that represents a contrast ('counterpoint') to the seriousness of the work. Melodic lines of this kind should on the whole be played legato. In order to achieve a flowing legato on keyboard instruments it is necessary to choose one's fingering carefully, to observe the difference between 'accented' and 'non-accented' notes, and above all to have supple wrists that rebound lightly between the notes, similar to the movement of the ankles when walking in an elastic manner. The contrast between these lines and the largely 'jagged' and rough melodic character of the preceding E flat minor Prelude is particularly striking; it is almost a conscious antithesis. For this reason, despite the climaxes in the strettos, the fugue should be played more cantabile than the prelude—softly, and with a full tone, though of course never in a feeble way. On no account should it end with a diminuendo. Rather, it must be played firmly and in a kind of liberating manner.

Ex. 10.21

The Structure of the D sharp minor Fugue

In a Bach fugue, suite, or concerto movement, the modulations to related keys are the corner-stones of the structure from which the performer has to take his bearings. In the D sharp minor Fugue they are as follows. After the surplus fourth entry of the subject in the exposition (bars 12–14) the fugue modulates, as might have been expected, to the nearest key, F sharp major (bars 15–16). Then, however, something unexpected happens. The last note in the treble, $e\sharp^2$, does not resolve on to $f\sharp^2$, leading instead with the help of a syncopation in the middle of bar 19 to another modulation, to A sharp minor. This marks the end of the first section of the fugue, and the tempo at the cadence may be slightly broadened (though this is not essential). Now the first stretto appears in the dominant key of A sharp minor.

Why, in bars 16–17, did Bach 'evade' the expected modulation to F sharp major? The reason is probably a psychological one. Even in the prelude it is noticeable that the first modulation is not to the relative major, G flat, as in many of Bach's works in the minor mode, but to the dominant minor, B flat minor (from bar 12, or arguably bar 14, to bar 16), and four bars later to the subdominant minor, A flat minor. Bach is obviously intent on avoiding the major mode, partly because it might be construed as a kind of 'cheap comfort' in this portrayal of sorrow.

In this respect there seems to be a genuine formal and emotional connection between the prelude and the fugue. However, Bach could not simply ignore the 'thwarted expectation' of the major mode in bars 16–17. The heralded F sharp major is, as it were, delayed until bar 30, coinciding significantly with the first entry of the inversion of the subject. This also leads to an inversion in the character of the music. Thus the fugue is not content merely to recapitulate the leaden mood of the prelude using different compositional means; it strives gradually to become brighter, or, to put it another way, to overcome the state of depression. The subject and its inversion are more than a contrapuntal device; they are almost programmatic in character. It is true that both forms occasionally appear in the opposite tonal mode (subject in the major, bars 24–30; inversion in the minor, bars 44 ff). However, this is only a passing phenomenon. The first climax is the entry of the inversion in the low, sonorous bass register in bar 44, exactly in the middle of the fugue, with a stretto in the treble. The most intense contest between the subject in its basic shape (in the minor) and its inversion (in the major) occurs within the space of a few bars in the middle of the fugue. The triple stretto of the fugue subject in the minor in bars 52–3 is answered—abruptly and yet with harmonic logic— by the triple reply of the inversion in the major. This is very dramatic indeed.

The second climax begins in the middle of bar 61 (at the imperfect cadence on the dominant, marking the beginning of the last section) and leads directly to the end. It is the thrice-repeated entry of the subject in double augmentation (ascending from bass to alto and treble), closely combined with the subject and its inversion. At the last entry (bar 77) they are joined by a special form peculiar to the fugue, an augmentation of one and a half (cf. bars 24, 48 ff.). The contrapuntal artistry with which these three forms are combined is so great that the correct harmonies seem to fall into place by themselves. This climax virtually exhausts the fugue's expressive content, and the work is brought forcefully to a major close by a three-quaver motif derived from the subject. The *tierce de Picardie* is not merely a conventional gesture; indeed, it might be construed as a symbol of salvation.

Finally a word about the keys Bach chose for the prelude (E flat minor) and the fugue (D sharp minor). This may well have been a way of showing that the circle of fifths is complete when there are six accidentals, in other words, that E flat minor and D sharp minor are identical in the *WTC*. A more plausible explanation for the unusual juxtaposing of the two keys is the view shared by Tovey, Keller, Müller, Palmer, and others that the fugue was originally in D minor, later being transposed into D sharp minor. From a notational point of view this was much simpler than transposing the work into E flat minor. Some editions (including that of Kroll, Peters edition) print both the prelude and the fugue in E flat minor. This is a perfectly reasonable thing to do.

EDITIONS OF THE PRELUDE IN E FLAT MINOR AND FUGUE IN D SHARP MINOR, *WTC* I

Explanation of Signs

∪	non-accented note
—	durational sign signifying tenuto or a certain emphasis (but less than >)
⨪	staccato that is not too short (*quasi détaché*)
∿∿∿	ritardando (∿∿∿ = slight, ∿∿ = marked ritardando)
⟶	accelerando
∿∿∿⟶	at first slightly slower, then accelerando
∧	with great emphasis
rubato	rhythmic licence between the beats while keeping strict time
sim., simile	continuation of a certain performance feature

All dynamic markings are editorial. They are merely intended as suggestions for performance—of course, only for instruments that permit inflected touch (clavichords, fortepianos, and pianos).

The present text is based on the BGA (edited by Kroll) and the Peters edition (Kreutz), with reference to Walther Dehnhard's Wiener Urtext edition, which reflects the latest state of research into the sources.[16]

---

[16] When this chapter was written the relevant NBA vol. had not yet appeared.

List of Some of the Sources consulted[17]

1. Autograph, P 415.[18] (A facsimile edition was published by the Bach-Archiv, Leipzig, 1964.) The autograph contains a number of emendations by Bach. These were made at various times. Walther Dehnhard, the editor of the Vienna Urtext edition, has labelled the various stages A1 to A4. A1 is practically coincidental with the first fair copy of 1722, and should thus really be termed A0. A2 probably dates from about 1732. A3 is a set of corrections corroborated by manuscript MS 6 in the Musikbibliothek der Stadt Leipzig. The A4 emendations, according to the Bach-Institut in Göttingen, come from the last years of Bach's life. According to Dehnhard, only Litt. XY (Brussels) can be regarded as a direct copy of this, though directly or indirectly P 402 and P 57 (see sources 3 and 4 below) also go back to this late version.

2. The P 202 copy. This incomplete copy by Anna Magdalena Bach was formerly considered to be an autograph. It is of particular interest to Bach research. The missing beginning was added up to bar 50 of the C sharp minor Fugue by an unidentified copyist (Müller?), the end, from bar 69 of the A minor Fugue, in 1739 by Bach's pupil J. F. Agricola. The main part, which corresponds to the A2 correction layer of the autograph, cannot have been written before 1732. It is unclear whether the copy was made from A2 itself or from a copy of A2. This manuscript, which used to be in the possession of Bach's eldest son Wilhelm Friedemann, contains a number of later emendations, especially in the E flat minor prelude (mainly in the shape of rests and ornaments), which, according to Kobayashi and Dürr, can almost certainly be ascribed to Wilhelm Friedemann. The embellishments are of great interest, for they appear in none of the other sources and yet seem to be eminently 'Bachian' (cf. the ornaments later added by Bach in stage A4 of the C sharp minor Prelude of *WTC* I). I have no doubt that they go back to J. S. Bach's verbal instructions, and have therefore included them in the main text in brackets. It is unlikely, however, that the minor cadences that Wilhelm Friedemann added in the prelude and the fugue would have found Bach's approval. Friedemann seems to have had a penchant for minor final chords, as is proved by other manuscript copies in his possession, such as that of the Chromatic Fantasia and Fugue, BWV 903.

3. The Altnikol copy P 402. One of the best copies of the final version, by Bach's son-in-law Johann Christian Altnikol.

4. The Kirnberger copy P 57, by Bach's pupil Johann Philipp Kirnberger, who later became a noted theorist. Also a copy of the final version with a number of variants.

---

[17] I am indebted to the staff of the Bach-Institut, Göttingen, in particular to Dr Alfred Dürr and Dr Yoshitake Kobayashi, for valuable information concerning sources and copyists.
[18] P is the abbreviation for Bach MSS (autographs or copies) held by the state libraries in Berlin (Staatsbibliothek Preußischer Kulturbesitz and Deutsche Staatsbibliothek).

5. The copy by Bach's cousin and friend Johann Gottfried Walther, P. 1074, which dates from before the emendations in source 1, and contains a number of important variants.

6 and 7. The two copies by Friedrich Gottlieb Schwencke, P. 203 and P 417. The later copy shows one of the earliest attempts to determine the differences between various versions. Kirnberger's variants in particular were noted in footnotes.

8. Hamburg. An important unidentified copy of *WTC* in the Staats- und Universitätsbibliothek, Hamburg (MB 1974).

9. Musikbibliothek der Stadt Leipzig, Pölitz collection, Pod. mus. MS 34. Another important copy of *WTC*. This was made by one of Bach's house copyists, and contains autograph corrections by Bach that editors have hitherto disregarded. The copyist inadvertently omitted the eleventh bar in the G major Prelude of *WTC* I; Bach later added it himself. He notated the (necessary) slur between the two quavers a^2–g^2, which is missing in all the other sources.

10. An incomplete copy by Heinrich Nikolaus Gerber dated 1725, though of later date from Prelude No. 7 (E flat major) onwards; at Riemenschneider Bach Institute, Baldwin-Wallace College, Berea, Ohio, CO 32. In 1985 a facsimile edition was published by the Riemenschneider Bach Institute.

Further sources of varying degrees of importance are listed in the Vienna Urtext edn. (app., pp. x–xi) and the Palmer edn. (pp. 5–6).

Prelude in E flat minor

Bar 9, etc. In the Griepenkerl edn. of the Chromatic Fantasia, BWV 903, said to go back to lessons with W. F. Bach, there are up-beat groups of 3 semiquavers in the recitative. The first of these notes are always shortened to demisemiquavers: instead of ♪ ♫♫ thus ♪♪ ♫♫. This rhythmic modification, which was surely not meant to be taken literally, is a way of stating that the 1st note should not be accented, being an up-beat

to the 2nd. On the harpsichord this is achieved by a very slight abbreviation of the initial note. The similarly structured up-beats in the E flat minor prelude, even when performed slightly later than stipulated, should be played lightly and very slightly faster than notated.

Bar 13, top line, last 6 notes. Possible variant in Kirnberger's copy:

Bar 15. The appoggiatura Bach probably intended—a typical *coulé* (see pp. 396 f.)—was inserted by W. F. Bach in Anna Magdalena's copy. The same is true of the appoggiaturas in bars 24 and 38 (the appoggiatura to bar 24 could perhaps be omitted). See comments on source 2 above.

Bar 19. As double dotting was not in common use during Bach's lifetime, the final note of the trill (in the autograph) is notated as a crotchet ab^2, although it is supposed to be struck later. In the copy made by Gerber (source 10) it is correctly notated as a quaver, though preceded by only 1 dot. Similarly incomplete notation is found elsewhere in Bach, e.g. in the Sarabande of Partita No. 1, bar 26.

Bars 20–2, 24–7. The broken-line slurs (entered by W. F. Bach?) occur only in source 2. The up-beat phrasing of the motif that is often played does not accord with the down-beat articulation that predominated in the 18th cent. This articulation principle was also preferred after the time of Bach, e.g. by Mozart: (see the 2nd movement of the Piano Concerto in C major, K. 467, or the 1st movement of the Piano Duet Sonata in C major, K. 521).

Bar 28. This trill sign, probably entered by W. F. Bach, appears only in P 202 (source 2).

Bars 30–4. The (self-evident) arpeggio signs in these bars are not in the autograph, though they appear in several important copies from the Bach circle.

Bar 39. Variant: last quaver *eb*[1] in place of *d*[1] (Altnikol P 402, Kirnberger P 57 by correction, Schwencke P 203, etc.: authenticity questionable).

Fugue in D sharp minor

Bar 1. As already mentioned in the commentary, the 1st leap of a 5th in the subject could be played legato or slightly detached. Here I prefer the legato execution, as in the case of the subject in *The Art of Fugue*, because separation could wrongly create the impression of an up-beat:

In the 2nd half of the subject, where no such danger exists, it would be better to play the leap of a 4th non-legato, especially in view of the rests (or written-out separations) in bars 21 and 22. However, this principle does not necessarily apply to all subsequent entries of the subject. Bach was often remarkably inconsistent when it came to the minutiae of articulation.

Bar 3. Whereas the long slurs seem designed for stringed instruments and in general correspond to 18th-century notational practice, the dotted slurs are valid for performances on keyboard instruments using modern notation.

Bars 5, 10, 11. Ornaments in round brackets come from secondary sources, and those in square brackets are editorial. According to Bischoff, Kreutz, and others, the trills (*Pralltriller*) in bars 5, 10, and 11 were added to Anna Magdalena Bach's copy at a later date by an unidentified scribe. However, despite their doubtful authenticity they are in keeping with the style. On the 4th beat of bar 11 a (short) trill is almost

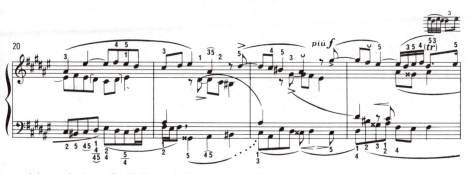

certainly required, or a *Pralltriller* above the upper voice. The dotted rhythm at this point does not appear in the original version, which had 2 quavers.

Bar 13. On the 4th quaver the autograph and some copies erroneously have ♮ instead of ♯. Many eds. believe that this is a mistake which crept in when the work was being transposed from a lost original in D minor, where the 4th note would of course have been *b*. An augmented 2nd *c*✗–*b* would go against the rules of part-writing.

Bar 16. Although the high *c*♯³ occurs only in Johann Gottfried Walther's copy (P 1074), one need have no qualms about playing this note. It would correspond to the *c*³ presumably notated in the lost D minor version. However, in D sharp minor Bach had to 'lop off' the tip of the preceding scale because at the time most keyboard instruments went only as far as *c*³. Nevertheless *b*² (in place of *c*♯³) has a charm of its own, for its syncopated rhythm corresponds to the tie across the barline in bars 16–17, and the missing top note *c*♯³ in bar 16 to the *e*♯²–*f*♯² resolution that is awaited in vain in bar 17.

Bars 20–1. Emended in the autograph. The original version read:

These emendations and the ones in bars 41, 52, 73, and 74 were made at a relatively late stage. This is

shown by the fact that the copies made by Anna Magdalena Bach, Fischhof, Gerber, Walther, Forkel, and Schwencke (P 417) still retain the earlier versions. The corrections in all these passages were adopted by, *inter alia*, Kirnberger, Altnikol, and Schwencke (in the later copy P 203).

Bar 23. The ornament required, usually notated as a *tr* sign, also occurs in the copies of Anna Magdalena Bach, Forkel, and Walther.

Bar 41. Original version in the bass (see n. to bars 20–1):

Bar 48. Original version in the bass:

When making corrections at a later stage Bach obviously forgot to notate the ♮ before *e* as required by the harmony. Only the P 207 copy adds it.

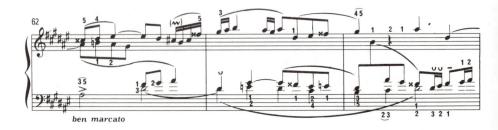

Bars 51, 69. According to Palmer the trill signs in these bars occur only in Walther's copy.

Bar 62. The *Pralltriller* sign above $c\sharp^2$ may originally have been in the autograph, though it later faded away or was erased. It is included in Ms 34, and was later added to the Hamburg copy.

Bars 73–4. The original version (see above, n. to bars 20–1) was:

The curious trill sign above the *b♯* in bar 74, which could also be a mordent (notated as such by Kirnberger with the lower auxiliary *a♯* as a small note), is a later addition to the autograph. Perhaps the embellishment was intended to create a rhythmic counterbalance to the two semiquavers (corrected version) in bar 73. I omit the embellishment at this point.

PART II

Studies in Ornamentation

The embellishments, or musical ornaments of the thorough-bass are innumerable, and vary according to the taste and experience of the player. Because this is not so much a matter of rules as of practice and much judiciousness, we can do no more in this restricted space than to give some *prima principia* and a brief introduction to the subject. The rest we must leave to the visual demonstration of a teacher, or to the student's own industry and experience. (Heinichen, *Der General-Baß*, p. 522.)

11

Introduction

Clothes are at the mercy of fashion, and so are performing styles. As Goethe once said, 'Erlaubt ist was gefällt' (One may do anything so long as it pleases). However, what pleases is largely determined by habit, fashion, and imitation. Significantly, the answer to the above statement in Goethe's *Torquato Tasso* is 'Erlaubt ist, was sich ziemt' (One may do anything so long as it is right and proper).

How in fact did the 'modern' view of Bach emerge? One thing seems certain: until about 1920 Bach was predominantly performed in a romantic manner, with a thick and massive sound and a predilection for unarticulated legato, as if he had been a contemporary of Liszt or Brahms.[1] In keeping with this, Bach's ornaments, where they were not omitted altogether,[2] were played in the style of the late nineteenth century. Trills and *Pralltriller* began on the note over which they were placed, the 'main note'. In an age which believed in progress, there was no interest in historically authentic interpretation, and the problem of performing music in a manner that befitted the style went unheeded. The works most in favour were those which approximated to the romantic aesthetic (such as the Chromatic Fantasia and Fugue). The others were usually considered dry, theoretical, and boring, at best suitable for study purposes. The situation changed after the advent of reformers such as Arnold Dolmetsch, whose book *The Interpretation of the Music of the XVII and XVIII Centuries* was widely read, and Wanda Landowska, who was particularly successful in restoring the harpsichord's reputation. There began to be a demand for authentic performances, and a new Bach style was forged on the basis of seventeenth- and eighteenth-century theorists and the manuscript sources. It is understandable that the zealous sometimes went too far, and that the 'baby', emotion, was often thrown out with the 'bathwater', romanticism.

---

[1] It is significant that e.g. the Chaconne for solo violin not only used to be performed with a piano accompaniment added in the 19th cent., but also, in Busoni's transcription, was invested with bombastic sonorities. It is also significant that bombastic piano transcriptions of organ works were far more common than the originals, and that the 'keyboard works' proper were deemed to be study material for children.

[2] See Busoni's edn. of the Goldberg Variations. When the Aria returns at the end it does so in 'purified' form, i.e. without ornaments.

Whereas the romantic and expressive aspect of Bach's works had been emphasized too strongly in the nineteenth century, the ostensible 'fidelity to the original' and 'objectivity' in favour in the middle of the twentieth century often tended to ignore it. 'It was wonderful, just like a sewing machine' used to be a witty way of describing performances rattled off in this way. It is easy to understand the emergence of two schools of thought among musicians: the romantics versus the adherents of stylistic fidelity. The execution of an ornament was no longer merely an aesthetic concern, but a part of one's philosophy of life. The way a trill began became a kind of 'uniform' that distinguished the members of the opposing camps. Beginning a trill or *Pralltriller* on the main note was the hallmark of the romantics, and beginning it on the auxiliary was the sign of the 'historical connoisseurs'.

Today, about half a century later, the historical and style-critical view, which has long since recognized that baroque music (even if it is not 'romantic') is replete with affections, has largely won the day. One reason for this may well be the fact that, just as a painting stripped of its varnish is more luminous than before, an authentic performance in all its immediacy is both more moving and more beautiful than a non-authentic one. However, when it comes to ornamentation, many musicians have not progressed beyond the stage arrived at about 1930. Thus an 'update' is required for musicians who strive for historical authenticity.

Apart from the study by Neumann already mentioned, *Ornamentation in Baroque and Post-Baroque Music*, there is another recent study of Bach's trills by the Australian musicologist John O'Donnell. He rightly notes

that the general lack of concern for authenticity which pervaded the earlier part of our century . . . has been replaced by the tyranny of a handful of rules which are frequently slavishly adhered to against all musical logic, despite a sizeable amount of evidence contrary to such standardized interpretations, and without sufficient consideration of historical aspects.[3]

The fact that there is little agreement and much controversy about the modern performance practice of Bach's works is probably due to the lack of an unbroken Bach tradition. Nor do we possess unambiguous and detailed information from Bach's contemporaries on how he wished to have his works performed. Yet it is still insufficiently recognized that the works themselves contain far more hard information on how to perform them in accordance with the style than is normally believed. However, in order to interpret Bach's information correctly, it is necessary to understand the mentality of his age and to become acquainted with contemporary music

---

[3] 'Bach's Trills: Some Historical and Contextual Considerations', *Musicology* (Musicological Society of Australia), 4 (1974), 14. Other studies that prepared the way for a change in the predominant view of Bach include Alfred Kreutz, *Die Ornamentik in J. S. Bachs Klavierwerken* (Leipzig, 1950), Walter Emery, *Bach's Ornaments* (London, 1953), and Bodky, *Interpretation*.

theory or, as it were, the musical notions of the eighteenth century. A detailed consideration of the music appears meaningful only against this background. Thus this part of the present study will first attempt to outline the historical development of the style.

One problem in particular emerged in the course of my investigations. This was the execution of the *Pralltriller*, an ornament which plays a large role in Bach's music (and in that of most other eighteenth-century composers). The name of this common and indeed indispensable ornament varies. However, as most descriptions are accompanied by music examples, it can hardly be denied that, despite differences in nomenclature, it is the same ornament. Furthermore, it is an ornament which occurs frequently in Bach in written-out form. At first I did not think that this was a problem, for eighteenth-century theorists were astonishingly unanimous in describing the *Pralltriller* as being an extremely short trill which, exceptionally, began on the main note. Yet I soon noticed that beginning on the main note was anathema as far as many Bach performers were concerned. They believed that it was an established fact that the three-note *Pralltriller* beginning on the main note did not occur in the music of J. S. Bach, and that it had been introduced by his successors. A much-quoted (pre-war) research finding stated that a *Pralltriller* beginning on the main note did not occur in Bach. The short trill, like the long trill, always had to begin on the upper auxiliary. The table of ornaments for Wilhelm Friedemann Bach showed, it was thought, that the sign $\wedge\!\!\wedge$ could not be short trill or have anything to do with the *Pralltriller* of a later period.[4]

Most musicians, and harpsichordists in particular, still share this view, believing it to be a fact that Bach never began the trill (whether long or short) on the main note. As late as 1983 Klotz, in his study of Bach's ornaments, referred to the *Pralltriller* as a 'post-Bachian' invention. 'Before Bach's death the French trill sign of the (short) wavy line was never taken to mean anything like a *Praller*. That the *Praller* has nothing to do with Bach's keyboard ornamentation has been clearly demonstrated in the recent literature.'[5]

Klotz and the authors cited by him arrive at this 'certainty' with regard to the execution of trills by ignoring all the documentary evidence capable of refuting their theory. For example, they forget to mention the following comment on Bach's playing in Ernst Ludwig Gerber's lexicon: 'On the pedal his feet had to imitate exactly every theme, every progression previously played by the hands. No appoggiatura, no mordent, no *Pralltriller* was omitted, or heard less clearly and distinctly.'[6] It is surprising, of course, to hear that Bach played ornaments which he is supposed not to have known!

---

[4] See Harich-Schneider, *Die Kunst des Cembalospiels*, p. 87.   [5] *Ornamentik*, pp. 45–8.

[6] *Historisch-biographisches Lexicon der Tonkünstler* (Leipzig, 1790–2), quoted in *Bach-Dokumente*, iii. 85 (my italics). E. L. Gerber was the son of Bach's pupil Heinrich Nikolaus Gerber. He obtained his information at first hand.

A thorough study of the sources has convinced me that my earlier willingness to accept the prevailing view on this matter simply did not do justice to eighteenth-century practice. One thing has become especially apparent. This is that one should not consider an ornament out of context. In order to achieve convincing results in a study of this kind one must take into account the florid melodic style, the aesthetics of the age, the doctrine of affections, and, above all, eighteenth-century principles of composition. Ornamentation is in fact as diverse as life itself, as language, music, or the various individual styles. It must always adapt itself to the flow of the music and to the claims of harmony, melody, and rhythm. It can scarcely be mastered with a few rules of thumb.

But why go to all this trouble? Is so much effort really necessary for an ornament as small as the *Pralltriller*? For the artist who strives for perfection the answer can only be an unequivocal 'yes'. What Thomas Mann says of the creative artist also applies, with certain reservations, to the 're-creative' performer:

Perfection—what a thought! It is closest of all to art and the artist. He always perfects. Always, from work to work, he is drawn on and tempted to live by the longing for perfection. It is unclear whether this urge is in fact directed at the work itself or at the individual and his salvation and justification, at his personal perfection. It is the urge towards what is 'good', both in the absolute and already in the symbolic sense of the word, which governs the artist, an urge whose dictates he obeys in serious and indeed symbolic play. All art is symbolic, by virtue of the double meaning of this urge, and even if eloquence is one of the means at its disposal, it still possesses the silent existence of the symbol, the sign, the image, into which or from which much can be read.[7]

Perfection can be attained only by those who also devote themselves to details.

After clarifying how eighteenth-century theory defined the *Pralltriller* (this will deal with some hitherto virtually unknown aspects which many musicians may find surprising), we shall examine, in Chapter 20, how all these insights can be applied to Bach's works.

Before this I consider it necessary to provide a brief account of the development of ornamentation in the Baroque era. The central figure in the section on theory is Bach's second son Carl Philipp Emanuel (1714–88), whose famous *Essay on the True Art of Playing Keyboard Instruments* is one of the most important Western treatises on music. It is representative of the middle of the eighteenth century, and still has much to say to the modern musician. C. P. E. Bach speaks to us in his own right, though at times in the name of the great tradition of his father, Johann Sebastian Bach. In an autobiographical essay the author stated: 'In composition and keyboard

---

[7] 'Ansprache im Goethe-Jahr', *Zum Thema Goethe* (Frankfurt-on-Main, 1982), 73.

playing I have never had any other teacher but my father'.[8] Thus there is good reason to believe that his theory of ornamentation was based on that of his father, or was at least strongly influenced by him. In many ways Carl Philipp Emanuel was his father's most loyal son, and we owe him a debt of gratitude for the fact that almost all of the Bach manuscripts he inherited (about a third of the total) have survived, unlike those given to his brothers. He repeatedly emphasized his father's greatness to Burney and others, and as late as 21 January 1786, in a passionate letter to Johann Joachim Eschenburg, he protested against the idolization of Handel and declared his father's music to be of greater stature.[9] Of course, as a composer C. P. E. Bach chose and indeed had to pursue a different path. However, the transition from the baroque to the *galant* style did not happen suddenly, and it certainly did not mean that the old rules of composition, part-writing, and ornamentation were discarded. In fact, the rules governing thorough-bass practice, the cantabile style in both composition and performance, the treatment of dissonance, and so on continued to be observed as before.

A valid objection to the application of C. P. E. Bach's ornamentation to J. S. Bach has been raised by Frederick Neumann:

Its [the German school's] headquarters was the Berlin of C. P. E. Bach, Marpurg and Agricola . . . Possibly influenced by the *genius loci* of Prussian militarism, these authors tried to regiment ornamentation into far more definite patterns than had ever before been envisioned. We search in vain for the counterpart to the French, and earlier German, apologies for the inadequacies of printed explanations and gain on the contrary the impression that the new ornament tables mean what they say in a more literal sense than all the preceding ones . . . One of the aspects of this rigidity was the new manner of regulating the precise rhythmical shapes of ornaments . . . However, the full measure of the new rigidity is only reached with C. P. E. Bach's unyielding insistence on the onbeat start of *every* small, symbol-prescribed ornament, regardless of its musical function or harmonic implications.[10]

Neumann is undoubtedly right. For the sake of uniformity and clarity, treatises have always tended to formulate strict rules 'permitting no exceptions'. Occasionally these are absurd and self-contradictory. However, if we read C. P. E. Bach's treatise more carefully, we soon notice that his artistic temperament had the upper hand, for all his apparent strictness. One is tempted to say 'it isn't that bad after all' when one reads that even the most discriminating performers 'without its being actually required, may depart somewhat from the written notes in introducing embellishments and variants' and that 'Such liberties spring not from faltering uncertainty but from a rational sovereignty' when one abandons oneself 'with complete freedom to

---

[8] In *Carl Burneys der Musik Doctors Tagebuch einer musikalischen Reise*, vol. iii, trans. J. J. C. Bode (Hamburg, 1773), p. 199.

[9] E. F. Schmid, 'Bach, C. P. E.', *MGG*, i. 935.   [10] *Ornamentation*, p. 39.

the affection of a piece'.[11] 'Play from the soul, not like a trained bird! A keyboardist of such stamp deserves more praise than other musicians.'[12]

In the eighteenth century a distinction was made between 'essential' and 'arbitrary' embellishments. The essential ornaments (appoggiaturas, trills, mordents, etc.) were expressed by means of symbols. The arbitrary ones, on the other hand, corresponded to our concept of free embellishment and were either improvised on the basis of a melodic skeleton, or written out in small notes.

In Bach the two kinds of embellishment, arbitrary and essential, merge to form an expressive kind of melody that reaches a climax in his embellished chorales. An example is the chorale prelude *O Mensch, bewein dein Sünde groß* from the *Orgel-Büchlein* (Ex. 11.1). This is no longer a series of baroque flourishes or 'topoi', but the personal and moving expression of Bach's art. It may be taken for granted that, as in the case of melismas written out in full, the 'essential' embellishments were intended to preserve the melodic flow and for this reason note-repetitions were to be avoided.

Ex. 11.1. Chorale prelude *O Mensch, bewein dein Sünde groß*, BWV 622, bars 1–2

After examining the very incomplete table of ornaments Bach wrote for his son Wilhelm Friedemann, explaining its significance and the misunderstandings to which it has given rise, and after some general remarks about Bach's method of embellishment, the symbols he employed for ornaments, and so on, the ensuing section will deal separately with the most common ornaments denoted by symbols ('essential' ornaments) in Bach, namely *Pralltriller*, appoggiaturas, *prallende Doppelschläge* (trilled turns),[13] mordents, and trills.

---

[11] *Essay*, p. 387.   [12] *Essay*, p. 150.

[13] The simple turn is dealt with only briefly because it always begins on the auxiliary (as in Haydn and in Mozart) and thus poses no problems. Furthermore, it has been discussed in detail by Emery, Neumann, Fries, and Klotz. Bach's arpeggio is also discussed in Chapters 4 and 18.

The discussion of the *Pralltriller* will take pride of place. The reason for this is straightforward: as we have seen, an execution of this ornament is currently taken for granted which in my opinion is simply 'wrong'. Someone who is intent on contesting a generally held view has to be well armed with arguments if he is to avoid being stamped a mad outsider. These investigations will show that it is above all the works themselves that provide insights into Bach's ornamentational practice. Particular attention must be paid to

written-out ornaments;

different notation of what appears to be the same embellishment in parallel passages (here a degree of caution is advisable, for inconsistency can also be intentional);

passages where the melodic character or the voice-leading suggests a certain execution;

information supplied by Bach's pupils and 'grand-pupils'.

Of course, it would be wrong to expect the results of historical research to be as compelling as a mathematical equation. The correctness of a certain kind of interpretation is always relative. Thus the results are not 'binding' in the mathematical sense, though they can lay claim to some artistic authority. Of course, what appears to me to be 'proof' in this sense may not seem convincing to some readers. But this objection is also valid the other way round. One should be cautious about using phrases such as 'the established execution of an ornament'.

The suggestions for free embellishment in Bach, which could be regarded as part of ornamentation (C. P. E. Bach calls them *willkürliche Manieren*, 'arbitrary ornaments'), are placed at the end because they demand from the performer not only good execution (*executio*), but also creative elaboration (*elaboratio*). Few performers are able to do this today. I hope, however, that through my own embellishments I may awaken and encourage hitherto dormant creative talents.

Quantz associated the two basic types of baroque embellishment, 'arbitrary' and 'essential', with the Italian and French styles:

The Adagio may be viewed in two ways with respect to the manner in which it should be played and embellished; that is, it may be viewed in accordance with the French or the Italian style. The first requires a clean and sustained execution of the air, and embellishment with the essential graces, such as appoggiaturas, whole or half-shakes, mordents, turns, *battemens*, *flattemens*, &c., but no extensive passage-work or significant addition of extempore embellishments. The example in Tab. VI, Fig. 26, played slowly, may serve as a model for playing in this manner. In the second manner, that is, the Italian, extensive artificial graces that accord with the harmony are introduced in the Adagio in addition to the little French embellishments. Here the example in Tables XVII, XVIII, XIX, in which all of these extempore embellishments are directly indicated with notes, may serve as a model; it will be treated more fully below. If the plain air of this example is played with the addition of only the essential graces already frequently named, we have another illustration of the French manner of playing. You will also notice, however, that this manner is inadequate for an Adagio composed in this fashion.[14]

What was Johann Sebastian Bach's view of the matter? He was of course familiar with the difference in styles, something that transpires from the frequent use of the epithets 'French' and 'Italian' in the titles of his keyboard works. However, this should not make us forget that he was a German composer all the same, a fact to which we shall have cause to return. When he arranged or composed works in the Italian style, he normally notated them in the German or French manner, that is, he usually wrote out the arbitrary ornaments in full. The most famous example of an arrangement of this kind with embellishments in the Italian style is the Adagio in D minor, BWV 974/2, after the second movement of an oboe concerto by Alessandro (?) Marcello. Less well known are Bach's arrangements of a sonata by Adam Reinken, BWV 966, and of a Vivaldi violin concerto in G major for harpsichord solo, BWV 973. Ex. 11.2 shows the beginning of the work's second movement of

Ex. 11.2. Vivaldi, Violin Concerto RV 299, and Bach's arrangement as the Harpsichord Concerto in G major, BWV 973: second movement, bars 1–5

---

[14] *On Playing the Flute*, p. 162. See Ex. 19.44.

the latter work in both versions. The fact that Bach usually wrote out embellishments of this kind in his own compositions, that is, that he did not wish them to be improvised by the performer, was the reason why he was criticized by Johann Adolf Scheibe. We shall return to this subject in Chapter 20.

No modern study of Bach's ornamentation can afford to ignore the comprehensive study by Frederick Neumann.[15] Although the greater part of the present study, in particular the section devoted to Bach's ornamentation, was written before the publication of Neumann's book, and my conclusions, which were finalized in 1978, were arrived at independently, I am indebted to Neumann's study insofar as it provided me with a large number of excellent examples that I was able to adduce in support of my views. Furthermore, Neumann's examples were of use in the historical survey. It is certainly gratifying to see that other musicians engaged in musicological research have come to conclusions that resemble my own.

Three virtually self-evident requirements form the basis for the correct understanding of ornamentation. They probably apply not only to the art of musical ornamentation, but also to other areas of life:

1. An ornament must embellish and beautify, that is, it should be beautiful and pleasing.
2. There must be a harmonious relationship between the ornament and the embellished object, and thus it should be light, indeed weightless. A necklace should not be larger than the body it adorns.
3. Although the application of an ornament must be regulated by tradition and compositional convention, it also requires a certain freedom. If a tyrant ordered all women to wear the same jewellery, it would no longer be jewellery, but a uniform.

These three principles will serve as the basis for the following investigations.

[15] *Ornamentation.*

12

The Development of Ornamentation in the Seventeenth and Eighteenth Centuries

INTRODUCTION

If we study the development of ornamentation symbols in the two centuries in which Bach lived, it becomes apparent that the same ornaments sometimes had different names in different provinces or countries, and that, vice versa, the same name could designate ornaments executed in a variety of different ways. This was the state of affairs in the Renaissance, and it did not change significantly in the Baroque era. Treatises written in neighbouring cities, or even in the same city, often contained different explanations of the same ornament. In Caccini's *Le nuove musiche* (printed in Venice in 1601) the modern trill was termed *groppo*.[1] *Trillo*, on the other hand, was Caccini's name for the quilismatic vocal tremolo on one note that was usually notated as in Ex. 12.1. (Bach employed the Caccini-style *trillo*, which was already old-fashioned in his day, only in the laughter aria of the 'Aeolus' Cantata, No. 205.)

Ex. 12.1

Unlike Caccini, Girolamo Diruta, whose treatise *Il Transilvano* was also published in Venice (Part I, 1593, Part II, 1609), only termed the modern trill *groppo* when it had a suffix. Otherwise he used the word *tremolo*. A *Pralltriller* beginning on the main note, which C. P. E. Bach later termed *Schneller*, Diruta called *tremoletto* (see Ex. 12.2).

In seventeenth-century Germany one can trace the use of ornament symbols of Italian and French origin, though these did not always have the same

---

[1] The term *groppo* was still being used in Germany in the 18th cent. However, Bach's cousin Walther (*Musikalisches Lexikon*, p. 292) stated that it was an embellishment on the *penultima* that resembled a turn. It appears in similar guise in Mattheson and Marpurg.

Ex. 12.2. From Neumann, *Ornamentation*, p. 288

meaning they had in Italy and France. This is an important observation, for it tells us that a French sign in Germany often had a similar, but not always exactly the same meaning as in its country of origin. For example, J. S. Bach adopted (from his predecessor Kuhnau?) the sign ⌇ for the slide. A similar sign also existed in France, though it had a completely different significance.

The recital of these facts is intended to emphasize that, whereas Bach's use of French ornament signs is an established fact and in many or the majority of cases the execution was the same or similar to that in France, it has not been demonstrated conclusively that the ornament symbols always had the same significance as in France. Internationally recognized symbols for the most common ornaments came into general use only towards the end of the eighteenth century. This had something to do with the development of music printing: from about 1780 onwards it became possible to print music in larger editions and indeed more cheaply, which in turn led to a decline in the earlier practice of selling manuscript copies. In the nineteenth century the musical world began to agree on the meaning of ornament symbols as a result of the international dissemination of the most common editions.

Another observation on the development of ornamentation in the Baroque era is worth emphasizing. Italy was always regarded to be the country with the most liberal art of embellishment. And yet the terminology used in France until the time of Rousseau tells us that individual taste played an important role in ornamentation. In France the art of ornamentation (not only of vocal, but also of orchestral melodies) was simply termed *goût du chant*, and with regard to ornamentation, *bon goût* was always required.

When we examine the most important ornaments and their development in the Baroque era, it becomes apparent that the appoggiatura, first termed *accentus* and later *Vorschlag*, had a particularly important role in Italian vocal music; that the trill underwent a number of modifications, whereas the mordent remained practically the same; and that the short trill or *Pralltriller* suffered from the fact that until 1750 it usually did not have a clearly defined name. Nor did it have a symbol of its own. In the seventeenth century it was often called *mordent*, and it was a matter of indifference whether the alternating note was above or below the main note. (To this day the terminology has survived in Italy, where the ornaments are called *mordente superiore* and *mordente inferiore*, and in Spain. In Britain the *Pralltriller* is known as the 'inverted mordent'.) At times the *Pralltriller* was considered to be a very short minimal trill, and often as the inversion of the mordent. For this reason alone we must include the longer trill and the mordent, the two closest relatives of the *Pralltriller*, in our investigation.

Ex. 12.3. From Santa Maria, *Libro llamado Arte de tañer Fantasia*

The earliest theoretical description of the *Pralltriller* is found in Fray Tomás de Santa Maria's *Libro llamado Arte de tañer Fantasia* (Valladolid, 1565), an astonishingly 'modern' treatise on how to play the clavichord. Here the *Pralltriller* is termed *quiebro senzillo* (see Ex. 12.3). Thus the claim that the *Pralltriller* did not exist before 1750 is quite wrong. On the contrary, it seems that it is a truly 'primeval ornament'. It occurs in Arab, Indian, and Chinese music, both instrumental and vocal, and appears repeatedly in Béla Bartók's collections of ancient Eastern European and Asian melodies. In vocal music it occurs most frequently in descending stepwise progressions. It even seems to be a fundamental musical instinct to repeat the penultimate note in the form of a short ornament (see Ex. 12.4).[2] Thus this ornament might also be termed *Rückschlag* (back-beat). On the other hand, it is astonishing that its inversion, the mordent, occurs less frequently in ascending lines (Ex. 12.5). It does not seem to lie so well for the voice. This observation may explain why the mordent (*mordente inferiore*) practically fell into oblivion in the Italian music of the next two centuries, which was primarily vocal. When the Italians use the word *mordente* today, they always mean the *mordente superiore*, the *Pralltriller*. The extent to which J. S. Bach thought in terms of Italian concepts, especially in his vocal works, is shown by the fact that he used the mordent only in works for keyboard instruments.[3] An indication that the mordent was less important than the *Pralltriller* is the fact that in German theory it is repeatedly

---

[2] It is perhaps significant that Stravinsky's *Rite of Spring*, an attempt to conjure up primeval rituals, has a *Pralltriller* of this kind in its very first motif:

[3] The same is true of Haydn, who employed mordents only in his early works and only in his piano sonatas at that. In the later Classical period the mordent fell out of fashion completely.

presented as an inversion of the *Pralltriller* (or half-trill, *Schneller*, etc., according to the terminology used). The *Pralltriller* is rarely stated to be the inversion of the mordent. Thus the less important ornament is derived from the more important one, and not vice versa. 'It should be observed that the mordent is the opposite of the *Pralltriller*. The latter may be used only over a descending step, precisely the situation which is unsuited to the mordent. The one element which they have in common is that both may be applied to the interval of a second; ascending in the case of the mordent and descending in the case of the short trill.'[4]

Ex. 12.4

Ex. 12.5

In the two baroque centuries the trill was performed in a number of different ways. Initially it seems to have started on the main note, at least in the case of descending melodic lines. If descriptions of ornaments such as trills, *Pralltriller*, mordents, and so on do not appear before the sixteenth century, this does not mean that they did not exist. They were merely beyond notation, like all diminutions probably of oriental origin.

In a strict sense *Pralltriller* and mordents have very little in common with the long trill. However, since it is well known that in the seventeenth century almost all trills began on the main note, it is understandable that theorists often termed the *Pralltriller* a short trill and the mordent an inverted short or long trill. This derivation of the other ornaments from the trill became a problem only when the longer trills began on the upper auxiliary, whereas *Pralltriller* and mordents still began on the main note. The confusion that resulted from this divergent development has continued to this day.

In the following account of the development of ornaments up to the time of Bach a distinction is drawn between Italian and French practice, and that of the increasingly independent German musical culture of the age of Schütz. In central Europe the three musical styles were in constant interaction. Many French and even more Italian musicians worked at German courts, and German musicians travelled to study in Italy and France. Sometimes they even settled in one of these countries.

---

[4] C. P. E. Bach, *Essay*, p. 131.

ITALIAN ORNAMENTATION—TRILLS AND *PRALLTRILLER*

The ornamentation of vocal melodies, the embellishment of lute and violin parts, and in particular the adaptation for keyboard instruments of Renaissance works by means of diminutions and embellishments led to a flowering of diminution practice, particularly in Italy, which towards the end of the sixteenth century evidently produced a rank growth of excessive virtuosity. Many composers would have found it difficult to recognize their own works, which were altered beyond belief. Just as Gluck, about 170 years later, was to criticize the practice of embellishment current in his time, there were those before and around 1600 who not only opposed the excessive use of ornamentation and variation, but in fact were concerned to forbid additions and alterations effected by the performers altogether. The strength of this reaction suggests that embellishment practice had indeed led to unwelcome excesses.

In addition to the monodists Bardi, Galilei, and Cavalieri, the opponents of arbitrary variation and embellishment included the organists Luzzaschi and Frescobaldi. On the other hand, we owe to the monodist Caccini, who achieved fame as a virtuoso singer and teacher, precise explanations for a series of desirable 'embellishments'. These could be added at the singer's discretion, and were represented by ornament symbols.

It seems that they helped to awaken an understanding in Germany for the new Italian vocal techniques. In the third volume of his *Syntagma musicum* Praetorius adopted many of the ornament symbols described by Caccini in the preface to his *Nuove musiche* of 1601.

We have already seen that the names of Caccini's ornament symbols do not always coincide with the modern names of the ornaments, or with those which other composers had already given to the same embellishments around 1600. Dadelsen[5] and Neumann[6] point out that Cavalieri's preface to *Rappresentatione di anima, et di corpo* contains what is probably the first table of ornaments in the modern sense of the word (see Ex. 12.6; 'm' and 'Monachina' signifies a mordent). The sign *t* for trill remained in use well into the eighteenth century. J. S. Bach usually wrote *t* instead of *tr*.

Ex. 12.6. After Cavalieri, *Rappresentatione di anima, et di corpo*, preface

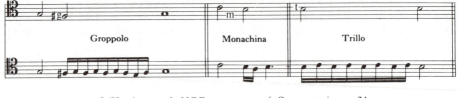

[5] 'Verzierungen', *MGG*.   [6] *Ornamentation*, p. 24.

Diruta's organ treatise also makes use of letters as symbols for small embellishments (*Manieren,* ornaments): G = *groppo,* T = *tremolo* (trill), A = *accento* (appoggiatura), M = *minuta.* Of these signs, Frescobaldi only employed the symbols *t* and *tr* to indicate where trills were to be added. However, Frescobaldi probably wrote out in large notes most of the ornaments required. In particular, the *groppo* (or suffixed trill) on the penultimate note is always written out in full.

Frescobaldi's instructions in the preface to the toccatas[7] are of great importance for the understanding of the rhythmical execution of all long trills. He expressly states that trills are not to be played as metrically notated, but more quickly and with greater freedom. Frescobaldi's reputation rested on his virtuoso organ and harpsichord playing, and in his century he was more famous than any other instrumentalist. As late as 1714 J. S. Bach made a hundred-page manuscript copy of Frescobaldi's *Fiori musicali* (published in 1635), in which he added a note in his own hand showing his ownership. He will have noticed that Frescobaldi was one of the handful of composers who preferred to write out the majority of embellishments in large notes, and it may well have been Frescobaldi who prompted him to do likewise. A close examination of the works of Frescobaldi shows that the majority of his trills begin on the main note. Presumably this was also true of other seventeenth-century Italian composers who, unlike Frescobaldi, did not write out their small ornaments in full, preferring to denote them by means of symbols.

Instead of *tr* Corelli employed a small cross, +, to indicate a trill. In his Op. 5 sonatas of 1703 most of the trills probably began on the auxiliary and not on the main note. However, hard and fast rules on how to begin the trill never existed in Italy; there were numerous exceptions, especially when the flow of the melody made it seem apposite.

It seems that in the eighteenth century the Italians still tended to prefer the main-note trill, though under the influence of French (and German) theorists they often paid lip-service to the auxiliary trill on the few occasions on which the treatises examined this problem. The discrepancy is seen most clearly in the case of Tartini. About 1750, in his *Regole per arrivare a saper suonar il violino*[8] he states that trills should begin on the auxiliary. Yet in his famous letter to Signora Maddalena Lombardini he expressly calls for main-note trills.[9]

A famous and important treatise by the eminent castrato Pier Francesco Tosi was written during Bach's lifetime. *Opinioni de' cantori antichi e moderni, o sieno Osservazioni sopra il canto figurato* was published in Bologna in 1723. Twenty years later an inadequate English translation by Galliard was

[7] Rome, 1615–16.
[8] MS, ed. E. R. Jacobi (with fac.) in *Traité des agréments de la musique* (Celle and New York, 1961), pp. 74 ff. (pp. 10 ff. of orig.).
[9] *Regole,* pp. 130 ff.

published in London,[10] and in 1757 a good German translation by Johann Friedrich Agricola in Berlin under the title *Anleitung zur Singekunst*. Unfortunately, Tosi's book contains no music examples. Agricola added his own comments and music examples to the *Opinioni*, thereby expanding the book to more than three times its original length.[11] However, his explanations often have little to do with the original, and reflect an attitude prevalent in Berlin around 1750. We shall return to this below.

Tosi described eight different kinds of trill, of which the long *trillo maggiore*, the *mezzo trillo*, and the *mordente* are of particular interest. Although he does not mention the beginning of the trill, he often seems to imply that it started on the main note. This may be deduced from the following remarks:

1. A trill may (but does not have to) begin with a 'support' (i.e. with an upper appoggiatura).
2. In the *trillo maggiore*, the main note (*tuono principale*) is heard more clearly than the upper auxiliary (*tuono ausiliare*).

Tosi's fourth, 'ascending' trill almost sounds modern. Beginning with a vibrato, the trill widens through an eighth-tone, a quarter-tone and a semitone until a whole tone is reached. This gradual increase cannot be expressed in musical notation.[12]

Tosi's *mezzo trillo* (literally 'half-trill') comes to a stop after a few alternations, which are quicker than in the long trill, and is given a little 'shine' (*brillante*) before it comes to an end. 'For this reason, this shake pleased more in brisk and lively Airs than in the Pathetick.'[13] It is thus a trill with a *point d'arrêt* (or halt) more or less half-way through the note, not a *Pralltriller*, as Agricola incorrectly assumed. But this translator's error is easy to explain, because in German until around 1750 the term 'half-trill' was employed for the *Pralltriller*, for which there was no separate term at the time.

Tosi's eighth trill is the *mordente*,

which is a pleasing Grace in Singing, and is taught rather by Nature than by art. This is produced with more Velocity than the others, and is no sooner born but dies. That Singer has a great advantage who from time to time mixes it in Passages or Divisions (of which I shall take Notice in the proper chapter). He, who understands his Profession, rarely fails of using it after the Appoggiatura.[14]

Of the 'divisions' (or coloratura) mentioned here Tosi says elsewhere that there are ascending and descending stepwise ones in addition to those 'that are

---

[10] *Observations on the Florid Song* (1742).

[11] Fac. edns. of both Tosi's *Opinioni* and Agricola's *Anleitung* ed. E. R. Jacobi (Celle, 1966).

[12] However, in his Eng. trans. Galliard provided a wholly abstruse music ex. which has nothing to do with Tosi's description. It looks like a study for a chromatic Chopin *étude*. The ex. shows that Galliard had totally misunderstood his master. Thus Robert Donington errs when, in *Baroque Music* (p. 129), he describes the music exx. in this trans. as typical for Tosi and 'correctly added'.

[13] Trans. Galliard, p. 45; trans. Agricola, p. 101.

[14] Trans. Galliard, p. 47; trans Agricola, pp. 102 f.

of difficult Intervals . . . Of all the Instructions relating to Divisions, The most considerable seems to be That, which teaches to unite the Beats and short Shake [i.e. *Pralltriller*] with them; and that the Master point out to him, how to execute them with Exactness of Time, and the Places where they have the best Effect.'[15] In a footnote Agricola wrongly declares the *mordente* to be an appoggiatura, whereas Tosi clearly considered the *mordente* to be a *Pralltriller*. Tosi's description means that this ornament 'taught rather by Nature' can only be as in Ex. 12.7. As we have seen, the word *mordente* (from *mordere*, to bite) does not mean the same in Italian as in German. The Italian mordent 'bites' upwards, the German mordent downwards. The mordent with the lower auxiliary, which never occurred in eighteenth-century Italian singing practice, and only rarely in instrumental music, is today, as we have seen, termed *mordente inferiore* in Italy.

Ex. 12.7

Neumann adduces numerous examples which show quite clearly that eighteeth-century Italian composers also began the majority of their long trills on the main note. Exx. 12.8 and 12.9 show these. Of interest is Scarlatti's notation of trills with very short appoggiaturas in the A minor Sonata K. 7 (L. 379, *Essercizi*, No. 7). Even if the trills in bars 3 and 5 should be applied to the imitation in the bass, as Kirkpatrick suggests in his edition, one wonders why Scarlatti notated about a dozen such appoggiaturas in this sonata— unless, of course, he considered the main-note beginning to be the norm (see Ex. 12.10). The notation of such appoggiaturas would have been completely superfluous if trills at the time always began on the auxiliary, as is often claimed and taught today. However, it seems more than likely that Maestro Domenico did not adhere to rules formulated in France and North Germany, of which he was probably unaware.

Ex. 12.8. From Vivaldi, Concerto del Gardellino, F XII/9, RV 428, after Neumann, *Ornamentation*, p. 355

Incidentally, such short appoggiaturas with trills do not only occur in Domenico Scarlatti. Other eighteenth-century Italian composers also wrote appoggiaturas of this kind, for instance the harpsichordist Giuseppe Paladini,

[15] Trans. Galliard, pp. 54 f; trans. Agricola, pp.129 f.

who worked at La Scala in Milan. In the second movement of his
Divertimento in D major, composed about 1740, he notated such appoggiaturas
before trills (in bars 9–14), whereas other trills were notated without
appoggiaturas (bars 15, 19), presumably because they began on the main note.
Similar examples also occur in the music of J. S. Bach (see p. 374).

Ex. 12.9. D. Scarlatti, Sonata K. 119, bars 34–5, after Neumann, *Ornamentation*,
p. 353

Ex. 12.10. D. Scarlatti, Sonata in A minor, K. 7, bars 1–8

In Scarlatti's Sonata K. 7, L. 379 there is a trill sign which, according to
Neumann, could also be interpreted as a mordent (see Ex. 12.11). The
practical musician is immediately convinced by Neumann's argument.

Ex. 12.11. D. Scarlatti, Sonata K. 7, bars 72–3, after Neumann, *Ornamentation*,
p. 354

The German and French mordent sign ⟋⟍ was not in use in Italy and thus
never occurs in Scarlatti. It is quite possible that when Scarlatti wrote 'tr',
he occasionally meant a mordent. However, this could also mean an 'ascending

trill' or an inverted turn B–C–D (on the beat, of course). As in Haydn and Mozart, the meaning of the ornament signs was fairly fluid and to a certain extent left to the discretion of the performer. However, in Scarlatti's E major Sonata K. 135, the mordent would seem to be the only possibility in bar 56 (Ex. 12.12) and in bar 60.

Ex. 12.12. D. Scarlatti, Sonata K. 135, bars 53–6

As the eighteenth century progressed the practice of beginning the trill on the auxiliary gained the upper hand, even in Italy. From Geminiani (1751) to Clementi (*c.*1800) several Italian authors demand this execution. However, they acknowledged some exceptions. Clementi required the trill to begin on the main note when the trill was preceded by the upper or lower auxiliary. Moreover, in Clementi the *Pralltriller* (half-shake) always began on the main note, and consisted of only three notes. However, not all theorists were in favour of beginning on the auxiliary. In his *Regole armoniche o sieno Precetti ragionati per apprendere i principii della musica*, published in Venice in 1775, Vincenzo Manfredini provided only a short explanation for the trill (see Ex. 12.13). Neumann pointed out that in Vincenzo Panerai's treatise, *Principi di musica* (*c.*1750–80), the trill also began on the main note (see Ex. 12.14).[16]

Ex. 12.13. Manfredini 1775, explanation of the trill

---

[16] *Ornamentation*, p. 350.

Ex. 12.14. From Panerai, *Principi di musica*

THE TRILL AND THE MORDENT IN FRANCE IN THE SEVENTEENTH AND EIGHTEENTH CENTURIES

Towards the end of the seventeenth century a main-note trill preceded by an anticipatory auxiliary note seems to have been common practice in French vocal music. Neumann adduces numerous examples, including that shown in Ex. 12.15 ('x' signifies a trill).[17] In his *Méthode claire, certaine et facile pour apprendre à chanter la musique* (Paris, 1683) Jean Rousseau (not to be confused with Jean-Jacques Rousseau) sanctions practically every kind of trill beginning on the main and auxiliary notes with long or short appoggiaturas.

Ex. 12.15. After Neumann, *Ornamentation*, pp. 247 ff. Bénigne de Bacilly, *Second livre d'airs* (1664)

On the other hand, from the first volume of Chambonnières' *Pièces de clavessin* (1670) onwards, beginning on the auxiliary was stipulated in music for keyboard instruments (see Ex. 12.16). Similar examples are also found in d'Anglebert (1689), whose table of ornaments was known to J. S. Bach, and in Saint-Lambert (1702) and others.

Ex. 12.16. After Neumann, *Ornamentation*, p. 259

In order to understand the French trill without a suffix it is important to consider the *point d'arrêt* (or halt) at the end, a short moment of repose before the arrival of the next note.[18] Ex. 12.17 shows some examples; the upper stem

---

[17] *Ornamentation*, pp. 247 ff.

[18] See Klotz, *Ornamentik*, pp. 13–16, 24 ff., 39, 57, and Table XXIV. *Inter alia*, Klotz quotes exx. from Chambonnières (1670) and André Raison (1688).

Ex. 12.17. Jean-Henri D'Anglebert (1689). After Brunold, *Traité des Signes*, p. 53

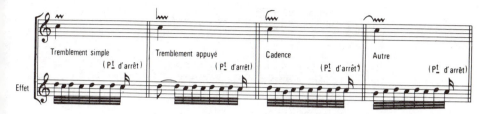

and the bracketed term *point d'arrêt* are not in the originals, but derive from tradition and the literal explanations provided in the tutors.[19]

The suffixed trill could be played in two ways, with and without a *point d'arrêt* before the suffix. For example, Pierre-Claude Foucquet describes the latter as *tremblement ouvert* (see Ex. 12.18). The version with a *point d'arrêt* (or halt) before the suffix also occurs in J. S. Bach, for instance in the E minor Prelude of *WTC* I, bars 10 and 12 (see Ex. 12.19). The Corrente of the A minor Partita, bar 17, should probably be played in a similar manner (Ex. 12.20). Performing the semiquaver suffixes as demisemiquavers (or faster still!) was common baroque 'French' practice (see the French Overture, BWV 831, first movement, bar 9, and the notation of the earlier version, BWV 831*a*). However, the flowing incorporation of the suffix is more common, and corresponds to the later classical execution. For example, it is described by Jean-Philippe Rameau in his second book of *Pièces de clavecin* (1731; see Ex. 12.21). In practice, for instance in Rameau's *Les Tourbillons*, this sounds as in Ex. 12.22.

Ex. 12.18. From Foucquet, *Méthode pour apprendre la manière de se servir des agréments utiles à la propriété des pièces de clavecin* (Paris, n.d. [c.1750])

With regard to J. S. Bach, the 'chopped-off' version described by Foucquet is primarily appropriate in French overtures and in similarly rhythmicized sarabandes, with their characteristic break before the short iambic notes at the end of the bar. The 'flowing' version is appropriate for cantabile pieces.

---

[19] See Paul Brunold, 'Observations essentielles', *Traité des signes et agréments employés par les clavecinistes français des XVIIe et XVIIIe siècles* (Lyons, 1925; reprint, Paris, 1986), p. 7.

Ex. 12.19. *WTC* I, Prelude in E minor, bars 12–13

Ex. 12.20. Partita No. 3, BWV 827, Corrente, bars 17–18

Ex. 12.21. Rameau, *Pièces de clavecin*, Book 2

Ex. 12.22. Rameau, 'Les Tourbillons': execution after Brunold, *Traité des signes*, p. 15

Rameau, Bach's great and underestimated contemporary, published two ornamentation tables. A short table appears in his first collection of *Pièces de clavecin* (Paris, 1706; see Ex. 12.23). A longer table was published in the editions of *Pièces de clavessin* of 1724 and 1731. It differs from the first only with regard to *pincé* and *port de voix*.[20] Facsimiles of both tables are given here on account of their importance; for the later one, see Ex. 12.24.

---

[20] Brunold (*Traité des signes*, pp.19, 58) interprets the difference as an engraver's error in the 1706 edn. In the 3rd ex. of the 1706 table the 2nd b should really be a quaver.

Ex. 12.23. From Rameau, *Pièces de clavecin*, Book 1, table of ornaments

Ex. 12.24. From Rameau, *Pièces de clavecin*, Book 2, table of ornaments

Translated into modern notation Ex. 12.24 reads as follows:

Slur   Execution   A slur embracing two   signifies that one may
                                 different notes, e.g.   only lift the finger from
                                                                the first note after the
                                                                second has been struck.

A note tied to one with a trill or a mordent serves as the beginning of these two ornaments.

Example   Execution

A slur over several notes signifies that all have to be held from one end of the slur to the other from the moment they have been struck.

Example   Execution

The thumb 1 should be in the middle of this *batterie*.

One can only admire the consistency with which for a whole century the French began each trill on the upper auxiliary, at least in theory. It is hardly possible to call this execution into question.[21] The sole exception, which was more common than one might suppose, occurred in the case of descending legato lines (see Exx. 12.22–4). This exception was particularly important when the note preceding the trill was a dissonance, because for centuries the legato link between a dissonant note and its resolution was a fundamental premiss of European music.

It is surely no accident that the practice of beginning the trill on the upper auxiliary was first introduced by French harpsichordists, thence embarking on its triumphal progress through European music. On the harpsichord, which cannot accent or emphasize a note by means of dynamics, beginning with a dissonance rather than a consonance sounds more brilliant. Furthermore, there is the fact that the dissonance increases the number of notes in the case of short, fast trills, which again creates the illusion of an accent. This might also explain the gradual return to the main-note trill as the harpsichord became unfashionable and was replaced by the dynamically more flexible fortepiano. It seems that, in the long run, the auxiliary trill is not as 'pleasing' as the main-note trill.

There are similarities between French practice and eighteenth-century English ornamentation. Some copies of the posthumously published edition of Purcell's *Choice Collection of Lessons for the Harpsichord or Spinnet* (1696) contain four pages of 'Instructions for beginers' (*sic*). These include a table of ornaments that was often reprinted up to around 1720. If we disregard the nomenclature, this table, which probably stemmed from Purcell himself, is largely synonymous with French practice, as described for instance by d'Anglebert in 1689. Certain obvious mistakes committed by the engraver have been convincingly corrected by Howard Ferguson.[22] Here again we find that the trill begins on the upper auxiliary and the *Pralltriller* (backfall and shake) only after a previous, higher note (like the *tremblement appuyé*). A detailed description of English ornamentation has been omitted because, despite the title of the 'English' Suites (which probably did not stem from the composer himself), Bach, as far as is known, was not subject to English influence.

The well-nigh total absence of the *Pralltriller* in French theoretical works is astonishing. It is only occasionally mentioned when discussing vocal works, as

---

[21] It would of course be possible to interpret this adherence to rules as a French peculiarity. See Quantz's comparison of the French and Italians, *On Playing the Flute*, pp. 334 ff., and p. 291 n. 64 below.
[22] *Keyboard Interpretation*, pp.149 ff.

in the case of the *cadence coulée* described by David (1737; Ex. 12.25) and the *cadence feinte* described by the Abbé Duval (1764; Ex. 12.26). In instrumental music the *Pralltriller* most closely approximates to Foucquet's *tremblement diézé* and *bémolisé* (see Ex. 12.27).

Ex. 12.25. From David, after Neumann, *Ornamentation*, p. 83

Ex. 12.26. From Duval, after Neumann, *Ornamentation*, p. 271

Ex. 12.27. From Foucquet, after Brunold, *Traité des signes*, p. 57

The normal *Pralltriller* appears much later, in Père Engramelle, who stated in 1775 that *Pralltriller* and mordents were interchangeable. In his famous book Dom François Bédos de Celles adopted Père Engramelle's account of ornamentation signs (see Ex. 12.28). French mechanical toys of around 1775, such as the keyboard-playing dolls of the Jaquet-Droz brothers, were already playing *Pralltriller* and *Schneller* beginning on the main note (see Ex. 12.29).[23]

---

[23] F. M. Ricci, *Androidi, le meraviglie meccaniche dei celebri Jacquet-Droz* (Milan, 1980), p. 64.

I am convinced that the normal short *Pralltriller* and mordent were often played, long before Père Engramelle and Bédos de Celles, especially when a rapid succession of notes left the player with no other choice. In this connection a discovery made by Kenneth Gilbert is of importance. In the preface to his edition of Couperin he proves that for the trill sign Couperin, like Bach and subsequently his son Carl Philipp Emanuel, made a typographical distinction between long and short wavy lines.[24] The short signs can actually only be executed as *Pralltriller*, as in Ex. 12.30. These are probably the *tremblements arbitraires*, which Couperin otherwise only described verbally: 'Some of them are supported [*appuyés*], others so short that they require neither support nor halt [*point d'arrêt*].'[25]

Ex. 12.28. Bédos, *L'Art du facteur d'orgues*, pt. IV/ii, Table 106

Ex. 12.29

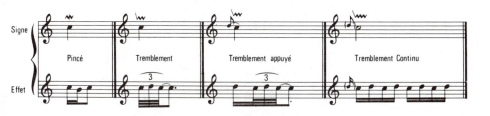

Only the *Schneller*, which is discussed below, does not seem to have been used in France before about 1750.[26] Circumstantial evidence that the French made use of the *Pralltriller* and *Schneller* after 1750 may have been provided by

[24] Prefs. to vol. i, p. xxi, vols. ii–iv, p. v.

[25] Harich-Schneider, *Die Kunst des Cembalospiels*, p. 84.

[26] One could also explain the omission of the *Pralltriller* and the *Schneller* by the unease felt by the authors of tutors when they began a short trill, contrary to their theory, on the main note. In the 19th cent., when Saint-Saëns, lacking such scruples, edited Rameau's harpsichord works for Durand, he suggested numerous *Pralltriller* (or *Schneller*) in the shape of small notes. His commentary to this edn. is still worth reading today, though this does not mean that one has to agree with his interpretations.

Ex. 12.30. Couperin, *Pièces de clavecin*: *a* book 2, ordre 6, 'Les moissonneurs', bars 1–12; *b* book 4, ordre 21, 'La reine des cœurs', bars 23–6

Marpurg. In his (anonymously published) *Kunst das Clavier zu spielen* (4th edn., Berlin, 1762) he also referred to the *Schneller* as *pincé renversé* (inverted mordent). As this term can hardly have come from Germany, it seems to indicate the use of this ornament in France.

Unlike the trill, the mordent (*pincé*) normally began on the main note, which alternated with the one below (see Exx. 12.31–3). The fact that the mordent was not redefined as an inversion of the auxiliary trill is a kind of illogicality that occurs repeatedly in the history of music. Rameau's example of 1706 (see Ex. 12.23, bar 2) is so unusual in French theory before 1750 that it may well be a mistake. In Germany only Quantz described an ornament of this kind,

Ex. 12.31. d'Anglebert (1689)

Ex. 12.32. Couperin

Ex. 12.33. Foucquet

though, as we shall see, he used a different name (*battement*). Later Bédos de Celles refers to the ornament as *pincé simple et détaché* (see Ex. 12.34).

In the preface to *L'Art de toucher le clavecin* François Couperin stipulated as early as 1716 that all trills should begin on the auxiliary. This is wholly in keeping with the French tradition. But in the first volume of *Pièces de clavecin* Paris, 1713) a table of ornaments contains an example of *tremblement continu* that has led to a variety of interpretations (Ex. 12.35). In his study of ornamentation Alfred Kreutz noted that a main-note trill remains after the barline, and that the 'surplus' note of the first bar has to be disposed of

Ex. 12.34. Bédos, *L'Art du facteur d'orgues*, pt. IV/ii, Table 108

Ex. 12.35. From Couperin, *Pièces de clavecin*, book 1

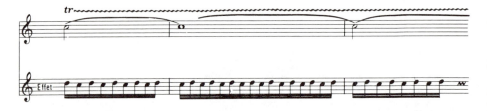

somehow or other.[27] Apart from the first note, this trill is nothing but an exact inversion of the *pincé continu* (see Ex. 12.36). In the case of the trill in the Ex. 12.35 it is a moot point whether a triplet ought somehow to be inserted before the barline or whether the first *d* should be lightly and quickly anticipated (cf. Neumann's 'grace-note trill'). In the light of Quantz's explanation of the trill (he was taught to play the flute by a French musician), Neumann's solution certainly seems plausible.[28]

Ex. 12.36. After Neumann, *Ornamentation*, p. 263 (pincé continu)

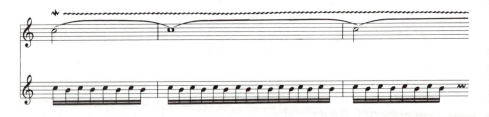

I myself consider that Couperin's long trill shows that he was an outstanding practical musician with a fine ear. In the case of *longer* trills one often notices that, even if the auxiliary is emphasized at the start, the lower note gradually begins to predominate. The laws of gravity seem to be at work. I have noticed the same phenomenon as in the Couperin example in the case of long Beethoven trills, for instance in the third movement of the Fifth Piano Concerto, bars 316–27, or in the second movement of the Piano Sonata Op. 111, bars 106 f. In both cases Beethoven's continuation after the trills shows that he was reckoning with a 'reversal' of this kind. Furthermore, there is an important remark by Couperin, which is very similar to one made by Frescobaldi: 'Although the trills in my first book are notated in equal note-values, they must nevertheless begin more slowly than they end; but this acceleration must be imperceptible.'[29]

---

[27] *Die Ornamentik* p. 5.   [28] See also Neumann, *Ornamentation*, p. 264, music ex.
[29] *L'Art*, p. 23.

Of importance for the understanding of the French way of playing trills is the distinction between detached and slurred trills in the case of descending lines. Couperin distinguishes between the *tremblement détaché* (Ex. 12.37), the *tremblement lié sans être appuyé* (Ex. 12.38), and the *tremblement appuyé et lié* (Ex. 12.39). The version in Ex. 12.38 goes back to d'Anglebert, whereas that in Ex. 12.39 seems more 'modern' (it comes from the second edition of 1717), being given, *inter alia*, by Rameau and J. S. Bach. The ear can hardly detect a difference. Yet it is significant that most of the German theorists after 1750 preferred the older form, because it retained, at least on paper, the auxiliary beginning of the trill considered (by them) to be so important.

Ex. 12.37. Couperin, *L'Art*

Tremblement détaché

Ex. 12.38. Couperin, *L'Art*

Tremblement lié sans être appayé

Ex. 12.39. Couperin, *L'Art*; execution, Neumann, *Ornamentation*, p. 266

Tremblement appayé et lié

The controversy about whether the ornaments in the above examples (Exx. 12.37–9) should be played on the beat or whether they should anticipate it is actually of no importance in this context. Neumann favours anticipation on account of the manner in which they are notated. However, Eta Harich-Schneider pointed out that in addition to consulting the music examples in the

Pièces one should read the explanations provided in *L'Art*, which instruct the performer to play on the beat.[30] Yet Couperin's explanations apply only to the long mordent and to appoggiaturas, not to the trill: 'Every mordent begins on the note on which it is notated. In order to make myself properly understood, I use the expression *point d'arrêt* . . . that is to say, the alternations of the mordent and the note which one is holding must all be contained within the value of the main note. . . . The lost small note of a *port de voix* or a *coulé* must be struck with the harmony, i.e. on the beat on which one should strike the following main note.'[31] On the subject of trills (see Ex. 12.39) he says: 'The trills of some considerable length comprise three aspects that must seem to be one in performance: 1. The support on the upper auxiliary 2. The trill alternations 3. The *point d'arrêt*.'[32]

Two possibilities appear in music examples provided by Dom Bédos de Celles,[33] who seems to be making the best of both worlds (see Ex. 12.40; the missing note in the original at 'Expression' has been added). Some readers will be surprised to learn that even the eighteenth-century French school knew the main-note trill. Neumann cites a number of examples that prove this, for instance by Dandrieu (1724, 1739) and the Belgian Van Helmont (1739; see Ex. 12.41).[34]

Ex. 12.40. Bédos, *L'Art du facteur d'orgues*

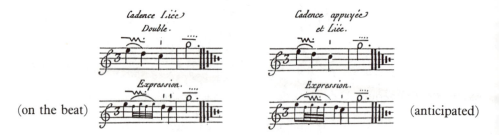

(on the beat)   (anticipated)

Ex. 12.41. Van Helmont, *Fuga prima*, after Neumann, *Ornamentation*, pp. 274 f.

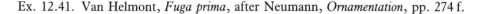

Version with spelled-out ornaments

---

[30] *Die Kunst de Cembalospiels*, pp. 82 f.   [31] *L'Art*, p. 17.
[32] p. 18.   [33] Table 106.   [34] *Ornamentation*, pp. 274 ff.

As we have seen, the *Pralltriller* (*Schneller*) also appears in France towards the end of the century, even in its anticipated form.[35] After about 1790 even the long trill begins with the main note. For example, in a music example in *L'Art de toucher le piano-forte* (1798) Bernard Viguerie only gives the main-note trill.[36] (Was this the reason for the French Revolution?)

TRILLS, *PRALLTRILLER*, AND MORDENTS IN GERMANY

The Thirty Years War (1618–48) had particularly disastrous effects in central Germany, where the population was in many places reduced by half. The terrors of war led the survivors, once they had recovered in economic terms, to espouse religious and cultural values, a phenomenon that is often apparent in post-war periods. In the towns and cities, some of which had been razed to the ground, there was a building boom; in the seventeeth century more new churches were built in Germany than at any time previously. The general upsurge in cultural activity in the second half of the seventeenth century is particularly apparent in the field of music. At no other time in German history was high-quality church and chamber music so widespread. In the decades before and after 1700 all sections of society, in both rural areas and cities, and even in the most humble village church, participated in the growth of musical culture.

At no other time did villages, small towns and small courts spend so much money on music; at no other time did they own and maintain so many instruments; at no other time was the average standard of music-making as high. Even if musical life at this time was a purely German affair, little of which was exported, it was still, in the context of German music history as a whole, on the highest level.[37]

Throughout this period German musicians displayed a great willingness to learn, eagerly seeking to study the achievement of other European countries, particularly that of Italy.

In the seventeenth and eighteenth centuries Italy was the leading musical country in Europe. Italian (and not French) musicians predominated in the orchestras of the German courts (with the exception of a few centres in the north-west such as Celle). Italian music was copied and played more than that of any other nation. Italian virtuosi travelled around Germany, and German musicians sought to study or complete their training in Italy. However much the French fashion in clothes and language began to spread from the time of Louis XIV onwards, until the end of the eighteenth century it was Italy that retained the musical leadership of Europe.

[35] See Neumann, *Ornamentation*, pp. 285 f.
[36] See William S. Newman, 'The Performance of Beethoven's Trills', *Journal of the American Musicological Society*, 29 (1976), 451.
[37] Friedrich Blume, 'Deutschland', *MGG*.

Even before the Thirty Years War German musicians had often travelled to Italy to study or complete their training, often with financial support from the Emperor or the local German prince. Thus Heinrich Schütz went to Venice to study with Gabrieli and Monteverdi, and Froberger received an imperial stipend to study with Frescobaldi in Rome for a year. Johann Joseph Fux, the first German to be appointed First Kapellmeister at the imperial court in Vienna (after a long line of musicians from Italy and the Low Countries), is known to have studied in Padua. Georg Muffat travelled to Corelli in Rome, and both Quantz and Handel spent a number of years studying in Italy. All three also visited France, though, with the exception of Muffat, they only did so for a relatively short time. Other composers who were drawn to Italy included Hasse, who almost ended up becoming an Italian, Gluck, J. S. Bach's youngest son Johann Christian, and Mozart.

The third volume of Michael Praetorius's widely read *Syntagma musicum*, which was published in Wolfenbüttel in 1619, contains symbols and explanations for a number of ornaments. Praetorius almost always referred to Caccini's *Nuove musiche*. But as other German theorists selected other Italian or German models the confusion with regard to concepts and terminology that had obtained in Italy around 1600 was perpetuated in German-speaking countries. In the seventeenth century the ornaments themselves, at least in southern and central Germany, corresponded to the contemporary Italian performance practice. In Dresden Schütz's pupil Christoph Bernhard compiled an interesting account of contemporary German vocal performance practice, which reflects the powerful Italian influence quite clearly. Neumann has pointed out that Wolfgang Caspar Printz in his various publications, which appeared mainly in Dresden and Leipzig between 1677 and 1714, also presented the old Italian ornaments, though in part he provided a new terminology for them. In Printz the terms *accentus* and *figura corta* are used to describe the *Pralltriller* and the mordent (see Ex. 12.42). At this time the trill and the *groppo* (or suffixed trill) almost always began on the main note. Some German theorists still made use of Printz's terminology at the beginning of the eighteenth century, that is, after 1700. Neumann points out that trills, *Pralltriller*, and mordents beginning on the main note are described by, among others, Franz Xaver Murschhauser (1703: Ex. 12.43) Johann Samuel Beyer (1703 and 1730), and Martin Heinrich Fuhrmann (1706, Ex. 12.44; 1715).[38] Thus it is not surprising that most German organists in the seventeenth and early eighteenth centuries evidently used main-note trills (and *Pralltriller*) almost exclusively. Frescobaldi's pupils Johann Jakob Froberger and Johann Kaspar Kerll wrote out trills in full, as their teacher had done, whereas Johann Pachelbel and others employed trill symbols. However, the use of embellishment symbols in northern and central Germany followed no single

---

[38] *Ornamentation*, pp. 302 f.

Ex. 12.42. From Printz, after Neumann, *Ornamentation*, p. 300

Accentus

Figura corta

Ex. 12.43. From Murschhauser, after Neumann, *Ornamentation*, pp. 302 ff.

Ex. 12.44. From Fuhrmann, after Neumann, *Ornamentation*, pp. 302 ff.

Trillo
tr

standardized pattern. At times the influence of the English virginalists still made itself felt in northern Germany, though from the end of the seventeenth century onwards that of France becomes noticeable (Georg Muffat, Johann Caspar Ferdinand Fischer). German organists developed a tradition of their own. Composers such as Buxtehude, Vincent Lübeck, and Georg Böhm probably construed their symbols similarly, and with only minute deviations. Perhaps also Kuhnau, who used some of his own symbols such as / or \ for the *accentus* (appoggiatura) and ⁄⁄ for the mordent. Reinken used two (straight) lines || for a (long?) main-note trill, and an X for the mordent with several alternations. It seems that even after 1700 the German organists continued to begin most trills on the main note. The French auxiliary trill was only occasionally propagated and applied. Neumann adduces a convincing example of why Dietrich Buxtehude (1637–1707) probably considered it normal to begin the trill on the main note (Ex. 12.45). In Buxtehude the *Pralltriller* in

Ex. 12.45. From Buxtehude, Fugue in E, after Neumann, *Ornamentation*, p. 308

'trillo longo'

the Exx. 12.46 and 12.47 probably begin on the main note—otherwise there would be 'forbidden' consecutive fifths.

Ex. 12.46. From Buxtehude, *Preludium con pedale*, after Neumann, *Ornamentation*, p. 308

Ex. 12.47. From Buxtehude, *Vater unser*, after Neumann, *Ornamentation*, p. 308

According to the 'Nekrolog' and a communication from C. P. E. Bach to his father's biographer, Forkel, J. S. Bach studied the works of these masters in his youth. Apart from this the journey on foot to Lübeck in order to hear Buxtehude says much about his great interest in this German composer's art of organ playing. O'Donnell is surely right when he remarks:[39]

Presently it is common to hear performances of 17th century German music with trills beginning invariably on the upper auxiliary. Except where French influence is evident, as in the works of Georg Muffat, such practice is contrary to all evidence. Even where a proliferation of French ornamentation signs occur, as in such an isolated instance as Bruhns's organ chorale-fantasia *Nun komm der Heiden Heiland*, this cannot be taken as proof of French practice. The parallels resulting from an upper-note start to the trill in bar 30 and elsewhere would never have been tolerated; this trill, and other trills in the work, must be interpreted in the traditional 17th century German manner:

An important contemporary of Bach, the theorist and composer Johann David Heinichen (1683–1729), has in the past tended to be neglected. However, the mere fact that two of his works, the *Fantasie* for harpsichord, BWV Anh. 179, and the *Kleines harmonisches Labyrinth* for organ, BWV 591, were for a long time erroneously ascribed to Bach[40] suggests that we ought to

---

[39] 'Bach's Trills' p. 17.
[40] See G. Hausswald, 'Heinichen, Johann David', *MGG*, vi. 46 f.

take him more seriously. In 1696 he entered St Thomas's School in Leipzig, where he was taught by Schelle and Kuhnau. In 1702 he began to study law at Leipzig University, but he soon devoted himself entirely to music, having taught music theory for some time previously. In 1709 he began to direct a collegium musicum in Leipzig; he also wrote operas for Leipzig and Weissenfels and completed his first theoretical work, *Neu erfundene und gründliche Anweisung*.[41] After a lengthy sojourn in Italy, where he stayed until 1716, meeting Vivaldi, Francesco Gasparini, and other musicians in Venice and witnessing successful performances of two operas, he returned to become Kapellmeister in Dresden (1717). Presumably he had met Bach by 1720 at the latest. At this time he engaged in a correspondence with Mattheson. His main theoretical work, the revised major thorough-bass school entitled *Der General-Baß in der Composition*, was published in Dresden in 1728. It is doubtless one of the most important theoretical works of the eighteenth century, and Bach himself accepted responsibility for selling the book in Leipzig.

Heinichen's treatise contains a chapter on ornamentation, from which the epigraph to Part II of this book is taken. It is relatively short, but contains some valuable information. The trills (which Heinichen obviously assumed were fairly familiar to his readers) are unfortunately dealt with rather briefly. Of importance to us are his remarks about the mordent.

§10. The mordent (or mordant, as people say) is also a well-known embellishment, but the following paragraphs will show that there is more to it than meets the eye, and that it must thus be examined more carefully. One speaks of a mordent when one plays a note almost at the same time as the one a semitone or a tone below, though releasing the latter immediately in order to remain on the main note. This execution can take three different forms.

§11. Taking as an example a mordent that is to be played on c^2, then one can play the semitone b^1 immediately below either

1. before it, adding the c^2 at almost the same tempo, but releasing the b^1 immediately, or
2. the c^2 is struck first, immediately followed by the b^1, and at the same tempo one returns to the first c^2 so quickly that all three notes impart as it were a single accent to the c^2. But this accent
3. some tend to repeat once or several times in the case of slow notes, playing as it were a half-trill below.[42]

This may well be the first time in the German literature that the mordent was described as an inversion of the half-trill ('a half-trill below'). Of course, Heinichen means a short trill with at least two alternations. Yet the main-note beginning clearly transpires from the description of the half-trill It may be

---

[41] *Neu erfundene und gründliche Anweisung . . . zu vollkommener Erlernung des General-Basses* (Hamburg, 1711).

[42] *Der General-Baß*, pp. 529 f.

assumed that, depending on the musical context, there were also a number of shorter half-trills. Perhaps this is even the case in the Ex. 12.48. Heinichen

Ex. 12.48. From Heinichen. *General-Baß*, p. 525

was also familiar with the slide ('die bekannte Schleiffung'), using Kuhnau's symbol, which was also adopted by Bach. He makes a point of advising against using the ornament where it 'leads to consecutive octaves and fifths with the bass'.[43] The accompanying music example shows such incorrect voice-leading. It demonstrates that, unlike the French, Heinichen considered this to be an up-beat ornament.

The auxiliary trill first came into use in Germany shortly before 1700, evidently as a result of French influence. In 1696 Johann Caspar Fischer, in *Musikalisches Blumen-Büschlein* (Augsburg),[44] provided the instructions quoted in Ex. 12.49. His successors included Johann Gottfried Walther (1708) and Georg Muffat's son, Gottlieb Muffat, who was active in Vienna. The latter's *Componimenti musicali per il cembalo* (Augsburg, n.d.) contains the table of ornaments quoted in Ex. 12.50. At this time French influence began to make itself felt in Vienna as a result of the marriage of Maria Theresia and Franz Stephan of Lorraine. This is reflected in the fact that the language of the court changed from Italian to French (though this was officially proclaimed only on the accession of Maria Theresia in 1740).

Ex. 12.49. From Fischer, *Musikalisches Blumen-Büschlein*, after Neumann, *Ornamentation*, p. 304

In conclusion, it should be emphasized once more that the non-uniform use of ornaments and symbols in Germany in the age of Bach makes it impossible in Bach's case to presuppose a one-sided adherence to French rules. Bach

---

[43] *Der General-Baß*, p. 527.
[44] The 2nd edn. of *Les Pièces de clavessin*, Op. 2 (Schlackenwerth, 1696).

grew up in the tradition of German organ playing, and thus Neumann is quite right to say that it is wholly unrealistic to claim that the French style replaced the old German tradition *at one fell swoop*.[45] This would contradict all historical and sociological experience.

Ex. 12.50. From Gottlieb Muffat, *Componimenti musicali*, after Neumann, *Ornamentation*, p. 365

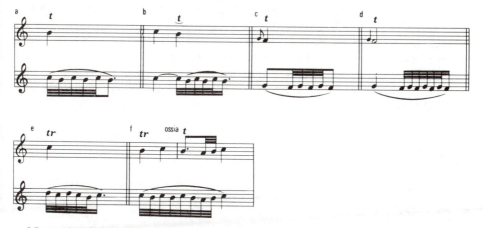

No early eighteenth-century German composer could of course predict that twentieth-century performers would misunderstand the German tradition's differing use of Italian, French, and German symbols, and that they would *automatically and without exception* execute trill and half-trill signs in the style of French clavecinistes.

C. P. E. BACH'S TREATISE

C. P. E. Bach's *Versuch über die wahre Art, das Clavier zu spielen* (*Essay on the True Art of Playing Keyboard Instruments*) is a key work for the understanding of eighteenth-century German music, including most of the music of J. S. Bach. On a number of occasions the author expressly refers to his father.[46] The modest title, *Essay*, conceals the fact that this is a comprehensive manual on keyboard playing, performance practice, figured bass, improvisation, and other matters. The title and some of the ideas no doubt derive from J. J. Quantz's *Versuch einer Anweisung, die Flöte traversière zu spielen* (*On Playing the Flute*), which was published a year earlier. Like C. P. E. Bach, Quantz worked at the court of Frederick the Great in Berlin. Up to the time of Beethoven, the *Essay* was used for keyboard and theoretical tuition, and often imitated. Part I was published in Berlin in 1753, going through three further

---

[45] *Ornamentation*, p. 309. [46] pp. 40, 42, 181, 426.

editions in C. P. E. Bach's lifetime.[47] Part II appeared in 1762 and was reprinted twice. In 1797 a posthumous edition of the whole *Essay* was published. During his lifetime C. P. E. Bach was more famous than his father, and around 1770 he was referred to as 'the great Bach'. It is an irony of fate that his fame rests more on his treatise—which he probably considered to be a by-product—than on his compositions. Even today, many of his oratorios, cantatas, and keyboard concertos have not been published.

The part of C. P. E. Bach's treatise that is of particular interest in the context of the present study is the long section devoted to ornamentation, above all his remarks about the trill and the *Pralltriller*. In Part I of the *Essay* he states that the normal (long) trill always begins on the upper note, the 'auxiliary' (see Ex. 12.51). Thus it was superfluous to indicate its beginning by means of a small note (as in Ex. 12.51*f*), unless a *long* appoggiatura was intended.[48]

Ex. 12.51. From C. P. E. Bach, *Essay*, p. 100. Below, *Essay*, p. 101, C. P. E. Bach explains the suffixed trill.

Like his father, C. P. E. Bach used the *tr* sign and the wavy line in current use in central Europe. The execution of the suffixed trill in *a* of the second system (with the irrational number of ten alternations) is similar to that of his father and of Rameau (see p. 267). He states that the versions notated in the second system under *b* and *c* indicate the same execution as *a*. If we are right in assuming that C. P. E. Bach largely followed the practice of his 'sole teacher', then his father may have preferred to execute trills in the French manner, at least in the second half of his life. However, the notion that this rule applies to Johann Sebastian Bach without exception is a modern fallacy, as we shall see.

In spite of a relatively comprehensive treatment of the subject, the *Essay* fails to discuss certain characteristic aspects of contemporary trill practice. For example, C. P. E. Bach does not mention the halt (*point d'arrêt*), though

[47] 1759, 1780 (unchanged, though it corrects printing errors), 1787 (with additions). New edns. of Part II appeared in 1780 and 1787.
[48] *Essay*, p.100. In Ex. 12.51*d* C. P. E. Bach departs from his main rule. According to his later description of the 'ascending trill' the trill here begins on the main note, d^2, and not on e^2.

he later makes a passing reference to it in a music example (see below, Ex. 12.52). Conversely, he mentions the tied trill (*cadence appuyée*) only in the text, without explaining its execution. Of importance is the remark that the alternations 'must be uniform and rapid', and that a 'rapid trill is always preferable to a slow one'. Trills over long notes always have a suffix, which 'must be played as rapidly as the trill proper', because a 'limp' suffix is 'ugly'.[49] The treatise does not mention the gradual acceleration of long trills found in Frescobaldi, Saint-Lambert, or Couperin.

The description of the 'ascending trill' is of interest:

Ex. 12.52. From C. P. E. Bach, *Essay*, p. 107

Because, aside from the keyboard, this symbol is not widely known, it is often notated in the manner of the asterisked examples; or the general abbreviation tr is written, the choice of trill being left to the *discretion* of the performer.[50]

Such 'discretion' is hardly ever in evidence today. The first of the asterisked trills is, surprisingly, a main-note trill, one of C. P. E. Bach's many inconsistencies.

Also of importance are the remarks concerning the execution of the trill over ascending dotted notes, where a (short) halt (or *point d'arrêt*) is required and a suffix advisable. C. P. E. Bach gives the 'approximate' execution quoted in Ex. 12.53, and makes a point of stating that the note separated from the suffix is to be played shorter than notated.[51] In J. S. Bach this execution is advisable in many trills over dotted notes.

Ex. 12.53. From C. P. E. Bach, *Essay*, p. 103

For the *Pralltriller*, which previous theorists had described as 'half-trill' or 'short trill', C. P. E. Bach invented the term still used today, and for this ornament made systematic use of the short zigzag line that previously had also been employed for the long trill. Originally all trill symbols (*tr*, ∿, ∿∿) could signify short and long trills depending on the musical context. (The symbols for short and long trills continued to be interchangeable even at the end of the eighteenth century. Thus Mozart, even in his late piano works, often writes *tr* where only a *Pralltriller* or *Schneller* (see below) is possible.)

---

[49] *Essay*, pp. 103 f.   [50] *Essay*, p.107 (my italics).

[51] *Essay*, pp. 103–4: 'Its length is dependent on the tempo; hence the execution of Example g is only approximately suggested by the time value of the last tone of the suffix, for the note following the dot is always shorter in execution than its notated length (a point which will be treated in Chapter III).'

The term *Pralltriller* may in fact have been invented by C. P. E. Bach. However, he did not invent the ornament itself, which has been in existence 'as long as anyone can remember'. Neither C. P. E. Bach nor his successors ever claimed that this was a new ornament which had never been used before. The *Pralltriller* is described thus in the first edition of the *Essay*:[52]

The half trill or *Pralltriller*, which is distinguished from the others by its acuteness and brevity, is notated for the keyboard in the manner of Figure XLV. Included in the figure is an illustration of its exception.

Ex. 12.54. From C. P. E. Bach, *Essay*, p. 110 [original printed version]

C. P. E. Bach continues:

Despite the upper slur, which reaches from the beginning to the end of the example, all notes are played except the last f, which is tied to its preceding tone by another slur which indicates that it must not be struck. The large slur merely specifies the necessary phrasing. . .

§31. This trill joins the preceding note to the decorated one and therefore never appears over detached notes. It represents in miniature an unsuffixed trill introduced by either an appoggiatura or a principal note.[53]

At first sight the above example and the appended commentary seem to suggest that the fifty-year-old 'modern' performance practice is correct, and that Bach's *Pralltriller* should all begin on the auxiliary. Performed as it stands, the first hemidemisemiquaver note g would have to be restruck. Thus the *Pralltriller* would have four notes (including the final one), and would begin on the upper auxiliary.

This version, which was still rejected about seventy years ago as being inappropriate for Bach, has been such a common feature of baroque performance practice in the last fifty years that since about 1950 it has almost become the norm, the 'correct' and 'pleasing' way of executing the ornament. For this reason it will come as a shock to some Bach performers to learn that C. P. E. Bach's description cited above contains a serious printing error. A printing error? How come?

In October 1974, while visiting Rudolf Serkin, my wife and I discovered in his collection a copy of the first edition of the *Essay* with an autograph dedication from C. P. E. Bach to Mademoiselle von Hürlimann. In this copy the above passage is corrected in C. P. E. Bach's own hand (see Fig. 5). It now reads: '. . . all notes are played except the second g and the last f, each of which is tied to its preceding tone by another slur which indicates that it must

---

[52] p. 110. Translation amended.   [53] *Essay*, p. 110. Translation slightly amended.

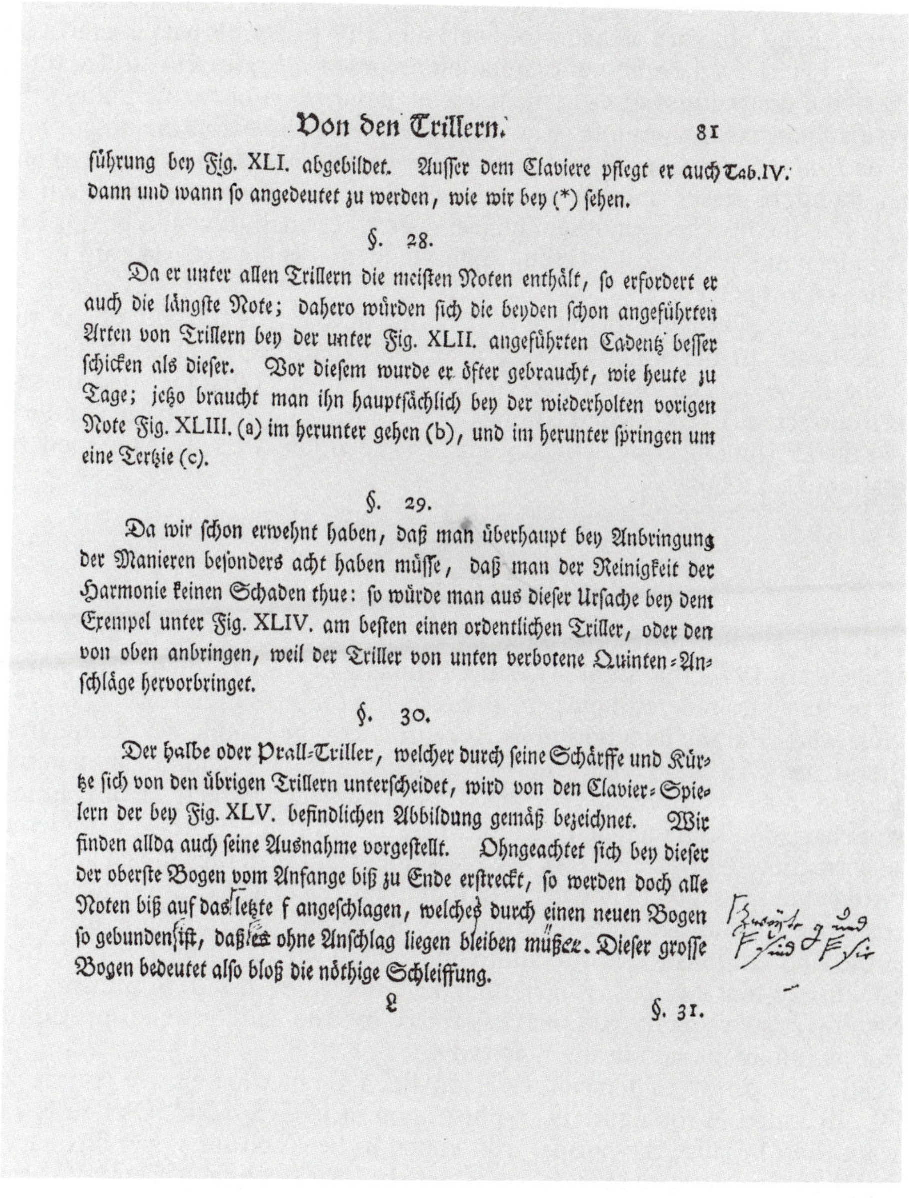

Von den Trillern.   81

führung bey Fig. XLI. abgebildet.   Auſſer dem Claviere pflegt er auch Tab. IV.
dann und wann ſo angedeutet zu werden, wie wir bey (*) ſehen.

§. 28.

Da er unter allen Trillern die meiſten Noten enthält, ſo erfordert er
auch die längſte Note; dahero würden ſich die beyden ſchon angeführten
Arten von Trillern bey der unter Fig. XLII. angeführten Cadentz beſſer
ſchicken als dieſer.   Vor dieſem wurde er öfter gebraucht, wie heute zu
Tage; jetzo braucht man ihn hauptſächlich bey der wiederholten vorigen
Note Fig. XLIII. (a) im herunter gehen (b), und im herunter ſpringen um
eine Tertzie (c).

§. 29.

Da wir ſchon erwehnt haben, daß man überhaupt bey Anbringung
der Manieren beſonders acht haben müſſe, daß man der Reinigkeit der
Harmonie keinen Schaden thue: ſo würde man aus dieſer Urſache bey dem
Exempel unter Fig. XLIV. am beſten einen ordentlichen Triller, oder den
von oben anbringen, weil der Triller von unten verbotene Quinten-An-
ſchläge hervorbringet.

§. 30.

Der halbe oder Prall-Triller, welcher durch ſeine Schärffe und Kür-
tze ſich von den übrigen Trillern unterſcheidet, wird von den Clavier-Spie-
lern der bey Fig. XLV. befindlichen Abbildung gemäß bezeichnet.   Wir
finden allda auch ſeine Ausnahme vorgeſtellt.   Ohngeachtet ſich bey dieſer
der oberſte Bogen vom Anfange biß zu Ende erſtreckt, ſo werden doch alle
Noten biß auf das letzte f angeſchlagen, welches durch einen neuen Bogen
ſo gebunden iſt, daß es ohne Anſchlag liegen bleiben müßet. Dieſer groſſe
Bogen bedeutet alſo bloß die nöthige Schleiffung.

L   §. 31.

Fig. 5. C. P. E. Bach's *Versuch über die wahre Art, das Clavier zu spielen*, vol. i (Berlin, 1753), 81. This signed presentation copy for Mademoiselle von Hürlimann contains holograph corrections by C. P. E. Bach

not be struck.'[54] That we are dealing with a printing error subsequently corrected and not with a change of heart on C. P. E. Bach's part is shown by the fact that the same ambiguous notation occurs in the case of the trilled turn, where the first edition already includes the description of the tie linking the first two notes. Furthermore, it would have been pointless in the description of the *Pralltriller* to note that it 'joins the preceding note to the decorated one and therefore never appears over detached notes'. If in the execution of Ex. 12.54 the first hemidemisemiquaver *g* were restruck, it would be difficult to understand why the preceding note could not be played staccato or be higher or lower.

This correction is all the more remarkable in that it is the only one in the whole book. In the appendix Bach also notes that the list of errata for the 'Probestücke' was no longer necessary in view of the fact that they had already been corrected. In the second edition (1759) of the *Essay* the passage is altered as in the Hürlimann copy. Thus the correct execution of Ex. 12.54 in modern notation is as follows:

In an afterword to the facsimile reprint of the first edition of the *Essay*, published in 1957, the editor, Lothar Hoffmann-Erbrecht, noted: 'The aim of the present facsimile edition is to publish, for the first time since 1797, the whole work and the later additions. It reproduces the original text of the first edition of 1753 and 1762, and, in an appendix, the additional material included in the editions of 1787 and 1797. However, corrections of printing errors have not been included.' Unfortunately Hoffmann-Erbrecht considered the correction of printing errors to be less important than they in fact are. The editor evidently failed to notice the 'minor detail' on page 81. Those using this reprint are thus misled into believing that the incorrect definition is also valid for the later editions. (It is difficult to understand why facsimile reprints often make use of first editions, which often have mistakes, instead of utilizing the second or subsequent editions corrected by the author, and providing information about significant alterations.)

Only now do we understand C. P. E. Bach's somewhat elusive remark in §30: 'Included in the figure is an illustration of its exception'. Obviously he meant that, because the normal trill tended to begin on the upper auxiliary, the *Pralltriller* was an exception which here became the rule. (As far as the ear is concerned, the first note of the ornament is *f*, the main note.)

---

[54] p. 110. Translator's note: the correct version of the *Pralltriller* is given in Mitchell's trans. of the *Essay* (1949), from which the extracts in this book are quoted.

The first 'victim' of the printing error seems to have been Johann Friedrich Agricola, who published a translation of the singing tutor by the Italian Tosi in 1757, four years after the appearance of the *Essay*.[55] He states in the preface that C. P. E. Bach was his model, and in his commentary on Tosi refers on a number of occasions (e.g. p. 61) to the 'great'—that is, C. P. E.—Bach. Whereas Agricola's translation is a good one, his comments, as we have seen, reflect the musical manners of Berlin in 1757 rather than Italian practice of 1723. For example, he provides the following incorrect explanation of Tosi's *mezzotrillo*:

Instrumentalists are apt to call this trill *Pralltriller*. Keyboard players have assigned to it a special symbol that looks like this: ⩗. In notes it could be written thus:

If an appoggiatura precedes a *Pralltriller*, it becomes its first note, so that this does not have to be played afresh.[56]

Copying exactly the mistake in the first edition of the *Essay* (and without referring to Tosi in any way) Agricola would have the performer restrike the preceding higher note, except when this is notated as a (long) appoggiatura. However, C. P. E. Bach never makes a distinction of this kind. He writes,[57]

The *Pralltriller* appears only in a descending second regardless of whether the interval is formed by an appoggiatura or by large notes.

Elsewhere C. P. E. Bach makes a point of stating that appoggiaturas, which can be written in large and small notation, are always joined to the following note 'in the absence as well as the presence of a slur'.[58]

Because the note preceding the *Pralltriller* happens to be in large notation in C. P. E. Bach and not an appoggiatura as in other theorists, Agricola recommended the four-note execution with a repetition of the first note.

[55] *Anleitung*: see p. 260 above.

[56] *Anleitung*, p. 99. One might conceivably say that Agricola, who was a pupil of Bach in his youth, had been instructed differently by him. But this is most unlikely. From 1741 onwards Agricola, as we have seen, was wholly under the influence of C. P. E. Bach and Quantz. Both his compositions and the *Anleitung zur Singekunst* reflect this. His quite isolated view of the *Pralltriller* is refuted not only by the later corrections to the *Essay*, but also by written-out performance instructions of other Bach pupils such as Gerber. Whereas Agricola in his commentaries to the *Anleitung* states that C. P. E. Bach was his model, he refers to J. S. Bach 14 years later (1769) in a controversy about the use of triplets in dotted rhythms. But nowadays Agricola's credibility is being questioned even here (see Albrecht, *Interpretationsfragen*, p. 128).

[57] *Essay* p. 111.   [58] *Essay*, p. 88.

However, his understanding of the embellishment was already criticized in the eighteenth century by Daniel Gottlob Türk.[59] This is in itself most revealing. C. P. E. Bach himself commented on the *Pralltriller* thus:

This trill is the least dispensable, the most attractive, but at the same time the most difficult embellishment. Played incorrectly, either it cannot be heard at all or else it sounds limp and ugly, which are attributes far from its true ones. Unlike other ornaments, it cannot be demonstrated slowly to students. It must literally crackle. In order to be truly effective the upper note must be snapped on its final appearance in the manner described in paragraph 7, but with such exceeding speed that the individual notes will be heard only with difficulty.[60]

Here C. P. E. Bach made an error—obviously he was referring to paragraph 8, not to paragraph 7, which states: 'When the upper note of a trill is given its final performance it is snapped; after the stroke the upper joint of the finger is sharply doubled and drawn off and away from the key as quickly as possible'.[61]

Modern harpsichordists pay too little attention to the 'snap' expressly demanded by C. P. E. Bach, even though this produces a quite charming effect. It is a muscular reflex comparable to the noise made by snapping the thumb and the third or fourth fingers. Try this out on a table-top with the second and third fingers (in a 2–3–2 sequence): the knocking sound made by the third finger must be considerably louder than that of the second. However, the snapping sound can be produced only *once* at this strength. This alone should put paid to the discussion about whether the *Pralltriller* has four or only three notes. The four-note execution usually played nowadays (fingering 3–2–3–2) makes it possible to snap the third finger on the first note, perhaps, but never, as C. P. E. Bach stipulated, on the penultimate note. His description suggests that he knew Tosi's treatise on singing of 1723. Both features—the emphasis on the last upper note of the trill and the fact that a *Pralltriller* should be executed faster than a normal trill—are already present in the *Opinioni de' cantori* (see above, p. 260). Tosi demands the *brillante* on the final note of the *mezzo trillo* and the greater speed of the *mordente*, which, as we have seen above, is the equivalent Italian term for our *Pralltriller*. Agricola translated the word *brillante* rather aptly as 'shimmer'. Another detail of C. P. E. Bach's description also resembles Tosi. Where the latter states that this ornament must be terminated as soon as it has been played, C. P. E. Bach writes: 'it must be played with such speed that the listener will not feel that the note to which it is applied has lost any of its length, but rather that it has entered precisely at the proper moment'.[62]

Thus C. P. E. Bach obviously did not 'invent' the *Pralltriller*. Rather, this is one of the ornaments of which he says in the introduction to his chapter on

---

[59] *Clavierschule*, p. 272.   [60] *Essay*, pp. 110–11.   [61] *Essay*, p. 101.
[62] *Essay*, p. 111.

embellishments: 'most of them have a long and close association with the keyboard and will undoubtedly always remain in favour'.[63]

THE TREATISES OF J. J. QUANTZ AND OTHER GERMAN THEORISTS

Johann Joachim Quantz (1697–1773) was one of the most fascinating musical personalities of the eighteenth century, a true cosmopolitan. Twelve years younger than J. S. Bach, he played nearly every instrument in common use at the time. As a member of the smaller Polish chapel in Dresden he took lessons on the flute from Pierre G. Buffardin; subsequently, in 1728, he joined the larger royal chapel. He also went on a grand tour of Italy in 1725–7, visiting a number of cities, including Naples, Florence, and Venice. Here he met many of the most important composers, including Mancini, Hasse, Alessandro Scarlatti, Vivaldi, Albinoni, and others. Thereafter he lived in Paris for seven months, where he befriended the flautist Michel Blavet. In 1727 he was in London, where he met Tosi and Handel. The latter tried to persuade him to stay in England. In 1741 he was called to the court of Frederick the Great in Berlin, where he received a handsome salary, directed an orchestra, and took part in house concerts with C. P. E. Bach and Franz Benda. His *Versuch einer Anweisung, die Flöte traversière zu spielen* (*On Playing the Flute*) was published in 1752. It reflects his great experience and culture, which were partly the result of his many travels. As might be expected, the book is more cosmopolitan and the view of music slightly 'older' than in the case of C. P. E. Bach's treatise. The lengthy final chapter, 'How a Musician and a Musical Composition Are to Be Judged', is of particular interest. Quantz gives a trenchant description of the Italian, French, and German styles, aspects of which remain true to this day, for example when he says: 'The Italian manner of singing is to be preferred to that of their playing and the French manner of playing to that of their singing.'[64] Quantz praises the German art of playing the organ, adding: 'Finally the admirable Johann Sebastian Bach in more recent times brought it to its greatest perfection'.[65] Elsewhere he mentions J. S. Bach's model way of placing his fingers on the keyboard.[66] This suggests that Quantz had met Bach, either while he was at Dresden or at least when the latter visited Potsdam in 1747.

---

[63] *Essay*, p. 80.

[64] *On Playing the Flute*, p. 334. He also states that 'The Italian manner of playing is arbitrary, extravagant, artificial, obscure, frequently bold and bizarre', whereas the French manner is 'slavish, yet modest, distinct, neat and true in performance'. The Germans 'sought to compose in an artful rather than in a comprehensible and pleasing manner, more for the eye than for the ear,' and through travel and study 'have appropriated the style' of other nations. 'The same can be said of neither Italian nor French musicians. The reason is not because they lack the talent to do it, but because they take few pains to learn foreign languages' (p. 341).

[65] *On Playing the Flute*, p. 339.   [66] *On Playing the Flute*, p. 260.

As might be expected, the trill described by Quantz is a combination of Italian and French practice. The basic form is an 'Italian' trill beginning on the main note:

Yet according to Quantz:

Each shake begins with the appoggiatura that precedes its note . . . and which may be taken from above or below. The ending of each shake consists of two little notes which follow the notes of the shake, and are added to it at the same speed. . . .

Sometimes the appoggiatura of the shake is just as fast as the other notes which form the shake; for example, when, after a rest, a new idea begins with a shake. Whether the appoggiatura is long or short, however, it must always be tipped with the tongue; the shake and its suffix, on the other hand, must be slurred to the appoggiatura.[67]

Despite the fact that it begins on the auxiliary, Quantz's trill differs from the French trill in that it is not the upper, but the lower note that is slightly emphasized (but compare what has been said about Couperin's trill).

What Quantz has to say about trills over dissonances is also of interest:[68]

If there are shakes upon notes which form dissonances against the bass . . . the appoggiaturas before the shakes must be very short, to avoid transforming the dissonances into consonances.

Here Quantz seems to have been referring to anticipated 'passing appoggiaturas', which are discussed below. I have added execution *e*, which is not by Quantz, though it complies with his instructions on passing appoggiaturas.[69]

Quantz refers to the *Pralltriller* using its old German name, 'half-trill', and derives it from the appoggiatura (see Ex. 12.55; execution *b*, also termed 'suffixed half-trill', was called 'trilled turn' by C. P. E. Bach. See p. 302.)

---

[67] *On Playing the Flute*, pp. 103–4. It is noteworthy that Quantz links the speed of the trill with the pulse beat (pp. 283 f.). He assumes a raised pulse-beat in the evening (probably due to the excitement of a concert) of 80 beats per minute, which in the example he gives would equal a metronome marking of ♩ = 80. At higher pitches the speed of the trill increases, at lower ones it decreases.

[68] *On Playing the Flute*, p. 96.   [69] *On Playing the Flute*, p. 154. See below, pp. 397 f.

Ex. 12.55. From Quantz, *On Playing the Flute*, p. 98

In the case of descending triplets Quantz states[70] that one

can always make a half-shake without a suffix (in which the finger falls only twice).

Thus in this case the trill sign can also signify a *Pralltriller*. The above description implies execution *b*. In other groups of triplets Quantz prefers to use short appoggiaturas. Repeated notes that would impair the smooth flow of the melody are obviously meant to be avoided (Ex. 12.56). On occasion Quantz uses certain terms for ornaments that depart from keyboard practice. For example, he terms *pincés battements*.[71]

Ex. 12.56. From Quantz, *On Playing the Flute*, p. 158

Friedrich Wilhelm Marpurg's *Anleitung zum Clavierspielen* was published in Berlin in 1755—before Agricola's *Anleitung zur Singkunst*. With regard to embellishments it had much in common with C. P. E. Bach's *Essay*. Marpurg had already published a small work on the subject in 1750, *Die Kunst das Clavier zu spielen*. (In *Der critische Musicus* of 1749–50 the French influence is unmistakable, whereas his publications of 1750 and 1751 contain nothing pertaining to ornamentation.) On the subject of the *Pralltriller*, Marpurg, who also knew J. S. Bach, disagrees with C. P. E. Bach in that he does not stipulate the minute delay created by the tie on the first note (see p. 288), thereby clearly describing the three-note execution beginning on the main note (see Ex. 12.57). Marpurg comments:

When in the tied simple trill the tied note is passed over and, contrary to the rules of the trill, starts at once on the main note, the alternations being shortened and restricted to three notes, this produces an imperfect trill which none the less is better

---

[70] *On Playing the Flute*, p. 154.   [71] *On Playing the Flute*, p. 98; cf. Ex. 12.63, p. 296.

in certain instances than the normal trill. These are (*a*) in fast stepwise descents and (*b*) when there is a long appoggiatura before a short note or (*c*) when a note is shortened on account of an appoggiatura . . . Herr [C. P. E.] Bach terms this trill a *Pralltriller* . . .[72]

Ex. 12.57. From Marpurg, *Anleitung*

Fig. 1

The tied note is deliberately excluded, and the extreme brevity of the ornament insisted upon. That the use of the tied first note is eschewed is noteworthy in that Marpurg, in the long tied trill, demands the 'old-fashioned' tie as described by d'Anglebert. This is as shown in Ex. 12.58.

Ex. 12.58

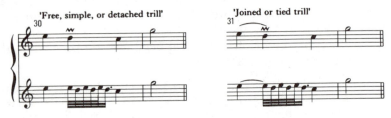

[72] *Anleitung*, p. 56. Marpurg makes no mention whatsoever of the fact that his version of the *Pralltriller* deviates rhythmically from that of C. P. E. Bach. Obviously he considered it to be an unimportant trifle.

With regard to the *Pralltriller*, Georg Simon Löhlein's *Clavierschule* (four editions, of 1765–82) follows Marpurg and not C. P. E. Bach, whereas Türk (1789) allows both exceutions while regarding the Bachian tie as 'more correct'.[73] However, it should be remembered that despite the varying theoretical explanations, the difference between the two executions of the *Pralltriller* consists in a delayed entry of less than a hundredth of a second in the case of the tied version, which as far as the listener is concerned is virtually inaudible.

Leopold Mozart came from Augsburg and thus did not belong to the northern or central German school. However, his views, which were influenced by his compatriot Georg Muffat, are so similar to those of his fellow musicians in Berlin that we will examine them briefly. As one might expect, in his *Versuch einer gründlichen Violinschule* of 1756 he follows his predecessors Muffat and Fischer with regard to the long trill. The two examples in Ex. 12.59 are also of interest with regard to trill endings that have a short *point d'arrêt*. But in Ex. 12.60 the trill obviously begins on the main note.

Ex. 12.59. From Leopold Mozart, *Violinschule*, Eng. edn., p. 188

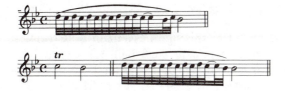

Ex. 12.60. From Leopold Mozart, *Violinschule*, Eng. edn., p. 188

Unlike C. P. E. Bach, Leopold Mozart also employed anticipatory and passing appoggiaturas. His 'half-trill' is similar to that of Quantz, and is played before the beat (see Ex. 12.61).

Ex. 12.61. From Leopold Mozart, *Violinschule*, Eng. edn., p. 185

[73] *Claverischule*, p. 272.

The term *Pralltriller* for a very short trill (*trilletto*) first makes an appearance in the second edition of the *Violinschule* in 1762, though it does not mean the same as in the works of the north German theorists. Had Leopold Mozart read the incorrect definition of the *Pralltriller* given in the first edition of the *Essay* in the mean time? At any rate, he and Agricola are the only writers at this time who begin the *Pralltriller* on the auxiliary (see Ex. 12.62).

Ex. 12.62. From Leopold Mozart, *Violinschule*, Eng. edn., pp. 195, 234

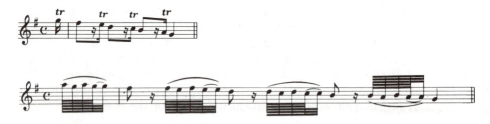

Leopold Mozart's remark about the long trill at the beginning of a piece is of importance: 'But when a passage commences with a trill, then the appoggiatura is hardly heard, and in such a case is no more than a vigorous start to the trill'.[74] In practical terms this signifies a main-note trill with a short anticipating appoggiatura. Neumann calls such trills 'grace-note trills'.

The executions of the mordent current in and after 1750 in Germany were as shown in Exx. 12.63 (Quantz) and 12.64 (C. P. E. Bach). C. P. E. Bach says[75] that there is 'an unusual manner of performing a very short mordent':

(The lower note is of course shorter than a quaver.)

Ex. 12.63. Quantz's *battements* (*On Playing the Flute*, p. 98)

Ex. 12.64. From C. P. E. Bach, *Essay*, p. 127

The mordent often occurs in stepwise ascending lines. If it is added to an appoggiatura (i.e. a dissonant suspension), then it 'is played lightly in

---

[74] *Violinschule*, §11.   [75] *Essay*, p. 127.

accordance with the rule covering the performance of appoggiaturas'.[76] However, it also occurs on initial notes and in leaps or detached notes—where its brevity is emphasized—to which it is designed to add 'brilliance'.[77] On this subject C. P. E. Bach notes:[78]

> It should be observed that the mordent is the opposite of the *Pralltriller*. The latter may be used only over a descending step, precisely the situation which is unsuited to the mordent. The one element which they have in common is that both may be applied to the interval of a second: ascending in the case of the mordent and descending in the case of the *Pralltriller*. Both employments are clearly illustrated in Fig. LXXVIII.

Marpurg follows C. P. E. Bach with regard to the exact inversion of the two ornaments (see Ex. 12.65). Agricola's description of the mordent also goes back to C. P. E. Bach, though he suggests that the tied mordent be delayed in exact analogy to the tied *Pralltriller*, thus going further than his model.[79] Quantz calls tied mordents *pincés* and the ones with leaps *battements*. The latter can begin both with the main note and the (lower) auxiliary 'on rather slow notes . . . but the demisemiquavers must still be produced with the greatest speed'.[80]

Ex. 12.65. From Marpurg, *Anleitung*, pp. 58 f.

---

[76] C. P. E. Bach, *Essay*, p. 128.   [77] C. P. E. Bach, *Essay*, p. 129.
[78] *Essay*, p. 131.   [79] Tosi–Agricola, p. 103.   [80] *On Playing the Flute*, p. 84.

ONCE MORE TO C. P. E. BACH'S TREATISE

How did C. P. E. Bach arrive at his explanation of the tied *Pralltriller*? If we assume that the *Pralltriller* was already being played in the first half of the eighteenth century as an 'inverted mordent' beginning on the main note, the difficulty lay in the fact that it did not have a name or a sign of its own. The same signs were used for the short and long trill and the *Pralltriller*: *tr*, ᴧᴧ, and ᴧᴧ. It was only towards the end of the eighteenth century that it became the practice to reserve the *tr* sign for the long trill, and the ᴧᴧ sign for the *Pralltriller*.

Perhaps practical musicians were not concerned about the fact that one sign was employed for two (or more) ornaments, or that two different signs were used for one embellishment. If what we surmised above is correct, then C. P. E. Bach was obviously confronted with a dilemma. In order to remain systematic, he felt moved to suggest a new interpretation of the ornaments, new signs, and a new terminology—and in this he was ahead of his time. He was obviously concerned to make a distinction between trill and *Pralltriller* signs that indicated a start on the main note and those that denoted a start on the auxiliary. Thus he may have invented the term *Pralltriller* in analogy to the *tremblement appuyé* (or *lié*) of the French theorists. By inventing the 'tied' *Pralltriller* he was presumably attempting to kill two birds with one stone. In theory the *Pralltriller* could begin on the upper note, and in practice on the lower note. Furthermore, it preserved the link with the long trill that in theory always began on the auxiliary.

The precondition for this kind of *Pralltriller* was the strict postulate that it could only occur when 'slurred' (i.e. to the preceding note) and that it was always preceded by the note immediately above—what else in fact could the *Pralltriller* be joined to? This rule proceeds from the correct observation that *Pralltriller* usually occur in descending stepwise motion (not only in baroque music), whereas, conversely, mordents often occur in ascending passages.[81] If the *Pralltriller* is over an unaccented note, such as the resolution of a dissonant suspension, then the minute delay suggested by C. P. E. Bach seems aesthetically satisfying because it increases the melodic tension and delays the expected resolution. However, this is not the case when the *Pralltriller* is over an accented note as in Exx. 14.19–23. Here the delay is unsatisfactory, partly for rhythmic reasons. Thus it is easy to understand why as early as 1755 Marpurg suggested the undelayed execution, even though he referred to the example of C. P. E. Bach on other occasions.

But in those cases where the note immediately above is not slurred, C. P. E. Bach could not very well have continued to use the old abbreviation

---

[81] See also Marpurg, *Anleitung*, p. 58 and Türk, *Clavierschule*, pp. 276 f.

Ex. 12.66

with a trill sign. For this reason he invented a new notation using small notes (Ex. 12.66) and the new term *Schneller*, or snap (a trill or 'short trill' would have begun on the upper note). The examples below illustrate his

unvariable notation of the short mordent in inversion, the upper note of which is snapped, the other notes being played with a stiff finger.

Its execution suggests that this ornament, not mentioned by other writers [noch sonsten nicht bemerckte Manier], might be called the snap. The snap is always played rapidly and appears only before quick, detached notes, to which it imparts brilliance while serving to fill them out.[82]

    C. P. E. Bach's remark that the term and the notation of the *Schneller* had not been mentioned by other writers has led some commentators to think that the ornament itself was invented by him. However, the equivalent phrase 'sonst nicht angemerckt' occurs in connection with the renaming of other ornaments that had been in use long before the *Essay* was written, such as the snapped turn. A Germanist of my acquaintance, Dr Rolf Pfister, has assured me that the phrase 'noch sonsten nicht bemerckte' does in fact mean 'not mentioned by other writers'.[83] In the 1787 edition of the *Essay* Bach added that the snap was 'identical' with the *Pralltriller* and that it was an inversion ('the opposite') of the mordent.[84]

    The most lucid description of the snap is given by Marpurg:

If one wishes to apply the *Pralltriller* on a note suddenly, the two notes before the main note, with which the alternation is made, must be notated either with small auxiliary notes, or written out in large notes, that is, to denote the length and the effect thereof. Table V, Fig. 5. Herr Bach calls this embellishment *Schneller*. That the latter, both in this case, where it is expressed in notes, and in the former, where it is an abbreviated slurred trill known as *Pralltriller*, is nothing other than a short mordent in inversion, will be recognized as soon as one has become acquainted with the

---

[82] *Essay*, p. 142.

[83] Before the time of Goethe *anmerken*, *bemerken*, and *vermerken* often meant the same thing, 'to mention'. *Sonsten* ('otherwise') could also be used to refer to a particular location.

[84] This important addition is also omitted in Hoffmann-Erbrecht's fac. edn. In England the mordent is sometimes called 'inverted mordent' (cf. Emery, *Bach's Ornaments*, p. 19).

mordent described in article 7 below. However, such a *Schneller* must never be termed mordent, as some keyboard players do in such a laughable manner. Ornaments must always be given their correct names.[85]

There can be no doubt then that *Schneller* and *Pralltriller*, both terms invented by C. P. E. Bach, are identical. The sole difference between them is their relationship to the preceding note. Yet in fact this was a problem for the theorists that the majority of practical musicians disregarded. Towards the end of the eighteenth century some minor writers on music, such as Johann Samuel Petri, adopted the term *Schneller* for this ornament, but the majority of musicians decided in favour of *Pralltriller*, and this was the only term to survive after the eighteenth century.

It would seem that the descriptions provided by C. P. E. Bach, Marpurg, Quantz, Türk, and others are unambiguous. Thus it is all the more surprising that a well-informed scholar, Robert Donington, in his book *A Performer's Guide to Baroque Music*[86] provides the following instructions for the execution of this ornament:

The half-trill (*Pralltriller*) consists of two repercussions: i.e. four notes [*sic*]. The last of the four is the main note, and is held on plain [*sic*]. . . . The half-trill, like the full trill, is an on-the-beat ornament, starting with the upper auxiliary, which is accented [*sic*] . . . But above a certain speed, the four notes have a natural tendency, for lack of time, to become three; i.e. the half-trill (*Pralltriller*) is turned into an inverted mordent (*Schneller*) [*sic*].[87]

Donington gives the illustration quoted in Ex. 12.67 and states that at a fast tempo, according to C. P. E. Bach [*sic*], version *c* should be played, and at a slow tempo version *d*. However, C. P. E. Bach never mentions such a break in a legato motif, the origin of the 'chopped-off' style of playing so typical of modern harpsichordists, either in fast or in slow tempos. On the contrary, he repeatedly emphasizes that the *Pralltriller* only occurs with slurred notes, and the snap only in the case of detached notes. It should be remembered that, in the case of the *Pralltriller* and in that of the snap, only three notes (including the final note) are heard. The four-note execution beginning with a restruck auxiliary never appears in the treatises of Quantz, Marpurg, and C. P. E. Bach, either verbally or in a music example. And C. P. E. Bach himself sometimes used the *Pralltriller* abbreviation in places where, according to his

Ex. 12.67. After Donington, *Performer's Guide*, p. 202

---

[85] *Anleitung*, p. 57.   [86] London, 1973.
[87] p. 202. [*sic*] indicates an error made by Donington.

own theory, the notation of a snap with two short notes would have been appropriate. This explains the following critical remark in Türk's keyboard tutor:

Although the *Pralltriller* (as Agricola and C. P. E. Bach tell us) should only be used after a preceding upper second, be it indicated by a normal (*a*) or a small note (*b*), even the best composers permit themselves an occasional exception in the matter as in examples *c*, *d*, and *e*. The *Pralltriller* in particular occurs in four-part figures, after a leap, over the middle note of a stepwise descent (*f*), and in the case of caesuras (*g*).

It is clear that in examples *c*, *d*, and *e*, which I have taken from the works of [C. P. E.] Bach, E. W. Wolf, and others, the *Pralltriller* has been confused with the snap that ought to have been used. I leave it to critics to decide how serious this transgression really is.[88]

Türk's remarks are of interest because today virtually no harpsichordist would play snaps in such passages, preferring short auxiliary trills. However, in a note on example *c*[1], showing note-repetition, Türk admits the possibility of using a short ('French') trill in such passages, perhaps modelling himself on Agricola. But this is more of an exception in late eighteenth-century theoretical literature. Türk states:[89]

In such cases some composers also place an invariable [i.e. short] appoggiatura before the note, which is better.

I have never come across this kind of notation in classical works; in Haydn and Mozart appoggiaturas before trills are nearly always *long* appoggiaturas.

For understandable reasons the distinction between *Pralltriller* and *Schneller* never became universally accepted. For example, Haydn and Beethoven, who

---

[88] Türk, *Clavierschule*, pp. 273 f. Unfortunately Türk fails to mention the source of his exx. As we shall see, the same confusion occurs in the *Essay* itself. [89] *Clavierschule*, note to p. 273.

were both acquainted with the *Essay*, continued to use the ⋀ sign for the snap. Not until the nineteenth century were both the small notes and the old abbreviation employed by a number of composers, though without making a distinction based on the pitch of the preceding note.

C. P. E. Bach used almost exactly the same words to describe the 'trilled turn', an embellishment that 'has no distinctive symbol'.[90] Again it is the notation and the nomenclature that are new, not the ornament itself, which had already been described by Quantz as a 'half-trill with suffix' (see Ex. 12.55 (p. 293)). It also occurs in Couperin and in late Bach in various notational guises, a subject to which we shall return below. As in the case of the distinction between *Pralltriller* and *Schneller*, C. P. E. Bach distinguishes two notational forms and names, according to whether the trilled turn 'is used only in a descending second, the first note of which is drawn into the embellishment'[91] or, as a 'snapped turn', after detached notes, leaps, and at the beginning and in the middle of phrases (see Ex. 12.68). The bracketed tie a^1-a^1 in this example corresponds to Bach's unmistakable description:

The effect of the combined ornaments can be most easily realized by thinking of a *Pralltriller* with a suffix. This ornament introduces a unique charm and brilliance to the keyboard. It is a miniature but lively, slurred and suffixed trill . . . It has no distinctive symbol. . . . With regard to the long slur over the last illustration, I refer the reader to the discussion of the *Pralltriller*.—This trilled turn occurs either with or without a preceding appoggiatura. However, like the *Pralltriller* it is used only in a descending second, the first note of which is drawn into the embellishment.[92]

Of note are the additions to the 1787 edition, where an alternative notation and execution for the trilled turn are suggested, 'so long as it does not create

Ex. 12.68. From C. P. E. Bach, *Essay*, pp. 121, 126

[90] *Essay*, p. 121. The execution and indeed the sign had long been in existence. In Couperin, for example, I have on numerous occasions noted the superimposition of these 2 symbols, e.g. in the very first of the *Pièces de clavecin*, book 1, 'Allemande l'auguste', bar 15, or in 'La Fleurie', bars 13 and 27. Thus C. P. E. Bach's statement that it 'has no distinctive symbol' refers simply to the nomenclature. This is of some importance, for it indicates that the *Schneller*, which also had no 'distinctive symbol' need not necessarily have been invented by C. P. E. Bach. What then, one is led to ask, are the 'new ornaments' he announces on pp. 80 and 85? Doubtless they are the 'ascending turn' (*Essay*, p. 127), the 'three-note slide' (*Essay*, p. 137), and in a way the 'compound appoggiatura', the 'dotted compound appoggiatura' (*Essay*, pp. 132–4), etc.

[91] *Essay*, p. 121.

[92] *Essay*, p. 121. Translation amended.

bad voice leading',[93] such as consecutive fifths (as at (3) in Ex. 12.69). As we shall see below, this kind of embellishment occurs frequently in J. S. Bach, and should probably be executed in a manner similar to that suggested by his son. In (1) of Ex. 12.69 C. P. E. Bach seems inadvertently to have used the *Pralltriller* sign for the *Schneller*—the first note is not preceded by the one

Ex. 12.69. From C. P. E. Bach, *Essay*, p. 122

immediately above. As this section of the *Essay* only deals with ornaments beginning on the main note, there can be no doubt that here the execution shown in Ex. 12.70 was intended.[94] However, the first ornament here is not a *Pralltriller*, but, going by the definition provided in the *Essay*, a *Schneller*,

Ex. 12.70

which, in C. P. E. Bach's own words, 'invariably' had to be notated with two small grace-notes. That by mistake he made use of the *Pralltriller* sign, which according to his own theory was unsuitable, is a lapse that is more important than it seems at first sight: the 'Freudian slip' points to the fact that this was an ingrained habit.

In the case of this ornament the snapped execution 'with a stiff finger' mentioned above also plays an important role:[95]

In performing the simple turn or the suffixed trill, at least three fingers must always be employed. Because, beyond this, the snap in these ornaments and particularly in the

---

[93] Addition to *Essay*, p. 122.
[94] It is one of the inconsistencies mentioned by Türk (see above, p. 301). However, it is virtually inconceivable that Bach meant the following:

For the auxiliary trill, even for the shortest, C. P. E. Bach invariably uses the longer wavy line or the *tr* sign in the *Essay*.   [95] *Essay*, p. 124.

trilled turn can be well executed by only certain fingers, there often arise great difficulties of performance, in the solution of which extreme expedients must be employed.

Of interest is the change of fingers on the (accented) appoggiatura note (quaver). The 'snapping' finger (see above) on the ornament is thus the third or fourth.

On the subject of the 'snapped turn' C. P. E. Bach writes that it 'is better suited to rapid notes than the trill' and that it occurs 'at the beginning of a passage, in the middle, before stepwise motion or a leap'.[96] Of importance is Bach's remark that 'aside from the keyboard', that is, in works for singers, strings, and winds, this ornament is indicated 'by the sign of a trill'.[97] This means nothing less than that a trill sign over a relatively short note can also be taken to signify a snapped turn—beginning on the main note. In those days musicians were not quite as obstinately consistent as we tend to think.

The music examples that C. P. E. Bach added to the 1787 edition[98] are also revealing. At this point the issue was that the length of a note and the embellishment applied to it had to be in proportion. Obviously, the faster a note, the fewer the number of embellishment notes that could be accommodated. The thrust of this argument in itself shows that which embellishment was applied to which note was often left to the discretion of the performer. However, it is interesting to note that as the speed of the note that was to be embellished increased, it was possible to begin the ornament on the main note or on the auxiliary. But precisely at the point where one might expect the four-part *Pralltriller* favoured by present-day harpsichordists (Allegretto), Bach wrote a turn. The last ornament in the music example that logically completes this series, that is, using a single appoggiatura as an embellishment, C. P. E. Bach mentions when discussing the execution of the trill.[99] Here he explains that at a very fast tempo one can replace the trill with an appoggiatura (see Ex. 12.71, which shows the execution of the ornaments as explained by C. P. E. Bach in the relevant sections).

To sum up: the manifold European developments in ornamentation led to a state of affairs where, from the middle of the eighteenth century onwards (though no earlier than that), all German theorists asked for the trill to begin

---

[96] *Essay*, p. 125.   [97] *Essay*, p. 126.   [98] *Essay*, p. 84.   [99] *Essay*, p. 105.

on the upper or lower auxiliary. However, in practice it was not always possible to adhere strictly to a rule that saw the trill primarily as a chain of appoggiaturas. The Italians perceived this most clearly of all, in both theory and practice, and they did not have immutable rules for trills (see p. 260 ff.). Mordents and *Pralltriller* continued to begin on the main note.

Ex. 12.71. From C. P. E. Bach, *Essay*, p. 84 (except last ex., by Paul Badura-Skoda)

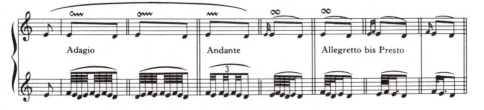

The *Pralltriller* as an ornament has always existed, and was repeatedly described in music theory between the sixteenth and seventeenth centuries. The common claim that it was invented only after the death of J. S. Bach, and that it can therefore not be used in his works, is historically untenable and therefore false. The *Schneller*—a *Pralltriller* that enters unprepared—is C. P. E. Bach's invention only as regards its theoretical description. His demand that the *Schneller* should be notationally distinguished from the *Pralltriller* was not complied with by the great composers. Even C. P. E. Bach sometimes transgressed against his own rules, occasionally designating *Schneller* with the *Pralltriller* sign.

13

J. S. Bach's Ornaments: Some General Remarks

It is often claimed that J. S. Bach used French ornamentation signs to the virtual exclusion of all others, and that for this reason all his embellishments ought to be executed in the French manner. This is a gross simplification of a rather complicated state of affairs. If conscientious performers were able to solve all problems of embellishment with the help of a few clear-cut instructions *à la française*, no one would be happier than those of us who perform the music of Bach.

It is of course correct that many of Bach's ornaments not only look the same as many contemporary French embellishments, particularly those employed by d'Anglebert, but also mean the same. However, when Hans Klotz claims: 'As we have seen, Bach's ornaments are identical with those of the French *clavecinistes*',[1] this is quite obviously incorrect. It is true that Bach himself made a copy of d'Anglebert's table of ornaments, which may in itself be taken as proof of his interest in French ornamentation. However, he made use of only some of the French symbols, and also employed ornaments of Italian origin, such as the Italian trill sign—and not as infrequently as certain commentators would have us believe. Bach's copy of d'Anglebert's table was made while he was in Weimar. Previously he had already notated signs with which his German contemporaries were familiar—and this was a mixture of French, Italian, and German symbols. In addition to the 'international' wavy line, he employed, as we have seen, the *t* or *tr* sign for the trill. Of Italian origin, the latter was used in Germany, though not in France. (Couperin introduced a combination of *tr* and wavy line for the long trill only in 1713.) For the slide, on the other hand, Bach mainly used the German sign ⌒ that came from his Leipzig predecessor Kuhnau, and only occasionally employed

---

[1] *Ornamentik*, p. 2. See my review of this book, 'Richtige Ausführung von Bachs Ornamentik?', *Üben & Musizieren*, 3 (1986), 21–7.

French symbols (small notes or an oblique stroke through a notated third). He repeatedly wrote out his ornaments in large notes.

The mixture of different kinds of notation suggests that Bach's ornamentation, like that of all the great composers, was not a carefully designed system, but a practical affair that came about spontaneously. In many cases different kinds of notation occur within a single work for one and the same ornament—a valuable lesson that helps us to understand Bach's intentions better.

Klotz has compiled a table of all the ornamentation signs that occur in Bach. In order to simplify matters it has been reproduced here virtually unchanged, though attention is drawn to certain problematical symbols (e.g. 16 and 17). Klotz's ornaments 25–7, 'staccato', 'aspiration', and 'liaison', are not included because they are in fact articulation marks.

TABLE 1. *Ornament Signs used by Bach (partly based on Klotz,* Ornamentik, *pp. 26 f.)*

1. Trill, short trill, *Pralltriller*

2. Mordent (see also 19)

3. Appoggiatura
   a descending   more rarely

   b ascending   more rarely

4. Turn
   a over one note

   b between two notes

5. Slide

6. Appoggiatura + trill

7. Turn + trill, descending trill

8. Appoggiatura + turn + trill (very rare)

9. Slide + trill (= ascending trill)

10. Trill + mordent (trill with suffix, often interchangeable with 19; often erroneously printed i places where the context makes it clear that only 2 is possible)

11. Appoggiatura + trill + mordent (trilled turn or a snapped turn without appoggiatura, both very rare)

12. Turn + trill + mordent (descending trill with suffix, a combination of 7 and 10)

13. Appoggiatura + turn + trill + mordent (combination of 8 and 10, very rare)

14. Slide + trill + mordent (ascending trill with suffix, combination of 9 and 10)

15. Appoggiatura + mordent

16. Turn + mordent (Klotz believes that Bach invented this combination. However, the examples he adduces (pp. 144 ff.) fail to convince. In the majority of cases normal mordents, trills, or turns were probably intended.)

17.   Slide + mordent (Klotz thinks that Bach invented this symbol. It does not occur in any of the MSS, and thus cannot be regarded as authentic. The example he cites (p. 146) from bar 29 of the Prélude of the A Major English Suite is probably an incorrect reading of a trill or a mordent)

18.   Continuous trill (longer form of 1, in reality not an ornament in its own right)

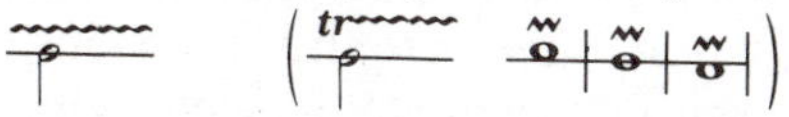

19.   Melodic continuous trill with suffix (usually identical with 10)

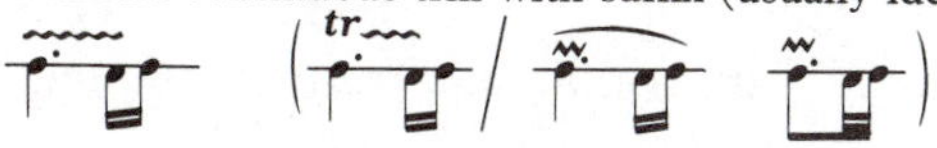

20.   Continuous mordent (long mordent, often no more than an imprecise version of 2 or 10)

21.   Suffix
      a ascending

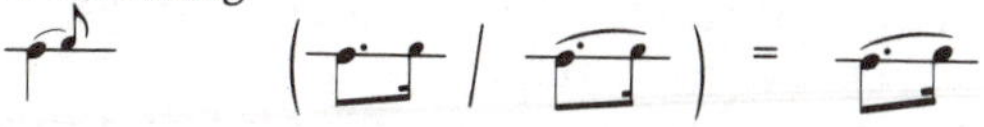

      b descending

22.   *Tierce coulée* (fairly rare in Bach: see *Ornamentik* p. 165)

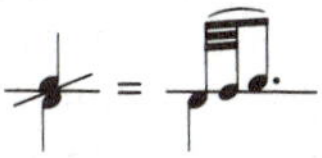

23.   Arpeggio
      a ascending

      b descending (?)

(It is impossible to prove the existence of this ornament in Bach. The examples adduced by Klotz (pp. 170 ff.) fail to convince, graphically and musically. There is no documentary evidence for the descending arpeggio often played in bar 10 of the Goldberg Aria. However, a descending arpeggio may have been intended in the Allemande of Partita No. 5, BWV 829, though this may also have been an engraver's error:

Finally we should mention the omission of two ornaments not found in Bach for which there is no logical explanation. These are the inversions of the turn (4) and of the 'trilled turn' (11), both of which would have been quite possible in terms of the systemization of all ornaments. The inversion of the turn ∞ = ♫♪ would be ♫♪. This ornament occurs frequently in Mozart, but in Bach only at the beginning of the trill formula (9). The inversion of the 'trilled turn' ♫♫♪ would be: ♫♫♪ , though it is nowhere to be found.[2]

THE INTERCHANGEABILITY OF DIFFERENT TRILL SIGNS

It has often been remarked that Bach's notation of trills and *Pralltriller*—particularly as regards the length of execution—lacks consistency.[3] A short wavy line can sometimes signify a long trill and, vice versa, a long mordent sign can signify a short mordent. This is quite in keeping with eighteenth-century usage. Marpurg comments:

To indicate a trill one makes use of either the two letters *tr*, a simple cross, or an *m* or *n*. The latter, being the most appropriate, are the ones most often used, and it matters little whether *m* or *n* is used. That some people indicate a long trill with an *m* and a short one with an *n* is simply a subtlety. The length of the trill is determined by the note-value, and the copyist or engraver may place an *m* for an *n* or vice versa only if the composer has not already made the difference clear in the original manuscript. So what is the point of it? The length or brevity of a trill is always determined by the value of the note to which it is applied.[4]

When writing *m* or *n* Marpurg meant the long or short wavy lines.

The 'short trill' mentioned here can of course be a *Pralltriller*; in theory and practice before the time of C. P. E. Bach it did not possess a symbol of its own, although it had long been in existence. To deduce from this that Bach and his contemporaries were not familiar with the *Pralltriller*—as still happens

---

[2] The term *prallender Doppelschlag* (trilled turn) is derived from the word *Pralltriller*. Thus its inversion, being derived from the mordent, might have been termed *mordender Doppelschlag* (translator's note: it is impossible to render this play on words in English. The literal translation would be 'murderous turn'). Obviously musicians were unwilling to use such dangerous ornaments.

[3] See e.g. Harich-Schneider, *Die Kunst des Cembalospiels*, p. 87; Bodky, *Interpretation*, p. 150.

[4] *Anleitung*, p. 54.

today—is almost certainly wrong (see the preceding section). The terminolog-
ical confusion that nowadays surrounds the *Pralltriller* is compounded by the
fact that some writers state that C. P. E. Bach's *Schneller* resembles
Griepenkerl's contraction of the word to *Praller* in 1837, though with quite a
different meaning.[5]

J. S. Bach's E flat minor Prelude from *WTC* I is an exceptional case. Here
the short wavy lines (e.g. in bars 4 and 19) stand for the long trill and the *tr*
sign in bar 15 (and bar 36 in some editions, a later addition to the autograph)
for the *Pralltriller*. (Both transpire from the musical logic and the part-writing.
Incidentally, it is a little-known fact that for the *Pralltriller* Mozart used the *tr*
sign almost exclusively.)

However, it must be pointed out that Bach was at pains to be as clear as
possible. In the majority of instances, above all in the fair copies of the
keyboard works, the short wavy line designates the *Pralltriller* and the long
wavy line or *t* (or *tr*) sign the normal trill. The extent to which Bach was
concerned to avoid all ambiguity with regard to ornament signs becomes
particularly apparent in the numerous corrections to the printed works,
which—and this has gone largely unnoticed—are particularly concerned with
ornamentation.

It is unfortunately often forgotten that Bach himself carefully revised some
of the printed copies of the *Clavier-Übung*. There are hundreds of these
corrections—usually carefully entered in black or red ink. Modern Bach
research is of the opinion that most of them are by Bach himself. Others were
undertaken at his behest, and may well have been entered by his wife or his
pupils.[6] These corrections by Bach were passed over by early editions, and
were first taken into account in the NBA. It is impossible to understand that
otherwise good editions simply ignore these emendations, with which
musicologists have long since been familiar. Thus most Bach performers,
without being aware of it, still continue to study and play his 'keyboard works'
in faulty versions.[7]

How are we to explain the care with which Bach made these corrections in
the printed editions? It stands in contrast to the notational practice adopted in
the manuscripts, where the symbols were often interchanged. The most
plausible conclusion is that in this handful of printed works, which were
destined for posterity, Bach was indeed concerned to make his intentions
absolutely clear, whereas from the mass of his other manuscripts, which often

---

[5] In the pref. to vol. i of his edn. of Bach's organ music (Peters, Leipzig) Griepenkerl speaks of
Pralltriller, though in the brief ornamentation table in the ensuing table of contents he uses the word *Praller*
in place of *Pralltriller* in the same music ex. Perhaps this was suggested by the printer in order to save space.

[6] See NBA V/1, Critical Report by R. D. Jones, pp. 26–7; and NBA V/2, Critical Report by W. Emery
and C. Wolff, pp. 26–8. See also Wolff, 'Textkritische Bemerkungen zum Originaldruck der Bachschen
Partiten', *BJb*, 65 (1979).

[7] See ch. 9.

differ significantly, it is often impossible to extrapolate a 'definitive version', much to the chagrin of the various editors.[8]

There are ornament corrections at the very beginning of the first part of the *Clavier-Übung*, in the Praeludium of Partita No. 1, BWV 825. In the first two bars and in bar 5, imperfections in the printing meant that the ornaments were rather longer than they should have been. In the copy at the British Library in London the imperfections were carefully scraped away, so that *Pralltriller* symbols remained. Further along, in bars 10–11, the engraver omitted the ornaments altogether. Here Bach added the missing short *Pralltriller* symbols in ink. A typical emendation is the addition of an (obvious) slur between bb^1 and a^1 at the end of bar 18.

Bach's emendations and corrections in the second part of the *Clavier-Übung*, specifically in the Italian Concerto (BWV 971), are even more revealing. With regard to the ornamentation, four versions of the work are of interest:

1. A hitherto unknown early version, which survives in a copy made by J. C. Oley.
2. The faulty first edition (copies in the Österreichische Nationalbibliothek (Vienna), British Library (London), and several other libraries).
3. Bach's personal copy (*Handexemplar*) of the first edition with holograph corrections (British Library, MS K 8 g 7).
4. The second printing of the first edition revised at Bach's behest (copies in the Österreichische Nationalbibliothek, Hoboken Archive, and elsewhere).

As might be expected, in the first and second movements Bach originally notated ∿ at numerous points (probably as signs for *Pralltriller*). This transpires from the early version of the work. The engraver of the first edition, who was obviously not wholly familiar with musical notation, reproduced all the wavy lines designating *Pralltriller* and trills as straight horizontal lines up to bar 13 of the second movement. In musical terms this was quite meaningless. On the other hand, he replaced the mordent symbols in the second movement with *tr*, which was even more ludicrous. Only after bar 13 of the second movement did he become aware of the fact that Bach's wavy lines were not supposed to be straight lines. From this point onwards he began

---

[8] See Dadelsen, 'Die Crux der Nebensache', p. 95: the majority of Bach's works '. . . from our point of view, lack the final redaction, the preparation for printing. If we wish to edit them, we have to make good this omission, with much circumspection and care, but with the necessary consistency. This contradiction cannot be resolved, only understood. Also, it cannot be circumvented by restricting ourselves in our historical and critical editions to a "diplomatic" reproduction of the source and—as is once more being recommended—leaving the required additions and modernizations to "practical" and "instructive" editions. As a rule an edition is based on several sources, such as a score and parts, which can complement (but also contradict) each other with regard to accidentals, ornaments, and articulation marks.' See also Dietrich Kilian, 'Über einige neue Aspekte zur Quellenüberlieferung von Klavier- und Orgelwerken J. S. Bachs', *BJb*, 64 (1978), 264.

to try and copy them.[9] The horizontal lines before bar 13 were too long to be replaced with *Pralltriller* signs. For this reason Bach, in a graphically rather adept manner, wrote a *t* at the beginning and a wavy line over the straight line. What else could he have done? However, it mistakenly led later editors to believe that Bach desired a longer trill even for the shortest of *Pralltriller*, for instance in bars 91, 93, and 95 of the first movement or bars 7 and 10 of the second. That this was not the case is demonstrated by Bach's correction in bar 156 of the first movement. Here the engraver had omitted the ornament altogether. Thus Bach, in his personal copy, was able to insert a normal *Pralltriller* sign. In the second edition Bach inserted *Pralltriller* signs at all the relevant places, and used wavy lines only to signify long trills (beginning on the lower auxiliary) in bars 112, 116, 135, and 137, where long trills were truly intended. It is a sign of ignorance when certain 'Urtext' editions still include trill symbols instead of *Pralltriller* signs, even in bar 156, where none of the printed editions has a trill sign. It is even more reprehensible when they print *tr* signs in place of mordents in bars 4 and 43 of the second movement.

Why did Bach entrust the engraving of such an important work to a completely inexperienced engraver? Christoph Wolff, the editor of the NBA, offers a plausible explanation: Bach probably confused the noted Nuremberg engraver and publisher Johann Christoph Weigel with his son, Weigel jun., who founded his own business in 1734 and devoted himself primarily to portraits and the like. It may thus be assumed that some of the younger Weigel's engravers, barely able to read music, tended to treat a page of music like a pictorial model that had to be copied.[10] There was of course one advantage—in purely graphical terms this edition is probably very similar to the lost autographs of BWV 971 and 831. The second edition also has a number of mistakes. Either Bach never received proofs, or he read them in a hurry.

Thus one conclusion is fairly obvious. If Bach went to such lengths to distinguish between long trills and *Pralltriller* in the printed works, then these signs must have signified different ornaments in the final versions. However, in the instances cited above the *Pralltriller* is often not preceded by the note immediately above; Bach seems to have meant the ornament that his son later termed *Schneller*. This view is taken by the (duly cautious) editors of the NBA.[11] In the works that have only survived in manuscript form this distinction is not always adhered to.

The notational distinction between trills and *Pralltriller* in fact only applies to keyboard works. In vocal pieces or those for other instruments Bach tended to make do with the uniform *t* (or more rarely *tr*) notation. In such works the performer had to deduce from the context whether a long or short trill or a *Pralltriller* was intended. A typical example of this is the Sarabande of the

---

[9] See NBA V/2, Critical Report, p. 45.   [10] NBA V/2, Critical Report, p. 17.
[11] NBA V/2, Critical Report, p. 46.

E flat major Suite for solo cello (Ex. 13.1). The same applies to the A minor Sonata for solo violin. The first two trill signs at the beginning of the first movement can practically only be played as *Pralltriller* beginning on the main note (see Ex. 13.2). In keyboard music, for example at the end of the G minor Prelude of *WTC* I, the *tr* symbol probably merely indicated a *Pralltriller* (Ex. 13.3). The rhythm of the last three bars is clearly striving towards a firm close on the fourth beat.

Ex. 13.1. Solo Cello Suite No. 4, BWV 1010, Sarabande

a

b   Suggested execution with *Pralltriller*:

Ex. 13.2. Solo Violin Sonata No. 2, BWV 1003, first movement

Ex. 13.3. *WTC* I, Prelude in G minor, bars 18–19

The difference in notation is particularly noticeable in works for harpsichord and solo instrument. Here Bach employed the normal *Pralltriller* notation in the harpsichord part, and the *t* abbreviation in the part for solo instrument. This is the case in the second movement of the G major Sonata for harpsichord and viola da gamba (see Ex. 13.4; note the careful articulation, which provides a valuable hint on how to play similar motifs in other works by Bach). However, at the beginning of this movement Bach seems to have made a

Ex. 13.4. Sonata No. 1 for harpsichord and viola da gamba, BWV 1027, second movement

Ex. 13.5. Sonata No. 1 for harpsichord and viola da gamba, BWV 1027, second movement, bars 1–4, harpsichord part

mistake, notating both forms of the ornament in the harpsichord part (Ex. 13.5). The two notations in fact signify the same.

Bach made a mistake of the opposite kind—again in the case of a sigh-motif—in the B minor Sonata for harpsichord and flute. At the beginning of the flute part he wrote the trill sign, later making use of the abbreviation he otherwise reserved for keyboard instruments (see Ex. 13.6). For the Bach performer, whether singer, keyboard player, or other instrumentalist, the choice of the 'best' ornament should be determined largely by the musical context and not the sign.

Ex. 13.6. Sonata in B minor for flute and harpsichord, BWV 1030, Andante

THE CONNECTION BETWEEN ORNAMENTATION AND COMPOSITION: PART-WRITING AND MELODIC PATTERNS

As we have seen, it is not enough to consider Bach's embellishments abstracted from the other principles that governed his compositional art. In fact the ornaments, called *Manieren*, were an important factor in the melodic, harmonic, and rhythmic structure of his music. From Bach's pupils—and these included his sons—we know that he attached great importance to correct part-writing. Like almost all his contemporaries, he considered consecutive fifths and octaves to be mistakes. His ear '. . . was so attuned to following the voice-leading, even of the most richly scored piece of music, that . . . in performances he noticed the slightest error immediately'.[12] Such sensitivity to incorrect voice-leading also applied to his own works, not only to those by other composers. Numerous later corrections to his works produce the stipulated purity of part-writing only by the elimination of open and concealed consecutive fifths and octaves, mistakes that even an experienced composer might make when first committing a work to paper. Of course it cannot be denied that in a handful of cases Bach deliberately left forbidden consecutives if they were either barely audible or inaudible. In his striving for correct part-writing Bach is wholly rooted in European music theory, whose rules on this point were deemed binding for centuries. Of particular interest in the present context are those corrections by Bach which transform 'forbidden' voice-leading into 'permissible progressions by the alteration or addition of ornaments. It is worth taking a closer look at the composer's workshop.

In the first version of Partita No. 6 in E minor, which is included in the *Notenbüchlein* for Anna Magdalena Bach, there were consecutive octaves b–d and c–e which were only slightly blunted by the rests in the upper voice (see Ex. 13.7). When Bach revised this partita before it was printed, he added two slides at this point, ostensibly in order to enrich the melody, but in fact more probably in order to improve the mistake in the part-writing mentioned above (Ex. 13.8).

Ex. 13.7. Partita No. 6, BWV 830, Toccata, bars 69–70, earlier version

---

[12] 'Nekrolog', p. 171, quoted in Spitta, *Johann Sebastian Bach*, ii. 601. For interesting information concerning Bach as a teacher of composition, see pp. 596 ff. of Spitta's book. See also *Bach-Dokumente*, iii. 87.

Ex. 13.8. Partita No. 6, BWV 830, Toccata, bars 69–70, later version

The second movement of the Harpsichord Concerto in F minor—probably a transcription of a lost instrumental concerto—has also survived in the shape of the introductory movement for solo oboe and strings in Cantata No. 156, *Ich steh mit einem Fuß im Grabe*. In bar 13 Bach at first transposed exactly the oboe part in the cantata from F major to A flat major (see Ex. 13.9*a*). He was obviously dissatisfied with the schematic sequence of the triplet figure, and so he changed it to read as in Ex. 13.9*b*. This version has hitherto been printed in all editions. However, as this leads to consecutive octaves by contrary motion, Bb–Ab, Bach changed the figuration a second time (Ex. 13.9*c*; see also Fig. 6). Unfortunately the correct reading of the autograph has never been included in any edition. But it was precisely the consecutive octaves that struck me as 'suspicious', and prompted me to discover Bach's emendation.[13]

Ex. 13.9. Harpsichord Concerto in F minor, BWV 1056, second movement, bars 13–14

[13] Important insights into Bach's method of composing and into his corrections are contained in Robert L. Marshall, *The Compositional Process of J. S. Bach* (Princeton, 1972). See vol. i, pp. 85 and 87 on voice-leading corrections.

FIG. 6. J. S. Bach, Harpsichord Concerto in F minor, BWV 1056, second movement, bars 12–15: part of the autograph manuscript with an important correction by Bach in bar 13, hitherto overlooked

A third example of correct voice-leading was not corrected by Bach, yet it demonstrates how much he valued correct part-writing. Ex. 13.10 shows bar 2 of the Sarabande of Partita No. 5 in G major. In the printed edition that he himself supervised, Bach made an unusual distinction between semiquaver and quaver appoggiaturas. The only reason for this can have been that he wished to avoid the consecutive fifths between the outer voices that would have come about if the treble and the bass were of equal length.[14]

Ex. 13.10. Partita No. 5, BWV 829, Sarabande, bar 2

[14] The succession of perfect and diminished 5ths is still the least objectionable form. This sarabande is also a good example of the execution of 'variable dotting': the quavers *after* the dotted crotchets in bars 9, 10, 11, 13, etc. are always printed exactly above the corresponding semiquaver, a subtlety that many editions have unfortunately done away with (see p. 58, Exx. 2.78, 2.79).

However, Bach's emendations usually aim at more than the mere elimination of incorrect or problematical progressions, being concerned with the flow of the melody and the rhythm. In the second movement of the Concerto in D minor for harpsichord (or fortepiano), BWV 1052, he made an emendation that has hitherto gone unnoticed. All the editions print bars 33–4 as in Ex. 13.11*a*. It seems that the early copyists and later the editors overlooked the subtle alteration in Bach's autograph manuscript (Ex. 13.11*b*). It is surprising how this minor improvement affects the flow of the melody.

Ex. 13.11. Concerto in D minor for harpsichord, BWV 1052, bars 33–4

Bach sometimes employs incorrect voice-leading in a symbolic manner, for example in the striking passage in the *St Matthew Passion* in which Peter falsely swears: 'Ich kenne des Menschen nicht!' (I do not know the man!) Here Bach puts wrong voice-leading in his mouth—consecutive fifths with the basso continuo (see Ex. 13.12). The subtlety of what Bach did is simply the work of a genius. Consecutive perfect fifths were forbidden by eighteenth-century theory, though they were tolerated in practice if both voices, as in this case, moved in semitone steps. Such 'permitted' semitone consecutives were later called 'Mozart fifths' after the voice-leading in the fugato of the *Magic Flute* overture. The 'correct' harmonization would have been B–C♯–F♯, instead of the B–D–C♯–F♯ bass. Thus Bach portrayed something that was 'incorrect' using means that were just about permissible.[15]

---

[15] Harnoncourt has made a similar observation with regard to the imperfect natural notes of the trumpet, which were often used to depict terror, horror, and the devil. These rough and slightly out-of-tune notes, which it is difficult to reproduce on modern valve trumpets, employ the 'ugly' sound for the truth of a

The harmonization of the final notes also provides food for thought—in terms of baroque operatic practice one could, according to Telemann, delay the final cadence (C♯–F♯ in the continuo).[16] If this were true, the 'incorrect' voice-leading would merely be an optical effect in the score.

Ex. 13.12. *St Matthew Passion*, recitative NBA No. 38c, BGA No. 46, bars 23–4

Ex. 13.13. *St Matthew Passion*, recitative NBA No. 26, BGA No. 32, bar 29

However, Christoph Albrecht points out that the only places in the *St Matthew Passion* where there are 'wrong' harmonies are Peter's phrase and Judas's kiss.[17] Thus Bach, as Albrecht rightly noted, makes expressive use of this 'incorrect' cadence (see Ex. 13.13). In other cases where Bach wished the cadence to be played after the singer's final note, he carefully notated a rest and then the continuo entry. (In the case of Peter's phrase it would be possible to avoid the clash of the singer's F♯ and the E♯ (the third of the dominant, C♯) by holding the G♯ appoggiatura a full crotchet, thereby delaying the F♯ resolution until the notated rest (Ex. 13.14).[18])

But it is hard to imagine that Bach would have put such a 'falsehood' in the mouth of Jesus, and at the opening words of the Eucharist at that (see

statement in terms of musical symbolism. The modern listener is rarely capable of noticing such subtleties. However, the performer should be aware of them. His performance gains in depth on the basis of such knowledge, and the listener can subconsciously sense this, even if he is incapable of explaining the facts in a rational manner (see *Musik als Klangrede*, pp. 116 f.).

[16] *Singe-, Spiel- und Generalbaßübungen*, cited in Gotthold Frotscher, *Aufführungspraxis alter Musik* (Leipzig, 1978), 148.

[17] *Interpretationsfragen*, p. 183.

[18] See C. P. E. Bach, *Essay*, pp. 90–1.

Ex. 13.15).[19] Thus to my mind at least this one trill or *Pralltriller*, in order to avoid consecutive fifths at intervals of a tone, where exceptions were not permitted, must begin with the main note, F, as version *c*.

Ex. 13.14.

Ex. 13.15. *St Matthew Passion*, recitative NBA No. 11, BGA No. 17, bar 31

Another example of tone-painting that makes use of 'wrong' notes occurs in the *St John Passion*. In the chorale, 'Christus der uns selig macht' (NBA No. 15; BGA No. 21), deceit and injustice are characterized by bitter harmonies. In bar 11 there is a hidden false relation between the bass (eb) and the soprano (e). Furthermore, the stresses in the text are incorrect: '. . . geführt vor Gottlose Leut' und fälschlich verklagt, verlacht, verhöhnt . . .'.[20]

Bach's part-writing, even in homophonic pieces, adheres to the laws of counterpoint. This is particularly noticeable with regard to the basses, which, in contrast to those in many classical works, are almost always melodic. March-like accompaniments and Alberti basses hardly ever occur in his

[19] Klaus Hofmann believes (and stated in an article, 'Noch einmal: Couperin and the Downbeat Doctrine for Appoggiaturas', *Acta musicologica*, 1971) that consecutive 5ths were permitted in conjunction with ornaments, and that they are impossible to avoid in ensemble music, the decisive factor being which of the notes is operative in terms of voice-leading (or harmonically).

[20] These observations do not of course exclude the possibility that Bach occasionally, though very occasionally indeed, made mistakes. A curious error occurs in the 1st movement of the 5th Brandenburg Concerto. In the viola part, bar 11, he 'emended' some harmless parallel voice-leading with the solo violin, and in the process created 'Puccini 5ths' with the harpsichord.

keyboard works. Nevertheless, he has in common with Haydn and Mozart, and to some extent with Beethoven, the singing quality of the instrumental works and the instrumental treatment of the voice parts, which makes great demands on the singer.[21] In the case of the characteristic coloraturas in homophonic and polyphonic works of both categories it is noticeable that, in accordance with an old contrapuntal rule, repetitions of notes that could impede the melodic flow are as a rule avoided.[22] One example among many of a similar nature occurs in the Aria of Partita No. 4 (see Ex. 13.16). In neither of the two voices are notes repeated. If ornaments are added in line with baroque practice, which regarded embellishment to be a self-evident right of the performer, they ought surely to retain the flow of the melody, indeed to enhance it. Apart from appoggiaturas (which 'occasionally repeat a preceding tone'),[23] the embellishments added by the performer should not impede the progress of the melody. Bearing this in mind, it would be quite possible, in Ex. 13.16, to improvise mordents on the crotchets in bars 9, 11, and 13, or *Pralltriller* (beginning on the main note) on the following notes and at the end. When C. P. E. Bach states that incorrect ornaments often ruin 'the finest

Ex. 13.16. Partita No. 4, BWV 828, Aria, bars 8–16

---

[21] The synthesis of vocal and instrumental music was a predominant 18th-cent. concept: 'Instrumental themes became vocal in character, or rather, they assumed a linguistic structure. On the other hand, vocal music is organized on instrumental lines. Replete with instrumental turns of phrase, it is deemed to be instrumental music. In Bach the itinerant musician, the organist, the cantor, and the court Kapellmeister are united in one person. It might be said that, since the independence of instrumental music, the inner reason for a division into vocal and instrumental music has disappeared. Vocal music is correctly performed only when it is treated as if it were instrumental music, that is, on account of its purely instrumental and motivic structure. And instrumental music should be performed as if it were vocal music, that is, in an eloquent manner, with the urgency of speech' (T. Georgiades, *Musik und Sprache* (Berlin, Göttingen, and Heidelberg, 1954), pp. 84 f. See also Karl Hochreither, 'Über die Wechselbeziehung zwischen Vokalem und Instrumentalem', *Zur Aufführungspraxis*, pp. 132 f.

[22] 'It is a well-known fact that in strict voice-leading repeating notes is forbidden': Harnoncourt, *Musik als Klangrede*, p. 169.

[23] C. P. E. Bach, *Essay*, p. 87.

legato passages' and that trills and mordents should be full and performed in such a way that 'the listener will believe he is hearing only the original note',[24] then he is also no doubt voicing the views of his father.

THE *CLAVIER-BÜCHLEIN* FOR W. F. BACH AND ITS SIGNIFICANCE FOR THE ORNAMENTATION AND PERFORMANCE OF BACH'S · KEYBOARD WORKS

Bach's manuscripts are far more for the musician than a mere source of information. They are objects of veneration. We contemplate with respect and astonishment those slightly browned sheets of paper, dumb witnesses of an inspiration that gave rise to masterpieces. However, the musical information of such manuscripts is much richer than would appear at first sight. Niceties of notation—so subtle they cannot be reproduced in print—sometimes give an indication of the kind of effect the composer had in mind when committing the work to paper, of which notes belong more closely together and which are to be separate, what is important and what is less important.[25] The difference between the impetuosity of a working manuscript and the calm, almost serene flow of a fair copy is clearly evident.

Corrections, which also occur in fair copies, show the endless possibilities that reside in the creative process in music. It is indeed astonishing that works whose inner logic seems to have the permanence of sculpture could in many places have quite easily taken a different turn, and that the version finally selected is usually the best one. Even for a genius such as Bach there was often no final solution to a compositional problem, merely a number of equally valid variants. And mistakes and slight moments of carelessness tell us something, if only that geniuses were at times all too human.

The paper also tells us much. Research into paper and watermarks often enables us to determine the date of a manuscript (which does not always coincide with that of the actual composition) to within a month. However important this and other information may be, the truly moving thing is the impression of the writing itself, of the hand which, like a 'tentacle' of the soul, has indelibly etched its traces into the paper. Bach's staunch faith and his firm and yet lovable character, which shine forth from every flourish of his beautiful energetic handwriting, have immortalized themselves in the autographs. The artistic energy and the typical curvature of Bach's beams—graphic works of art in their own right—continue to move one; they are a clear sign that these lines suggested to him a performance that was full of life.

---

[24] *Essay*, pp. 106, 150.
[25] See Harnoncourt, 'Was ein Autograph sagt', *Musik als Klangrede*, p. 237. I wrote this chapter before Harnoncourt's book was published, and am gratified to see that our views on this subject coincide.

In spite of retaining a firm basic rhythm there was nothing angular, sharp-edged, or machine-like about his music.

These and similar thoughts and emotions ran through my mind when, in March 1982, while visiting Yale University, I was briefly able to hold in my hand the *Clavier-Büchlein* for Wilhelm Friedemann Bach about 260 years after it had been written. It is perhaps the most precious gift that any child has ever received. The volume also contains the two-part Inventions and three-part Sinfonias (in a sequence that is perhaps even more convincing than that of the 'final version')[26] in addition to some preludes from *WTC* I with interesting variants. All this has an ideal intellectual value that far exceeds the astronomical material worth. As a particular gem among all these treasures the volume contains some pieces with fingering, and above all Bach's only extant table of ornaments, the 'Explication unterschiedlicher Zeichen, so gewiße manieren artig zu spielen, andeuten' (see Ex. 13.17 and Fig. 8).[27]

Although this table is of great interest on account of the light it sheds on Bach's ornamentation, it has caused a certain amount of confusion. Bach could not have foreseen the controversies it has occasioned. If he had, he might well have preferred to restrict himself to instructing his son by word of mouth, as he did with his other children and pupils.

How did these controversies arise? What is the reason for this confusion? The facts are that:

1. some musicians have considered and still consider that this short, two-line table suffices to solve all the problems of ornamentation in the works of Bach;
2. certain important Bach ornaments are not included in the table;
3. the first sign for the long trill with a halt (*point d'arrêt*) is the very short wavy line that was later exclusively used for the *Pralltriller* and *Schneller*;
4. Bach's table bears a certain resemblance to an old table by d'Anglebert, which Bach himself copied (see Fig. 7). This has led to the facile assumption that Bach's ornamentation is 'French'.

With regard to the final point, which also appears in Dolmetsch, Harich-Schneider, and Kreutz, the best thing to do is to compare the facsimile of the complete d'Anglebert table (Fig. 9) with Bach's 'Explication' (Fig. 8). Certain similarities do exist, of course. Yet even the first trill is different, and the second d'Anglebert ornament is completely different to the last and last-but-one Bach ornaments. D'Anglebert's fifth and sixth ornaments do not appear at all in Bach's table; nor does the seventh. The signs for the mordent (on d'Anglebert's second line) are completely different from those used by Bach. In short, this cannot be a straightforward copy.

---

[26] See Ellwood Derr, 'Bach's "Composer's Vademecum" or the "Strong Foretaste of Composition" in the Two-Part Inventions Explain'd', *Music Theory Spectrum*, 3 (1981), 26–48.

[27] The claim that the title should really be 'Explicatio' (see e.g. Neumann, *Ornamentation*, p. 126), and that the 'n' was added later, probably by Bach himself, is unfounded.

Ex. 13.17. J. S. Bach's 'Explication' of ornaments for his son Wilhelm Friedemann

Fig. 7. J. S. Bach's copy of d'Anglebert's table of ornaments

FIG. 8. J. S. Bach's 'Explication' of ornaments for his son Wilhelm Friedemann

Let us briefly examine the other points that could cause confusion. With regard to the first point, a list compiled for a child will, for pedagogical reasons, tend to simplification. Bodky makes the following comment:

Unfortunately, for practical purposes the table is not as helpful as we would like it to be; it covers only average problems, revealing nothing about the subtleties of the art of embellishment for which C. P. E. Bach needs sixty pages. However, it seems obvious that the elder Bach did not want to go into more detail because his table was written for a boy of nine who would have been more confused than enlightened by anything more than the basic information.[28]

As Bach himself stated in the title, he wished to give only an indication of the ornaments concerned, and it would surely be wrong to accord too much importance to these hints. A 'hint' of this kind tells the experienced player that the first trill can also have seven notes instead of five, that the second one can have ten, twelve, or fourteen notes instead of eight, and that in the turn, the *cadence*, the notes do not have to be of equal length and can be played rubato. And in the penultimate example one pair of notes could easily be omitted, which would give us a *Pralltriller* as described by Marpurg.

Concerning the second point, the missing ornaments do not only include the *Pralltriller*, slide, and long mordent, as has often been noted, but also, as Neumann correctly points out, the most important of all ornaments, the small

[28] *Interpretation*, p. 150.

FIG. 9. D'Anglebert's printed table of ornaments

appoggiatura note. There are also no trills with notated suffixes, turns after dotted notes, acciaccaturas, arpeggios, and so on. To explain all these missing ornaments is not within the scope of this study. However, one word about the slide. Bach uses two different abbreviations, namely two small notes, and the German slide symbol ⌃. Both signs were explained by his son in the *Essay* (see Ex. 13.18). Marpurg gives only the second form (see Ex. 13.19); it is sometimes played as in Ex. 13.20, though this is quite wrong.

Ex. 13.18. From C. P. E. Bach, *Essay*, p. 137

Ex. 13.19   Ex. 13.20

Emery and Neumann provide a great deal of interesting information about this ornament, for example that the slide sometimes has to be anticipated, as in Kuhnau and Heinichen, and that in the old German form it can also appear in a dotted rhythm.[29] The long mordent, which also does not appear in the table, was probably only rarely used by J. S. Bach.

The third possible cause of confusion, namely that short wavy lines can signify long trills and trill signs short trills or *Pralltriller*, has been discussed above. Concerning the fourth point, the fact that Bach copied something does not mean that he agreed with its contents. In this case in particular it could also mean that he was trying to familiarize himself with French ornamentation. It is important to emphasize the differences between Bach's and d'Anglebert's tables. Bach almost always used different names and, above all in the case of the *mordant*, and the *accent* and *trillo*, different symbols, both deriving from the German tradition.

However, one would descend to the level of a nine-year-old child if one thought that by concentrating solely on the 'Explication' one could solve all problems of Bach ornamentation. It is in the nature of such short tables that they do not contain the most common embellishments. I am personally of the opinion that Bach did not have to explain the 'half-trill' to young Wilhelm Friedemann, for he was quite familiar with it.[30] Evidence that the 'Explication' itself cannot wholly explain Bach's ornamentation is immediately provided by the piece that follows it, the 'Applicatio' (application, or fingering). It only contains a small selection of the ornaments previously described, and also calls for executions not provided for in the preceding table (see Ex. 13.21). Not only the note symbols have a profound significance; so do Bach's titles, such as the three letters 'J.N.J.' (In nomine Jesu), which apply not only to the 'Applicatio', but probably to the whole *Clavier-Büchlein*. On account of this superscription it cannot come as a surprise that the 'Applicatio' concludes with a melodic formula taken from early church music: an embellished resolution of the suspended *penultima* (f), which has always been a traditional cadential feature. An earlier technical term for suspension was *Vorschlag* (appoggiatura) or *Akzent* (accent), and thus we would not go far wrong in suggesting an execution of the final embellishment in the last bar on the lines of Bach's *accent* and *trillo*, though with two notes fewer than in the 'Explication'—after all, it is the ornament that by common consent is supposed to be so short that it does not impede the progress of the notes (see

---

[29] Emery, *Bach's Ornaments*, pp. 24 ff.; Neumann, *Ornamentation*, pp. 217 ff. On Heinichen, see above, p. 282.

[30] O'Donnell rightly observes that a table written in Cöthen in 1720 does not necessarily apply to works written in Arnstadt in 1703 or in Weimar in 1712 ('Bach's Trills', p. 17). The turn between 2 notes, which is not mentioned in the 'Explication', is examined by Emery, *Bach's Ornaments*, pp. 32 ff., Werner J. Fries, 'Bachs Doppelschlag', *BJb*, 57 (1971), 98, and Neumann, *Ornamentation*, p. 474.

Ex. 13.21. *Clavierbüchlein* for W. F. Bach, 'Applicatio'

J. N. J.

1. Applicatio

Ex. 13.22).[31] However, the number of alternations is not as important as the fact that the ornament begins on e.

Ex. 13.22

This should really be self-evident. Yet the instructions by Willard Palmer quoted in Ex. 13.23 are unfortunately typical of a whole generation of harpsichordists and pianists.[32] This separation of suspension and resolution is surely wrong. The French, who are usually cited in such cases, did not execute the ornament thus: compare Rameau's *cadence appuyée* (p. 267), the last bar of Ex. 1.2, and a table provided by Dom Bédos. The numbers and signs in the lower system refer to the construction of organ-barrels, the upper system provides an exact transcription into normal notation. I have taken from this table the extracts shown in Exx. 13.24–5, which show *Pralltriller* and trills beginning on the main note (even in the case of unslurred notes).

---

[31] See ch. 12, the statements of Tosi (p. 260), C. P. E. Bach (p. 288), and Marpurg (p. 298). Formulas of this kind have survived for centuries. What is virtually the same formula appears even in a *galant* work such as Mozart's F major Sonata K. 332/300k (1st movement, bars 7–8).

[32] Equally incorrect instructions are found in the edns. of Tureck and Aldrich.

Ex. 13.23. *Clavierbüchlein* for W. F. Bach, 'Applicatio', bar 8, ed. W. Palmer, *J. S. Bach. An Introduction to his Keyboard Music* (Sherman Oaks, Calif., n.d.), 28

Ex. 13.24. Bédos, *L'Art du facteur d'orgues*, vol. ii, Table 119

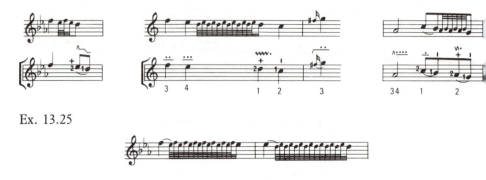

Ex. 13.25

They come from a romance by Claude-Bénigne Balbastre. Balbastre, a pupil of Rameau and an imitator of Couperin, carried out this exact notation at the behest of Père Engramelle or Dom Bédos.[33] Of course it also contains examples of auxiliary trills. Of interest is a gradually accelerated long trill in bars 19–20 of the romance.

As baroque composers used legato slurs very sparingly, it is certainly legitimate to play a slurred *Pralltriller* in similar cases, no matter whether a slur is included or not. If one plays an auxiliary trill on the second note the effect shown in Ex. 13.26 results, especially on old instruments with sluggish actions. This completely contradicts the usual 'suspension and resolution' articulation. The auxiliary trill always creates a sharp accent—and is thus out of place on an unaccented note.

Ex. 13.26

---

[33] See Bédos, *L'Art du facteur d'orgues*, i. 527.

In J. S. Bach, there is a *Pralltriller* in the F minor Fugue of *WTC* I (sixth and penultimate bars) that is related to the 'Applicatio' of the *Clavier-Büchlein*. Again it embellishes a *penultima* note (see Ex. 13.27). This also is

Ex. 13.27. *WTC* I, Fugue in F minor, bars 1–6

an embellishment of a suspension (Ex. 13.28). For this reason Bach wrote a *Pralltriller* over the b and not a mordent, as one might have expected on account of the preceding lower note a. And for the same reason it would be

Ex. 13.28

wrong to begin the *Pralltriller* on c (see Ex. 13.29). A leap of a third from a to c would run counter to the old principle that compound ornaments should comprise only conjunct steps (i.e. intervals of a second). Here again the performer's feeling for 'natural' melody should help him to come to the right decision even without such special knowledge. However, experience teaches us that this cannot be taught.

Ex. 13.29

A particularly valuable aspect of the 'Applicatio' is the fingering. As in the old organ and keyboard tablatures Bach does his best to avoid the thumb, and often causes the other fingers to cross, as Chopin was later to do. This produces a singing style of playing, especially on the clavichord, because the upper fingers can depress the keys more softly than the thumb. It is charming to see how Bach, in the cadential formula mentioned above, took into account the small size of the child's hands. Unfortunately he did not extend the fingering to the ornaments—it would have solved some of our problems. However, at least the execution of the mordents can be regarded as certain: in the first two bars the only possible fingering is 3–2–3. In such cases this means that the number refers to the *first* note of the ornament.[34] In the fifth note of bar 1 the lower note could be either f or f♯. Going by a rule laid down by Heinichen,[35] f♯ seems preferable. In bar 6 the ascending trill must surely begin with g♯ (instead of g), the leading note in A minor.

The second part of the 'Applicatio' begins in true Bachian style with an inversion of the beginning. I would not hesitate to include the ornament in this, by playing a c–d–c *Pralltriller*. The 3–4–3 fingering would be an analogy to the fingering of the mordent in bar 1. However, harpsichordists in the last fifty years have been quite happy to play a short auxiliary trill, d–c–d–c, here, though this would mean that the ensuing b cannot be played with finger 2 as Bach recommends.

The following chapters attempt to ascertain which of the two executions is most probably the correct one. I use the word 'probably' because absolute proof can only be attained in a very few cases. However, an argument in favour of the literal inversion of a motif seems to be provided by a final version of the Gigue from the A minor Partita that has hitherto gone unnoticed.[36] In this piece the second part also begins with an inversion of the theme, though initially this does not incorporate the melodic patterns on the second and fourth beats (see Ex. 13.30). On the second and fourth beats of the bar both versions have a written-out mordent. However, in the 'final' version Bach

Ex. 13.30. Partita No. 3, BWV 827, Gigue, bars 1–2, 24–6

---

[34] In the 18th cent. it was common practice in Germany to give only the fingering for the 1st note of an ornament (e.g. in C. P. E. Bach, Türk, A. E. Müller). Couperin on the other hand provides fingering in a trill exercise in *L'Art*, p. 20, for chains of trills. These obviously refer to the unembellished notes. Thus it is wrong to jump to conclusions about the execution of the ornaments on the basis of Bach's fingering. The trill over f^2 in bar 2 of the 'Applicatio' is problematical. Fingering 4–5 or 5–4 could hardly be countenanced (not only in the case of a child). Either Bach meant a 4–3 fingering (g–f), or he wrote a mordent that turned out to be longer than intended, something I consider to be more plausible.

[35] *Der General-Baß*, p. 531.

[36] Wolff, 'Textkritische Bermerkungen', pp. 70 ff. I share Wolff's view that these corrections were most probably made by Bach himself.

transformed the mordent in the second section into a 'slow *Schneller*', making several changes in the other voices to accommodate the voice-leading (Ex. 13.31).

Ex. 13.31. Partita No. 3, BWV 827, Gigue, bars 24–8, 41–2

Let us look briefly at the next piece of the *Clavier-Büchlein*, the Praeambulum, which concludes with a lengthy pedal-point. There is another *Pralltriller* in the fourth bar before the end. If this ornament begins on the main note it fits in snugly into the flow of the music; if, on the other hand, one treats it as a short auxiliary trill, it leads to a repetition of c^2, which would be not only musically rather clumsy, but also difficult to play from a fingering point of view (see Ex. 13.32). Would Bach really have confronted his little son

Ex. 13.32. *Clavierbüchlein* for W. F. Bach, Praeambulum, bars 10–18

with difficulties of this kind? Although this has little to do with ornaments, it is worth noting that on the organ the held G in the bass is heard throughout all eight bars. But on all other keyboard instruments it must be restruck from time to time (see p. 141). In the autograph Bach may well have omitted the dotted ties in this example deliberately. The F natural at the end of bar 15, which is included in the Griepenkerl edition, is omitted in most modern editions, possibly due to an oversight on the part of the editors. As is well known, Bach's accidentals applied only to the notes they immediately preceded, and did not remain in operation for the whole bar. If Bach had wanted an F sharp at this juncture, he would have written another sharp sign, as indeed he did before the seventh note. Thus F natural is the only permissible reading (see also p. 496, n. 12).

14

Pralltriller

SUMMARY: THE TWO FORMS OF THE *PRALLTRILLER* IN THEORY AND
PRACTICE FROM THE SEVENTEENTH CENTURY TO THE TWENTIETH
CENTURY

(*a*) *Beginning on main note*   (*b*) *Beginning on auxiliary*

1. In theory before J. S. Bach

Repeatedly described, also with several alternations as long trill	Non-existent (longer form with several alternations described on a few occasions)

2. In theory at the time of J. S. Bach

Repeatedly described	Non-existent

3. In theory after J. S. Bach

Repeatedly described	Sporadically described. The earliest description in 1753 by C. P. E. Bach is based on a printing error that was corrected in later editions

4. In written-out form in J. S. Bach

Several instances	Non-existent

5. Relationship to the rules of part-writing

Almost always leads to correct voice-leading	Sometimes produces consecutive fifths and octaves

6. In written-out form in Haydn, Mozart, and Beethoven

Several instances	Non-existent

7. In musical practice since *c*.1930

Becoming increasingly rare	Becoming increasingly common

PRALLTRILLER AFTER PRECEDING UPPER SECOND

As we have seen, especially in Chapter 12, a stepwise descending succession of notes is the classic instance of where a *Pralltriller* occurs; and here it almost always has to begin on the main note. Here even confirmed devotees of the 'auxiliary' admit the main-note execution, though with the wrong proviso that there must be a slur.[1]

Thus our first task will be to prove that this restriction deriving from the notation is not normally true in Bach. This is simply because he rarely notated slurs in his keyboard works. The performer had to supply them on the basis of the rules of part-writing valid at the time. There is *always* a legato slur of this kind when a dissonant appoggiatura is followed by a consonant resolution. The rule from the *Essay* cited above to the effect that the note following an appoggiatura has to be linked to it 'in the absence as well as the presence of a slur' also applies to J. S. Bach.[2] It makes no difference whether the preceding appoggiatura accent is notated as a small hook, a small appoggiatura note, or a large note. The legato slurring of appoggiatura and main note was a rule to which there were no exceptions right into the nineteenth century. A good example of the interchangeable nature of different ways of writing the appoggiatura is found in the E major Prelude from *WTC* II, where Bach, in passages that are otherwise identical, once (bar 21) writes a large quaver, and later (bar 43) a quaver appoggiatura. In the autograph the *Pralltriller* sign above the second note is missing in both instances, though it appears in copies, including those made by Bach's pupils Altnikol and Kirnberger. These contain many later changes and emendations by Bach and thus, as final corrected versions, are often to be preferred to the autographs themselves. However, as repeated notes make slurs impossible, the execution often heard (Ex. 14.1) is almost certainly incorrect. Slurring two adjacent notes can and should be further intensified on keyboard instruments by legato—the first of two notes is released only after the second has been played.[3] The legato effect

Ex. 14.1

---

[1] See Harich-Schneider's remarks concerning Rameau's *tremblement appuyé* (*Die Kunst des Cembalospiels*, p. 85).

[2] The rule which states that a harmonic suspension, no matter how it is notated, has to be linked to its resolution is thus explicitly stated by C. P. E. Bach (*Essay*, p. 88). Indeed, it has been a feature of European music for centuries, as Harnoncourt pointed out in *Musik als Klangrede*, p. 168. In the above passage (*Essay*, p. 88) C. P. E. Bach states that appoggiaturas are normally louder than the following note. Later he notes: 'But in general it can be said that dissonances are played loudly and consonances softly, since the former rouse our emotions and the latter quiet them.' (*Essay*, p. 163.)

[3] See Rameau's description of the *liaison* (slur) in *Pièces de clavecin*, p. 41.

is further emphasized by the addition of an ornament. However, if the first note were repeated, there would be a gap between notes that belong together (note-repetition entails re-activation of the same note, and this in itself contradicts the slur). Appoggiaturas of this kind in Bach must thus be 'slurred' to the following resolution, as for example in the recitative and arioso 'Immanuel, o süßes Wort' in the Christmas Oratorio, Part IV (see Ex. 14.2). Not only the (self-evident) slur in the violin part, but also the word-underlay in the soprano, 'Kreu-zes Stamm', excludes a repetition of c^2, 'Kreu-eu-zes Stamm'.

Ex. 14.2. Christmas Oratorio, Part IV, recitative and arioso No. 38, bar 17

An incorrect repetition of this kind with the ornament on the resolution of a dissonance has unfortunately often become the rule in modern harpsichord playing. Thus in his edition of the Goldberg Variations, Ralph Kirkpatrick gave the executions of the *Pralltriller* in the theme as shown in Ex. 14.3. This execution would be justified only if the melody of the Aria were not intended to be played cantabile, but in a kind of hopping manner.[4]

Ex. 14.3. Goldberg Variations, Aria, ed. R. Kirkpatrick (Schirmer, New York, 1938)

[4] On the embellishment of this theme see below, pp. 466 f.

Similar repetitions in the case of *Pralltriller* or short trills that Bach probably did not want are contained in certain modern editions of the Inventions and Partitas (see Exx. 14.4–14.6). It should be noted that J. S. Bach himself added the bracketed slur in Ex. 14.6 as a correction in some copies of the first edition. The correct execution of this passage from the B flat Partita is shown in Ex. 14.7.

Ex. 14.4. Invention No. 1, BWV 772, bars 1–2

Bach's autograph

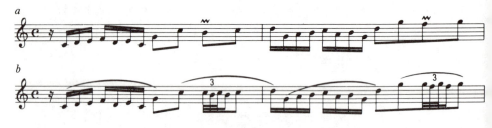

ed. P. Aldrich; W. Palmer (Alfred Ed.); and many modern harpsichordists

Ex. 14.5. Partita No. 1, BWV 825, Allemande, bar 12, ed. Palmer

Ex. 14.6. Partita No. 1, BWV 825, Praeludium, bar 18, ed. Palmer

The importance that Bach attached to the legato slur between suspension, dissonance, and resolution is also demonstrated by the genetic history of the six Partitas, which appeared singly from 1726 onwards until they were collected in 1731 to form the first part of the *Clavier-Übung*. Even in the first single edition the handful of slurs that do occur are between dissonances and their resolutions, and are intended to clarify matters compared with the early versions, where they are usually missing. When the Partitas were finally gathered together in the second edition Bach had a number of corrections

Ex. 14.7. (*a*) according to Marpurg, Quantz, and others; (*b*) according to C. P. E. Bach (the best solution); (*c*) according to the 'Explication'[5]

made, which again included legato slurs of this kind. And finally, in his *Handexemplar* (personal copy)[6] and in other copies Bach himself again added slurs between suspensions and resolutions.[7] In the Goldberg Variations Bach added several slurs in his personal copy, for instance in variation 12 between the first two notes in bars 4 and 5, top system. He could hardly have been more forthright about making it plain that he did not wish his works to be performed in a 'chopped-off' manner!

We will now consider the *Pralltriller* in the context of descending voice-leading.

Pralltriller *on an Unaccented Note after a Suspension*

Pralltriller of this kind often occur on the final note of a sigh-motif, as for instance in the Allemande of the Partita No. 2 in C minor, bars 9–10 (see Ex. 14.8). As a conclusion of a sigh-motif this form occurs frequently not only in the works of J. S. Bach, but also in those of later composers (e.g. C. P. E. Bach, Haydn, Chopin). Ex. 14.8 is particularly instructive in that the slurs in

Ex. 14.8. Partita No. 2, BWV 826, Allemande, bars 9–10

---

[5] Elsewhere Quantz advises against using more than 3 notes (*On Playing the Flute*, p. 154).

[6] British Library, MS Hirsch II/37. J. S. Bach, 'Clavierübung I, 6 Partiten'; fac. repr. in 'The Composer's Edition', ed. D. Kinsela (Basingstoke, 1985).

[7] A cursory examination revealed no less than 7 such additional slurs.

brackets and the fourth *Pralltriller* sign do not appear in the first edition, but were added in ink in the Hirsch copy referred to above. They show the importance Bach attached to the 'slurred' execution of this combination of notes. Furthermore, the addition of the fourth ornament in the Hirsch copy shows that in sequences of this kind ornaments should also be repeated, even if they were originally not notated. The same holds true of the A minor Duet, BWV 805, bars 18–20, 22–4, and so on (Ex. 14.9); however, the preceding note in this case is not a suspension.

Ex. 14.9. Duet No. 4, BWV 805, bars 17–20

Such *Pralltriller* also occur in longer groups of notes, for instance in the C sharp minor Prelude from *WTC* II. Ex. 14.10 shows the suspension in bar 4 notated as a small appoggiatura note (in other sources it appears as a little hook, the meaning of which is identical). Ex. 14.11 shows bar 11 in Altnikol's reading. (On the possible short execution of these appoggiaturas see below, p. 410.) In bar 61 the appoggiatura is notated as a large note (see Ex. 14.12). Ex. 14.13 shows a further instance, from the Duet in A minor, BWV 805. The slur missing from the dissonance *a* to *g♯* in the original is absolutely essential, according to the rules of part-writing. The execution of the ornament often played (Ex. 14.14) is thus to be deplored (the note *a* occurs three times on the strong beat).

Ex. 14.10. *WTC* II, Prelude in C sharp minor, bar 4

Because the accented dissonance preceding the *Pralltriller* definitely has to be slurred to the following resolution, there can be no reasonable doubt in these instances about an execution as in Exx. 14.3 and 12.57. Thus the

Ex. 14.11. *WTC* II, Prelude in C sharp minor, bar 11, Altnikol's reading

Ex. 14.12. *WTC* II, Prelude in C sharp minor, bar 61

Ex. 14.13. Duet No. 4, BWV 805, bars 39–42

Ex. 14.14

tripartite *Pralltriller* enters either on the beat (as suggested by Marpurg) or is slightly held back (as suggested by C. P. E. Bach). One should be wary of the anticipation that is unfortunately rather common. C. P. E. Bach makes a point of stating: 'All embellishments notated in small notes pertain to the following tone. Therefore, while the preceding tone is never shortened, the following tone loses as much of its length as the small notes take from it. This observation grows in importance the more it is neglected . . .'[8]

----

[8] *Essay*, p. 84. On rare exceptions to this rule see pp. 396 ff.

Pralltriller *over an Accented Note*

Ex. 14.15. Italian Concerto, second movement, bar 7

The g^1 dissonance in Ex. 14.15 must be slurred to the following consonance, f^1. In such passages even the French used to begin the *Pralltriller* on the main note in the eighteenth century (see Ex. 14.16). As there is no slur at this point in the first edition of the Italian Concerto, some Bach performers are of the opinion that it should be played non-legato, and that a *Pralltriller* beginning on the auxiliary is intended. However, this is unlikely, for two reasons:

1. The notes preceding the trill signs are dissonances.

2. Slurring the three descending notes corresponds to Bach's normal articulation, for which there is much evidence, for instance in the first movement of the Harpsichord Concerto in E major, bars 5, 22, 59, 112, 135, 172 (see Ex. 14.17) and bar 89 (Ex. 14.18). For this reason it is very unlikely that the *Pralltriller* in the same movement of BWV 1053, bars 52 and 166, were conceived in a non-legato context, quite apart from the technical difficulty in the Allegro tempo (see Ex. 14.19).

Ex. 14.16. Bédos, *L'Art du facteur d'orgues*, vol. ii, Tables 114, 117

Ex. 14.17. Harpsichord Concerto in E major, BWV 1053, first movement, bar 5

Ex. 14.18. Harpsichord Concerto in E major, BWV 1053, first movement, bar 89

Ex. 14.19. Harpsichord Concerto in E major, BWV 1053, first movement

It is also remarkable that in almost all later theoretical works it is this formula that is cited as a model example for the application of a *Pralltriller*, for instance, in C. P. E. Bach (see Ex. 14.21) or Marpurg (see Ex. 14.20). Klotz cites an identical example from Bach's son Johann Christoph Friedrich (b. 1732), though unfortunately without revealing the source. Finally, in J. S. Bach, legato slurs occur in similar figurations, for instance in the Courante of English Suite in A major (Ex. 14.22) and in the Sarabande (Ex. 14.23).

Ex. 14.20. Marpurg, *Anleitung*, p. 56 n. 2 and Table V, Fig. 1

Ex. 14.21. C. P. E. Bach, *Essay*, p. 112

Ex. 14.22. English Suite No. 1, BWV 806, Courante, Double I, bar 21

Ex. 14.23. English Suite No. 1, BWV 806, Sarabande, bar 1

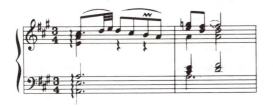

In descending lines with *Pralltriller* the question is whether or not it is right to add legato slurs even if they are not in the text. If the preceding note is a dissonance, the legato slur is certainly correct. However, what happens when there is a consonance before the ornament? Here a short trill beginning on the auxiliary on the lines of the *tremblement détaché* may well be meant. The execution shown for Invention No. 1 in Ex. 14.24, which is now played by the majority of harpsichordists, would perhaps be justified (e.g. on the lines suggested by Agricola) if the motif of the last three quavers (c–b–c and g–f–g) were construed as being separate. The original grouping of twice two quavers in bar 1 might in this instance really suggest an articulation of the kind shown in Ex. 14.25. For this articulation there would even be corroborative evidence in the case of a similar melodic figure in the *St Matthew Passion* in

Ex. 14.24

Ex. 14.25

the aria with chorus 'Ich will bei meinem Jesu wachen' (see Ex. 14.26*a*). But in this case Bach changed the original articulation consistently in the flute and upper string parts that he wrote out himself. The last three quavers of the motif were slurred, namely in bars 14, 19 f., 27 f., 55 f., 63 f., 71 f., and 77 f. (see Ex. 14.26*b*). This is all the more remarkable because it means that the instrumental parts deviate from the declamation of the (identical) vocal line— surely a convincing piece of evidence for the kind of articulation that Bach favoured in instrumental works.[9]

Ex. 14.26. *St Matthew Passion*, aria NBA No. 20, BGA No. 26

Reading of the autograph score

a

Reading of parts corrected by Bach

b

[9] In the score the NBA has rightly adopted the later articulation from the authentic performance material. Harnoncourt (*Musik als Klangrede*, p. 54) has made the same observation with regard to Cantata No. 47.

Recently some evidence has come to light that almost seems to prove the use of the *Pralltriller* in Invention No. 1. In a recently discovered letter written in 1801 to the Leipzig publishers Hoffmeister & Kühnel in connection with the publication of the Inventions, Bach's biographer Johann Nikolaus Forkel comments on the embellishments:

The embellishments therein must be precisely distinguished, and as I now see in the fourth volume that you are as yet not wholly familiar with the distinction peculiar to the Bach school, I am putting the main points in writing. The ∿ is a *Pralltriller* that is used in descending melodies, whereas in ascending ones the short mordent ∿ is employed. The two embellishments consist of two notes only; the former takes the note above, and the latter the note below the main note. The ∿ sign indicates a simple trill, the ∿ sign an ascending trill, and the ∿ sign a descending trill. The ∾ signs refer to turns . . .'[10]

As is well known, Forkel had written and spoken to Bach's eldest sons a quarter of a century before the publication of his biography. C. P. E. Bach's letters to Forkel afford evidence of the fact that the latter was at pains to include in his biography all the information supplied.[11] As Forkel, according to Griepenkerl, was a pupil of Wilhelm Friedemann Bach (from whom he borrowed for a time a cycle of Bach cantatas now no longer extant), he probably owed his knowledge of Bach's ornaments to the son into whose *Stammbuch* Bach had written the Inventions.[12]

The execution shown in the C major Invention also applies to the start of the Sarabande of Partita No. 3 in A minor. Ex. 14.27 shows the autograph reading.[13]

Pralltriller on accented notes often occur in figuration that derives from the old German organ and harpsichord performance practice (e.g. Froberger,

Ex. 14.27. Partita No. 3, BWV 827, Sarabande, bars 1–2, autograph reading

[10] Again I am grateful to George B. Stauffer for allowing me to consult his MS 'A Bach Biographical Source Recovered', and his transcription of Forkel's letter of 21 Dec. 1801. Forkel's letters to this publisher have now been published in Arthur Mendel, 'The Forkel–Hoffmeister & Kühnel Correspondence—A Document of the Early 19th-Century Bach Revival', *Essays on J. S. Bach*, ed. George Stauffer (New York, 1990), pp. 5 ff.

[11] See *Bach-Dokumente*, iii, Nos. 785, 791–5, 801–4, 807.

[12] See Stauffer, 'Biographical Source', pp. 1 and 8.

[13] The *Pralltriller* sign occurs in the *Notenbüchlein* for Anna Magdalena Bach. In the *Clavier-Übung* version there is a sign here (and at parallel passages) which could signify both a somewhat drawn-out mordent and a suffixed trill. However, a mordent (the BGA reading) is unlikely.

Kerll, Buxtehude, Pachelbel), where the main-note beginning is also well documented. There are analogies to this in the Allemande of Partita No. 3 (Ex. 14.28) and in the C minor Toccata (Ex. 14.29). For technical reasons an execution other than the three-note (unretarded) one is hardly possible in instances of this kind. Circumstantial evidence for this execution is supplied

Ex. 14.28. Partita No. 3, BWV 827, Allemande, bars 6–7

Ex. 14.29. Toccata in C minor, BWV 911, bar 1

by a passage in the C sharp minor Fugue of *WTC* II (Ex. 14.30). Yet if, in these examples, one were to follow posthumous rules (such as those of Agricola) blindly and begin the ornament none the less with the auxiliary, one would be offending not only against the rules of part-writing, but against that main rule of embellishment, which requires of ornaments that they should link the melody (and not tear it apart). As we have seen, '. . . the primary aim of all embellishments is to connect notes'.[14]

Ex. 14.30. *WTC* II, Fugue in C sharp minor, bar 26

Kirnberger's version   Altnikol's version

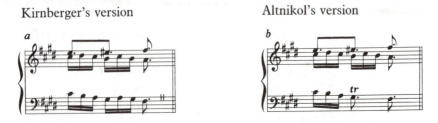

This way of executing the *Pralltriller* is probably even more valid for Handel than it is for Bach. Handel's style was decisively influenced by the Italian school during his long sojourn in Italy, though in his youth he had been trained in the German organ tradition by his teacher Zachow (and by his meetings with Buxtehude). Both the Italian and German schools adapted the start of the trill to the melodic context, and began the *Pralltriller* on the main note.

---

[14] C. P. E. Bach, *Essay*, p. 84.

Just how widespread the fashion of beginning the *Pralltriller* on the upper auxiliary (which is historically unprovable) was even fifteen years ago is shown by the following remark and example by Peter Northway in the preface to the second volume of the keyboard works in the Hallische Händel-Ausgabe:

When the trill sign appears over a short quaver or semiquaver note it is frequently impossible to play more than a *Pralltriller*.

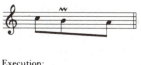

Execution:

This view, proferred without any source-based evidence, is no longer tenable from a historical point of view. Evidence to the contrary includes the many written-out trills beginning on the main note, such as those in Handel's Organ Concerto in B flat major (see Ex. 14.31).

Ex. 14.31. Handel, Organ Concerto in B flat major, Op. 7/1, first movement, Andante, bar 37 after Adolf Beyschlag, *Die Ornamentik in der Musik* (Berlin, 1908; repr. Leipzig, 1953), 108

PRALLTRILLER ON THE SECOND OF TWO REPEATED NOTES (*ACCENTUS* FORMULA)

With regard to this sequence of notes, performers in the recent past have almost always played short four-note trills beginning on the auxiliary. The prevailing view continues to be that a tripartite *Pralltriller* should not be played here because Bach supposedly did not know the ornament. But as we have seen, C. P. E. Bach's innovation (see Chapter 12, pp. 298 f.) did not consist in the invention of this ornament. He only labelled and divided it into two similar embellishments (*Pralltriller* and *Schneller*), whose sole difference is the presence or absence of a preceding higher note.

That Bach knew the seventeenth-century German three-note trill described in Chapter 12 (p. 279) is demonstrated by similar notation in his own works, often in written-out form (see below, pp. 369 f.). O'Donnell comments:

The main musical influences of Bach during his early years were neither French nor Italian, but German. His various harpsichord and organ toccatas and partitas are emphatically German, influenced no doubt by other members of the Bach family, as well as such composers as Froberger, Kerll, Pachelbel and Buxtehude. There are indeed works of French influence, such as the *Fantasien* BWV 562 and 572, as there are works of Italian influence, including the *Alla breve, Canzona*, fugues on themes of Corelli, Legrenzi and Albinoni, and transcriptions of Vivaldi concertos, most of them dating from his Weimar years. But Bach was trained essentially as a German musician of a great line of keyboard performers and composers. Most of his early works belong to this tradition and, not surprisingly, his ornamentation conforms to German practice . . . The *Pralltriller* in the form of an inverted mordent was also commonplace at this time, occurring especially on the third semiquaver of groups of four. To commence this ornament in this context with the upper note, either struck or tied, is to mistake its ancestry. It is common late 17th century German form, particularly in harpsichord music, and is not a form of *tremblement lié*.[15]

It is important to note that numerous examples can be adduced to corroborate O'Donnell's observation. On the other hand, the four-note 'mini-trill' that is the one most commonly played today never appears in written-out form in Bach. We shall have occasion to return to this below. But first we must examine the three combinations in which a Bach *Pralltriller* or trill is preceded by a note of the same pitch. This formula occurs most frequently in so-called sigh-motifs, though it also appears over the second note of a tie, and in rapid runs.

Pralltriller *on the Penultimate Note of Sigh-motifs*

In the extract shown in Ex. 14.32 the (self-evident) articulation in the sigh-motif is missing. But compare Bach's dots and legato slurs in the wholly similar motif in the second movement of the G major Sonata for viola da gamba and obbligato harpsichord, BWV 1027 (see above, p. 315, Ex. 13.4).

Ex. 14.32. Partita No. 6, BWV 830, Toccata, bars 26–9

---

[15] 'Bach's Trills', pp. 17–18.

It is apparent to any musician that sigh-motifs often lead to 'forbidden' consecutive fifths and octaves if *Pralltriller* are executed as short auxiliary trills.[16] Only two conclusions can be drawn from these findings: either wrong voice-leading was tolerated in the case of certain embellishments, or the ornament that has to be played here cannot have been a trill beginning on the auxiliary. A third possibility, namely beginning with an extremely short anticipating appoggiatura auxiliary, is discussed on pp. 379 ff.

With regard to the first possibility, some Bach players seriously believe that on account of the speed of the ornament it does not matter whether one plays consecutive fifths or octaves (thereby suggesting that the rules of part-writing depend on speed). The dogma of beginning on the auxiliary is so universally and uncritically accepted nowadays that even good part-writing is unthinkingly sacrificed in the process. The fact that even fast consecutive fifths were not tolerated in the eighteenth century is shown by the example from the *Essay* quoted in Ex. 14.33, where C. P. E. Bach remarks that an ascending trill cannot be used because 'it creates forbidden fifths' (starting the trill with e–f–g–f would create the fifths f–e to the bass bb–a).

Ex. 14.33. From C. P. E. Bach, *Essay*, p. 110

This view can probably be explained only by the fact that the music of the last hundred years has accustomed us to consider as beautiful chords consisting of consecutive fifths, octaves, and other intervals. However, it is not legitimate to project our modern feelings on this matter on to past centuries. The surest way of refuting such erroneous views is the remarkable fact that the classical literature contains virtually no instances of two voices a fifth apart with trills on both. The reason for this is obvious. If the same ornament, for instance a trill beginning on the auxiliary, were executed, it would create a whole series of consecutive fifths.

However, there is a rare exception that made such a strong impression on me that I remembered it for well over thirty years. It occurs in the second movement of the G major Sonata for two pianos by Bach's youngest son, Johann Christian Bach (see Ex. 14.34). To our classically trained ears the passage sounds decidedly exotic. I have never been able to establish whether

[16] See also A. Kreutz, comm. to the English Suites, BWV 806–808 (Leipzig, 1950); Bodky, *Interpretation*, p. 375; Emery, *Bach's Ornaments*, pp. 147 f.; O'Donnell, 'Bach's Trills', p. 17; Neumann, *Ornamentation*, p. 316.

this is simply an inaccuracy on the part of the edition I was using, or a witticism on the part of the composer.

Ex. 14.34. J. C. Bach, Sonata in G major for two pianos, second movement

In those days I would not have believed that there is a unique instance of this kind in the music of J. S. Bach. However, Klaus Hofmann has pointed out that in the fourth movement of Cantata No. 199, *Mein Herze schwimmt in Blut*, there are trills a fifth apart. Moreover, even without these trills the first and second violins create consecutive fifths. That this may have been an error on the part of Bach is virtually ruled out, for the 'bad voice-leading' appears three times, in bars 19–20, 61–2, and 135–6 (see Ex. 14.35). How is one to account for this intentional 'error'? The answer seems to be suggested by the text of the aria, which reads:

> Tief gebückt und voller Reue
> lieg ich, lieber Gott, vor Dir.
> Aber habe doch Geduld mit mir,
> ich bekenne meine Schuld.

> [Bowing deep, and all repenting
> Dearest God, I lie before thee.
> But have patience yet with me
> All my sins I do confess.]

Ex. 14.35. Cantata No. 199, fourth movement, bars 16–21

The consecutive fifths are probably a symbol of the recognition of personal fallibility. Something of this kind never occurs in Bach's instrumental music where the verbal explanation is lacking.

Ex. 14.36. Invention No. 2, BWV 773

Bars 3, 13, 23, 25:

Probably incorrect execution of bar 3:   Suggested execution:[17]

Consider the instances of sigh-motifs with trills or *Pralltriller* shown in Exx. 14.36–14.40. In all these examples the *Pralltriller* must begin on the main note in order to avoid incorrect voice-leading. There would be particularly obtrusive consecutive fifths if the *Pralltriller* beginning on the auxiliary were used in bars 1 and 2 of the second movement of Flute Sonata with obbligato harpsichord No. 3 (see Ex. 14.41).[18]

---

[17] On *one* manual the passage can only be played in this way. 'Collisions' of this kind, where 2 voices touch the same note (key) shortly one after the other, occur fairly frequently in Bach's keyboard music, e.g. in bar 13 of the Courante from the C minor Partita, BWV 826:

Execution:

(simplified execution: mordent with $f \sharp^1$).

[18] I am grateful to Konstantin Restle of Munich for pointing this out to me.

Ex. 14.37. Invention No. 15, BWV 786, bars 14–15

Ex. 14.38. Canonic Variations, BWV 769, variation 4, bars 38–9

Ex. 14.39. Concerto in C major for two harpsichords, BWV 1061, third movement, bars 42–3

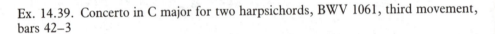

Ex. 14.40. Christmas Oratorio, Part VI, final chorale, bar 2 (repeated in bar 4).

One thing is certain. There are too many examples of this kind to enable us to assume that they were merely slips of the pen.[19] Bach certainly did not

[19] The great composers did sometimes write consecutive 5ths and octaves by mistake. Brahms, for example, assembled a collection of such errors. An instance in Bach (see p. 320) occurs in the 5th Brandenburg Concerto, where a new mistake in the part-writing came about after a correction had been made. Dr Rolf Pfister has drawn another interesting ex. to my attention: the recitative 'Behalte nur', No. 5 in Cantata No. 8, *Liebster Gott*, bars 6–7.

Ex. 14.41. Sonata No. 3 for flute and harpsichord, BWV 1032, second movement, bars 1–2

produce incorrect part-writing intentionally. C. P. E. Bach was equally severe in this respect, and repeatedly warned against applying ornaments that would lead to 'ugly' fifths.[20] The examples of incorrectly applied ornaments that he proceeds to give are also very revealing:

Fig. 81

Hence, as with all embellishments, the introduction of an appoggiatura (and of all other ornaments) must not corrupt the purity of the voice leading. For this reason the examples of Figure 81 had better not be put into practice.[21]

And as we have seen above, C. P. E. Bach was particularly against 'forbidden consecutive fifths' occasioned by starting the trill on the wrong note. Most probably this was due to 'His Master's Voice'; after all, J. S. Bach had been his only teacher. But why did C. P. E. Bach not warn about an analogous incorrect execution of the *Pralltriller*?[22] Surely because this was something he simply did not expect. At places of this kind a *Schneller* had always been played. According to C. P. E. Bach, this ornament

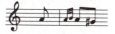

[20] *Essay*, p. 95.   [21] *Essay*, p. 95.
[22] A warning of this kind could have been: 'Hence, as with all embellishments, the introduction of short trills must not corrupt the purity of the voice-leading.'

'is often used at caesurae [imperfect cadences]'.[23] An instance of this kind occurs in the theme from J. S. Bach's E minor Partita (see Ex. 14.32). The similarity between this theme and the A minor example from the *Essay* is hardly an accident: C. P. E. Bach owned the manuscript of the first part of the *Clavier-Übung* that has since disappeared. He will certainly have known this, the most important of his father's keyboard suites apart from the B minor Overture and the Sixth English Suite, rather well. His reply to Burney cited above shows how highly he valued his father's works.

As the anticipation of an ornament was out of the question as far as C. P. E. Bach and many of his contemporaries were concerned, the execution of the *Schneller* shown in Ex. 14.42 is the only possible one. It was probably intended in the examples from J. S. Bach cited above. The pronunciation of the Italian word *ac-cén-to* (or, more precisely, *addio*) may serve as a model for the performance of such sigh-motifs. The final note should be unaccented, but should not be too short.

Ex. 14.42

ac · · cen · · to

There are practical as well as historical arguments in favour of starting on the main note in sigh-motifs. According to O'Donnell[24] and other musicologists, these motifs were of Italian origin, being employed particularly by the Venetian and Bolognese schools. The dissonance on the strong beat was rhythmically and dynamically emphasized by the addition of a three-note ornament—hence the term *accentus* used by W. C. Printz[25] and other baroque authors. O'Donnell quotes a number of sigh-motifs from Bach, some of which are identical with the above examples, and notes that they occur in works with a pronounced Italian character (e.g. *Aria variata alla maniera italiana*). What, then, is the point of playing the ornaments in the 'French' manner?

Of course, when applying an auxiliary trill the creation of forbidden consecutives depends primarily on the accompanying voices. Wherever there is no danger of faulty part-writing, there can be no fundamental objection to beginning the trill on the upper auxiliary. In the eighteenth century there seems to have been a certain freedom with regard to the choice of ornaments in sigh-motifs.[26] In a paragraph added to the third edition of the *Essay* C. P. E. Bach writes trills throughout on a sigh-motif of the same kind (see

[23] *Essay*, p. 143.   [24] 'Bach's Trills', p. 21.

[25] *Phrynis Mitilenaeus oder Satyrischer Componist* (Quedlinburg, 1676–7), and *Musica modulatoria vocalis oder Manierliche und zierliche Sing-Kunst* (Schweidnitz, 1678).

[26] See pp. 11 ff. and 305.

Ex. 14.43); according to the rules these have to begin with the upper note (c^2 and d^2).[27] 'Where [the trill] is difficult to perform'[28] he suggests a simplification in the shape of turns, though this cannot be applied in the case of J. S. Bach (see Ex. 14.44). By transposing Ex. 14.43 from G major to F minor we obtain the beginning of Bach's Prelude No. 12 from *WTC* II (Ex. 14.45).[29] Here one could play either *Schneller* or auxiliary trills on the lines suggested in the 1787 edition of the *Essay*, though in the case of the latter we would, in bars 12–13 and 14–15 be confronted once again with the 'forbidden' consecutives criticized above, albeit in the milder form of diminished and perfect fifths (see Ex. 14.46).

Ex. 14.43. From C. P. E. Bach, *Essay*, p. 115

Ex. 14.44

Ex. 14.45. *WTC* II, Prelude in F minor, bars 1–2

From this point of view the varying interpretation of the *Pralltriller* sign— sometimes a *Schneller*, sometimes a trill—becomes a problem in such passages. The player either decides to use *Schneller* in such motifs, or he must

[27] There is a good reason why this 'French' manner of playing is so popular with harpsichordists nowadays—the start on the upper auxiliary and the greater number of notes makes it possible to suggest a 'sharper' accent than with only 3 notes. If it were not for the voice-leading problems, I would also far rather play trills of this kind.

[28] *Essay*, p. 115.

[29] In older copies of this prelude (the MS is no longer extant) there are no ornaments, yet later ones (Altnikol I, Schwencke, etc.) doubtlessly contain authentic *Pralltriller* signs. In the lost autograph Bach probably did not write down ornaments which to him were self-evident. In the Toccata of the E minor Partita, BWV 830, the *Pralltriller* sign in the fugal section is missing from the earlier version (in the *Notenbüchlein* for Anna Magdalena Bach).

Ex. 14.46. *WTC* II, Prelude in F minor, bars 12–14

from the start relinquish the hope of sight-reading Bach without making voice-leading mistakes. In this prelude the consecutive fifths are hardly noticeable. Christoph Albrecht rightly notes, when discussing a similar problem—whether or not to anticipate in the case of slides—that, particularly in ensembles, the singer or instrumentalist only had the one part in front of him, and could not embark on a critical comparison with the other players' music.[30] In practice, then, one has to decide in favour of one of the two forms and adhere to it consistently. The use of short auxiliary trills in the F minor Prelude is suggested by the execution on musical clocks and organ-barrels (though these come from the latter part of the eighteenth century) in similar passages. However, there is some evidence to the contrary. For example, in J. S. Bach it is noteworthy that he sometimes notated written-out ornaments similar to the *Schneller* after an up-beat repeated note, for instance, in the first movement of the A minor English Suite (Ex. 14.47). It would have been quite possible for Bach to write a different ornament at this point, such as that in Ex. 14.48. Why, in this and similar passages, did Bach never write the second ornament, an embellishment that performers of his music would have regarded as 'the only correct one' 250 years later? The answer is surely that he did not care for it, and that therefore it never occurred to him. This is something worth thinking about. Those who cannot be persuaded by rational

Ex. 14.47. English Suite No. 2, BWV 807, Prélude, bars 55–7

Ex. 14.48

argument to depart from the auxiliary-trill principle have at their disposal an elegant way out of the dilemma in the shape of the 'grace-note trill' mentioned by Frederick Neumann.[31] The auxiliary is played immediately before the beat, and the main note on the beat, thereby circumventing consecutives and other technical problems. This kind of trill is certainly not foreign to the baroque style (see the description of the trill by Quantz[32]). However, it does not seem to have been in favour in Bach's circle: compare for instance C. P. E. Bach's polemics against the anticipating appoggiatura (see Chapter 15).

Pralltriller *on Tied Notes*

Such *Pralltriller* can only begin on the main note. An example of this kind occurs at the beginning of the Third Organ Sonata in D minor (Ex. 14.49). Today many organists would play a short trill beginning on the auxiliary at this point (see Ex. 14.50). But this way of executing the ornament would lead

Ex. 14.49. Organ Sonata No. 3, BWV 527, first movement, bars 1–2

Ex. 14.50

to untenable consecutive octaves, and these, coming at the beginning of the sonata, would be particularly noticeable on account of the two-part texture. Here Neumann suggests using his 'grace-note trill' (Ex. 14.51). This would

Ex. 14.51. After Neumann, *Ornamentation*, p. 329

---

[31] *Ornamentation*, pp. 327 ff.   [32] *On Playing the Flute*, p. 103.

overcome the incorrect voice-leading, though it would not do justice to the prescribed tie. After all, a tie is meant to prolong a note, yet this way of playing the ornament would in practice shorten the first d^1, which does not make sense at this juncture. If it did, Bach could have saved himself the trouble of writing the tie here and at similar places. The ornament was probably meant to be played as in Ex. 14.52. This execution is confirmed by the fact that Bach often wrote out this formula in large notes, as for instance in bar 44 of the aria 'Glorificamus te' in the B minor Mass (see Ex. 14.67 below).

Ex. 14.52

There is a further example in Cantata No. 14, *Wär' Gott nicht mit uns diese Zeit*. In the aria with obbligato violin 'Unsere Stärke, bist zu schwach' there are a number of instances of a tied note with a trill (or *Pralltriller*) after the barline, for example in bars 2–4 and 7–8 (see Ex. 14.53). The tie means that the entry of the ornament is delayed. On account of the suspended dissonance on eb^2 the short trill (or *Pralltriller*) should not accent the upper note(s).

Ex. 14.53. Cantata No. 14, aria 'Unsere Stärke, bist du schwach', from obb. violin part *a*, bars 2–4; *b*, bars 7–8; *c, d*, execution

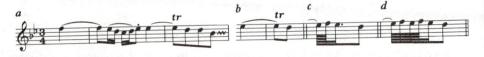

The tied trills in the transposed C minor keyboard version, BWV 1062, of the D minor Concerto for two violins, BWV 1043, are also of interest. In the second movement Bach wrote *Pralltriller* or trills on the tied notes in bars 13–15 and 14–46, which could also be adopted by violinists playing the original version (see Ex. 14.54). Here the *Pralltriller* have to be short because the longer versions would lead to consecutives (eb–db) with the other harpsichord.

Pralltriller *on the Same Short Repeated Note*

In contrast with the instances discussed above, in the case of a *Pralltriller* on the same short repeated note, beginning the ornament on the upper auxiliary is unobjectionable because it hardly ever creates consecutives. And here the *Pralltriller* commencing on the auxiliary fits smoothly into the figuration (see

Ex. 14.54. Concerto in C minor for two harpsichords, second movement

Exx. 14.55 and 14.56). But perhaps in order to avoid misunderstandings we should always speak of a 'short trill' in this context. Two ascending notes followed by a trill over the repeated second note form a frequent formula in which the trill always commences on the auxiliary regardless of its length, both in baroque music and later in Beethoven and Chopin (see Exx. 14.57 and 14.58). In Ex. 14.58 the choice of short or long trills is left to the discretion of the performer. Yet on account of the French character of this sarabande, longer trills should come to a stop shortly before the suffix (*point d'arrêt*).

Ex. 14.55. Chromatic Fantasia, bars 55–6

Ex. 14.56. Partita No. 6, BWV 830, Allemanda, bar 11

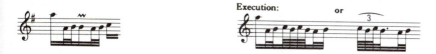

The main-note execution of Ex. 14.59, beginning on d^2, would even create hidden consecutive fifths (f♯–c♯ and g♯–d). It is perhaps no accident that this particular example is written in the 'French style'; thus there is the possibility of introducing a *cadence* with four or six notes in the manner of Rameau.

Ex. 14.57. Invention No. 2, BWV 773, bar 2

Even more revealing is a passage in Prelude No. 7 of *WTC* I. Here the ornament that Bach did not notate in bar 41 must be added, because in unembellished form the outer voices would produce hidden consecutive fifths,

Ex. 14.58. Partita No. 6, BWV 830, Sarabande, bars 27–8

f–c and g–d (see Ex. 14.60; fifths of this kind were sometimes tolerated in the inner voices). When the added shorter or longer trill begins, as it should, on the upper auxiliary, the 'forbidden' fifths have as if by magic been

Ex. 14.59. Partita No. 4, BWV 828, Ouverture, bar 7

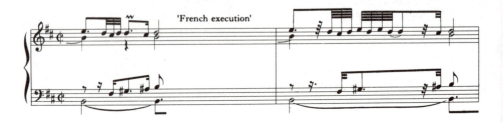

transformed into 'permitted' sixths. In contrast with this passage we recall the excerpt from the *St Matthew Passion* quoted above (Ex. 13.15), where beginning the *Pralltriller* on the auxiliary leads to 'forbidden' consecutive fifths. This is so conclusive that nowadays I consider the *Schneller* version to be a possibility even in Ex. 14.60.

Ex. 14.60. *WTC* I, Prelude in E flat major, bar 41

THE TRILLED (OR SNAPPED) TURN

Because this ornament, which is related to the *Pralltriller*, often occurs in Bach preceded by a note at the same pitch, it will be briefly discussed at this juncture. As we have seen in the previous chapter, it was described in the middle of the eighteenth century by a number of theorists. C. P. E. Bach invented two terms for the ornament, which he wrongly stated to be new, and used three different symbols for it, namely the turn sign placed over the *Pralltriller* sign; a turn with a preceding short appoggiatura on the same note (this was new!); and a normal *Pralltriller* sign followed by a lower semiquaver (or demisemiquaver) note. (He did not mention a fourth possibility, which plays a fairly important role in J. S. Bach, namely writing out the ornament in large notes.)

The first symbol, *Pralltriller* plus turn, was used fairly often by Couperin. As far as I have been able to establish, J. S. Bach used it only twice: in the small C major Praeludium, BWV 933, and in bar 6 of the Allemande of Partita No. 3, in the version preserved in the *Notenbüchlein* for Anna Magdalena Bach (see Ex. 14.61).[33] Here, oddly enough, the sign is used in a melodic context for which, according to Bach's son, it was not intended. C. P. E. Bach stated that this ornament had to be preceded by the note immediately above. In this case it is the one immediately below.

---

[33] After completing my MS I discovered that Neumann quotes the same passages (*Ornamentation*, p. 340).

The second abbreviation never occurs in J. S. Bach. In fact it never came into common use. Of the great composers, apart from C. P. E. Bach himself, it was used only by Haydn, for instance at the start of the D major Piano Sonata (Hob. XVI/39).[34] Thereafter it fell into oblivion.

Ex. 14.61. Partita No. 3, BWV 827, Allemande, bar 6, earlier version

The third abbreviation, a *Pralltriller* sign followed by a lower semiquaver or demisemiquaver, occurs frequently in Bach, both in descending passages, as in bar 14 of the first three-part Sinfonia (Ex. 14.62) and in the Italian

Ex. 14.62. Sinfonia No. 1, BWV 787, bar 14

Concerto, first movement, bars 45–6 (Ex. 14.63), and in cases of repeated notes, for instance in the same movement, bars 91–5 (Ex. 14.64). The tied version of this ornament has been described on pp. 357 ff.

Ex. 14.63. Italian Concerto, first movement, bars 45–8

[34] See my art. 'On Ornamentation in Haydn', *Piano Quarterly*, 34 (1986), 38–48. Chopin used a similar notation (appoggiatura plus the same note) for a trill beginning on the main note, e.g. in Opps. 53 and 58. Such appoggiaturas do not imply repeating a note.

Ex. 14.64. Italian Concerto, first movement, bars 90–5

Of course, the most revealing version of all is the written-out one. In Bach this occurs in all combinations: it enters freely or after leaps, as in the first bars of the thirteenth of the Goldberg Variations (Ex. 14.65),[35] in ascending lines, as in the second movement of the D minor Harpsichord Concerto, bars 40–1 and 59 (Ex. 14.66), and in the case of tied or descending notes, as in the 'Glorificamus' from the Gloria of the B minor Mass, bars 44–5 (Ex. 14.67) and in the E minor Prelude of *WTC* I, bars 10, 12, and 20 (Ex. 14.68).

Ex. 14.65. Goldberg Variations, variation 13, bars 1–3

Ex. 14.66. Harpsichord Concerto in D minor, BWV 1052, second movement

a   bars 40–1: the written-out and abbreviated versions are combined

b   bars 59–60

[35] In this variation, as in other parts of the *Clavier-Übung*, Bach demonstrates a great affection for this relatively new ornament. It is a remarkable fact that Gustav Mahler rediscovered this expressive figure, as it were, in 'Abschied' in *Das Lied von der Erde*. Incidentally, the free entry at the beginning of a phrase is, according to C. P. E. Bach, the most favoured place for the application of the 'snapped turn' (*Essay*, pp. 125–6).

Ex. 14.67. Mass in B minor, Gloria, 'Glorificamus', bars 43–6

Ex. 14.68. *WTC* I, Prelude in E minor, bars 12, 20

It is indeed remarkable that Bach always began this ornament on the main note. If he had been prescient enough to foresee twentieth-century baroque practice, he would surely have composed the excerpt from the Goldberg Variations in Ex. 14.65 as in Ex. 14.69. But perhaps he avoided this notation because beginning a piece with a dissonance (or an appoggiatura) was not common practice at the time.

Ex. 14.69

Let us turn now to the combination of repeated note and snapped turn. As in the case of sigh-motifs, the combination of 'same note plus snapped turn or trill' often leads to 'forbidden' consecutive fifths or octaves when it begins on the auxiliary. A case of this kind was noted in the recitative of Christ mentioned at the start (see p. 321); another is in the recitative and arioso 'Wohlan' in Part IV of the Christmas Oratorio, five bars before the end (see Ex. 14.70). Beginning the trill on c would create consecutive fifths with the bass. Apart from such hidden consecutive fifths there are also rhythmical

Ex. 14.70. Christmas Oratorio, Part IV, recitative and arioso No. 40, 'Wohlan'

reasons that practically exclude the auxiliary beginning in the bass aria 'Grosser Herr' in the Christmas Oratorio, Part I, bars 31–2 and 35–6. There are limits to the agility of the bass voice. At best it would be possible to use a 'snapped' turn at this juncture (Ex. 14.71). The same is true for the end of the aria's middle section (Ex. 14.72). A 'legitimate' alternative to the use of the *Pralltriller* in such passages is to play a short, unaccented (and at times anticipated) appoggiatura. The possibility of exchanging *Pralltriller* and appoggiaturas will be dealt with in greater detail below (pp. 379 and 381). For all these reasons I now begin many 'snapped turns' on the main note, for

Ex. 14.71. Christmas Oratorio, aria No. 8, 'Grosser Herr', bars 35–6

Ex. 14.72. Christmas Oratorio, aria No. 8, 'Grosser Herr'

Execution:

instance in the second movement of the Italian Concerto, bar 16 (see Ex. 14.73).

Ex. 14.73. Italian Concerto, second movement, bar 16

Discussion of a Problematical Case: The Trilled Turns in the Praeludium of Partita No. 1, BWV 825

Ex. 14.74. Partita No. 1, BWV 825, Praeludium, bars 1–2

The notation suggests that the *Pralltriller* in this Praeludium are 'snapped turns' of the kind described by C. P. E. Bach which, apart from the small note-values, are exactly identical to the above examples. As a baroque performer one is none the less tempted to play a short 'French' auxiliary trill, especially where this does not create incorrect voice-leading. Today almost all harpsichordists and pianists play the first ornaments beginning on *c*. For about twenty-five years I also played this execution, which is certainly permitted by baroque rules. Recently, however, theoretical and musical considerations have led me to doubt whether this version is the 'only' correct one.

It is instructive to imagine how a discriminating French musician of the stature of Rameau might have reacted to this piece and its *ornements* if he had known it. He would probably have commented negatively on the strict part-writing—'très allemand'—in such a graceful work, and then on the fact that the ornaments are placed over the shortest note-values, demisemiquavers. 'C'est étrange, on ne peut pas les exécuter proprement avec netteté!' he would have been prompted to remark. In fact, the theoretically correct version with demihemidemisemiquavers (Ex. 14.75) is totally impossible to play. So is the compromise formula (Ex. 14.76), which is still so fast that the listener can hardly distinguish between the notes, particularly in later appearances in the

Ex. 14.75

Ex. 14.76

bass.[36] 'C'est bousculé' (It's a bit on the fast side) our friend would have exclaimed, and indeed it goes against the fundamental requirement that embellishments should not be rushed. In 1702 Michel de Saint-Lambert emphasized: '. . . qu'il ne faut jamais se presser pour faire un agrément, quelque vite qu'il doive passer: Qu'il faut prendre son temps, préparer ses doigts, et l'executer avec hardiesse et liberté'.[37]

Similarly, in 1731, Rameau remarked in the second edition of the *Pièces de clavecin*: 'Il faut bien se garder de précipiter la cadence sur la fin pour la fermer: elle se ferme naturellement, lorsqu'on a une fois acquis l'habitude.'[38]

The French did not teach that *Pralltriller* and *Schneller* could exceptionally be played faster than other ornaments. This was recommended only by the Italians (Tosi) and the Germans (C. P. E. Bach). A good eighteenth-century musician would not have accepted the executions usually played today (Ex. 14.77).

Ex. 14.77

The first of these would water down the basic rhythm with its characteristic

detached semiquaver B♭ to or

---

[36] An experienced performer, Gustav Leonhardt, side-steps the issue best of all. In his recording of the Praeludium (Harmonia Mundi HMS 30882) the slow, ponderous tempo means that the correct rhythm is maintained in spite of the fact that he begins on the auxiliary. It is doubtful, however, whether a slow tempo of this kind does justice to the graceful character of this piece, which, as is well known, Bach placed in the cradle of the newborn Prince of Cöthen with a charming dedicatory poem (see App. 5).

[37] *Les Principes du clavecin* (Paris, 1702), 57. Translation: 'One should never hurry the execution of an embellishment, however fast it is supposed to be. One should take one's time, prepare one's fingers and execute the ornament with assurance and freedom.'

[38] p. 19. Translation: 'One must guard against accelerating the trill at the end. It comes to a close naturally once one has acquired the habit.' See also the similar warning about overly fast ornaments in Quantz, *On Playing the Flute*, p. 127: 'Execution is poor if the graces . . . are rushed'.

 whereas the second creates the impression that the piece begins with a rhythmically imprecise main-note trill. For these reasons a French contemporary of Bach would probably have decided to play short appoggiaturas (*ports de voix*) instead of *Pralltriller* or trills (see Ex. 14.78). This is an excellent solution, and can even be regarded as possible in terms of Bachian practice (compare Bach's substitution of appoggiaturas for *Pralltriller*, pp. 379–80).

Ex. 14.78

That it is possible to apply only a *Pralltriller* (actually a *Schneller*) to a demisemiquaver note, and not a trill, was in fact stated by none other than Bach's 'grand-pupil' Johann Nikolaus Forkel, not by an imaginary French musician. His comments refer to the passage we are discussing: 'You will see from this that in the first Präludio of the *Clavierübung* no ⚬ or long trill could stand over the demisemiquaver. Who can play a long trill on a demisemiquaver? It should be a *Pralltriller*.'[39] Immediately before this Forkel had written that a *Pralltriller* comprises only two notes.

Thus a musician trained in the Italo-German tradition at the time of Bach would not have had the slightest compunction about beginning the *Pralltriller* in this prelude on the main note (see Ex. 14.79 and the quotation on p. 363,

Ex. 14.79

Exx. 14.65–6). In addition to its pleasing sound, this execution, which I have also adopted recently, has the advantage that in the case of the ninth chords in bars 10[40] and 17, the 'German' version *b* creates better voice-leading than *a* (see Ex. 14.80). Furthermore, the function of a bass trill, be it short or long, is to emphasize the root of a chord by beginning on the main note.[41]

---

[39] Letter dated 21 Dec. 1801. See Arthur Mendel, 'The Forkel–Hoffmeister & Kühnel Correspondence'.

[40] In bars 10 and 11 the *Pralltriller* symbols are missing in the 1st edn. However, Bach later added them in at least 2 copies. See NBA V/1, Critical Report, p. 55. They can therefore be regarded as being authentic. If, in order to avoid the ugly *e*–*eb* discord on the 2nd quaver, one plays the embellishment with *eb* instead of *e*, one introduces into the principal motif a chromatic step from *eb* to *e* between the 1st and 2nd crotchets, which can hardly have been intended: at the beginning the 1st ornament is played with an auxiliary *C*, not *Cb*. Bach liked to introduce major and minor 6ths simultaneously in different voices, e.g. in the C minor Toccata, BWV 911, bar 49; or in the Italian Concerto, 1st movement, bars 77 and 112, and 2nd movement, bar 10; and, in a particularly 'harsh' manner, in the 2nd movement of the 1st Brandenburg Concerto.

[41] See also O'Donnell, 'Bach's Trills', pp. 19 f., and Ex. 16.18.

Ex. 14.80. Partita No. 1, BWV 825, Praeludium, bar 10

PRALLTRILLER AFTER LEAPS

In keeping with the view that has predominated since about 1930, *Pralltriller* signs on notes after leaps have been played as short trills beginning on the auxiliary. Of course, in many cases an execution beginning on the auxiliary in the 'French' manner is quite 'correct'. However, ornamentation in the eighteenth century was much richer and freer than has hitherto been believed. Musical clocks and organ-barrels—and C. F. Colt's barrel-organ is in no way exceptional in this regard—show that many ornaments missing from contemporary tables were in fact played. The tables hardly ever concerned themselves with exceptions to the rules. In this connection the remarks by Heinichen are very revealing: 'The embellishments . . . are innumerable, and vary according to the taste and experience of the player. Because this is not so much a matter of rules as of practice and much judiciousness. . . .'[42] Bach, who knew Heinichen personally, would no doubt have agreed.

One of the ornaments seldom mentioned by the old rules, though J. S. Bach would not have found it strange, was the *Schneller* (or main-note *Praller*). It was identical with the *Pralltriller*, though not 'supported' like the latter by the preceding upper auxiliary. Some *Schneller* in Bach's works are written out in large notes, for instance in the A minor Fugue of *WTC* I, bar 17 (Ex. 14.81); in unornamented form this would be as shown in Ex. 14.82. The reason why

Ex. 14.81. *WTC* I, Fugue in A minor, bars 17–18

Ex. 14.82

---

[42] See above, p. 244. The original has the old form of the word for 'practice', *praxin* (experience).

Bach wrote out the ornament in full was probably not that he wished to depart from the ostensibly strict rule. Why here and not in a hundred similar passages? Rather, it was the only way in which he was able to stipulate the F♯ accidental. The notation ♯ had not yet become common practice. Incidentally, it is noticeable that he did not employ the notation shown in Ex. 14.83. On the fourth beat of this example (bar 7) I also play the beginning of the trill f♯–g, not because I am disturbed by the repeated g, but because the f♯–g leading-note character of this cadence would otherwise be lost.

Ex. 14.83

As mentioned above, it is rather strange that the formula that is nowadays considered to be 'self-evident'  was never written out by Bach or by any other great eighteenth-century composer. It first appears occasionally in the nineteenth century, for instance at the beginning of Liszt's Second Hungarian Rhapsody (Ex. 14.84). Were Hungarian gypsies the only musicians to preserve the 'true' baroque tradition?

Ex. 14.84. Liszt, Hungarian Rhapsody No. 2, bars 1–2

In the fifteenth of the Goldberg Variations Bach again wrote out a *Schneller* in full (see Ex. 14.85). Here Bodky rightly notes that Bach was presumably trying to integrate the ornaments into the canon *in moto contrario* in a way that

Ex. 14.85. Goldberg Variations, variation 15, bars 13–15

was visible on paper.[43] Furthermore, it was not usual to ornament the first note of a motif with a *Pralltriller* instead of a mordent. There is also a written-out *Pralltriller* in the G minor Prelude of *WTC* I, bar 8, fourth beat.

---

[43] Bodky, *Interpretation*, pp. 154 f.

On the basis of these examples, to which others could be added,[44] it would on occasion not be wholly wrong to play *Pralltriller* (i.e. *Schneller*) beginning on the main note. In the Corrente of Partita No. 1 there is a *Pralltriller* of this kind after a leap of an augmented fourth (see Ex. 14.86). One hears this leap as a b♭–a–g–f♯ progression, which corresponds to the similar one in bars 4–5 (see Ex. 14.87). For this reason a *Pralltriller* sounds more natural here than an auxiliary trill. The preceding note, as far as the ear is concerned, is the g^2 of bar 32, and thus the 'normal rule' applies. Beginning bar 33 with the dissonance g^2 is also unadvisable. In the motivically similar bars 35 and 37 I also add a three-note *Pralltriller* beginning on a consonance.

Ex. 14.86. Partita No. 1, BWV 825, Corrente, bars 32–3, 4–5 (outline)

Ex. 14.87

In the C sharp minor Prelude of *WTC* II there are, in bar 19 and the following bars, a number of *Pralltriller* signs after leaps (Ex. 14.88). Although beginning the trill on the upper note is not 'wrong' at this point, I prefer a *Schneller* because at this juncture the intervallic leap of a diminished fifth is melodically of importance, and would be diluted by the insertion of a $c♯^2$, however short.[45]

Ex. 14.88. *WTC* II, Prelude in C sharp minor, bars 18–19

[44] See Bodky, *Interpretation*, pp. 155 ff.

[45] For the same reasons Albrecht (*Interpretationsfragen*, pp. 139 f.) suggests beginning the trill on the main note in the F minor Organ Fugue, BWV 534:

But Emery (*Bach's Ornaments*, pp. 48 f.) was of the opinion that in such passages one could begin on the auxiliary, citing as evidence bar 8 of the B minor Organ Prelude, BWV 544, where there is an appoggiatura before the 2nd note of leap of a 7th downwards. Both views seem plausible. (David Humphreys ('Did J. S. Bach Compose the F minor Prelude and Fugue, BWV 534?', *Bach, Handel, Scarlatti*, ed. P. Williams, pp. 173–84) has cast doubt on the authenticity of this fugue.)

In Ex. 14.88 there is another reason for beginning on the main note. In the first sixteen bars of the prelude there are before this only *Pralltriller* that begin unequivocally on the main note. It would be quite illogical if the same sign were to have a different meaning in bars 16–20 from its meaning before and afterwards.

Ex. 14.89. Partita No. 3, BWV 827, Gigue, bars 44–5

In Bach *Pralltriller* (and trills) sometimes occur in ascending chromatic lines, for instance in bars 44 and 46 of the Gigue of Partita No. 3 (Ex. 14.89).[46] Although there are no leaps, the progression is remarkable for the fact that one would initially expect mordents, not *Pralltriller* (or *Schneller*). However, a chromatic mordent g♯–g–g♯ does not come into question, and a diatonic one, g♯–f♯–g♯, would 'obstruct' the line. Thus an 'inverted mordent' g♯–a–g♯ is surely the best solution. An auxiliary trill would also lead to concealed consecutive fifths.

Particularly after leaps, the performer is to a certain degree free to decide whether to use a *Schneller* or a short trill beginning on the auxiliary. The point of this book would be misunderstood if the strait-laced interpretation that has hitherto prevailed were to be replaced by another that is equally constricted. The player's taste and the character of the piece, be it German, Italian, or French, play a role. One passage where I always play short auxiliary trills (of four to six notes) is the early version of the Toccata of the E minor Partita. In bars 5 and 6, where in *Clavier-Übung*, Part I, there are (surely short and accented) appoggiaturas, the earlier version in the second *Notenbüchlein* for Anna Magdalena Bach of 1725 has *Pralltriller* signs (see Ex. 14.90). Beginning on the main note would seem decidedly bland here.

Ex. 14.90. Partita No. 6, BWV 830, Toccata, bars 5–6, earlier version

---

[46] Bach added the 2nd *Pralltriller* in some copies at a later date.

PRALLTRILLER ON DETACHED NOTES AND IN RAPID PASSAGES

On Detached Notes

In the Gigue of the B minor French Overture we encounter a rhythmic pattern in which *Pralltriller* and mordents alternate. If this were a piece that was legato in character one could easily slur the *Pralltriller* to the preceding note and begin on the main note. However, this gigue is surely supposed to 'skip along', that is, it should be played detached (see Ex. 14.91).[47] Thus we have the choice between a short *cadence* (i.e. the version beginning on the auxiliary that is so common today,) and the *Schneller* as described by C. P. E. Bach and other theorists and recommended for staccato figuration from about 1750 onwards (Ex. 14.92). In my opinion both forms are historically accurate and feasible in this passage, though the 'French' version commencing on the auxiliary is somewhat more brilliant than the 'Italo-German' one with the *Schneller*.

Ex. 14.91. French Overture, BWV 831, Gigue, bars 1–10

Ex. 14.92. From C. P. E. Bach, *Essay*, p. 142

The example from the French Overture shows the consummate skill with which Bach integrated the ornaments into the melodic and rhythmic structure of a work. In the first two bars, where the motion has not as yet got under way—long notes at the beginning of the bar—there are two appoggiaturas, one from below and one from above, which of course have the effect of standing in for a mordent or a *Pralltriller*. This 'delay' in the opening bars is

---

[47] See ch. 4, p. 114.

also expressed by the inversion of the up-beat motif b–a♯ at the very beginning, which leads to the repetition of a note across the barline that is later avoided (from bar 2 to bar 3, etc.). If the appoggiatura in bar 1 is regarded as a 'substitute' for a mordent (cf. bar 5) then it would be tempting to play the following mordents in the same way, from below—that is, with a total of four notes. However, the 'normal' three-note version of mordents is to be preferred at this point.

In its later embellished form, the Gigue from the French Suite No. 2 in C minor is related to the above theme (see Ex. 14.93). In contrast with the Overture there are appoggiaturas preceding the *Pralltriller* at various points in this version which, on account of the dotted rhythm, can only be very short.[48] These appoggiaturas before *Pralltriller* are unusual for Bach (there are ten in all and one from below before the mordent in bar 75) and therefore raise new questions. What is the point of this tenfold 'superfluous' notation of appoggiaturas if these *Pralltriller* (as received opinion would have it) have to begin on the upper auxiliary in any case? Why are these appoggiaturas missing in the case of the other *Pralltriller*? Should they be played here as well?

Ex. 14.93. French Suite No. 2, BWV 813, Gigue, bars 1–5, later version

The fact that, in this gigue, appoggiaturas not in the earlier version were also added to a number of unembellished notes suggests that Bach wished to accentuate the first beat in a particular way. In other words, this was not an obvious execution. Therefore, in the unmarked parallel passages in bars 7, 11, 19, 38, 41, 45, 49, 57, 61, and 73, short appoggiaturas should be added to the *Pralltriller*, though perhaps not in the left hand. Unfortunately the Henle and Peters Urtext editions omit all the appoggiaturas without comment. Yet they are in two of the most important sources, which also contain the other embellishments, namely in the copy made by an unidentified Bach pupil (formerly mistaken for an autograph)[49] and in the very reliable copy made by Ernst Ludwig Gerber.[50] It is hardly possible to doubt that these ornaments go back to Bach himself. It is simply wrong to omit a group of ornaments merely because it is assumed that performers will automatically begin on the auxiliary. The sporadic appoggiaturas in bar 4 or before the mordent in bar 75

[48] Cf. Quantz, *On Playing the Flute*, pp. 289 ff. and 168, §22.
[49] See NBA V/8, Critical Report, pp. 14–18, 78–81, 95.
[50] See NBA V/8, Critical Report, pp. 38–41.

may well have been a mistake. On the other hand, the *Pralltriller* in the bass in bar 29 must begin on the main note, otherwise there would be consecutive fifths with the mordent in the upper voice.

In variation 7 of the Goldberg Variations (Ex. 14.94)[51] the symmetry of rhythm and ornamentation is once again unmistakable. The odd bars have mordents, and the even bars *Pralltriller* signs (after a higher note and stepwise descending line). The way in which this is normally played today, with the mordent beginning on the main note and the *Pralltriller* on the auxiliary

Ex. 14.94. Goldberg Variations, variation 7, bars 1–4

(Ex. 14.95), is inconsistent and asymmetrical. In historical terms this execution is of course not wrong, though it is rather inconsistent. Short trills beginning on the upper note did exist, but so did mordents beginning on the lower auxiliary, even if they were less frequent. Mordents of this kind were described by Heinichen, Quantz, and others. The logical consequence of the way the ornaments are performed in the even bars of the above example would be to play the mordents beginning on a dissonant note (Ex. 14.96). Even this would be possible when we consider the limitless wealth and variety of baroque ornamentation. However, there would be one slight disadvantage—

Ex. 14.95

Ex. 14.96

Bach rarely employed the 'ascending' (or 'auxiliary') mordent, which is also missing from the 'Explication'. Thus it would be preferable to play normal mordents and *Pralltriller* with a total of three notes (see Ex. 14.97). This view is also shared by Emery.[52]

---

[51] The marking 'al tempo di giga' was later entered by Bach in his personal copy (*Handexemplar*), now in the Bibliothèque Nationale, Paris.
[52] *Bach's Ornaments*, p. 74.

Ex. 14.97

However, we are not so much concerned with the problem of historical accuracy as such, but, as was noted in the introduction, with the psychological attitude of twentieth-century performers and listeners. In spite of its lack of musical logic, the form employed in the first version (Ex. 14.95) is thus felt to be pleasing because it has become familiar through countless similar performances. The vast majority of those who play or listen to this version have never troubled to think about historical accuracy at all, preferring to pursue the habits they have grown accustomed to. This attitude would hardly matter if it did not often lead to 'dogmatic' intolerance.

Thus, for the twenty-first century I would like to suggest a simpler solution to this little problem. In its most concentrated form this juxtaposing of mordents and *Pralltriller* is found in an example also quoted by Neumann,[53] namely at the beginning of the chorale prelude for organ *Christ lag in Todesbanden*, BWV 718 (Ex. 14.98). Here again the two ornaments alternate. An articulation in keeping with the style suggests separating the individual figures. To preserve the rhythmic consistency it would be best to play the *Pralltriller* as 'inverted mordents' (see Ex. 14.99). (In this particular case ornaments should probably be played before the beat, preceding the semiquavers. See below.) A similar alternation of the two ornaments is also found at various points of the E flat major Prelude, BWV 552/1.

Ex. 14.98. Chorale prelude *Christ lag in Todesbanden*, BWV 718, bars 1–3

Ex. 14.99

Proof that the execution shown here is not only a hypothesis but reflects Bach's own feeling for melody is provided by the Gavotte of Partita No. 6. The earlier version of this piece from the *Notenbüchlein* for Anna Magdalena Bach has the melody line shown in Ex. 14.100. It is not difficult to see that the unembellished 'fundamental' melodic line consisted of crotchets and triplets

---

[53] *Ornamentation*, p. 327.

Ex. 14.100. Partita No. 6, BWV 830, Gavotte, bars 24–6, earlier version

(Ex. 14.101). When fleshing out this line Bach replaced the crotchets with triplets (e–d♯–e, etc.), and these could be termed 'slow mordents'. Bach included the E minor Partita in the *Clavier-Übung*, Part I. In this printed version he achieved an even greater variety in the figuration by modifying it as in Ex. 14.102. It would never have occurred to him to write the version in Ex. 14.103, yet this kind of rhythmic variety would have contributed to the interest of this gavotte, in which triplets and semiquavers alternate in other passages as well.

Ex. 14.101

Ex. 14.102. Partita No. 6, BWV 830, Gavotte, bars 24–6, later version

Ex. 14.103

In Rapid Passages

Bach often wrote *Pralltriller* or trill signs in passages that are so fast that only three notes can be accommodated if one does not wish to slow down the tempo to a point where the other, unembellished notes would begin to drag.

A typical example of this occurs in the Corrente of Partita No. 6 (Ex. 14.104). As the note *g* that precedes the *Pralltriller* in this example is longer than the one that follows it, it might even be possible to make an exception and anticipate the ornament.

Ex. 14.104. Partita No. 6, BWV 830, Corrente, bars 27–9

A second example occurs in the second movement (Allegro) of the E major Violin sonata with obbligato harpsichord (Ex. 14.105). Even at a moderate Allegro tempo of ♩ = 100 this *Pralltriller* (to be exact, a 'trilled turn') can only be played before the beat (anticipating), if, that is, one does not prefer the solution of substituting a short f♯ appoggiatura.

Ex. 14.105. Sonata No. 3 for violin and harpsichord, BWV 1016, second movement, bars 66–7, 82–3

The execution of such ornaments on certain wind instruments is even more of a problem than on the keyboard. In bars 7–8 of the aria with solo flute 'Wo wird in diesem Jammertale' from Cantata No. 114, *Ach liebe Christen seid getrost*, as Neumann rightly observes, only a three-part *Pralltriller* (to be precise, a 'snapped turn') is possible—for purely technical reasons (see Ex. 14.106).

In all these examples the four-note version would seem too fast. 'Care must be taken, however, that the air is not overburdened or crushed by them [embellishments] . . . Observance of this rule is particularly important in very

Ex. 14.106. Cantata No.114, aria 'Wo wird in diesem Jammertale', bars 7–8, after Neumann, *Ornamentation*, p. 341

quick passages, where the time does not permit many additions, if they are not to become indistinct and distasteful . . . Execution is poor . . . if the graces are poorly concluded, or rushed.'[54] The other extreme, ornaments in an Adagio that were too slow, was also considered undesirable: 'Execution is poor if the graces in the Adagio are too drawn out (slow), and do not accord with the harmony'.[55]

THE INTERCHANGEABILITY OF THE *PRALLTRILLER* AND THE SHORT APPOGGIATURA

It often happens that in the same configuration of notes Bach sometimes writes appoggiaturas, and sometimes *Pralltriller* or trills, apparently for no good reason. In this respect it is particularly revealing to compare the fourth movement of Cantata No. 140, *Wachet auf, ruft uns die Stimme*, with the organ version in the 'Schübler' chorales. As O'Donnell has noted, at certain places the cantata version has trills where the original version has appoggiaturas, and vice versa.[56] Stranger still, Bach failed to correct inconsistencies within the chorale prelude itself, which was one of the few works printed in his lifetime (see Ex. 14.107). Kreutz has drawn attention to a similar inconsistency in the chorale prelude *Nun komm der Heiden Heiland*, BWV 659.[57] The earlier version, BWV 659a, has *Pralltriller* in bar 5 (see Ex. 14.108a), whereas the later one has appoggiaturas (Ex. 14.108b). On top of this the later version has *Pralltriller* in the parallel passage in bar 29, where the first version has no ornaments at all. Bach could hardly have demonstrated with greater clarity that certain ornaments were interchangeable and that it is occasionally necessary to add ornaments that are not notated—a subject to which we will return below.

Ex. 14.107. Chorale prelude, *Wachet auf, ruft uns die Stimme*, BWV 645, after Albrecht, *Interpretationsfragen*, p. 141

---

[54] Quantz, *On Playing the Flute*, p. 127. Saint-Lambert states: 'One should never hurry the execution of an embellishment . . .' (*Les Principes du clavecin*, p. 57). See above, p. 367. Rameau's comments on the subject are similar.

[55] Quantz, *On Playing the Flute*, p. 127.   [56] 'Bach's Trills', p. 22.   [57] *Ornamentik*, p. 8.

Ex. 14.108. Chorale prelude *Nun komm, der Heiden Heiland*, BWV 659, bar 5

earlier version, BWV 659*a*

later version

For the Bach performer this means that in many passages where even the execution as a *Schneller* would seem too ungainly it is perfectly possible to play a short unaccented appoggiatura. There are good examples for this in the Gigue of the English Suite in A major (Ex. 14.109), at several places in the F major Duet, such as bars 44–5 (Ex. 14.110), and at the end of the A flat major Prelude of *WTC* I (Ex. 14.111). In all these cases a short unaccented appoggiatura is the best solution. The motif that was left unembellished

Ex. 14.109. English Suite No. 1, BWV 806, Gigue, bar 11

earlier in the prelude Bach enriched with ornaments in order to underline the effect of the ending. (For this reason I would be against adding ornaments to its previous appearances.) Appoggiaturas (b♭ and a♭) sound much better here than even the shortest *Pralltriller* (*Schneller*).

Ex. 14.110. Duet No. 2, BWV 803, bars 44–6

Ex. 14.111. *WTC* I, Prelude in A flat major, bars 41–4

It is noteworthy that Mozart, in the case of a similar motif in the second movement of the A minor Sonata, K. 310, was probably also thinking of an execution using an appoggiatura (Ex. 14.112). In an almost identical passage in the second movement of the Duet Sonata K. 521 Mozart later wrote appoggiaturas, which sound better and are easier to play than *Pralltriller*.

Ex. 14.112. Mozart, Piano Sonata K. 310, second movement, bar 12

Why did Bach and Mozart not write appoggiaturas in such passages in the first place? Perhaps because an appoggiatura required three strokes of the pen, whereas trill or *Pralltriller* signs could be written with one. The great composers considered abbreviations and anything that made writing easier to be of paramount importance.

The substitution of appoggiaturas for trills is even more important in instrumental and vocal music than in keyboard works. In the introduction to the aria 'Sehet, Jesus hat die Hand' from the *St Matthew Passion* Bach wrote trills for the two alto oboes (oboes da caccia) that are unplayable at a moderately fast tempo (see Ex. 14.113). Here is is advisable to play unaccented short appoggiaturas instead of *Pralltriller* or trills. The vocal line of the aria 'Laudamus te' from the Gloria of the B minor Mass begins with a motif that is similar to the one in bar 2 of Ex. 14.113 (see Ex. 14.114). Here again the way this is usually sung, with short unaccented appoggiaturas in the first bar and a *Pralltriller* in the second, is the best solution (Ex. 14.115).

Ex. 14.113. *St Matthew Passion*, aria, NBA No. 60, BGA No. 70, bars 1–2

Ex. 14.114. Mass in B minor, Gloria, aria 'Laudamus te', bars 12–15

Ex. 14.115

Another possibility would be to sing a *Schneller* (Ex. 14.116).[58] Yet these *Schneller* would have to be very light, quasi-anticipating embellishments, so that the prayer of adoration is indeed a graceful one. The modern harpsichordist's formula (Ex. 14.117) is certainly out of place. Even if a virtuoso soprano were able to sing such figures precisely, these ornaments would sound 'fussy' and thus offend against one of the fundamental rules of ornamentation, namely that the function of embellishments is to enhance the beauty of a passage.

Ex. 14.116

Ex. 14.117

[58] This execution is recommended by Quantz: 'Here I would like to note in addition that if shakes are indicated above several quick notes, the appoggiatura and termination are not always possible, because of the lack of time; often only half-shakes are performed.' (*On Playing the Flute*, p. 229, §24.)

In the violin solo at the beginning of the aria it is possible to play an appoggiatura instead of a *Pralltriller* in bar 9 (see Ex. 14.118). (As we have seen, Bach usually used the *Pralltriller* sign only for keyboard instruments. See above, p. 313.)

Ex. 14.118. Mass in B minor, Gloria, aria, 'Laudamus te', bars 9–10

The trumpet theme in the third movement of the Second Brandenburg Concerto, quoted in Ex. 4.11, also belongs to this category. It can be played only with a *Schneller* or an appoggiatura. Finally it should be added that in the Praeludium of Partita No. 1, substituting short up-beat appoggiaturas for *Pralltriller* is possible and sounds excellent.

CONCLUDING REMARKS

Although all the important aspects of the execution of the *Pralltriller* have been dealt with above, it will be useful to restate them at this point. As we have seen, the genuine *Pralltriller* begins on the main note. (For the sake of clarity the figure ⎓ that is often termed *Pralltriller*—it also appears in baroque practice—should be called 'short trill'.) It is faster and sharper than a normal trill and is usually played on the beat. And it should always be played legato.[59]

Yet which note should be accented, the first or the last? The answer to this common question may seem surprising: 'Neither. The middle one!' Many eighteenth-century authors of harpsichord and piano tutors agree that the penultimate note should crackle, that is, be played with a 'geschnellter Finger' in a manner resembling the movement made when snapping one's fingers. Authors such as Tosi and Agricola or Quantz aptly term this slight 'emphasis' on the penultimate note 'shimmer' or 'shine'. The slight emphasis produced by 'snapping' can also be heard on a good harpsichord.

---

[59] Glenn Gould's staccato execution of the *Pralltriller* and other ornaments is historically unfounded.

Apart from the accentuation of the penultimate note there none the less remains the question of which of the two remaining notes should receive the greater emphasis, the first or the last. Here I should like to suggest a personal observation that has proved its worth in practice. If the *Pralltriller* is over a note that is emphasized by the metre or the rhythm, then the first note should be accented, as in the case of the mordent. However, if it is over an unaccented note, such as a resolution of a suspension on the second quaver, then it should be the last note. Within faster passages there will inevitably be a slight accent on the last note. The best description of its execution after that of C. P. E. Bach is that of Türk:[60]

The half-trill (short trill) or *Pralltriller* is a very agreeable and necessary ornament, though by no means an easy one. For much precision and snapping power of the fingers is needed in order to execute a *Pralltriller* clearly and with the required sharpness and speed. . . . True, the *Pralltriller* is usually 'slurred' and thus with regard to performance different to the *Schneller*. Yet the last auxiliary note, which I have marked below at *a* with ', must be brought out by means of snapping (extremely fast withdrawal of the finger from the key) so that the *Pralltriller* is given the sharpness it requires. For this reason one can most conveniently use the second and third, or third and fourth fingers, granted that in certain cases one would also have to employ fingering that is usually not allowed, as in examples *b*, *c*, *d*, and *e*.

With regard to the tied execution Türk follows C. P. E. Bach, though he also allows the undelayed execution described by Marpurg, Quantz, and others. As has already been established, this version is often to be preferred in J. S. Bach. With the exception of the delay or non-delay of about a hundredth of a second, there is no difference in the execution, and for this reason Türk's description can also be applied to Bach's *Pralltriller*:

When the *Pralltriller* is placed above a note with a pause, as in *a* and *b*, the preceding note is long. After the *Pralltriller*, which in this case must be performed lightly (with

[60] *Clavierschule*, p. 274.

Abzug decrescendo), the finger must be lifted from the key immediately. Thus the execution would be roughly as in the second system:

[In J. S. Bach, as we have seen, the first tied note can be omitted.]

This weak *Pralltriller* in particular requires much practice, if it is to be performed with the required clarity and sharpness. I would only have the pupil practise it if he could clearly play this ornament at the normal dynamic level.[61]

But there is a still shorter version, which is mentioned by C. P. E. Bach and others, though only in connection with the explanation of the mordent. This entails simultaneously striking both notes and then releasing the upper note before the lower one. A (better) variant of this is to strike the upper note very slightly after the main note. Though hardly possible on the organ, this execution sounds excellent on the harpsichord or the piano. As we have seen (p. 256), it was described by Tomás de Santa Maria as early as 1565 (!): 'One must observe two things. First, that the finger which plays the first note must not release the key after it has struck it. Rather, it must adhere firmly to it; and the finger which strikes the second note must then be withdrawn from the key, whereby it glides along as if one were scratching it . . .' This manner of playing is recommended even as late as the fifth edition of Ignaz Pleyel's piano school (*c*.1805) 'if precision demands it'.[62] It also sounds excellent on modern pianos and can be recommended for works by Bach such as the Courante and the Gigue from the C minor French Suite, and also for certain works by Mozart and Beethoven.

Ornaments, particularly those with very fast notes, must be softer than long unembellished melody-notes. On the piano in particular 'snapped' ornaments can easily be too loud. C. P. E. Bach was already aware of this problem. What he has to say about playing the fortepiano is still valid for the modern grand piano:

With regard to the execution of this trill, it must be pointed out that it is almost insuperably difficult to play it lightly at the fortepiano. Because the snap requires pressure, its performance on this instrument increases the volume. Yet it is impossible

---

[61] *Clavierschule*, pp. 271 ff. NB: the prolongation occasioned by the pause refers to the preceding note.
[62] See Kreutz, *Ornamentik*, p. 8.

to perform our trill without this characteristic element. Hence the performer is faced with a dilemma, worsened by the fact that the short trill either by itself or combined with the turn often follows an appoggiatura and therefore, according to the rules governing the execution of appoggiaturas, must be played softly. The problem arises in all snaps, but particularly here, where it assumes its most radical form. I doubt that the most intensive practice can lead to complete control of the volume of the short trill at the fortepiano.[63]

This quotation is of note for a variety of reasons. First, it shows that the fortepiano must have been relatively widespread at the time (1753), probably in the form of the square piano, because the wing-shaped version was still rather rare and thus fairly expensive. The statement that *Pralltriller* and *Schneller* over unaccented notes should be played quietly is of particular importance. Naturally this also applies to the other ornaments. Embellishments that are too heavy and obtrusive, in music and elsewhere, are felt to be ugly intrusions. The reason why C. P. E. Bach hardly mentions this more sensitive performance of ornaments elsewhere is of course the fact that dynamic inflections of this kind were virtually impossible on a harpsichord. The greater brevity of final detached notes (*Abzug*) in the case of *Pralltriller* is probably a harpsichordist's substitute for playing piano—a shorter note is felt to be a quieter one.

The subsequent perfecting of the piano's action, particularly of double escapement, made it possible to play ornaments very fast and yet lightly and gracefully. Yet pianists still find fast trills and mordents difficult to execute softly. It is often necessary to half-depress the keys, but to do this swiftly. A passage where soft, slurred *Pralltriller* are appropriate occurs in the Allemande of Partita No. 2, BWV 826, bars 9–10 (see Ex. 14.8). On the clavichord and the fortepiano it would sound rather ugly if the last notes of this sigh were cut off short.

To sum up. With regard to the *Pralltriller* we have returned, albeit in a roundabout way, to the execution that was employed at the beginning of the Bach Renaissance in the first half of the nineteenth century. Perhaps this is a good sign. When, in the early nineteenth century, Friedrich Conrad Griepenkerl was preparing his monumental edition of Bach's organ works a number of 'grand-pupils' or 'great-grand-pupils' raised in the Bach tradition were still alive. Precisely because the organ was very much neglected in the hundred years after Bach there is reason to believe that 'modern' stylistic developments had little impact on the tradition of organ playing.[64] This would explain why on the subject of the long trill the organists consulted by Griepenkerl were in favour of beginning on the auxiliary, a view that deviated from the contemporary norm:

[63] *Essay*, p. 112. Translation amended.
[64] On the decline of organ playing after 1750 see Hochreither, *Zur Aufführungspraxis*, p. 10.

To perform Bach's trill properly it is necessary to ensure that it never begins with the note over which the sign is placed, but with the one immediately above, a tone or a semitone according to the key. Bach considered the trill to be a multiple repetition of an appoggiatura, seeing its aesthetic charm in the multiple recurrence of appoggiatura and resolution. This also explains the suffix, without which the final resolution could not come about. Younger musicians would do well to regard the matter from the same point of view.[65]

With regard to the *Pralltriller* and the mordent Griepenkerl received the following information from the same source:

With regard to the signs used for the ornaments and their execution, they should be understood to signify the following:

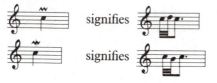

---

[65] Pref. to *Bachs Orgelwerke*, vol. i (Leipzig, 1844), n. 49. As we shall see there are a number of exceptions even to this basic rule.

15

Appoggiaturas

Appoggiaturas, which could be either short or long, were the most common eighteenth-century ornaments. Significantly, C. P. E. Bach calls the short appoggiaturas 'unvariable', thus revealing that the duration of the other appoggiaturas was not always precisely determined: it was variable.

The length or brevity of an appoggiatura cannot be deduced from the way it is written in Bach (and his contemporaries), who normally notated a small quaver or a little hook. Rather, the length or brevity of the appoggiatura note was determined by the musical context and by convention, and, as we have seen, it could not always be precisely established. This 'imprecision' was probably felt to be part of its charm and a challenge to the performer. Thus, when executing appoggiaturas we are concerned with their length, their accentuation (or lack thereof), and their position within the bar (on the beat or before it).

LONG APPOGGIATURAS

The majority of long appoggiaturas are dissonant harmonic suspensions that stand on the strong beat. The following (large) main note is thus delayed, and its duration is shortened by that of the appoggiatura (suspended) note. In addition to this, being a resolution of a dissonance, it should be played piano. This is always a problem for inexperienced players, because they are used to playing small notes quietly, and large notes more loudly.

On the other hand, in the case of shorter and short appoggiaturas almost everything was possible in the eighteenth century. They could be accented or unaccented, and played on the down-beat or on the up-beat. The latter, such as an appoggiatura played before the barline, is not tolerated by C. P. E. Bach, at least in theory. Yet in practice many appoggiaturas could not be played in any other way.

J. S. Bach often wrote out long appoggiaturas in large notes, thus giving us valuable advice on how to perform them. One of the most beautiful and expressive examples of such an appoggiatura occurs in the last bar of the *St Matthew Passion* (see Ex. 15.1). The painful b–c dissonance in the flutes makes an unforgettable impression on the listener. I owe to Frank Martin the interesting information that this striking dissonance probably had its origins in the restricted range of transverse flutes at the time. In the final chorus they usually double the violins, but here they are unable to play the final c. To cut out the flutes entirely in the final bar was unthinkable; and a leap of a seventh upwards to c^2 would have seemed much too coarse. Thus Bach was virtually forced to write this appoggiatura figure in this way.

Ex. 15.1. *St Matthew Passion*, chorus, NBA No. 68, BGA No. 78, bars 122–8

But why did he not follow the normal practice at this point and write a small note (a quaver)? Surely because at this juncture the length had to be clearly defined. In 3/4 time at least two other ways of playing the appoggiatura would have been possible—as a quaver or as a minim (see Ex. 15.2). By writing a crotchet Bach probably stipulated the maximum duration of an appoggiatura

Ex. 15.2

in such passages. If he did not wish to have an overly long dissonance at a moment of great pathos such as the end of the *St Matthew Passion*, it would have been even shorter in pieces in a lighter vein. In the keyboard music there are similar dissonances using appoggiatura notation, for instance at the end of the theme of the Goldberg Variations (Ex. 15.3) and at the end of the Gavotte

Ex. 15.3. Goldberg Variations, Aria

in the E minor Partita (Ex. 15.4). In Ex. 15.3 one could play an accented semiquaver or quaver; and in Ex. 15.4 either a quaver triplet or a d♯ crotchet. It is noteworthy that this appoggiatura is missing in the first version of the Gavotte in the *Notenbüchlein* for Anna Magdalena Bach. I am of the opinion that the later addition of the appoggiatura is not a compositional emendation. Rather, it prescribes an ornament that was often improvised or added in similar passages.

Ex. 15.4. Partita No. 6, BWV 830, Gavotte, bars 31–2

In his edition of the Goldberg Variations Ralph Kirkpatrick, at the beginning of his career, suggested some ways of playing the appoggiaturas that were certainly too long. An example of this occurs in bar 8 of the theme itself (Ex. 15.5). Playing the f♯ as a crotchet is surely wrong for the following reasons:[1]

1. Played thus, the appoggiatura would be proportionally longer than the comparable appoggiatura in the *St Matthew Passion*. Here we are only dealing with an Aria (i.e. air), which hardly justifies a pathos of this kind.
2. The resolution of the dissonance with the bass would come about only after the bass itself had already moved on, thus clouding the harmony.
3. In this suggested execution two identical ornaments would be heard at the same time in the outer voices, which is not in keeping with Bach's keyboard style.

Ex. 15.5. Goldberg Variations, Aria, bar 8

For all these reasons the appoggiatura should be an accented quaver at the most, especially if the second note in the bass is delayed and played as a semiquaver in the style of a baroque sarabande. However, Bach probably wished the appoggiatura note to merge with the mordent in the manner of a *battement* (see pp. 297 and 449).

In many long appoggiaturas it is a rule of thumb that they should be half as long as the following note, if this is not longer than a crotchet.[2] A perfect example of this is a passage in the E major Prelude of *WTC* II that has already

---

[1] See also Neumann, *Ornamentation*, pp. 147–9.
[2] Shorter appoggiaturas are almost always envisaged in the case of longer notes, such as minims or semibreves.

been mentioned above. Here Bach wrote a large quaver in bar 21 (Ex. 15.6) and an appoggiatura in the corresponding passage in bar 43 (Ex. 15.7). If there is an ornament over the note of resolution (a♯ or d♯), this always has to begin on the main note (e.g. mordents in the case of ascending appoggiaturas, and trills, *Pralltriller*, and trilled turns in the case of descending ones).

Ex. 15.6. *WTC* II, Prelude in E major, bar 21

Ex. 15.7. *WTC* II, Prelude in E major, bar 43

In bars 2 and 4 of the G sharp minor Prelude of *WTC* II, Bach wrote the sigh-motif in small notes (see Ex. 15.8), whereas he wrote similar motifs, for instance in bar 16, in large quavers (Ex. 15.9). Performers often come to the seemingly obvious conclusion that both passages should be played in the same way. I am unable to share this view, because here, unlike in the previous example, we are not dealing with an exactly identical passage. Rather, I believe that the sighs which are consistently written in small notes should be

Ex. 15.8. *WTC* II, Prelude in G sharp minor, bars 1–4

played with particularly intense expression. This is achieved by emphasizing the appoggiaturas and playing the following notes piano (with *Abzug*). The painful affection, which is reminiscent of the flute sighs in the duet 'So ist mein Jesus nun gefangen' from the *St Matthew Passion*[3] is further emphasized

Ex. 15.9. *WTC* II, Prelude in G sharp minor, bars 16–17

by playing the appoggiatura slightly shorter than a quaver, thus about a triplet quaver in duration. Evidence for these shortened sighs is provided in the harpsichord version, BWV 1054, of the E major Violin Concerto. In the second movement, at one of the most expressive points of the violin concerto, Bach wrote out sigh-motifs in regular semiquavers (see Ex. 15.10). In the D major keyboard version, which otherwise does not depart significantly from the original, Bach changed the written rhythm at this point, replacing it with demisemiquavers and dotted semiquavers. I believe it is possible that both versions may mean practically the same, namely a slightly abbreviation of the first note to about the value of a triplet.

However, it would be wrong to shorten the first of two notes in all motifs where groups of 2 + 2 notes have slurs. Ex. 15.10 should be regarded as something of a special case, brought about perhaps by the motivic material.

Ex. 15.10. Violin Concerto in E major, BWV 1042, second movement, bars 23–4

[3] NBA No. 27a, BGA No. 33.

As a rule the exact opposite is the case; according to the theory of *notes inégales* described by Couperin and Quantz, the first note should be slightly prolonged. Shortening the first note of each two-note group in the B minor Fugue of *WTC* I would sound decidedly mannered, whereas an imperceptible prolongation would sound good, the polyphony permitting (see Ex. 15.11).

Ex. 15.11. *WTC* I, Fugue in B minor, bars 1–4

In Bach's works there are a few rare cases of appoggiaturas in the form of a small crotchet (longer values do not occur). This obviously indicates an execution as a long, accented appoggiatura in the style of the Viennese Classical period. A good example of this occurs in the last bar of the Polonaise of the E major French Suite (Ex. 15.12). This execution is suggested not only by Bach's unusual crotchet notation, but above all by the characteristic polonaise cadence, which remained rhythmically unchanged for centuries, as a comparison with Chopin's E flat minor Polonaise, Op. 26 No. 2, demonstrates (see Ex. 15.13).

Ex. 15.12. French Suite No. 6, BWV 817, Polonaise (NBA), bars 23–4

Ex. 15.13. Chopin, Polonaise Op. 26 No. 2

A peculiarity of ornamentation practice around 1750 was the fact that under certain circumstances some appoggiaturas could take the whole value of the following note. A case of this kind was given when the notes were followed by a rest. Quantz remarks:[4]

---

[4] *On Playing the Flute*, p. 96.

If a rest follows a note, the appoggiatura receives the time of the note, and the note the time of the rest, unless the need to take breath makes this impossible.

C. P. E. Bach also adopted this convention, though he notated the small notes as minims or crotchets (which correspond to their real value).[5] However, he criticized this notation as being incorrect, 'since in performance the rests are filled in'.

A possible application of this rule in J. S. Bach might be in bar 2 of the E flat major Prelude of *WTC* II (Ex. 15.14), and also in bar 4. The fact that Bach had no scruples about writing out long accented dissonances in large notes speaks against this execution. If he had really wished a long execution of this kind, notating the eb^2 as a dotted crotchet would have been easier and more precise. (It is of course possible that around 1744 he wished to comply with the newly fashionable notation of long appoggiaturas before rests.) More probably he intended the appoggiatura to be an accented quaver (Ex. 15.15). But it would be quite wrong to play the appoggiatura as a crotchet: this would create consecutive fourths with the bass, and a dissonant resolution of the suspension.

Ex. 15.14. *WTC* II, Prelude in E flat major, bars 1–2

[5] *Essay*, pp. 90–1.

A similar baroque rule applies to appoggiaturas before tied notes. The example in the *Essay* (see Ex. 15.16) is revealing—the appoggiatura 'swallows' the note before the tie. A possible application suggests itself in Prelude No. 19 of *WTC* II, bar 19, where the a^1 quaver appoggiatura of the autograph could be executed as a dotted crotchet. However, in view of the initial quavers in

Ex. 15.15

the prelude (e.g. bars 5, 15, 25), I believe the shorter execution was intended. (Surprisingly, the Henle edition prints this appoggiatura, which Bach notated in the autograph, in parentheses.)

Ex. 15.16. From C. P. E. Bach, *Essay*, p. 90

PASSING APPOGGIATURAS (*COULÉS*) AND SHORT APPOGGIATURAS (*PORTS DE VOIX*)

Few musicians nowadays know the very common form of the short appoggiatura used all over Europe in the late Baroque era that was also known as *coulé* or *tierce coulée*.[6] These terms describe the habit of filling descending intervals of a third with unaccented, as it were improvised intermediate notes in order to make them more pleasing, or 'flattering'. Quantz refers to these notes as 'passing appoggiaturas' (see Ex. 15.17) and comments:

Ex. 15.17. From Quantz, *On Playing the Flute*, p. 93

Notes of this kind must not be confused with those in which a dot appears after the second, and which express almost the same melody:

---

[6] Türk also describes such appoggiaturas anticipated 'in the French manner' as passing appoggiaturas (*Clavierschule*, pp. 223, 230 ff.). The term *tierce coulée* had a different meaning to the French than to the Germans, namely the introduction of an intermediate note in arpeggiated ascending 3rds in the manner of a slide. In the case of descending progressions they used the word *coulé*. For this reason Quantz's term deserves to be given precedence; it is unequivocal.

Fig 8

In this figure . . . the short notes . . . as dissonances against the bass are executed boldly and briskly, while the appoggiaturas discussed here require, on the contrary, a flattering expression.[7]

In the course of his explanations Quantz makes a point of warning against the habit of playing the appoggiaturas in the above example as (accented) quaver appoggiaturas, because this 'would be opposed to the French style of playing, to which these appoggiaturas owe their origin'.[8] With regard to anticipation Quantz is not in agreement with C. P. E. Bach, who makes out a case for short appoggiaturas in descending thirds,[9] but wishes to have these played on the beat.[10] In practice, however, the two ways of playing them can hardly be told apart.

In the music of J. S. Bach, as we shall see, both versions occur. Yet his short passing appoggiaturas (anticipated and non-anticipated) are often confused with accented long appoggiaturas, which are unfortunately notated the same way.[11] In most cases it is possible to establish whether an accented or a passing appoggiatura is intended by deducing the best version from the *musical* context. 'Flattering' appoggiaturas come into question where a long accented note follows one or more short notes in a descending third. In certain cases the voice-leading can help us to discover the correct version. Neumann cites a good example of this (see Ex. 15.18). If the A in the bass were sung as a 'normal' quaver appoggiatura, there would be no less than three consecutive fifths with the soprano. The A of the bass *must* be performed as a *coulé* (before the second crotchet).[12]

[7] *On Playing the Flute*, p. 93.   [8] *On Playing the Flute*, p. 94.   [9] *Essay*, p. 92.
[10] *Essay*, p. 97.
[11] This confusing of appoggiaturas and intermediate appoggiaturas was often bewailed in the 18th cent., e.g. by Türk, *Clavierschule*, p. 230.
[12] That this is not an isolated case is shown by a similar passage in the A major Mass, BWV 234, 1st movement, bar 87:

(see B. Billeter, 'Die Verzierungen bei Johann Sebastian Bach', *Schweizerische musikpädagogische Blätter*, 75 (1987), 103 f., 152 f.; 76 (1988), 160 f.

Ex. 15.18. Cantata No. 137, third movement, bar 42, after Neumann, *Ornamentation,*
pp. 127, 133 ff.

For keyboard players this insight is of considerable value because the
beginning of the Loure in the Fifth French Suite in G major consists of the
same motif as the bass-line in Ex. 15.18. Bach probably had in mind a passing
or anticipating appoggiatura. The long appoggiaturas that are normally played
do not, it is true, lead to 'forbidden' consecutives, but they dilute the dance
rhythm (see Ex. 15.19).

Ex. 15.19. French Suite No. 5, BWV 816, Loure, bar 1

As early as 1908 Adolf Beyschlag, in his study of ornamentation, cited
another convincing example of the fact that Bach occasionally wished to have
such passing appoggiaturas performed in an anticipating manner (Ex. 15.20).
This surely requires simultaneous execution, with an anticipating appoggiatura
in the violins. Another example of passing appoggiaturas that is often quoted
is found in Invention No. 3, bar 4 and the corresponding passage in bar 46
(see Ex. 15.21).[13] Played on the beat this would produce three consecutive
fourths. This would be a serious error according to the eighteenth-century
rules of composition (see Ex. 15.22). For this reason these appoggiaturas *must*
be anticipated. In bar 46 of the early autograph of 1720 (in the *Clavier-
Büchlein* for Wilhelm Friedemann Bach) Bach even wrote out the anticipation
in large notes (Ex. 15.23), though in the later manuscript of 1723 he wrote

---

[13] See Landshoff, ed., *Bach Inventionen,* Beilage II; Emery, *Bach's Ornaments,* 97; W. Palmer, *Bach
Inventions and Sinfonias,* p. 91.

Ex. 15.20. Christmas Oratorio, No. 42, bars 12–13, after Beyschlag, *Ornamentik*, p. 121

Ex. 15.21. Invention No. 3, BWV 774, bars 1–4

Ex. 15.22

Ex. 15.23

Ex. 15.24

appoggiatura hooks (Ex. 15.24). The correct execution can only be one of those shown in Ex. 15.25.

Further indirect evidence for the anticipation of such appoggiaturas is provided by a passage in the second movement of the Italian Concerto, bars 5–6, which in the hitherto unknown early version reads as in Ex. 15.26*a*; Ex. 15.26*b* shows the final version with a written-out passing appoggiatura. A similar

Ex. 15.25

Ex. 15.26. Italian Concerto, BWV 971, second movement, bars 5–6

Earlier version   Final version

passage, where the anticipating *coulé* sounds much better than an accented appoggiatura, occurs in the third movement of the A major Harpsichord Concerto, BWV 1055 (Ex. 15.27).[14] Another typical example of a passage

Ex. 15.27. Harpsichord Concerto in A major, BWV 1055, third movement, bars 24–7

where this execution of the appoggiatura and no other comes into question is to be found at the beginning of the Sarabande of the G major Partita (Ex. 15.28).

Ex. 15.28. Partita No. 5, BWV 829, Sarabande, bars 1–4

The NBA quite rightly adds the appoggiaturas to the initial motif in bar 4 and in parallel passages; however, by mistake it omits the tie in the inner voice (bars 2–3).

[14] For the sake of consistency the appoggiatura b in bar 3 should be played as a *port de voix*, i.e. short and unaccented.

Bach's unusual differentiation between small semiquavers and quavers, which has already been mentioned in another context (p. 318 (Ex. 13.10)), leads to varying executions. The execution in Ex. 15.29 shows that not all *coulés* have to be anticipated. In bar 2 the on-beat version is certainly the better one. There are a number of options in bar 4. At first sight a short appoggiatura on account of the series of thirds would seem possible. However, in view of the parallel passage in bar 34 where Bach wrote out crotchets in full, a long crotchet appoggiatura might exceptionally be the better solution. The other appoggiaturas, particularly in the left hand, bar 2, are not passing ones, but the normal, short on-beat appoggiaturas that the French call *ports de voix*.

Ex. 15.29. Partita No. 5, BWV 829, Sarabande, bars 1–4: possible execution

It is noteworthy that in a number of works Bach did not initially write passing appoggiaturas: he later added them himself, or had them inserted by his pupils. Appoggiaturas of this kind are to be found in the C sharp minor Prelude of *WTC* I, bar 13 (Ex. 15.30*a*); the E flat minor Prelude of *WTC* I, bar 15 (*b*); and the Capriccio of the C minor Partita, BWV 826, two bars before the first double bar (*c*). In such instances Bach would hardly have overlooked or 'forgotten' to notate this ornament. Thus a plausible explanation may be that in order to avoid misunderstandings, he preferred to have it improvised, adding it at a later stage when he noticed that some of his pupils were simply not musical enough to understand his intentions.

Those who have acquired a taste for this ornament through the preceding examples will add passing (and other) appoggiaturas elsewhere, particularly in cantabile pieces. The Sarabande of the Third English Suite is a case in point (see Ex. 15.31). In this example I have replaced ties by dotted lines where they should not be taken literally on the harpsichord and piano, and where long notes

Ex. 15.30

Ex. 15.31. English Suite No. 3, BWV 808, Sarabande

ought to be restruck (see p. 141). The appoggiaturas that I have added at
'NB' are not in the original. They are justified by their use in other works by
Bach as well as by contemporary theory:

When the melody descends by thirds one must normally add passing appoggiaturas.[15]

[Exemples du coulé]

Explication

Further examples of essential embellishments are given in Chapter 17. The
prolongation of the dotted notes in bars 4, 7, and 12, which would be equally
possible in bars 1, 2, 5, 6, and 9, also corresponds to baroque practice, as
Quantz states when discussing sarabandes: '. . . the quavers that follow the
dotted crotchets in the loure, sarabande, courante, and chaconne must not be
played with their literal value, but must be executed in a very short and sharp
manner.'[16]

The first part of this sarabande also provides a good example of the need to
restrike the bass note G. This has already been mentioned above (see p. 401).
C. P. E. Bach and Quantz ask for this, because otherwise 'without the
fundamental note the dissonances are transformed into consonances by the
ear . . .'.[17] In the second section the tied eb^2 in the top voice should be restruck
for the same reason.

Nowadays long accented appoggiaturas of about a quaver in length are
usually played in bars 8 and 9 of the Andante of the Italian Concerto (Ex. 15.32),
which often sounds as in Ex. 15.33. Thus bb and a, which in fact are the
structural sustained notes, are played as unaccented appoggiatura resolutions.
This produces a melodic 'vacuum'. However, the small note e^1 in bar 2 is not
an appoggiatura at all; it is merely a portamento. No singer would emphasize a
note of this kind! This appoggiatura should thus be played as a semiquaver or
even shorter.[18] But the c^2 in bar 8 follows Quantz's definition, and should be
construed as a passing note. It should also be played short and unaccented. It
is unimportant whether these appoggiaturas anticipate or are played on the
beat as long as the 'accent' falls on the long notes. Following the example of
bars 14 and 16, the on-beat version is actually to be preferred (Ex. 15.34).

[15] Sébastien de Brossard (1699), quoted in David Fuller, 'An Unknown French Ornament Table from
1699', *Early Music*, 9 (1981), 56 f. The original text is: 'lorsque le chant descend de trois degrez il faut faire
ordinairement des coulez sur les degrez qui ne sont pas remplis.' Performers are warned against a too-liberal
application of this French rule to the works of Bach.
[16] *On Playing the Flute*, p. 290. I do not share Frederick Neumann's view that the words 'short and
sharp' signify staccato execution (normal quavers).
[17] Quantz, *On Playing the Flute*, p. 263.
[18] According to Oley's copy there were semiquaver appoggiaturas at this point in the original MS (no
longer extant).

The passing appoggiaturas in bar 12 of the Sarabande of the French Overture are of interest because Bach, using what was then a 'modern' manner of notating semiquaver appoggiaturas, clearly stipulated the short

Ex. 15.32. Italian Concerto, second movement, bars 8–9

Ex. 15.33

Ex. 15.34. Italian Concerto, second movement, bars 14, 16, preferred execution

execution, which would here be better on the beat (see Ex. 15.35). Otherwise it would have been possible to construe them as long appoggiaturas (of crotchet duration). That a short on-beat appoggiatura G♯ should be prefixed to the *Pralltriller* in the repeat would have seemed self-evident to Bach's contemporaries.

Ex. 15.35. French Overture, BWV 831, Sarabande, bars 11–12

A very similar melodic pattern occurs in the famous Air from the Orchestral Suite No. 3 in D major, BWV 1068 (see Ex. 15.36). The modern habit of omitting this appoggiatura simply because it is missing in certain old editions reflects an ignorance of baroque style. That the two appoggiaturas in bar 2 should also be played in a 'gliding' manner (anticipating as described by Quantz) should have become apparent by this stage (Ex. 15.37).

Ex. 15.36. Orchestral Suite No. 3, BWV 1068, Air, bar 10

Ex. 15.37. Orchestral Suite No. 3, BWV 1068, Air, bars 1–2

Two instances of the use of *coulé* in the *St Matthew Passion* deserve to be mentioned inasmuch as well-known performers of Bach's music sometimes execute them incorrectly. The first is at the end of the aria 'Blute nur' (see Ex. 15.38). In this passage the solo voice is doubled by the solo flute. However, at the final note on 'Herz!' the flute cannot hold the long B because it immediately has to join in the ritornello of the first violins. Thus the flute *cannot* play a long appoggiatura. If the singer turns the c♯ into a crotchet, it will clash with the other notes in a way that might be considered impeccable modern counterpoint, but which is quite foreign to the baroque aesthetic. Here again the solution can only be a passing appoggiatura. This would fit in with the harmony of the preceding dominant chord. At the very most one might play the c♯ as an accented semiquaver.

Ex. 15.38. *St Matthew Passion*, aria 'Blute nur', NBA No. 8, BGA No. 12, bars 20–2

The second example comes from the end of the bass aria 'Gerne will ich mich bequemen'. The execution of the appoggiatura A as a crotchet may sound very expressive in melodic terms, but it produces 'Bartókian' consecutive seconds with the continuo bass (see Ex. 15.39). Here again the only possible solution is to play a 'passing' or an accented semiquaver (or quaver) appoggiatura.

That Bach considered the use of the *coulé* wholly natural in the works of other composers transpires from his transcription of a Couperin rondeau, 'Les Bergeries' (*Pièces de clavecin*, book 2, ordre 6). Ex. 15.40 shows Couperin's

Ex. 15.39. *St Matthew Passion*, aria 'Gerne will ich mich bequemen', NBA No. 23, BGA No. 29, bars 60–5

Ex. 15.40. Couperin, 'Les Bergeries', bars 1–4, original notation Naïvement

Ex. 15.41. Couperin, 'Les Bergeries', bars 1–3, in Bach's transcription, BWV Anh. 182.

original notation, and Ex. 15.41 shows Bach's transcription of this rondeau in the *Notenbüchlein* for Anna Magdalena Bach, with certain embellishments written out in full.

Yet it would be wrong if one were to play all of J. S. Bach's descending appoggiaturas that fill a third on the up-beat and unaccented. In this connection I would like once more to refer to Neumann, who quotes some instances of *accented* appoggiaturas in descending thirds.

Such expressive accented appoggiaturas occur in the second movement of the D minor harpsichord concerto, BWV 1052 (Ex. 15.42*a*) and corresponding passages; Ex. 15.42*b* shows the execution according to C. P. E. Bach.[19] If

---

[19] *Essay*, p. 92: 'However, in an Adagio their expression is more tender when they are played as the first eighth of a triplet rather than as sixteenths.' (C. P. E. Bach's music example corresponds to the execution I have suggested.)

Bach had wanted passing appoggiaturas at this point, he would probably have written them out in large notes as in Cantata No. 84 (see Ex. 15.43).

Ex. 15.42. Harpsichord Concerto in D minor, BWV 1052, second movement

Execution according to C. P. E. Bach

Ex. 15.43. Cantata No. 84, after Neumann, *Ornamentation*, p. 133

Even where there are no thirds to be filled, many of Bach's appoggiaturas should also be short. This is especially true of those small notes or little hooks that were often added at a later stage. They were intended so to speak to add a little extra flavour to a melodic line that is in itself expressive, as for instance in the Fantasia of Partita No. 3, bars 101–3. This originally had no ornaments; Bach added the appoggiaturas at a later stage (see Ex. 15.44). Playing long appoggiaturas of about a quaver in length would be tantamount to distorting this expressive phrase, which in unembellished form is reminiscent of the 'Qui sedes' from the B minor Mass.

Ex. 15.44. Partita No. 3, BWV 827, Fantasia, bars 100–3

Short anticipated appoggiaturas should also be played where the main note already has the character of a suspension (e.g. in sigh-motifs). Quantz gives a good example of this, and expressly states that in such cases the small note is tipped briefly and reckoned in the time of the previous up-beat note (see

Ex. 15.45).[20] In Bach such appoggiaturas occur at various places in the Goldberg Variations (variations 13, 25) and in the Canonic Variations for organ on 'Vom Himmel hoch'. Walter Emery quotes an interesting example from the third variation, bars 16–17 (cf. also bar 23), where only the Quantzian up-beat execution can ensure correct voice-leading. Any other version would create consecutive fifths (see Ex. 15.46). In bar 17 of the thirteenth of the Goldberg Variations the on-beat execution would even create consecutive octaves. That Bach had these appoggiaturas printed as small demisemiquavers reflects his desire to differentiate, something that is rarely in evidence in baroque music. The appoggiatura notated as a small quaver with a diagonal stroke through the tail was never used by Bach, though it is employed in many later editions.

Ex. 15.45. From Quantz, *On Playing the Flute*, p. 94

Ex. 15.46. Canonic Variations BWV 769, variation 3, bars 16–17, after Emery, *Bach's Ornaments*, p. 78

In conclusion, with regard to the difficult question of whether appoggiaturas should be long or short—today the majority are *too* long—we should bear in mind that the essence of ornamentation is to enhance the beauty of something, not to detract from it. Thus an ornament, if it is not to distract us from what is essential, must be small, light, and graceful in comparison with the object to be embellished. Another function of an ornament is to enliven empty spaces or surfaces (as in the case of stucco, wallpaper, and floral decorations). Yet here again a surfeit of ornamentation has a detrimental effect. In other words, it is a good idea to approach ornamentation as an aesthetic phenomenon and not merely a historical one. A jewel on a ring that is larger than the finger itself is not felt to be an adornment, but a vulgar display of wealth.

[20] *On Playing the Flute*, p. 94.

With regard to music this observation leads us to a simple rule of thumb. If an unembellished melody is felt to be beautiful, then appoggiaturas, turns, trills, and so on should be played or sung as short and lightly as possible. Only where an ornament enhances the music's expressivity and where its absence creates a vacuum should it obtrude itself on our attention by being long and accented.

COULÉ FOLLOWED BY A *PRALLTRILLER*

From what has just been said it transpires that the appoggiaturas in the above extracts from the C sharp minor Prelude of *WTC* II (Exx. 14.10–11) should actually be construed as *Zwischenschläge*, or passing appoggiaturas (see Ex. 15.47).[21] Particularly in *b* this execution is decidedly preferable. As it is normally played, as an accented quaver appoggiatura, the b^1 (bar 11) in the top voice would sound simultaneously with the B in the bass, and this would lead to an unwelcome doubling of the third in G sharp minor. Ex. 15.48 shows three possible executions of the two extracts: *a*, with passing appoggiaturas as suggested by Quantz; *b*, with accented quaver appoggiaturas; and *c*, with 'unvariable' short appoggiaturas as stipulated by C. P. E. Bach.

Ex. 15.47. *WTC* II, Prelude in C sharp minor, bars 4, 11

The improvised addition of *coulés* that are not notated mentioned above can often be used where, after a leap of a third, there is a note with a *Pralltriller*, as in the Sarabande of Partita No. 2, bar 4 (see Ex. 15.49). The second passing appoggiatura *a* at 'NB' is omitted by all editions to date (including NBA). However, it is an authentic addition in one of the copies of the first edition corrected by Bach, namely in source G25.[22] In the Corrente of Partita No. 1, the introduction of a passing appoggiatura at the end of the first and second sections seems advisable (see Ex. 15.50). These two interpretations are evidently very similar to the 'modern' conception (Ex. 15.51). Clearly the

---

[21] It is significant that Bach, in bars 10 and 56 of this prelude, wrote a *Pralltriller* without appoggiatura, and in bar 55 a descending 3rd without any ornament at all. In later copies an f♯ appoggiatura was added in these places.

[22] Library of Congress, Washington, DC. See also Wolff, 'Textkritische Bemerkungen', p. 73.

Ex. 15.48. *WTC* II, Prelude in C sharp minor, bars 4, 11, possible executions

Ex. 15.49. Partita No. 2, BWV 826, Sarabande, bar 4

Ex. 15.50. Partita No. 1, BWV 825, Corrente, bars 59–60

Ex. 15.51

boundary lines often were and are indistinct. If in Ex. 15.51 one plays a long trill, which would also be in keeping with the style, two similar executions are possible. The listener can hardly tell the difference. The anticipating version

(Ex. 15.52*a*) corresponds to that of Quantz, the on-beat version (*b*) to that of C. P. E. Bach. The fact that these passing appoggiaturas can be applied ad lib does not mean that they should be used every time there is a descending interval of a third. The mind boggles at the idea of what Bach's music would sound like if all the thirds were 'filled in'.

Ex. 15.52

It is difficult to decide whether or not passing appoggiaturas should be added in the passage from the Aria of Partita No. 4 quoted in Ex. 15.53. The *coulé* execution—which should subsequently be applied to all corresponding passages in this Aria—will sound beautiful and elegant only if it is used very discreetly.[23] I play this passage with the fingering given at *a*. In order to play the ornaments in a light and elastic manner it is important to have an instrument with a good action (no matter whether it is a harpsichord or piano) and reliable finger-technique. However, versions *b* and *c* are easier to play.

In the E major Prelude of *WTC* I, there is a similar option (see Ex. 15.54). In the case of the *coulé* execution at *a* it would be logical to 'improvise' a similar unaccented appoggiatura in bar 2 of this prelude. It would not be a *coulé*, but a suffix or a *port de voix*. But here I prefer version *b*, because it is more 'Italian' and cantabile, and because this prelude is Italian in character (in

---

[23] The free addition of appoggiaturas designed to fill in descending 3rds is also suggested by Agricola in the case of singers: 'Before a note that makes an accented leap of a third downwards . . . one sometimes adds an appoggiatura from the upper auxiliary, and, in tender passages, accompanies the same with a soft *Pralltriller*' (*Anleitung*, p. 154).

Normal 18th-cent. notation:

Execution suggested by Agricola:

Ex. 15.53. Partita No. 4, BWV 828, Aria, bars 1–3

Ex. 15.54. *WTC* I, Prelude in E major, bars 1–2

Ex. 15.55. Schubert, 'Ständchen', D. 957/4

the style of a pastorale). A comparison from a later period may clarify this point: a similar motif reappears, almost note for note, in Schubert's 'Ständchen' ('Leise flehen meine Lieder') (See Ex. 15.55). Fortunately, Schubert decided to use small notes, which means that there can be no doubt about its execution.

16

The Longer Trill

As we have seen, there was a great deal of variety in the seventeenth century and at the beginning of the eighteenth century with regard to the execution of the trill. The French trill beginning on the auxiliary gradually gained the upper hand, especially in the second half of the eighteenth century. In the course of the nineteenth century this trill then went out of fashion. At no time, however, was one of the two forms entirely displaced by the other.

With regard to J. S. Bach, there is good reason to believe that, particularly in his later years, he preferred the 'French' way of playing the trill that began on the auxiliary. It would none the less be wrong to equate Bach's ornamentation practice with the French manner. Of course, Bach's interest in French music is beyond doubt; he knew works by Raison, Grigny, Marchand, Nivers, Couperin, and Dieupart, and copied d'Anglebert's table of ornaments (see Fig. 7, p. 325). Yet in general terms the Italian tradition was stronger in Thuringia than the French. O'Donnell has pointed out that it would be possible to compile an equally impressive list to suggest that the most important influence on Bach was Italian or German.[1] A number of German composers before Bach had studied in Italy, and were so strongly influenced by their models that it is almost possible to speak of an Italo-German school. Italian composers whose works Bach knew, studied, or performed included Palestrina, Frescobaldi, Peranda, Legrenzi, Bassani, Conti, Corelli, Pasquini, Caldara, Lotti, Vivaldi, Benedetto or Alessandro Marcello, Albinoni, Locatelli, Porpora, and Pergolesi.[2] With regard to German music, the 'Nekrolog' states that Bach copied out many keyboard works by Froberger and Kerll (both pupils of Frescobaldi) and Pachelbel; and that in his organ works, in addition to French composers, he modelled himself on Bruhns, Reinken, J. C. F. Fischer, and Buxtehude.[3]

[1] 'Bach's Trills', p. 23 n. 1.
[2] Christoph Wolff, 'Bach und die italienische Musik', *Bach-Tage Berlin* (Neuhausen and Stuttgart, 1985), 225 ff.
[3] *Bach-Dokumente*, iii. 81 f.

This suggests that Bach was not primarily indebted to the French style. His music contains elements that are doubtless of French origin, but it is also very much influenced by the Italian style, for instance genres such as the Vivaldi concerto and the sonata (*da chiesa*). Yet in his polyphony he is doubtless German. Sometimes there are even links back to the Franco-Netherlands school, as in his riddle canons. Ornamentation being an integral aspect of composition, there is reason to believe that Bach's 'Italian' and 'German' works suggest an execution of the embellishments that differs from those in the French style.

In his study O'Donnell lists several organ and harpsichord works by Bach with written-out trills that reflect the influence of the Italo-German organ tradition (see Exx. 16.1–16.4). O'Donnell also cites the following: for organ: Prelude and Fugue in D major BWV 532, bars 12–14 of the Prelude (organ); Toccata in C major, BWV 564, bars 45, 47, and 49; and for harpsichord or organ *manualiter*: Toccata in E minor, BWV 914, bar 49.[4]

Ex. 16.1. Prelude in A minor, BWV 551, bars 84–7

With regard to trills that are not written out, O'Donnell rightly notes that they should be played in a manner resembling the ones that are written out. He adduces as examples the Chromatic Fantasia and Fugue, BWV 903, bar 59; Toccata in E minor, BWV 914, bar 15 and similar passages; and Prelude and Fugue in A minor, BWV 551, bar 10. Instances of this kind show that the seventeenth-century German organ and harpsichord tradition survived into

---

[4] See Marshall, 'Organ or "Klavier"?'

Ex. 16.2. Fugue in C minor, BWV 574, bars 111–12

Ex. 16.3. Prelude in E minor, BWV 533, bars 6, 10–11

Ex. 16.4. Toccata in D major, BWV 912, bars 68–9 (for harpsichord or organ *manualiter*: see Marshall, 'Organ or "Klavier"?')

the first two decades of the eighteenth century.[5] However, in spite of the clear-cut evidence that the old seventeenth-century German way of playing trills still obtains in several works by Bach, there is good reason to believe that the normal form of his trill, particularly in his later works, was the French one. The well-known table for Wilhelm Friedemann supports this view, as do the instructions of C. P. E. Bach and other Bach pupils. Thus we should regard the auxiliary beginning as the rule and the main-note beginning as an exception, albeit not an infrequent one. We shall return to this subject below. However, first to the rule.

Ex. 16.5 shows the execution of two extracts from the Chromatic Fantasia and Fugue (the number of alternations in this and the following examples may vary). These trills are sometimes played beginning on the main note. This is characteristic of the late nineteenth century, and has no foundation in historical fact.

Ex. 16.5. Chromatic Fantasia and Fugue

a   Fantasia, bar 69

b   Fugue, bars 12–14

c   Execution

[5] See O'Donnell, 'Bach's Trills', p. 18.

However, in the Allemande of the E minor Violin Sonata with basso continuo, BWV 1023, Bach wrote out a similar Frescobaldian trill in order, it seems, to emphasize the leap of a sixth in the melody: it would have been a seventh if the trill had started on the auxiliary (see Ex. 16.6).[6] On account of the similarity with the above passage from the Chromatic Fugue it could be argued that it might also be historically justified to begin on $g\sharp^2$.

Ex. 16.6. Violin Sonata in E minor, BWV 1023, Allemande, bars 12–13

As we have seen, beginning on the auxiliary is particularly common in the case of the frequent formula . There is a good example of this in the Sarabande of the Fourth Cello Suite in E flat major (Ex. 16.7). If the trill began on the main note there would be hidden consecutive fifths between f and c^1 and g and d^1. However, a few bars further on, at the beginning of the Bourrée II, Bach in fact wrote hidden fifths of this kind, and in an unembellished piece at that (see Ex. 16.8). But here the whole point is that the second note, f, is long enough to be perceived as part of the sixth ab–f.

Ex. 16.7. Solo Cello Suite No. 4, BWV 1010, Sarabande, bars 18–20

Ex. 16.8. Solo Cello Suite No. 4, BWV 1010, Bourrée II, bars 1–2

---

[6] See Bodky, *Interpretation*, p. 158.

If a trill is preceded by the upper auxiliary, a decision has to be reached about whether the articulation entails a legato slur or a break. In the case of the former we arrive at something resembling the French *tremblement lié*, in that of the latter at the *tremblement détaché*. But Bach rarely notated legato slurs. They have often to be deduced and added on the basis of the musical context, above all after a dissonance when the trill is on the note of resolution, as for instance in Ex. 16.9a. Bach stated in the 'Explication' how such trills were to be played (see Ex. 16.9b).

Ex. 16.9

 (number of alternations optional)

The theme of the Gigue of Partita No. 6 contains a good example of the *tremblement détaché* in a descending line (Ex. 16.10). The rest before the trill precludes a slur. It should be played as in Ex. 16.11 (number of alternations optional, possibly with a *point d'arrêt* on the penultimate f♯; see below). In the second part of this gigue Bach, in his personal copy, drew the start of the trill into the inversion of the theme (see Ex. 16.12). In the case of the 'skipping' theme of the E flat major Fugue of *WTC* I, the *détaché* execution is merrier than the somewhat 'lame' one beginning on the main note (see Ex. 16.13).

Ex. 16.10. Partita No. 6, BWV 830, Gigue, bars 1–3

Ex. 16.11

Ex. 16.12

 (number of alternations optional)

Ex. 16.13. *WTC* I, Fugue in E flat major, bars 1–2, ed. Palmer (Alfred Ed.)

Even if it were impossible to prove Bach's occasional recourse to the old Italo-German organ tradition mentioned above, it would still be going too far to require the auxiliary beginning for all his trills without exception, as is still often the case today.[7] For example, consider the case of a conductor who asked for an execution of the trill by the flute according to contemporary rules, thus beginning on the auxiliary, in bar 45 of the aria 'Blute nur' from the *St Matthew Passion* (see Ex. 16.14). In the final bar this would mean that the soprano would have to sing a trill slurred to the preceding note (in terms of tone-painting a symbol of the serpent's tail), that is, an *accento con trillo* as described in the 'Explication' (Ex. 16.15). Going by the rules, the flute trill would begin on the auxiliary, which would lead to an absurd contradiction (see Ex. 16.16). In practice the two musicians come to an agreement, whereby the soprano usually wins and the flautist plays a main-note trill. But why did Bach write this musically unnecessary and indeed troublesome quaver rest for the flute? Presumably because, being a practical-minded musician, he wished to give the flautist a chance to breathe. With regard to the vocal part, he either thought that the boy treble did not need to take a new breath, or he wished to prevent the flautist and the chorister from interrupting the phrase to take a breath at the same time.

Ex. 16.14. *St Matthew Passion*, aria 'Blute nur', NBA No. 8, BGA No. 12, bars 42–5

[7] e.g. Putnam Aldrich, Robert Donington, Hans Klotz.

Ex. 16.15

Ex. 16.16

Bach's pupil Gerber, a familiar figure on account of his many accurate copies of his teacher's works, notated executions of certain ornaments in the Inventions which almost certainly go back to Bach himself, and demonstrate his superior attitude to the conventions of his time.[8] Ex. 16.17 shows an example; on this basis it is not difficult to prove the necessity of many main-note trills in Bach's later works.[9] This is illustrated by Exx. 16.18–16.20. It is

Ex. 16.17. Invention No. 7, BWV 778, bar 9 (NBA)

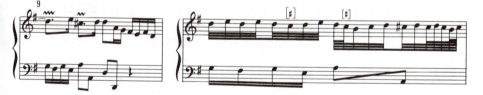

Ex. 16.18. 'Dorian' Toccata and Fugue, BWV 538, Fugue, bars 178 ff.

[8] Bach's independence of the given norm transpires above all in the compositions themselves. For example, the 1st fugue of *The Art of Fugue* transgresses many didactic rules.

[9] Some of the following exx. have previously been cited by Beyschlag, Emery, Bodky, Neumann, and others.

Ex. 16.19. Solo Cello Suite No. 3, BWV 1009, Prelude, bars 85–6

Ex. 16.20. Organ Fugue in C major, BWV 531, bars 70–1

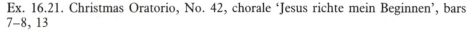

rather unlikely that baroque instrumentalists would have begun the trills shown in Exx. 16.21 and 16.22 on the upper auxiliary. The penultimate bar of the A minor Fugue of *WTC* II is of interest in that the upper voice has a 'French' trill and the middle voice a 'German' one (see Ex. 16.23). The bass trill in the following final bar should probably begin on the main note. That even strict adherents to the auxiliary-note principle find it difficult at this point to begin the second trill on the upper note and with a repeated d becomes apparent in a recording by Gustav Leonhardt. He 'rewrote' the passage, playing it as in Ex. 16.24. Yet this is unjustified and unnecessary interference with Bach's composition. Both in the autograph and in the best copies, the middle voice begins on b, presumably because Bach wished on the one hand to avoid the false relation with the c in the bass and on the other to create the chromatic line c–c♯.

Ex. 16.21. Christmas Oratorio, No. 42, chorale 'Jesus richte mein Beginnen', bars 7–8, 13

Ex. 16.22. Christmas Oratorio, final chorale 'Nun seid ihr wohl gerochen', bars 14–15

Ex. 16.23. *WTC* II, Fugue in A minor, bars 27–8

Ex. 16.24

On the basis of these observations there is no longer any need to fight shy of playing a main-note trill in the F sharp major Fugue of *WTC* I instead of doggedly repeating the $d\sharp^2$ (Ex. 16.25). Bach himself wrote a 'trill substitute' in the F sharp major Fugue of *WTC* II, which corresponds to an old German trill formula. It also begins on the main note: compare the beginning (Ex. 16.26)

Ex. 16.25. *WTC* I, Fugue in F sharp major, bars 1–3

Ex. 16.26. *WTC* II, Fugue in F sharp major, bars 1–5

with bars 20–1 (Ex. 16.27). Here technical reasons probably excluded a normal trill (in most of his works Bach placed great emphasis on writing playable music). On the basis of bar 20 one would be tempted to start the initial trill on e♯ as well. This would be in keeping with the desire to heighten the leading-note character of the beginning and the motivic relationship between e♯–f♯ and d♯–e (bars 1–2). However, in bar 32 Bach wrote the trill in a context that practically only allows it to begin on the upper note (see Ex. 16.28). Faced with such contradictions one is minded to say with Faust, 'Da steh' ich nun, ich armer Tor, Und bin so klug als wie zuvor!' (Now here I stand, a fool and more, No wiser than I was before.) However, Bach and his contemporaries would probably have laughed heartily about our scruples and attempts to provide clear-cut solutions in each and every case. Whether we like it or not, contradictions are a part of life.

Ex. 16.27. *WTC* II, Fugue in F sharp major, bars 20–3

Ex. 16.28. *WTC* II, Fugue in F sharp major, bars 32–4

Nevertheless, in the case of trills played *ex abrupto*, that is, at the beginning of a piece or a phrase, it is possible to approximate to a historically correct solution that also corresponds to modern views on the subject. We must simply bear in mind that this is an instance where two fundamental late baroque rules conflict, namely, the 'old' one that a piece should not begin on a dissonance, and the 'new' one that a trill should not begin on the main note.[10] Here the compromise solution suggested by Quantz and Leopold Mozart (see above, pp. 292 and 296) is surely the best. The trill begins on the auxiliary,

[10] A rule that a trill on a leading-note should exceptionally begin on the main note did not exist in the 18th cent., though *mi-fa*, the leading-note, was a well-known concept.

but this is played very lightly and quickly, so that, on the lines suggested by Tosi (see p. 260), the main note is heard as the 'master' and the upper note as a 'less powerful assistant'. I should like to suggest the same solution for the beginning of the G minor Prelude of *WTC* I (Ex. 16.29). However, in the case of the bass trills later on in this piece it is probably better to begin on the main note.

Ex. 16.29. *WTC* I, Prelude in G minor, bars 1–3

ASCENDING AND DESCENDING TRILLS

These trills are described in the 'Explication' as 'Doppelt Cadence und Mordant'. They occur frequently in Bach, often in alternative versions as variants of the normal trill. A good example of the 'ascending trill' is the more richly embellished version of the Allemande of the French Suite No. 5 in G major (see Ex. 16.30). In works like this suite that have survived in two or more versions one can repeat the more richly embellished version as a 'varied recapitulation' of the simple one. (C. P. E. Bach considered such *variierte Reprisen* to be repeats (mostly in slow movements) in which richer embellishments or slight melodic and rhythmic modifications were made, though the original form continued to be discernible.)

But even where there are no known alternative versions to the normal trill one can still play an 'ascending trill'. A good place to do this is in the Chromatic Fugue, bar 53. This execution obviates the need to repeat the g^2 at the beginning of the trill (see Ex. 16.31). In this connection it may perhaps be of interest that the long trills in the first movement of the Italian Concerto, BWV 971, were replaced by ascending trills in the second revised edition.

Ex. 16.30. French Suite No. 5, BWV 816, Allemande, bars 1–2

(the number of alternations can be increased)

Ex. 16.31. Chromatic Fugue, bars 52–4

(number of alternations optional)

This trill formula was also very popular with later generations of composers. The different ways of notating them always mean the same thing (see Ex. 16.32). Türk warned against possible misinterpretations of these trills, such as those shown in Ex. 16.33.[11]

All these symbols for the 'ascending trill' have in common the fact that they do not begin before the beat; examples are in Mozart's Piano Sonata in F

[11] *Clavierschule*, p. 267. In general terms it is possible to say that compound trills (and not only in Bach) only consist of stepwise intervals (of a 2nd). Repeated notes or leaps of a 3rd would impair the melodic flow of these ornaments.

major, K. 280/189*e*, first movement, bar 47 (Ex. 16.34), and in the second movement of Chopin's Piano Concerto in F minor, Op. 21, bar 7 (Ex. 16.35).

Ex. 16.32

Ex. 16.33

The 'descending trill' that C. P. E. Bach described as being rather old-fashioned[12] occurs far less frequently than the ascending trill, and is also less well suited to being substituted for the normal trill than the latter. It is found, for example, in bar 17 of the second movement of the Italian Concerto (see Ex. 16.36). In view of the syncopated delayed initial notes (rubato) in these bars one could delay the entry of the ornament slightly, as for instance in Ex. 16.37. C. P. E. Bach's term 'descending trill' is often misunderstood to mean a normal trill beginning on the auxiliary, and 'ascending trill' a main-note trill.

Ex. 16.34. Mozart, Piano Sonata K. 280/189*e*, first movement, bar 47

Ex. 16.35. Chopin, Piano Concerto No. 2, Op. 21, second movement, bars 6–7

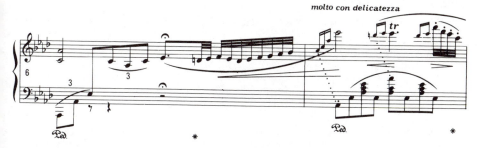

---

[12] *Essay*, p. 109.

Ex. 16.36. Italian Concerto, second movement, bars 17–18

Ex. 16.37

On account of the graphic similarity the descending trill ⌐⌐ is often confused with the *accento con trillo* ⌐⌐. However, they signify quite different things. In the latter the trill is preceded by a more or less lengthy appoggiatura, as in bar 65 of the Fantasia of Partita No. 3, BWV 827. In certain instances neither of these meanings applies. The older Bach was in the habit of beginning the wavy line for the normal trill in a somewhat flamboyant manner, for example ⌐⌐. The engravers immediately reproduced this as ⌐⌐ or ⌐⌐, and it is printed thus to this day. Musically meaningless descending trills of this kind occur at the end of the E flat major Fugue, BWV 552/2, at the end of the F major Duet, BWV 803, and in the second section of the Gigue of Partita No. 5, BWV 829. This formula is particularly obtrusive at the end of the subject of the three-part ricercar in the *Musical Offering*. Here Bach surely meant only a normal suffixed trill (beginning on the main note, d).

TRILL SUFFIXES

Although the majority of Bach's trills are notated without a suffix, most long trills should be performed with one (see below). Bach himself in fact notated suffixes in three ways:

1. The wavy line with the vertical stroke at the end given in the 'Explication': ⌐⌐
2. Two suffix notes written out in full:[13]

[13] *Small* suffix notes first came into common use after the time of Bach. However, Neumann *Ornamentation*, p. 340 n. 31) found a single authentic passage with small suffix notes, in the 1st movement of the E major Harpsichord Concerto, BWV 1053, bar 63.

3. The notation of a single note as an anticipation of the final note:

However, this way of ending the trill is usually termed an anticipation, not a suffix.

In the case of this anticipatory formula the application of a trill was so self-evident that ornament symbols were frequently omitted, as at c above. It is quite wrong to play such concluding phrases unembellished, as is unfortunately often the case, for instance at the end of the Chromatic Fugue, BWV 903, penultimate bar (see below, p. 478).

The wavy line with a vertical stroke at the end was seldom used by Bach, presumably because it could easily be confused with the mordent sign. Thus the performer must exercise caution when he comes across it, deducing from the context whether it designates a mordent or a trill. However, there is clearly a trill of this kind in bar 3 of the Air of Partita No. 6 (see Ex. 16.38).[14]

Ex. 16.38. Partita No. 6, BWV 830, Air, bars 3–4

Examples of written-out suffixes are to be found in the Chromatic Fugue, bar 35 (Ex. 16.39) and in the Ouverture of Partita No. 4, bar 33 (Ex. 16.40). The notation continually tempts one to play such suffixes as if they were integrated into the metrical scheme (here as semiquavers). Yet this would be wrong, for C. P. E. Bach makes a point of stating that the 'suffix must be played as rapidly as the trill proper' and mentioning 'the usual extremely rapid motion into the following note'.[15] And a 'limp' suffix he considered to be an 'ugly' error.[16] The seemingly slower suffixes in the music of J. S. Bach are of

Ex. 16.39. Chromatic Fugue, bar 35

Ex. 16.40. Partita No. 4, BWV 828, Ouverture, bars 33–4

[14] Klotz (*Ornamentik*, pp. 28 and 131) interprets this symbol differently. See also n. 17 below.
[15] *Essay*, pp. 103–4.   [16] *Essay*, p. 106.

course connected with the fact that double dotting (for the preceding note) had not yet been introduced. Ex. 16.40 is remarkable in that it contains a *Pralltriller* symbol. However, the written-out suffix is an indication that a longer trill was intended. The same obtains in the case of bars 3 and 4 of the E flat minor Prelude of *WTC* I, though in the case of the first trill a *point d'arrêt* is to be recommended.

A baroque peculiarity that 'disappeared' in the Classical period is the occasional halt and break before the suffix in pieces in the French style, particularly in overtures and sarabandes. The notation that has already been mentioned (see p. 266) in bars 10 and 12 of the E minor Prelude of *WTC* I is of interest in this respect, as is a particularly characteristic example, bars 8 and 45 of the French Overture (Ex. 16.41). Earlier versions of both works in simpler notation have survived. The C minor version of the French Overture shows that Bach had the demisemiquaver suffix in mind from the very start

Ex. 16.41. French Overture, BWV 831, bars 8–9

despite the semiquaver notation: compare the lower voice (Ex. 16.42). 'Chopping off' the suffix in this way represents a special case and must not be done in flowing, cantabile pieces.[17]

[17] Klotz (*Ornamentik*, pp. 27, 58 f.) stipulates the rule that there has always to be a break before the suffix. However, at the beginning of the 5th French Suite, BWV 816, a piece that is surely meant to be legato, the Klotzian ending would not only interrupt the flow, but also lead to 3 consecutive 5ths:

An execution on the lines suggested by C. P. E. Bach would avoid both these pitfalls:

Ex. 16.42. French Overture, C minor version, BWV 831*a*, bars 8–9

If only one note (anticipation) follows the trill, care should be taken to ensure that it is not too long, and that the trill comes to a halt shortly before. A typical example of this occurs in bar 13 of the Praeludium of Partita No. 1 (Ex. 16.43), which one normally hears played as in Ex. 16.44. It does not sound very graceful and, furthermore, it differs from the similar embellishment in bar 18, which ends with a demisemiquaver. Thus I think it is much better to apply literally the rule quoted by C. P. E. Bach (see Ex. 16.45).[18] The additional suffix (here d^2) recommended by C. P. E. Bach can also be omitted, particularly when the anticipation takes place in a descending line; an example is in the last two bars of the Courante of Partita No. 2 in C minor (Ex. 16.46).[19] This execution with a suffix played later than notated is particularly important in ensemble playing, where the impression of rhythmic imprecision might otherwise arise, for instance in the last movement of the E major Sonata for violin and harpsichord, bar 91 (Ex. 16.47). Earlier in this

Ex. 16.43. Partita No. 1, BWV 825, Praeludium, bars 13–14

Ex. 16.44

---

[18] See p. 285 (Ex. 12.52). Other ways of playing this are given by Neumann, *Ornamentation*, p. 333: the executions under *e* and *f* can also be recommended.

[19] Bach later added the appoggiatura before the trill in his personal copy (British Library, London). Thus it would also be possible to play a normal trill without a long appoggiatura.

Ex. 16.45

Ex. 16.46. Partita No. 2, BWV 826, Courante, bars 23–4

Ex. 16.47. Sonata No. 3 for violin and harpsichord, BWV 1016, last movement, bar 91

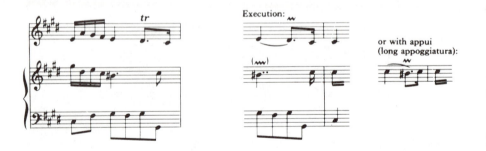

movement (bar 66) there would even be consecutive fifths between harpsichord and violin if the suffix were played 'limply' in the nineteenth-century manner (Ex. 16.48). At the end of the first movement of this sonata the suffixes should surely be synchronized. As an example of the shortening of the last note and the *point d'arrêt* Bodky cites Jean Rousseau's *cadence pleine* (Ex. 16.49).

Even if none is notated, most trills should be performed with a suffix, mostly in the usual two-note form. 'Trills on long notes are played with a

Ex. 16.48. Sonata No. 3 for violin and harpsichord, BWV 1016, last movement, bar 66

correct execution:

Ex. 16.49. From Jean Rousseau, after Bodky, *Interpretation*, p. 160.

suffix regardless of a subsequent stepwise descent or ascent.'[20] This rule was so obvious for the majority of composers up to Beethoven and Brahms that they often did not notate suffixes. Thus in Haydn and early Mozart in particular most trills are notated without a suffix, which nowadays often leads to ludicrous interpretations.

However, there are certain instances where suffixes are not necessary. C. P. E. Bach listed them precisely:[21]

The unsuffixed trill is best used in descending successions, Fig. XXVIII. (a), and principally over short notes (b). The suffix is omitted from successive trills (c) and from trills followed by one or more short notes which are capable of replacing it (d). If this substitution is made, the asterisked example must not be played in the slowest tempo. Further, the suffix is not employed over triplets (e).

---

[20] C. P. E. Bach, *Essay*, p. 103. See also Quantz, *On Playing the Flute*, p. 103: 'The ending of each shake consists of two little notes which follow the notes of the shake, and are added to it at the same speed (see Tab. VII Fig. 2). They are called the termination. This termination is sometimes written out with separate notes (see Fig. 3). If, however, only a plain note is found (as in Fig. 4), both the appoggiatura and termination are implied, since without them the shake would be neither complete nor sufficiently brilliant'.

[21] *Essay*, pp. 104–5.

'Successive trills' are of course chains of trills, which also occur in J. S. Bach on a number of occasions, for instance in the last movement of the F minor Harpsichord Concerto, bars 73 ff. (and 81 f., 165 ff., 173 ff.) (see Ex. 16.50). There is an even longer chain of trills (also descending) in the second movement of the Fourth Organ Sonata, BWV 528, bar 38. In both instances I believe it is correct to begin the trill on the main note (at least from the second one onwards), because trills automatically imply a slur (*tremblement lié*). However, it is also possible to end each trill with a *point d'arrêt* and to start the next one on the auxiliary. In this connection we should remember that the *Pralltriller* symbol can also signify a long trill, for example in the Invention in G major, bars 20–3 (Ex. 16.51).

Ex. 16.50. Harpsichord Concerto in F minor, BWV 1056, last movement, bars 73–7

Ex. 16.51. Invention No. 10, BWV 781, bars 20–2

A special case are the trills that finish with a tie over the barline. They occur frequently in Bach. Here I value Emery's suggestion to end the trill shortly before the barline (with or without suffix) in the manner of a *point d'arrêt*, so that the ensuing syncopation becomes audible.[22] However, C. P. E. Bach

---

[22] *Bach's Ornaments*, p. 65.

suggests a different solution, which also sounds good: the trill continues uninterrupted and the suffix is played after the barline (Ex. 16.52). He also adds that the suffix can be omitted if it is followed by a descending series of notes. An instance of the trill with tied final note occurs in the first movement of the Italian Concerto, bars 114–15 (see Ex. 16.53). However, the last version accents the (unaccented) note g that follows. For this reason I prefer versions *a* and *b*. See also Ex. 16.59.

Ex. 16.52. From C. P. E. Bach, *Essay*, p. 108

Ex. 16.53. Italian Concerto, first movement, bars 114–15

THE SPEED OF THE TRILL

The notion that in Bach and other baroque composers trills ought sometimes to be played slowly seems impossible to eradicate. Yet the treatises are virtually unanimous in stating that trills, as indeed most of the ornaments expressed by means of signs (with the exception of long appoggiaturas), should be played fast, flowingly, and lightly. Rameau speaks repeatedly of the 'speed and lightness' of trills.[23] Marpurg remarks: 'The trill . . . is in fact nothing more than a series of appoggiaturas repeated one after the other with the greatest speed',[24] and C. P. E. Bach comments:

Trills are the most difficult embellishments, and not all performers are successful with them. They must be practiced industriously from the start. Above all, the finger

---

[23] See Harich-Schneider, *Die Kunst des Cembalospiels*, p. 25.
[24] *Anleitung*, p. 53.

strokes must be uniform and rapid. A rapid trill is always preferable to a slow one. In sad pieces the trill may be broadened slightly, but elsewhere its rapidity contributes much to a melody. With regard to the amount of pressure, the performer must be guided by the nature of the passage, be it forte or piano, in which the trill appears.[25]

Not only these descriptions, but also the words themselves in various languages point to speed: *tremulo, tremblement*, shake. I have never seen anyone trembling, or indeed an object shaking, slowly.

The most refined and thus the most valuable remarks on this subject are those by Quantz pertaining to the tempo of the trill:

If the shake is to be genuinely beautiful, it must be played evenly, or at a uniform and moderate speed. Upon instruments, therefore, the fingers must never be raised higher at one stroke than at another. To fix precisely the proper speed of a good regular shake is rather difficult. Yet I believe that a *long* shake which prepares a cadence will be neither too slow nor too quick if it is so struck that the finger makes not many more than about *four* movements in the time of a pulse beat, and thus makes *eight* notes, as illustrated in Tab. VII, Fig. 1.

In fast and gay pieces, however, brief shakes can be struck a little more quickly. Here the finger may be raised, in the time of a pulse-beat, once or at most twice more. But this latter type is permissible only upon short notes, and when there are several short notes in succession.[26]

The 'moderate' speed of the Quantzian trill has nothing in common with the slow trills criticized above, but must be regarded from the point of view of the faster feeling for tempo that obtained in the eighteenth century. As Quantz states elsewhere that the pulse-beat is eighty per minute, this moderate tempo of ♩ = 80 is, as far as we are concerned, a normal fast tempo. It is very suitable for many of Bach's trills. The possible acceleration by one to two alternations that Quantz mentions leads to extremely fast trills. This can be seen quite clearly if instead of ♩ = 80 we set the metronome to ♪ = 160 and practise trills as in Ex. 16.54.

Ex. 16.54

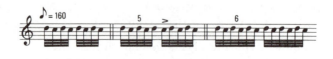

[25] *Essay*, p. 101.   [26] *On Playing the Flute*, pp. 102–3.

An exception to the stipulated evenness of the trill can occur when a trill continues for some time. Here a slight acceleration towards the end is to be recommended (see p. 274, bottom). Whereas a singer or a wind player can progressively increase the loudness of a long note, this effect can be achieved on tonally inflexible keyboard instruments such as the harpsichord or the organ only by increasing the number of notes. Michel de Saint-Lambert (1702) remarked: 'If the trill has to be long it is more pleasing to play it slowly at the beginning and to accelerate towards the end; but if it is short it must always be fast'.[27] Quantz also says that the speed of a trill depends on the acoustics of the room, the pitch, and the character of a piece. An unduly fast trill becomes indistinct in a room where the sound reverberates.

In a small or tapestried room, on the other hand, where the listeners are close by, a quicker shake will be better than a slower one. In addition, you must be able to distinguish the character of each piece you play, so that you do not confuse those of one sort with those of another, as many do. In melancholy pieces the shake must be struck more slowly, in gay ones, more quickly. Slowness or quickness, however, must not be excessive.[28]

In J. S. Bach a relatively slow trill of this kind is a possibility at the end of the Andante of the Italian Concerto (see Ex. 16.55). I believe this trill should begin slightly faster than the preceding *tirata* and should then slow down to

Ex. 16.55. Italian Concerto, second movement, bars 48–9

the point where the final figure corresponds roughly to the demisemiquavers of the rest of the movement; Ex. 16.56 shows an approximate notation. However, a trill of this kind is more the exception than the rule.

Ex. 16.56

---

[27] Quoted by Harich-Schneider, *Die Kunst des Cembalospiels*, p. 79. An acceleration of this kind is also inherent in the notation of certain Bach trills mentioned above (pp. 421–2, Exx. 16.18–19). I also believe that the trills in the D major Toccata, BWV 912, bars 68–70, should not be played as written, but accelerated in the manner of Frescobaldi (and with more alternations than notated).

[28] *On Playing the Flute*, p. 101.

Finally it should again be emphasized that it is part of the essence of the trill that it preserves a certain independence of the metre even where it is metrically notated in the textbooks (e.g. as demisemiquavers). The legato execution of almost all trills is also so self-evident that most treatises do not even mention it.[29]

ACCIDENTALS AND TRILLS

The fact that Bach never notated accidentals in trills sometimes causes problems. For example, in bar 33 of the E minor Prelude of *WTC* II, Tovey, Emery, and O'Donnell suggest c as the upper alternating note of the trill on the lines of the preceding g–f♯ bass trill (see Ex. 16.57). However, this section of the prelude is in B minor, a key in which the semitone step f♯–g (dominant) corresponds to a whole-tone step b–c♯ (tonic). I have no qualms about starting the trill with b–c♯, and regard the preceding c♯ (bar 32) to be a 'support' to the trill on the lines described by Rameau.

On this subject Christoph Albrecht comments:[30]

In baroque fugues the rule which states that the trill has to comply with the key means that different forms of the trill may have to be used for the subject and the answer. This is because the leading-note (a semitone) lies beneath the tonic, whereas there is a whole tone beneath the dominant. The Organ Fugue in E minor (BWV 533) is a classic example of this:

(If the mordent were b–a♯–b the beginning of the fugue would sound as if it were in B minor, not in E minor.)

In the first movement of the Italian Concerto, the trill in bar 112 is usually and inexplicably played starting on c^2 instead of $c♯^2$, which sounds wrong for melodic and harmonic reasons because of the false relation with the c♯ in the lower voice (see Ex. 16.58). It should really be played as in Ex. 16.59. Compare this with the trill shown in Ex. 16.60 where, oddly enough, everyone begins correctly with *b*.

---

[29] See Donington, *A Performer's Guide*, p. 200.   [30] *Interpretationsfragen*, pp. 144 f.

Ex. 16.57. *WTC* II, Prelude in E minor, bars 31–6, after W. Emery, *Bach's Ornaments*, pp. 53–4

Execution after O'Donnell and W. Emery

Execution after Emery

Ex. 16.58. Italian Concerto, first movement, bars 110–14

Ex. 16.59

Ex. 16.60

TECHNICAL PROBLEMS ASSOCIATED WITH PLAYING TRILLS

Trills still cause problems for many pianists, harpsichordists, and organists. Surprisingly little has changed in this respect in the last 300 years. For this reason C. P. E. Bach's advice[31] is still of great value today and deserves to be cited:

In practising the trill, raise the fingers to an equal but not an excessive height. Trill slowly at first and then more rapidly but always evenly. The muscles must remain relaxed or the trill will bleat or grow ragged. Many try to force it. Never advance the speed of a trill beyond that pace at which it can be played evenly. When the upper tone of a trill is given its final performance it is snapped; after the stroke the upper joint of the finger is sharply doubled and drawn off and away from the key as quickly as possible.

The trill must be practised diligently with all fingers so that they will become strong and dexterous. However, let no one believe that all of the fingers can be made to trill equally well. For one thing, there are natural differences among them, and for another, compositions usually offer more trills for certain fingers than for others; hence these are unwittingly given more practice. Yet prolonged trills appear at times in outer parts and preclude a choice of fingers, most of them being engaged in performing the inner parts. In addition certain passages are extremely difficult to perform unless the little finger has learned to trill rapidly, as illustrated in Fig. XXV [Fig. 93].

No one can succeed without a minimum of two good trills in each hand: the second and third, and the third and fourth fingers of the right hand; and the thumb and second, and second and third fingers of the left. It is because of this normal fingering of trills that the left thumb grows so agile and along with the second finger becomes about the most active of the left hand.

Some performers practise double trills in thirds with one hand. Various examples of these may be constructed from Fig. XLII. Such exercise, pursued as far as one wishes, is beneficial to the fingers, but aside from this it is better not to employ double trills unless they can be made to sound even and distinct, the two desiderata of good trills.

When the upper tone falls on a black key, and the lower on a white key it is not incorrect to perform a trill with the second finger of the left hand crossed over the thumb as illustrated in Fig. XXVI [Fig. 94].

C. P. E. Bach's last piece of advice can also be applied to the right hand with good effect, as in the case of the *a–g♯* trill (see Ex. 16.61). The following comment is remarkably modern: 'Also, some find it convenient to trill with

[31] *Essay*, pp. 101–2.

Ex. 16.61

the third and fifth or the second and fourth fingers of the right hand when the action of the keys is stiff.'[32]

Rameau's instructions in *De la méchanique des doigts sur le clavessin* (1724) are similar to those of C. P. E. Bach, though in contrast to the latter he states that the fingers should be lifted higher still: 'When one practises trills one must lift the fingers one is using singly and as high as possible. Yet the more this movement becomes a matter of habit, the less one lifts them, and the large movement is in the end transformed into a swift and light movement'.[33]

[32] *Essay*, p. 102.
[33] See Harich-Schneider, *Die Kunst des Cembalospiels*, p. 25.

17

Bach's Mordent

INTRODUCTORY REMARKS

Two factors are characteristic of the mordent: it occurs only in keyboard music (at least in J. S. Bach),[1] and, unlike the trill, it adheres to the main-note beginning even in the early eighteenth century. In view of the fact that it mirrored the (short) trill it should, going by the 'auxiliary note' rule, have begun on the lower auxiliary. In retrospect it seems illogical that this happened in only a handful of exceptional cases. The reason for it may have been that (accented) appoggiaturas from below have always played a far less important role than ones from above. This in turn is due to the fact that the resolution of a suspended discord downwards is felt to be more *natural* than upwards, for the simple reason that downwards there is a relaxation of strings or vocal cords. Thus the resolution shown in Ex. 17.1 occurs more frequently than that in Ex. 17.2. The rules of strict part-writing did not allow the latter resolution of a dissonance, though in free composition it was at the most tolerated in the case of semitone steps.

Ex. 17.1

Ex. 17.2

The fact that Bach's mordents begin on the main note has never been called into question. Bach himself made the execution quite clear in the 'Explication',

---

[1] Recently a well-known cellist asked me whether he could introduce mordents (in ascending lines) in the solo cello suites in addition to the required trills and *Pralltriller*. My answer tends to be no. Neumann (*Ornamentation*, p. 44) also regards the mordent as a typically 'keyboard' embellishment, though in France it made an appearance in music for the viola da gamba.

though he did not mention the longer mordent (a repeated alternation with the note immediately below). Bach rarely seems to have used this ornament, which often occurs in French music. However, Kreutz cites an interesting example from the Gigue of the Sixth English Suite in D minor, where bars 30–31 are an exact inversion of bars 6–7 (Ex. 17.3; NBA also prints long mordents here). This probably means that a longer mordent alternating with the note a semitone below (a–g♯) should be played at this point and in parallel passages. Neumann complements this example with a passage in the Gavotte of the Third English Suite in G minor, where the long mordent in the bass imitates a drum-roll (Ex. 17.4). Neumann similarly cites an example from the harpsichord version, BWV 1054, of the E major Violin Concerto, BWV 1042, where Bach notated a long mordent in the style of Couperin in place of the first held note of the violin (see Ex. 17.5).[2]

Ex. 17.3 English Suite No. 6, BWV 811, Gigue, bars 6–7, 30–1, after Kreutz edn., p. 7

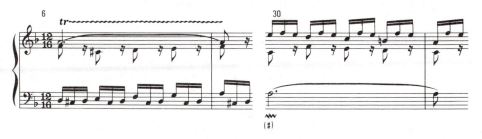

Ex. 17.4. English Suite No. 3, BWV 808, Gavotte, bars 18–21, after Neumann, *Ornamentation*, p. 443

According to C. P. E. Bach the mordent is 'an essential ornament which connects notes, fills them out, and makes them brilliant'.[3] The 'connection' occurs in the case of ascending legato lines, and leads to forms that may be regarded as mirror images of the *Pralltriller*.[4] This means that, if possible, the mordent should be played swiftly. If it is placed over an unaccented note, for instance after an ascending accented suspension (or appoggiatura), it is played

[2] See the MS of BWV 1054 in Deutsche Staatsbibliothek, Berlin (P 234).
[3] *Essay*, p. 127.   [4] *Essay*, p. 131.

Ex. 17.5. Violin Concerto in E major, BWV 1042 (*a*) and Harpsichord Concerto in D major, BWV 1054 (*b*), second movement, bars 7–9, after Neumann, *Ornamentation*, p. 443

lightly.[5] The mordent in Ex. 17.6 should be played in this way. The manner of performing the 'very short' mordent given in the *Essay* is also of interest (see Ex. 17.7). Here the top note is held, and the lower note released immediately.

Ex. 17.6. Partita No. 4, BWV 828, Allemande, bar 28

Ex. 17.7. From C. P. E. Bach, *Essay*, pp. 127–8

In a handful of cases Bach actually wrote out the mordents in full, for instance in the C minor Fantasia, BWV 906, bars 21–2 (Ex. 17.8). It is difficult to say why Bach did this. Written-out mordents of this kind are also found in the introduction to aria No. 5, of Cantata No. 186, bars 3–5.[6]

---

[5] *Essay*, p. 128.   [6] Communication from Klaus Hofmann.

Ex. 17.8. Fantasia in C minor, BWV 906, bars 21–2

MORDENTS ON INITIAL NOTES

A special feature of Bach's mordent is the fact that it often marks the beginning of a melody, where it imparts to a long held note a certain brilliance.[7] Exx. 17.9–17.11 show some instances. Initial mordents of this kind permit the starting transient of a note that enters 'brilliantly' to be heard more clearly than in the case of one that begins unembellished.

Ex. 17.9. Toccata in D minor, BWV 565, bars 1–2

Ex. 17.10. Harpsichord Concerto in F minor, BWV 1056, second movement, bars 1–2

In Ex. 17.11 one could also play a longer mordent with two or three alternations on the lines suggested by C. P. E. Bach (see Ex. 17.12). However, this would hardly be possible in Ex. 17.9 and 17.10, because 'a liberal

---

[7] Cf. C. P. E. Bach, *Essay*, p. 127.

application of trills' of this kind would reduce the effect of a sustained initial note. One could term such mordents 'medium-length mordents'. C. P. E. Bach makes a point of warning against too many alternations:

To lessen the possibility of such an error, strike a tone with due pressure and hold it. In so doing, one realizes that our instrument sustains tones longer than generally believed. In using mordents the performer must be careful not to destroy the beauty of a sustained tone. Hence, as with other ornaments, he must not apply them to every long note nor overextend them. When mordents serve to fill out a note, a small fraction of the original length must remain free of decoration, for the most perfectly introduced mordent sounds miserable when, like the trill, it speeds directly into the following tone.[8]

Ex. 17.11. Italian Concerto, second movement, bar 4

Ex. 17.12

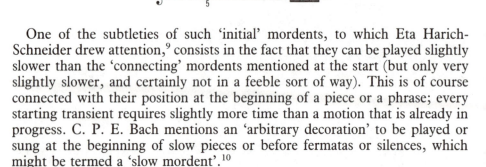

One of the subtleties of such 'initial' mordents, to which Eta Harich-Schneider drew attention,[9] consists in the fact that they can be played slightly slower than the 'connecting' mordents mentioned at the start (but only very slightly slower, and certainly not in a feeble sort of way). This is of course connected with their position at the beginning of a piece or a phrase; every starting transient requires slightly more time than a motion that is already in progress. C. P. E. Bach mentions an 'arbitrary decoration' to be played or sung at the beginning of slow pieces or before fermatas or silences, which might be termed a 'slow mordent'.[10]

Another reason for not playing ornaments quite so fast as the player may imagine they should be is, in the case of organs, the size of the building. Yet even here the retardation must be minimal.

A serious mistake that often occurs when a mordent is placed over an initial note is that it is played too soon, therefore sounding like an up-beat (see Ex. 17.13). The reason for this anticipation is probably to be sought in the fact that the player involuntarily wishes to emphasize the long note. However, the same intensity should apply to the first three (or five, seven, or nine) notes, thus emphasizing the sustained melody-note, which should unfold and wax like a *messa di voce*.

---

[8] *Essay*, p. 129.   [9] *Die Kunst des Cembalospiels*, p. 87.   [10] *Essay*, p. 132.

Ex. 17.13

The added brilliance provided by the initial mordent also makes it possible to accent rhythmically important notes in dance-like pieces. For this reason the mordent, unlike other ornaments, is often to be found in the bass. Mordents of the kind at the beginning of the D minor Prelude of *WTC* II (Ex. 17.14), as indeed mordents on short notes, should always be played sharp, fast, and aggressively (Ex. 17.15).

Ex. 17.14. *WTC* II, Prelude in D minor, bars 1–3

Ex. 17.15

MORDENTS AFTER LEAPS

According to C. P. E. Bach the mordent often occurs in conjunction with leaps (mostly on the target-note), particularly with upward leaps. Rules of this kind are of interest because they can probably be traced back to J. S. Bach, his son's 'sole teacher'. They help us to add the right mordents and other ornaments where they are missing in the text (see below). Exx. 17.16 and 17.17 show instances of such mordents. The mordent is also used in the case of downward leaps, though here J. S. Bach often prefers the *Pralltriller*, which should probably be played as an inverted mordent (*Schneller*) in such passages (see Exx. 17.18 and 17.19). Here, however, many Bach performers tend to play, without exception, a *cadence simple détachée* beginning on the auxiliary as

Ex. 17.16. Partita No. 3, BWV 827, Corrente, bars 34–6

Ex. 17.17. Partita No. 6, BWV 830, Allemanda, bars 13–14

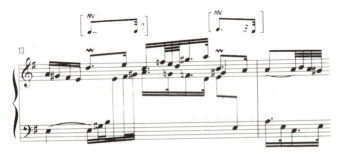

Ex. 17.18. Partita No. 1, BWV 825, Corrente, bars 21–2

Ex. 17.19. Chorale prelude *Wenn wir in höchsten Nöten sein*, BWV 641, bar 2

described by Dom Bédos de Celles (1776; see below). Both forms were current in the eighteenth century (see p. 305).

FURTHER USES OF THE MORDENT

The mordent after an accented appoggiatura (or suspension) mentioned above can, if the appoggiatura is short, lead to an ornament beginning on the auxiliary. Here again the chorale prelude *Wenn wir in höchsten Nöten sein* provides good examples (Ex. 17.20). In *a* the appoggiatura could be rather longer (e.g. an accented semiquaver); but in *b* it can only be short, possibly anticipatory.[11] Only when it is written in this way (with preceding small hook or lower appoggiatura) should Bach's mordent begin on the lower auxiliary.

Ex. 17.20. Chorale prelude *Wenn wir in höchsten Nöten sein*, BWV 641, bars 1–2, 3

In eighteenth-century theory this ornament certainly occurs, though infrequently. It is found in Heinichen and Quantz (as *battements*), and in Dom Bédos de Celles as *pincé simple et détaché*, in contrast to *pincé simple et lié* (Ex. 17.21).

Ex. 17.21. Bédos, *L'Art du facteur d'orgues*, Part II, Table 108

---

[11] See Neumann, *Ornamentation*, p. 348.

C. P. E. Bach is rather vague with regard to accidentals, saying that they adjust themselves 'to circumstances'.[12] It is in fact only possible to follow one's musical instincts when it comes to deciding when to alternate with a major or a minor second. The leading-note (lower minor second) should always be played in the case of the mordent on the tonic.[13]

Though up-beat anticipation must be ruled out in the case of mordents on initial notes, there are, in the case of 'connecting' mordents, a number of instances where anticipation is not only possible, but desirable. There is a good example of this in the Sarabande of the E minor Partita, where, in bar 17, Bach had a mordent sign printed in the middle voice, and, two bars later, in what is almost the same passage, a written-out mordent on the up-beat (Ex. 17.22). This is a mordent preceded by an ascending appoggiatura (written in large notes). The on-beat execution corresponds to Bach's 'Explication', the up-beat one on the other hand to Muffat's instructions,

Ex. 17.22. Partita No. 6, BWV 830, Sarabande, bars 17, 19

Ex. 17.23

which Bach no doubt knew (see Ex. 17.23). Even when mordents are placed over relatively unaccented up-beat notes, anticipation as recommended by Muffat is perhaps preferable, for otherwise such up-beat notes would almost always be accented. A case of this kind is to be found in the first arioso of the *Capriccio sopra la lontananza del suo fratello dilettissimo*. Here I am in agreement with Neumann's interpretation (Ex. 17.24). But even here an on-beat execution is possible (see Ex. 17.25).

---

[12] *Essay*, p. 130.

[13] See also Albrecht, *Interpretationsfragen*, pp. 144 f., who recommends the diatonic execution ('tonic and semitone', 'dominant and whole tone').

Ex. 17.24. *Capriccio sopra la lontananza del suo fratello dilettissimo*, BWV 992, after Neumann, *Ornamentation*, p. 446

Ex. 17.25

18

Arpeggios

In the preceding chapters I have referred on a number of occasions to arpeggio, a technique that is very common in the case of stringed instruments. Because the art of arpeggiation is deemed to be an aspect of embellishment in older and newer treatises, it seems apposite to sum up some of the relevant rules that pertain to Bach, and to discuss a number of special cases.

It is a well-known fact that the term 'arpeggio' is derived from 'harp' (or *arpa*), an instrument on which triadic chords tend to be played in sequence. As every musician knows, on the harp the majority of 'Harpeggien' begin on the lowest note (there is no need to discuss the acoustical reasons for this). This basic rule has always applied to arpeggios played on other instruments such as the lute, the guitar, the keyboard, the violin, and so on. An arpeggio beginning at the top of the chord must thus be regarded as an exception to the rule. It was so uncommon that its sign fell into oblivion in the nineteenth century. New symbols for descending arpeggios were introduced in the twentieth century, for example by Bartók in the second of the Two Elegies, Op. 8b.

I have been unable to find a sign for the 'inverted arpeggio' in the music of J. S. Bach. It occurs in French music, being notated thus ʃ. Klotz errs when he attempts to prove that Bach made use of this symbol[1]—graphic and musical reasons speak against his reading of the passage in question. Bach's sign for a normal arpeggio was the wavy line still in use today ∤ (see the E flat minor Prelude of *WTC* I). However, in southern Germany and in Italy an arpeggio was indicated by a diagonal line through the middle of a chord—a sign that Haydn, Mozart, and occasionally even Beethoven (e.g. Piano Concerto No. 5, Op. 73, third movement) employed. For this reason it would be absurd to play all the arpeggios written by these composers as acciaccaturas, something that is still occasionally suggested.

With regard to the descending arpeggio in the music of J. S. Bach, the lack of hard evidence for a sign of this kind does not of course mean that it was an

---

[1] *Ornamentik*, pp. 169 f.

ornament Bach did not know or wish to use. However, there is much to suggest that it was to be applied with discretion, and rather infrequently.

In the case of the normal ascending arpeggio, there are two different kinds of execution: (1) the fast, as it were guitar-like plucked arpeggio, which is designated by a vertical wavy line placed in front of the chord, and (2) the less dramatic version, usually designated by the word 'arpeggio', which corresponds closely to the style of the harp. There are of course a number of intermediate forms. With regard to the first form, it should be noted that it was almost certainly played far more frequently than indicated. A full chord played all at once often sounds ugly on the harpsichord and the piano; it sounds aggressive, like a mere 'lump' of sound. If a longer arpeggio begins on the lowest note, it can be played on the up-beat, so that the top note arrives on the beat. However, if a chord is arpeggiated in a higher register, the first arpeggio note should usually be played on the beat as in the case of an appoggiatura.

With regard to the second form, the longer harp-like arpeggio, there is an acoustic rule for the production of a beautiful sound, though this applies only to instruments with an action capable of inflection (the clavichord and piano). After playing the bass note to its full length (it 'carries' the harmony), one plays the second note fairly softly in order to make possible a stepwise crescendo to the top note (i.e. the melody-note), as in Ex. 18.1.

Ex. 18.1

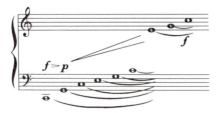

In his commentary to the Chromatic Fantasia and Fugue von Dadelsen provided some hints on how to perform the passages marked 'arpeggio'. These can also be applied to other works:

There is no compulsory way of arpeggiating the arpeggio chords here and in the following passages. One is at liberty to do as one pleases. A general rule would be to arpeggiate the chords up and down once, whereby the fingers remain lying on the keys. Where there are two crotchets, the one should be arpeggiated upwards, and the other downwards. If the next chord has the same bass note, the preceding arpeggio should only be taken to the penultimate note. The chords that conclude the various arpeggio passages should only be arpeggiated upwards once.[2]

---

[2] *Fantasien, Praeludien und Fugen*, Henle edn., p. 135.

FIGURED ARPEGGIOS

Strictly speaking these are not the same as arpeggios proper. Rather they comprise various kinds of broken chords, sometimes even with non-harmonic passing notes, which serve as a model for the execution of various different harmonies. Occasionally this kind of performance is described using the term *Präludieren*. A characteristic example of this occurs in the *Clavier-Büchlein* for Wilhelm Friedemann Bach. On folio 14 there is an early version (BWV 846a) of the C major Prelude that Bach later placed at the start of the *WTC* (see Ex. 18.2); compare the simple harmonic scheme of the final line with that of the *WTC*. Ex. 18.3 shows the Fantasie BWV 944; the similarity in the notation makes us assume that these arpeggios are also to be treated motivically, though with a different and more variegated figuration than in the prelude.

Ex. 18.2. Prelude in C major, BWV 846a, bars 5–27

Ex. 18.3. Fantasie, BWV 944

PLAYING THE ARPEGGIOS IN THE CHROMATIC FANTASIA AND FUGUE

It is difficult to disagree with Kreutz when in his edition of the Chromatic Fantasia and Fugue (Schott) he writes:

H. Schenker and later G. Mantel (*Bach-Jahrbuch* 1929) were of the opinion that the arpeggios in the Chromatic Fantasia ought not, as taught by contemporary theoretical works and oral tradition, to be played with the normal upwards and downwards arpeggiation of the chords, but rather in a more sophisticated, more 'artistic' manner. Instead of simple arpeggiation they recommended free figuration permeated with suspensions and passing and auxiliary notes. This view is unjustified. It was the task of the arpeggios to create moments of repose between the passage-work and figures of toccatas, preludes, and fantasias. The chordal pillars of the arpeggios were supposed to convey a static effect, not to continue or to anticipate the melodic motion. Arpeggios of this kind were used by all baroque composers. That their task in the Chromatic Fantasia was precisely this is confirmed by three old manuscripts in the Berlin library, in which they are written out in full.[3]

Furthermore, it is worth bearing in mind that if Bach really had been interested in elaborating these arpeggios motivically, he would surely, being the passionate pedagogue that he was, have shown at least one of his pupils what this might have looked like. However, none of the copies made by the inner circle of pupils—at least five have survived—contains the slightest indication for a motivic elaboration of the arpeggios. (Apart from bar 27 they are only notated as chords.) This does not mean of course that one had to simplify matters on the lines of the late copyist of P 551 (probably not a member of the circle of pupils), whose version of bars 33–4 reads as in Ex. 18.4. The expressive passing note d^2 bar 33 is much too short (as is the d^2 in bar 40). (The written-out arpeggios of this version are printed in the Schott and Ricordi editions, with minor modifications.) How can and should we play these arpeggio passages?

First of all it is a good idea to determine the formal function of the arpeggio passage in the fantasia as a whole. As is immediately apparent, the arpeggiated chords form the central section of the fantasia, framed by the virtuoso toccata

[3] A. Kreutz, preface, [p. 5].

Ex. 18.4. Chromatic Fantasia, bars 33–4

section and the instrumental recitative (this in turn is interrupted by toccata-like passages), which round off the form.

The arpeggio passage is clearly divided into three parts:

1. Bars 27–30. D minor I–V (or VII). Three-bar toccata-like interlude modulating from D minor VII to G minor VII.
2. Bars 34–42. Extensively modulating section (G minor VII–B flat major I^7); three-bar recitative-like run (similar to bars 71–3), modulating from B flat to E, the dominant of A.
3. Bars 45–9. Cadence in A minor ending in A major, which at the beginning of the following recitative section is redefined as the dominant of D.

In order to understand the harmonic and rhythmic design, it is a good idea at first to ignore the arpeggios and to play the chords as they stand in the manner of a chorale, with an expressive treble. This will demonstrate that the first and third sections have a harmonic goal, whereas the harmony of the central section moves 'indecisively' through several keys. With regard to the barring, the central section eschews the clear structuring of the outer sections. A three-bar group (A minor) is followed by five bars (2 + 3), which, after enharmonic redefinition, remain in the key of D minor. The major seventh chord on B♭ thus arrived at marks the beginning of the recitative-like passage that leads to the four-bar concluding arpeggio section (bars 43–8), which ends on the chord of A major at bar 49.

What does the enharmonic redefinition in the middle of the second arpeggio section consist of? The fact that bar 38 in context is felt to be in B flat minor, and that the c♯ in the treble is understood to be d♭. Thus in bar 39 one expects the 'logical conclusion', an F major chord with c in the treble (Ex. 18.5). However, this expectation is thwarted; what appears to be d♭^{2} in bar 38 is redefined enharmonically as c♯^{2}, and this leads surprisingly to a D minor sixth chord (Ex. 18.6).

It would be wrong to 'make light' of a bold modulation of this kind. Thus it is absolutely necessary to hold back slightly before the surprising entry of the D minor chord. Furthermore, on the piano one should emphasize the leading

Ex. 18.5

Ex. 18.6. Chromatic Fantasia, bars 38–9

note $c\sharp^2$, playing the D minor chord slightly more softly than the preceding passage. Enharmonic modulations are rare in Bach, and when they occur they have a certain significance. Of course, it is not necessary to suppose at once that they have a profound symbolic significance, as at the end of the Credo of the B minor Mass, where the enharmonic change symbolizes St Paul's words about the resurrection: 'We shall all be changed'. However, it is meaningful to play the central part of the arpeggio passage of bars 34–42 softly and tenderly, as Edwin Fischer used to do in a very personal and yet thoroughly convincing manner. (The 'transformation' passage in the B minor Mass, 'Confiteor', bars 138–44, is usually played softly and mysteriously.) On the other hand, Edwin Fischer built up the last part of the arpeggio passage into a mighty crescendo, and this was artistically most convincing. I myself do not play the central section from bar 34 onwards piano, preferring poco forte e agitato, something that probably corresponds more to the original conception of the work for harpsichord. At the end, bars 45–9, I then progress to forte with a continual but not exaggerated crescendo. Although the Chromatic Fantasia was not conceived in terms of the piano, certain dynamic gradations can also be reproduced on the harpsichord: for instance, the effect of a crescendo can be created by playing more and faster notes in a given length of time.

The beginning of the arpeggio poses the smallest problem; Bach himself supplied the figuration, which should surely be retained for the following bars. A basic observation: all chords are written so that the fingers can remain on the keys throughout. The reason for this is the fact that the harpsichord does not have a damper pedal. (For more detailed description of this execution see Chapter 4, p. 123.) But on the piano, where there are no handicaps of this kind, one can at certain places fill out the intermediate spaces occasioned by the harpsichord action: the harmonies continue to sound if the pedal is depressed.

Many pianists add an octave D in the bass in the first arpeggio section. This can hardly be faulted. We should bear in mind that in many of his transcriptions Bach himself chose a lower octave than the original, as for instance in the transcription for harpsichord of a movement from the C major Sonata for solo violin. (It must be added that there are doubts about the authenticity of this piece.) However, I dislike 'entering' this octave by means of a leap of a tenth. I therefore suggest the solution shown in Ex. 18.7. On the other hand bar 33 is somewhat more difficult for the performer. The manuscript P 626 (now P 1152) and Griepenkerl's edition (1819), which goes back to his teacher Forkel, are the only sources to reproduce the text given in Ex. 18.8. This no doubt sounds good (was it Wilhelm Friedemann's interpretation?). However, one should be clear in one's own mind that this is pure piano writing (with pedal), and on the harpsichord this would go against the legato principle because one of the two hands would have to release the keys.

Ex. 18.7. Chromatic Fantasia, bars 26–7, 28–30: suggested execution

Thus, to do as J. S. Bach would have done, I tend to favour the execution shown in Ex. 18.9.

There are two possible ways of playing bars 34–42: rhythmically freely, as notated in some of the manuscripts of about 1770, or with figuration

Ex. 18.8. Chromatic Fantasia, bars 33–4

Ex. 18.9. Chromatic Fantasia, bars 33–4: suggested execution

throughout, either semiquaver triplets or demisemiquavers. With regard to the latter, Bach provides excellent examples of his own, for instance, at various points in the D minor Harpsichord Concerto, and in the Prelude in A minor, BWV 894, bars 77 ff. (see Ex. 18.10). According to Schenker, Bach could also have notated these harmonies as in Ex. 18.11; in analogy to this I sometimes play the figuration shown in Ex. 18.12. However, if one selects the simpler, unfigured version, which in the light of the above comments is probably most in keeping with Bach's intentions, then it is probably best to play the harmonies in bars 40–2 as in Ex. 18.13.

From bar 37 onwards Edwin Fischer began the arpeggios an octave lower, an excellent idea on the modern piano. In the final arpeggio section Fischer added a lower octave, and introduced a significant crescendo. The 'increase in

Ex. 18.10. Prelude in A minor, BWV 894, bars 77–85

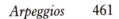

Ex. 18.11

Ex. 18.12. Chromatic Fantasia, bars 34–43: possible execution

Ex. 18.13. Chromatic Fantasia, bars 40–2: suggested execution

the number of notes' designed to achieve a crescendo is effective both on the harpsichord and the piano. One possibility is the execution shown in Ex. 18.14. Finally it should be noted that at the final arpeggio chord (bar 49) the topmost note a^1 must be clearly audible in order to do justice to its 'bridging' function: the end of the arpeggios becomes the beginning of the recitative.

Ex. 18.14. Chromatic Fantasia, bars 41–5: possible execution

19

The Application of Ornaments that are not Notated

ERRONEOUS ORNAMENT SIGNS IN BACH'S TEXTS

Although Bach's ornamentation is far more precise than that of the majority of his contemporaries, he is sometimes guilty of unclear or ambiguous notation. Quite a number of mistakes have crept in, especially in works that have survived only in copies or in printed form. Some signs have been mistaken for others, and some are in the wrong place. An instance of this is bar 28 of the Allemande of Partita No. 4, where the first edition printed the ornaments shown in Ex. 19.1. According to C. P. E. Bach this accumulation of ornaments on adjacent notes is undesirable.[1] For this reason Bach himself made the necessary correction in his personal copy (see Ex. 19.2).

Ex. 19.1. Partita No. 4, BWV 828, Allemande, bar 28, first edition

Ex. 19.2. Partita No. 4, BWV 828, Allemande, bar 28

---

[1] '. . . it would be wrong to play the mordent directly after the trill, for ornaments must never be crowded against each other' (*Essay*, p. 131).

But in many other cases the choice of the right ornament in the right place is left to the performer and his understanding of the style. Mordents, *Pralltriller*, and longer trills were often confused by copyists. For example, one only has to omit by mistake the vertical stroke of a mordent or to place it too far to the right, and one has a *Pralltriller* sign or a suffixed trill. To this day mistakes of this kind have been 'bequeathed' from one edition to the next. For example, the very first bar of the Aria at the beginning of the Goldberg Variations has an ornament that has led to contradictory explanations (see Ex. 19.3). Yet it can in fact only be a short mordent, and this transpires quite clearly from Anna Magdalena Bach's copy (see Ex. 19.4; on account of the legato slur a slightly delayed execution of the mordent on the lines of C. P. E. Bach's *Pralltriller* is to be recommended).[2]

Ex. 19.3. Goldberg Variations, Aria, bars 1–7, first edition

Ex. 19.4. Goldberg Variations, Aria, bars 1–6, *Notenbüchlein* for Anna Magdalena Bach

The notation in the first edition of the *Clavier-Übung*, Part IV (Ex. 19.3) probably corresponds exactly to the lost autograph manuscript. In fair copies Bach was often in the habit of writing the ornaments with rather more of a flourish. The sign was immediately reproduced either as a long mordent or as a suffixed trill (which would be quite wrong here), the latter even in the otherwise excellent NBA (see Ex. 19.5; see also p. 530, n. 10). In the first edition the mordents are not particularly long. Above all, the stroke is usually in the middle of the mordent sign.

In bars 10, 20, 21, and 22 of the Aria the *Pralltriller* for the left hand were erroneously printed as long trills in the NBA and other editions (see also

[2] The ornaments in this MS used to be ascribed to Bach, though recent research is of the opinion that they were written by his wife, Anna Magdalena.

Ex. 19.5. Goldberg Variations, Aria, bars 1–6, as in NBA

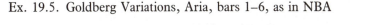

p. 337). Here the *Notenbüchlein* also has the correct version in this context. On the other hand, the opposite is true of the start of the second part of the Aria: here the *Notenbüchlein* has a *Pralltriller* (surely a mistake in this context), whereas the first edition clearly has a mordent, which the NBA considers to be a long trill. However, this simply *has to be* a mordent, because in Bach only this ornament (and not the *Pralltriller*) could be used for the beginning of a phrase. At the very most one could play a long trill. Yet this would entail going against the sarabande rhythm, and is thus wholly improbable.

The Goldberg Aria also contains, in bar 17, a strange combination of different ornaments intended to be played simultaneously (see Ex. 19.6). In synchronized form this produces faulty voice-leading (see Ex. 19.7). The problem can be overcome by playing the mordent more slowly (Ex. 19.8); slowing down the start of the trill would also be possible. However, it is more than likely that the mordent in the inner voice was not really what Bach intended, and that it goes back to a mistake made by the engraver. It does not appear in the version in the *Notenbüchlein* for Anna Magdalena Bach, which otherwise coincides very closely with the printed text of *Clavier-Übung*, Part IV. In the majority of cases considerations of this kind tend to limit the choice of the correct ornament.

Ex. 19.6. Goldberg Variations, Aria, bars 17–18

A further guide-line for the correct application of mordents and *Pralltriller* is the repeatedly cited fact that *Pralltriller* tend to prefer descending lines and mordents ascending ones.[3] Caution should thus be exercised when the reverse (i.e. ascending *Pralltriller* and descending mordents) is found.

[3] This restriction does not apply to long trills, which occur in all kinds of contexts.

Ex. 19.7

Ex. 19.8

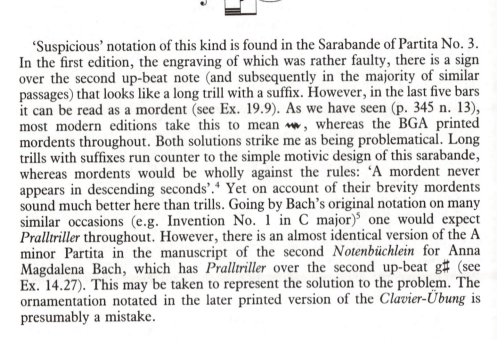

'Suspicious' notation of this kind is found in the Sarabande of Partita No. 3. In the first edition, the engraving of which was rather faulty, there is a sign over the second up-beat note (and subsequently in the majority of similar passages) that looks like a long trill with a suffix. However, in the last five bars it can be read as a mordent (see Ex. 19.9). As we have seen (p. 345 n. 13), most modern editions take this to mean ∿, whereas the BGA printed mordents throughout. Both solutions strike me as being problematical. Long trills with suffixes run counter to the simple motivic design of this sarabande, whereas mordents would be wholly against the rules: 'A mordent never appears in descending seconds'.[4] Yet on account of their brevity mordents sound much better here than trills. Going by Bach's original notation on many similar occasions (e.g. Invention No. 1 in C major)[5] one would expect *Pralltriller* throughout. However, there is an almost identical version of the A minor Partita in the manuscript of the second *Notenbüchlein* for Anna Magdalena Bach, which has *Pralltriller* over the second up-beat g♯ (see Ex. 14.27). This may be taken to represent the solution to the problem. The ornamentation notated in the later printed version of the *Clavier-Übung* is presumably a mistake.

Ex. 19.9. Partita No. 3, BWV 827, Sarabande, bars 1–8, first edition

The reverse of this, strokes inadvertently omitted, thereby turning mordents into *Pralltriller*, is found in the Courante of Partita No. 4, bars 20–2

---

[4] C. P. E. Bach, *Essay*, p. 128.
[5] Some old copies and edns. of Invention No. 1 erroneously substitute mordents for *Pralltriller*.

(ascending line). Here Bach himself made the necessary corrections in bar 20 and bar 22 (see Ex. 19.10).[6]

Occasionally the trill or *Pralltriller* sign can also signify a turn. Howard Schott cites an example of this from the Second Sonata for viola da gamba BWV 1028 (see Ex. 19.11). There is another *Pralltriller* sign in the first bar of the Rondeau of the C minor Partita, BWV 826. In bar 33 of his personal copy Bach 'explained' that it is really ∾. (On a piano this ornament tends to sound 'clumsy' and it would be better to omit it.)

Ex. 19.10. Partita No. 4, BWV 828, Courante, bars 16–22

a   First edition

b   Bach's personal copy (now in the British Library, London)

Ex. 19.11. Sonata No. 2 for viola da gamba and harpsichord, BWV 1028, last movement, bars 51–2, after Howard Schott, *Playing the Harpsichord* (London, 1971), 128

Sometimes it is not the ornament that is at fault, but its place in the text. Mordents that do not occur in ascending lines, but, for example, after leaps, are *never* placed over unstressed notes in Bach. Thus in the Allemandes of

[6] A good fac. edn. of Bach's personal copy was pub. in 1985 by Gregg International (Godstone, Surrey): *J. S. Bach, Part One of the Clavier Übung 1731* (The Composer's Edition, i), ed. D. Kinsela.

Partitas No. 5 (bar 1) and No. 6 (bar 4) their location in the unrevised first edition is certainly wrong, and in fact revisions by Bach have survived (see Exx. 19.12 and 19.13). Bach himself corrected the mistakes by scraping away the faulty ornaments and writing in the correct ones (see Exx. 19.14 and 19.15; note also the appoggiatura added in bar 2 of the E minor Allemanda). Only the most recent editions have begun to take into account these and other corrections by Bach. Apart from NBA these are the new Henle edn. (from 1979) and Editio Musica (Budapest).

Ex. 19.12. Partita No. 5, BWV 829, Allemande, bars 1–3, first edition

Ex. 19.13. Partita No. 6, BWV 830, Allemande, bars 1–4, first edition

Ex. 19.14. Partita No. 5, BWV 829, Allemande, bars 1–3, corrected first edition

Ex. 19.15. Partita No. 6, BWV 830, Allemanda, bars 1–4, corrected first edition

The choice between trills and *Pralltriller* is not always easy to make, for in certain passages both are possible. The most suitable ornament usually transpires from the context. In instances where a suffix is notated the long trill is preferable. Bar 65 of the Fantasia of the A minor Partita should be played in this way (see Ex. 19.16). Conversely, if a two-note suffix is not notated, the use of the *Pralltriller* is often a likely option. This is the case at certain points in the Sarabande of the E minor Partita, for instance in bar 23 (see Ex. 19.17).

Ex. 19.16. Partita No. 3, BWV 827, Fantasia, bars 65–6

Ex. 19.17. Partita No. 6, BWV 830, Sarabande, bars 23–4

C. P. E. Bach's remark that the mordent 'never appears in descending seconds',[7] which has been cited a number of times above, holds true in 98 per cent of all cases in J. S. Bach. With regard to the other 2 per cent, about half, as we have seen, can be traced back to imperfect copies and editions (e.g. copyist's mistakes). However, there are a handful of authentic mordents in Bach's manuscripts that are applied to descending seconds, for example at the end of the chorale prelude *Wenn wir in höchsten Nöten sein*, BWV 641. My first reaction to this was to consider the mordent a slip of the pen, for 'that which is not permitted cannot be'. But then I discovered that this irregular mordent sounds very good indeed (see Ex. 19.18).

The reverse, a *Pralltriller* sign on ascending lines, occurs in bar 5 of the F minor Prelude of *WTC* I. The rather elongated sign in the autograph is no different to the trill sign in bar 2 (no doubt a long trill). It seems that a long trill is also intended in bar 5.

---

[7] *Essay*, pp. 128 and 131.

Ex. 19.18. Chorale prelude *Wenn wir in höchsten Nöten sein*, BWV 641

There is a problematical ornament in bar 26 of the Allemande of the C minor Partita. Above the final note, d^2, in the right-hand part a trill with suffix was added in the otherwise reliable source G 23, and all recent editions have included it (see Ex. 19.19); in the first edition there is no ornament at this point. There are three reasons why this emendation is unsatisfactory. A trill of this kind represents a link between the single up-beat d and the following down-beat that is uncharacteristic of Bach. Apart from this it distracts the listener's attention from the principal motif in the lower voice, which should take pride of place at this juncture; and furthermore it produces consecutive fifths. The equally reliable sources G 24, G 26, and G 28 have a turn here, and the effect of this is excellent.[8] In source G 23 Bach's instructions were probably misconstrued. At the most one could play a mordent. Ex. 19.20 shows the execution of the turn in the baroque manner; Ex. 19.21, which produces consecutive fifths, is incorrect.

Ex. 19.19. Partita No. 2, BWV 826, Allemande, bars 26–7

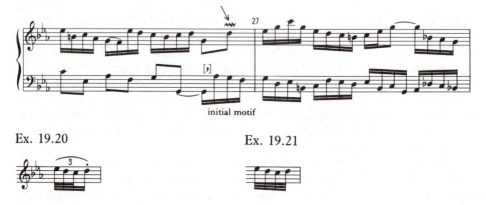

initial motif

Ex. 19.20   Ex. 19.21

---

[8] See NBA V/1, Critical Report, p. 31. In 'Textkritische Bemerkungen' (p. 73), Wolff fails to mention this turn.

ADDING ORNAMENTS THAT ARE NOT NOTATED

Ex. 19.22. *WTC* I, Prelude in C sharp minor, bars 1–3, earlier version

Ex. 19.23. *WTC* I, Prelude in C sharp minor, bars 1–3, later version

Ex. 19.24. French Suite No. 2, BWV 813, Gigue, bars 1–5, earlier version

Ex. 19.25. French Suite No. 2, BWV 813, Gigue, bars 1–5, later version

If we consider the 'keyboard works' by Bach that have survived in two or more versions, we notice that in virtually every case the later version is the more richly ornamented one. It would be naïve to think that the earlier

versions represent simpler 'original' forms to which Bach later imparted a 'final shape'. We now know that the free addition of ornaments was one of the self-evident tasks of a baroque performer. Yet the very fact that Bach's keyboard works were used for teaching the clavichord, the harpsichord, and the organ, as well as composition (which is also the reason why a large number of copies have survived) suggests that there may have been a pedagogical reason for this. The versions with few ornaments might be construed as a kind of compositional practice, exercises in the richer kind of elaboration envisaged by baroque theory; and the later versions show how the master himself solved the problem. But even here we should not forget that we are often dealing with one of several solutions which is not necessarily the only valid version. Furthermore, if in didactic pieces the ornamentation seems excessive compared with that of other works, this may well mean that Bach wished to use them as models to demonstrate several ways of embellishing a single piece, one of which one could choose at will. Its appropriateness to a certain instrument (harpsichord, clavichord, or fortepiano) and its attendant characteristics (sustaining power, the response of the action) need to be borne in mind, as does the player's musicianship and taste. The Sinfonia in E flat, BWV 791, seems to be an instance of this kind. Bach later entered embellishments in his own fair copy of this piece and in the copies made by his pupil Gerber (see Ex. 19.26); P 219 is a copy made by one of Bach's pupils. The two versions, which start out by being virtually identical, diverge slightly as the piece progresses. The turn between two notes used here, a rare occurrence, has not yet been discussed. Bach himself provided an indication of how he wished this to be performed in the French Overture (first movement) by first writing it out in full (bar 19) and abbreviating it as a sign when it recurs later on (bar 162) (see Ex. 19.27).[9] Applied to Ex. 19.26 this would suggest the execution shown in Ex. 19.28,[10] or, in a slightly less accented form, that in Ex. 19.29. The best solution is the execution given in the copy made by Bach's pupil Gerber (see Ex. 19.30).[11]

Another execution of the turn between dotted notes occurs in the earlier version of the F minor Invention (in the *Clavier-Büchlein* for Wilhelm Friedmann Bach), bar 16 (see Ex. 19.31a); Ex. 19.31b shows the later version. The two versions of this piece are otherwise identical, and thus we may assume that the written-out ornament 'explains' the turn. A counterpart to this work is the remarkable Organ Trio in D minor BWV 583, where some of the ornaments can easily be omitted.

All these observations show that it is a mistake to select one version arbitrarily and disregard the others, as in the majority of editions. Bischoff's

[9] See Emery, *Bach's Ornaments*, p. 33.
[10] See C. P. E. Bach, *Essay*, pp. 119–20.
[11] See the Wiener Urtext edition of the Inventions and Sinfonias, p. 103.

Ex. 19.26. Sinfonia No. 5, BWV 791, bars 1–4

P219

Gerber

Autograph
(P 610)

Ex. 19.27. French Overture, BWV 831, first movement, bars 19–20, 162–3

Ex. 19.28

Ex. 19.29

Ex. 19.30

Ex. 19.31. Invention No. 9, BWV 780, bar 16

Earlier version

Later version

a 16

b 16

editions (Steingräber) and the NBA are welcome exceptions to this unfortunate habit, as is Palmer's edition of *WTC* I (*WTC* II has not yet appeared).

As the vast majority of ornaments appear in slow movements, one might think that the baroque predilection for the embellishment of such passages derived from the fact that the harpsichord and the clavichord were capable of producing only a short-winded and not a 'sustained' or 'singing' tone. Although it is widely held, this view ignores the fact that decoration or ornamentation was a fundamental baroque trait. After all, works for organ and violin and, above all, vocal pieces were repeatedly embellished.[12]

An interesting form of added embellishment that sometimes borders on free embellishment is represented by the varied movements of suites, mainly sarabandes, which immediately follow the simpler versions in the form of *agréments*. Today it is generally agreed that these *agréments* were intended to be varied repeats of the sarabande. In section 1 the simple version precedes the embellished one. The same procedure is then applied to section 2.[13] The technique of the 'varied recapitulation' was very widespread at the beginning and in the middle of the eighteenth century. C. P. E. Bach complemented the *Essay* with sonatas with varied repeats, which were intended to be an introduction to this art of variation. Clearly the real intention was to stimulate a pupil with a talent for composition to improvise on the same lines in those cases where the composer had only provided a single version. I do not doubt that J. S. Bach also expected this kind of improvisation from his performers, and that his *agréments* are masterly models of an art that should also be applied to other, similar pieces. However, in the course of the Classical era the role of the performer declined; from being a free collaborator he became a mere executant carrying out orders. The ability to improvise gradually disappeared.

Doubles, of which the Courante of the First English Suite in A major, BWV 806, has two for good measure, should not be confused with *agréments*. They are real variations, not merely embellished variants. For this reason I believe that they should be played as independent variations after the whole of the *simple* has been played. The fact that certain *doubles* have written-out bridge passages before the double bar (with brackets for first-time and second-time bars) seems to confirm this. If the *double* were intended to be the repetition of the corresponding first or second section there would be little point in repeating it a second time.

The intention of this and the following chapter is to encourage the modern performer to add ornaments and embellishments with discretion and good taste. This of course entails studying Bach's own art of ornamentation. There is certainly no dearth of examples. Apart from the works already mentioned, I recommend studying the C sharp minor Prelude from *WTC* II with its

---

[12] See Hochreither, *Zur Aufführungspraxis*, p. 132.

[13] Gustav Leonhardt and Ivo Pogorelich play the movements with *agréments* as separate, self-contained '2nd' sarabandes.

beautiful variants.[14] The art of embellishment reaches a peak of perfection in variation 25 of the Goldberg Variations. Here the ornaments are so expressive and at the same time so carefully balanced that we sense an inner affinity to the ornamentation in Beethoven's late works (the Diabelli Variations and late quartets). Adding further ornaments would seem to be out of the question. However, Bach himself thought otherwise. In his personal copy (Bibliothèque Nationale, Paris) he added further ornaments, both in this and in other variations.[15]

In this connection we are confronted repeatedly by an important question. Where can and where should we add additional embellishments? We should, indeed we must, in passages where the application of ornaments was expected of the performer as a matter of course. One of these, as we have seen, was the penultimate note in cadences, which, according to the context, had to be supplied with a trill, a *Pralltriller*, or, more rarely, a mordent (see Ex. 19.32). A case of this kind occurs at the end of the Chromatic Fantasia and Fugue (Ex. 19.33); the probable intended execution is shown in Ex. 19.34.[16]

Ex. 19.32

Ex. 19.33. Chromatic Fugue, bars 158–61

---

[14] The Henle and Wiener Urtext edns. have excellent fingering, but unfortunately they disregard virtually all of the variants. Best in this respect are the old Bischoff edn. (Steingräber) and BGA (with Editorial Commentary). The new Peters edn. also includes a number of variants. (*WTC* II has not yet appeared in NBA.)

[15] Reproduced in NBA and Henle edn. (1975).

[16] Jörg Demus has come up with an original solution for this ending. It may not be justified in historical terms, but it works well in practice. He plays the last run doubled at the lower octave, in strict time, emphasizing in the penultimate bar the latent final notes of the subject $e^2–a^1–c\sharp^2–d^2$. Here it is of course impossible to play a trill.

Ex. 19.34. Chromatic Fugue, bars 160–1, probable intended execution

Another progression where a trill was usually applied, going by unanimous statements made by C. P. E. Bach, Marpurg, Türk, and others, was the *Einschnitt* or caesura, in modern parlance an imperfect cadence on the dominant coupled with a suspension. A caesura of this kind occurs in the F sharp minor Prelude of *WTC* II, before the return of the initial motif (Ex. 19.35).

Ex. 19.35. *WTC* II, Prelude in F sharp minor, bars 29–30

Finally it should be noted that in every work where a theme occurs a number of times, the embellishments added to it should be retained when it reappears, provided of course that they are playable. In a number of works Bach notated the ornament signs only at the first entry of a theme. This rule is also mentioned in his son's treatise: 'Moreover, all imitations must be exact to the smallest detail.'[17] This is true, for example, of the final trills in the subjects of the Fugue in B minor in *WTC* I and the Fugue in F sharp minor in *WTC* II; and, provided they can be played, of the *Pralltriller* in the fugato of the introductory Toccata of Partita No. 6, BWV 830.

Sporadically applied ornaments such as those in the D sharp minor Fugue of *WTC* I and the F sharp minor Fugue of *WTC* II, bar 15 (only in later versions), can also be taken as confirmation of the fact that more ornaments of this kind should be added. Thus, at the end of the D sharp minor Fugue, upper voice, bars 83–5, there is a good opportunity to introduce passing

---

[17] *Essay*, p. 86.

appoggiaturas (*coulés*). In his recording Friedrich Gulda did this in a convincing and tasteful manner.

Ex. 19.36. From Quantz, *On Playing the Flute* pp. 97–9

Quantz provides valuable information on how and when to embellish a melody (see Ex. 19.36). His comments on these examples are:

If you wish now to mix the graces described in the fourteenth and fifteenth paragraphs with the pure appoggiaturas used in Tab. VI, Fig. 26, and introduce them after the appoggiaturas, you may do so in the following manner at the notes that have letters above them. The grace in Fig. 27 may be introduced at the notes beneath (c), (d), (f), (i) and (n). That in Fig. 28 is proper with the note at (k). That in Fig. 29 is made at the notes beneath (g) and (m). That in Fig. 30 should be heard at (e), but that in Fig. 31 at (b). That in Fig. 32 may be joined to the notes beneath (a) and (l), and that in Fig. 33 to the note under (h). It is obvious that the graces must everywhere be transposed to the notes indicated by the appoggiaturas.[18]

Quantz was of course not trying to suggest that all these embellishments should be played. This would have been too much for this pretty melody, and would have run counter to his own aesthetic position.

In this mixture of the simple appoggiaturas with the little graces . . . it will be found that the melody is much more lively and brilliant with the latter than without them.

[18] *On Playing the Flute*, pp. 98–9.

The mixture, however, must be undertaken with discernment; for a considerable part of good execution depends upon it.

Some persons greatly abuse the use of extempore embellishments as well as the appoggiaturas and the other essential graces described here. They allow hardly a single note to be heard without some addition, wherever the time or their fingers permit it. They make the melody either too weak, through an excessive load of appoggiaturas and *Abzüge*, or too variegated through a superabundance of whole and half shakes, mordents, turns, *battemens*, &c. These they frequently introduce upon notes which even an insensitive musical ear recognizes as inappropriate. . . . It is true that the ornaments described above are absolutely necessary for good execution. But they must be used sparingly, or they become too much of a good thing. The rarest and most tasteful delicacies produce nausea if over-indulged. The same is true of musical embellishments if we use them too profusely, and attempt to overwhelm the ear. . . . They are, so to speak, bored with noble simplicity. Those who would avoid such blunders should early accustom themselves to singing and playing neither too simply nor too colourfully, always mixing simplicity and brilliance. The little embellishments should be used like seasoning at a meal; if the prevailing sentiment is taken as the guiding principle, propriety will be maintained, and one passion will never be transformed into another.[19]

I will now attempt to give some hints on how to add embellishments to the E major Prelude of *WTC* II (see Ex. 19.38). Bach seems to have been particularly fond of this beautiful work, for in the course of time he made more minor modifications to it than to any other part of the *WTC*. I play this prelude in its unembellished form, and apply ornaments in the repeat.

Two of Bach's variants deserve to be singled out for special mention. There are three different versions of bar 50 (bass), all equally convincing; and as regards the final chord, there is a version without a mordent and one with a mordent, where the upper voice merely has e^2. I was prompted to add some of my own ornaments because in certain suites Bach later added *Pralltriller* in figures containing three descending semiquavers, for instance in the first bar of the D minor French Suite and in the Allemande of Partita No. 2 (see Ex. 19.37). This and other embellishments entered in a copy of the first edition now in the Library of Congress, Washington, DC, have never previously been published.[20]

Ex. 19.37. Partita No. 2, BWV 826, Allemande, bar 1

---

[19] Quantz, *On Playing the Flute*, pp. 99–100.
[20] MS Music 3233, item 5. See Wolff, 'Textkritische Bemerkungen', p. 74 n. 18.

Ex. 19.38.*WTC* II, Prelude in E major: ornaments, fingering, and performance marks by Paul Badura-Skoda

Some Hints on How to Play this Version of the E major Prelude

All mordents and *Pralltriller* should be played on the beat, that is,

not like this: but like this:

The *Pralltriller* should be played lightly and swiftly,[21] and should begin on the main note, that is,

not like this: but like this:

The bracketed *Pralltriller* in bars 2–4 and 6–8 are optional and can be omitted. These *Pralltriller* and the mordents in bars 3 and 7 are mutually exclusive. This means that when *Pralltriller* are played, the mordents must be omitted, and vice versa. In general fewer ornaments should be added on the piano than on the harpsichord.

I should also like to suggest richer embellishment in the case of the repeats in Minuet II of Partita No. 1 (see Ex. 19.39). The repeat of Minuet I after the Minuet II, which Bach did not in fact stipulate, seems to be required for formal reasons, because a short movement of only sixteen bars seems out of place in this Partita. Minuet II is nothing other than a trio, to use the later term for it, even if it is in four parts. In the French Overture (*Clavier-Übung*, Part II), which is more carefully marked than the Partitas (*Clavier-Übung*, Part I), Bach himself stated that the first movement of a pair was to be repeated after the second.

In the embellishments suggested above I have deliberately restricted myself to the simplest ornaments. Bach himself, as we have seen, went much further in this respect. In this connection I should like to draw attention to one of his favourite forms of embellishment: filling in intervals of a third. In the autograph of Invention No. 1, Bach entered changes of this kind, thereby intensifying the expressivity of the piece (see Ex. 19.40). It is a pity that this final version is hardly ever played.[22]

---

[21] See C. P. E. Bach, *Essay*, pp. 110–11.

[22] These triplets should not be applied to all the other notes of this invention as certain commentators have suggested, e.g. W. H. Bernstein, 'Freiheit in Bachs Musik. Eine aufführungspraktische Studie über Ornament und Rezitativ', *Bach als Ausleger der Bibel* ed. M. Petzoldt (Berlin, 1985), 225. A glance at the F sharp minor Prelude of *WTC* II, or at the 3rd movement of the Sonata in E major for violin and harpsichord, BWV 1016, is enough to convince us that Bach considered the juxtaposition of duplets and triplets to be completely natural.

Ex. 19.39. Partita No. 1, BWV 825, Minuet II, ed. Paul Badura-Skoda

Ex. 19.40. Invention No. 1, bars 1–2

a Early version, BMV 772

b Final version, BMV 772*a*

A further example of this kind, which is largely unknown, deserves to be mentioned here. In the Courante of the C minor Partita, Bach, in a personal copy (source G 25), systematically added third-filling appoggiaturas in the theme, thereby creating a motivic connection with its subsequent inversion (see Ex. 19.41).[23] The mordent required to mirror bar 2 was also added in this copy. The inversion of the theme in bar 13 is shown in Ex. 19.42.

[23] See Wolff, 'Textkritische Bemerkungen', pp. 65 f.

Ex. 19.41. Partita No. 2, BWV 826, Courante, bars 1–2, as in Bach's personal copy

Ex. 19.42. Partita No. 2, BWV 826, Courante, bars 12–14

Recently Georg von Dadelsen, in the preface to the NBA volume containing the Inventions and Sinfonias, has made the following noteworthy comments on the subject of embellishment:

A correct performance will include the various kinds of trill, mordent, appoggiatura (accent), turn (cadence), and slide—the *Manieren* [embellishments] that enliven the cantabile line, link the intervals, and emphasize the principal notes. It is an old, though probably ineradicable prejudice to dismiss them as 'baroque flourishes' that impair the pure and powerful counterpoint of Bach's voices. True, they are a matter less for the composer than for the player, who has to proceed on an individual basis using his taste and musicianship. As a rule Bach provided him only with what was absolutely essential.

Here again he did not proceed systematically like a modern editor, but by means of allusion. He assumed, in a theme that had initially been ornamented, or in passages that bore no ornamentation, that the player would proceed on the basis of analogous passages or would change the kind of embellishment employed. The normal cadential trills on the (often dotted) last but two melody-notes of the cadences are prescribed in only a few instances.[24]

In this connection it seems apposite to remark that Bach's understanding of concepts such as 'natural' and 'noble simplicity' was not the same as that of the early Viennese Classical period. Bach would have considered it to be just as 'unnatural' to play a slow melody in unembellished form (as in late Mozart, or Beethoven) as to go out of the house without his wig. In other words, what

[24] NBA V/3 (1972), pp. iii–iv.

sometimes strikes us, the heirs of the Viennese Classical and Romantic periods, was still perfectly 'natural' as far as Bach was concerned.

The freedom to add embellishments can of course be understood in an inverted sense when we decide to play a work in a less embellished version. This is to be recommended in the case of the C sharp minor Prelude of *WTC* I (see Ex. 19.22). The virtually unembellished earlier version has a greater immediacy, and the modern listener will find its clear, noble arioso lines more moving than the embellished version. In the case of this beautiful prelude it is the embellished version that is normally played,[25] and usually the original melody is virtually unrecognizable. The embellishments, which, to use a simile, should be placed on the melodic line like small, gleaming precious stones, are as heavy as bricks in many modern renditions. The beginning of the prelude then sounds something like *a* in Ex. 19.43.

Ex. 19.43. *WTC* I, Prelude in C sharp minor, bars 1–2

A negative feature of the 'incorrect' execution (Ex. 19.43*a*) is the overly long execution of the quaver appoggiatura a^2 in bar 2 (and in corresponding passages). It has already been noted that Bach tended to write out long appoggiaturas in large notes, and that for this reason most of the appoggiaturas notated in small notes or hooks should be short. Here we are concerned with the principle of free embellishment of given melodies. The addition of long appoggiaturas is undesirable from the composer's point of view because it is too much of an intrusion on the melody and harmony. In this context it is very instructive to examine Quantz's suggested embellishments to his own melodies. Long appoggiaturas are not added, and the original melodic line can also be discerned in the embellished version (see

---

[25] One reason for this one-sided treatment is that almost all editions of *WTC* I print only the later version. The earlier version is included in the Palmer edn. of *WTC* I, in the NBA edn. (Bärenreiter) of the *Clavier-Büchlein* for W. F. Bach, and, with some errors, in the Czerny edn. (Peters).

Ex. 19.44). The dynamic markings, indicated in the original by other abbreviations, have been translated into modern notation on the basis of Quantz's instructions (see also Ex. 5.1, p. 132).

Ex. 19.44. Quantz, *On Playing the Flute*, p. 171, Table XIX, after Perl, *Rhythmische Phrasierung*, p. 253

The mistake of adding long appoggiaturas is unfortunately rather widespread. An example from a later period of music history shows how a melody can be severely distorted by the application of long appoggiaturas (Ex. 19.45). In the first version, where short appoggiaturas have been added, the well-known theme is easy to recognize; it is not in the second version with its long appoggiaturas.

Ex. 19.45

In Bach's C sharp minor Prelude there are other arguments in favour of the unembellished version. The latest research, particularly that shown in Dehnhard's Wiener Urtext edition, has revealed that Bach added the embellishments to his autograph only in the final correction, A 4, which was made about twenty years after the work was composed. In other words, they constitute an afterthought. The fact that Book I of *WTC* was studied by almost all advanced pupils under the composer's guidance suggests that this prelude may initially have been played only in the simpler version. It is found unaltered in numerous copies by friends and pupils. If Bach in his lessons had recommended as many additional embellishments as in fact occur in the final version, they would appear at least in part in the pupils' copies, as is the case with many other keyboard works. This is not to say that Bach's embellishments are worse than the simple version. However, some of them pose virtually insurmountable problems for many modern performers.

20

Free Embellishments in Bach's Keyboard Works

INTRODUCTORY REMARKS

One of the most noticeable differences between the music of the Baroque era and that of the Classical period is the fact that in the former richly decorated melodic lines predominated, particularly in slow movements, whereas towards the end of the eighteenth century there gradually arose a predilection for cantilenas and long sustained singing notes. Of course these melodic forms have always existed side by side, yet it is possible to state in general terms that in slow baroque pieces straightforward sustained lines were the exception, whereas in the Classical and Romantic epochs they tended to be the rule.

There have always been great composers who, no doubt disillusioned by negative experiences, preferred not to trust the performers and to write out as much as possible, even if this was not generally accepted practice. Bach was probably an exception in his time, as Frescobaldi had been before and Mozart after him. He tended to notate much more precisely than Handel and other baroque composers, and wrote down almost all the notes he wished to have played. This led to the often-cited reproach of the critic Johann Adolf Scheibe:

This great man would astonish whole nations if he were more pleasing, and if he did not distort the natural character of his pieces by being overblown and confused, obscuring their beauty by an excess of art . . . All ornaments, all small embellishments and everything which is understood as being played according to the method he expresses with real notes. This robs his pieces not only of the beauty of harmony, but also makes the singing incomprehensible.[1]

---

[1] *Der Critische Musicus* (Hamburg), 14 Feb. 1737, quoted in *Bach-Dokumente*, ii. 286, 298. In reality Bach did not write out every single ornament. Bodky states: 'On the one hand he omits quite a few essential ornaments, such as trills at cadences . . . He also very often puts down an ornament only at the first appearance of a phrase (for example, in the Sinfonia in F major), leaving it to the interpreter to add it again wherever the phrase reappears' (*Interpretation*, p. 148). A remarkable feature of Scheibe's publication is the fact that it eschews the conventional German use of capitals for substantives.

It is a well-known fact that Scheibe failed to pass an organ examination at which Bach was examiner. A 'critical musician' does not forget something like that in a hurry. Perhaps there would be no 'Scheibe v. Bach' case if Bach had adhered to the unwritten law which says that one must be friendly and accommodating to critics even if they are fairly ignorant. Scheibe's unjust criticism (also in regard to other matters)[2] led the Leipzig Professor of Rhetoric, Johann Abraham Birnbaum, to publish a brilliant reply in 1738, from which a further controversy about Bach developed:

Furthermore, experience teaches us that the application [of ornaments] is usually left to the singer's and instrumentalist's discretion. If they were sufficiently acquainted with what is truly beautiful in the method . . . it would be superfluous for the composer to write out in notes what they know already. However, few know enough about the matter, and yet spoil the principal melody by means of an injudicious application of their method, indeed often adding passages which . . . could be reckoned to be errors committed by the composer. Thus every composer, and also the Herr Court Composer, has the right, by prescribing the correct method that corresponds to his intentions, to point the erring in the right direction, and thereby to ensure the preservation of his own honour.[3]

In 1739 Birnbaum wrote:

That the Herr Court Composer no less possesses the ability to move his hearers' hearts by his artful and pleasing playing is emphasized by the testimony of many foreign and native musicians, who almost daily admire the combination in him of two so important qualities. . . . The parts and advantages that the elaboration of a work of music has in common with the art of oratory, he knows so perfectly, that one not only listens to him with perfect pleasure when he discusses the similarity and agreement of the two, but also one admires the adept application of this in his works.[4]

Strangely enough, Scheibe shortly afterwards praised Bach's Italian Concerto in a review as a 'perfect example of a well-written concerto for one solo instrument'.[5] And yet in the Andante Bach had written out in full all the arbitrary embellishments. It would be a fascinating task to notate Bach's melody in the way one of his Italian contemporaries might have written it. Ex. 20.1 is an attempt to do this, which reveals how 'pathetically Italianate' the unembellished melody might have sounded. The unembellished melody might be notated as in *a*; *b* shows Bach's 'arbitrary' (i.e. free) embellishments.

A similar reconstruction of a fictitious Italian original was made a

---

[2] As a representative of a philosophy of music which, unlike that of Bach, postulated the undemanding and pleasing, Scheibe was not altogether wrong (see G. Wagner, *BJb*, 68 (1982)). However, it is impossible to overlook the fact that this criticism was written not in order to arrive at the objective truth, but with slanderous intent. This transpires from the fact that Scheibe does not refer to Bach as a composer (or *compositeur*), but as a *Musikant*, a term that had a derogative tinge even in those days.

[3] *Bach-Dokumente*, ii. 304.

[4] *Bach-Dokumente*, ii. 347, 352.

[5] 22 Dec. 1739. *Bach-Dokumente*, ii. 373.

Ex. 20.1. Italian Concerto, second movement, bars 4–7

Possible notation of unembellished melody

Bach's embellished version

generation ago by Wanda Landowska.[6] Recently Rosalyn Tureck has suggested that the accompaniment of this movement should also be embellished. However, this would be wholly out of keeping with Italian baroque practice, for which there is plenty of evidence. The fact that the accompaniment in the concerti grossi by Vivaldi, Corelli, Geminiani, Tartini, Albinoni, and others was played by an ensemble of several musicians excludes the use of free embellishments in the accompanying voices.

Bach's contemporaries considered 'essential' and 'arbitrary' embellishments to be indispensable. They adorned the melody just as stucco added interest to a baroque building. C. P. E. Bach is surely speaking for his 'deceased father' when he says:

No one disputes the need for embellishments. This is evident from the great numbers of them everywhere to be found. They are, in fact, indispensable. Consider their many uses: They connect and enliven tones and impart stress and accent; they make music pleasing and awaken our close attention. Expression is heightened by them; let a piece be sad, joyful, or otherwise, and they will lend a fitting assistance. Embellishments provide opportunities for fine performance as well as much of its subject matter. They improve mediocre compositions. Without them the best melody is empty and ineffective, the clearest content clouded.[7]

We will now proceed to examine certain free ornaments with a view to discovering how, in Bach's music, their correct application connects and enlivens the notes, and heightens the expression.

Today the works of the Classical and Romantic epochs play a predominant role in the training of musicians all over the world. For this reason baroque embellishments present modern musicians with a series of problems. They are used to playing slow movements in such a way that (virtually) every note is

---

[6] 'On Ornaments', *Landowska on Music*, pp. 118 ff. See also Konrad Wolff, *Masters of the Keyboard* (Bloomington, Ind., 1983), 59.

[7] *Essay*, p. 79.

replete with expression and 'feeling', and so they are ill at ease when confronted with baroque melodies and the many small notes that hardly permit the expression of individual emotion. This stems from the fact that they often 'cannot see the wood for trees', and are unable to distinguish between the pillars of the melody and the harmony, which are as unruffled as classical melodies, and the surrounding ornamentation, which should be played more lightly, weightlessly, as it were. In their striving for profound expression they often cling to every semiquaver or demisemiquaver and thus forget the appropriate basic tempo and the musical context. However, the attempt to sustain a flowing tempo can also lead to the melody being played without expression, or 'rattled off'. In both cases there is often a slavish adherence to the note-values that stifles any attempt at rubato or rhetorical freedom. In reality musical rhythms can be only roughly expressed using traditional note-values. The normal division into either two, four, eight, and sixteen or three, six, and nine units says little compared with the unending diversity of the spoken word. An instructive example of seemingly equal note-values that should on no account be played as they stand is the Viennese waltz. If it is executed correctly, the second crotchet is played earlier than notated, and the third seems to be held back as a result of this. Similar observations can be made in the non-notated music of other cultures, a phenomenon to which no transcription into our system of notation can ever do justice.

In view of this vitality, the march rhythms that predominate in many classical orchestral works strike one as rhythmic impoverishment. It was the price that had to be paid for the development of music that was largely homophonic, that often constructed large forms on the basis of simple thematic material, that was supposed to be easy to grasp, and that posed few problems for the ensemble. But in classical concertos and solo works by major composers the 'four-square' look of the notes on the page is deceptive. We know that Mozart and Beethoven often preferred a freely floating, 'eloquent' manner of performance, which, especially in slow movements, certainly left room for rubato. In baroque music the insistence on rhetoric and rubato holds true to an even greater extent. Baroque music, it has to be admitted, also has serene and 'classical' lines that should not really be embellished. This is always the case in an ensemble when the same part is played by more than one player, and where for this reason free embellishment is wholly out of the question. The famous Air from Bach's Third Orchestral Suite in D major, BWV 1068, is a typical example of this, and it is surely no accident that this beautiful, exceptionally serene melody was particularly popular in the Romantic period. In the nineteenth century, Winckelmann's famous definition of classical antiquity as 'noble simplicity and quiet grandeur' seemed just as applicable to the music of the Baroque and Classical epochs. What those who 'rediscovered' baroque music could not know, of course, was the fact that the 'wonderfully serene' largo movements of Handel and Corelli were richly embellished. They were not as serene as the notation suggested, and in reality were played with pathos and emotional involvement.

Many baroque composers considered the melodic skeleton sufficient, placing their trust in the performer's ability to improvise flowing melodic embellishments. But almost all of them, in a few exemplary works, provided a number of models of how it could and should be done in order to help less gifted and inexperienced musicians to approach the subject of free ornamentation. These instructions, some of which were lost for more than a century, are now available in numerous editions. Yet practical musicians have been slow to apply the results of musicological research in this area.

A good example of rich—one might even say overly rich—embellishment is the Air from Handel's great D minor Harpsichord Suite, which he himself published in embellished form as the theme of a set of variations. An older version of the variations has been preserved, in which the theme is notated in unembellished form (see Ex. 20.2). There is a superficial resemblance between this simple version and Schumann's 'Nordisches Lied' from the *Album for the Young*, Op. 68. However, Handel's embellishments are wholly 'unromantic' (see Ex. 20.3)! In this edition the distinction between large and small note-heads most probably does not stem from Handel, but from the editor, Rudolf Steglich, who wished in this way to emphasize the melodic skeleton mentioned above. Unfortunately he failed to explain why the melody-notes highlighted in this way do not quite coincide with the unembellished version of the theme. There may well have been a slightly more elaborate intermediate version.

Ex. 20.2. Handel, Harpsichord Variations in D minor, theme, bars 1–4, after Hallische Händel-Ausgabe, vol. IV/17/4

Naturally this comparison of two versions does not necessarily imply that all plain melodies were embellished in this way. Handel also wrote many tranquil movements that were almost certainly not embellished, particularly in his choral and orchestral works, though this was more exceptional in his solo and chamber music works.

The skeleton notation of the melodic structure mentioned above corresponded, as we have seen, to contemporary Italian practice. In the French style the melody and the embellishments were laid down fairly precisely.

J. S. Bach differs from the majority of his contemporaries in that he

Ex. 20.3. Handel, Harpsichord Variations in D minor, bars 1–4, after Hallische Händel-Ausgabe, vol. IV/1/1

habitually wrote out embellishments and ornaments, both in works in the French style, and, as we have seen, in works in the Italian style. This kind of notation already expresses a tendency to mingle the two styles that was widespread during Bach's lifetime. Finally, there was the German style, the significance of which is often underestimated in modern musicological research. To this style belong many of those Bach preludes that consist partly of organ polyphony, and partly of passages that foreshadow the character-piece or impromptu of later epochs—pieces for which there are hardly any parallels in non-German music at the time (with the possible exception of early English keyboard music). In the German style the music was on the whole written as it sounded, sometimes even (as in English and early Italian keyboard works) including written-out trills and other ornaments—a notational habit that enables us to draw certain conclusions about the performance of embellishments abbreviated by means of signs.

From this point of view there are, thankfully, only a few instances in Bach where something has to be added to the written text. As far as we are concerned this is a gratifying fact, because every addition and every embellishment runs the danger of conveying something to the music that is foreign to the style or capable of distorting it. Conversely, of course, a performance of a 'note skeleton' without ornaments is even more foreign to the style than a not wholly successful modern attempt at embellishment. Apart from this, modern cadenzas and ornaments in baroque or classical vein, as I have noted elsewhere,[8] are, objectively speaking, better at times than

[8] See E. and P. Badura-Skoda, *Interpreting Mozart*, pp. 177 ff. and 214 ff., and E. Badura-Skoda, 'Über die Anbringung von Auszierungen in den Klavierwerken Mozarts', *Mozart-Jahrbuch* (1957), 186.

contemporary ones, because we have at our disposal the whole of a composer's work and are thus able to find suitable models for every embellishment.

Yet even if the opportunities for embellishment are few and far between in Bach, he was and remains a baroque composer who took the creative co-operation of his performers for granted.[9] Such co-operation could range from working out the articulation and the rhythmic style to the addition of ornaments that were not notated and even to 'arbitrary embellishments'. The latter are of particular interest to us at this juncture, and can be subdivided into two categories, namely

1. cadenza-like embellishments of fermatas;
2. embellishment of the melody whenever the notes are 'bare', so to speak.

FERMATA EMBELLISHMENTS

When in a concerto or an aria, and occasionally in a solo work, the music comes to a standstill at the end of a section, which is marked by a long chord, often with a fermata or its equivalent, the indication 'adagio' combined with a trill sign, this has traditionally been regarded as an invitation (or a summons) to the solo singer or instrumentalist to introduce passages, runs, *tiratas*, and so on, enabling her or him to demonstrate her or his virtuosity and also inventive ability. This was still true in Mozart and Haydn, where even today fermatas in da capo arias or solo concertos unfortunately remain unembellished in spite of numerous written-out models.

Of course not all fermatas should be embellished, for in the eighteenth century the fermata sign had a variety of meanings. The only one of these to survive is the pause (which extends the note to about twice its value). That the fermata sign used to have more than one meaning was quite clearly stated by one of Bach's last pupils, Johann Friedrich Doles, in his unpublished singing tutor of about 1760:[10]

The ⌒ sign signifies (1) a pause . . . (2) a cadenza, that is, an arbitrary embellishment by the singer as he thinks fit at the end of a piece above the penultimate note of the bass. (3) A final cadence . . . (4) When *tenuta* is written over a long note, which the Italians call *messa di voce*, this note begins softly and increases to be sung loudly, and vice versa, for the duration of the note . . . (5) The *custos* . . .[11]

To begin with let us examine some of Bach's own fermata embellishments. There is an instance in the Chromatic Fantasia (later version), bar 30

---

[9] See P. Badura-Skoda, pref. to performing edn. *Haydn: 4 sonates pour piano* (Paris, 1982).

[10] See *Bach-Dokumente*, i, pp. 121 f., 123 f., 272.

[11] Extract quoted in A. Schneiderheinze, 'Johann Sebastian Bach, Johann Friedrich Doles und die *Anfangsgründe zum Singen*', *Beiträge zur Bachforschung*, 4 (1985), 51. The word *custos* refers to the fermatas that indicate the end of lines in chorales.

(Ex. 20.4).[12] Unembellished this passage could look like Ex. 20.5. Another example of an original fermata embellishment occurs at the end of the Andante section of the Sinfonia of the C minor Partita (see Ex. 12.6).[13] In less embellished form these bars might possibly sound as shown in Ex. 20.7. The extent of such fermata embellishments in Bach can be seen in the cadenza at the end of the infrequently played Fugue in D minor for harpsichord, BWV 948.[14] This example is particularly instructive, for two versions of the work have survived—with and without cadenza (see Ex. 20.8).

Ex. 20.4. Chromatic Fantasia, BWV 903, bars 30–3

Ex. 20.5

---

[12] Accidentals as in the sources. In the Baroque era it was normal practice to repeat accidentals within a single bar.

[13] The version quoted here is based on Bach's holograph corrections in a copy of the 1st edn. (now in the Library of Congress, Washington, DC). Hitherto it has been correctly reproduced only in the Wiener Urtext edn. See Wolff, 'Textkritische Bemerkungen', p. 69.

[14] The authenticity of this fugue used to be called into question, and even the volume editor of BGA (pref. to vol. xxxvi) expressed his doubts about the work. However, it was printed in NBA with no mention of these doubts, and is now obviously regarded as genuine.

Ex. 20.6. Partita No. 2, BWV 826, Sinfonia, bars 28–30

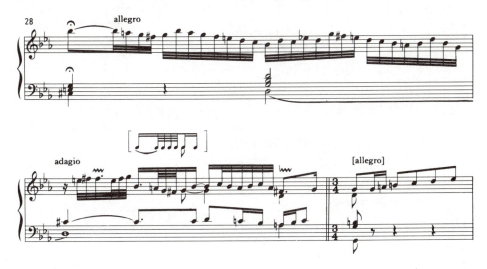

Ex. 20.7

Ex. 20.8. Harpsichord Fugue in D minor, BWV 948

Without cadenza   With cadenza (and extended ending)

It is not impossibly difficult, using Bachian models, to provide stylistically accurate embellishments for plain fermatas and caesuras. My own attempts to do this do not claim to be particularly original, though they may perhaps serve as a model for musicians who wish to do the same. 'Monstrous cadenzas' on the lines of BWV 948 should be avoided; only Bach himself could take such liberties (if indeed this cadenza is by him—see n. 14). Exx. 20.9 and 20.10 suggest some further embellishments for fermatas and caesuras.

In the Adagio of the C major Concerto for three harpsichords, BWV 1064, there are three fermatas in bars 36, 37, and 41 (according to NBA there is also one in bar 38), which would sound fairly thin if they were not embellished. Bach wrote the demisemiquavers after the fermatas in bars 37 and 38 in *small* notes. Presumably they were intended as cues to tell the other players when the improvised runs had come to an end. These fermatas should also be embellished with a number of runs. Every gifted musician can improvise these himself, and an example is therefore superfluous.

Ex. 20.9. Harpsichord Concerto in E major, BWV 1053, first movement, bars 113–14

Original notation

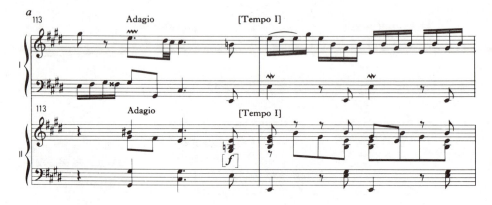

Embellishment by Paul Badura-Skoda

Ex. 20.10. Harpsichord Concerto in F minor, BWV 1056, third movement, bars 194–9

Original notation

a

Embellishment by Paul Badura-Skoda (1984)

b

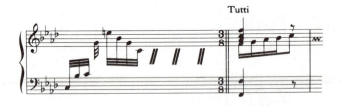

With an adagio cadenza similar to that in the Concerto in D minor, BWV 1052, third movement

The application of a cadenza-like embellishment in the Adagio of the first movement of the Sixth English Suite, BWV 811, is rather more difficult. The unusually large dimensions of this suite suggest a lengthier cadenza (see Ex. 20.11).

Ex. 20.11. English Suite No. 6, BWV 811, Prélude, bars 37–8

Original notation:

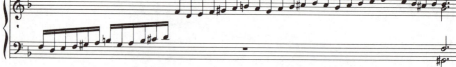

However, it would be wrong to prettify each and every fermata and general pause. In the final analysis we know too little, in instrumental music, about where a real point of repose was intended, and where a cadenza-like solo improvisation was desired. In the *WTC* and *The Art of Fugue* none of the fermatas should be embellished.[15] Indirect proof of Bach's intentions in the case of the *WTC* is the fact that not a single run was added in any of the numerous copies and revisions.

EMBELLISHMENT OF SLOW PIECES

We have seen that opportunities for embellishments of this kind are rare in Bach because he wrote most of his works out in full. For this reason we must even approach the embellishment of relatively simple pieces with great care, for their simplicity and tranquil voice-leading may well have been intentional. Yet in a few instances this was probably not so. C. P. E. Bach describes the necessity of this kind of embellishment thus:

The harpsichord lacks the power to sustain long notes and to decrease or increase the volume of a tone or, to borrow an apt expression from painting, to employ chiaroscuro. These conditions make it no small task to give a singing performance of an adagio without creating too much empty space and a consequent monotony due to a lack of sonority; or without making a silly caricature of it through an excessive use of rapid notes. However, singers and performers on instruments which are not defective in this respect also do not dare to deliver an undecorated long note for fear of eliciting only bored yawns . . . Hence, satisfactory and successful examples of the art of performance can be presented to all but those who bear a strong prejudice against keyboard instruments. A golden mean is difficult but not impossible to discover, particularly in view of the fact that our most usual sustaining devices, such as the trill and the mordent, are also well known to other instruments and the voice. Such embellishments must be full and so performed that the listener will believe that he is hearing only the original note. This requires a freedom of performance that rules out everything slavish and mechanical. Play from the soul, not like a trained bird. A keyboard player of such stamp deserves more praise than other musicians.[16]

A case in point, to which Neumann has drawn attention,[17] is the Sarabande of the Sixth English Suite, BWV 811. Even a cursory examination of the six English Suites reveals that the sarabandes, for whatever reason (perhaps a didactic one), have progressively fewer and fewer notes. Whereas the Sarabande of the Fifth Suite seems rather thin, the one in the Sixth Suite is

---

[15] In *The Art of Fugue*, Contrapunctus 1, bars 70–2, G. Leonhardt added cadenza-like runs to the fermatas, not a bad idea in itself. However, I cannot recommend it, for it is precisely this interruption of the even flow, the almost unbearable tension during the rests finally resolved in the final cadence, that Bach probably intended. Cf. the similar fermatas and rests at the end of the A minor Fugue of *WTC* I and the E minor Fugue of *WTC* II.

[16] *Essay*, pp. 149–50.   [17] *Ornamentation*, p. 548.

decidedly austere. Of course the harmonies and the basic melodic line are so striking that even here one is justified in asking whether, as in the A minor Suite (BWV 818), the intention was to juxtapose a *Sarabande simple* and an ensuing *Sarabande double*. Or was this simplicity deliberate, on the lines of a tranquil chorale?—To ask such questions in this context is almost synonymous with negating them. It is precisely the harmonic poverty of certain bars, such as bar 13, which militates against a chorale-like *simple* execution. This occurs in none of Bach's chorales.

The abrupt advent of the richly ornamented bars 10 and 23 speaks in favour of embellishment. They convey the impression that Bach wished to say: 'Dear performer, at these points let me do the embellishing myself so that things do not become too arbitrary'. Another argument in favour of ornamentation is the theme of the Goldberg Variations, also a sarabande, the first variation of which resembles the *double* of the D minor Sarabande. It is ornamented throughout, even in the early version found in the *Notenbüchlein* for Anna Magdalena Bach. If the Goldberg Aria were reduced to the notation of our D minor Sarabande its opening bars would sound like Ex. 20.12. This would simply not make 'Bachian' sense.[18] That is why I have attempted to construe the D minor Sarabande as an exercise for 'those desirous of learning',[19] to enable them 'to obtain a strong foretaste of composition'. I have produced two versions: a simple one that restricts itself to amplifying the melodic line (Ex. 20.13*a*) and a second one that also draws in the middle and lower voices (Ex. 20.13*b*).

Ex. 20.12

---

[18] According to Frederick Neumann, *Musical Quarterly*, 71 (1985), 281–94, this aria may not be by Bach. However, Marshall has refuted this rather convincingly (*The Music of Johann Sebastian Bach*, pp. 54–8).

[19] See Bach's own pref. to the Inventions.

Ex. 20.13. English Suite No. 6, BWV 811, Sarabande: two embellished versions by
Paul Badura-Skoda (1984)

Embellishment of the melodic line

Embellishment of melodic and lower voices

Of course there are also passages in non-keyboard works that require improvisational amplification. One of these has often puzzled commentators: the chords between the movements in the Third Brandenburg Concerto. Taken by themselves, they seem meaningless, and for this reason are rightly omitted in many performances. Neumann suggests an embellished fermata to be played by the solo violin.[20] Yet even this seems insufficient in the context of the concerto's formal balance. The two chords, I believe, are an invitation to a creative and talented violinist to improvise a more or less extended cadenza-like fantasia for violin solo in place of a slow middle movement, which by all appearances should be in E minor. The two accompanied chords would form

---

[20] *Ornamentation*, p. 548.

the conclusion of this fantasia, which could be modelled on the opening movement of the G minor Sonata for solo violin, BWV 1001.[21]

The method demonstrated of going back, as it were, from richly embellished passages in the original to simpler Baroque notation can also provide important information, even in longer pieces, about how they were composed and about how they should be performed. I should like to attempt a reduction of this kind in the case of the well-known Sarabande from Partita No. 1. Reduced to its basic substance the design of the Sarabande looks something like Ex. 20.14. Notated thus, Bach's Sarabande looks like the twin sister of Handel's famous D minor one, which, as in the case of Bach, was almost certainly not intended to be played in the form of a simple chordal skeleton (Ex. 20.15). The choice of crotchets or minims as notational units has no bearing on the basic tempo. The idea sometimes voiced that a work by Bach or Handel should be played more slowly because it is written in 3/2 or 4/2 time is not always right. On several occasions Bach wrote the same piece in each of two time signatures, as in the cases of the B minor Prelude from *WTC* II and the Gigue from Partita No. 6, where the versions in the *Clavierbüchlein* for Anna Magdalena Bach are notated in 4/4, and those in the *Clavier-Übung* in 4/2. However, only one of Bach's sarabandes, that of the Sixth English Suite, is written in 3/2.

Ex. 20.14

Ex. 20.15. Handel, Sarabande in D minor, bars 1–4

---

[21] According to Klaus Hofmann, Fritz Neumeyer realized another possibility in the 1950s and 1960s, playing a large-scale improvisation on the harpsichord. However, in this work, which is so obviously conceived in terms of string sonorities, it is difficult to see the logic of a harpsichord improvisation, particularly in view of the fact that in the 5th Brandenburg Concerto Bach assigned to the harpsichord a solo role of a previously unknown magnitude.

If we played these movements in their unembellished form in the tempo of a slow dance, we would hardly select anything slower than ♩ = 50–2. At this speed the dance character is still preserved, and the formation of four- and eight-bar periods will remain perceptible to the listener (and the dancer), just as much as the bass-line in its capacity as the 'basic' element. This speed does not drag, and yet the majestic character of the sarabande, whose solemn harmonies and octave leaps in the bass betray an inner affinity to the Sanctus of the B minor Mass, will become clearly apparent (see Ex. 20.16). Once this has been grasped it will not be difficult to understand that the ornamented version should not detract from the majestic character of this sarabande. (After all, according to the dedicatory poem, this particular partita was a present for a new-born prince. See Appendix 5.) In other words, the small fast notes must take their bearings from the basic rhythm, and not the other way round. These melodic garlands can be compared with the flowery festoons that are coiled around the regularly constructed pillars of a temple. Unfortunately many performers have lost the feeling for this kind of structure. The majority of modern performances are almost twice as slow as a normal sarabande, and rather unrhythmical at that.

Ex. 20.16. Mass in B minor, Sanctus, bars 1–6

The recognition of the basic compositional substance mentioned above shows the extent to which the harmonic design, which is based on that of the bass-line (thorough-bass composition), determines the structure of a work. The same or a similar design could be used in works that are very different in character. Using the harmonies of this sarabande, Bach (or another baroque composer) could easily have composed quite different works, for example a Kyrie for chorus and orchestra (see Ex. 20.17) or a suite for solo violoncello (Ex. 20.18), and, of course, other keyboard works (such as Ex. 20.19).

Ex. 20.17

Ex. 20.18

Ex. 20.19

Does this mean that we should not consider the notated form to be the only possible one? Yes and no. On the one hand, by choosing this version and no other, Bach decided once and for all in favour of a certain harmonic and melodic shape. It is astonishing that he 'only' made use of such a monumental idea in a modest keyboard work. On the other hand, even the notated ornamented version can serve as a starting-point for further discreet embellishment. This is the case when, in the repeat, one plays 'varied repetitions' of the melody, though these must not depart too much from the original and must be in keeping with the style. In certain works, such as the three-part Sinfonias and some of the sarabandes in the English Suites, Bach himself provided model examples of this kind of 'mini-variation' (i.e. discreet and hardly noticeable embellishment).

The fact that Bach, particularly.in the case of sarabandes, sometimes wrote down more richly ornamented repeats has led me to attempt something similar in the case of the Sarabande of Partita No. 1. I believe that this ornamented version corresponds more closely to Bach's intentions than slavish repetition. Apart from writing out certain ornaments in full I have adhered strictly to precedents in other works by Bach. The upper stave of Ex. 20.20 shows the embellished version.

Ex. 20.20. Partita No. 1, BWV 825, Sarabande: suggestion for the application of varied repeats by Paul Badura-Skoda (1984)

Original text:

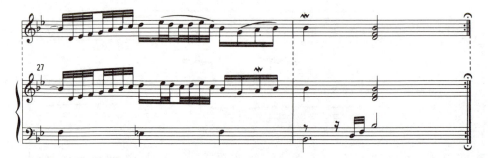

However, it would be completely wrong to embellish every slow movement by Bach in which there are long held notes. In the moving Adagio of the E major Violin Concerto, BWV 1042, or the tragic and serious opening movement of the F minor Sonata for violin and harpsichord, adding notes would only spoil the effect (see Ex. 20.21). Quantz also states that themes beginning with long notes should not be ornamented.[22]

Ex. 20.21. Sonata No. 5 for violin and harpsichord, BWV 1018, first movement

There is now sometimes a tendency to overshoot the mark when embellishing works by Bach and to play hardly a single line the way it was written. This leads to a 'distortion' of beautiful lines and to an effeminacy that contradicts the straightforwardness and strength of Bach's message. For example, what some performers add in the way of runs and ornaments is on occasion quite pleasing, but, taken as a whole, goes far beyond what eighteenth-century tutors say on the subject of embellishment. In this connection it is a good idea to remember that Couperin said it was his express wish that his works should be performed exactly as written and that nothing ought to be added to them.[23]

An anecdote about Josquin related by Mattheson may not be authentic, but it shows that Bach's Hamburg contemporary did not entertain a high opinion of excessive ornamentation:

---

[22] *On Playing the Flute*, p. 277.   [23] *Pièces de clavecin*, book 3, pref.

When Josquin was still at Cambrai and someone introduced an improper ornament that Josquin himself had not written in one of his pieces, he was so enraged that he said to him: 'Thou fool, why didst thou add an ornament? If the same had been pleasing to me I would have added it myself. If thou art minded to correct well composed songs, why, go and make thine own, and leave mine unbesmirched'.[24]

According to Forkel, Bach rejected the habit of enveloping single notes in a drapery of runs,[25] and considered the works of French keyboard composers to be affected 'because they make too great a use of ornaments'.[26] In conclusion we return to Bach's son Carl Philipp Emanuel, who considered the question of embellishment to be of such importance that at the end of Part I of his great didactic work he wrote:

Not everything should be varied, for if it is the repeat will become a new piece. Many things, particularly affettuoso or declamatory passages, cannot be readily varied. . . . All variations must relate to the piece's affection, and they must always be at least as good as, if not better than, the original. . . . Simple melodies can often be made into elaborate ones and vice versa. All this must be done with no small deliberation. Constant attention must be given to preceding and succeeding parts; there must be a vision of the whole piece so that the variation will retain the original contrasts of the brilliant and the simple, the fiery and the languid, the sad and the joyful, the vocal and the instrumental. In keyboard pieces the bass too may be modified so long as the harmony remains unchanged. Despite the present popularity of elaborate variations, it is of first importance always to make certain that the lineaments of a piece, by which its affection is recognized, remain unobscured.[27]

[24] Quoted in Albrecht, *Interpretationsfragen*, p. 150.
[25] Albrecht, *Interpretationsfragen*, p. 153.
[26] Forkel, *Bachs Leben*, p. 37; Eng. trans. p. 310.
[27] *Essay*, pp. 165–6.

EPILOGUE

'Gott ist unsere Zuversicht' (God is our refuge and strength) is a cantata text that could serve as a motto for all of Bach's works. His music is imbued with a faith in God, an inner composure, and gentle strength that impress themselves on listeners and performers even if they know nothing of Bach's personality. This music does not aim to excite, but to delight the heart, 'das Gemüt ergötzen', as Bach himself put it.

At the age of ninety-four Pablo Casals used to begin the day by playing Bach at the piano. Visitors and friends have described the effect this had on him. From being a frail old man who could hardly walk, he seemed to become rejuvenated, full of life and energy. Casals himself described this experience thus:

> For the past eighty years I have started each day in the same manner. It is not a mechanical routine but something essential to my daily life. I go to the piano, and I play two preludes and fugues of Bach. I cannot think of doing otherwise. It is a sort of benediction on the house. But that is not its only meaning for me. It is a rediscovery of the world of which I have the joy of being a part. It fills me with awareness of the wonder of life, with a feeling of the incredible marvel of being a human being. The music is never the same for me, never. Each day it is something new, fantastic and unbelievable. That is Bach, like nature, a miracle.[1]

The liberating and invigorating effect of Bach may well be sensed more by the player than the listener. My teacher Edwin Fischer once gave me a piece of advice that I have remembered ever since: 'If you're in trouble, play Bach'. I have often found this to be true.

But was religious piety really a pronounced trait in Bach's character? Bach research took this for granted for a hundred years, though our sceptical age has cast doubt on the idea that he was a musician largely motivated by his faith. Today this merely seems to be a modish view adopted by musicologists around 1960, which in turn reflected the post-war Protestant theology of 'de-mythologizing', a theology that owed much to materialistic ideologies. In 1962 Friedrich Blume, a respected musicologist and Bach scholar, asserted that Bach had accepted the post of cantor in Leipzig unwillingly, because it merely

---

[1] Pablo Casals and Albert E. Kahn, *Joys and Sorrows: Reflections by Pablo Casals as Told to Albert Kahn* (London, 1970), 17. Stravinsky, too, started his old days with Bach's preludes and fugues. (Lillian Libman *And Music at Close: Strawinsky's last years*, (Norton, New York, 1971), p. 207.

happened to be the best he was able to obtain; that he composed a large part of his church music only because it was required of him; that he had cobbled together works such as the Christmas Oratorio, the B minor Mass, and even the *St Matthew Passion* with large sections lifted from secular works to which different words had been added—in other words, that they were not written at the dictates of an inner need or the desire to proclaim the Gospel. In short, the 'arch-cantor Bach', the composer in the service of Holy Scripture, the ardent believer in Lutheran Christianity, all this was merely a romantic fiction.[2]

Very little of this has survived. Today, about a quarter of a century later, Blume's theory has become remarkably unpopular, partly because some of his claims were quite simply untenable in historical terms, which is why—and this must be said in defence of Blume's musicological colleagues—they immediately caused a great deal of controversy. The most entertaining riposte came from Hans Joachim Moser. Using the language of Bach's time, he depicted him in heaven protesting vigorously that a lowly mortal was suggesting that he be relegated from the area reserved for composers of sacred music to one destined for town pipers. Moser placed arguments in Bach's mouth that stand up to scrutiny in terms of music history.[3]

The controversy about Bach's religious beliefs sheds light on the problem of historical research itself, for the handful of documents from the past that have survived, with all their faults and errors, can often be interpreted in different ways. A 'correct and true' picture of the past—inasmuch as such a thing is at all possible—can be obtained only by examining all the relevant facts in a meaningful and psychologically convincing context.

Bach's true attitude is revealed by a document that has recently come to light: the composer's annotations to his copy of the Bible. This was not available to scholars twenty-five years ago:

NB Erstes Vorspiel, auf 2 Chören zur Ehre Gottes zu musicieren. [NB First prelude, to be performed on 2 choirs to the glory of God.]

NB Dieses Capitel ist das wahre Fundament aller Gottgefälligen Kirchen Music etc. [NB This chapter is the true foundation of all sacred music etc.]

NB Ein herrlicher Beweis, daß neben anderen Anstalten des Gottesdienstes, besonders auch die Musica von Gottes Geist durch David mit angeordnet worden. [NB Wonderful evidence that, apart from other kinds of worship, music in particular was commanded by the Holy Ghost through David.]

NB Bey einer andächtigen Musique ist allezeit Gott mit seiner Gnadengegenwart. [NB In devout music God is at all times present with his grace.][4]

---

[2] See Friedrich Blume, 'Umrisse eines neuen Bach-Bildes', *Syntagma musicologicum: Gesammelte Reden und Schriften von Friedrich Blume*, ed. M. Ruhnke (Kassel, 1963), 466 (some of Blume's arguments are given in App. 6 below).

[3] This linguistic and musicological *tour de force* is given in App. 6.

[4] *Bach-Dokumente*, iii. 636. These 4 glosses refer to Exod. 15: 20, 1 Chr. 25 (ch. heading 'Von den

It is impossible to cast reasonable doubts on the matter. If Bach had displayed a lack of interest in religious matters he would hardly have read the Bible, and he would certainly not have annotated it in this way. Thus Bach's well-known statement that music exists for 'the glory of God and the recreation of the spirit'[5] was more than mere lip-service.

Do we have to be religious in order to be able to understand Bach's music?[6] In the final analysis the answer to this question depends on how we define the word 'understand'. If, as is customary nowadays, we take it to mean intellectual perception and nothing else, the answer could well be no. In the numerous works that were not written for ecclesiastical use the main thing is to achieve a musical, beautiful, and expressive performance, and to understand the style correctly.[7] True, where we are dealing with arrangements of sacred works it will be of use to know the text and the mood of the original work in order to enter into the spirit of the piece. Being aware of such interrelationships, for instance that the slow movement of the F minor Harpsichord Concerto, BWV 1056, appears in Cantata No. 156, *Ich steh mit einem Fuß im Grabe*, and the Siciliano of the E major Harpsichord Concerto, BWV 1053, in the aria 'Stirb in mir, Welt', Cantata No. 169, does not by any stretch of the imagination mean that a good performer must be prepared to die a Christian death.

The theory behind this is that, no matter whether it is sacred or secular, the message is always expressed with purely *musical* means, not only in the case of Bach. For this reason the performer should first of all become acquainted with the musical grammar of a given age. Subsequently he should study the extramusical dimension, which in the Baroque era in particular was admittedly full of symbols and allusions (such as number symbolism). When studying musical tone-painting,[8] emotional and sign symbolism, and the relationships between words and music, it transpires that so-called religious emotions and the manner in which they are mirrored in music have their roots in common human experience. Whether the joy expressed refers to the birth

Sängern und Instrumentisten' ('Of Singers and Instrumentalists')): 7, 31, 1 Chr. 28: 21, and 2 Chr. 5: 13 (title: 'Der Dritte theil. Wie auff die schöne Music die Herrligkeit des Herrn erschienen sey' ('The Third Part. How the Glory of the Lord appeared after the playing of Beautiful Music)). Bach almost certainly made further glosses in his copy of the Bible that are no longer extant.

[5] See Spitta, *Johann Sebastian Bach*, ii. 916.

[6] We take musicality for granted, for it is obvious that a pious, though unmusical religious person will experience difficulties when attempting to understand the message conveyed through the medium of music.

[7] In this connection it should be emphasized that not all of Bach's works were written in the spirit of the Lutheran creed. After all, Bach dedicated the B minor Mass to the Catholic king in Dresden (which, 3 years later, earned him the title of a Royal Saxon Court Composer); he wrote works for the Calvinist court of Cöthen; and for the free-thinking Frederick the Great of Prussia. His compositions include the secular family idyll of the 'Coffee' Cantata, the earthy 'Peasant' Cantata, the short opera (yes, opera) inspired by antiquity *Der Streit zwischen Phoebus und Pan*, and a host of secular instrumental music.

[8] In this respect there is a similarity with 19th-cent. programme music; Richard Strauss's jocular remark that he could even portray a glass of beer musically could almost have stemmed from a baroque composer.

of Christ or to an heir to the throne, whether a real human tragedy or the Passion of Our Saviour are portrayed in musical terms, in essence we are dealing with the same indivisible feeling of joy and pain. Even love for God can be expressed only in language that tells of our love for another human being. For this reason mystics have always expressed their love for God in terms of poetry that seems to be addressed to a human beloved.[9] Even the 'numinous' state, the reverential awe in the face of that which cannot be understood, or the experience of having complete faith in God, has its roots in human experience (a child has faith in its mother's love), even if it can grow 'into the firmament of heaven'. Devotion, prayer, and meditation are nothing but stepping-stones from everyday human life to eternity. But is there not, some may be prompted to ask, a specifically religious element in music, for instance in Gregorian chant or the Protestant chorale? Of course there is. However, we must admit that even this specifically religious element arose on account of its virtually exclusive ecclesiastical use. One of the most moving and beautiful hymns, the chorale 'O Haupt voll Blut und Wunden', strikes us as the musical embodiment of the Passion of Christ. Yet it was originally a dance-like song in 6/4 time by Hans Leo Hassler, 'Mein Herz ist mir verwundet von einem Mägdlein zart' (My heart is wounded by a tender maiden). The change in meaning is very great indeed, though there is a common root in the expression of pain denoted by the words 'wound' or 'wounded'. The greater profundity of the chorale melody is due to the change in the rhythm and the slower tempo.

Let us sum up what we have said so far. From a purely intellectual point of view—assuming that one knows the style and is sufficiently musical—it is useful, indeed perhaps even necessary, to be as aware of the religious element in Bach's music as it is to sense the seriousness, the profundity and greatness of his personality. But to understand all this one does not, it seems, have to be religious oneself.

However, understanding in the deeper meaning of the word is much more than a mere intellectual exercise. True understanding also encompasses a kind of emotional and spiritual comprehension that discerns the secrets that lie beyond the surface of words. Goethe described this mystery in a poem, 'Die Geheimnisse' ('The Mysteries'):

> Doch glaube keiner, daß mit allem Sinnen
> Das ganze Lied er je enträtseln werde:
> Gar viele müssen vieles hier gewinnen,
> Gar manche Blüten bringt die Mutter Erde . . .

---

[9] St John of the Cross, to take but one example, wrote some of the most beautiful love poetry in world literature. However, without his detailed commentaries we would hardly know that he was speaking metaphorically.

[Let none imagine that with all their thinking
They'll ever pierce the mystery of all the song.
Here many minds are many things a-gaining
And Mother Earth brings forth a flowery throng . . .]

Even if we cannot 'pierce the mystery of all the song' with 'thinking' or reflection, we can attain to an intuitive empathy with the composer who also wrote his secular works under the motto 'ad maiorem Dei gloriam'—to the greater glory of God.[10] The important thing is not what and how one believes, but the almost absurd fundamental trust in the world as meaningful creation, the trust that for the love of God utters: 'Thy will be done'. How else would it be possible to grasp the mystic fervour of an aria such as 'Mache dich, mein Herze, rein'?[11] Those who are not imbued with the desire to cleanse their souls will no doubt fail to grasp the deeper significance of such a work.

Edwin Fischer expressed in beautiful terms this striving on the part of the artist for inner perfection:

But no amount of studying, no amount of talent, no amount of industry suffices if one's whole life is not dedicated to the idea of being the mediator of great thoughts and emotions. Every deed, and indeed every thought leaves its mark on the personality. The purity of one's life should even extend to the food one eats. Thus prepared, that which cannot be taught will come, the grace of the tranquil hour in which the spirit of the composer speaks to us, that moment of the subconscious, of rapture—call it intuition, grace, or what you will—when all ties are loosened, all constraints disappear. One seems to hover. One no longer feels: I am playing. Rather, IT is playing. And lo, everything is right, as if led by the hand of God the melodies stream from your fingers. It streams through you, and you allow yourself to be carried along, humbly experiencing the greatest joy of the recreative artist, of being nothing but a medium, a mediator between the Godly, the Eternal, and human beings.[12]

However, it would be wrong to equate religious feeling with the ability to believe. 'Re-ligio', the 're-connection' with the feeling of safe haven in God that is often thought to be lost, can also be experienced and lived by non-believers. None other than the great 'heathen' Goethe wrote these deeply religious lines:

In unsres Busens Reine wogt ein Streben,
Sich einem Höhern, Reinern, Unbekannten
Aus Dankbarkeit freiwillig hinzugeben,
Enträtselnd sich den ewig Ungenannten;
Wir heißen's fromm sein! . . .

---

[10] See the quotation 'To the glory of God in the highest', above.
[11] *St Matthew Passion*, NBA No. 65, BGA No. 75.
[12] *Musikalische Betrachtungen* (Frankfurt-on-Main, 1964), 31; Eng. trans., p. 22.

[Surging in our chaste breast is a desire
In thankfulness quite freely to surrender
To something that's unknown, purer, and higher,
The eternal Unnamed One in words to render;
We call it piety . . .][13]

It is no accident that this great poem originated in a deeply felt and tragic love:

. . . In solcher seligen Höhe
Fühl' ich mich teilhaft, wenn ich vor ihr steh'.

[. . . In such blissful heights
I feel at one with it when I am near her.]

This is the continuation of the above lines. Love and devotion—this is perhaps the essence of religious life. 'And though I have all faith, so that I could remove mountains, and have not charity, I am nothing.'[14] Loving devotion, the creative urge, and a desire to communicate—in the end it is this which leads a composer to spend long nights and weeks creating a great work without giving a thought to material rewards. Loving devotion should thus also be the main motive of the performer. Whoever is guided by this urge to achieve inner perfection will find that Bach's music is a source of joy and inner peace; for it has an appeal transcending that which can be understood in rational terms. 'Beauty unites.'

[13] 'Marienbader Elegie'.
[14] 1 Cor. 13: 2. Translator's note: in Luther's trans. of the Bible the word is *Liebe*.

APPENDIX 1

Some Recommended Editions of Bach's Keyboard Works

For understandable reasons a performer cannot assess the merits and demerits of every single edition. However, on the basis of my long experience as a performer, scholar, editor, and teacher I believe I can give a relatively objective idea of the good and bad qualities of certain editions. Under each work, genre, or collection in the following list, what I consider to be the best edition has been listed first. As I am exclusively concerned with the correct reproduction of the musical text, I have omitted the names of those who have provided the fingering, restricting myself to listing the publishers and the editors.

NOTES ON EDITIONS

BGA (Bach-Gesamtausgabe): *J. S. Bach: Werke*, ed. Bach-Gesellschaft, Breitkopf und Härtel (Leipzig), 1851–99: the 'old' Bach complete edition, available in a number of reprints.

Kalmus (New York): photographic reproduction of Hans Bischoff's Steingräber edition, with commentaries translated into English.

NBA (Neue Bach-Ausgabe): *J. S. Bach: Neue Ausgabe sämtlicher Werke*, ed. Johann-Sebastian-Bach-Institut, Göttingen, and Bach-Archiv, Leipzig, Bärenreiter (Kassel and Basle), and VEB Deutscher Verlag für Musik (Leipzig), 1954– . Separate issues are also available.

Peters (Leipzig, Frankfurt, New York, and London).

Steingräber: *Kritische Ausgabe der Bachschen Werke*, ed. Hans Bischoff (Offenbach-on-Main, formerly Leipzig, Hanover, and New York, 1880–8).

Wiener Urtext: published by Universal Edition (Vienna), Urtext Edition Schott (Mainz), and Editio Musica (Budapest: licensed edition for Eastern Europe).

EDITIONS OF MAJOR WORKS

BWV 772–801: *Inventions and Sinfonias*

—— NBA V/3, ed. G. von Dadelsen).[1] Critical Report forthcoming.

---

[1] In the G minor Sinfonia No. 11, bar 50, the reading of the *Clavier-Büchlein* for W. F. Bach is probably better: last note in the bass eb instead of f. Palmer's arguments in favour of eb are plausible.

—— Wiener Urtext.[2] With formal analysis by E. Ratz and interesting remarks on ornamentation by K. H. Füssl.
—— Alfred Ed. (Sherman Oaks, Calif.), ed. W. Palmer.[3]
—— Peters, ed. L. Landshoff.
—— Steingräber, ed. H. Bischoff.
—— Kalmus, ed. Bischoff.

BWV 802–805: *Four Duets (from* Clavier-Übung, *Part III)*

—— NBA IV/4, ed. Tessmer. Bärenreiter (Kassel and Basle) is identical.
—— Henle (Munich), ed. R. Steglich.
—— Peters, ed. K. Soldan.
—— Peters, ed. F. C. Griepenkerl, in *Orgelwerke: Clavier-Übung III*. This oblong edition is rather convenient from a pianist's point of view (fewer pages to turn).

BWV 806–811: *English Suites*

—— NBA V/7, ed. A. Dürr.
—— Editio Musica (Budapest), ed. Zászkaliczky.
—— Peters, ed. A. Kreutz. With supplement on ornamentation.
—— Wiener Urtext, ed. Dehnhard (forthcoming).

BWV 812–817: *French Suites*

—— NBA V/8, ed. A. Dürr. To be recommended, because early and late versions are printed separately.
—— Wiener Urtext, ed. Müller. Good, but does not include enough variants.
—— Steingräber, ed. H. Bischoff. Includes numerous variants.
—— Kalmus, ed. H. Bischoff.
—— Peters, ed. H. Keller.

BWV 825–830: *Six Partitas* (Clavier-Übung, *Part I*)

There is no satisfactory edition.
—— Wiener Urtext, ed. Engler (forthcoming).
—— Henle (Munich), ed. R. Steglich. New edition, 1979.
—— NBA V/1, ed. Jones and A. Dürr. Unfortunately there are faults in the first book of the *Clavier-Übung*, the six Partitas, even in the NBA.[4]
—— Editio Musica (Budapest), ed. Pertis. Based on NBA, with all its errors, and adds inaccuracies of its own.[5]

---

[2] See n. 1.   [3] See n. 1.
[4] The most important errors are: p. 5, Allemande, bar 25, 4th note, upper system: the flat belongs to the 7th note; p. 66, mvt. 2, bar 19: 4 slurs to be added above the repeated notes (in P 215); p. 82, mvt. 3, bar 5: 3rd note should be g^2 and not $f\sharp^2$; p. 105, bar 30: 1st note, right hand, and 2nd note, left hand, should be *e* and not *d*. Furthermore, many of Bach's later corrections in Partitas Nos. 2 and 3 were disregarded due to the editors' excessive caution. See Wolff, 'Textkritische Bemerkungen', p. 65.
[5] e.g. missing sharp in Partita No. 6, p. 104, bar 64, right hand, 2nd note.

BWV 831: *French Overture in B minor* (Clavier-Übung, *Part II/2*)

In many editions with the Italian Concerto, BWV 971 (*Clavier-Übung*, Part II/1), and
often with the Goldberg Variations, BWV 988 (*Clavier-Übung*, Part IV).
—— NBA V/2, ed. Emery and Wolff. With the early version, BWV 831*a*.
—— Peters, ed. Soldan.
—— Henle (Munich), ed. Steglich.
—— Steingräber, ed. H. Bischoff.
—— Kalmus, ed. H. Bischoff.
—— BGA.

BWV 846–893: The Well-Tempered Clavier, *Parts I and II*

Part I (BWV 846–869)
—— NBA, ed. A. Dürr (1989). Small error in Prel. No. 22, bar 3: the tie f^2–f^2 is not
authentic.
—— Alfred (Sherman Oaks, Calif.), ed. W. Palmer.
—— Wiener Urtext, ed. Dehnhard. Excellent in part, but does not include enough
variants.
—— Steingräber, ed. H. Bischoff. Includes many variants.
—— Kalmus, ed. H. Bischoff.
—— BGA, ed. Kroll. With editorial commentary unfortunately omitted in most
reprints.
—— Associated Board (London), ed. D. F. Tovey.
—— Peters, ed. Kroll. Not identical with the version Kroll prepared for BGA, which
appeared later.
—— Editio Musica (Budapest), ed. Lantos.

Part II (BWV 870–893)[6]
—— NBA (forthcoming).
—— Alfred (Sherman Oaks, Calif.) (forthcoming).
—— Peters, ed. Keller.
—— BGA, ed. Kroll. With editorial commentary.
—— Wiener Urtext, ed. Dehnhard.
—— Peters, ed. Kroll. Excellent with regard to Prelude No. 4.
—— Steingräber, ed. H. Bischoff. With many variants.
—— Kalmus, ed. H. Bischoff.
—— Associated Board (London), ed. D. F. Tovey.

BWV 903: *Chromatic Fantasia and Fugue in D minor*[7]

—— NBA (forthcoming).

---

[6] For reasons impossible to understand, many modern Urtext editions simply omit the many
considerable variants, which 100 years ago were given by BGA and Bischoff. To name only a few: Prelude
No. 4, C sharp minor, bar 2, turn over 1st note $d\sharp^2$ (Altnikol copy). Prelude No. 12, F minor, bars 1, 2,
etc., *Pralltriller* symbols over 1st note in Schwencke, Altnikol II, and others. Fugue No. 20, A minor, bars
2–3, 3–4, staccato strokes from the Kirnberger copy (or dots in Schwencke) are mentioned only by Keller.
[7] For a more detailed discussion of variants see App. 2, pp. 533–9.

—— Henle (Munich), ed. G. von Dadelsen and K. Rönnau in *Fantasien, Präludien und Fugen.*[8]
—— Universal edition (Vienna), ed. Huber.
—— BGA.
—— Hansen (Copenhagen), ed. Edwin Fischer.
—— Universal Edition (Vienna), ed. H. Schenker. The commentary is of particular interest, though the text is rather old-fashioned.

BWV 910–916: *Toccatas*

—— NBA (forthcoming).
—— Henle (Munich), ed. Steglich.
—— Peters, ed. Keller.
—— Steingräber, ed. H. Bischoff.
—— Kalmus, ed. H. Bischoff.
—— BGA.

BWV 971: *Italian Concerto in F major* (Clavier-Übung, *Part II/1*)

—— NBA V/2, ed. Emery and Wolff.
—— Hansen (Copenhagen), ed. Edwin Fischer.
—— Wiener Urtext, ed. Engler. There are a few minor errors.[9]
—— Peters, ed. Soldan.
—— Schott (Mainz), ed. Kreutz.
—— Steingräber, ed. H. Bischoff.
—— Kalmus, ed. H. Bischoff.

BWV 988: *Goldberg Variations* (Aria mit verschiedenen Veraenderungen, Clavier-Übung, *Part IV*)

—— NBA V/2, ed. Wolff.[10]
—— Henle (Munich), ed. Steglich.[11]
—— Peters, ed. Soldan.
—— Schirmer (New York), ed. Kirkpatrick.
—— BGA.

---

[8] Printing errors: Fantasia, bar 62: 4th note should be e^1 instead of $d\sharp^1$. By notating g$\sharp$ Bach suggests that the beginning of this bar is already in E major, and no longer in A flat minor. Thus the mordent's lower auxiliary should probably be f$\sharp$ and not f$\times$.

[9] 1st movement, bar 146, missing natural before b (left hand); 2nd movement, bar 33, missing tie linking g^1–g^1; 2nd movement, bar 17, *Pralltriller* (left hand) should be omitted; 3rd movement, bar 27, 5th note of right hand should be g^2.

[10] Only mistakes: incorrectly reproduced mordents in the theme, bars 1, 3, 5, 8, 9, 17, 19; variation 2, bars 1, 3; variation 7, bars 1, 3, 9, 10, etc. (see p. 466). The majority of Bach's *Pralltriller* symbols are given as long wavy lines.

[11] Variation 8, bar 3, top 2nd semiquaver: in all edns except NBA d^1 mistakenly for e^1. I am grateful to Gerhard Schuler (Vienna) for drawing this to my attention.

BWV 992: Capriccio sopra la lontananza del suo fratello dilettissimo *in B flat major*

—— NBA V/10, ed. Eichberg.[12]

—— Henle (Munich), ed. G. von Dadelsen in *Suiten, Sonaten, Capriccios und Variationen.*

—— Schott (Mainz), ed. Kreutz.

—— Steingräber, ed. H. Bischoff.

—— Kalmus, ed. H. Bischoff.

—— BGA.

BWV 1080: Die Kunst der Fuge (The Art of Fugue)

—— NBA, ed. Hofmann (forthcoming).

—— Henle, ed. D. Moroney.

—— Peters. Facsimile edition with commentary by Wolff.

—— Muzïka (Moscow), ed. Kopchevski. Keyboard arrangement.

—— Breitkopf & Härtel (Wiesbaden and Leipzig), ed. Graeser. Study score with piano reduction.

—— Oxford University Press, ed. D. F. Tovey. A fascinating commentary, *A Companion to Bach's 'Art of Fugue'* (London, 1931), was published separately.

—— Boosey & Hawkes (London), ed. Hans Gál.

—— Peters, ed. Czerny.

COLLECTIONS

Clavierbüchlein *for Anna Magdalena Bach (1722 and 1725)*

—— NBA V/4, ed. G. von Dadelsen.

—— Bärenreiter (Kassel and Basle), ed. G. von Dadelsen. This bibliophile's edition is not identical to NBA.

Notenbüchlein *for Anna Magdalena Bach (1725)*

—— Henle (Munich), ed. Heinemann. Does not include early versions of Partitas Nos. 3 and 6.

Clavier-Büchlein *for Wilhelm Friedemann Bach*

—— NBA V/5, ed. Plath.

—— Da Capo Press (New York). Facsimile edition with commentary by Ralph Kirkpatrick.

---

[12] NBA and Henle are almost equally good, the only real difference being in the fugue, bar 52, where the sources are imprecise. Here the reading given by Kreutz (Schott) is certainly a possibility.

Little Preludes and Fughettas

—— NBA (forthcoming).
—— Wiener Urtext, ed. Dehnhard.
—— Alfred (Sherman Oaks, Calif.), ed. W. Palmer.
—— Peters, ed. Keller.
—— Henle (Munich), ed. Steglich.

Suites, Sonatas, Capriccios, and Variations

—— Henle (Munich), ed. G. von Dadelsen.
—— Steingräber, ed. H. Bischoff.
—— Kalmus, ed. H. Bischoff.
—— BGA.

Die kleinen Klavierstücke: Bärenreiter (Kassel and Basle), ed. Doflein. Twenty-seven pieces, mainly from the *Clavierbüchlein* for Anna Magdalena Bach and the *Clavier-Büchlein* for Wilhelm Friedmann Bach, and with the Six Little Preludes BWV 933–8.

Einzelne überlieferte Klavierwerke II und Kompositionen für Lauteninstrument: NBA V/10, ed. Eichberg and Kohlhase. Contains the capriccios BWV 992 and 993, Aria variata BWV 989, Sonata BWV 963, single suites BWV 820, 822, 823, 832, and 833 (ed. Eichberg), and compositions for lute instruments (ed. Kohlhase), including the Prelude, Fugue, and Allegro in E flat for lute or harpsichord, BWV 998.

Fantasien, Präludien und Fugen: Henle (Munich), ed. G. von Dadelsen and Rönnau. Fantasias, preludes, and fugues.

Italienisches Konzert, Französische Ouvertüre, Vier Duette, Goldberg-Variationen: Henle (Munich), ed. Steglich. The Italian Concerto, French Overture, Four Duets, and Goldberg Variations.

Neues Bach-Heft: Bärenreiter (Kassel and Basle), ed. Doflein. Five little-known pieces for harpsichord or piano.

APPENDIX 2

Some Textual and Interpretational Problems in Bach's Chromatic Fantasia and Fugue, BWV 903

The autograph of the Chromatic Fantasia and Fugue is no longer extant. However, scholars know of the existence of numerous copies of this important keyboard work. About twenty-five of these can be regarded as source material because they were made during Bach's lifetime or by people who were close to him.[1] The many copies that have survived testify to the fact that this work soon became very popular. Recently a French copy from the eighteenth century has come to light, one of the very few pieces of evidence for Bach's music in France at this time.[2]

It is of course a difficult task to 'sort the sheep from the goats' in this plethora of sources (they often differ from one another) in order to discover Bach's intentions. Georg von Dadelsen, on the basis of work published by Hans David in the *Bach-Jahrbuch* in 1926, undertook an examination and evaluation of the principal sources, and established their probable interrelationship. It is important to determine the copyists and the provenances of the various sources, in other words, who copied what from whom. The plausibility of this can often be demonstrated with the help of a subtle system that traces 'perpetuated errors'.

Dadelsen's research enabled him to prepare a performing edition of the Chromatic Fantasia and Fugue for the publishing firm of Henle, and in fact this edition is superior to all the others currently available. Of particular interest is the fact that Dadelsen demonstrated that the surely unauthentic dynamic markings of the manuscript P 577, which unfortunately continue to appear in new editions, are bad later additions and thus have to be rejected.[3] Apart from P 577 no early source contains dynamic markings. That P 577 cannot be an authentic source is also demonstrated by certain pedal marks for octave doublings in entries of the subject in the bass, which proves that they are of later origin.

If certain textual problems in the Henle edition remain unresolved despite Dadelsen's systematic and thorough approach, then this is mainly because a more

---

[1] A good survey is given by George B. Stauffer in his essay ' "This fantasia . . . never had its like": on the enigma and chronology of Bach's Chromatic Fantasia and Fugue in D minor, BWV 903', *Bach Studies*, edited by Don O. Franklin, (Cambridge University Press, 1989), pp. 160 f.

[2] See Mary Cyr, 'Bach's Music in France: A New Source', *Early Music*, 13 (1985), 256.

[3] As late as 1976 Maria Tipo included one of these dynamic markings in her edn. (Ricordi, Milan).

detailed commentary would have exceeded the limits of a practical edition. Dadelsen established a seven-branched stemma for the BWV 903 version, to which, as an eighth branch, should be added the special version BWV 903a, where bars 3–20 are replaced by twenty-one bars that are differently figured, more straightforward, and less varied than the principal version. Hitherto the so-called 'Rust Manuscript' (dated 'Bernburg 1757') was the only known source for this longer version. It is no longer extant, but was included in the BGA (vol. xxxvi) in incomplete form, and in full in the old Peters edition (edited by Griepenkerl), with diplomatic accuracy, it seems. Dadelsen was probably unaware of the almost identical copy of this version (Darmstadt, Hessische Landesbibliothek, Mus. ms. 69); at any rate he does not mention it. This copy is also a special case inasmuch as, in contrast with all other old sources, in which the fantasia has no key signature, it is notated in 'modern' D minor (this may have been a decision taken by the copyist). Apart from this it is almost the same as the Rust copy, though it contains more copyist's errors. For example, some accidentals are missing, such as the sharp before the f in the final chord, which in Rust is D major. If the harmony in bar 37 (see below) were the same, one might consider Mus. ms. 69 to be a copy of the Rust version. However, it is more probable that Mus. ms. 69 was copied from the lost autograph independently of Rust. The earliest owner of this copy was Johann Samuel Endler, who is known to have played in Bach's collegium musicum in Leipzig in 1736. Most Bach scholars are now of the opinion that this version of BWV 903 is the earliest state of the Chromatic Fantasia, though only as regards bars 3–24, whereas the rest of the fantasia bears stylistic traces of a later version.

However, might it not be possible that BWV 903a, despite the seemingly primitive character of bars 3–24, represents a relatively late intermediate version? The following reasons speak for this hypothesis:

1. The remarkably small range, $D–c^3$, of the Chromatic Fantasia and Fugue—with two exceptions, the d^3 in bar 27 of the Fantasia and the B_1 in bar 96 of the Fugue, though the latter does not occur in certain early sources such as Mus. ms. 20136—is exceeded in the BWV 903a variant by a fourth downwards (bar 24). If Bach's early harpsichord really had a larger range than a later one, then one could assume that Bach, in bar 58 of the fantasia (BWV 903 numbering) would have written a low $C\sharp$ as a continuation to the chromatic bass-line in bars 54–8, and would have written lower basses elsewhere as well.

2. The BWV 903a version is three bars *longer* than BWV 903, which tends to suggest that BWV 903a was written at a later date (cf. the various versions of the C major Prelude of *WTC* II, where the longer version is surely the later one).

3. It seems highly unlikely that a copyist would of his own accord have patched together a text of the fantasia from two different manuscripts, an earlier and a later one. In such a situation it would be more logical to copy either an immature 'early version' BWV 903a in full, or to base the copy on the 'more mature' version.

4. According to the latest research, Mus. ms. 69 (BWV 903a) cannot be earlier than 1731, whereas the earliest copy of the Chromatic Fantasia and Fugue, the familiar P 421 version, is dated 1730.[4]

---

[4] See Stauffer, 'This fantasia . . .', p. 171.

There is therefore reason to believe that, in a creative moment, Bach once improvised as it were the rhythmically unified version, BWV 903*a*, perhaps writing this on a single sheet of paper and giving it to his pupils to copy, but then not recognizing it as the 'final' version after all. Otherwise far more copies of BWV 903*a* would have survived.[5]

The version published by Peters in 1819 is certainly not authentic and thus of little importance to modern Bach interpretation. Griepenkerl, who had been taught by Forkel ten years earlier, prefaced it with the following words: 'New edition with an indication of true execution as transmitted from J. S. Bach to W. Friedemann Bach, from him to Forkel, and from Forkel to his pupils'. Heinrich Schenker, in his edition of 1909, which continues to be of value, convincingly demonstrated the lesser artistic value of this version compared to the original.[6] The frequent use in the Griepenkerl edition of the 'trilled turn' over demisemiquavers ℘ makes Johann Sebastian Bach's authorship impossible. Nevertheless, this edition also contains some interesting pieces of information, for instance that the first page and a half should be played forte throughout. Another 'Bachian' touch is the added semiquaver accented passing appoggiatura d^2 before $c\sharp^2$ on the third beat of the penultimate bar of the fugue.

But now to textual matters. Dadelsen quite rightly treated P 651 as the principal source, a 'particularly reliable copy made by Bach's pupil J. F. Agricola . . . going by the writing, it was probably made in Leipzig 1738–40'—the title is in the hand of C. P. E. Bach. Dadelsen consulted other equally reliable sources with which to compare it.[7] In this regard the version in manuscript P 803, which contains two related copies by Bach's pupils Johann Tobias Krebs and Samuel Gottlieb Heder, proved to be particularly useful. Yet here bars 21–4 appear in a version that is two bars shorter. Was this run the result of a whim similar to BWV 903*a*? As far as Bach was concerned, a fantasia was in some respects improvisatory in character, and thus could not be precisely notated in a single manuscript.

There is some doubt about the authenticity of manuscript P 212 (source F of the Henle edition), a copy made by Forkel. It contains a number of interesting variants, which otherwise occur only in copies or printed editions derived from it, in other words, which do not appear in any other early source. In P 212 both the fantasia and the fugue end on a D minor chord; this can hardly have been Bach's intention. Nevertheless, in some respects this version could also be authentic.

In several copies (P 421, dated 1730; P 551; P 887) the Chromatic Fantasia and Fugue is expressly stated to be a work for harpsichord, whereas C. P. E. Bach, in the heading to P 651 that was probably added at a later stage, assigned it to the 'clavier', which in his case (in contrast with his father and other contemporaries) probably meant the clavichord.

I am grateful to Yoshitake Kobayashi (of the Bach-Institut, Göttingen), who helped me in the compilation of the following list of problematical passages.

---

[5] Stauffer, 'This fantasia . . .' p. 181, argues that the triplet version, BWV 903*a*, may have been written in Cöthen. Here Bach may have had at his disposal a Mietke harpsichord with a larger range, an instrument he had to leave behind when he moved to Leipzig. But *WTC* I and other Leipzig keyboard works have a larger range than BWV 903.

[6] Universal Edition (Vienna), pref., pp. 29–31.

[7] See the commentary in his Henle edn. of Bach's fantasias, preludes, and fugues (Munich), pp. 133–5.

LIST OF SOME PROBLEMATICAL PASSAGES IN THE CHROMATIC FANTASIA
AND FUGUE

The Fantasia

1. Bar 4, fourth crotchet:

Version *a* is usually notated in all early copies (including P 651, P 421, P 295, P 212) with a flat, which should be incorporated into modern editions. Version *b* appears only in BWV 903*a*, the other version mentioned above.

2. The last note in bar 14 should obviously have been B♮ and not B♭. All earlier sources were notated in the 'Dorian' manner without an initial flat. Certain sources (e.g. P 228, P 1083) even have an unnecessary natural before the B.

3. There are several variants for bars 37–8:

Version *a* occurs in sources P 651, P 803, P 887 and Mus. ms. 69. In P 289 it was later altered to *e*.

Version *b* occurs in sources P 275 and P 421.

Version *c* occurs in source P 626 (now P 1152), later addition.

Version *d* occurs in source P 320.

Version *e* occurs in sources P 289, P 295, P 551 (where *eb*^{1} was changed to *e*^{1}), P 577 (copied from P 551), and P 1152 (copied from P 577).

Version *f* occurs in P 212 (*eb*^{1} changed to *e*^{1}). Derived from this: P 1083, P 228, and the first edition of 1803.

Version *g* occurs in the Rust copy of BWV 903*a*.

Version *h* occurs in manuscript LM 4838, Yale University Library, New Haven.

The unusual number of variants in this passage is surely due to the fact that many copyists did not understand the passing nature of the harmony in bar 37, deeming it necessary to correct what they considered to be a mistake. In reality the harmonic progression in version *a* is quite simple:

There can be no doubt that this reading, which is corroborated by the most reliable manuscripts, is the best one. Originally P 577 also had this harmony, though it was later changed to version *e*. In Mus. ms. 69 the flat before the first g♭ in the bass was inadvertently omitted.

With regard to other variants, version *b* tones down the harsh quality of the passing harmony in bar 37, but in the process creates a 'Schubertian' altered chord of a kind that occurs nowhere else in Bach. After all, P 275 stems from Müthel, one of Bach's last pupils, who is justly referred to as an 'early Romantic'. Version *c*, which the BGA took from P 626 (P 1152), is harmless enough, but does not occur in any of the reliable early copies, not even in P 551 and P 577, as certain editors, such as Kreutz (Schott), wrongly state. Version *d* and a number of other deviations have long been considered to be arbitrary changes made by Bach's pupil J. C. Kittel. Version *e* from P 577, where all arpeggios were written out, and from other later copies in part derived from it, can hardly be regarded as authentic on account of the consecutive fifths with the following bar. Version *f*, presumably derived from *a* (originally with e♭¹ in the second chord!), occurs only in Forkel's copy and the sources based on it. Version *g* comes from the Rust version, BWV 903*a*.

4. Bar 50:

The vast majority of all copies (including the version contained in BWV 903*a*) reproduce the text of *a*, including P 275, P 289, P 295, P 421, P 551, P 577 (lower system: wrong chord Eb–Bb–eb), P 651, P 803/1, P 803/2, P 887, P 1152, Am B 56, Am B 548, Bologna DD 78, Darmstadt Mus. ms. 69, Yale University LM 4838, Eisenberg private collection (Göttingen), and Spitta Estate Mus. ms. 10487 (Staatsbibliothek Preussischer Kulturbesitz).

The variant *b*, on the other hand, comes from only one strand of the stemma, namely the copy made by Forkel (probably from W. F. Bach), from which P 1083 was copied, the basis of the first printed edition by Hoffmann & Kühnel (Leipzig, 1803). In turn this first printed edition is the source of P 228 and the Brussels copy (Conservatoire Royal de Musique 12.209). Schenker preferred this version, because in bars 49–54 it cements as it were the semitonal step $Bb^1–a^1$.[8] Even if version *b* goes back to Bach, it can hardly be regarded as his favourite version, for otherwise it would have occurred in other parts of the stemma.

5. Bar 59:

Version *a* occurs in P 295, P 320, P 551, P 577 (with added appoggiaturas), P 804/1, P 803/2, Am B 56, Am B 548, Berlin Hochschule für Musik 6138/20 Darmstadt Mus. ms. 69, Yale University LM 4838, and Spitta Estate Mus. ms. 10487.

Version *b* occurs in P 275, P 289 (dot and semiquaver beam very indistinct: erasure?), P 421, P 651, and P 887.

Version *c* occurs in P 212 and the sources based on it (see commentary to bar 50).

Version *a* is probably the best. The dotted rhythm of *b*, lower system, does not sound like Bach and could be a slip of the pen. Version *c*, which has an *Anschlag* (compound appoggiatura—the term comes from C. P. E. Bach), an ornament which occurs nowhere else in J. S. Bach, is surely not authentic.

6. Final chord of the Fantasia, bar 79. In the vast majority of sources this is a major chord. It is a minor chord in only P 212 and copies based on it (see above), and in P 577 and Darmstadt Mus. ms. 69 (slips of the pen?).

The Fugue

There are only a handful of important variants in the fugue.

---

[8] In the pref. to his edn., pp. 28 f.

1. Bars 64–6:

(Slurs in brackets from P 295. They are missing in P 651 and other older copies.)

Version *a* occurs in P 289, P 421, P 535, P 577, P 651, P 1152 (contamination?), and Berlin Hochschule für Musik P 6138/20. All the others have version *b*. But in Darmstadt Mus. ms. 69, P 212, and P 228 the ornament in bar 66 is missing. P 535 combined *a* and *b* at a later stage.

Here there is reason to believe that version *a* is the older one. When bringing bar 66 into line with bar 64 the original rhythm of bar 64 could not be retained for reasons associated with the voice-leading. Thus Bach probably changed the expressive rhythm of bar 64 from ♪♪♪ ♪ to ♪♪ ♪ , which corresponds to a written-out slide.

2. Bar 85. All the sources have g and not the g♯ that is sometimes printed. This was certainly intentional. For Bach it was obviously more important to determine the E minor tonality (subdominant of the preceding B minor, bars 80–3) than to write a chromatic line come what may. Similar diatonic passages in highly chromatic pieces occur repeatedly in Mozart. Here again certain editors make unauthorized changes to masterpieces, for instance in Mozart's A minor Rondo, K. 511, where, in bar 169, many an editor has added a flat before the B in the treble.

3. Bar 93. In all the sources the last note in the treble is a crotchet a^2, which corresponds to the crotchet c^1 in bar 134.

4. Bar 157, third crotchet. In P 212 and the copies and editions based on it, there is a crotchet g^2 in the treble in place of the two quavers g^2–a^2 of all the other sources. This could indicate that the more primitive version of this branch of the stemma, F, reproduces an early state of the work.

The Trills in the Fugue. Most of the trills in this fugue, except in bars 13, 24, 35, 71, and 144, occur only sporadically in the sources, probably because it was a self-evident right of the performer to decide when to apply them and when not. However, P 651 is one of the few manuscripts to have trill signs in bars 23, 46, and 80. The trills in bars 53 and 101 (the latter is omitted by von Dadelsen) occur mainly in the F branch of the stemma (P 212: ascending trill in bar 53!) and in P 887 (trill sign only in bar 53), the trill in bar 111 only in C, F, and G (P 803). None of the manuscripts adds trills to the long bass notes in bars 91, 107, and 155, which may possibly mean that trills were not desired. Strangely, a trill sign is missing on the third crotchet of the penultimate bar in almost all sources except P 887 ('Anonymous 300', a copyist close to C. P. E. Bach, Berlin) and the very late copy P 1152. The rhythmically similar passage in the penultimate bar of the Sinfonia from the C minor Partita, BWV 826, permits us to assume that Bach also intended a *Pralltriller* or trill at this point.

APPENDIX 3

J. M. Gesner,
'Johann Sebastian Bach as Conductor, Keyboard Player, and Organist' (Göttingen, 1738)

Johann Matthias Gesner was elected to the post of Rector at the St Thomas's School in Leipzig in 1730, thereby becoming Bach's direct superior. In 1734 he accepted a post at the University of Göttingen, where he died, a respected classical philologist, in 1761.

In his edition of Marcus Fabius Quintilianus' *Institutio oratoria*, which was published in 1738, he added a commentary to the passage in which the author remarks that a human being is able to survey and do many things simultaneously, pointing to the example of a kithara player. The translation (the original is in Latin) reads as follows:

This, Fabius, you would deem to be wholly unimportant if, recalled from the underworld, you were able to see Bach—to mention only him, for not so long ago he was my colleague at St Thomas's School in Leipzig—playing with both hands and all fingers our clavier, for example, an instrument that comprises many kitharas. Or that fundamental instrument, the innumerable pipes of which are supplied with air by bellows, how here he hurries with both hands over the keys, and there with swift feet, and alone produces as it were hosts of quite different and yet fitting notes. If you saw him, I say, how, in a manner never attained by many of your kithara players and innumerable flautists, he not only sings one melody like the kithara player and maintains his own part, but also pays attention to all simultaneously, and encourages from thirty to forty musicians to observe the rhythm and the beat, this one with a nod, the next by stamping his feet on the ground, the third with a threatening finger, giving the one his note in the top range, the other in the low range, and the third in the middle. How all alone in the midst of the loudest passages played by the musicians, though having the most difficult part himself, he notices none the less if something is amiss; how he holds them all together, giving a helping hand everywhere; and if they are assailed by doubt, he immediately restores order; how he feels the beat in arms and legs, scrutinizing the harmonies with a sharp ear, alone bringing forth all the voices with his own limited throat. In all other things a passionate admirer of antiquity, I believe that friend Bach alone, and those who resemble him, surpass Orpheus several times, and Arion at least twenty times.[1]

---

[1] *Bach-Dokumente*, ii. 332 f.

APPENDIX 4

Excerpt from the Article 'Takt' in J. G. Sulzer's *Allgemeine Theorie der schönen Künste*, vol. ii (Leipzig, 1774)

As the final note of a piece or a period must always be an important note, it can, in all the even metres listed here, occur only on the first note of the bar, and last throughout the bar if the ending is to be perfect. In any case the main accents of a piece must always occur on the first note of the bar, the less important accents on the first note of the second half of the bar; and on the other beats, according to their inner length and brevity, the unaccented notes and the passing or very short notes . . .

The treatment of these beats with regard to their varying different importance and the accents that have to be placed on them is easy after what has just been said of even metres. Yet with regard to triple time it should be noted that the second beat can also be long. However, this only when the caesura occurs on the first beat, as here:

Mur · re   nicht,   lie · ber   Christ ! . . . "

. . . In order to get a clear idea of all this, one should try placing above the words 'Ewig in der Herrlichkeit!' notes of appropriate length and brevity, observing the accents and the weight of the beat. As they are all spondees, duple time would seem to be the best, for instance 2/4. Thus the notes would be arranged as follows:

E · wig   in   der   Herr lich   keit !

The long and short syllables of the poetic metre would be observed precisely; the final note would fall on the first beat of the bar; and the rhythm would be wholly correct. But note that the word 'in' and the last syllable of 'Herrlichkeit', which are not important when spoken, are here given the greatest weight because they occur on the first beat of the bar. This can only be avoided by drawing together two of these bars to make one, that is:

E · wig   in   der   Herr · lich · keit !

In this way the two syllables are assigned to the middle of the bar, to its weak or short beat, where, it is true, they still retain an accent, though one that is by no means as heavy as the first, and in the case of the last, being a final syllable, is necessary. . . .

We will start by discussing the various kinds of duple time, beginning with those that have two beats. They are:

2/2 or alla breve time, whose beats consist of two minims, which is indicated by the ₵ sign at the beginning of a piece, to which one customarily adds the words 'alla breve'. It is performed heavily, but twice as fast as its notes suggest, and is thus most suited to serious and fiery expression, above all to fugues, and in this, the style and movement peculiar to it, can take no notes faster than quavers. . . .

2/4 time. Unless a special movement is indicated, it has the movement of the preceding time, though it is much more lightly performed, and can take all kinds of notes from minims to semiquavers, and in the case of a handful of successive notes, demisemiquavers. It is suited to all lighter and pleasant states of mind, which according to the kind of expression can be toned down by andante or adagio and so on, or made more lively by vivace or allegro, etc. . . .

The varieties of quadruple time are as follows:

1. Great quadruple time, where the bar consists of crotchets, and which is indicated either by ₵ or better still by 4/4, in order to distinguish it from the following ₵. Its fastest notes are quavers, which like the crotchets and the other longer notes are performed on the violin with the whole weight of the bow without the slightest shading of piano and forte apart from the special emphasis on each first beat of a bar, which is necessary in all kinds of time. . . .

2. Small quadruple or common time. It is indicated normally with ₵ and differs from the previous time through the lighter performance and through the movement, which is twice as fast. Crotchets are its main notes, which in performance apart from the special emphasis on the first beat of the bar are equally marked as in great 4/4 time, that is:

Uneven or triple time is similar to even time. Performance and speed are determined by the longer and shorter notes peculiar to each kind of time, that is, heavy and slow in the one, and light and lively with the other. On the whole uneven time, on account of the triple succession of its main beats, produces a greater liveliness in every kind of expression, and is thus more suited to the portrayal of lively states of mind than even time. It consists of the following metres:

1. Three-two time, 3/2;
2. Three-four time, 3/4; and
3. Three-eight time, 3/8; to which
4. Three-sixteen time, 3/16, could be added. Although not in common use, it is in fact the only one capable of correctly rendering the extremely light and swift execution of many English dances, which are usually written in 3/8.

APPENDIX 5

The Dedication of Partita No. 1 (BWV 825) and the Dedicatory Poem

Dem durchlauchtigsten Fürsten und Herrn
Herrn *Emanuel Ludewig,*
Erb-Printzen zu Anhalt, Hertzogen zu Sachßen,
Engern und Westphalen, Grafen zu Ascanien,
Herrn zu Bernburg und Zerbst, etc. etc.
    Widmete diese geringe Musicalische Erstlinge
    aus unterthänigster *Devotion*
Johann Sebastian Bach.

Durchlauchtigst
    Zarter Prinz
                  den zwar die Windeln decken
    Doch Dein Fürsten Blick mehr als erwachsen zeigt,
Verzeihe, wenn ich Dich im Schlaffe sollte wecken
    Indem mein spielend Blatt vor Dir sich nieder beugt.
Es ist die Erste Frucht, die meine Saiten bringen;
    Du bist der erste Printz den Deine Fürstin Küst
Dir soll sie auch zuerst zu Deinen Ehren singen,
    Weil Du, wie dieses Blatt, der Welt ein Erstling bist,
Die Weisen dieser Zeit erschrecken uns und sagen:
    Wir kämen auf die Welt, mit wünzeln und Geschrey
Gleichsam als wolten wir zum vorauß schon be Klagen,
    Daß dieses Kurtze Ziel betrübt und Kläglich sey.
Doch dieses Kehr ich um, und sage, das Gethöne,
    Das Deine Kindheit macht, ist lieblich, Klar und rein,
Drum wird Dein Lebens Lauff vergnügt, beglückt und schöne,
    Und eine Harmonie von eitel Freude seyn.
So Hoffnungs-Voller Prinz will ich Dir ferner spielen
    Wenn Dein Ergözungen noch mehr als tausendfach.
Nur fleh ich, allezeit, wie jetzt, den Trieb zu fühlen
    Ich sey
        Durchlauchter Prinz
            Dein
                tieffster Diener
                Bach.

To His Royal Highness
Emanuel Ludewig
Crown Prince of Anhalt, Duke of Saxony,
Engern and Westphalia, Earl of Ascania,
Lord of Bernburg and Zerbst, etc. etc.
  These slight first fruits of music are
  dedicated with most humble devotion
  Johann Sebastian Bach.

Most High and Tender Prince
            out of your swaddling clothes you peep,
  And yet your Princely visage shows that you're a man.
Forgive me if I venture to disturb your sleep,
  While this, my sheet of music, bows as best it can.
These are the first fruits of my lyre's string,
  You are the first Prince that your mother's kisses meet,
To honour you the work shall first resound and sing,
  For you are first-born, like this sheet.
The wise men of our time do fright us, claiming
  We come into the world and mewl and whine and cry
As if we wished at once to start bewailing
  That this short goal is dark and just a sigh.
I turn this round and say, the sound
  Your childhood makes is charming, clear, and pure
With cheer and beauty shall your life abound,
  And greatest bliss, and harmony secure.
Auspicious Prince, I hope for you to play
  When your amusements cross the thousand mark
That always I may feel the wish, I pray,
  To be, Most Gracious Prince,
    Your humble servant
      Bach.

Bach's dedicatory poem to Partita No. 1 is full of gentle humour and flowing rhythms. We will not go far wrong if we play the whole partita in the spirit of these lines, which suggest a tender performance suited to a small child. (One is prompted to say 'Mozart is not far away!' In fact many of Mozart's elegant keyboard works in the 'smooth' key of B flat major display a certain affinity, such as the Sonata K. 281/189f or the Variations K. 500. However, in Mozart's case the 'rhythmic flow' is never as continuous as it is here.) The Sarabande, the most majestic in the six Partitas, should probably be played forte. It is a symbol of nobility.

  If this pretty poem really is by Bach—and I see no reason to doubt it—then, over and above the occasion for which it was written, it would be a remarkable example of his linguistic skill. The humorous intent is clearly apparent when Bach refers to the new-born prince's 'erwachsenen Blick' (your Princely visage shows that you're a man). However, this partita can be regarded as 'first fruits' only inasmuch as it is his first *printed* keyboard work. In short, Bach makes play with baroque linguistic formulas and eschews the pompous turgidity that was otherwise the rule (as indeed he did in his music). In formal terms the poem, and in particular the ending with its diminishing lines that conclude with the single syllable, 'Bach', is rather striking. It is reminiscent of the preface to *WTC* I, which is also written in the shape of a funnel.

APPENDIX 6

Friedrich Blume and Hans Joachim Moser

In a lecture given early in 1963—the newspaper headline was 'The Downfall of the Fifth Evangelist'[1]—Friedrich Blume made the following claims:

If one looks at the sources of Bach's life objectively, then Bach was no more of a church musician than his handful of great and numerous minor contemporaries. . . . In 1708 Bach turned his back on the Church with the declared intention of taking on a court post, and fifteen years later once more donned the cantor's gown with great reluctance: the circumstances made it imperative. The Erdmann letter of 1730 provides clear and incontrovertible evidence of the extent to which he was disappointed by Leipzig. Did Bach have a heartfelt attachment to his ecclesiastical office? Was it a need dictated by his religious beliefs? Hardly. At least there is no evidence to suggest that this was the case. The arch-cantor Bach, the creator in the service of God's word, the sturdy confessor of the Lutheran creed—all this is a legend. We will have to bury it with all the other romantic ideas we have inherited and grown to love. . . .

There has been an earthquake in Bach research due to the new chronology of the Leipzig vocal works recently established by Georg von Dadelsen and Alfred Dürr on the basis of new source-critical methods. Bach's activities in church music during his total of twenty-seven years in Leipzig now look completely different. When Bach assumed the Leipzig post he first began with a number of impressive church works (*St John Passion*, Magnificat). Then for three years in succession (from the first Sunday after Trinity 1723 to Whitsun 1726), as if in a creative frenzy, he supplied a new cantata for Leipzig on every Sunday and feast-day (it is immaterial that, burdened as he was with many duties, these were repeats or new arrangements). From this point on, however, the chronology becomes doubtful. Whether in addition to these three cantata cycles Bach actually composed the fourth and fifth that his son C. P. E. Bach and his pupil J. F. Agricola ascribed to him in the 'Nekrolog' has become debatable. A small number of cantatas can be assigned to the years after 1726, but evidently these were mainly occasional works which are of minor importance in the context of a twenty-four-year period. However, this signals the end of Spitta's image of the arch-cantor who for decades supplied his Leipzig congregations with church works with unremitting toil. Bach's Leipzig activities as a composer of

[1] *Christ und Welt*, 26 and 29 June 1963.

cantatas are restricted to the first three (possibly five) years of office, and what followed were works written at irregular intervals. With this his career as a composer of church music came to an end. For, apart from their predominantly parodic character, the Passions and oratorios were reluctantly composed works, an 'onus' (burden), as Bach once put it.

The Christmas Oratorio, apart from the recitatives and chorales, is exclusively a parody of earlier secular works. The so-called Ascension Oratorio is wholly or largely a work of parody. The smaller masses are probably all parody, even if in the case of some of the movements this has not been conclusively proven. The B minor Mass is full of parody movements. Perhaps the only original parts are the Kyrie, parts of the Gloria, the Credo, and the Sanctus (the latter already existed in 1724) . . .

The sole remaining pillars of the old view of Bach among the oratorios are the *St John Passion* and the Magnificat. The *St Matthew Passion* has been under attack for a long time. It has nine movements in common with the Funeral Music for Prince Leopold that Bach composed for the funeral ceremony in Cöthen in March 1729. At all events, the chorale movement 'O Mensch, bewein dein Sünde groß' is earlier. Ten years ago Friedrich Smend, summoning up all the courage of his convictions and his ability to argue in a subtle and persuasive manner, sought to rescue the *St Matthew Passion* as an original composition and to banish the Funeral Music to the ranks of parody. However, his arguments are not wholly convincing, and the danger that this pillar will come crashing down cannot be ignored. Are you, honoured listeners, aware of what this means? At least that numerous works, oratorios, masses, cantatas, which we have grown to love as works that are an expression of Christian belief, works on the basis of which the classical and romantic tradition taught us to know and admire the image of a churchman, the mighty word of a Christian herald, the moving pious confession of a Lutheran, have fundamentally nothing to do with such contents and emotions. Bach simply arranged them for reasons of compositional economy, and did not write them because he wished to preach the Gospel, or because it was a deeply felt need.

The few allusions to recent research that I have been able to make may have shown you that with regard to the 'contours of a new view of Bach' we are not dealing merely with the gradual change that always comes about in the course of history, but that something has happened that could be likened to an earthquake.[2]

Naturally Blume's 'earthquake' theory did not go unchallenged. Perhaps the wittiest response was that of Hans Joachim Moser, who, in a fictitious letter, poked fun at Blume's theory that Bach was more of a secular than a sacred composer.

'BACH SELBER NIMMT DAS WORT' (BACH SPEAKS OUT)

Open letter from the former Leipzig Director of Music, J. S. Bach, to St Peter, apportioner of nooks in the musicians' heaven.

Your Apostolic Holiness has conveyed to me a copy of a journal for comment, noting in the margin that, if the journalistic rhetorician concerned be right, it would be a matter for serious debate whether I could any longer retain the warm nook honorably

---

[2] 'Umrisse eines neuen Bach-Bildes', pp. 466 ff.

conceded to me for well on 212 years here among the masters of sacred music, and whether it would not be more appropriate to demote me to the vile level of secular town pipers (it being a suspicious fact my father having been one of them)—against which hereby I duly protest, having every reason to contest the matter.

I am joined in this most warmly by all my fellow inmates of the aforementioned organists' and church musicians' cubicle, Dufay, Ockeghem, Josquin, Schütz, etc.

I come to the point. In a lecture given at Mainz an emeritus professor of musicology with lodgings at Schlüchtern felt moved to tell all and sundry that there was something decidedly fishy about my Facultas organisandi or organist's art because *a* my teachers be not known and *b* our colleague Caspar Ferdinand Fischer and others besmeared a number of pounds more of music-paper with organ music than I did.

With regard to *a*, I humbly ask Your Apostolic Holiness to note that Georg Böhm and Dietrich Buxtehude were among my professors in person and Froberger, Pachelbel, Hauff, and all good earlier masters in spirit, so that on this count I cannot be accused of being any old incompetent layman. With regard to *b* it is new to me and rather surprising that one's work is to be measured by the weight of the paper, on top of which it should be said that (and this does not seem to have reached the ears of South Hessen folk) the name 'C. F. Fischer' refers to a family business, half of which falls to the Kapellmeister of Turkish Louis (His Highness the Duke, no less), and half to his son of the same name—and how the dickens can Professor Flosculus[3] tell how much in fact I wrote for the organ when my pupils may well have lost some of the stuff?

The aforementioned selfsame principle of quantity also applies to my industry in composing cantatas for Leipzig, whereby he attempts to assert that I had not at all times honoured God and all he stands for with sufficient learning.

Did I write 'Jesu juva' and 'Soli Deo gloria' on my manuscripts out of sheer boredom and hypocrisy? Some learned young men may be right in claiming that I was writing chorale cantatas at the beginning of my time in Leipzig (it was high time someone modernized the existing repertoire that survived from Kuhnau's time!)— but these are mere details of biography and in no way touch on my piety.

Even if this debunker of my Christianity explains away the existence of my fourth and fifth cantata cycles, which may well have encompassed the harvest of my last years (it ain't my fault if Friedemann squandered his patrimony, but before he did so Forkel had a good look at these pieces, and C. P. E.'s collection of my chorales contains quite a number of examples taken from them), the 'earthquake orator' from Mainz (as he has styled himself) should leave the distortion of my letter to Erdmann to the Communists of 1950, who attempted to make of me a hater of clergymen and indeed an enemy of the Church.

In this I clearly set out the fact that I was pretty fed up about changing from being a Kapellmeister to becoming a cantor, in other words, from being a servant of a princely court to becoming the servant of a municipality. And I have had it confirmed that I was in a better position with my friend the late Prince Leopold, God bless him, than later with mayor, consistory, university, and other authorities. But what was the point of my missive to Erdmann? He was to help me get a better job in Danzig, which in

---

[3] Allusion to Blume's surname.

those days could only have been the post of Cantor at St Mary's Church, another ecclesiastical office!

With regard to Prince Leopold: the learned professor who hails from Schlüchtern is intent on secularizing my *Passio secundum mattäum* (not to say, on devaluing it) by harping on about the fact that I incorporated into it the funeral music for His Highness Leopold—but this was surely not a secular work, it was a sacred one . . .

And with regard to the parodies or contrafacta in my other great sacred works, I won't stand people who are younger than I am using such 'secular' models as a pretext for insinuating that they were not in a Christian spirit. I hope that my whole being and work was always *in nomine Dei*, even if written for a Professor Müller, Squire von Dieskau, Goldberg, or the Elector of Saxony and His Majesty the King of Poland.

Thus I conclude with something that is wholly fundamental. I know not why and wherefore the gentleman down there quaked his earthquake—for him it will likely be nothing but to effect a remarkable descent in the esteem of my pupils in spirit. That he has shown himself to be a bad historian is clearly apparent. He should not impute to those who met their Maker in the year of Our Lord 1750 nonsensical ideas that were first brought to the fore by Frenchmen and other skepticks a fully thirty years later.

In my lifetime at any rate there was no difference between a churchgoer and a mere *homini religiosi vel pio*. Rather, whosoever had been a cantor without an inner longing for the Trinity would have been despised as a d— false Christian and cynick by such as myself, detested and driven away.

I conclude, dear St Peter, let not your ire be directed against such learned scribblers of novelties at all costs, they know not what they do, driven by their earthly ambition, and leave me safely in the nook I have occupied hitherto. I know not what was supposed to be 'romantic' and therefore outmoded about the truism that as a churchgoer with a thousand tongues I praised my Saviour. Amen!

Your most obedient servant,

Joh. Seb. Bach
Cantor at St Thomas and Director of Music in Leipzig[4]

---

[4] *Christ und Welt*, 13 July 1963.

BIBLIOGRAPHY

ADLUNG, JAKOB, *Anleitung zur musikalischen Gelahrtheit* (Erfurt, 1758); fac. repr. (Kassel, 1963).
—— *Musica mechanica organoedi*, ed. J. L. Albrecht (Berlin, 1768).
AFFILARD, MICHEL L', *Principes très faciles pour bien apprendre la musique* (Paris, 1694; 5th edn., 1705).
AGRICOLA, JOHANN FRIEDRICH, *Anleitung zur Singkunst* (Berlin, 1757): trans. of and comm. to Pier Francesco Tosi, *Opinioni de' cantori antichi e moderni* (Bologna, 1723); fac. edn. of both works ed. E. R. Jacobi (Celle, 1966).
AHLGRIMM, ISOLDE, 'Bach und die Rhetorik', *ÖMZ* (1954), 342.
—— 'Zur heutigen Aufführungspraxis der Barockmusik', *Organa Austriaca*, 2 (Vienna, 1979), 1–36.
AHRENS, CHRISTIAN, 'Zur Geschichte von Clavichord, Cembalo und Hammerklavier', *Ausstellungskatalog der 10. Tage alter Musik in Herne* (Herne, 1985), 44–68.
ALBRECHT, CHRISTOPH, *Interpretationsfragen. Probleme der kirchenmusikalischen Aufführungspraxis von Johann Walther bis Max Reger (1524–1916)* (Berlin, 1981).
ALDRICH, PUTNAM, 'On the Interpretation of Bach's Trills', *Musical Quarterly* (1963).
AMMERBACH, ELIAS NICOLAUS, *Orgel- oder Instrument-Tabulatur* (Leipzig, 1571).
Atti del XIV Congresso della Società Internazionale di Musicologia. Bologna, 1987, ii, Study Session XII (Turin, 1990).

BACH, CARL PHILIPP EMANUEL, *Versuch über die wahre Art, das Clavier zu spielen* (Berlin, 1753 and 1762); fac. repr. ed. L. Hoffmann-Erbrecht (Leipzig, n.d.); trans. W. J. Mitchell as *Essay on the True Art of Playing Keyboard Instruments* (London, 1949).
—— 'Autobiography', in *Carl Burneys der Musik Doctors Tagebuch seiner musikalischen Reisen*, iii, trans. J. J. C. Bode (Hamburg, 1773), 208 ff.; 'Autobiography' trans. W. S. Newman in *Musical Quarterly*, 51 (1965), 366–72.
Bach-Dokumente, i: *Schriftstücke von der Hand Johann Sebastian Bachs*, ed. W. Neumann and H.-J. Schulze (Leipzig, 1963).
—— ii: *Fremdschriftliche und gedruckte Dokumente zur Lebensgeschichte Johann Sebastian Bachs 1685–1750*, ed. H.-J. Schulze (Kassel and Leipzig, 1969).
—— iii: *Dokumente zum Nachwirken Johann Sebastian Bachs 1750–1800*, ed. H.-J. Schulze (Kassel and Leipzig, 1972).
BADURA-SKODA, EVA, 'Besaitete Tasteninstrumente um und nach 1700: Pantalone, Lautenwerk und Cembal d'amour' (forthcoming).
—— 'Komponierte J. S. Bach "Hammerklavier-Konzerte"?', *BJb* 77 (1991), 117–29.

BADURA-SKODA, EVA, 'Prologomena to a History of the Viennese Fortepiano', *Israel Studies in Musicology*, 2 (1980), 77–99.

—— 'Über die Anbringung von Auszierungen in den Klavierwerken Mozarts', *Mozart-Jahrbuch* (1957), 186.

—— 'Zur Frühgeschichte des Hammerklaviers', *Festschrift für Hellmuth Federhofer zum 75. Geburtstag*, ed. C. Mahling (Tutzing, 1988).

—— and BADURA-SKODA, PAUL, *Mozart-Interpretation* (Vienna, 1957); enlarged Eng. ed. trans. Leo Black, *Interpreting Mozart on the Keyboard* (London, 1962).

BADURA-SKODA, PAUL, 'Auf dem Weg zum richtigen Verständnis von Bachs Ornamentik', *Schweizerische musikpädagogische Blätter*, 76 (1988).

—— 'Fehlende Takte und korrumpierte Stellen in klassischen Meisterwerken', *NZfM* 119 (1958), 635–42.

—— *Haydn, 4 Sonates pour clavier* (performing edn., Paris, 1982–5).

—— 'Noch einmal zur Frage Ais oder A in der Hammerklaviersonate op. 106 von Beethoven', *Gedenkschrift für Günter Henle* (Munich, 1980), 53–8.

—— 'On Ornamentation in Haydn', *Piano Quarterly*, 34 (1986), 38–48.

—— 'Playing the Early Piano', *Early Music*, 12 (1984).

—— 'Um den Chopin'schen Urtext', *NZfM* 121 (1960), 82–8.

—— 'Von den Vieldeutigkeit der musikalischen Notation', *Logos musicae. Festschrift für Albert Palm* (Wiesbaden, 1982).

—— 'War Beethoven unfehlbar?', *Hifi-Stereophonie*, 12 (1973).

BASSO, ALBERTO, *FRAU MUSIKA: La vita e le opere di J. S. Bach* (Turin, 1979 and 1983).

BECKING, GUSTAV, *Der musikalische Rhythmus als Erkenntnisquelle* (Augsburg, 1928).

BÉDOS DE CELLES, FRANÇOIS, *L'Art du facteur d'orgues* (Paris, 1766–78); fac. repr. (Kassel, 1936).

BERNSTEIN, WALTER HEINZ, 'Freiheit in Bachs Musik. Eine aufführungspraktische Studie, über Ornament und Rezitativ', *Bach als Ausleger der Bibel*, ed. M. Petzoldt (Berlin, 1985).

BEYSCHLAG, ADOLF, *Die Ornamentik der Musik* (Berlin, 1908); repr. (Leipzig, 1953).

BILLETER, BERNHARD, 'Antwort an Paul Badura-Skoda', *Schweizerische musikpädagogische Blätter*, 76 (1988).

—— 'Die Verzierungen bei Johann Sebastian Bach', *Schweizerische musikpädagogische Blätter*, 75 (1987).

—— 'Zahlensymbolik bei Bach', *Schweizerische musikpädagogische Blätter*, 76 (1988).

BLUME, FRIEDRICH, 'Johann Sebastian Bach', *MGG*.

—— 'Umrisse eines neuen Bach-Bildes', *Syntagma musicologicum: gesammelte Reden und Schriften*, ed. M. Ruhnke (Kassel, 1963).

BODKY, ERWIN, *The Interpretation of Bach's Keyboard Works* (Cambridge, Mass., 1960).

BOWERS, QUENTIN DURWARD, *Encyclopedia of Automatic Musical Instruments* (New York, 1972).

BRUCHHÄUSER, WILFRIED W., 'Zur Aufführungspraxis der Werke Johann Sebastian Bachs—Forschung–Tradition–Willkür', *Bach-Tage Berlin* (Neuhausen and Stuttgart, 1985).

BRUNOLD, PAUL, *Traité des signes et agréments employés par les clavecinistes français des XVIIe et XVIIIe siècles* (Lyons, 1925); repr. (Paris, 1986).

BUTLER, GREGORY, 'Ordering problems in J. S. Bach's "Art of the Fugue" 69 The Resolved', *Musical Quarterly* (1983), 44–61.

CACCINI, GIULIO, pref. to *Le nuove musiche* (Venice, 1601).

CANDÉ, ROLAND DE, *Jean-Sébastien Bach* (Paris, 1984).

CARRELL, NORMAN, *Bach the Borrower* (London, 1967).

CASALS, PABLO, and KAHN, ALBERT E., *Joys and Sorrows: Reflections by Pablo Casals as Told to Albert Kahn* (London, 1970).

CHAILLEY, JACQUES, *L'Art de la Fugue de J. S. Bach* (Paris, 1971).

—— *Les Chorales pour Orgue de J. S. Bach* (Paris, 1974).

—— *Les Passions de J. S. Bach* (Paris, 1963).

CHAMBONNIÈRES, J. CHAMPION DE, *Les pièces de clavessin* (Paris, 1670); fac. edn. (New York, 1967).

COOKE, MAX, *Bach at the Piano* (Melbourne, 1985).

COSSART-COTTE, FRANÇOISE, '"Documents sonores" de la fin du XVIIIe siècle: leurs enseignements pour l'interprétation', *L'Interprétation de la musique française au XVIIème et XVIIIème siècles* (Paris, 1974), 131–41.

COUPERIN, FRANÇOIS, *L'Art de toucher le clavecin* (Paris, 1716; 2nd edn., 1717); repr. (Wiesbaden, n.d.).

—— *Pièces de clavecin* (Paris, 1713); repr. (Paris, 1969).

CUMMING, ALEXANDER, *A Sketch of the Properties of the Machine Organ Invented, Constructed, and Made by Mr. Cumming, for the Earl of Bute, and a Catalogue of the Music on the Various Barrels, Numbered from One to Sixty-four* (London, 1812).

CZERNY, CARL, *Complete Theoretical and Practical Piano Forte School* (London, 1839).

DADELSEN, GEORG VON, 'Die Crux der Nebensache: editorische und praktische Bemerkungen zu Bachs Artikulation', *BJb* 64 (1968).

—— 'Die "Fassung letzter Hand" in der Musik', *Über Bach und anderes* (Laaber, 1983).

—— pref. to *Inventionen und Sinfonien*, NBA (Kassel and Leipzig, 1972).

—— 'Von den Quellen zur Neuen Bach-Ausgabe', *300 Jahre Johann Sebastian Bach: eine Ausstellung der Internationalen Bach-Akademie, Stuttgart* (Tutzing, 1985), 29–50.

DENIS, CLAUDE, *Nouveau système de musique pratique* (Paris, 1747).

DERR, ELLWOOD, 'Bach's "Composers' Vademecum", or the "Strong Foretaste of Composition" in the Two-Part Inventions Explain'd', *Music Theory Spectrum*, 3 (1981), 26–48.

DICHLER, JOSEF, 'Bach auf dem modernen Hammerklavier', *ÖMZ* (1962), 574–9.

DIRUTA, GIROLAMO, *Il Transilvano. Dialogo sopra il vero modo di sonar organi, & istromenti da penna*, 2 vols. (Venice, 1593 and 1609).

DOLMETSCH, ARNOLD, *The Interpretation of the Music of the XVII and XVIII Centuries* (London, 1916); 2nd edn. (London, 1946).

DONINGTON, ROBERT, *A Performer's Guide to Baroque Music* (London, 1973).

—— *Baroque Music: Style and Performance* (London, 1983).

—— *Tempo and Rhythm in Bach's Organ Music* (London and New York, 1960).

DREYFUS, LAURENCE, *Bach's Continuo Group. Players and Practices in his Vocal Works* (Cambridge, Mass., 1987).

Dürr, Alfred, 'Neue Forschungen zu Bach's "Kunst der Fuge"', *Die Musikforschung* (1979).

—— 'Tastenumfang und Chronologie in Bachs Klavierwerken', *Festschrift G. von Dadelsen* (Stuttgart, 1978), 73.

—— 'Zur Entstehungsgeschichte des 5. Brandenburgischen Konzertes', *BJb* 61 (1975), 63 ff.

Eggebrecht, Hans Heinrich, *Bachs 'Kunst der Fuge', Erscheinung und Deutung*, 2nd edn. (Munich, 1985).

Ehrlich, Heinrich, *Die Ornamentik in Joh. Seb. Bachs Klavierwerken* (Leipzig, n.d. [1900]).

Emery, Walter, *Bach's Ornaments* (London, 1953).

—— *Editions and Musicians* (London, 1957).

Ernst, Friedrich, 'Bach und das Pianoforte', *BJb* 48 (1961).

—— *Der Flügel Johann Sebastian Bachs* (Frankfurt-on-Main and New York, 1955).

Faulkner, Quentin, *J. S. Bach's Keyboard Technique: A Historical Introduction* (St Louis, Mo., 1984).

Ferguson, Howard, *Keyboard Interpretation* (London, 1975).

Fischer, Edwin, *Musikalische Betrachtungen* (Wiesbaden, 1950); trans. as *Reflections on Music* (London, 1951).

Fischer, Johann Caspar Ferdinand, *Musikalisches Blumen-Büschlein* (Augsburg, 1696).

Forkel, Johann Nikolaus, *Über Johann Sebastian Bachs Leben, Kunst und Kunstwerke* (Leipzig, 1802); repr. (Berlin, 1968); fac. edn. (Frankfurt-on-Main, 1950); trans. in H. T. David and A. Mendel (eds.), *The Bach Reader* (New York, 1945); 2nd edn., (London, 1966).

Foucquet, Pierre-Claude, *Méthode pour apprendre la manière de se servir des agrémens utiles à la propriété des pièces de clavecin* (Paris, n.d. [c.1750]).

Franklin, Don (ed.), *Bach Studies* (Cambridge, 1989).

Fries, Werner J., 'Bachs Doppelschlag', *BJb* 57 (1971).

Frotscher, Gotthold, *Aufführungspraxis alter Musik* (Leipzig, 1978).

Fuhrmann, Martin Heinrich, *Musicalischer Trichter* (Frankfurt an der Spree [Berlin], 1706).

Fuller, David, 'Analyzing the Performance of a Barrel Organ', *Organ Yearbook*, 11 (1980).

—— 'An Introduction to Automatic Instruments', *Early Music*, 11 (1983).

—— 'Dotted Rhythms', *The New Grove*.

—— 'Dotting, the "French Style" and Frederick Neumann's Counter-Reformation', *Early Music*, 5 (1977).

—— *G. F. Handel: Two Ornamented Organ Concertos, Op. 4 Nos. 2 and 5, as Played By an Early Barrel Organ* (Hackensack, NJ, 1980).

—— 'Mechanical Instruments as a Source for the Study of *notes inégales*', *Bulletin of the Musical Box Society International*, 20 (1974).

—— 'The "Dotted Style" in Bach, Handel and Scarlatti', in P. Williams (ed.), *Bach, Handel, Scarlatti: Tercentenary Essays* (Cambridge, 1985), 99–118.

GÁL, HANS, pref. to *J. S. Bach, Musical Offering* (London, 1952).

GECK, MARTIN (ed.), *Bach-Interpretationen* (Göttingen, 1969).

GEORGIADES, THRASYBULOS, *Musik und Sprache* (Berlin, Göttingen, and Heidelberg, 1954).

GERMANN, SHERIDAN, 'The Mietkes, the Margrave and Bach', in P. Williams (ed.), *Bach, Handel, Scarlatti: Tercentenary Essays* (Cambridge, 1985).

GILBERT, KENNETH, *Couperin: Pièces de clavecin*, 4 vols. (Paris, 1969).

GOULD, GLENN, *The Glenn Gould Reader* (New York, 1985).

GRIEPENKERL, FRIEDRICH, pref. to *Bachs Orgelwerke*, i (Leipzig, 1844).

—— pref. to *Klavierwerke von Joh. Seb. Bach*, viii (Leipzig, 1835).

HAHN, HARRY, *Symbol und Glaube im 1. Teil des Wohltemperierten Klaviers von J. S. Bach* (Wiesbaden, 1973).

HARICH-SCHNEIDER, ETA, *Die Kunst des Cembalospiels*, 2nd edn. (Kassel, 1939).

HARNONCOURT, NIKOLAUS, 'Bachforschung und Bachinterpretation heute—Wissenschaftler und Praktiker im Dialog', *Bericht über das Bach-Symposion 1978* (Marburg and Kassel, 1981).

—— *Musik als Klangrede*, 2nd edn. (Salzburg and Vienna, 1983).

HEINICHEN, JOHANN DAVID, *Der General-Baß in der Composition* (Dresden, 1728).

—— *Neu erfundene und gründliche Anweisung . . . zu vollkommener Erlernung des General-Basses* (Hamburg, 1711).

HENKEL, HUBERT, 'Bach und das Hammerklavier', *Beiträge zur Bachforschung*, ii (Leipzig, 1983).

HERMANN-BENGEN, IRMGARD, *Tempobezeichnungen. Ursprung—Wandel im 17. und 18. Jahrhundert* (Tutzing, 1959).

HICKS, ANTHONY, pref. to *Handel, eight great suites*, p. 63 Klaviersuiten I–VIII (Munich, 1983).

HILLER, JOHANN ADAM, *Anweisung zum musikalisch-zierlichen Gesange* (Leipzig, 1780); repr. (Leipzig, 1976).

HOCHREITHER, KARL, *Zur Aufführungspraxis des Vokal- und Instrumentalwerkes Joh. Seb. Bachs* (Kassel, 1983).

HOFMANN, KLAUS, 'Noch einmal: Couperin and the Downbeat Doctrine for Appoggiaturas', *Acta musicologica* (1971).

HOTTETERRE, JACQUES, *L'Art de préluder sur la flûte traversière, sur la flûte-à-bec, sur le haubois, et autres instruments de dessus* (Paris, 1719).

HOULÉ, GEORGE, *Meter in Music 1600–1800: Notation, Perception and Performance* (Bloomington, Ind., 1987).

HUBER, ANNA GERTRUD, *Takt, Rhythmus, Tempo in den Werken von Johann Sebastian Bach* (Zurich, 1958).

JACOBI, E., and BILLETER, BERNHARD (eds.), *Albert Schweitzers nachgelassene Manuskripte über die Verzierungen bei Johann Sebastian Bach* (Bach Studien, 8; Leipzig, 1984).

KAUSSLER, INGRID, and KAUSSLER, HELMUT, *Die Goldberg-Variationen von J. S. Bach* (Stuttgart, 1955).

KELLER, HERMANN, *Die Orgelwerke Bachs* (Leipzig, 1948).
——*Phrasierung und Artikulation. Ein Beitrag zur Sprachlehre der Musik* (Kassel, 1955).
KELLNER, HERBERT ANTON, 'Neue Perspektiven der Bach-Forschung—das Rätsel von Bachs Cembalostimmung', *ÖMZ* 40 (1985), 73 ff.
KILIAN, DIETRICH, 'Über einige neue Aspekte zur Quellenüberlieferung von Klavier- und Orgelwerken J. S. Bachs', *BJb* 64 (1978), 264.
KIRKENDALE, URSULA, 'The Source for Bach's Musical Offering: The Institutio Oratoria of Quintilian', *Journal of the American Musicological Society*, 33 (1980), 88–141.
KIRKPATRICK, RALPH, *Domenico Scarlatti* (Princeton, NJ, 1953; rev. 1955, 1982).
KIRNBERGER, JOHANN PHILIPP, *Die Kunst des reinen Satzes in der Musik* (Berlin, 1771–9); repr. Hildesheim, 1968).
KLOTZ, HANS, *Die Ornamentik der Klavier- und Orgelwerke von J. S. Bach* (Kassel, 1984).
——'L'Interprétation de la musique française aux 17e et 18e siècles', in *L'Interprétation de la musique française aux 17e et 18e siècles* (Paris, 1974).
——*Studien zu Bachs Registrierkunst* (Wiesbaden, 1983).
KREUTZ, ALFRED, *Die Ornamentik in J. S. Bachs Klavierwerken*, supplement to Peters edn. of Bach's English Suites (Frankfurt-on-Main, 1950).
KRICKEBERG, DIETER, 'Einige Cembalotypen aus dem Umkreis von Johann Sebastian Bach und die historisierende Aufführungspraxis', *Ausstellungskatalog der 10. Tage alter Musik in Herne* (Herne, 1985).

LANDOWSKA, WANDA, 'Bach's Keyboard Instruments', in D. Restout (ed. and trans.), *Landowska on Music* (New York, 1964).
LANDSHOFF, LUDWIG, *Bach-Inventionen*, Peters edn., Beilage II, p. 343.
LEINSDORF, ERICH, *The Composer's Advocate* (New Haven, Conn. and London, 1981).
LINDLEY, MARK, 'Keyboard Technique and Articulation: Evidence for the Performance Practices of Bach, Handel and Scarlatti' in P. Williams (ed.), *Bach, Handel, Scarlatti: Tercentenary Essays* (Cambridge, 1985).
LÖHLEIN, GEORG SIMON, *Clavierschule* (Leipzig and Züllichau, 1765–81).

MALLOCH, WILLIAM, 'The Earl of Bute's Machine Organ: A Touchstone of Taste', *Early Music*, 11 (1983), 172–83.
MANFREDINI, VINCENZO, *Regole armoniche, o sieno Precetti ragionati per apprendere i principii della musica* (Venice, 1775).
MANN, ALFRED, 'Bach and Handel as Teachers of Thorough Bass', in P. Williams (ed.), *Bach, Handel, Scarlatti: Tercentenary Essays* (Cambridge, 1985).
MARPURG, FRIEDRICH WILHELM, *Anleitung zum Clavierspielen* (Berlin, 1755).
——*Die Kunst das Clavier zu spielen* (Berlin, 1750; 4th edn., 1762).
MARSHALL, ROBERT L., 'Organ or "Klavier"? Instrumental Prescriptions in the Sources of J. S. Bach's Music', in G. B. Stauffer and E. May (eds.), *J. S. Bach as Organist: His Instruments, Music & Performance Practices* (Bloomington, Ind., 1986), 212 ff.
——'Tempo and Dynamic Indications in the Bach Sources: A Review of Terminology',

in P. Williams (ed.), *Bach, Handel, Scarlatti: Tercentenary Essays* (Cambridge, 1985).

—— *The Compositional Process of J. S. Bach* (Princeton, NJ, 1972).

—— *The Music of Johann Sebastian Bach. The Sources, the Style, the Significance* (New York, 1989).

MATTHESON, JOHANN, *Critica musica* (Hamburg, 1722–5); fac. repr. (Amsterdam, 1964).

MELKUS, EDUARD, 'Bach-Interpretation zwischen Scylla und Charybdis', *ÖMZ* 42 (1987).

MENDEL, ARTHUR, 'The Forkel–Hoffmeister und Kühnel Correspondence—A Document of the Early 19th-Century Bach Revival', in George Stauffer (ed.), *Essays on J. S. Bach* (New York, 1990), 5 ff.

MIEHLING, KLAUS, 'Die Wahrheit über die Interpretation der vor- und frühmetronomischen Tempoangaben', *ÖMZ* (1989).

MOSER, HANS JOACHIM, 'Bach selber nimmt das Wort', *Christ und Welt* (13 July 1963).

MOZART, LEOPOLD, *Versuch einer gründlichen Violinschule* (Augsburg, 1756); fac. edn. (Vienna, 1922); trans. E. Knocker as *A Treatise on the Fundamental Principles of Violin Playing* (London, 1948).

MUFFAT, GEORG, *Florilegium secundum* (Passau, 1698); ed. H. Rietsch, Denkmäler der Tonkunst in Österreich.

MUFFAT, GOTTLIEB, *Componimenti musicali per il cembalo* (Augsburg, n.d. [1736]).

MÜLLER, WERNER, *Gottfried Silbermann: Persönlichkeit und Werk* (Leipzig, 1982).

NEUMANN, FREDERICK, *Essays in Performance Practice* (Ann Arbor, Mich., 1984).

—— 'Facts and Fiction about Overdotting', *Musical Quarterly*, 63 (1977), 155–85.

—— 'La note pointée et la soi-disant "manière française"', *Revue de la musicologie*, 51 (1965); trans. in *Early Music*, 13 (1985).

—— *Ornamentation in Baroque and Post-Baroque Music. With Special Emphasis on J. S. Bach* (Princeton, NJ, 1978).

NEUMANN, WERNER, 'Probleme der Aufführungspraxis im Spiegel der Geschichte der Neuen Bachgesellschaft', *BJb* 53 (1967).

NEWMAN, WILLIAM S., 'The Performance of Beethoven's Trills', *Journal of the American Musicological Society*, 29 (1976).

NIEMÖLLER, HEINZ HEINRICH, 'Polonaise und Quodlibet: der innere Kosmos der Goldbergvariationen', *Musik-Konzepte*, 42 (1985).

NOE, GÜNTHER VON, *Der Vorschlag in Theorie und Praxis* (Vienna, 1986).

O'DONNELL, JOHN, 'Bach's Trills: Some Historical and Contextual Considerations', *Musicology* (Musicological Society of Australia), 4 (1974).

—— 'The French Style and the Overtures of Bach', *Early Music*, 7 (1979), 190, 336.

ORD-HUME, ARTHUR W. J. G., *Barrel-Organ* (London, 1978).

—— *Joseph Haydn and the Mechanical Organ* (Cardiff, 1982).

—— 'Ornamentation in Mechanical Music', *Early Music*, 11 (1983), 185–93.

PALMER, WILLARD, *Bach Inventions and Sinfonias* (Sherman Oaks, Calif., n.d.).

—— *J. S. Bach, Das wohltemperierte Klavier* (Sherman Oaks, Calif., 1982).

——*J. S. Bach. An Introduction to his Keyboard Music* (Sherman Oaks, Calif., n.d.).

PANERAI, VINCENZO, *Principi di musica* (Florence, n.d. [*c*.1750–80]).

PERL, HELMUTH, *Rhythmische Phrasierung in der Musik des 18. Jahrhunderts* (Wilhelmshaven, 1984).

PESTELLI, GIORGIO, 'Bach, Handel, D. Scarlatti and the Toccata of the Late Baroque', in P. Williams (ed.), *Bach, Handel, Scarlatti: Tercentenary Essays* (Cambridge, 1985).

PETZOLDT, MARTIN (ed.), *Bach als Ausleger der Bibel* (Berlin, 1985).

PONT, GRAHAM, 'A Revolution in the Science and Practice of Music', *Musicology*, 5 (1979).

—— 'French Overtures at the Keyboard: How Handel Rendered the Playing of them', *Musicology*, 6 (1980), 29.

—— 'Handel and Regularization: A Third Alternative', *Early Music*, 13 (1985), 500–5.

—— 'Handel's Overtures for Harpsichord or Organ: An Unrecognized Genre', *Early Music*, 11 (1983), 309–22.

—— 'Rhythmic Alteration and the Majestic', *Studies in Music*, 12 (1978).

PRAETORIUS, MICHAEL, *Syntagma musicum*, ii (Wolfenbüttel, 1619).

PRAUTSCH, LUDWIG, 'Figuren und Symbole in der "Kunst der Fuge"', *Bach-Tage Berlin* (Neuhausen and Stuttgart, 1985), 75 ff.

PRINTZ, WOLFGANG CASPAR, *Musica modulatoria vocalis oder Manierliche und zierliche Sing-Kunst* (Schweidnitz, 1678).

—— *Phrynis Mitilenaeus oder Satyrischer Componist* (Quedlinburg, 1676–7).

QUANTZ, JOHANN JOACHIM, *Versuch einer Anweisung, die Flöte traversière zu spielen* (Berlin, 1752); trans. Edward R. Reilly as *On Playing the Flute* (London, 1966); refs. are to the pbk. edn. (New York, 1975).

RAMEAU, JEAN-PHILIPPE, *Pièces de clavessin avec une méthode pour la méchanique des doigts* (Paris, 1724, 2nd edn. 1731); fac. edn. ed. Erwin R. Jacobi (Kassel, 1958); fac. edn. (New York, 1967).

—— *Premier livre de pièces de clavecin* (Paris, 1706).

RASCH, RUDOLF, 'Does "Well-Tempered" Mean "Equal-Tempered"?', in P. Williams (ed.), *Bach, Handel, Scarlatti: Tercentenary Essays* (Cambridge, 1985).

REICH, WILLI, *Alban Berg* (Zurich, 1963); trans. Cornelius Cardew (London, 1965).

ROUSSEAU, JEAN, *Méthode claire, certaine et facile pour apprendre à chanter la musique* (Paris, 1683).

ROUSSEAU, JEAN-JACQUES, *Dictionnaire de musique* (Paris, 1768).

SADIE, STANLEY (ed.), *The New Grove Dictionary of Music and Musicians* (London, 1980).

SAINT-LAMBERT, MICHEL DE, *Les Principes du clavecin* (2nd edn., Paris, 1702).

SCHEIBE, JOHANN ADOLF, *Der critische Musicus* (Hamburg, 1737).

SCHERING, ARNOLD, *Musikgeschichte Leipzigs*, ii: *von 1650 bis 1723* (Leipzig, 1926); iii: *Johann Sebastian Bach und das Musikleben Leipzigs* (Leipzig, 1941).

SCHLOEZER, BORIS DE, *Entwurf einer Musikästhetik. Zum Verständnis von Johann Sebastian Bach*, trans. Horst Leuchtmann (Hamburg and Munich, 1964); 1st pub. in French (Paris, 1947).

SCHMIDT, MARTIN-CHRISTIAN, 'Instrumentenkundliche und konservatorische Aspekte einiger ausgewählter "Claviere" der Carl Philipp Emanuel Bach-Zeit', *Frankfurter Konzepte* (Frankfurt-on-Oder, 1986).

SCHMIEDEL, PETER, 'Zum Gebrauch des Cembalos und des Klaviers bei der heutigen Interpretation Bachscher Werke', *BJb* 58 (1972), 95.

SCHMIEDER, WOLFGANG, *Thematisch-systematisches Verzeichnis der musikalischen Werke Johann Sebastian Bachs* (BWV) (Leipzig, 1950).

SCHMITZ, HANS-PETER, *Die Kunst der Verzierung im 18. Jahrhundert* (Kassel, 1955).

SCHNEIDERHEINZE, A., 'Johann Sebastian Bach, Johann Friedrich Doles und die *Anfangsgründe zum Singen*', *Beiträge zur Bachforschung*, 4 (1985).

SCHOTT, HOWARD, *Playing the Harpsichord* (London, 1971).

SCHÜTZ, HEINRICH, pref. to *Auferstehungs-historia* (Dresden, 1628); repr. (Leipzig, n.d.).

SCHWEITZER, ALBERT, *J. S. Bach* (Leipzig, 1908); trans. Ernest Newman (London, 1911).

SCHULZE, HANS-JOACHIM, *Studien zur Bach-Überlieferung im 18. Jahrhundert* (Leipzig, 1984).

SIEGELE, ULRICH, *Bachs theologischer Formbegriff und das Duett F-Dur* (Neuhausen and Stuttgart, 1978).

SIMON, ERNST, *Mechanische Musikinstrumente früherer Zeiten und ihre Musik* (Wiesbaden, 1960).

SMEND, FRIEDRICH, *Bach bei seinem Namen gerufen* (Kassel, 1950).

SPITTA, PHILIPP, *Johann Sebastian Bach* (Leipzig, 1873 and 1880); trans. Clara Bell and J. A. Fuller-Maitland (London 1884–5).

STAUFFER, GEORGE B., 'Bach's Organ Registration Reconsidered', in G. B. Stauffer and E. May (eds.), *J. S. Bach as Organist: His Instruments, Music and Performance Practices* (Bloomington, Ind., 1986), 193 ff.

—— 'Über Bachs Orgelregistrierpraxis', *BJb* 67 (1981).

—— '"Diese Fantasie . . . hat nie ihres Gleichen gehabt". Zur Rätselhaftigkeit und zur Chronologie der Bachschen Chromatischen Fantasie und Fuge BWV 903', *Bericht über die wissenschaftliche Konferenz zum V. Internationalen Bachfest der DDR* (Leipzig, 1985), 253 ff.

STEGLICH, RUDOLF, *Tanzrhythmen in der Musik Johann Sebastian Bachs* (Wolfenbüttel and Zurich, 1960).

SULZER, JOHANN GEORG, *Allgemeine Theorie der schönen Künste* (Leipzig, 1771–4).

TARTINI, GIUSEPPE, *Regole per arrivare a saper ben suonar il violino* (MS), ed. E. R. Jacobi (with fac.) in *Traité des agréments de la musique* (Celle and New York, 1961).

TELEMANN, GEORG PHILIPP, *Singe-, Spiel- und Generalbass-Übungen* (Hamburg, 1733–4).

TOSI, PIER FRANCESCO, *Opinioni de' cantori antichi e moderni, o sieno Osservazioni sopra il canto figurato* (Bologna, 1723); trans. with comm. by Johann Friedrich Agricola as *Anleitung zur Singkunst* (Berlin, 1757); fac. edn. of both works ed. E. R. Jacobi

(Celle, 1966); *Opinioni* trans. J. E. Galliard as *Observations on the Florid Song* (London, 1742).

TOVEY, DONALD FRANCIS, *Bach: 48 Preludes and Fugues, Books I and II* (London, 1924).

TROEGER, RICHARD, *Technique and Interpretation on the Harpsichord and Clavichord* (Bloomington, Ind., 1987).

TURECK, ROSALYN, *An Introduction to the Performance of Bach*, 3 vols. (Oxford, 1960).

—— *Concerto in the Italian Style* (Tureck/Bach Urtext Series, New York, 1983).

TÜRK, DANIEL GOTTLOB, *Clavierschule* (Leipzig and Halle, 1789); fac. repr. (Kassel, 1962).

VEILHAN, JEAN-CLAUDE, *Die Musik des Barock und ihre Regeln* (Paris, 1977).

WALTHER, JOHANN GOTTFRIED, *Musicalisches Lexicon* (Leipzig, 1732).

—— *Praecepta der musicalischen Composition* (Weimar, 1708).

WIEMER, WOLFGANG, *Die wiederhergestellte Ordnung in J. S. Bachs Kunst der Fuge* (Wiesbaden, 1977).

WILLIAMS, PETER, 'A New Approach to Bach's Well-Tempered Clavier', *Early Music*, 11 (1983).

—— 'Figurae in the Keyboard Works of Scarlatti, Handel and Bach: An Introduction', in P. Williams (ed.), *Bach, Handel, Scarlatti: Tercentenary Essays* (Cambridge, 1985).

WOLFF, CHRISTOPH, 'Bach und das Hammerklavier' (forthcoming).

—— 'Bach und die italienische Musik', *Bach-Tage Berlin* (Neuhausen and Stuttgart, 1985).

—— 'The last Fugue: Unfinished? in Bach's Art of the Fugue. An examination of The Sources', *Current Musicology* 19 (1975), 71–77.

—— *Johann Sebastian Bachs Klavierübung*. Kommentar zur Faksimile-Ausgabe (Leipzig/Dresden, 1984).

—— 'Textkritische Bemerkungen zum Originaldruck der Bachschen Partiten', *BJb* 65 (1979), 65.

WOLFF, HELLMUTH-CHRISTIAN, 'Das Metronom des Louis-Léon Pajot, 1735', *Festskrift Jens Peter Larsen* (Copenhagen, 1972), 205–17.

ZIELINSKA, TERESA, 'Nieznany autograph Jana Sebastiana Bacha', *Muzyka* (1967).

INDEX OF J. S. BACH'S WORKS

GENERAL INDEX